At the dawn of the 1970s, GLAM smashed through the faded denim dream of the hippie era – an eruption of alien glamour, gender mayhem and thrilling music that changed pop for ever.

SHOCK AND AWE takes the reader on a wild tour of the glam era, chronicling the exploits of its flamboyant personalities against a backdrop of social upheaval and political disillusion. Spearheaded by David Bowie, Alice Cooper and T. Rex, the glam movement revelled in artifice and spectacle. Simon Reynolds explores how artists such as Roxy Music, New York Dolls and Lou Reed celebrated illusion over truth and self-invention over authenticity. The book also tracks the reverberations of glam themes – fame, decadence, extreme fashion, theatrical excess – as they continue to influence contemporary pop.

SHOCK AND AWE is a defining work that stands alongside Reynolds's classics RIP IT UP AND START AGAIN and RETROMANIA as a milestone in cultural criticism.

D1339685

SHOCK AND AWE

by the same author

BLISSED OUT: THE RAPTURES OF ROCK

THE SEX REVOLTS: GENDER, REBELLION AND ROCK 'N' ROLL (WITH JOY
   PRESS)

ENERGY FLASH: A JOURNEY THROUGH RAVE MUSIC AND DANCE CULTURE

RIP IT UP AND START AGAIN: POST-PUNK 1978–1984

BRING THE NOISE: TWENTY YEARS OF WRITING ABOUT HIP ROCK AND HIP
   HOP

TOTALLY WIRED: POST-PUNK INTERVIEWS AND OVERVIEWS

RETROMANIA: POP CULTURE'S ADDICTION TO ITS OWN PAST

SHOCK AND AWE

GLAM ROCK AND ITS LEGACY
from the Seventies to
the Twenty-First Century

SIMON REYNOLDS

BAINTE DEN STOC

WITHDRAWN FROM
DÚN LAOGHAIRE-RATHDOWN COUNTY
LIBRARY STOCK

ff

FABER & FABER

First published in 2016
by Faber & Faber Limited
Bloomsbury House, 74–77 Great Russell Street
London WC1B 3DA

Typeset by Ian Bahrami
Printed and bound by CPI Group (UK) Ltd, Croydon, CR0 4YY

All rights reserved
© Simon Reynolds, 2016

The right of Simon Reynolds to be identified as author
of this work has been asserted in accordance with Section 77
of the Copyright, Designs and Patents Act 1988

A CIP record for this book
is available from the British Library

ISBN 978–0–571–30171–3

10 9 8 7 6 5 4 3 2 1

To my late father Sydney,
who gave me a touch of madness

To my mother Jenny,
who raised me sane

In memory of Jessica Maynard,
17 April 1964 – 27 April 2016

CONTENTS

For footnotes and related material, go to
shockandawesimonreynolds.blogspot.com

ILLUSTRATIONS

PLATES

Bryan Ferry at the EG management office in Chelsea, London, 1972 (© Barrie Wentzell)

New York Dolls perform on Dutch TV, 6 December 1973 (© Gijsebert Hanekroot/Redferns/Getty Images)

Wayne County, *c*.1973 (© Joe Stevens)

The Rocky Horror Picture Show's star Tim Curry and its creator Richard O'Brien (© *Evening Standard*/Stringer/Getty Images)

Roy Wood, 1973 (© Gijsbert Hanekroot/Redferns/Getty Images)

Russell and Ron Mael, 1975 (© Jorgen Angel/Redferns/Getty Images)

Rodney Bingenheimer surrounded by Les Petites Bonbons and other LA glitter scenesters (© Julian Wasser)

The Tubes in concert in New York City, 1975 (© Images Press/Getty Images)

Iggy Pop lashed by Ron Asheton at The English Disco, Los Angeles, 11 August 1974 (© Julian Wasser)

David Bowie's infamous 'Nazi salute' at Victoria Station, London, on 2 May 1976 (© Chalkie Davies/Getty Images)

'Everything without tells the individual that he is nothing, while everything within persuades him that he is everything.'

Anonymous (from D. T. Suzuki, *Lectures on Zen Buddhism*, 1957)

INTRODUCTION

Somewhere between 'All You Need Is Love' and 'Hot Love', between The Beatles and T. Rex, pop music began for me.

And it began primarily on the television screen, reaching me through kids' TV shows and *Top of the Pops*.

During most of the show's four decades of existence, *Top of the Pops'* jumble of chart entries and rising hits made for a fairly motley parade of middle-of-the-road fare, novelty singles and merely professional pop. During the early seventies, though, the balance at *Top of the Pops* tilted sharply towards the freaky and far-out. British pop was overrun by the absurd, the excessive and the grotesque. The show seemed *garish*, even for that majority of UK households who would still have been watching in black and white.

That's what we had: a small black-and-white set. My family went without television until I was around the age of eight, which was 1971, so glam is pretty much the first pop music I can remember clearly. I didn't know glam as *glam*, a distinct and defined era of pop. What I saw on the TV screen was simply what pop *was* then: extreme and fantastical, silly and scary all at once.

One of my absolute earliest pop memories is being shaken by the sight and sound of Marc Bolan on *Top of the Pops* singing 'Children of the Revolution', or maybe 'Solid Gold Easy Action'. It was the look of Bolan even more than the ominous sensuality of T. Rex's sound that transfixed me. That electric frizz of hair, the glitter-speckled cheeks, a coat that appeared to be made of metal – Marc seemed like a warlord from outer space.

The spark that ignited the glam explosion, Marc Bolan had company very soon. The plastic insurrection of The Sweet. Gary

Glitter's barbarian bubblegum. The jubilant stomp and roar of Slade. Wizzard's gaudy blare of horns and hair dye. Roxy Music's romping noise and mannered poise. Alice Cooper, a demonic Pied Piper. Sparks' swashbuckling histrionics. And right in the midst of it all was David Bowie, set to straddle the decade like The Beatles had the sixties, a sustained presence of elegant strangeness in the pop charts. 'Space Oddity' – re-released in 1975, when it gave him his first #1 – made the deepest impression on the mini-me.

This glam-derived idea of what pop is and should be – alien, sensationalistic, hysterical in both senses, a place where the sublime and ridiculous merge and become indistinguishable – never left me.

I rediscovered glam in the mid-eighties, by which time I had become a serious follower of music and fledgling critic. Those first impressions, burned into my dazed child-mind, were now joined by a more considered and conceptual overlay of ideas: the sense that something had been lost when punk and post-punk fatally demystified the process and exposed the mechanisms behind the spectacle. Playing battered seven-inch singles that my friends and I had dug out from charity shops and jumble sales – songs by The Sweet, Glitter, Hello, Alice Cooper – I felt the pull of a time when pop was titanic, idolatrous, unsane, a theatre of inflamed artifice and grandiose gestures. This long-gone, real-gone era seemed the opposite of what pop had become in the post-post-punk eighties: adult, responsible, caring and socially concerned.

Glam – also known as glitter in the US – refers to a cluster of artists and bands who are often connected by relationships of collaboration and shared management, and energised by friendly rivalry with each other. Glam also describes a sensibility, a spirit of the age that emerged around the start of the seventies and flourished for about four years, before petering out shortly prior to the punk explosion. Beyond this generally accepted historical reality of glam – as era, genre, scene, movement – it can also be seen as a continuum that encompasses both precursors within rock itself (Rolling Stones, Velvet Underground, Little Richard and others) and ancestors who predate rock'n'roll and form a lineage stretching back deep into the nineteenth century, or even earlier. Today, there are fans, critics and contemporary artists for whom glam is a creed, a cosmology almost: the prism through which they perceive everything they revere in music and pop culture.

In *Shock and Awe*, glam serves as an elastic label that covers all the obvious candidates but also some less usual suspects from art pop and theatrical rock, including The Sensational Alex Harvey Band, The Tubes and Queen. Like most music genres and scenes, glam is fuzzy, overlapping with other blurry-edge categories like teenybop, prog rock, singer-songwriter and hard 'n' heavy rock. As a historical era, glam is fuzzy at each end too: artists like Bowie, T. Rex, Alice Cooper and Roxy Music emerged out of the longhair underground and took a while to shake off their post-psychedelic traits; many of the late-period glam figures either point towards punk or would actually enjoy a second phase of existence during the new-wave late seventies. Rather than get hung up on definitions, I have interpreted 'glam' generously and loosely, following where the music, storylines and leading personalities seem to want to go.

That said, one larger definitional issue does warrant addressing: what is it that makes the glamorousness of glam different from the standard-issue razzle-dazzle of pop music? After all, varying degrees of elegance, choreographed stagecraft and spectacle are core features of pop in particular and showbiz in general. One crucial distinction is the sheer self-consciousness with which the glam artists embraced aspects like costume, theatrics and the use of props, which often verged on a parody of glamour rather than its straightforward embrace. Glam rock drew attention to itself as fake. Glam performers were despotic, dominating the audience (as all true showbiz entertainers do). But they also often engaged in a kind of mocking self-deconstruction of their own personae and poses, sending up the absurdity of performance.

Glam rock also drew attention to its glamorousness because it was reacting against what came before it. *Unglam rock*, the all-grown-up, all-dressed-down rock of 1968–70, made the glam gesture both possible and pointed: a defiant embrace of flash, frivolousness and folly. The three-year period of 1968–70 – the epoch of *Abbey Road*, *Music from Big Pink*, *Atom Heart Mother*, *At Fillmore East*, *Déjà Vu*, *Tommy*, *Blind Faith* – was when rock matured, leaving behind childish things like seven-inch singles and pop image. Arenas and airwaves alike were dominated by mellow country rock, earnest singer-songwriters, earth-toned hippy jam bands and countless nondescript-looking bluesy boogie outfits. Whether rootsy or expansive, all these groups agreed that rock was all about the music and nothing but the music. Caring about image or putting on a show was seen as juvenile, square, commercial.

Flaring up against this drab backdrop of beards and denim, glam was the first true teenage rampage of the new decade. In some respects it was the resurrection of the original spirit of the fifties, when rock'n'roll was something to look at as well as listen to: Little Richard's camp flamboyance, Jerry Lee Lewis's thunderous showmanship. To achieve an equivalent audio-visual impact, the glam rockers had to go much further. Amplifying the androgynous and homoerotic currents already present in fifties and sixties pop, flirting with new frissons of deviance and decadence, the glam performers used luridly over-the-top costumes and staged outrage to stun audiences into awestruck submission.

Glam was a sonic reversion too, a rediscovery of the simplicity of fifties rock'n'roll and the hard-hitting attack of the early-to-mid-sixties beat groups. Glam, in fact, staged a complete inversion of the hairy 'n' heavy rock that preceded it: instead of flashy playing plus unflashy clothing, glam splayed image excess over stripped-down rock.

What stopped glam from being regressive rock, a mere revival or re-enactment of the past, was the way its sound was sluiced through the studio advances of the second half of the sixties, which saw huge changes in how guitars sounded and drums were recorded. The result was a merger of primitivism and production that thrillingly combined the subhuman and the superhuman. At once a fifties flash-back and a preview of punk, glitter rock was at its most innovative in the hands of hit-factory bosses like Mike Chapman, Mike Leander, Phil Wainman and Jeff Wayne. Their records were so sculpted and burnished they seemed to have a visual quality, every smash single impacting listeners like a drama staged on the radio. Music 'styled to be watched as well as listened to', as Chapman put it.

Glam also inverted the political and philosophical principles that underpinned late-sixties hippy-era rock. Discarding the ail-ing communal ethos of the underground, glam performers weren't interested in uniting to change the world but instead sought to achieve a personal escape from reality into a never-ending fantasy of fame and freakitude. They were driven by a half-ironic, deep-down deadly serious obsession with stardom and all the trappings of ostentatious luxury that came with it. Breaking with the pieties of the long-haired liberation generation, glam celebrated illusion and masks instead of truth and sincerity. Glam idols like Bowie, Alice Cooper, Gary Glitter, Bryan Ferry and others espoused the notion that the figure who appeared onstage or on record wasn't a real person but a constructed persona, one that didn't necessarily have any correlation with a performer's actual self or how they were in everyday life.

This celebration of image and play-acting represented a com-plete reversal of the guiding instincts and governing ideals of the sixties. The tone was set right at the start of the decade with Daniel J. Boorstin's 1962 book *The Image*, a widely read analysis of what its author described as 'the menace of unreality' creeping into every area of American life and mass culture. Written during the early days of John F. Kennedy's administration, the book coolly appraised the new politics of photo ops and publicity stunts, which Boorstin caustically termed 'pseudo-events'. Teeming with imagery of mist, fog, shadows and phantoms, *The Image* diagnosed a social-cultural malaise of 'nothingness', in which 'the vacuum of our experience is actually made emptier by our anxious straining with mechanical devices to fill it artificially'. Celebrities, whom Boorstin famously defined as people 'well-known for being well-known', were nothing but 'receptacles into which we pour our own purposelessness . . . ourselves seen in a magnifying mirror'. The media – in particular news and advertising – stoked excessive expectations for life and an insatiable appetite for stimulation, an unsustainable rate of novelty. So the void got filled with pseudo-events: opinion polls, political theatre, photo ops, award ceremonies. This fatal blurring of the border between true and false, real and artificial, had injected 'a new elusiveness, iridescence, and ambiguity' into everyday life.

Paralleling the insights of the sociologist Erving Goffman in his 1959 book *The Presentation of Self in Everyday Life*, Boorstin wrote about the rise of the term 'public image', as used by everyone from entertainer-celebrities to corporations to the nation itself (America's projection of strength to other countries). The notion filtered down into the ordinary lives and self-conception of regular folks too. So widespread was the concept that by the end of the sixties Muriel Spark used it as the title of her novel *The Public Image*, about an English actress whose balance between her cinematic persona and her equally staged private life is capsized when her mentally unbalanced husband kills himself – but not before engineering a scandal that will destroy her.

This negative concept of the 'image' that spread during the sixties was part of a growing view of public life as a realm of falsehood and facade. Against this rallied the conviction that 'the truth will set you free' – the motor behind nearly all the forms of bohemian expression and radical dissent that bubbled up during that decade. Cut off from all that was real and raw, bourgeois existence was felt to be shackled by taboos, censorship and conditioning, and thus condemned to inauthenticity and repression. Abrasive honesty and an appeal to 'reality' and the 'natural' were the most formidable weapons in the counterculture's armoury.

This compulsion to show and say the unpretty truth had first started to stir in the mid-fifties, with the Angry Young Men playwrights and novelists in Britain, and the Beats in America. Fellow travellers in America included Norman Mailer and Jackson Pollock, whose 'I am Nature' spontaneity splashed across his canvases (but also into the fireplace of his benefactor Peggy Guggenheim when he unzipped and urinated during a dinner party). Teenage icon Holden Caulfield in *The Catcher in the Rye* rails constantly against the phoniness of grown-ups, a plaint echoed within a few years by Bob Dylan with 'All is phony.' However, the patron anti-saint of the 'truth will set you free' era was not a painter, poet or rock singer, but a comedian. Lenny Bruce's brand of stand-up wasn't just about blue jokes but about standing up for his right to say whatever he wanted. According to his biographer Albert Goldman, Bruce worshipped 'the gods of Spontaneity, Candor and Free Association', seeing himself as the comedy equivalent of Charlie Parker. His improvised routines approached automatic writing.

In the sixties, theatre itself was under assault from reality, as playwrights like Joe Orton introduced content and language that strained against the leash of propriety. The quest for honesty was the explicit subject of many plays, like *Who's Afraid of Virginia Woolf?*, whose title, Edward Albee said, translated as 'Who's afraid of living life without false illusions?' Some radical theatre groups like the Living Theatre attempted to bring reality onto the stage itself with improvised action, nudity and confrontation with the audience. Meanwhile, a post-Method school of actors and directors aspired to a de-theatricalised form of naturalistic acting, all mumbling and tics, that inevitably spawned a new set of mannerisms that today look as stagey and trapped in time as the Hollywood golden age of poise and elocution. In all the arts, in fact, every attempt at realism, no matter how stringently stripped down or crude, seems to birth a new repertoire of stylised conventions and stock gestures. Bowie, for one, was acutely aware of this in relation to rock, which he precociously grasped was a *performance* of real-ness rather than a straightforward presentation of reality onstage.

The Realist was the name of one of the earliest and most important magazines of the emerging counterculture. Launched in 1958 by Paul Krassner, this 'Angry Young Magazine' dedicated itself to the pursuit and unveiling of 'reality', in opposition to 'the land where dreams come true' (i.e. the mainstream America of Hollywood and sanitised TV). Soon Krassner and co. were joined by fellow travellers like foul-mouthed freaks The Fugs (with their barely disguised expletive of a band name) and *Screw*, the porn paper launched by Al Goldstein. Aimed directly at *Playboy*'s swinging-bachelor-pad dream world of 'hairless women and cockless men', Goldstein's mission statement in the November 1968 debut *Screw* proclaimed that 'fantasy runs rampant over reality in the world of sex' and declared war on all forms of 'hypocrisy, sham and deceit'.

Despite *Screw*'s rampant sexism, the magazine became an unlikely ally to the feistier elements of radical feminism – raunchy libertines like Germaine Greer, who co-founded an equally no-holds-barred, everything-bared sex paper with a four-letter title starting with 'S': *Suck*. First-wave feminism was driven by a hunger to reveal the plain truth: strip away the mystique of femininity and all its cosmetic enhancements; expose the reality of the war of the sexes as female misery and male misogyny. Flashpoints in the feminist war against illusion included protests at beauty contests such as Miss America 1968, where Women's Liberation activists hurled bras and make-up into a Freedom Trash Can.

History does not record whether the feminists threw razors into the bin, but hair – armpit and leg, as well as on scalps and men's faces – became the decade's most potent symbol of natural honesty, along with nudity. Hairiness suggested a reversion of the body to an Edenic wilderness. *Hair*, a hit musical that co-opted the counterculture, culminates with mass nudity onstage. Nudity became a fixture of radical theatre works of the era like *Dionysus in 69* and *Paradise Now*. Likewise, free festivals such as Woodstock and Glastonbury Fayre invariably involved naked hippies gambolling unsexily in pools of mud or innocently humping in idyllic meadows. Perhaps the single most emblematic image of the late sixties is the naked photograph of John Lennon and Yoko Ono on the front of their album *Two Virgins*: the long lank locks of hair, the pendulous private parts poking through lugubrious pubic bush. After exploring the regression-to-childhood-trauma therapy of Primal Scream – a form of emotional nudism – Lennon boiled down the core longing of the counterculture into the desperate protest song 'Gimme Some Truth'.

Glam's soul-cry was 'Gimme some *un*truth' – it believed fantasy would set you free, not reality. Shunning the natural, organic and wholesome in favour of the unnatural, plastic and artificial, glam essentially rehearsed the sensibility of what we would later know as postmodernism. In the early seventies, the term 'postmodern' was very far from common parlance, barely existing outside a rarefied circle of architecture theorists. However, the attitude and artistic techniques had already been prefigured in certain renegade zones within sixties culture, in particular the gay underground and Pop Art. Glam drew from these vanguards of sensibility, from camp and

Warholism. But glam's ironic and self-referential traits also came out of pop's intrinsic tendency to fold back on itself, paying homage to and re-enacting its own youth, the virgin exhilaration of its moment of emergence. That stems from nostalgia, but also from irreverence, an impulse to make fun of itself through parody and caricature.

My own experience with glam – experiencing it in stunned, pre-conceptual wonder as a child, then rediscovering it and enjoying it in a more self-aware, analytical way later – replicates what was going on in glam itself. Most of the major figures – Bolan, Bowie, Mott the Hoople, Roxy, Gary Glitter, Slade, New York Dolls, Roy Wood – were knowingly invoking and recreating their own primal encounters with pop and rock in the fifties or mid-sixties. What for me, in 1972, was pure thoughtless sensation was for its perpetrators already distanced and ironic, an *idea* of 'innocence' or 'wildness'.

Glam is a divisive concept. In its own time it was celebrated by some for bringing back a spirit of image-conscious entertainment and spectacle to rock after the earnest artistry of the late sixties. But it was also deplored by others as precisely the relapse of rock back into showbiz. One of the things I find so intriguing about glam as a moment – and why I think it resonates especially at the present time – is the way it wove together strands of the radical and the reactionary. On the one hand, it teemed with innovation on the level of style, visual presentation, theatrics and sexual experimentation; on the other, it was regressive in terms of its escapism, its flirting with decadence, its nostalgia. Musically, too, glam often seems to hark backward and step forward at the same time. It can't be coincidental that glam principles become ascendant in pop culture during periods when politics moves to the right – the early seventies of Nixon and Heath, the eighties of Reagan and Thatcher, and, most recently, during the first decade of the twenty-first century.

For all its compelling characters, legendary exploits, outsize gestures and marvellous records, glam rock was a movement rooted in disillusionment. It was a retreat from the political and collective hopes of the sixties into a fantasy trip of individualised escape through stardom. Depending on the performer, the realisation of that fantasy could take the form of a nouveau riche caricature of regal splendour (in the tradition of Graceland) or a dandy aesthete's existence dedicated to exquisiteness and elegance – collecting antiques and *objets d'art*, visiting exotic places, feasting your eyes, experiencing every kind of sensation and pleasure.

Modelling themselves on their idols, glam fans formed a self-created elite, albeit one that accessed the aristocratic fantasy vicariously, through records and concerts and reading about it in music-paper interviews. Glam introduced a syndrome new to pop: fans who turned up to concerts dressed like the star performer (something that happened with Bolan, Bowie and Roxy, but also with Gary Glitter, Slade and The Sweet). Instead of standing onstage as a representative of an existing community (as The Who did with mod, say), the star now commanded a tribe shaped in his own image. This dynamic cuts to the essence of glam, which is its blend of exhibitionism and authoritarianism: the star en*thralls* the fan, who is midway between voyeur and vassal.

Shock and Awe is about the power of make-believe. A good number of the protagonists in this story were delusional narcissists who created a bubble of unreality around themselves and then convinced large numbers of people to join them inside. Because it's pop music, this process is arguably harmless, apart from the damage to a handful of unhealthily obsessed fans, and to the idols themselves, when they can no longer step outside the fantasy cocoon they've built. Still, it's worth noting that the same charismatic techniques are used by political leaders with a messianic or utopian message (as opposed to those who merely graft and finagle their way up through the machinery of power) and by the founding figures of cult religions.

Pop is a personality cult: it's based on the belief that some people are extraordinary and that the ordinary can achieve elevation either by direct contact or through emulation. And some of those who are best at playing this role are born liars. Glamour could be defined as the lie you tell so well you believe it yourself, and make others believe it too.

Shock and Awe is about sensation and mania as social facts, about mass hypnosis and mass hysteria as real phenomena in which thousands get swept up. But it also examines the realities behind these phenomena: the engineering of excitement, the planning of controversy, the manipulations and deceptions, the trickery behind the magic. To return to the performer with whom I started, the one that startled me most as a child: Marc Bolan seemed to come out of nowhere, a wizard, a fully formed star. But Bolan, of course, paid extensive dues; he slowly, fitfully constructed an artistic self from an array of precursors and inputs. Both the appearance and the reality have equal weight, equal interest and equal value to me.

The impression of Bolan as a comet streaking across the pop firmament is what you might call a true illusion.

1:

BOOGIE POET: MARC BOLAN AND T. REX

John's Children – Tyrannosaurus Rex – T. Rex

At the giddy pinnacle of Marc Bolan's superstardom, *Melody Maker* ran a feature on T. Rex's concert at Birmingham Odeon on 9 June 1972. They presented positive and negative perspectives on both the show and the phenomenon. Representing the anti-Bolan position was Barry Fantoni, a cartoonist and jazz critic identified here – satirically, no doubt – as *Melody Maker*'s Classical Reviewer. Fantoni archly offered that his 'overall impression was that the music . . . displayed an almost unprecedented achievement in that every item sounded exactly alike, not only in tempo, melody and harmony, but in texture, orchestration and use of dynamics'. Adjusting his invisible bow tie, Fantoni confessed that for the first time in his life he envied Beethoven for his deafness.

The pro-Bolan response came courtesy of fifteen-year-old Noelle Parr, from Kilsby, Northamptonshire. Although less a review than comments woven out of an impromptu interview conducted by *Melody Maker*'s reporter at the venue, Noelle's thoughts were far more telling than Fantoni's arid irony because they were alert and alive to the visual components of T. Rex as total pop experience:

> There's his fuzzy hair for a start. The way he moves it really gets me. The curls stick to his forehead with the perspiration. It's so sexy.

> Then there is the way he wriggles. His body actually ripples. It's too much. He pumps feeling into you. You just let yourself go.

And his clothes are fantastic. He dresses to suit his body and his beautiful face. People knock him for wearing women's shoes but he wears what suits him. He doesn't care about anybody else.

T. Rex's music came last, if not least:

His music is original – fancy, he writes most of his material in the bath – and he puts it over so well. He goes with it and he puts himself into it. He's living it . . .

Noelle's review ended with a saucy-but-sweet anecdote about how she and her four Bolan-fan friends brought 'a large pair of pink bloomers' as a devotional offering to their idol. They embroidered a message for Marc and T. Rex's willowy percussionist Mickey Finn, signed 'from five vamporators – Suzanne, Noelle, Judith, Beverley, Adaline' – 'vamporators' referring to the line about being a 'vampire for your love' in T. Rex's recent hit 'Jeepster'. The five girls split the 45 pence cost of the panties between them.

Dry and distanced as his take was, Fantoni wasn't wrong, exactly. The T. Rex songbook is samey, for sure, and slight, if you like. It certainly doesn't stretch anywhere near as far and wide as The Beatles', whose own fan craze, Beatlemania, was invariably mentioned as the precursor to T. Rextasy, with Bolan celebrated for triggering teen screams on a scale last heard during the Fab Four's early years. Actual classical critics like Wilfrid Mellers praised Lennon–McCartney for their pentatonic whatnot, but nobody then or since has gone that deep into Bolanological song analysis.

T. Rextasy was not the sort of phenomenon that results in something as solidly quantifiable and validated as a legacy. It was too quicksilver. What Bolan left was not so much a substantial body of work (compositions, songs for the ages) as a nubile body of performances. The songs don't tend to cover well (see The Power Station's brawny mauling of 'Get It On') because so much depended on Bolan's personality and presence.

Even at his height Bolan was hardly ever considered a heavyweight. When he talked about being a poet – boasting, accurately, that he was Britain's best-selling bard, thanks to fan-propelled sales of his verse volume *The Warlock of Love* – nobody took him seriously. Well, apart from Noelle and her peers: in the *Melody Maker* piece she gushed that Marc was 'a brilliant poet . . . He believes in the little people and reminds you of a different world,' and she prophesied that 'in years to come, when the world reaches the peak of knowledge, they will realise what Marc Bolan has written'.

Bolan didn't have the art-school credentials of a Roxy Music, or the autodidact intellectual aspirations of a Bowie; his reading ran to J. R. R. Tolkien and C. S. Lewis, rather than Burroughs or Nietzsche. He went from a hippy cult oddball to a teenybop pin-up without an intervening period of credibility or respect. In America especially, where T. Rex's only Top 10 hit was 'Get It On' – retitled 'Bang a Gong' to avoid confusion with a similarly titled hit – he's seen as a trifling figure.

Yet it is precisely as a lightweight that Bolan was a marvel. T. Rex took the ponderousness and grit out of blues-based rock, made it lithe and succulent. At a time when the spectrum of male sexual expression in rock ranged from ballsy strut (Free's 'All Right Now') to Viking conquest (Led Zep's 'Whole Lotta Love'), Bolan androgynised rock – but without sacrificing urgency or heat. Cock rock became coquette rock. Instead of wham-bam bombast, T. Rex songs moved to a reciprocal groove, a gentle grind he dubbed 'the slide'. Active and passive roles slipped and flipped around: Bolan figured in his songs as prey or plaything (had any male singer before gasped 'take me' in the fey way he did in 'Get It On'?) as often as predator. Even in that mode he was playful, as with the hissed 'And I'm gonna *suck you'* that follows the vampire-for-love routine in 'Jeepster'.

T. Rex shunned heaviness in another sense. Unlike the down-tuned, downcast sound of Black Sabbath and their heavy-metal brethren, there's no sense of ordeal or struggle in Bolan's music. T. Rex bypassed the pall of post-sixties gloom that enveloped rock culture in the first years of the new decade. The stance of 'Cosmic Dancer' and 'Life's a Gas' – the closest things to mission statements Bolan ever wrote – recalls the light-of-spirit philosophy of Nietzsche's *Thus Spoke Zarathustra* and *The Gay Science*. 'Gay' here means merry rather than homosexual; it's a translation of the German word *'fröhliche'*, the root of our English 'frolic'. Song and dance were central and essential for Nietzsche, the expression and external sign of existential health, inner rightness. 'Now I am nimble, now I fly, now I see myself under myself, now a god dances through me,' Friedrich rejoices in *Zarathustra*.

The denigrators are right, in a sense: T. Rex is not for adults, it's not a fully grown-up music. It speaks to the skipping inner child within: inquisitive, wide-eyed, easily fascinated; maintaining a porous border between daydream and reality; yet to make the acquaintance of lack and loss, disappointment and decay.

'I'm still the same little boy I was,' Bolan told *Melody Maker* at the apex of his fame. 'I don't think I've changed since I was four years old. I think I was hipper when I came out, when I was born.' The modern myth of Peter Pan springs to mind. Marc Bolan was a Peter Pan*theist*, a modern pagan who found wonder and enchantment everywhere. 'I think that I am a child. Everything blows my mind,' he told *Star* magazine. And Bolan was Peter Pan*sexual*: not so much bi-curious as the polymorphous perverse child of Freudian lore, open to erotic possibility.

In practice, most of his relationships were with women, but Bolan left some people, like his early manager Simon Napier-Bell, convinced that he was 'fundamentally gay'. His attitude to sex was the same as his approach to clothes: he grabbed and enjoyed anything that attracted him, regardless of gender.

Four things defined Marc Bolan's personality and world view: androgyny, dandyism, magic and a fourth category that could be designated with various 'F' words – fantasy, fabulism, fancy, what Tolkien called 'faerie'. These four aspects don't necessarily always overlap: it's quite possible to be androgynous and have no particular interest in clothing or self-beautification. 'Faerie', though, does connect to androgyny via 'feyness'. Once upon a time, 'fey' meant that you had a changeling aura, that you came from and truly belonged in the world of elves, pixies, goblins and other supernatural creatures. And, of course, 'fairy' is a quaint derogatory term for an effeminate gay man.

Foppish effeminacy was a current in rock'n'roll from the beginning, most blatantly with Little Richard. But it was particularly pronounced in British pop. This came about partly because of a Tin Pan Alley tradition of gay managers with a flair for finding pretty boys whose non-threatening sexuality appealed to teenage girls. But it also had something to do with the art-school system, which infused the British rock scene with a bohemian laxness as regards appearance and sexual conduct. In his 1969 book *Bomb Culture*, Jeff Nuttall recalls the mid-sixties moment when art-school attitudes filtered into the beat-group scene: 'Shoes were painted with Woolworth's lacquer. Both sexes wore make-up and dyed their hair ... "Kinky" was a word very much in the air. Everywhere there were zippers, leathers, boots, PVC, see-through plastics, male make-up, a thousand overtones of sexual deviation ...'

Sixties British rock oozed a quality that American critic Andrew Kopkind identified as 'not a variety of sexuality but a sensation of the ambiguous'. It wafted pungently off The Kinks, from Ray Davies's camp demeanour to the oblique sexual subtexts of songs like 'See My Friends' and 'Fancy', which eventually became overt with 1970's trans-anthem 'Lola' – Davies singing as a not-very-masculine man whose lover looks like a lady but most likely isn't one.

The ambiguity was most upfront and outrageous with The Rolling Stones. More than any other claimants to the throne, the Stones were glam's prime precursors: Brian Jones with his blond pageboy hair and foppish unisex dress, his enigmatic smiling and effetely pursed lips; Mick Jagger's pouting and prancing. Jones and Jagger copped moves and gestures from girls of their acquaintance, and in Jagger's case, from the hyper-sexual performance style of Tina Turner.

The Stones' gender games edged towards anarchy and the grotesque. In the promo film for 'Jumpin' Jack Flash', the band are plastered in thick make-up. But this is mild compared to the earlier promo/single sleeve for 'Have You Seen Your Mother, Baby, Standing in the Shadow?', in which the group are dragged up as stereotypes of British womanhood – old biddies in fur and gloves, tarty Second World War servicewomen. At the same time, the nasty parodic edge evident in this visual framing of the song (itself one of the Stones' most malicious anti-love songs) shows how the band's gender-havoc coexisted with callous misogyny. The androgyny was surface deep; underneath the cosmetics-caked skin and dandy plumage beat cold, hard hearts that had assimilated and amplified the toughness of blues performers like Muddy Waters and Howlin' Wolf.

Male pop performers annexing for themselves the feminine province of fashion and beautification, then, was not necessarily an indicator of respect for women. It was an extension of vanity, a new terrain for the male ego.

'[Bolan] had the biggest ego of any rock star ever. No one in his own mind was greater than Marc Bolan.' So claimed Mark Volman, who – with fellow ex-Turtle Howard Kaylan – supplied the falsetto backing vocals that brought such a feeling of fruity overload to T. Rex's hit singles. According to another close associate who worked with Bolan during a crucial phase of T. Rex's rise – John Gaydon of E. G. Management – 'when Marc did *Top of the Pops*, he always used to look up at the monitor – rather annoying me, because I thought it was a real giveaway – to see how he looked'. Like Volman, Gaydon emphasises Marc's sweetness, warmth, generosity – 'he was a lovely man' – but admits that the vanity was central and upfront, and adds: 'I've always likened pop singers, in a way, to whores – they're selling bits of themselves, and they always have to look good enough to buy, if you like.'

If dandyism offers one means of peacock display, self-mythology is another form of 'costuming the ego'. Are the actual facts dull and dreary? Dress them up. Not content with looking fabulous, Bolan was a fabulist. Right from the start of his career – before the start of it, really – he told tall tales, offering journalists grossly inflated accounts of real events and circumstances, while talking up future projects that would never be delivered and in most cases never got beyond being an idle fantasy: TV cartoon series based around him and scripted by him; screenplays for 'three European pictures . . . including one for Fellini'; several science-fiction novels supposedly on the verge of UK publication. He boasted of having painted 'enough for an exhibition' and having 'five books finished which I've been sitting on for a long time'. Even on the downward slope of his career, he unfurled fantastical plans for a 'new audio-visual art form'. Music journalists ate it up because it was good copy. PR man Keith Altham compared him to Walter Mitty: 'He knew that people always wanted something larger-than-life, so he always exaggerated. And sometimes he actually began to believe that himself.'

Bolan came from a humble background (lorry-driver father, market-stall-holder mum) in the East End of London. He escaped through make-believe and making things up. First and foremost, Bolan made up himself. 'I am my own fantasy,' he told *Petticoat* magazine. In classic showbiz style, he changed his surname, swapping the Jewish Feld for Bolan. He chose it because he thought it looked French, and somewhere in his background there was supposed to be French ancestry. Confusingly, though, initially he spelt it with a not-very-Gallic umlaut: Bölan.

Bolan's most extravagant fiction was a kind of self-creation myth: he said he spent a long period living with a wizard in France, claiming it was a profoundly formative experience during which he was exposed to various forms of magic and esoteric wisdom. The details changed from telling to telling. Sometimes the stay lasted five months; on other occasions it was a year, even eighteen months. Sometimes he and the wizard lived in a wood, under a tree or even *up in* a tree. At other times he stayed at the wizard's forty-room chateau on Paris's Left Bank. In one version, Bolan was the sorcerer's chauffeur – this despite the fact that he never learnt to drive.

The nature of the sorcery varied too: sometimes Bolan spoke of white magic; at other times he characterised it as black magic of the most gruesomely malign kind. In one early interview, Bolan told a reporter from the *Evening Standard* that 'they crucified live cats. Sometimes they used to eat human flesh just like chicken bones. From a cauldron.' As if aware he was stretching the interviewer's credulity, Bolan added: 'I don't care whether you believe it or not. It's a bit scary, however false it sounds.' On other occasions he talked of having witnessed levitation; of learning how to conjure spirits and demons, and how to be invisible; of discovering that his poetic gifts came from a previous life as a bard. Bolan recalled writing out 'a rite to Pan' in order to change himself into a satyr, but losing his nerve before casting the spell: how would he live in mutated form? Would he end up in a zoo, or dissected in a hospital?·

His own version of the Robert Johnson legend – soul sold to the devil in exchange for bluesman musical mojo – Bolan's confabulation inspired the song that became his first single, 'The Wizard' (1965), which would later be revisited on the first T. Rex album in

1970 and transformed into a frenzied, incantatory epic. The humdrum reality underneath the inflated tale appears to be that 'wizard' was Bolan's nickname for an actor friend called Riggs O'Hara,
who took him to Paris for the weekend. Bolan's mid-sixties manager
Simon Napier-Bell insists that the magician was a real person, a con-
juror that Bolan met in a gay club and with whom he had had a brief
affair. 'It was very difficult for Marc to separate calculated bullshit
and reality,' Napier-Bell says. 'He liked to live in a mystical cloud,
but he also knew that the mystical cloud was good imagery.'

The concept of magic – and the conception of himself as a magical
being – was central to Bolan's outlook and work. Words like 'magic'
and 'spell' crop up continually in his interviews and frequently in his
lyrics. Bolan once argued that 'a successful hit rock'n'roll record is
a magic spell'. Speaking to *NME* in 1972, he declared, 'There's no
such thing as a pop star. It doesn't exist. But when you're making a
record, there's a certain magic that comes down from the spheres.'
The remark shows a fascinating capacity for double-think, oscillat-
ing between demystified and mystical viewpoints: simultaneously
seeing through the pop process, yet seduced by mystique and myth.
It suggests that glamour itself is a trick for which we all willingly fall,
a game we play on ourselves.

Glamour is a concept that Bolan's favourite writer Tolkien used
in his scholarly writings on legend and lore. As used in the phrase
'cast the glamour', the old-fashioned, original meaning of the word
referred specifically to visual illusions, spells that bewitch and
deceive the eye. Or, as *Webster's* dictionary has it: 'A kind of haze in
the air, causing things to appear different from what they really are.'
The word was popularised by Sir Walter Scott, who used it in various writings, including his 1830 treatise *Letters on Demonology and
Witchcraft*: 'This species of Witchcraft is well known in Scotland
as the glamour, or *deceptio visus*, and was supposed to be a special
attribute of the race of Gipsies.'

There is an etymological connection between glamour and word-magic: 'glamour' is believed to derive from or be related to 'gram-arye' – occult learning, books of spells. Bolan always saw himself as a poet as much as a musician: a 'Weilder of Words', as one of his Tyrannosaurus Rex songs is titled (and misspelt). His lyrics for Tyrannosaurus Rex and, to a lesser extent, T. Rex often resemble spells and magic speech, as described by Daniel Lawrence O'Keefe in his study of magic *Stolen Lightning*: riddled with 'archaisms, neologisms and nonsense syllables . . . repetitious, alliterative and full of figures', and chanted in 'a peculiar tone of voice', a sing-song or whine or mumble.

Defending his story of cat-murdering, people-eating magicians to the *Evening Standard*, Bolan insisted, 'It sounds ego; yet it's true.' The phrasing is peculiar – 'ego' used as an amorphous adjective, perhaps shorthand for egocentric or egomaniacal. And it's reveal-ing. Magic and narcissism are intimately connected. The idea of extraordinary powers, acquired as birthright or imposed as destiny, goes hand in hand with a superiority complex. 'I've always known I was different, right from the moment I was born,' Bolan informed *Melody Maker* in 1971. In another interview the following year, he declared, 'When I was younger I certainly thought I was a superior sort of being. And I didn't feel related to other human beings.'

Children's books and young-adult fiction are often based around identifying with a hero who is different: gifted with unique facul-ties, at once ennobled by and burdened by a higher purpose. Just think of the Harry Potter books, or in a different way, the onerous missions bestowed upon Bilbo and Frodo in *The Hobbit* and *Lord of the Rings*. The appeal of this to pre-teens and adolescents is obvi-ous: feeling special in the face of a world that makes you feel insig-nificant and powerless, at a time when the still-forming ego is brittle and insecure. But as the sales of fantasy fiction and movies attest, many adults never grow out of these wishful daydreams.

Magic and self-aggrandisement go together. Aleister Crowley's dictum 'Do what thou wilt shall be the whole of the law' enshrines the egocentric world view of the disobedient child. In *Stolen Lightning*, O'Keefe argues that magical thinking actually plays a primary role in the formation of the ego itself. While 'significant others' such as family members are the first mirrors of the emerging ego, the process continues as the self simultaneously projects and reflects in relation to figures in its non-immediate surroundings. 'The ego has to make itself, "magically", out of other things' – heroes, influences, icons of popular culture and so forth. 'All its life, ego collects objects. It sucks them in like a black hole.' This ravenous, still-forming self is vulnerable to idealising identifications, from worship of political leaders to fanatical obsession with pop heroes. These cults of personality can be sites of fantasy and spurs to wishful thinking that bears more than a tinge of magic.

Talking to one interviewer in 1975, Bolan characterised his self – at this point, in his late twenties, usually a long way past adolescence – as malleable and impressionable: 'I'm not the same person 24 hours a day, I'm always changing. It's like when you're a kid and you go to the pictures to see a cowboy film, then when you come out you're pretending to shoot everyone 'cos you're a cowboy.' Memories of family members bear this out, from his brother Harry, who spoke of how as a movie-loving child Bolan adopted the characters of screen heroes as a form of self-protection, to his wife June, who described Marc as 'a wonderful, wonderful sponge'.

Talking about his song 'Mirror Freak', Cockney Rebel's messianic frontman Steve Harley described Bolan as 'the original "Mirror Freak"'. David Bowie – like Harley, a friend of Bolan's, but also a rival – observed that '[Marc's] so terrifically aware of image . . . he really is engrossed in his own image.' Talk about the kettle calling the pot black, you might well think. Still, Bolan's enjoyment of his own image – initially reflected back in mirrors or passing shop windows, later in the audio-visual mirror of an admiring audience – takes us to the essence of glam.

Bolan's pop journey began in 1956: for his ninth birthday he was given an acoustic guitar, but instead of learning to play it, 'I used to just look in the mirror and wiggle about,' miming the risqué hip grind of Elvis the Pelvis. 'From the moment the first rock'n'roll acts came along, that's what they all did,' says Napier-Bell of the early British imitators of American rockers. 'They practised in front of a mirror. Not necessarily narcissistic, but certainly to get an image right. The bedroom mirror was the forerunner of the television camera.'

A few years after acquiring his first guitar, Bolan encountered a book at the public library that had a profound effect on him: a biography of the Regency-era dandy Beau Brummell, whose fastidious attention to grooming and strict ideas about dress enthralled the English aristocracy of the early nineteenth century, elevating him to an unofficial but influential position as counsellor in elegance to the Prince Regent. Falling out of favour and into serious debt, Brummell was forced to relocate to Calais, where he eked out a faded parody of his former grand lifestyle thanks to the support of a few loyal friends. In Jules Barbey d'Aurevilly's 1845 monograph *Of Dandyism and George Brummell*, the disgraced and increasingly delusional exile is described as sometimes staging imaginary dinner parties, at which he would announce the entrance of notable but not-actually-there nobles with a flourish.

D'Aurevilly's book – a celebration of Brummell and a defence of vanity, extravagance and frivolity – influenced Baudelaire and the later French decadents, who succumbed to a nostalgia for the aristocratic age now fading. Baudelaire wrote that dandyism was 'like a sunset', a 'last spark of heroism'. Other nineteenth-century literati denounced dandyism. Thomas Carlyle had Brummell and his ilk in his sights when he wrote 'The Dandiacal Body' chapter of his

1836 satirical work *Sartor Resartus*. Carlyle defines the dandy as 'a Clothes-wearing Man', someone whose 'every faculty of . . . soul, spirit, purse and person' is dedicated 'heroically' to 'the wearing of Clothes wisely and well: so that as others dress to live, he lives to dress'. All the dandy cares about is 'the glance of your eyes'. Carlyle detects a quasi-religious impulse at work: the 'Dandiacal Sect' is an eruption, adapted to the present day, 'of that primeval Superstition, *Self-worship*'.

From Brummell through Baudelaire and Oscar Wilde up to Brian Jones, dandyism is one long discontinuous revolt against a 'very ugly and sensible age' – Wilde's verdict on the fact-not-fancy world created by the Industrial Revolution and the Protestant work ethic. This great divide in sensibility dates back earlier than Brummell, though, at least as far back as the Roundheads and Cavaliers of the seventeenth century. When Cromwell's New Model Army defeated the Royalist noblemen defenders of Charles I, the Puritans not only abolished the monarchy, they also closed the theatres and restricted ungodly entertainments like dancing. Finery and frivolity were restored in 1660, along with the executed king's heir Charles II (whose mistress Nell Gwyn was an actress). Dandyism is Royalist in essence because the dandy aspires to a form of royalty through aesthetics. Dandies ruled over a realm of cold exteriors and stylised manners: social life itself as theatre. Aristocrats disdainful of the Protestant work ethic, they shunned the ignoble realm of production and profit, and instead dedicated themselves to ever-shifting codes and ceremonies, frittering energy and wealth away on cavalier displays of conspicuous consumption.

Growing up in a post-Second World War Britain where rationing had only just come to an end, amid the drab environs of an East End scarred with uncleared bomb sites and sooty with the by-products of industry, young Bolan must have thrilled to the vision presented by the Brummell biography: life governed only by the imperatives of elegance and extravagance. In interviews he often talked about coming from a working-class background, with parents who were 'so poor'. Bolan rhapsodised about how fame and fortune had 'commuted my sentence of working in a factory for the rest of my life'.

From Brummell's life story Bolan derived the concept of self-reinvention. 'The only philosophy I had as a kid is that a human being is an art form,' he told *Petticoat* magazine. This explains the apparent discrepancy between Bolan's frequent references to his working-class origins and his posh accent. At some point in the early to mid-sixties, he developed the de-cockneyfied voice that you hear in his TV and radio appearances during his later success, or in the snippets of studio chat in recording-session out-takes and demo versions: smoothly enunciated and thespian rather than born-bourgeois. This kind of vocal self-transformation was the showbiz norm in those days: upper-class-sounding radio and TV personality Frank Muir liked to surprise people by pointing out, 'I was educated in E10, not Eton.'

Bolan himself grew up in an adjacent east London postcode, E5. And it was there – the Hackney/Stamford Hill area – that he found his own underworld of modern-day dandies in the form of the mods. Baudelaire had written of how, in times of transition, men 'socially . . . ill at ease' will conceive 'a new kind of aristocracy'. That was the mods all over. Nearly always upper working class and lower middle class in origin, these were young men who never made it into higher education and onto the ladder of the meritocracy, but who were ill suited for a life of labour. Intellectually ravenous, but autodidacts rather than academics (indeed mods *despised* university students), they constructed their own hierarchy based around taste and knowledge, a status system completely separate from society's existing structures and snobberies. Mod enabled these hungry, angry young men to live an aristocratic existence oriented entirely around clothing and activities that displayed the clothes to advantage (like dancing or riding a moped).

Bolan caught the spirit of mod in his 1977 song 'The London Boys', a flashback to his early-teenage time running with a gang of flash boys: 'Mighty mean mod king / Dressed like fame.' As he told the *NME* in 1972, 'In those days I created a world where I was king of my neighbourhood.' Just fourteen, he was hanging with 'guys that were twenty or twenty-four years old' and 'known through the East End . . . But that was an illusion I created.' In another interview, he recalled being 'completely knocked out by my own image, by the idea of Mark Feld.'

As with the original dandies, mod was all about a strictly maintained facade of icy impassivity. Its chill thrill was 'the joy of astonishing others, and the proud satisfaction of never oneself being astonished' (Baudelaire). Nik Cohn recalled how the mod Marc 'used to change his clothes maybe four times each day. He was very image then, arrogant and cold and he couldn't even nod to anyone who wasn't hip.' He took being cool to an extreme, admitting years later, 'I had 40 suits when I was a kid but I never had any friends.'

So renowned as a face was the fourteen-year-old Marc Feld that he featured prominently in a 1962 feature about mods in *Town* magazine. He boasted of wild, implausible spending patterns: 'I've got 10 suits, eight sports jackets, 15 pairs of slacks, 30 to 35 good shirts, about 20 jumpers, three leather jackets, two suede jackets, five or six pairs of shoes and 30 exceptionally good ties.' He claimed he knew all the best tailors in the East End and would give them detailed instructions on lapels, stitching, pockets and all the latest criteria of mod styling. He even got his shoes hand-made. How on earth did Bolan afford it? He claimed, later on, that it was through petty crime, stealing motorcycles. 'I was quite a villain . . . Clothes were all that mattered to me.'

In the photo spread for the *Town* article, Bolan and the two much older mods featured stare haughtily and unsmiling in their polished shoes, three-piece suits and ties, set against a backdrop of shabby

Stamford Hill streets. They look for all the world like a junior version of East End gangsters the Kray twins. When asked by the interviewer about politics, all three express support for the Conservative government of the day: 'They're for the rich so I'm for them.' Cyril Connolly argued that dandyism was inherently capitalist because of its love of 'beautiful things and decorative people'. Being 'deaf to the call of social justice', dandies 'celebrate things as they are' rather than attempt to 'change them'. Mod, too, wasn't just rampantly consumerist but inegalitarian: 'You got to be different from the other kids,' Bolan told *Town*. 'I mean, you got to be two steps ahead. The stuff that half the haddocks you see around are wearing I was wearing years ago.'

Mods were effeminate in certain respects – some even wore make-up – without necessarily being in touch with their feminine side or having much time for actual women. Bolan's 'The London Boys' captures the male-dominated vibe of the movement, which was all about boys dressing to impress other boys, not attract girls. Modettes were peripheral figures, never faces. Boy mods 'simply were not interested . . . too self-absorbed', writes mod scholar Kevin Pearce. Pills played a part, overriding libido (along with other biological needs like food and sleep) in favour of self-admiration and a tribal feeling of collective glory.

Bolan's reign as mod king was interrupted when, in late 1962, his parents moved across the city to a no less dreary hinterland of south-west London called Summerstown. Cut off from his cohorts, stripped of his status, Bolan retreated inwards.

During this period of what he later called 'spiritual crisis', books displaced clothes: he devoured the British Romantic poets, moved on to Rimbaud ('the first poet that really rocked me. When I read him I felt like my feet were on fire'), and eventually reached the American Beats. When he turned to music as an escape route, it was Dylan who provided the model: poet plus acoustic guitar. His first approach to the record industry was as a folk singer with a peaked cap called Toby Tyler. But the gap for a 'British Dylan' was already being filled by Donovan.

Around this time Bolan developed his second artificial voice. Not the well-spoken and deceptively well-brought-up-sounding accent, but a highly mannered mode of singing: a warbly whine with an exaggerated vibrato. Bolan once claimed he had acquired the style by playing records by the black American crooner Billy Eckstine at 45 rpm instead of 33 rpm and copying the sound. Simon Napier-Bell says it was actually Bessie Smith: 'Play her albums at 45 and you heard Marc Bolan.' If that's true, then Bolan's voice came not just from technologically achieved artifice, but from a kind of trans-gendering – albeit one in which he sounded more high-pitched than his female model.

When Bolan visited the home of Napier-Bell, the young manager was enthralled by Marc's strange singing style and intrigued by his unusual songs. But he was taken even more by Bolan's image, the canny way that he exploited his smallness by climbing 'into the biggest armchair, crossing his legs' and creating an effect 'like a Dickensian orphan'. By the time someone gets to the age of fifteen or so, argues Napier-Bell, 'you've usually worked out how to get the best of what you are. And Marc had done that with his image. Everything was very worked-out.'

In pop, Napier-Bell insists, 'the image is more important than the music'. You can 'falsify the sound', with songs written by others, played by session musicians and whipped into shape by a producer. Visual allure can be enhanced by others but, Napier-Bell argues, it can't be created where it doesn't exist. Using what they innately possess, stars fashion this raw X-factor – presence, charisma, magnetism

– into an image. Ultimately, the process of self-manufacture has to originate with the artist. 'If you take someone and tell them, "I want you to have this voice, dress this way," and you send them off to a voice coach, you'll get a load of rubbish,' says Napier-Bell. 'Real images come from real, unusual people.' On the face of it, this is a curious definition of pop-star authenticity: the 'true' fake is in control of the masks he or she wears. But it fits figures like Bolan and his competitive friend Bowie. Both invented a series of personae before finding one that clicked with the public.

The distinction Napier-Bell makes between manufacture and self-manufacture points to a divide running through pop history. On one side, the tradition of the assembled group: styled, choreographed, in some cases passed through a showbiz finishing school similar to the Hollywood studio system. On the other, the tradition of the pop group or performer who operates as an artistically autonomous unit, controlling their own image, presentation and packaging, as well as steering the musical direction.

The sixties had seen the rise of artistically autonomous groups in the UK: a wave of art-school and increasingly middle-class bands with little interest in being moulded or given new names, as typically happened with the first wave of British rock'n'roll performers. Napier-Bell had a foot in both camps. Previously he had managed The Yardbirds, a key group in the transition from flashy pop to serious-minded rock. But John's Children – his other main client – were a mixture of chaotic charisma and manufactured provocation.

As was the case with quite a lot of groups in the sixties, John's Children didn't even play on their early singles – 'Smashed Blocked' and 'Just What You Want – Just What You'll Get' – because their skills were so poor. The sessions for their debut LP produced such dire results that Napier-Bell only salvaged them by creating a fake live album. He paid a small fortune ('£20,000,' he says) to purchase teen-girl screams from the soundtrack of the Beatles movie *Help!* and spliced them all over the LP, which would be provocatively titled *Orgasm*. But John's Children wrote almost all their songs and they possessed an innate instinct for mischief and mayhem, as well as intelligence and charm. Napier-Bell's role evolved into an uneasy mixture of friend and Svengali.

His biggest intervention was his decision to implant Marc Bolan into John's Children as a guitarist and backing vocalist. The group needed a halfway-capable musician and a dose of songwriting talent, but Napier-Bell also believed that success with John's Children would speed up Bolan's path to solo fame. 'The idea was this funny, wavery voice of Marc's, if it was behind Andy Ellison's lead vocal, was something the public and the record companies would get used to. They'd come around to him eventually.'

Today, John's Children get filed under 'freakbeat', a term that wasn't actually used in the mid-sixties but was retroactively invented by record collectors. Freakbeat refers to bands like The Eyes and The Creation who operated at the frenzied cusp between mod and psychedelia. Their template came from The Who, whose sound – white R&B so amphetamine-uptight it came apart at the seams – was arguably the first uniquely English contribution to rock, shifting its emphasis from dance and desire to social-existential unrest. The music – Keith Moon's free-flailing cymbal crashes and tom-tom rolls, Pete Townshend's slashed and scything power chords, John Entwistle's bass lunges – fuelled a pent-up tension that demanded explosive release. It came, orgasmically, with The Who's climactic onstage instrument smashing.

John's Children took The Who's live chaos to the next level. Soundtracked by a howling wall of feedback that masked their ineptness, the group staged fake but gorily convincing fights between band members. Ellison would leap off the stage and embroil himself in assaultive interactions with the audience, anticipating the confrontational performances of The Stooges' Iggy Pop and Suicide's Alan Vega.

What really made John's Children the ultimate in freakbeat was their music's volatile cocktail of mod aggression and psyche-delic gentleness. Like Syd Barrett and Donovan, Ellison's singing was choirboy pure, almost effete in its exaggerated Englishness. Summer of Love themes of nature and childhood blossomed in songs like 'Come and Play with Me in the Garden'. For one photo shoot, Napier-Bell had John's Children pose naked in a field, their privates concealed by plants.

'We really looked almost like angels,' recalls Ellison, blond and pale in those days. 'Dressed all in white. But put us onstage and we'd turn into this monster. You really had no idea what you were getting. On the way to gigs, we used to pull lots of flowers from people's front gardens, then we'd throw them onstage and just leap on them. It was the opposite of flower power for us.'

In February 1967, at Napier-Bell's encouragement, Ellison vis-ited Bolan at his home in south London to see if they could forge any kind of musical connection. 'He played cross-legged on a sofa, strumming these strange songs to me, and I thought, "There's no way that he's going to fit in with this extremely wild band, with all our huge amplifiers."' As well as the gulf between the acoustic-folky Bolan and electric-feedbacky John's Children, there was a social gap too: unlike working-class Bolan, Ellison and drummer Chris Townson knew each other from boarding school.

Still, at an early rehearsal Bolan showed promise: he arrived with sound baffles he'd made out of tinfoil draped over vanity screens, most likely from his mother's bedroom, and placed them around the group's monstrous amps, declaring that he would use them to control his guitar feedback. Soon he was supplying the group with material, writing their classic songs 'Desdemona' and 'Midsummer Night's Scene', along with two other tunes that were among the best of the group's slender output, 'Sarah Crazy Child' and 'Go Go Girl'.

One of the sixties' true why-wasn't-this-a-hit? mysteries, the single 'Desdemona' features the risqué chorus 'lift up your skirt and fly' over Townson's flailing Moon-style drums, with Bolan's goat-like bleat audible as backing vocals. 'Midsummer Night's Scene' is a feverish fantasy landscape painting of Dionysian revels in an after-dark park: hippy chicks with faces 'disfigured by love' strew flowers and prance the rites of Pan. The one-note bass riff, monstrously engorged with fuzz-tone, is like staring into a furnace. On 'Midsummer Night's Scene' – as well as thrilling non-Bolan tunes like 'Jagged Time Lapse' and 'Remember Thomas A Beckett' – there's barely anything you could call a proper chord, let alone a riff; just spasms of distortion, staccato jolts, drum-roll gear shifts, swathes of sustained feedback that appear and disappear without good reason, blissed-out moans and gasps.

Not content with out-Who-ing The Who sonically, John's Children took theatricalised destruction further too. In one interview with the group, Bolan described a typical gig as 'a 45-minute happening. Sometimes we're barely conscious of what we're doing. It's like a big turn-on séance between us and the audience. I've seen Andy go quite mad like a witch-doctor in a tribal dance.' Demurring from the word 'happening' – in the sixties a big buzzword in the art world and radical theatre – Ellison today says, 'I didn't really ever think of it as any kind of art form. But we did take it to the limit. Almost destroyed ourselves.'

This tendency reached its climax on a spring 1967 West German tour supporting The Who, appropriately enough. The mod gods were comprehensively upstaged, not just in musical and onstage anarchy, but in terms of sheer volume, thanks to John's Children's acquisition of a massive wall of Jordan amplifiers, which Ellison claims were 'made by NASA' and bought with the proceeds of the American success of 'Smashed Blocked', a regional Top 10 hit in both California and Florida. John's Children worked up a stage routine involving whips, fights using fake blood capsules for added verisimilitude, and a huge number of feathers scattered through the concert hall.

'I used to have a silver whip at the time,' Bolan told the NME in 1972. 'I'd chain up whole banks of amplifiers and drag them across the stage and whip the guitar . . .' While the band blasted out deafening decibels, Ellison would dive into the hostile German audiences, charging through the jungle of angry fists while gaily ripping open pillows and hurling clouds of feathers. After one particularly wild night, The Who came on and were forced to start the set with 'My Generation', the climactic number that usually closed their performances. As Bolan recalled, 'They could only pick it up from there. The stage was wrecked with feathers and brassieres and stuff all over the place.' Who manager Kit Lambert warned John's Children that if they carried on 'doing the act that you're doing, you're going to be thrown off the tour', recalls Ellison. 'But we couldn't stop. We wanted to see how far we could take it.'

John's Children's pyrrhic triumph arrived at the next concert, in Ludwigshafen. 'The riot police were called. Twenty thousand people were going berserk,' Ellison says. 'We got badly injured. People were attacking us onstage. We had to escape. As we were trying to get out of there, all I could see was water cannons being fired in through the windows as chairs were being thrown out.' Forced to flee West Germany in a hurry, the band left all their equipment behind.

Almost immediately upon arrival back in Britain, Bolan quit. Perhaps he realised that for all its thrills, a group like John's Children was too unfocused to make it. The failure of 'Desdemona' to be a hit added to the sense of a group on the fast track to nowhere.

Music was changing too. The rough-hewn attack of the early Who and Stones gave way to increasingly accomplished musicianship and studio polish, as displayed by the post-Yardbirds careers of

Eric Clapton and Jeff Beck, outfits like Procol Harum and Traffic, the moustache-wearing 'mature' Beatles and The Jimi Hendrix Experience's fusion of violence and virtuosity. John's Children were considered gimmicky.

Still, Bolan considered his brief stint in the group to be foundational. He told *ZigZag* in 1971 that with T. Rex 'all I've done really [is] re-create John's Children, or what I wanted John's Children to be when I was with them at the beginning'. In between John's Children and T. Rex, though, Marc Bolan took a long detour into the underground, with his new band Tyrannosaurus Rex.

Supposedly witnessing sitar guru Ravi Shankar play in Luxembourg on the way back from the catastrophic tour of West Germany is what inspired Bolan to form the all-acoustic duo Tyrannosaurus Rex. Bolan and the rest of John's Children were still wearing their white stage clothes stained with blood (fake and real) from the riotous Ludwigshafen concert. 'Marc was entranced. Shankar sat on a rug, playing his sitar, and nothing could destroy his act,' says Napier-Bell.

If this was really such a 'Eureka!' moment, though, it's puzzling that on his return to London, Bolan immediately attempted to form his own fully electric band. Hastily pulled together via an ad placed in *Melody Maker*, the group played a single, disastrous gig at the Rock Garden in Covent Garden. 'Marc auditioned by their names and their looks, as he always did,' says Napier-Bell. 'Didn't rehearse them either. He just believed that cosmic magic would produce something wonderful.'

It was only after this debacle that Bolan settled on the acoustic concept for Tyrannosaurus Rex. He retained one of the people who'd answered the *Melody Maker* ad, a seventeen-year-old 'flower child' who'd taken the name of a hobbit character in Tolkien's *Lord of the Rings*. Steve Peregrin Took – for reasons unknown he kept his first name, somewhat undermining the fairy-tale aura – was a drummer, but he was soon forced to sell off his kit to pay the rent. It was through happenstance, then, that Tyrannosaurus Rex settled on a sound based around Bolan's singing 'n' strumming over Took's hand percussion and background yelps.

The duo's quirky style appealed to the emerging hippy audience, and the duo swiftly became in-demand performers, earning £50 a gig. Napier-Bell, his faith in Bolan's talent vindicated, wanted to push the price up. But Bolan – who had adapted with chameleonic speed to the underground's anti-commercialism – wasn't into it. 'Marc said, "Oh no, man, I don't want to do that. It's not the right thing to do. I'm part of this culture and we're not a money culture,"' Napier-Bell recalls. So Bolan and his first manager went their separate ways, amicably enough. Tyrannosaurus Rex then took up with Blackhill, a rising management outfit right at the heart of the UK counterculture.

Founded by Peter Jenner and Andrew King to look after the country's leading psychedelic group, Pink Floyd, the company was based in Ladbroke Grove. Among the Blackhill team was Jenner's flatmate June Child, who started out driving Pink Floyd to gigs, graduated to looking after their finances and became the fledgling company's first employee, working as office receptionist and all-purpose assistant. She and Bolan were soon besotted with each other. Pale, willowy, her long oval face framed by flaxen locks, June Child had not just the classic look of the female flower child, but the name too. But she was also more adult than Bolan, being several years older. Child became his adviser, virtually his manager, as well as his soulmate, muse, lover and eventually wife.

Possibly adding to Child's allure was the fact that she'd briefly been Syd Barrett's paramour. There was a slight physical resemblance between Bolan and the Pink Floyd singer/guitarist, a dark and curly-haired handsomeness, with a hint of gypsy. But there was a deeper resemblance between Bolan and Barrett: a preciously English vocal style and lyrics that plunged into a children's storybook world of idyllic innocence. 'One of the few people I'd actually call a genius,' Bolan gushed. 'He inspired me beyond belief.' Barrett's pop success with Pink Floyd – hits like 'See Emily Play' and *The Piper at the Gates of Dawn*, one of the big albums of the UK's Summer of Love – encouraged Bolan to explore what was already in him.

Barrett shunned drawling American intonation in favour of a crisply enunciated refinement that sounded positively upper class at times, flashing the listener back to a children's nursery room in Edwardian England. This was presaged in pop only by The Rolling Stones' mock-medieval courtly love song 'Lady Jane' and the exaggeratedly precise, genteel diction of Donovan's 'Mellow Yellow'. Full of nursery-rhyme-style assonance and internal rhymes, Barrett's lyrics took psychedelia's exaltation of childhood – broached first in British pop by The Beatles with 'Strawberry Fields' and 'Yellow Submarine' – further with 'See Emily Play', 'The Gnome' and 'A Candy and a Currant Bun'. On *The Piper at the Gates of Dawn*, 'Matilda Mother' evokes the halcyon daze of the bedtime story, the maternal voice magically turning 'scribbly lines' on the page into wonderlands of the mind's eye; 'Bike' features a friendly mouse called Gerald. The anthropomorphism and animism (Barrett believed in tree spirits) relate to the pantheistic consciousness common to many LSD users. But there were also dark glints of the supernatural ('Lucifer Sam', about a spooky feline – 'that cat's something I can't explain'), which foreshadow the psychotic breakdown that claimed Barrett, as the barrage of psychedelics wore down his psyche's fortifications.

The Piper at the Gates of Dawn takes its title from the seventh and most mystical chapter of *The Wind in the Willows*, in which Water Rat and Mole glimpse the nature god Pan, having been lured upstream by the tantalising sounds of his primordial music. Associated with rustic rites and forest groves, and usually accompanied in mythology by frolicsome maiden sprites known as nymphs, Pan became an obsession for Bolan. A little green statue of the half man/half goat, which he nicknamed Poon, sat on the mantelpiece of Bolan and Child's home, and later appeared on the sleeve of Tyrannosaurus Rex's *Beard of Stars* LP. Pan's presence flickers through the entire Tyrannosaurus Rex discography, especially songs like *Beard of Stars'* 'Woodland Bop' and the demo-only 'Puckish Pan'.

Pan is also the source of Peter Pan, the 'Wild Boy' of J. M. Barrie's story who never grows up (and who onstage is always played by an androgynous young woman). In the sixties, a new type of young British man emerged, characterised by the refusal of mature manhood and the embrace of pursuits conventionally deemed feminine. Bolan and Barrett belonged to this new breed of 'soft males', alongside other late-sixties underground figures like Kevin Ayers and Robert Wyatt of The Soft Machine. This was the first generation since before the forties not to go through the 'character-building' rigours of military service. (National Service had been discontinued by the start of 1961.) The 'soft males' were also part of the first generation of sons to benefit from permissive child-rearing practices, which for some meant never fully breaking away from their indulgent mothers and identifying with the patriarchal order.

With neither the state (through conscription) nor their families (through discipline and emotional deprivation) affixing the traditional stiff upper lip to their beardless faces, this generation of male youths never really put away childish things, even when they added sex and drugs and rock'n'roll to their leisure activities. 'I am still waiting to grow up, I am still waiting to be a man,' Bolan told the teen-girl readership of *Jackie*. 'Bolan was someone that girls wanted to mother, rather than the person they wanted to be fucked by,' recalls Blackhill's Peter Jenner. 'He played to being a pretty boy. And very much a boy, not a man.'

'What the Pink Floyd do electronically, we do acoustically,' Bolan once said of Tyrannosaurus Rex. Lyrically and vocally that certainly applies, but sonically it seems a reach. The parallel is more with the incantatory fast-strummed folk of Richie P. Havens, or The Incredible String Band if they'd been rooted in rock'n'roll more than folk. Bolan and Took's sound was bass-less and backbeat-free, dominated instead by high-frequency tones: bright jangled acoustic guitar, shrill vocals and a tinkling array of exotic percussion, including African talking drums, finger cymbals and the Pixiephone, a 'little kid's xylophone' that Took found in Harrods' toy department.

As well as hand percussion, Took's department was improvised backing vocals – harmonies, but also chants and interjections. His menagerie of whinnies, whoops, hisses, sighs, gasps and mouth-percussion flurries is heard at its most out-there on 'Scenes of Dynasty', a track that consisted of just voices and loosely synched handclapping. 'I was never excited that much about Steve's drumming,' Bolan admitted. 'The one thing he did really well was sing . . . He really had harmony.'

Tyrannosaurus Rex songs often feel like spontaneous jams captured by a surreptitious microphone tucked beneath a toadstool in a forest glade. There's virtually nothing in the way of trendy psychedelic effects like phasing or the tape trickery that Abbey Road engineers provided for *The Piper at the Gates of Dawn*. One of the only exceptions is on the second album, 1968's *Prophets, Seers & Sages, The Angels of the Ages*: 'Deboraarobed'. As the disconcerting title hints, the song is an audio palindrome: exactly halfway through, it flips into reverse and ends with the beginning. It takes the listener a while to cotton on: at first, it just sounds like Bolan is incanting a lost, or newly invented, tongue.

At the core of each Tyrannosaurus Rex song is what sounds like a cosmic busker, whose strumming and warbling find the exact middle point between folk and rockabilly. The more percussively chittering songs resemble the clattery hippy jams that broke out spontaneously at free festivals or squat-land parties, the stoned-to-say-the-least throng picking up bongos, tambourines, bottles, saucepans and anything else at hand to clink.

More than Syd Barrett or The Incredible String Band, the biggest influences on Bolan at this time were literary: J. R. R. Tolkien and C. S. Lewis, the most widely read fantasy writers of the twentieth century, both of whom belonged to The Inklings, an Oxford cabal of like-minded scholars affronted by the modern world.

Some accounts suggest Bolan was a voracious reader; others assert he was dyslexic and June read Tolkien's work aloud to him. In one interview, Bolan spoke of listening to recordings of the books recited by Tolkien himself. Whatever the case, Tyrannosaurus Rex's debut album *My People Were Fair and Had Sky in Their Hair . . . But Now They're Content to Wear Stars on Their Brows* derived its ridiculously elongated title from a saying of Tom Bombadil from *Lord of the Rings.* And the album is dedicated to 'Aslan and the Old Narnians' – a reference to the Christ-like lion in C. S. Lewis's series of novels set in the magical world of Narnia.

In one of the first Tyrannosaurus Rex interviews, for the debut issue of underground paper *Gandalf's Garden*, Bolan explained that the group's name came from a childhood bout with measles: while confined to bed, he'd read about prehistoric dinosaurs and decided that it was plausible that 'they could have breathed fire and smoke', which proved that dragons could actually have existed. 'I relive my childhood through my songs, because I get inside things, like records and books, and live them.'

Ornately encrusted with arcane language, Bolan's early lyrics are a long way from the hit singles of T. Rex, the group that Tyrannosaurus Rex became. Instead of the succinct sexiness of 'Get It On', Bolan's

Tyrannosaurus Rex

My people were fair and had sky in their hair... But now they're content to wear stars on their brows

Steve Peregrin Took (left, in shades) and Marc Bolan (right, an eruption of ringlets) lurk amidst the fantastical illustrated cover of Tyrannosaurus Rex's 1968 debut

hippy-era songs resemble random collections of exotic-sounding or ancient words, faraway in time and in place. Words are ransacked from archaeology and anthropology, mythology and zoology. There's a profusion of bards and damsels, allusions to lost civilisations like the Incas and near-extinct tribes like the Shawnee. A panoply of antiquated weapons and vehicles (chariots were a favourite), garments and fabrics reel across your mind's eye, along with exotic substances like damask and chalcedony.

'The textures of the past interest me,' Bolan told *Gandalf's Garden*. 'I never write for the future. Names, strings of words, odd

books . . . names of herbs just break me up, freak me out completely.
I can groove a whole story out of just the name of a herb.' Rather
than telling tales, Tyrannosaurus Rex songs are braided together
through a non-narrative illogic, using tongue-twisty verbal-musical
effects like assonance, sibilance and internal rhyme: 'chants a crooning moon rune'; 'a tusk of boar with dwarfish awe'. And everywhere
there are creatures, some real, some extinct and some mythological:
ravens, dolphins, storks, pterodactyls, fauns.

All these areas out of which Tyrannosaurus Rex songs are woven –
archaeology, the animal kingdom, dinosaurs, fairy tales and fantasy
literature – are consuming passions and escape routes for children
(or used to be, before the Internet and video games). Perusing the
lyrics of the four Tyrannosaurus Rex albums, I realised that Bolan's
early songbook constituted an almost complete cross-section of my
interests between the ages of six and ten. My first ambition was
to be an archaeologist, parting fronds of Central American jungle
to uncover Mayan temples. Next I wanted to be a zoologist/orni-
thologist, observing ospreys through binoculars, making plaster
of Paris imprints of paw tracks. Then I decided to become a children's author, because I wanted to grow up to be a writer and that's
what I read at the time. *The Hobbit*, *The Lord of the Rings* and *The
Chronicles of Narnia* were particular passions: I must have reread
all of these three or four times each, before graduating to science
fiction and grown-up literature.

The back cover of *Prophets, Seers & Sages* features the text: 'in
the head of a man is a woman, in the head of a woman is a man,
but what wonders roam in the head of child'. The idea is that pre-
pubescence is a lost paradise of the imagination; the fall into sexuality clouds the mind, diminishing the capacity for visionary awe.
But given that Tyrannosaurus Rex's audience was post-pubescent
– hippies and student-age bohemians – and that sexual liberation
was an article of faith for the counterculture, what was the appeal

of innocence? 'Juniper Suction' may be the only Tyrannosaurus Rex song that's about making love, but it's oblique and oddly apprehensive in tone – something that would change when Bolan graduated to the raunch 'n' grind of T. Rex.

But even within the realm of pre-adolescent fantasy, the Tyrannosaurus Rex songbook shies away from the darker corners of children's literature: the English tradition of ghost stories and tales of the uncanny. It leaves out the scary parts of Tolkien too: the reality of evil and the grim necessity of girding one's loins to defeat it.

What Bolan seemed to take from Tolkien and Lewis was the idea of escaping the here-and-now, and the notion of world-creation. In his essay 'On Fairy Stories', Tolkien discusses the making-up of imaginary worlds as a form of playing God. The writer mirrors the Maker of all things by building 'a Secondary World'. Inside this 'sub-creation', everything that happens 'accords with the laws of that world' as invented by the writer. Tolkien, a professor of philology, went as far as devising several completely invented languages for the races of Middle Earth.

For Bolan, imagination provided a haven for his own bruised grandiosity, the humiliations imposed by reality. He described himself as 'a weird kid, very fucked up', who'd been 'very much into my own little world . . . I didn't boogie with people very much . . . I used to read a lot.' The books of Tolkien and Lewis inspired him to conjure up his own magical land, Beltane. This became the setting for a book Bolan wrote in early 1968 titled *The Krakenmist* (derived from John Wyndham's science-fiction novel *The Kraken Wakes*, whose own title came from Alfred Tennyson's poem, in turn inspired by Norse legends). At one point Bolan planned to write an entire concept album based around Beltane, but the only finished product was the song 'Beltane Walk', which appeared on the self-titled first album by T. Rex in 1970.

The appeal of these imaginary worlds for readers (or listeners in the case of Tyrannosaurus Rex) is that they create a sanctuary for the inner child, a mind garden secured and secluded from the cynical ways of the real world. Adult existence, organised around careerism and consumption, eroded the soul and callused the heart: in his correspondence as well as in interviews Bolan often referred to 'the *hard* world' or complained about how so-called real life was 'very harsh', a place of 'twitchy hang-ups' where 'most anything that is tender . . . is suspect'.

Perennial complaints, these, but they were especially prevalent and plangently felt in the late sixties. Tolkien's un-modernity was what made his books so huge with the hippies. He believed fantasy could offer both remedy and resistance in the face of disenchantment: a haven of 'freedom from the domination of observed "fact"'. *Lord of the Rings*, as literary critic Jenny Turner observed, was 'written to keep the modern world at bay'. Tolkien himself noted that 'the reader or the maker of fairy-stories' need not 'be ashamed of the "escape" of archaism, of preferring not just dragons but horses and not just elves but knights and kings to progressive things like factories . . . machine-guns . . . bombs'.

Despite deploying electric guitars, massive stacks of amplifiers, light shows and state-of-the-art studio technology, psychedelic rock distrusted technological progress outside the realm of its own art form. Bands like Traffic talked of 'getting our heads together in the country'; the new rock festivals chose pastoral settings for their tribal gatherings. Chiming with the back-to-nature spirit of the burgeoning commune movement, Bolan told the *NME* in 1968 that he disliked 'cities and the realities of modern life; I find plastic things repellent'. Speaking to *Fusion*, he claimed that the debut *My People Were Fair* consisted of 'wood-land songs . . . I wrote most of them in the country.'

On that album Bolan's friend John Peel – the British underground's leading DJ – recited a 'Woodland Story' in the vein of *The Wind in the Willows*. The protagonist, Kingsley Mole, daydreams about 'sunken galleons and pirate pictures of rusted doubloons and deep-water cabins stacked to the brim with musty muskets and goldfish gauntlets'. Peel also penned a tribute to the duo on the back sleeve: 'Tyrannosaurus Rex rose out of the sad and scattered leaves of an older summer. During the hard, grey winter they were tended and strengthened by those who love them. They blossomed with the coming of the spring, children rejoiced and the earth sang with them. It will be a long and ecstatic summer.'

Peel was Tyrannosaurus Rex's biggest supporter, playing their records on his radio shows and inviting them to perform at his DJ gigs. 'Peel was really hammering Marc and his music,' recalls Peter Jenner. 'And Peel was the tastemaker of the underground. He was a very strong live DJ, making really good money, and he gave half of it to Bolan and Took.' The constant exposure from these gigs and from sessions recorded for Peel's radio shows turned Tyrannosaurus Rex into one of the underground's leading groups.

Peel and his junior counterpart at the BBC's Radio One, Bob Harris, were crucial figures operating at the threshold between the underground and the overground. Other key mediation points were the weekly music magazine *Melody Maker* and the monthly *ZigZag*, along with the biggest-selling counterculture papers, such as *International Times* and *Oz*, and London listings magazine *Time Out* (at that time operating as a collective). The British counterculture's spiritual and geographical centre – approximately equivalent to Haight-Ashbury – lay in the west London neighbourhoods of Ladbroke Grove and Notting Hill Gate. In those days a funky, run-down part of London where immigrants and bohemians mingled uneasily, the area was home to the offices of underground magazines like *Frendz* and progressive labels like Island, hairy rockers like Hawkwind and The Pink Fairies, and to Marc Bolan himself, who lived with June Child in an attic flat on Blenheim Crescent.

There were outposts of counterculture similar to Ladbroke

Grove all across the UK: head shops, groovy clothes boutiques, record stores, arts labs and communal squats. The longhair community converged at the outdoor festivals, some of which were free and anarchic, while an increasing number were commercial and relatively well organised. Tyrannosaurus Rex played the first of a series of free concerts in Hyde Park, the brainchild of Peter Jenner.

The underground was more or less synonymous with university students. The college-gig circuit was crucial, providing progressive bands with direct access to a relatively open-minded audience, or at least one whose primary concern was not dancing. College gigs paid well too: the undergraduates in charge of booking had entertainment budgets flush with funds thanks to the dues paid automatically by every student to the National Union of Students. Regular club promoters complained bitterly that the university circuit was pricing certain bands out of the market.

Musically, the term 'underground' referred to a wide spectrum of music: bombastic heavy rock, the convoluted structures of prog-rock outfits who drew on classical or jazz influences, trippy space rock, folk-blues troubadours, and many other flavours. But despite the diversity, there were common traits and biases. Underground groups didn't bother themselves overly with image; or rather, they cultivated a studious anti-image. Increasingly, they didn't appear on their own record covers, which featured instead surreal or abstract artwork. With a few exceptions, these bands didn't go in for showmanship much either, preferring to let the music speak for itself and exuding an inwardly focused air during their extended solos and lengthy jams.

Above all, as far as the underground was concerned, rock was opposed to pop. 'Commercial' was a dirty word. This disdain went hand in hand with a lack of interest in the creative possibilities of the seven-inch single. Which worked out well, given that there was rarely anything remotely radio-friendly or succinct enough on their long-players to qualify as a single release. In some cases (notably post-Barrett Pink Floyd and Led Zeppelin) bands didn't bother to put out singles at all. Singles were for dancing and disco-theques; albums were for serious listeners. Bolan, in 1968–9, went along with this underground orthodoxy. When labels looked to sign Tyrannosaurus Rex, he recalled, his stance was 'I don't want to do a single, I want to do an album.'

As for image, by 1968 the underground's anti-pop attitude meant that a new, gritty, earth-toned look replaced the psychedelic fop-pishness of the swinging mid-sixties. The anti-style was defined by natural materials and ethnic fabrics, handcrafted garments, tie-dyed shirts and, above all, faded denim. Bell-bottom jeans were patched even when there was no hole to cover up. A heavy-handed signi-fier of make-and-mend folksiness, patched jeans communicated a distance from the mass-produced world of mainstream fashion. Symbolising practicality and informality, denim became the uni-form of the counterculture.

Perhaps the most revealing stylistic sign of the transition from mod to hippy aesthetics was hair: long and straight for women, shaggy or frizzed out into fake Afro for men. Beards suggested both a return to nature and an ascent to adulthood. For musicians it announced that you had left behind such pop fripperies as image and the requirement to appeal to teenage girls. The ultimate in anti-glam might be the drawings of a hippy couple – bearded nature-man and his bushy-pitted woman – getting it on in Alex Comfort's guide *The Joy of Sex*.

Steve Peregrin Took had a wispy little beard, but Bolan never grew one. (He looked like he was incapable, frankly.) But in other respects, Bolan the one-time mod went along with the hippy style. Photos of Tyrannosaurus Rex show him dressed down in scooped-neck shirts, jeans, floppy hats and other raggle-taggle garb.

Ideologically, too, Bolan completely adapted to underground

principles. He presented his creative process as uncalculated and intuitive, the songs coming from some higher plane. 'When I write the words and music come together, normally very roughly, but I start getting high on it and I just can't stop, until I blow my head off and it all comes bubbling up,' he told *Gandalf's Garden*. Bolan espoused the reigning shibboleths of authenticity and sincerity: 'I am saying what I am. I look like what I am, because it's too much of an effort to keep up an image.' He professed a complete indifference to commercial success or publicity. Tyrannosaurus Rex, he said, were starting to get paid for gigs now, 'but we are still doing it for free this summer. We have permission from the council to use the bandstand in certain parks known to us all, as long as we don't advertise it.' He was happy to talk to *Gandalf's Garden* because it was 'a nice scene', but otherwise Tyrannosaurus Rex would not be 'doing interviews at all, ever, as far as I'm concerned'.

Given that he went to the absolute other extreme with T. Rex – releasing singles, chasing stardom, revelling in luxury, doing countless interviews – it's tempting to assume that Bolan was simply biding his time in the underground, opportunistically playing the hippy role. But I think it's more likely that he had a situational relationship with belief. Impressionable and chameleonic, Bolan's course through the sixties sees him bending like a reed in the prevailing winds of fashion and zeitgeist. Yet deep within his seemingly malleable character lay the intractable inner steel of self-belief. This combination of flexibility and will-to-fame is a syndrome shared by many of the key figures in glam, something manifested even more clearly with Bowie – a fellow traveller with the underground, and similarly convincing in playing the part of true believer.

In her memoir *Real Life*, Marsha Hunt – briefly a UK pop star with 'Walk on Gilded Splinters' – remembers a dalliance with the hippy-era Bolan, a love affair she characterises as an attraction of opposites. 'I personified things which Marc rejected. He was reclusive, macrobiotic . . . He had no money and acted as though he was opposed to it on social grounds . . . He teased me about my success. I almost believed he spurned it . . . To Marc, my visibility was commercial, and this wasn't appropriate for the serious art of music which he implied was validated by obscurity.'

If Marc-the-hippy was just a role he was playing, a form of pandering to his underground cult, surely he would have felt comfortable enough to drop the facade with his pop-star girlfriend? Bolan's prickly teasing of Hunt suggests that at that moment he believed in what he was saying with all his fickle heart. This isn't hypocrisy as we commonly understand it, more a case of someone entering into an act so totally it becomes real. For his part, Steve Took – who eventually left Tyrannosaurus Rex to pursue more street-radical music with The Pink Fairies – never believed that Bolan had only ever been pretending. 'I guess for a while Marc was a good hippy,' Took recalled at the height of T. Rex's success. 'We used to sit around and rap about what needed changing.'

Whatever the case, in just a few years' time Marc would sound a totally different tune: singing songs about the Rolls-Royce he'd bought (despite not being able to drive!) and boasting to *The Weekly News* that 'today I'm not making 40 pounds a week but 40 pounds a second'. (An astronomical exaggeration typical of Bolan, since it would amount to annual earnings of £1 billion.)

When someone asked him where Steve Took was these days, he quipped heartlessly: 'Oh, in a gutter somewhere.'

Tyrannosaurus Rex were actually pretty successful commercially: they even scored two Top 40 hits with 'Debora' and 'One Inch Rock' (before Bolan took against singles), and *My People Were Fair* and the third album, *Unicorn*, both reached the Top 15 of the album chart. But by the end of 1969, the group had hit an album-sales ceiling of somewhere between 13,000 and 17,000. That lust for grander fame – dampened for a while by the underground ethos – began to build up inside Bolan again, inspiring an original move later copied by subsequent cult figures such as Adam Ant: the strategic sell-out, the underground/overground flip. A gamble, because you could end up alienating the original cosy cult following without winning a wider audience.

Bolan started making tentative steps in this direction with the fourth – and, it would turn out, final – Tyrannosaurus Rex album, 1970's *Beard of Stars*. He started playing electric guitar again. Took had left, and his replacement on percussion, Mickey Finn, while not nearly as creative with the exotic textures, brought a funkier feel to the music. Electric bass featured on some songs too, played by Bolan. But these changes didn't quite amount to a full-blown rhythm section. Tyrannosaurus Rex weren't radio ready yet, but 'By the Light of a Magical Moon' hinted at the bubblegum-boogie future. Bolan and producer Tony Visconti tacked on the sound of girls screaming, as if invoking – even magically summoning – the fandemonium to come. Probably Bolan remembered Simon Napier-Bell doing the same trick on John's Children's *Orgasm*.

By the end of 1970, Tyrannosaurus Rex had condensed their name to T. Rex and released a self-titled album, as if to highlight the sense of a fresh start. *T. Rex* still had one foot in the underground, but the other stepped confidently towards the studio stage of *Top of the Pops*. On 'Seagull Woman' and 'Beltane Walk', the classic T. Rex sound is present and correct: the groove struts, the Visconti-arranged strings sashay, the guitar riff grinds thick and bluesy, and the chorus is pure sugar. But there are also songs like the eldritch 'Children of Rarn', a fragment from Bolan's never-completed concept album/book about prehistoric Earth and primordial races with names like the Dworns and the Lithons. Somewhere between these poles of pop concision and rambling acid rock lay Bolan's remake of 'The Wizard', his very first single. The new version sounds like it has chart potential until it takes off into a choppy, ragged groove, with Bolan's endlessly looping chant 'He was a wizard and he was my friend he was' devolving into shrieked babble and yapping. It's a thrilling valediction to the underground.

The year 1970 is often described as a pause: the null lull before the glam storm. It was a treading-water year, with most major groups of the sixties either recently split up ('divorces' in some cases caused by marriage, as with The Beatles) or ailing. The supergroups vaunted as their replacement, such as Blind Faith, lacked the organic (precisely because accidental) gang bond to make them lasting propositions. During 1970, impatience began to build for the new decade to get going – for a seventies sound that would slice through the stale ideas and congealed ideals still hanging around from the previous decade like leftovers in the fridge.

In the UK, it would be T. Rex who would kick-start the new era of pop.

Somewhere between *Beard of Stars* and *T. Rex*, Bolan totally reversed his attitude to singles, deciding that far from a commercial distraction they were 'energy bursts', missives propelled into the wider world that could 'turn people on'. He told *ZigZag*, 'I see no reason why the freaks shouldn't be represented in the charts.' This shift in attitude was provoked by inner restlessness, his ego's need for a larger stage than that offered by the cult audience. But it was also a response to external developments: the return of rock'n'roll to the pop marketplace. Bolan's twitchy antennae sensed which way the culture was moving, how and where he needed to position himself.

Norman Greenbaum's 'Spirit in the Sky', a glorious fuzzed-up stomper that reached #1 in the UK in early 1970, was an example of this proto-glam sound. Around the same time, John Lennon's

'Instant Karma!' was a Top 5 hit on both sides of the Atlantic. Lennon had asked Phil Spector for a fifties sound, but the producer had pushed Alan White's bashy drums way further up front than would have been acceptable or even possible in the original rock'n'roll era. 'Instant Karma!' and the Spector-produced solo album *John Lennon/Plastic Ono Band* that followed later in 1970 'influenced me incredibly', Bolan would later admit. 'The drum sound . . .' Finally, there was Mungo Jerry's 'In the Summertime', an old-timey strum-along topped with a quavery vocal not a million miles away from Bolan's. 'Summertime' reached #1 in nineteen countries and spent seven weeks at the top of the UK charts. 'It killed Marc that Mungo Jerry got a #1 with his voice,' says Napier-Bell. 'That was the moment, really, when he couldn't wait another minute.'

'The Fifties rock era is where my head is at . . . The feel of the Fifties is very important,' Bolan told the *NME* a few years into his pop stardom. In truth, it had always been part of his DNA, even in Tyrannosaurus Rex, but it had been cloaked by the hippy-dippy acoustic folksiness, peeping out now and then in songs like 'Hot Rod Mama' and 'One Inch Rock'. As soon as he plugged in an electric guitar again, his love for and indebtedness to Eddie Cochran, Chuck Berry, Ricky Nelson's guitarist James Burton and others became more apparent. If you've a mind to, it's possible to forensically break down T. Rex tunes and trace their riff components to songs by Little Richard, Chuck Berry, Howlin' Wolf, Jimmy McCracklin and more. Sometimes Bolan liked to work in the equivalent of citations, lyrical lifts that pointed to the original song he was remaking: 'Meanwhile, I'm still thinking' during the fade of 'Get It On' nods to Berry's 'Little Queenie', while 'Telegram Sam' doffs its hat to 'Smokestack Lightning' with the line 'I'm a howlin' wolf.'

But the end product didn't come across like studious replication: T. Rex were the fifties if it had somehow come *after* the sixties. Rock'n'roll, but with everything that historically followed folded into it: the hallucinatory Englishness of 'Strawberry Fields' and 'See Emily Play'; the folkadelic whimsy of Donovan's 'Jennifer Juniper' and The Incredible String Band's *The Hangman's Beautiful Daughter*.

A fantasy version of the fifties filtered into Bolan's lyrics too, which started to lose their flowery verbosity. 'A lot of people think that because I've got away from long visual descriptions that I'm no longer a poet,' Bolan told *ZigZag*. 'But what I'm writing now is poetry of the heart really.' Antiquity was displaced somewhat with science fiction (the flying saucer of 'The Planet Queen'), but mostly there was a new emphasis on the post-Second World War Americanised present. As glam scholar Philip Auslander has observed, Bolan had always shown a decidedly non-pastoral penchant for cars ('Mustang Ford', 'Hot Rod Mama') that would have made J. R. R. Tolkien frown. In Tyrannosaurus Rex, he compared his paramours to exotic fauna; in T. Rex, the paeans started to include lines such as 'Like a car you're pleasing to behold' ('Jeepster') and 'You're built like a car / Hubcap diamond star halo' ('Get It On'). In 'Children of the Revolution', he invented bling a quarter of a century ahead of schedule, boasting, 'I drive a Rolls-Royce / 'Cos it's good for my voice.'

'Ride a White Swan', T. Rex's first hit, has still not completely shaken off the hippy era: the vehicle in question is powered by wings rather than the combustion engine, while Druids pop up in the lyrics. T. Rex were sending out mixed messages. They embarked on a big tour with ticket prices kept to a low 50 pence as a move to court impoverished teenyboppers, yet the concert ads described the band as the 'Last of the Great Underground Groups'. But unlike the Tyrannosaurus Rex days – when Bolan strummed cross-legged – the singer was now up and boogieing onstage, riding the groove supplied by the newly acquired rhythm section of Steve Currie (bass) and Bill Legend (drums). Although 'Ride a White Swan' was recorded before they joined, the single had a boppy insistence perfect for the discotheque floor. The single rose slowly and steadily, taking two months to reach its peak of #2 in late January 1971. It was blocked from the top spot only by the sentimental novelty single 'Grandad', by Clive Dunn and a chorus of schoolgirls.

Those tweenage girls were soon screaming at Marc Bolan, the first real pop idol of the new decade. 'Hot Love', released in February 1971, was the decisive blow. Curiously, it was a twelve-bar blues at bottom. 'I wanted to make a twelve-bar record a hit, which hasn't been done since "Hi-Heel Sneakers" really,' Bolan told *ZigZag*, referencing the 1964 tune by Tommy Tucker. He claimed 'Hot Love' took just ten minutes to write: 'We got very lushed one night, had about four bottles of brandy, it was about 4 in the morning, and we just did it.' The song was certainly simple, but there was nothing throwaway about the honeyed glisten of Visconti's production, the honed details of the arrangement. 'Hot Love' was the first Bolan record to feature back-up from Howard Kaylan and Mark Volman, formerly of The Turtles and later, as Flo & Eddie, associates of Frank Zappa and The Mothers of Invention. Swoony and swaying, Kaylan and Volman's backing vocals brought a creamy pitch of hysteria to the T. Rex sound, taken to the dizzy limit on the long 'Hey Jude'-like fade of 'Hot Love'.

From its chugging bluesy groove to the vaguely doo-wop backing vocals, there was essentially nothing new about 'Hot Love'. And yet everything about it is new, or at least fresh: the feel, the slink, the lightness. That comes down partly to Visconti's production, but most of all to Bolan's personality and presence, proving that you can be an original without being innovative in any measurable way. Talent borrows, genius steals.

Bluesy but not ballsy, 'Hot Love' teases the budding sexuality of girls between the ages of eleven and fifteen. Bolan plays a soft-voiced, almost gentlemanly vassal, 'a labourer of love', offering the coyest of come-ons: 'I don't mean to be bold but may I hold your hand?' When he utters the title phrase, he sounds like it's he who's melting in surrender. 'Hot Love' is the song where Bolan starts to introduce his repertoire of choked gasps and muttered moans – sounds that in concert elicited the biggest screams from the girls.

Just as vital for Bolan's successful seduction of the mass teen-girl audience was his newly feminised image: satin jackets, feather-boa scarves, a fur coat borrowed from June's mother and, for the *Top of the Pops* performances that inaugurated the whole glam era, a speckle of glitter on his cheekbones. Legend disagrees on where this bright idea originated: June, or his new manager Chelita Secunda, or a sudden impulse from Marc himself. Bolan expert Dave Mantell pinpoints the second of T. Rex's 'Hot Love' appearances on *Top of the Pops* as the turning point. Bolan wore a 'shiny silver sailor suit . . . made of velvet but looking like satin or even lamé', with a 'plunging neckline', and kept 'erupting into girlish giggling' throughout the performance. During the long, scarf-waving, la-la-la-la-la-la-la outro, girls from the studio audience danced onstage and this 'image was superimposed onto that of the smiling silver-clad pretty-boy' – symbolically sealing Bolan's identification with his new audience.

Bolan knew that his look, and good looks, played a mighty role in T. Rex's crossover; he grasped that unlike rock, pop worked as an audio-visual phenomenon, experienced by most young fans as a flash of sensations, with image, sound, words and gestures indivisible. 'Ninety-five percent of my success is the way I *look*,' he told *Creem*, adding that it had been no different with The Beatles or the Stones, as much as they now claimed to have outgrown the pop audience. Look and presence was 'what people pick up on. The music is secondary. You do have to have good music . . . but initially, it's got nothing to do with music.'

Yet if you look at live footage of T. Rex at their peak, such as the huge London concerts of spring 1972, it's remarkable how untheatrical and glitz-free they are compared with later glam stars or your average pop performer in the twenty-first century. There's no stage set or props, apart from a life-size cut-out of Marc at the edge of the stage. The lighting is poor and the rest of the group look pretty scruffy; even Bolan's glam is limited to a satin jacket and feathery scarf.

At the Wembley mega-concert, T. Rex play like a scrappy garage band, barely holding it together. Bolan's bopping and jiving is unchoreographed, based simply around his own innate funkiness and a flair for copping moves from his precursors: Chuck Berry's duck walk, guitar-wielding gestures from Pete Townshend and Jimi Hendrix. His only real 'routine' was the Jimi-like manoeuvre of frenziedly frotting his fretboard with a tambourine, generating a scree of scraped noise, and then hurling it up the neck of his guitar and into the audience: a mime of masturbation, with the tossed tambourine as an arc of ejaculate.

Bolan's effeminate clothing (he was petite enough to wear women's shoes) raised questions about his sexuality. Rumours circulated, like the one about Bolan wanting to have a sex change and marry percussionist Mickey Finn, himself a fey figure with his long dark hair, slender build and Pre-Raphaelite pallor. Bolan enjoyed the confusion his ambiguity invited. He told one interviewer a tale about being approached by girls at the Speakeasy club asking if he was 'a fag'. Nodding yes, he asked, 'Had they got any little brothers at home?' and gleefully mimed for the journalist the horrified expressions of the girls.

In March 1970, Bolan talked to *ZigZag* magazine about his comfort with homosexuality and his own bi-curious leanings: 'Sexually, I believe that one should love what one loves, and I quite enjoy the Greek idea of two warriors going to war and mentally being very close – they didn't actually screw each other on the battlefield, but mentally they were really into each other.' Later, in the twilight of his idol-hood, Bolan defined his sexual make-up with an endearingly down-to-earth specificity, telling *Record Mirror* that he was 'bisexual, but I believe I'm more heterosexual 'cos I definitely like boobs. I always wished that I was 100 per cent gay, it's much easier . . . as I say I've checked it all out, and I prefer chicks.'

Sex – and dancing, its public surrogate – had never played a prominent part in Tyrannosaurus Rex. But they became virtually everything with T. Rex. Explaining the departure of Steve Took and T. Rex's new danceable direction, Bolan told the *NME*, 'I've always been a bit of a wiggler . . . Really, the split with Peregrin was partially due to the fact I wanted to boogie.'

'Boogie' was the word of the hour: Marc described his songs as 'boogie mind poems'; the T. Rexploitation movie was titled *Born to Boogie*; and Fly, his old label, rushed out a compilation called *Bolan Boogie*. The word has a long history, traceable back to boogie-woogie, a piano-oriented style of blues designed for dancing that emerged in the early decades of the twentieth century. It filtered into numerous corners of American popular and roots music, as far apart as The Andrews Sisters and John Lee Hooker, whose 'Boogie Chillen' may be where Bolan picked it up. Although most seem to believe it comes from the same murky etymological past as 'boogeyman', an alternative explanation roots it in French Louisiana and the word *'bouger'*, meaning 'to move'. That's an attractive notion given boogie's whole other life in the late seventies and eighties as a disco buzzword: 'Boogie Nights', 'Blame It on the Boogie', 'Boogie Wonderland' . . .

But in the early seventies, ironically enough, boogie was just about the least glam music around, purveyed by bands like Humble Pie, British sweat-hogs who were huge on the American arena circuit and whose debut single, 'Natural Born Bugie', reached #4 in the UK in late 1969. Beardy American blues scholars Canned Heat recorded 'Refried Boogie', a single riff stretched over forty minutes and *both sides* of a disc from the double LP *Livin' the Blues*.

Although boogie is technically defined by a 4/4 rhythm subdivided by twelve rather than sixteen notes, most listeners can detect its presence by feel: a black-and-bluesy swing, a syncopated funky shuffle. Boogie was rock you could dance to, appealing on a tactile or even reptilian-brain level at a time when too much rock was getting overly sophisticated or laidback. In America, 'Boogie!' became the bleary rallying cry of the denim-clad arena hordes wasted on booze and Quaaludes.

Bypassing the ham-fisted heterosexism of the boogie boors, Bolan made the idiom his own: slinky, almost daintily androgynous. His most beautiful boogie was 'Get It On', the #1 single that followed hard on the heels of 'Hot Love'. That exquisite flick-of-the-wrist riff, with horns gently pummelling underneath as support. The chorus, shadowed by backing vocals like a ghostly echo. The immortal line 'You're dirty and sweet and you're my girl.' To find another song with such a perfect balance of erotic urgency and ethereal languor, you'd have to look outside rock altogether, to the songs of Al Green or the Marvin Gaye of 'Got to Give It Up'.

This sublime blend of dirty grind and elfin delicacy stretched itself cat-like across both sides of *Electric Warrior*, the second T. Rex album – Bolan's finest album by far, an almost perfect platter. Although the ominous, murky cover shows Bolan grappling with an axe next to a speaker stack, it's not a heavy album. Electric guitar is used sparingly, in fact. Instead, tracks like 'Planet Queen' and 'Cosmic Dancer' share a peculiarly translucent sound. Full-kit drums, choppy acoustic guitar, rambling bassline and strings supply the propulsion, but the absence of a driving central riff conjures a sense of empty expanse.

'Cosmic Dancer' is a mixture of memoir and mission statement – 'I danced myself right out the womb / Is it strange to dance so soon?' – that abandons mystic doggerel for an exquisite guitar solo, billowing eerily like a film of cigarette smoke run in reverse. 'Life's a Gas' is Marc's 'eternal boy' manifesto, in which Bolan impishly glides right past all the bring-down spoilers of good vibe, all those scolding allies of the reality principle. Like 'Hot Love', but sidling along at ballad tempo, 'Life's a Gas' is blues-without-the-blues, climaxing with another gorgeous solo that finds nothing in the world to worry about.

Elsewhere on *Electric Warrior* things get more raunchy. 'Jeepster' contains some of his best sexy nonsense and love poesy ever: 'You've got the universe reclining in your hair.' Released as the follow-up single to 'Get It On', 'Jeepster' was another massive hit. Most of Bolan's biggest singles were paeans to a foxy female, a role that every teen girl could imagine herself playing. He very consciously turned his attention to the '95% of our audience', by his own estimate, that were girls going through sexual awakening and looking for an erotic but unthreatening fantasy object. 'Motivate', meaning 'to turn on', was one of his favourite words, as in 'Your motivation is so sweet' in 'Jeepster', or 'The Motivator', which declared, 'I love the clothes you wear,' among them a 'velvet hat . . . the one that caused a revolution'.

Revolution might be overstating it, but there was certainly something insurrectionary about the delirium incited by Marc. 'Return of the Scream-Age Idol' shrieked the front cover of *Melody Maker*'s 20 November 1971 edition. Inside, the feature bore the headline 'Prophet of a New Generation'.

Pundits rushed to identify Bolan as 'that fabled commodity: A Successor To The Beatles', something the record business had dreamed of for years now, with particular pangs during 1969–70, when single sales sank to unheard-of lows as the mature-but-dowdy album scene took over. Industry insiders worried that the coming demographic of teens and pre-teens would lose interest in pop altogether if nothing stepped in to supply their need for raw excitement, instant-impact singles, danceable beats and visually stimulating heroes to lust after, or identify with. It was with a combination of relief and vicarious excitement, then, that people like promoter Tony Smith invoked the Stones and Beatles when celebrating the way Bolan 'speaks to a whole new generation of young kids, whose average age seems to be about 15, if not younger'.

The statistics bore out the comparison with The Beatles' exploits. In their first year of chart-topping success, T. Rex sales accounted for 3.5 per cent of the entire British record market. They had three #1 albums in the same year – *Electric Warrior*, the *Bolan Boogie* comp and another release that repackaged the first two Tyrannosaurus Rex LPs as a two-fer – a feat previously achieved only by, you guessed it, The Beatles. In further Fab Four flashbacks, Bolan belatedly shifted 20,000 copies of his 1969 poetry book *The Warlock of Love*, an echo of Lennon's success with *In My Own Write*, and soon he had so much clout he was able to form his own Apple-like label through EMI, the T. Rex Wax Co. (although unlike the Beatles' imprint, it would never release anything apart from Bolan's own records).

More gratifying still, Lennon and McCartney anointed Bolan as a worthy successor. Lennon hailed T. Rex as 'good rock 'n' roll; it has a good beat and it really swings'. He pinpointed Bolan's way with words as particularly praiseworthy: 'His way of writing is new and I have never read lyrics as funny and as real as his.' Ringo Starr became a bosom buddy of Bolan's, copped some Marc moves with his solo hit 'Back Off Boogaloo' and directed the debut T. Rex movie, *Born to Boogie*. Commentators noted the symbolic chang-ing of the pop guard when, at the 1972 Wembley concerts, Starr was completely ignored by the screaming young fans as he stood in the photographers' pit filming the gig.

What really sealed the comparison between T. Rextasy and Beatlemania was the fervour of the fans. Bolan-believers even imi-tated his look: the hair, the clothes, the eye make-up, the glitter and gold stars affixed to cheekbones.

How did Bolan do it? Why him? Considered coldly, he was a quirky, rather limited singer; a middling guitarist by the standards of his time; a sometimes inspired but erratic songwriter and lyricist. But he had 'it', the X-factor that entertainment industries sift through a mass of hopeful contenders in hope of finding, the star quality that they control and mass-market and exploit but can never manufacture out of thin air. Tony Visconti described Bolan as possessing more personal magnetism than anyone he'd ever met: 'light emanated from him'. He overflowed with charm, a word that nowadays simply means attractive but which carries a magical undertone. He had an amazing smile – so cartoon-wide it seemed to twinkle at each corner of his mouth – that hovered just the right side of the line between charm and smarm, not spoiled one bit by his awareness of its dazzling power.

In *Revolt into Style*, his 1970 history of 'the pop arts', George Melly insists that magic is far more important than talent, adding that 'magic is more precisely described as "charisma", a form of magic halo emanating from objects, people or places which gives them power over and above their measurable qualities'. 'Charisma' itself is an utterly devalued word today, as empty as 'iconic'. But its original meaning was thoroughly mystical. As a word it goes back as far as the Ancient Greeks (*'charis'* means grace, glow, a divinely bestowed gift). But it was really codified as a religious concept by St Paul in the Epistles circa AD 50. Charisma could be the attribute of a gifted preacher, a miracle-worker, someone endowed with gifts of oratory or oracular utterance. But charisma could also be possessed by the congregation itself, which in the early days of the Christian church was more like a band of outcasts than the hierarchical bureaucracies of subsequent centuries. It is arguable that charisma of this kind – collective single-mindedness – is a 'vibe' that generates itself within any cultic group that shares a marginal world view and renegade value system.

T. Rextasy peaks with two concerts at Wembley on the same night,
18 March 1972. Ringo Starr – there filming *Born to Boogie* – finally
experiences Beatles-level fandemonium as an outside observer

Bolan himself used charisma in this way when reminiscing about
the mod mid-sixties. 'There was a great charisma about that time,'
he told the *NME* in 1972. Charismatic energy emerged from the
cult and was then projected onto a focal figure: the mods came first,

then the mod bands like The Who and Small Faces. Time and again you see this process play out within music subcultures, from rock to rave: the people (meaning always a particular tribe rather than the general public) have the power, but they transfer it voluntarily to leaders produced from their own ranks.

According to Len Oakes, author of *Prophetic Charisma*, the typical candidate for the role of cult leader has a narcissistic personality, combining 'grandiose self-confidence', enormous energy, skills of seduction and manipulation, and a striking lack of self-doubt. Okay, that sounds like most pop stars, or indeed just about everybody involved in the performing arts. But when Oakes lists the characteristics of charismatic sects – congregations that erupt into frenzy, abandon, raising of hands, shaking, rocking and fainting; believers possessed by 'dreadful Tremblings in their Bodies' who emit shrieks and roars – it sounds an awful lot like rock'n'roll, like disco, like rave and other eruptions of enthused dance culture. Look at the Wembley footage documented on *Born to Boogie* – the teenage girls (and occasional teenage boy) spasming and jacking at the waist, mouths screaming so wide you see the fillings and stringy filaments of saliva, hands outstretched and beseeching to the god-man. That's some ole-time religion.

Commentators at the time picked up on this born-again aspect of T. Rextasy. The *NME*'s Tony Tyler noted 'the almost mesmeric control' Bolan had over his fans at concerts. 'For thousands of Rexmaniacs, secure in their fundamentalist faith, it burned with all the fervour of a religio-sensual experience. A Dionysian Rite of Spring in which they flocked to pay frenzied devotive offerings.' The delirium could get dangerous. At the Boston Gliderdrome, a 6,000-capacity venue in Lincolnshire, thirty-three fans fainted. One girl was taken to hospital, with confused reports claiming she'd either tumbled over the balcony in her excitement or had her shoulder broken when a TV light on the balcony fell onto her.

As with earlier and later examples of fandemonium, an industry of exploitation sprang up instantly, offering T. Rex merchandise of every kind. The official T. Rex Fan Club soon swelled to 6,000 members and received thousands of letters every week, many of them enquiring as to the truth of the gruesome rumours that tend to swirl around pop idols: 'Is it true that Marc is dying of leukaemia or kidney disease?' In one profile of Bolan, June reads out a fan letter: 'I will do anything, any time, for/to/or with you. Delete whichever is inapplicable. Please send me any food, nail cuttings, clothes, anything you may have touched.'

'Is there an anti-T. Rex fan club anywhere in Britain?' asked Gerald Levy of Middleton, Lancashire, writing in to *Melody Maker*'s letters page in early 1972. The music papers were convulsed with letters decrying or defending Bolan. Some of the irritation stemmed from the overkill coverage Marc was receiving, with barely a week going by without some kind of Bolan story (even his publicist extraordinaire B. P. Fallon got profiled). Other complaints came from prog-rock believers, who denounced Bolan's 'banal chord progressions' and described him as 'the worst disaster ever to befall the British pop music scene', singlehandedly undoing 'the whole progression and maturity drive of the last decade'. And then, of course, there were the old Tyrannosaurus Rex fans wishing he would change his mind and go back to singing about runes and Rarn. *International Times* spoke for the embittered underground flock when they ran a special 'Bolan – Who Needs Him?' cover.

Nineteen seventy-two was when T. Rextasy peaked, with massive concerts, a string of #1 and #2 singles and the release of the *Born to Boogie* film. But by the end of the year, there was a definite feeling of exhaustion – creative, mental, physical on the part of the idol himself, and in terms of the phenomenon itself having crested and begun its descent.

Number 1 in May 1972, 'Metal Guru' was in some ways the ultimate T. Rex song: a jingle, really, a verse-chorus looping endlessly amid a caramel swirl of sickly-sweet sound. But it was the first indication of a thinness to Bolan's new material. It also showed signs of messianic navel-gazing. As music critic Neil Kulkarni observes, the question 'Metal guru / Is it you?' seemed to be Bolan talking to himself, assessing his own candidacy as generational leader. In interviews he talked hazily about the song being about the 'godhead' and isolation, and further claimed that he was hatching a film script around the concept of 'a cosmic messiah . . . a messenger from God who has to check up on planet Earth . . . God has not returned to the planet since [Eden]. He expects a race of gods and what he finds is this mess.'

'Metal Guru' was the lead track on *The Slider*, which Bolan boasted had achieved a new sound 'totally different from anything we've done . . . softer but harder. Like liquid concrete.' But apart from the sexy, languid title track and the earlier single 'Telegram Sam', the album was patchy. *The Slider* stalled at #4 in the UK album chart, a dismaying sign of a different sort of slide.

Ironically, just as fans and observers began to accuse Bolan of repetitiousness and self-plagiarism, he rallied with a spurt of three of T. Rex's most original and different-sounding singles. The lyrics showed further evidence of a messianic complex, but musically 'Children of the Revolution' was drastically slower than his previous hit singles, its strings-propelled lurch-groove making it a sort of bubblegum precursor to Led Zeppelin's 'Kashmir'.

Described by its creator as 'a very fast rockaboogie', the next single, 'Solid Gold Easy Action', was the missing link between The Dave Clark Five's 'Bits and Pieces' and Captain Beefheart's 'Sun Zoom Spark': a jarring sawtooth riff, followed by a jolting 'Hey! Hey! Hey!' chant synched to bash-bash-bash beats, followed by a

Bo Diddley shuffle, then a chorus so cloying it's like Black Forest gateau squooshed into your ear canal.

Then came '20th Century Boy', Bolan's punkest statement ever. He described this single as 'erection rock . . . purely an energy record . . . some of it quotes Muhammed Ali . . . I think that every man in the 20th Century is a superstud and the record's meant for him.' Kicked off with a blasting riff, the song struts with near-parodic machismo, Bolan virtually rapping lines like 'sting like a bee' but still offering himself as a plaything ('I wanna be your toy'). Backed with raspy female soul vocals that recall Merry Clayton on 'Gimme Shelter', the song heads out in a Stooges/*Funhouse*-like bedlam of honking sax, pummelled rhythm, tambourine and garbled, or even gargled, vocals from Bolan, an absurd caricature of menace that nonetheless is a little disturbing.

A few years before T. Rextasy, George Melly argued that a primitive religious impulse underlay the erotic frenzy of teen-fan mania: 'Throughout history religious enthusiasm at this level is frequently indistinguishable from sexual hysteria. Equally mysterious is the sudden extinction of dangerous divinity in any one artist or group . . . the screaming stops, the crowd dissolves . . .' Melly is right about the arbitrary fall of idols in pop, but in the case of Bolan there are mundane explanations for the vertiginously swift decline. Unlike The Beatles or the Stones, Bolan was entirely dependent on his own creative resources: his band were subordinates, not foils off which he could spark or who could take up the slack when it came to songwriting.

And for all his talk of stretching out into other avenues of artistic expression, Bolan was not a polymath like his friend David Bowie. He couldn't act, or script-write, to save his life. *Born to Boogie* was a farrago, interweaving electrifying footage from the Wembley concerts with pseudo-surreal, semi-improvised interludes filmed on John Lennon's estate. Talking to the *NME*, Bolan raved about a scene in which Ringo Starr (as the Dormouse) and Bolan (as the Mad Hatter) declaim 'Byron type poetry in a bright red Cadillac – all very camp – and we end up singing "Tutti Frutti".' Be warned: a pissed-off dwarf also appears, munching the Caddy's wing mirror.

Bolan was also feeling the pressure of fame, which he compared to being pinned against the wall by hundreds of invisible people. Already in April 1972, he talks in interviews of being reclusive, about how fame gives so much but what it takes away is irreplaceable, like brain cells. 'I've never felt so insecure, or such pain as I do now, because I'm so exposed musically,' Bolan complained. 'What I'm playing and singing is a projection of my real self.' One of the better tracks on *The Slider*, 'Main Man' contained the revealing lines: 'As a child I laughed a lot . . . now it seems I cry a lot.' Elaborating to *Melody Maker*, he confessed, 'I've never cried so much in my whole life as this last year.'

Premonitions of death darkened his thoughts: 'I don't know whether I'm going to be around for much longer as a human being . . . I honestly feel it could all end tomorrow. Not just the band thing – I mean life.' He fantasised about giving it all up, perhaps becoming an archaeologist in Egypt.

A huge blow to Bolan's ego came with T. Rex's failure to duplicate their British success in America. 'Get It On', retitled 'Bang a Gong', made the Top 10. But T. Rex's sound tumbled into the Grand Canyon-sized chasm between FM and AM radio in America. FM was the domain of the progressive underground, the hairy freaks, and they found T. Rex too lightweight and poppy. The AM stations were pure pop, the home of The Carpenters or boy bands like The Osmonds; T. Rex still had too many cosmic trappings for this market.

T. Rex toured the States repeatedly during 1972–4, with variable reactions. A new breed of glitter fans in Los Angeles flocked to their gig in Santa Monica, but San Francisco's longhairs – still hung up on the city's acid-rock heyday – greeted Bolan's pop-star antics with indifference. *Melody Maker's* Roy Hollingworth, reporting on a late-1972 American tour, noted the awkwardness: the seductive ploys that worked so well at home when Bolan was dealing with TV-converted kids just fell flat with an older audience 'that don't move, groove, wet themselves, dance, or get up and scream'. When Bolan threw a towel into the audience, 'nobody caught it'. It was humiliating. And it's proof that charisma is a gift bestowed by the congregation as much as an inherent property of the prophet or priest, a mutually reinforcing confidence trick that loops back and forth between audience and star.

Stung by the reviews from America, Bolan launched into damage-limitation mode, with a November 1972 *Melody Maker* interview that the paper cruelly titled 'Marc: I Wasn't a U.S. Flop!' He denied reports that a packed gig in New York was really what people in the concert-promoter world call a 'papered house', i.e. partly achieved through giving away free tickets. He boasted that there was interest in America in a thirty-nine-week TV series in the style of the Jackson 5 cartoons, with Bolan himself writing the script. It was premium Bolan bullshit, and no one was buying it.

By early 1973, it was essentially all over.

But let's not dwell too long on the decline and falter. The cocaine and champagne. The weight gain and the terrible haircut. The rising paranoia and the undignified jibes at Bowie, who ascended to a level of artistic credibility and respect that Bolan would never achieve. There were sporadic glimmers of the old brilliance on later albums like *Tanx* (1973) and *Dandy in the Underworld* (1977). A smatter of killer singles: the elegiac 'Teenage Dream' and the goofy 'New York City', both decent-sized hits, and the proto-punky 'Laser Love', an undeserved flop.

Wipe the years of decay from your mind and dwell on his peak. What can be made of the Bolan phenomenon? Pop-cult analyst

Pete Fowler complained that T. Rextasy, unlike Beatlemania or rock'n'roll in the fifties, wasn't 'pure'. Bolan, like Bowie, was too self-conscious, too aware of the mechanics of fan identification and the rise-and-fall cycles of stardom. In 1965, in one of his first interviews, Bolan was already looking ahead to the serenity and wisdom of post-stardom life: 'Besides, once I get over the fame, I will know where I stand.' Bolan was schooled in the music press, which he'd read devotedly since 1962, and had kept all the back copies for reference purposes, to find out, say, what guitar a certain artist had used. 'It's normally pictures. I'm very into pictures, and hand movements, all that sort of jive.'

But what of the phenomenon itself – the sensational experiences of fans like Noelle Parr? That *was* pure (while also impure in thought – sweetly dirty). The sheer youth of the T. Rexstatics made for a certain unknowingness. If Bolan himself stood slightly outside his own myth, his fans were fully immersed. Lost in star lust.

Today, we can't access the phenomenon, only read about it in historical reconstructions or watch the surviving clips of documentary footage. What's really left for us is the body of work. Three or four fabulous John's Children songs. The curiosity of Tyrannosaurus Rex, whose records would have remained among the least influential of all time if they hadn't been belatedly seized upon by Animal Collective and other freak-folk artists of the noughties. Two close-to-perfect albums: *T. Rex* and *Electric Warrior*. Above all, that run of nine smash singles, from 'Ride a White Swan' to '20th Century Boy'.

The words teem with flashes of juvenile genius. But they'd be nothing without the delivery, without Bolan himself. T. Rex, in the end, was not so much a body of work as the work of a body. It all emanated from Marc. That voice. That face. The twinkle in the eye. The Cheshire Cat grin.

Glamour that ultimately didn't have anything to do with spangles on the cheek or a jacket made of satin, with things that you could buy or apply. Glamour as a spooky insistence of self, the spark of sheer caprice.

Tolkien might have been describing Marc when he wrote that 'Faërie cannot be caught in a net of words; for it is one of its qualities to be indescribable, though not imperceptible.'

Or as Syd Barrett might have put it: that cat's something I can't explain.

2:

THE LONDON BOY: BOWIE'S EARLY YEARS

David Bowie – Anthony Newley – Lindsay Kemp – Oscar Wilde

Years before David Bowie made it, he had a brush with fame when, aged seventeen, he appeared on the BBC current-affairs programme *Tonight* in November 1964 as leader of the Society for the Prevention of Cruelty to Longhaired Men. Flanked by young men with girlish locks similar to his own, Bowie – then still known by his birth name, David Jones – denounced the prejudice and indignities they faced: 'For the last two years we've had comments like "Darlin'!" and "Can I carry your handbag?" thrown at us. And I think it just has to stop . . . We don't see why other people should persecute us.'

Several things about the TV clip stand out, among them Bowie's startling beauty: pale skin, delicate features and dazzling blond shoulder-length locks. Then there's his manner: polite, demure, a grin cracking up his face that may be defensive shyness and certainly defuses the supposed militancy of the SPCLM. There's also the fact that so early in the career of rock's most famous gender bender – before it had really started – androgyny and sexual confusion were at the forefront of Bowie's presentation of himself to the public. It was only a year or two since The Beatles' own long hair had started the whole 'Are you a boy or a girl?' furore.

But what's really striking – and something that viewers in 1964 can be forgiven for missing – is that the whole thing is patently a charade: the Society for the Prevention of Cruelty to Longhaired Men is a non-existent organisation. When a BBC researcher approached the aspiring pop star in a cafe in Denmark Street (the centre of London's music industry at the time) and asked Bowie if he'd ever been hassled over his long hair, the unknown singer came up with the idea of the pressure group as a publicity stunt. And the BBC fell for it, or opted, perhaps, not to poke too hard and deep into the background of what had all the makings of a fun, topical *Tonight* item.

After the TV appearance, Bowie milked the non-story hard. Speaking to the *Evening News*, he declared, 'It's time we united and stood up for our curls,' and complained that 'Everybody makes jokes about you on a bus, and if you go past navvies digging in the road, it's murder!'

His manager Les Conn drummed up further fake controversy around the issue when Bowie and his band The Manish Boys were lined up to perform on the pop show *Gadzooks!* Conn – whose catchphrase aptly enough was 'Conn's the name, con's the game' – propagated the rumour that the BBC were insisting that Bowie cut his hair. He even orchestrated a demonstration, with fans parading 'Let's Be Fair to Long Hair' placards outside the television studio. A huge amount of publicity was wrung out of this spurious dispute, with stories appearing in the *Daily Mail*, the *Evening Standard*, the *Mirror* and the *Daily Telegraph*, bearing headlines like 'Get Your Hair Cut BBC Tells Pop Man' and 'Long Suffering', and featuring Bowie quotes like, 'I would rather die than get my hair cut.' There were equally fabricated follow-up stories about the ban having been lifted but only on condition that, should viewers complain, The Manish Boys' fee would be donated to charity.

Bowie did not live in a fantasy world to anything like the same extent as his on-and-off friend Marc Bolan. But fibbing would play a crucial role at key stages of Bowie's career. For a sixties-generation figure, he was unusually comfortable with the strategic deployment of falsehoods, the mechanics of hype, and the concept and practice of selling oneself.

Perhaps it ran in the family: his father, Haywood Jones, worked as a public-relations officer for the charity Barnardo's, and prior to that had been involved in showbiz, using inheritance money first to buy a theatre troupe, and then, when that failed, investing in a West End nightclub (also unsuccessful). At Barnardo's, Jones Sr applied his showbiz connections to procure top entertainers for charity events. His PR skills also came into play in the early stages of his son's career. Together they came up with a pitch letter to a highly successful entrepreneur called John Bloom, arguing that 'if you can sell my group the way you sell washing machines you'll be on to a winner'. Bloom was tickled by the chutzpah but he had no interest in diversifying into pop management, so he passed the letter on to an aspiring showbiz Svengali he knew, Les Conn.

Anticipating contemporary political techniques of spin, 'optics' and 'controlling the narrative', Bowie quickly learnt to charm and intrigue the press. Kenneth Pitt, the manager who took over from Conn and became Bowie's most important mentor during the sixties, advised the singer on 'exactly what the interviewer's interests were . . . I told him you've got to try to anticipate the interviewer, tell him or her what they want to hear, and adopt a different style according to the different types of media.'

Another formative influence that contributed to Bowie's flexible relationship with the truth was his early exposure to the world of advertising. Leaving school at sixteen, he got a job as a paste-up artist in the London office of the Yorkshire agency Nevin D. Hirst, whose principal client at the time was the company behind a brand of slimming biscuits called Ayds (a name that would surely have had to be changed had the product survived to the eighties). Later on in the sixties, Bowie and the guitarist of one of his many bands earned money on the side writing music for commercials for products like Youthquake Clothing.

Advertising had an ambivalent status in the sixties. On the one hand, it was bound up with the post-war bounty of consumerism; on the other, it represented everything phoney in Western life, since it essentially involved the art of telling lies, propaganda for corporations rather than the state. In Britain, advertising also connoted America: commercial television – TV with ad breaks – had only arrived in 1955 with the launch of ITV and was regarded by puritanical left-wingers and snooty conservatives alike as another pernicious US import alongside supermarkets and rock'n'roll itself. *The Hidden Persuaders*, an exposé by American social critic Vance Packard of advertising's psychological manipulation tricks, was widely read and discussed when published in the UK by Penguin in 1960. Among its readership was the young Bowie.

Yet the ad industry increasingly exerted fascination too, as a glamorously happening, creative realm, with the rise of cult copywriters like David Ogilvy, the British-born author of *Confessions of an Advertising Man* and a figure often mentioned as the possible inspiration for *Mad Men*'s Don Draper. Advertising added to the pep and colour of everyday life (especially in a Britain only just emerging from post-war austerity), and its graphic invention and optimistic aura influenced the Pop Art of Richard Hamilton and Andy Warhol. The pirate-radio stations that supplied British youth in the sixties with the pop they craved – and that the BBC's Light Programme rationed out in stingy portions – were commercial, funded by ad breaks whose hyped-up, faux-American energy matched the faux-American informality of the disc-jockey patter.

In years to come, Bowie would look back with some pride on his brief association with advertising, an industry that – he argued – had affected the late twentieth century as profoundly as rock had done. But in the sixties itself he had a more conflicted attitude. Bowie participated in the era's bohemian quest for authenticity, the search for a true self that led him and his contemporaries to black music (blues, soul, jazz), to the Beat writers, to the cult of Bob Dylan as poet-seer, to Eastern spirituality. But he was also consistently adaptable and incredibly ambitious, repositioning the Bowie brand (a term no one used in that way then) according to the fluctuations of fashion. Ultimately, any beatnik hang-ups about 'selling out' were eclipsed by his fervent drive to sell and be sold.

As well as being a time of self-discovery and spiritual seeking, Bowie's sixties was also a fitful trial period of self-manufacture and self-marketing, a spasmodic sequence of product relaunches, played out across interviews, recordings, performances and image makeovers. The three albums and thirteen singles Bowie released during 1964–70 were not so much 'advertisements for myself' as attempts to fashion a self that the public might want to buy.

Some kind of magical motivation carried Bowie through these seven years of flops and flip-flopping, false starts and limbos of irresolution. Like Bolan, underneath the chameleonic surface burned a core of pure will.

Born on 8 January 1947, Bowie spent his early childhood in Brixton, an area of south London that had traditionally been a favoured neighbourhood for theatricals and showbiz people. As his father's career at Barnardo's prospered, the family moved further south to the true suburbs of Bromley.

Throughout his career Bowie alternated between describing himself as middle class and working class. Like so many vital figures in British pop history, from Pete Townshend to Paul Weller, Bowie came from a blurry region of British society that encompasses the educated working class, the socially precarious petite bourgeoisie and what could be called the uncomfortably-off middle class, i.e. professional or office workers whose income didn't quite match their aspirations.

Bowie's parents mixed upward mobility and social slippage. Raised in the north, his father Haywood lost nearly all of his inheritance from his family's footwear company in failed showbiz ventures. His mother Peggy was a former waitress with a born-out-of-wedlock son much older than half-brother David. She was an ex-working-class Tory whose sour outlook on life was shaped by post-Second World War privations and the history of mental illness in her family line.

'An awful lot of emotional, spiritual mutilation goes on in my family,' is how Bowie described his upbringing. Although he admired and adored his father, the relationship with his mother was frosty. The tense domestic atmosphere, along with the family's uncertain place in the class structure and Bromley's peripheral location in relation to Greater London, must all have contributed to his feeling of growing up 'on the outside of everything'. For much of his childhood he was the classic dreamer – a loner who would 'retreat into my room'.

As with so many British kids in the mid-fifties, Bowie's first foray into music came during the skiffle boom: a UK reinterpretation of a rough-hewn blues-folk sound originally popular in twenties America. Lonnie Donegan's hit singles, like 'Rock Island Line', inspired a do-it-yourself explosion as thousands of youths across the land picked up basic instruments (acoustic guitar or, in Bowie's case, ukulele) and household implements (the washboard, strummed percussively), as well as cobbling together crude surrogates like a makeshift double bass made from a broomstick, string and a tea chest that served as resonator. These skiffle combos soon mutated into rock'n'roll groups as Elvis Presley, Little Richard, Buddy Holly and the rest impacted the UK. But it took until the summer of 1962 before Bowie joined his first real group, The Kon-Rads, by which point he was playing the saxophone.

Towards the end of that same year, Beatlemania erupted. One result was that the beat-group format took over as the dominant force in British pop, eclipsing the previously reigning templates of solo performer or singer plus backing band (as in Vince Taylor and the Playboys, Johnny Kidd and the Pirates, et al.). Backing bands tended towards anonymous proficiency, versatility, doing what they were told. Beat groups were more 'organic', which meant that they could grow. Usually brought together by some mixture of happenstance and friendship, the members typically had different skill levels, influences and tastes; the relatively narrow zone where these converged became the group's distinctive sound, the basis from which they could evolve.

The groups came across externally as gang-like entities and they functioned internally as quasi-families. The band as internally combustible creative engine heading off on a musical journey: this is the basis of British rock achievement in the sixties. Nearly all the forces that pushed music forward – The Beatles, The Rolling Stones, The Kinks, The Who, The Yardbirds, Pink Floyd – had stable yet flexible band structures that allowed for collaboration with outsiders (producers, guest players) or the replacement of key members taken out by drugs or mental problems (as with Brian Jones and Syd Barrett). But the core of these groups, based on musical chemistry and personal loyalty, endured.

David Bowie played and sang in bands for much of the sixties, but on a fundamental level he had very little truck with the British beat-group revolution. Instead, he operated as if he was a solo artist, abandoning bandmates when his career progress stalled and moving on to another set-up. Between 1963 and 1968 he passed through a staggering number of groups – The Kon-Rads, The Hooker Brothers, who then merged with The King Bees, The Manish Boys, The Lower Third, The Buzz, The Riot Squad, Feathers. Thereafter, as a solo artist, he continued to move rapidly through shifting line-ups of backing musicians and collaborators.

It's hard to think of another major artist in the sixties – or indeed the seventies – whose career was marked by such mobility, this chronic reluctance to stick with a style or a set of accomplices. Other important artists of the era changed with the shifting styles, for sure: Steve Winwood, as he moved from The Spencer Davis Group to Traffic, also evolved through mod-era R&B into psychedelia and then to folky-jazzy progressive rock. But Bowie switched styles abruptly and absolutely. It became the hallmark of his career, something for which he would eventually be praised and admired. In the sixties, though, it just looked like a wannabe hopscotching from one failed gambit to another. Bowie similarly leaped from role model to role model – The Yardbirds' Keith Relf, Bob Dylan, Anthony Newley, and more.

Out of that list of names, by far the most fundamental influence – almost the foundation of Bowie's early style – was Anthony Newley. 'I was the world's worst mimic . . . I was Anthony Newley for a year,' Bowie recalled in a 1973 *NME* interview, discussing the way that impressionable young performers necessarily start out doing impressions, impersonating the artists they're so impressed by. '[Newley] was once one of the most talented men that England ever produced,' gushed Bowie, still a diehard fan in '73. Now largely forgotten, in the late fifties and sixties, Newley was indeed one of the most well known and highly regarded figures in showbiz. Partly, what Bowie admired in Newley and aspired to was simply the shape and range of his career, which spanned singing and recording, songwriting for other performers, composing musicals and acting in the theatre, television and film. This served as Bowie's model and ideal.

Bowie's biographers, critics and fans usually move quickly past the subject of his debt to Newley, as if perplexed or embarrassed. They acknowledge the undeniable – the uncanny resemblance of vocal styles, the exactness with which Bowie replicated Newley's cockney vowel sounds, his un-rock'n'roll clarity of enunciation and stagey delivery – but they hardly ever probe deeply into what made the young singer so fixated on the older star, or what he might have gleaned from him beyond vocal mannerisms. His contemporaries were equally bemused: Bolan recalled going round to Bowie's place in south London, where 'he always played Anthony Newley records', which filtered into Bowie's early solo recordings, with their 'very theatrical flavour' and 'very square backings'.

Yet Newley wasn't actually square, a middle-of-the-road performer catering to the middle-aged. He had one of the more outlandish imaginations in the showbiz realm. Mentored during the Second World War by a music-hall veteran, he had been a child performer, playing the Artful Dodger in a film version of *Oliver Twist* and appearing in TV shows. Newley also scored a string of hit singles that jumped on the rock'n'roll bandwagon, but exhibited scant real feel for the new youth music. By the early sixties, he was starring in musicals he'd written with partner Leslie Bricusse, such as *Stop the World – I Want to Get Off* and *The Roar of the Greasepaint, the Smell of the Crowd*. Their success in America established him as a hugely popular cabaret performer, both onstage and in TV specials.

What characterised all of Newley's work was the combination of arch Englishness (prissy yet self-mocking gestures) and mime elements that were often compared to Marcel Marceau (as with the Pierrot-like tragic clown figure Littlechap, the everyman protagonist of the life-as-circus allegory *Stop the World*). Other hallmarks were an absurdist-existentialist humour tinged with fatalism, and performance that comments on itself, characters that step in and out of persona, action that breaches the fourth wall. A classic example of these traits is Newley's song 'The Man Who Makes You Laugh', the blues of a comic who feeds 'the monster with the thousand eyes' – the insatiable, fickle audience. Performing the song on a British talk show, Newley hams it up in his inimitable style, miming putting on make-up in the dressing-room mirror of the audience's gaze.

All of these elements – mime, meta, music hall, mugging – were intensely present in *The Strange World of Gurney Slade*, a remarkable TV series broadcast in the autumn of 1960 that starred Newley and was devised by him, although actually written by Dick Hills and Sid Green. 'Remember the "Gurney Slade" series? That was tremendous,' burbled Bowie in the 1973 interview. 'A friend of mine has a collection of them, and there's a lot of Monty Python in there.'

The opening episode starts with Newley as Gurney Slade – an actor in a TV soap opera – walking off the set, to the consternation of his fellow performers and the studio technicians, and then out into the street, where he breaks free of all role play and capers manically down the street. *Gurney Slade* constantly disrupts realism: Newley addresses the viewer directly, but also converses with a stone, a dustbin, a coquettish cow and a dog. The latter tells him he's a fan of Lassie but not Rin Tin Tin, who's 'too exaggerated . . . not true to life' because he runs past too many trees without taking a pee. The series parodies television itself, offering a running commentary on the conventions of what Slade mordantly refers to as 'the golden age of British entertainment'. Later in the first episode, the camera cuts back to the soap opera from which Slade went AWOL: the family are huddled around the TV watching *The Strange World of Gurney Slade*.

These self-reflexive tendencies culminate in two hilariously subversive episodes that cast back to Pirandello's 1921 play *Six Characters in Search of an Author* and ahead to Tom Stoppard's *Rosencrantz and Guildenstern Are Dead* (which follows the plight of two minor *Hamlet* characters exiled to the margins of the plot). In the penultimate episode, Slade is tried in court for appearing 'on a TV screen' in front of 'seven million viewers . . . for the purpose of amusing said viewers' but having raised 'not one titter'. His clown-like defence lawyer is Archie Rice, the decrepit music-hall performer portrayed by Laurence Olivier in the 1960 movie of John Osborne's *The Entertainer*. The final episode takes television-about-television further still: Slade is confronted by the characters he created in earlier episodes, who fret about what will happen to them when the series is over, until someone from the Characters Bureau turns up with roles for them in other series. For Gurney Slade himself it's all over: he gradually transforms by stages into a ventriloquist's dummy, and Anthony Newley strides onstage and carries away his now wooden alter ego.

The seeds of 1972's *The Rise and Fall of Ziggy Stardust and the Spiders from Mars* are visible in this 1960 TV series. There's a premonition, too, of 1975's 'Fame', Bowie's chilling exposé of stardom's paranoia and hollowness, in *Gurney Slade*'s ambivalence about the business of show. In one scene, TV executives are shown a 'new design' performer, an 'all-purpose model' who'll 'do practically anything . . . singing, comedy . . . recording'. It's Gurney Slade, who bitterly mutters to himself, 'They think I'm a machine . . . I'll show them . . . I'll just sit here and refuse to move.'

For most of the sixties, even while fronting a series of rock bands, Bowie aspired to be 'an all-purpose model' – the adaptable all-round entertainer of variety and vaudeville tradition, proffering 'a song, a dance, a laugh' in the small boxed ad section of *The Stage*. Performing-arts schools have always instructed their pupils in the full range of theatrical skills – tap, mime, singing, acting – to maximise their employment prospects. Likewise Bowie's manager Kenneth Pitt – a second father figure, with whom the young singer cohabited for several years – saw his protégé as a versatile star with potential not just in the pop arena, but in cabaret and film (Pitt secured him a small role in the movie *The Virgin Soldiers*, for instance).

'Those who judge him and me and, in doing so, take as their yardstick rock and roll, fail to understand that David never was a devotee or exponent of rock and roll,' the manager wrote in his memoir *Bowie: The Pitt Report*. 'Whenever he rocked and rolled he did so in the context of theatre, as an actor,' he continued, quoting Bowie's own claim that 'rock does not play an important part in my life'. Bolan recognised this lack of gut connection to rock'n'roll, observing that Bowie 'was very Cockney then . . . We were all looking for something to get into . . . I wanted to be Bob Dylan, but I think David was looking into that music hall humour. It was the wrong time to do it, but all his songs were story songs.'

Talking to *Melody Maker* in 1966 – the year of *Revolver, Blonde on Blonde, Pet Sounds* and half a dozen other masterworks, the year when rock indisputably emerges as the defining popular art form of its time – Bowie talked about his plans to write a musical (called *Kids on the Roof*) with middle-of-the-road arranger/songwriter Tony Hatch. He declared that his long-term ambition lay in acting. 'I'd like to do character parts. I think it takes a lot to become somebody else.'

Songs from that never-realised musical made their way into Bowie's self-titled debut album for Deram, the 'progressive' subsidiary of the huge major label Decca. Recorded at the end of 1966 and in early 1967, *David Bowie* saw the singer abandon his band of the moment, The Buzz (apart from bassist Dek Fearnley, who stayed on to work on the arrangements), in favour of session musicians. The sound was a jaunty, wittily embellished style typically found on the comedy records of the era, by artists like Ken Dodd and the Diddymen and The Bonzo Dog Doo-Dah Band: bouncy basslines, a frisky skitter of drums, trumpet parps and huffing-and-puffing tubas, whimsical tweets of piccolo or recorder, perhaps the jangly scrabble of ukulele or rinky-dinky tinkle of a piano. The non-album single 'The Laughing Gnome' – a daft ditty about a leprechaun-like lodger – resembles nothing so much as comedian Charlie Drake's later hit single 'Puckwudgie', also about a benign household troll. Full of painful if ingenious puns and featuring the sped-up voices of Bowie and engineer Gus Dudgeon as gnomes, 'The Laughing Gnome' was an utter flop in 1967.

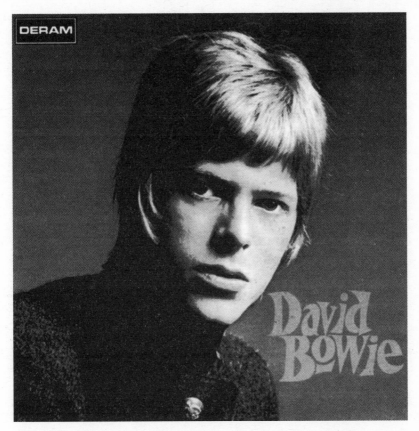

Boy child: David Bowie's debut album, released on 1 June 1967

'The Laughing Gnome' and the self-titled debut very much belong to the tradition of comedy pop, where the music is definitely *backing* music. Sound is kept in its place, as support and dramatic counterpoint to the singer; hearing the words is paramount, and these are clearly enunciated and full of dramatic emphases. Writing about the music-hall tradition of the character song, Simon Frith notes that 'the singer is playing a part, and what is involved is neither self-expression . . . nor critical commentary'. Instead, it's all 'a matter of acting'.

This applies totally to the album *David Bowie*. The single 'Love You Till Tuesday' is a delightful romp of exaggeratedly English pronunciation ('hoping for a little romance' is rendered nasally as 'romarnnnce' as opposed to the American 'romaaanse') and comedy histrionics, with Bowie seemingly imitating Kenneth Connor or Jim Dale from the knockabout *Carry On* films. 'We Are Hungry Men' – an ostensibly serious dystopian warning about a coming crisis of overpopulation – is full of comic turns: a posh Peter Sellers-like voice reads out astronomic population figures for cities of the near future (New York has 80 million inhabitants), while later a German Nazi caricature proposes mass abortion and legalised infanticide and threatens slaughter for 'anyone found guilty of consuming more than their allotted amount of air'.

Rock'n'roll is generally a first- or second-person art form: it speaks as an 'I' or sometimes a 'we'; it addresses a 'you'. But in 1966–7, there was a vogue in the UK for third-person vignettes and satirical portraits of 'types': The Beatles and The Kinks led the way with 'Eleanor Rigby' and 'Dedicated Follower of Fashion' respectively, which were soon followed by huge hits like Cat Stevens's 'Matthew and Son' and Keith West's 'Grocer Jack'. Bowie's debut LP was squarely on trend with its predominance of third-person portraits. The opening track, 'Uncle Arthur', tells of an emotionally retarded shopkeeper, unmarried and still living with his mother, while 'Little Bombardier' is about a lost, damaged war veteran whose friendship with small children is regarded, unfairly, as questionable by a hostile and uncomprehending world. 'Join the Gang' is a satire on the Swinging Sixties that runs through stock characters, like the sitar-playing existentialist Johnny, the model turned acid freak Molly, and Arthur, the blues-croaking, booze-swigging singer in a 'heavy' band.

Even when he uses 'I' on the album, Bowie is playing a part, as with the closing 'Please Mr Gravedigger'. Recited rather than sung and decorated with sound effects (church bells, distant thunder, pouring rain and dripping water, sneezes and, naturally, the scrape of a spade through soil), 'Please Mr Gravedigger' is more like a miniature radio play than a song. The plotline doesn't quite make sense – the narrator kills a little girl, confesses it to the gravedigger, then digs a grave for the poor workman so as to keep the secret safe – but the atmosphere of macabre whimsy makes this piece the most startling and original song on *David Bowie*.

Unsuccessful at the time, the album and various singles and B-sides released by Deram during this early phase of Bowie's career were repackaged in 1973, following his rise to stardom, as the double LP *Images 1966–1967*. (Deram also reissued 'The Laughing Gnome' as a single, without Bowie's consent, and it made the Top 10, to his mortification.) The *Images* liner notes describe the assemblage as 'the original cast album of show tunes that do not belong to any show'. Although *Characters* would actually suit better the contents of the album, *Images* is a suggestive title, capturing something essential about the sixties that shaped Bowie and would eventually enable him to dominate the British seventies.

Like Bolan, Bowie was caught up in mod, the most image-conscious youth movement so far. His early groups, like The Lower Third and The Manish Boys, were all in the mod/Brit R&B mould. Subcultural analyst Dick Hebdige has written about a special mod way of standing, a posture struck to draw the gaze of others (impressed or outraged, it hardly mattered). This stiff pose – which Hebdige described as 'auto-erotic' in his essay 'Posing . . . Threats, Striking . . . Poses: Youth, Surveillance, and Display' – turned 'the fact of being under scrutiny into the pleasure of being watched . . . Fractions of youth now aspire to the flatness and stillness of a photograph. They are completed only through the admiring glances of a stranger.'

This intensified enjoyment of one's own image on the part of young men in the sixties – something that was regarded as 'effeminate' and 'poofy' by old-fashioned menfolk – owed a huge amount to the ascent of the photographer to star status. 'The pop photographer . . . has transferred those qualities which, until the 60s, were thought of as essentially homosexual and made them available to what used to be known as "red-blooded males",' wrote George Melly in *Revolt into Style*. Star photographers like David Bailey not only celebrated but in some sense created the new classless aristocracy of Swinging England, in which rank was determined by looks and style.

Spearheaded by the mods and disseminated through the quality magazines' fashion spreads and clothing advertisements by the new photographers, male dandyism reached the mainstream with figures like Simon Dee, a pirate disc jockey turned TV talk-show host. Where television presenters had previously been dowdy, respectable-looking figures, Dee was self-consciously 'with it'. Writing in 1968's *The Simon Dee Book*, he enthused about the changing attitudes:

> Twenty years ago, for a man to think about fashion was considered effeminate and a huge joke. Your actual stepping-out gear consisted of a shapeless grey or blue suit with turn-ups, a white shirt and the kind of tie elderly aunties always give you for Christmas . . . By the time Carnaby Street came along, nobody blinked an eye at lilac frock coats, pink shirts and suede bootees. Suddenly it was smart to take an interest in your appearance. None of your mates thought you were soft at all – they were too busy hunting among the boutique belt themselves . . . Up the revolution – banish all drab greys and pinstripes of the 'Rolled Brolly Brigade'. Let's see the pastels, voiles and mohairs of the whiz kids take over.

Bowie was a product of this shift in sartorial ideas as much as an agent of it. 'I remember asking once about his time as a mod,' says *Melody Maker* journalist Michael Watts. 'I said, "Well, what were you like?" And Bowie said, "Well, I wore the eyeliner and the Cossack hairspray, which everybody had . . . I guess you could say I was *camp with balls*."'

It was this androgynous quality that captivated the various managers and mentors who guided Bowie during his long apprenticeship for fame, including Kenneth Pitt and the mime artist Lindsay Kemp. He had the look of a potential idol well before he nailed down the sound.

Marc Bolan believed that Bowie's interest in mime was first piqued by Anthony Newley's use of it in *Stop the World – I Want to Get Off*. But when Bowie was introduced to the work of Lindsay Kemp and his small troupe in 1968, he encountered a form of mime that was vastly more experimental and transgressive, infused and enflamed with the influence of Jean Genet and Oscar Wilde, along with Japanese theatrical forms like Kabuki.

It was Kemp who approached Bowie first, however. A copy of Bowie's debut album had come into his possession; he was so enchanted by the songs – and the singer – that he worked 'When I Live My Dream' (one of Bowie's more cloying Newley-style tunes) into his current show. Then he sent Bowie an invitation to see it performed in a tiny attic space tucked away in an alley in the heart of London's theatre district. Bowie was both flattered and blown away by Kemp's Pierrot-based performance. Invited back to Kemp's Soho flat after the show, Bowie was plunged into the mime's outré milieu. Soon he was taking dance classes with Kemp, but had also joined the troupe and was collaborating with Kemp on the performance *Pierrot in Turquoise*. They were lovers too.

'Everything I thought Bohemia probably was, [Kemp] was living,' Bowie recalled years later. 'Everything in his life was theatrical . . . The stage thing was just an extension of himself . . . his day-to-day life.' Kemp had learnt what he called 'the art of mesmerism' during boarding school, as a survival tactic: 'It was never enough to entertain them,' he recalled. 'I had to enchant them.'

Through Kemp, Bowie encountered many of the things that would inform his later music and performance, from Kabuki to

Genet. *Flowers*, the Kemp troupe's 1968 interpretation of Genet's
Our Lady of the Flowers – a 'hallucinatory tale of drag queens,
pimps, murderers and sailors', according to journalist Rupert
Smith – became one of the mime troupe's most famous performance pieces, 'orgiastic, violent, teetering constantly on the verge
of bathos, and thoroughly homosexual'. Kemp completed an education in gay aestheticism for Bowie started by Kenneth Pitt, who had
introduced him to the work of Oscar Wilde, Aubrey Beardsley and
the Weimar Berlin novels of Christopher Isherwood.

Under Kemp's tutelage, Bowie learnt how to use his physical
presence to mesmerise the audience. 'I taught David to free his
body,' Kemp told *Crawdaddy* in 1974. 'I taught him to exaggerate
with his body as well as his voice . . . Ever since working with me
he's practiced that, and in each performance . . . his movements
are more exquisite . . . The mime uses gestures to convey his inner
beauty . . . Bowie does that with his voice.'

Kemp also worked on burnishing Bowie's outer beauty, telling
Nova magazine that he'd taken the still-diffident singer in hand: 'I
knew he was wonderful but I wanted other people to see it. I found
myself having to push him. I painted his face and dyed his hair to
get people to notice him . . . to color him in to let people see just
how sexy and beautiful he was.'

Although probably exaggerated – Bowie already knew the effect
his looks had on other people – Kemp's account of his self-image-
boosting role in the singer's life eerily resembles 'I'll Be Your
Mirror', the Velvet Underground song written by Lou Reed and
sung by Nico: specifically the lines about not being able to believe
'you don't know the beauty you are' and the promise to reflect back
the truth. Bowie had actually heard that song and the debut album
on which it appeared – 1967's *The Velvet Underground & Nico* –
before almost anyone else in the UK, thanks to Kenneth Pitt. On a
business trip to New York in November 1966, Pitt had visited Andy

Warhol's Factory and been given an acetate promo version of The Velvet Underground's debut album. The band's songs and music – along with the camp, decadent milieu surrounding the band's patron, Warhol – would hugely influence Bowie's music and image in the seventies. But in 1968, he was seriously considering abandoning the music biz altogether and concentrating on becoming a dancer.

'The Mirror' was the title of a new song Bowie wrote for *Pierrot in Turquoise* when the mime play was adapted as a TV special in early 1970. Broadcast on a Scottish channel and retitled *Pierrot in Turquoise, or, the Looking Glass Murders*, the half-hour show saw Bowie resume his role of narrator, despite a period of estrangement from Kemp after an amorous tiff (Bowie had two-timed Kemp by sleeping with one of the troupe's female dancers). In 'The Mirror' sequence, Bowie's lines about a 'fay troubadour' and 'gay harlequin', his references to packing up your face and a mirror that's 'hung up on you' are accompanied by a surreal spectacle in which Harlequin gyrates and capers in a courtship dance with Columbine, amid a dream-like stage set of nude, armless mannequins and stepladders. Harlequin is bald, black and naked except for gold earrings, glitter-encrusted eyes and a bizarre half-leotard that's like suspenders attached to swimming trunks; Columbine is mad-eyed and mad-haired in a green frock with ruffled sleeves. Bowie, as the narrator Cloud, is glimpsed briefly, atop a stepladder, his face panstick white, his hair frizzy and powdery. The camera pulls back to frame Harlequin and Columbine in proscenium arches, with a stage curtain closing and reopening to the sound of applause, and images from a painting of a Victorian theatre audience.

Central to mime is the idea of the mask: the feature-flattening white greasepaint serves to depersonalise, creating a blank canvas on which stylised expressions are depicted, according to a universal and timeless grammar of emotion. Descending from medieval dumbshow, mummers and masques, paralleling Japanese forms like Noh and Kabuki, and seeping into twentieth-century popular culture with tragicomic silent-movie stars like Buster Keaton, mime is all about escaping one's actual self and donning the costume of a persona. Mime is theatre in its most pure and distilled form. The Germans have a word for it: '*Maskenfreiheit*', 'freedom in wearing masks'. This release – from the burden and challenge of having to represent his true self onstage – would be crucial for Bowie going forward.

Towards the tail end of the period when he was most intensely involved with Kemp, Bowie composed a mime piece called 'The Mask'. This would become one of the segments of a promo film that Kenneth Pitt funded in early 1969, in hope of boosting his client's stagnant career. Garbed in Marcel Marceau-like get-up, Bowie plays a young man who finds a mask in a junkshop. Initially just putting it on to show off to family and friends, the boy soon finds he has a career on his hands. At the height of the performer's fame – a concert at the London Palladium – he discovers to his horror that he can no longer remove the rictus grin of the stage persona and dies, writhing hopelessly in the cruel spotlight. Bowie's voiceover narrates drily: 'The papers made a big thing out of it . . . "Strangled on Stage", they said . . . Funny, though . . . they didn't mention anything about a mask.' Although Bowie's marionette-like movements are clumsy and jejune, 'The Mask' is an astonishingly self-aware preview of the costs of stardom and the psychological dislocation caused by having a public image. Not that rehearsing the process in 'The Mask' did anything to deflect Bowie from ardently pursuing his destiny.

'Man is least himself when he talks in his own person. Give him a mask, and he will tell you the truth,' declared Oscar Wilde in 'The Critic as Artist', one of his most famous aesthetic-manifesto essays, alongside 'The Decay of Lying' and 'The Truth of Masks: A Note on Illusion'. Wilde is the first philosopher of glam, expounding its tenets eighty years in advance. He did this through critical essays, but above all with *The Picture of Dorian Gray*, which is less a novel than a scaffold over which Wilde drapes his theories and aesthetic stances in the form of exquisitely wrought, mordantly witty epigrams and aphorisms. Speaking largely through the character of Lord Henry, Wilde scorns authenticity and artlessness as tedious humbug: 'Being natural is simply a pose, and the most irritating pose I know'; 'the value of an idea has nothing whatsoever to do with the sincerity of the man who expresses it'. He celebrates the theatricality and facades of social life: 'It is only shallow people who do not judge by appearances'; 'I love acting. It is so much more real than life.'

Bowie's entire career is predicted – and the carping distrust of his critics deflected in advance – with Wilde's rhetorical question: 'Is insincerity such a terrible thing? I think not. It is merely a method by which we can multiply our personalities.' But what really makes Wilde the prophet of glam is not the finely reasoned paradoxes and impish inversions of common sense in his writings, so much as the irrationalism that bubbles to the surface like intoxicating fumes. A pagan paean to the cult of youth and beauty, *The Picture of Dorian Gray* is criss-crossed with idolatrous currents. 'You are made to be worshipped,' says Basil the artist to the delicate Dorian. The text is riddled with words like 'poison' (in the sense of intoxicant) and 'influence' (as in something insidious, corrupting). Above all, Wilde uses the concepts of fascination and charm – words that, like 'glamour', 'charisma' and 'prestige', have a magical undertone, referring to sinister powers to lead astray, deceive, fool. The repetition of similar phrases throughout *The Picture of Dorian Gray* – 'an exquisite poison in the air', 'a curious influence over me', 'his strange and dangerous charm' – brings an incantatory insistence to the prose.

For those bestowed with it, charm is a licence: 'I never interfere with what charming people do,' quips Lord Henry. Wilde often makes an analogy with music, another power that operates outside of rationality or practical necessity, that overpowers and bewitches. 'Beauty is a form of Genius,' a force that rules by 'divine right', Wilde writes. 'It makes princes of those who have it.' Beauty is atavistic and anti-modern, an enclave of aristocratic intransigence in the face of the ugly nineteenth-century England – that 'dim, dull abyss of facts' – birthed by the Industrial Revolution and the mercantile middle classes.

This modern world spawned its own literary and dramatic mode: realism. In 'The Decay of Lying', Wilde rails against the 'prison-house of realism'. Art, he demands, should be 'a veil, rather than a mirror', and facts must be 'kept in their proper subordinate position' or banished altogether for dullness. Art need concern itself only with 'beautiful and impossible things', miracles and monsters, as opposed to everyday life or social conditions. 'We must cultivate the lost art of lying,' Wilde implores.

In 1967, Bowie made a tentative step towards fulfilling his dream of breaking into entertainment forms other than pop and 'starred' in *The Image*, a short film that resembles a Hammer Horror twist on *The Picture of Dorian Gray*. Director Michael Armstrong described it as 'a study of the illusionary reality world within the schizophrenic mind of the artist at his point of creativity'. Made on a budget of nearly nothing, *The Image* is a fourteen-minute, black-and-white slice of ghoulish camp, in which an artist paints a portrait of a beautiful boy, who then comes alive (or undead). The painter has to kill the Bowie-zombie over and over again, in increasingly gory ways, with spasming stabs that have a stylised sexual charge, climaxing with the boy impaling himself erotically on the artist's blade. The film ends with the artist frenziedly slashing the canvas and collapsing in a weeping heap on the floor, while the camera pans to a framed photograph of, you guessed it, the boy – clearly the lost love object of a doomed affair whose ghost-pest of a memory insists on being repainted repeatedly.

N

In 1968, in the wake of his ignored debut album, Bowie remained hopelessly at odds with the vital currents of late-sixties music and culture. Rock in 1968–9 was as earnestly uncamp as it has ever been: these were the years when things got heavy and bluesy, rootsy and backwoodsy. Meanwhile, Bowie was still thinking in terms of musical theatre and mime.

For a while, he dithered, directionless. When his father expressed concern about his lack of income, Bowie impulsively responded: 'Okay, so I'm doing cabaret. When do we start?' With Kenneth Pitt's help, he worked up a set that mixed his own songs with some by The Beatles and actually involved him appearing onstage with cardboard cut-outs of the Fab Four from the cartoon movie *Yellow Submarine*. The set was auditioned to various agents, one of whom praised it highly ('better than Cliff Richard'). But it was deemed too clever for the cabaret circuit.

So Bowie changed course – the first of many grand swerves in his musical career – and threw himself wholeheartedly into the hippy trip. (Almost wholeheartedly – he didn't grow a beard.) Discarding Newley and comedy pop, Bowie shifted his music in a folky, singer-songwriter direction, with increasingly verbose and allegorical lyrics. Like Bolan in the Tyrannosaurus Rex era, his interviews at this point feature the litany of counterculture pieties. And Bowie reached out to the underground audience, playing free festivals.

Festivals were the totemic events of the counterculture, especially when held outdoors, amid nature. Bowie played at some of the major festivals of the period, like Atomic Sunrise at the

Roundhouse, London, in early 1970, where he appeared on a bill weighted down with heavy bands like Fat Mattress and Hawkwind, while Living Theatre members moved among the audience, breaking down the barrier between stage and spectators.

Bowie also played at dawn during the second Glastonbury Fayre in 1971. Captured in Nicolas Roeg's documentary film, the Fayre was a fiesta of spiritual seeking and antic whimsy. The communal vegetarian food was the same colour as the mud in which nude hippies cavorted. Raggle-taggle hordes of hairies banged drums, blew recorders and whooped it up in spontaneous cavalcades of collective music-making. A kooky cat from Ladbroke Grove called Mighty Michael caterwauled trouser-less onstage, his genitals flailing with each wail and holler. Glastonbury was anti-glam, the opposite of everything Bowie would become. But as late as 1971, he still fitted in there, playing alongside progressive heavyweights like Family, Gong and Quintessence, and folkies like Melanie and the fiddle-driven Fairport Convention.

So committed was Bowie to the Revolution that he opened his own arts lab in Beckenham. As the word 'laboratory' suggested, arts labs were experimental spaces suited for artistic activity that blurred the boundaries between disciplines and forms, and increasingly erased the gaps between art and everyday life. They were places where happenings happened. The first arts lab was founded by Jim Haynes, whose countercultural pedigree included being involved in the founding of both the fringe theatre The Traverse and leading underground paper *International Times*. In summer 1967, Haynes rented a building in London's Drury Lane. He set up an all-night cinema in the basement (with a soft floor that soon became a crash pad for hippies), a gallery on the ground floor, a film workshop upstairs (later mutating into a restaurant) and a theatre space in an adjacent warehouse. In the first *Arts Lab Newsletter*, Haynes defined the concept: 'A lab is a non-institution. We all know what a hospital, theatre, police station and other institutions have in the way of boundaries, but a lab's boundaries should be limitless.'

Haynes's invention spawned imitators across the country: some fifty of them by 1969, including the Beckenham Arts Lab. Launched in spring 1969 and based out of the Three Tuns club, it was the brainchild of Bowie (who had performed and rehearsed at the Drury Lane space) and some local like-minds, including a young woman called Mary Finnigan, with whom he'd started cohabiting. Together they formed an organisation named Growth, whose slogan was 'Growth is people, Growth is revolution'.

Less involved in the lab's week-to-week administration, Bowie became its public spokesperson, telling *International Times* that its goal was to have a wider appeal, reaching the parent generation and squares rather than just the already-hip converted. 'Arts Labs should be for everybody, not just the so-called turned-on minority. We need energy from all directions, from heads and skin-heads alike.' Unlike other 'pseud places', Beckenham Arts Lab drew people who were 'real – like labourers or bank clerks', he told *Melody Maker*. Bowie came across as a true believer in the 'Arts Lab movement', describing it as 'extremely important . . . [It] should take over from the youth club concept as a social service.'

The logical next step for Bowie and his arts-lab comrades was staging their own free festival. 'The Growth Summer Festival and Free Concert in Beckenham' took place on 16 August 1969 in the town's recreation grounds. Coinciding with the historic events at Woodstock, several thousand miles away, but blessed with far better weather, the festival's attractions – which drew some 3,000 over the course of the day – included stalls for exotic teas, herbs, jewellery, ceramics, posters and original artwork, along with street theatre, a Tibetan shop and traditional village-fete and carnival fare, like candy floss, an assault course and a coconut shy. There was also the Brian Cole Puppet Theatre presenting a 'rather drug-influenced version of a children's puppet play', according to puppeteer David Bebbington. Live music performed on the old Victorian bandstand included the folky likes of Bridget St John and The Strawbs. Bowie himself did a turn. The Beckenham Free Festival's idyllic vibe was marred only by Bowie's foul mood, probably the result of being shattered by his father's recent death. At the end of the day, he lashed out at his Growth colleagues for being 'mercenary pigs' when he stumbled upon them totting up the takings.

During his hippy phase Bowie also went along with the musical vibe of the day. Through an ad in *International Times* he recruited Tony Hill, the guitarist of The Misunderstood, a psychedelic outfit favoured by John Peel on his pirate-radio show *The Perfumed Garden*. Together with Hermione Farthingale – Bowie's girlfriend before he hooked up with Finnigan – they formed the multimedia trio Turquoise, although that name only lasted one gig before they changed it to Feathers. When Hill left to form the acid-rock band High Tide, Bowie replaced the guitarist with one of his old bandmates in The Buzz, and this new trio persevered with an uneasy mixture of mime, ballet, poetry and song: a sort of LSD-era version of cabaret, featuring covers of Jacques Brel songs, along with Bowie originals like the fey and flimsy 'Ching-a-Ling'.

Feathers faded away. Bowie drifted along, writing songs in the acoustic-guitar-centred style of hippy minstrels like Shawn Phillips and Tom Rapp. Kenneth Pitt disapproved of this development, and in his memoir describes Bowie as 'comparatively aimless' during this period: 'His direction was that in which he happened to be facing in any given week.' An April 1969 letter from Bowie to his manager shows how confused the singer was. It rambles across a number of vague and contradictory plans for the future. Bowie writes of wanting to do an album of country pop, while also pursuing a trad-folk direction running in parallel with a contemporary-folk series at the Sir Christopher Wren pub. But he also raises the possibility of writing a musical and doing TV commercials. At this time he also contemplated a Simon and Garfunkel-like partnership with a guitarist called John Hutchinson.

Unfocused and half-hearted as the period was, it wasn't fruitless. For this was when Bowie wrote and recorded the song that would be his breakthrough: 'Space Oddity'. Conceived after watching Kubrick's *2001: A Space Odyssey* in a chemically altered state, 'Space Oddity' was written for the same multi-song promo film in which 'The Mask' featured, devised and financed by Pitt to win Bowie TV exposure in Britain and on the Continent.

'Space Oddity' could hardly have been more archetypally late-sixties. It played off the huge success of the Kubrick movie (especially popular with the heads, as something to watch stoned or tripping) and capitalised on the flurry of NASA missions during 1968, which pointed to a landing on the Moon at some point in 1969. Outer space and cosmic imagery were staples of acid rock, from The Byrds' 'Mr Spaceman' to Jimi Hendrix's 'Third Stone from the Sun' and Pink Floyd's 'Astronomy Domine'. Musically, 'Space Oddity' pressed many of the right contemporary buttons, managing to be both folky (Bowie's lonesome voice and acoustic guitar at the core) and cinematically orchestrated in the post-*Sgt Pepper's* style. Bowie's demo was sombre and gaunt, but once embellished by producer Gus Dudgeon and a team of session musicians, the finished record was close to the psychedelic easy listening of The Moody Blues (who later in 1969 released their own symphonic concept album about the Moon landing, *To Our Children's Children's Children*). Appropriately spacey touches were added to 'Space Oddity' using the Stylophone (a rudimentary synthesizer) and strings, some of which were real and some of which were simulated using a new instrument called the Mellotron, almost a proto-sampler in so far as swatches of tape provided ersatz orchestral timbres.

Yet in other respects 'Space Oddity' undercut the mood of summer

1969, skipping right past the wonderstruck collective euphoria about the Moon landing and moving straight to the post-lunar trist-esse: the 'so what?/what now?' comedown of still being stuck on planet Earth with all its mounting problems. As Bowie recalled to the *NME* eleven years after his first hit, 'Here we had the great blast of American technological know-how shoving this guy up into space, but once he gets there he's not quite sure why he's there. And that's where I left him.'

Far from celebrating a technological triumph that has opened a new frontier for mankind, the song-story concerns a mission gone wrong. The melody shifts from a two-note dirge in the verses to a sighing yet serene chorus that conjures the passive fatalism of Major Tom, adrift in his 'tin can', resigned to his doom: 'Planet Earth is blue and there's nothing I can do.' The astronaut is done for but he's also free of his home planet's mundanity – like the newspaper reporters jabbering to know what brand of shirt he wears.

Topicality was the song's major appeal to the record company, Mercury, which timed its release for the July Moon mission. 'A gim-mick was a big deal then . . . Mercury took him on specifically for that,' Dudgeon would recall. When after two months as a sleeper it finally ascended to #5 in the UK chart that autumn, 'Space Oddity' had something of the aura of a novelty single. Tony Visconti, Bowie's principal producer at this time, had actually passed on working on the single precisely for this reason – feeling that the tie-in with the Moon shot was a cheap shot – and handed it over to an eager Dudgeon. An engineer with little production experience, and unable to read or write music, Dudgeon devised his own unique pictorial system to convey his ideas to arranger Paul Buckmaster: a colour-coded score that looked like 'a kid's map, covered in little drawings and stars', with particular symbols or zigzaggy lines signi-fying 'a stylophone swoop or a mellotron part'.

Like a movie, 'Space Oddity' was a collaborative work of art,

with Bowie as scriptwriter and leading man, Dudgeon as director, Buckmaster as cinematographer and the musicians (including
future Yes man Rick Wakeman on Mellotron, drummer Terry Cox
from the folk-rock outfit Pentangle, and Herbie Flowers, soon to
become the leading bassist-for-hire of the glam era) providing vivid
details akin to costume and scenery. As a child I was entranced by
'Space Oddity': the whooshing take-off sounds (which nod to The
Beatles' 'A Day in the Life'), the guttural detonations of bass and,
my favourite thing of all, the way Bowie sang 'tpeculiar', enjambing
the last letter of 'most' onto 'peculiar' in the line 'floating in a most
peculiar way'. It *sounded* peculiar, like language in zero G.

What's really odd about 'Oddity' is that Bowie seemed almost
instantly embarrassed by its success. It did take on the air of the
novelty single, saddling him for years with a one-hit-wonder reputation. The accompanying album, confusingly titled *David Bowie*
just like the debut (but also released as *Man of Words/Man of Music*
in America and later re-released as *Space Oddity*), was a half-writ-
ten and noncommittal affair. Rush-recorded, with Visconti back at
the helm, and centred around Bowie's twelve-string guitar, this may
well be his worst album, at least until the mid-eighties. The debut,
charming and tuneful, conveys that Bowie's heart is in it, his delight
in the jokes and play-acting palpable. None of that comes through in
the second album. Its interest now is mainly archaeological, something to sift through for hints of future greatness or clues to Bowie's
state of mind in this period of irresolution.

Bowie is still searching for a self to sell, and coming up mostly
with wan forgeries of others' styles, from the harmonica-laced
Dylan mimicry of 'Unwashed', to folky rambles not far from what
The Faces would work up in a few years' time and pallid, wittering,
Donovan-esque nothingness such as 'An Occasional Dream'. 'Wild
Eyed Boy from Freecloud' possibly aspires to the symphonic gran-
deur of solo-album Scott Walker (another recent musical crush of

Bowie's), but is closer to the orchestrated vanity-project album put out by *Man from U.N.C.L.E.* star David McCallum.

Still, there are two deeply intriguing songs on *David Bowie* the Second: 'Cygnet Committee' and 'Memories of a Free Festival'. Redolent of Roy Harper's 1971 masterpiece *Stormcock* but nowhere near as realised or commanding, 'Cygnet' is a ten-minute-long opaque allegory about the decay of the hippy underground. In an October 1969 interview with *Disc & Music Echo*, Bowie explained that 'It's basically three separate points of view about the more militant section of the hippy movement. The movement was a great ideal but something's gone wrong with it now. I'm not really attacking it but pointing out that the militants have still got to be helped as people – human beings – even if they are going about things all the wrong way.' The final section of the song is merciless in its caricaturing of the counterculture's radical-chic postures, Bowie now impersonating the freaks who 'stoned the poor on slogans', which escalate from the merely faddish ('Love Is All We Need', 'Kick Out the Jams') to the borderline fascist ('Kick Out Your Mother', 'We Can Force You to Be Free'). While the lyrics are interesting both as a reflection of their time and a glimpse into Bowie's evolving world view, this cavalcade of scrabbled-out folk is a failed epic. 'Memories of a Free Festival' is a fonder and more focused adieu to the hippy dream. An idealised recollection of the mini-Woodstock in Beckenham Recreation Grounds, it drops epochal keywords like 'love' and 'ecstasy' and 'satori' as it heads into its 'Hey Jude'-like singalong coda.

In the summer of 1969, Bowie was wont to profess that, rather than being a singer, running the Beckenham Arts Lab was his 'chief occupation, something that matters to me more than anything else'. Yet within just a few months of the Free Festival, he was expressing deep doubts about the whole counterculture project. In December '69, he confessed that 'the whole revolution bit drives me mad . . .

These people, they're so apathetic, so lethargic. The laziest people I've met in my life. They don't know what to do with themselves. Looking all the time for people to show them the way. They wear anything they're told, and listen to any music they're told to.' Alternative culture had become a new conformity, a market.

Whether or not he had ever been genuinely dedicated to the scene's values, Bowie was far from alone in his disillusionment with hippy culture. By 1970, in the wake of Altamont and the Manson murders, the dream of a mass youth bohemia was in disarray. The movement split into factions. A hardcore political element still strove to construct utopia either by seceding from the mainstream (the back-to-the-land drive of the communes) or by attacking the architects and symbolic figureheads of the Establishment (as with the terrorist acts committed by apocalyptic guerrilla outfits like the Weather Underground, the Angry Brigade, Germany's Red Army Faction). A larger swathe ditched the politics of the counterculture but kept faith with the attitudes, aesthetics and newly invented customs: the music, the drugs, the dress.

Bowie seemed to find it hard to break with the underground completely, if only because in 1969–70 it was the only scene going. So he carried on playing free festivals and parroting in interviews the progressive party line about commercialism and the unimportance of singles. At the end of 1969, he claimed not to care about the hit parade at all, dismissing 'Space Oddity' – his greatest achievement to date – as 'only a pop song after all'. In 1970, he sniffed to *Melody Maker* that the hit song 'served its purpose but I hope I'm not going to be expected to write and record a whole lot of stuff that is so obvious as "Space Oddity".'

Bowie was in a funk, no longer really believing in the underground but equally turned off by his taste of pop stardom. 'David eventually got what he wanted, but it drove him to the depths of despair,' Kenneth Pitt recalled. But the manager attributed some of the disillusionment to 'affectation': Bowie still trying to fit in with the counterculture, conform to its nonconformism. 'The putting down of the single and pretending he wasn't a pop star and hating all these people wanting to take his photograph . . .' all came from what Pitt saw as the misguided influence of the Beckenham Arts Lab crowd. 'They were very anti-success, anti-hit record, anti-pop star.'

This sense of the hollowness and transience of worldly success was enlarged by Bowie's explorations of Tibetan Buddhism. His interest in Eastern spirituality was deep and long-standing, predating its fleeting embrace by the likes of The Beatles. It began after Bowie encountered Zen concepts in Beat writers like Jack Kerouac and really blossomed when he read the memoir *Seven Years in Tibet* by Heinrich Harrer. Bowie's fascination with Tibet was evident in some of his earliest interviews. 'I'd like to take a holiday and have a look inside the monasteries,' he told *Melody Maker* in 1966. 'The Tibetan monks, Lamas, bury themselves inside mountains for weeks and only eat every three days . . . It's said they live for centuries.'

Bowie talked earnestly of the spiritual poverty of 'Western life', describing 'the life we live now' as 'wrong', but admitted he found it hard to work these beliefs into the songs he was writing about London. Perhaps a hint of emptiness shadowed one of his best early songs, the 1966 single B-side 'The London Boys', a glimpse into the anxious inner life of a young lad at the amphetamine heart of the mod scene.

Bowie was a regular visitor to London's Tibetan Buddhist Institute, also known as Tibet House. It was here that he met a man clad in saffron robes, Chime Yong Dong Rinpoche. Through his new guru, Bowie learnt about plans for the establishment of a Scottish haven for other refugees from Maoist oppression in Tibet: Johnstone House in Eskdalemuir, Dumfriesshire. The singer became involved in the project, which soon became a destination for pop stars on a spiritual-awakening trip – Lennon and Ono, Leonard Cohen, The

Incredible String Band – as well as various actors and actresses. Eskdalemuir has been described as 'more like a rest home for burned out hippies than a religious institution', with sex and drugs competing with spiritual contemplation for the visitors' time.

Bowie, though, was serious. He was torn between an impulse to leave behind the fame chase altogether and renewed surges of desire to make it in the pop biz, throwing himself into strategising and the wooing of movers and shakers who might help him get to the top.

'I'm thinking of chucking it in. Really, I'd like to become a Buddhist monk,' he told one interviewer in late 1967. Recalling this period many years later in a published dialogue with William S. Burroughs, Bowie spoke of a time when 'I wanted to become a novice monk', only to blow it by getting drunk two weeks before the final commitment. In another account, he claimed that his guru Rinpoche advised him that Buddhism was not his true calling or heart's desire, saying, 'You should follow music.' In yet another set of possibly embroidered memories, it was Lindsay Kemp who dissuaded him from shaving off his beautiful locks.

One of Bowie's Kemp-influenced mime pieces, 'Jetsun and the Eagle' – which he performed a number of times in 1968–9, including during concert dates supporting Tyrannosaurus Rex – took its name from the eleventh-century Tibetan yogi Jetsun Milarepa, whose writings were canonical in the Mahayana strand of Buddhism to which Bowie adhered. The piece was based on the legend that Milarepa was originally an adept of black magic, which he used to avenge himself upon wicked relatives. But he then abandoned the dark arts for a higher path, achieving enlightenment and mastery over himself, as well as supernatural powers, like the ability to change the shape of his body and fly like a bird. Buddhist notions fed into certain early Bowie songs like 'Karma Man' and the debut album's 'Silly Boy Blue'. The latter, which also served as the backing track to performances of 'Jetsun and the Eagle', is a panorama across the wondrous strangeness of Tibet and refers to 'yak-butter statues', as well as concepts like reincarnation, the Over-Soul and *chela*, a word that means 'disciple' and usually pairs with 'guru'.

If the musical expressions of Bowie's earnest interest in Eastern spirituality seem somewhat jejune, it's worth bearing in mind that in 1969 he was only twenty-two. Like many adolescent autodidacts, his awakening mind was attracted to disparate bodies of thought – Buddhism, Nietzsche, Wilde's aestheticism, Warhol and more – and wove often incompatible threads into a world-view-in-progress. While many of us, as youths, jotted down provisional thoughts about life and art into our journals or, later on, wrote essays for college mags that were swiftly and mercifully consigned to oblivion, Bowie's juvenilia has stuck around. It is permanently engraved in vinyl that circulates to this day; it's also been extensively reissued and rendered universally accessible through YouTube, Internet lyric sites and fan webzines containing exhaustive archives of his early interviews.

To his credit, Bowie was under no illusions that he had worked anything much out, admitting in a 1972 interview that 'I'm not an intellectual by any stretch of the imagination . . . I would describe me as a tactile thinker. I pick up on things . . .' In another earlier profile he dismissed the aspirations to profundity of his entire profession: 'We're not the great thinkers of our time, as you might believe from all the interviews we have to do.' He suggested that musicians and their critic-hagiographers were no closer to 'real thinking' than the right-wing detractors of rock who saw it as degenerate trash: 'We're . . . just as naïve and bigoted.'

There was an intensity to Bowie's engagement with Buddhism, though: he was really searching for answers. What was it that drew him to Mahayana, the branch of Tibetan Buddhism that he mostly studied? Mahayana is a complicated, varied set of principles and concepts, full of paradoxes, confusing to the uninitiated outsider.

Still, certain themes do have a striking resonance with how Bowie conducted his career. 'The Songs of Milarepa', as the yogi's writings are often known, stressed the necessity of non-attachment, including to one's physical body. Bowie has said that 'the idea of transience' never left him: the self as a figment, a will-o'-the-wisp illusion, the thinnest of membranes masking a profound emptiness. But in Buddhism this interior void is not troubling or nihilistic: the true self *is* the no-self, a positive emptiness that is distinguished from the puffed-up 'substance' of the public person. Reality, the world of appearances, is *maya*, a word that means variously illusion, magic and dream. But in Mahayana, the self too is a 'magic show', a trick done with mirrors.

These ideas – the everyday world as illusion, the true self as a deathless essence – have certain resemblances to Gnosticism, something that Bowie would later explore in his spiritual questing. Both mystical creeds have an anti-worldly bias, seeing so-called reality as either vaporous vanity or the botched creation of a false god. Renouncing the world is a way of escaping passion (in Christian mysticism a word that signifies both desire and suffering) and achieving serenity.

Hurling oneself into the glamour chase of pop stardom would seem the absolute opposite of such ascetic withdrawal from the worldly. But at the same time, the Buddhist idea of 'self-empty' lends itself to a blank-slate view of personality, a career based around constant change and image makeover. This is where Buddhism makes an unlikely convergence with the performative notion of gender and self-construction that underpins camp and drag.

Blending Mahayana and the camp theatricality of Lindsay Kemp, Bowie developed a psychology of flux and mutability. This idea was emblazoned in the title of the 2013 Victoria and Albert Museum retrospective of his career and work: 'David Bowie Is . . .' This hanging predicate, initially left blank, was then completed by a variety of verbs, nouns and adjectives in different sections of the exhibition. The truly telling variation was 'David Bowie Is . . . Making Himself Up'.

Sixties Bowie, still a creature of that decade and its obsession with truth and the real, sometimes fretted about the absence of an authentic core to his self. But increasingly he found solace in the idea that if every image and public persona is fake, a put-on, then that freed you up to put them on and take them off, just like costumes. 'It's much more a realism for me to think that this (clothes, hair, gestures, the room) is all me; that there's nothing else in here,' Bowie said in one interview. 'It's all outside. I prefer that way of existence.'

Bowie had grasped a problem that recurs throughout the history of rock, and is common to all art forms based on the idea of reality or naturalism. Every once shockingly 'real' form of expression eventually becomes a set of mannerisms, emptied out by repetition and the passage of time. This process would play out in music time and time again: rock'n'roll, punk, hip hop – each became a code replicable by inauthentic outsiders, a tradition that outlived its original function or context. The same sort of syndrome can also be seen at work in acting, where every attempt to introduce a new level of reality in performance reveals itself in time to be as theatrical as the gestural codes it attempted to disrupt and outdate.

If trying to represent truth onstage or in song is a fool's errand, and the performance persona can only be a mask, telling lies becomes more honest; openly being a charlatan or poseur is to be authentic. In the 1974 dialogue with Burroughs, Bowie confessed without embarrassment that 'I change my mind a lot. I usually don't agree with what I say very much. I'm an awful liar . . . People are always throwing things at me that I've said . . . [but] you can't stand still on one point for your entire life.' Integrity – sticking to principles, being internally consistent in your opinions and values – was a mirage. We are all making it up as we go along, unmaking our minds and remaking our selves.

The hodgepodge of philosophical and spiritual ideas that Bowie was ingesting coalesced into a winning strategy, something that would establish not just a successful pop star, but the dominant, sensibility-defining figure of seventies rock. The strategy was the serial identity makeover, what we'd nowadays call 'rebranding'. Inspired by the 'David Bowie Is . . .' exhibition, a copywriter and design journalist called Jude Stewart penned a paean entitled '6 Things David Bowie Taught Me About Branding'. Among the life lessons were 'authenticity is overrated', 'root your brand in verbs, not nouns' (in other words, don't get fixed in terms of genre or approach) and 'brands multiply their power by intersecting with culture' (meaning it's okay to steal ideas from other regions of the popular and highbrow arts).

This sort of approach, and the idea of changing your sound and image with every album, is now such a commonplace practice in pop – thanks largely to Bowie – that it can be hard to reconstruct how sacrilegiously new it was at the start of the seventies. Serious rock culture in both Britain and America regarded hype with great suspicion and expected bands to pay their dues with years of slogging on the live circuit. The artists who were respected in those days almost always did a certain thing and evolved it in a steady, gradual fashion: think the Stones, Clapton, Fleetwood Mac or The Grateful Dead . . . or anybody really. Integrity meant consistency and commitment.

One of Jude Stewart's other Bowie-derived morsels of wisdom was that 'great brands lead culture'. But that wasn't particularly true for Bowie: often he was just quick off the mark at picking up on what was already happening in a more obscure region of the culture. And in the early phase of his career, Bowie was actually lagging a little behind the times.

Take his third album *The Man Who Sold the World*, released late in 1970 in America and early in 1971 in Britain. The music world had been undergoing a concerted shift back to basic rock'n'roll for a year or two by that point, led by figures as high profile as John Lennon, Creedence Clearwater Revival and Bowie's own friend Marc Bolan. Yet *The Man Who Sold the World* offered a behind-the-curve precis of the late-sixties sounds: Cream, Hendrix, Jefferson Airplane, Jethro Tull.

Bowie didn't hide his lack of commitment to this style, talking openly about the direction as a strategy: 'I probably needed a heavier sound behind me, and obviously it's worked. It's not that I have a very strong feeling for heavy music – I don't. In fact, I think it's fairly primitive as a music form.' But even as a strategic move, it was hopelessly mistimed: the underground was in decline and raw rock'n'roll was topping the charts. The results were unconvincing – Bowie shrieking shrill and reedy over endless solos, bombastic jams and time-signature shifts – in part because he was so uninvolved during the process. He ceded the initiative to producer Tony Visconti and, above all, to his new accomplice, Mick Ronson, who in addition to playing lead guitar took charge of the arrangements and became the de facto musical director.

Initially titled *Metrobolist*, a play on Fritz Lang's *Metropolis*, *The Man Who Sold the World* continued some of the science-fiction leanings evident in 'Space Oddity' and 'Memories of a Free Festival' (in which Venusians land, hang out with the hippies, then take off). Here Bowie was in tune with tendencies elsewhere in the hippy underground: the Jefferson Airplane side project Jefferson Starship, with its *Blows Against the Empire* fantasy of hippies purloining a government spaceship and fleeing Earth to create a paradise of 'free minds, free bodies, free dope, free music'; or the similar freaks-versus-fascism allegories of Ladbroke Grove cosmic rockers Hawkwind. 'Saviour Machine' is the only explicitly science-fiction song on the album, virtually merging two Kubrick movies about technology gone wrong – *Dr Strangelove* and *2001: A Space Odyssey* (specifically, the supercomputer H.A.L. going insane) – to tell a tale of a supercomputer designed to eradicate war and famine using logic and planning, but which grows increasingly demented by boredom, until it contemplates exterminating humanity altogether just to liven up its existence.

The title track has been interpreted by some critics as a ghost tale or uncanny conundrum: men who aren't there meeting on the stairs, speaking without words, confusion of time, swapping identity. Being a teenage science-fiction fan, the image of 'the man who sold the world' always made me think of Frederik Pohl and C. M. Kornbluth's *The Space Merchants*, or Alfred Bester's *The Demolished Man* and *Tiger, Tiger*, with their themes of telepathy and mega-corporations carving up the solar system; while others point to Robert Heinlein's *The Man Who Sold the Moon* as a possible influence. Far and away the best song on the album, 'The Man Who Sold the World' would later become a hit single when redone by Lulu, with Bowie overseeing; decades after, Kurt Cobain popularised the tune with an acoustic rendition for Nirvana's MTV *Unplugged* show.

Close behind 'Man Who Sold' as the album's other redeeming moment is 'The Supermen', a slow stampede of processed drums that sound like an orchestra's tympani, over which Bowie shrieks about a lost primordial race of demigods. Here sci-fi is less the reference point than pulp paperback sword 'n' sorcery folded into *Thus Spoke Zarathustra*. 'I was still going through the thing where I was pretending I understood Nietzsche,' Bowie admitted in a 1976 BBC radio interview. 'A lot of that came out of trying to simplify books that I had read . . . I had tried to translate it into my terms to understand it.'

Sounding at various points like bombastic proggers Van Der Graaf Generator and the compellingly grotesque acid-folk group

Comus (fixtures of the Beckenham Arts Lab scene), *The Man Who Sold the World* was Bowie trying to pass for an underground band. The question is, why? He'd already stopped believing in hippy values and had broken away from the Beckenham Arts Lab crowd. Impetus to that parting of the ways came from the powerful new force in his life: Angela Barnett, a vivacious, dynamic American girl he'd met in 1969 through Mercury's head of promotion, Calvin Lee, a Swinging Sixties dude whom Bowie later claimed he and Angie had both been seeing separately. By the autumn of that year, he and Angie were shacked up in Beckenham, in a grand house called Haddon Hall. In March 1970, they married.

Bowie has talked about how he was still 'looking for myself' in this period. Yet there were signs of a new direction, most prominently the cover of *The Man Who Sold the World*, on which Bowie wore a velvet frock designed by Michael Fish, the boutique owner who had also created a 'man-dress' for Mick Jagger. Bowie had always been androgynous, but his image now moved well beyond the standard-issue sixties pretty-boy zone into drag-level provocation. The *mise en scène* – Bowie reclining languidly on a chaise longue, wearing the floral-pattern dress over knee-length leather boots in the classic 'fuck me' style, iron-curled locks tumbling over the plunging neckline – has been described as Pre-Raphaelite by some, while others mention Lauren Bacall as an analogue. Either way, while there had been any number of girlishly pretty rock singers, no one had splayed themselves in such a blatantly feminine posture before.

Another herald of glam was Bowie's formation of a short-lived group with Mick Ronson and Tony Visconti called The Hype, the name deliberately chosen to chafe against the underground's anti-commercialism. In a further provocation, with Angie's encouragement and assistance the group decked themselves in over-the-top costumes representing stage characters: Bowie, clad in scarves and Lurex, was Rainbowman; Ronson was the fedora-wearing

Gangsterman; bassist Visconti sported a Superman costume in his role as Hypeman; and drummer John Cambridge dressed buccaneer-style as Pirateman.

Bowie was groping his way towards the sound and visuals that would make him a star. But he was still not seen as any kind of sure bet even by those closest to him. In fact, shortly after the recording of *The Man Who Sold the World*, but before it was released in the UK, Bowie's band on that record – Visconti, Ronson and drummer Woody Woodmansey – took off to make a record without him. Initially they used the name Hype, but then changed it to Ronno – after Ronson – and brought in Benny Marshall, an old associate of the guitarist's from Hull, as their singer. In November 1970, the group entered the studio to make an LP. They struggled to generate song material, but Ronno did release one single, 'Fourth Hour of My Sleep', released on the progressive label Vertigo in early 1971. This odd episode – revealing both lack of loyalty and lack of foresight, given that Bowie was set to be the most important rock performer of the seventies – shows how little promise the singer seemed to possess in 1970–1.

The Man Who Sold the World made some waves in America, but in the UK it came out to minimal impact. Shortly before its March release, Bowie released a single unaided by Visconti (now busy with Bolan), 'Holy Holy', a slight, uncatchy Xerox of T. Rex. It sank without trace.

By the spring of 1971, Bowie had been in the music biz for nearly nine years. From The Kon-Rads to The Hype, he'd been in or fronted some eight or nine bands, depending on how you define that word. Bowie had been through four or five distinctive stylistic phases. There had been three unsuccessful albums and a long line of flop singles that would have been perfectly unbroken if not for

'Space Oddity', a work of genius that saddled him with the reputation of one-hit wonder, not least in his own mind.

The notion of 'overnight success' is almost always a myth, hiding years of preparation and graft. Still, there can't be many examples of success that are less overnight than Bowie's, and even fewer where the success, when it came, was so total. What kept him going? What was the source of his unflagging self-belief? Simply that same magical self-motivational power that both he and Bolan possessed.

But that's not all he had. Like Bolan, he also had the ability to motivate other people, to make them believe he was destined for stardom. That was why such a long string of managers, mentors, accomplices, music-biz movers-and-shakers placed such faith in his gifts, when the evidence was fairly thin on the ground. It had a lot to do with his personal charm and the unusual quality of his beauty – that enigmatic visual allure conjured by his gaunt features, those disconcerting, differently coloured eyes (from an injury caused by a childhood scrap), the hint of vampire to his smile. If David Bowie had looked like . . . well, Mick Ronson, a solidly decent-looking British bloke, would he have been extended all that time in which to find himself, to fashion a self that could sell?

Bowie had this effect on people – gay and straight, men and women. Many of those who helped him on his long, fitful way to the top were more or less in love with him, or otherwise transfixed by his latent star quality. One thinks again of Dorian Gray and his 'curious charm'. Perhaps, as Wilde wrote, beauty *is* a form of genius – one that was working for Bowie long before any other kind of genius made an appearance.

3:

ELECTED: ALICE COOPER AND SHOCK ROCK

Alice Cooper

Alice Cooper is reminiscing about the days when he killed himself for a living. 'Any time you have moving parts onstage, you are asking for *Spinal Tap*,' he says of the gallows and the guillotine that were climactic fixtures of his early-seventies concerts. 'And when it doesn't work, you have to play it for comedy.' But the time the gallows broke in England was no laughing matter. 'There was a wire connected to my back, it stopped the noose from hitting my neck, and we'd done the trick one hundred times, never thinking, "Maybe that wire is getting brittle." And then it snapped and the noose grabbed me for real.' Cooper was quick-witted enough to tilt his chin up and slip through the noose. He was lucky to escape with a nasty rope burn down his throat and bruised knees.

Four decades after this close shave, Cooper sits serenely in a downtown LA hotel suite. Wearing white jeans with an excess of zips, a plain black T-shirt and a vaguely sepulchral medallion nestled in a thicket of chest hair, Alice looks much the same as he did in his seventies heyday, give or take a few wrinkles and some paunch.

But when you look at the old footage of Alice onstage, it's striking how even in his twenties he never really seemed like a young man. From his swarthy, crow-like countenance to his scrawny body, Cooper was never going to become a rock star through sexual magnetism, nor through the strength and beauty of his voice. Instead, he became one of the best 'bad' singers rock'n'roll has ever known, his haggard rasp equally suited to the proto-punk snarl of 'I'm Eighteen' and the megalomaniacal bombast of 'Elected'. Rather than a sex symbol, Cooper achieved stardom as a death symbol. Abandoning 'erotic politics' as a faded relic of the idealistic sixties, Cooper based his act around gore and gruesomeness: songs like 'Dead Babies', 'Under My Wheels' and the necrophilia love song 'I Love the Dead'; LPs with titles like *Killer* and *Love It to Death*; and, above all, the infamous stage routines involving molesting mannequin women, chopping up baby dolls and hair-raisingly realistic executions, starting off with a chrome electric chair that Cooper himself built.

Even more than the lyrics or the theatrics, it was Alice Cooper's image that perturbed: the ratty frizz of black hair, the stooped posture, the down-turned gashes of black make-up at the corners of his mouth and from the centre of his eyes that made him resemble Pierrot in hell. His acrid voice and abject aura – intensified by the use of snakes in the act and in photo sessions – made him seem like a grown-up version of that spiteful, nasty neighbourhood kid that parents fear as a Bad Influence. Cooper's physical presence suggested a figure of unimaginable depravity who took impure delight in evil-doing. And it was this as much as the songs and the shows that attracted his vast following of 'sick things', Cooper's nickname for the fans: young kids looking for something definitively seventies, a nihilistic new sensibility of bad taste and black humour as repellent to fans of earlier rock – their older brothers and sisters, in other words – as it was threatening to their parents.

Alice Cooper – confusingly the name of the band as well as the adopted alias of its lead singer, Vincent Furnier – evolved from its early sound of chaotic psychedelia into a hard-riffing machine. But unlike the other strutting arena bands of the era, like Led Zeppelin, they weren't cock rock but shock rock. The foundation of Alice Cooper's appeal was the pubescent boy, one lacking sexual confidence or (most likely) experience. The group found a constituency of early-adolescent males into all things grisly and precociously cynical – horror movies, books about the Third Reich and serial killers, fantasies about nuclear destruction – as well as comic books and pulp fiction of all kinds. 'We affect the little teenage boys between the ages of twelve and fifteen more than anybody,' Cooper once said. 'They consider us the heroes of our time for some reason.'

Today, Cooper tends to be seen as one of the godfathers of heavy metal, an Ozzy Osbourne-like revered elder still hauling his haggard carcass onstage to huge crowds across the world. But Cooper has as much of a claim to be a central innovator in glam as Bolan or Bowie. Simultaneous with the British pioneers – even slightly ahead of them – Alice Cooper explored cross-dressing, deployed outrage as both titillation-lure for the audience and attention-getting strategy in the media, embraced decadence as a concept, an atmosphere, even an 'ideal', and talked openly about his use of lies for the purpose of both self-reinvention and self-promotion.

Although often dismissed as a cartoon figure, Alice Cooper has received a measure of recognition as a pioneer of theatrical rock and as the inventor of shock rock. In Cooper, theatricality and outrage are synonymous, but they don't have to be. Rock bands have been theatrical without necessarily being offensive, instead opting for the fantastical, the surreal, the magical-mystical, the whimsical and just plain daft, as has often been the case with progressive rock: Jethro Tull's prancing flute player Ian Anderson; Peter Gabriel of Genesis costumed as a fox or as the bulbously deformed Slipperman; Kate Bush's 1979 'Tour of Life' concerts, which incorporated mime, magic and modern dance. Equally, performers like Iggy Pop, Suicide, James Chance and GG Allin have shocked audiences without resort to props, stage sets or choreographed routines, but through premeditated yet improvised confrontations with the audience, acts of onstage destruction or obscenity.

Alice Cooper didn't invent either rock theatre or rock shock, but he escalated existing tendencies to the point where some of the more overheated contemporary commentators wondered how long it would be before a rock performer killed himself, or someone else, onstage.

Fifties rock'n'roll was for the most part energetic but at a distance from showbiz razzle-dazzle. The big exceptions are Screamin' Jay Hawkins, with his exotic costumes and macabre props, like a smoking skull and a coffin; and Jerry Lee Lewis, who'd douse his piano with gasoline during 'Great Balls of Fire' and transform it into a pyre, all the while pounding the blazing keys. By the mid-sixties, though, this flashy vaudevillian side to rock'n'roll had almost completely died out in America, as rock became an earnest affair with aspirations to artistic weight and countercultural edge.

Again, there were exceptions. Strawberry Alarm Clock sometimes got carried onstage by their roadies on magic carpets, while the drummer rigged up gas jets to his wrists to wreathe his hands in flames. Dr John developed a hoodoo-voodoo shtick of witchdoctor robes and ceremonial incantations illuminated by flickering torches. The Doors instinctively deployed the power of portentous gesture and musical drama with epic song suites like 'The Celebration of the Lizard'. 'Jim Morrison was a better actor than a singer, and he was a fantastic actor,' Alice Cooper has said, acknowledging The Doors as an influence, but adding 'they didn't go to the next step, which is props'. But for the most part, serious rock groups in America shunned visual showiness, associating it with, well, showbiz – which in the bohemian mind equated with phoney. Instead, wrote Albert Goldman, rock bands in America modelled their stage performance on 'the tradition of the singing vagabond, the country bluesman, and other artists of the road'.

In Britain, though, the theatricality of early rock'n'roll acts like Johnny Kidd and the Pirates and Nero and the Gladiators – both dressed in the costumes their names suggest – continued with the spectacles of orgiastic destruction staged by mid-sixties groups like

The Who, The Creation and John's Children. Many of the new British beat groups had a heightened awareness of image and presentation through being products of art school. 'Most people thought we were British at first,' says Cooper. 'Me and Dennis Dunaway, our bassist, were both art majors and probably the two strongest forces as far as the image and the staging. We were Salvador Dalí fans.'

Alice Cooper's three prime precursors in terms of theatrical rock and shock rock are British performers: Screaming Lord Sutch, who copied and intensified Screamin' Jay Hawkins's act and added a prankster public persona with his forays into electoral politics; The Move, with their extravaganzas of onstage demolition and use of contrived controversy as PR; and The Crazy World of Arthur Brown, with their pyromania, outlandish costumes and grotesque make-up.

Screaming Lord Sutch offered what his manager called a 'unique blend of singing, comedy and horror', and what Sutch himself called 'vaudeville but put into rock and roll'. From 1960 onwards, backed by his band The Savages and sporting fourteen-inch-long green hair, Sutch entertained audiences with songs like 'Jack the Ripper' and 'Big Black Coffin' that were set-ups for stage routines: fake disembowelment with internal organs hurled into the audience; Sutch emerging from, you guessed it, a big black coffin. He would do themed tours like 'Sutch and the Roman Empire', the whole band garbed as Roman infantry. Sutch pre-empted and surpassed Cooper on another front: whereas in the video for 'Elected' the latter only posed as a candidate in the 1972 US presidential election, Sutch actually stood for political office repeatedly, starting in 1963, when he campaigned to be an MP for the National Teenage Party. A few years later he campaigned in the seat of then prime minister Harold Wilson. His youth-friendly platform included lowering the age of voting to eighteen. Later, Sutch founded the Official Monster Raving Loony Party and continued running for office under the banner 'Vote for insanity, you know it makes sense.'

'The most obnoxiously contrived image-peddlers in the history of English pop' – that's how critic Andrew Weiner described The Move, a group willing to resort to any stunt in order to wage and win what he called 'the Image War'. Manager Tony Secunda had worked with Johnny Kidd and the Pirates, whose gimmick was dressing like buccaneers, and he had also been a wrestling promoter briefly. Although Roy Wood, the musical genius behind The Move and, later on, the mastermind behind glitter-pop sensation Wizzard, felt embarrassed by the publicity ploys hatched by their manager, singer Carl Wayne spoke for the rest of The Move when he declared, 'We were always willing to be Secunda puppets.' Soon they were taking axes to TV sets and smashing up cars during concerts, performing alongside effigies of Hitler and Harold Wilson, bringing strippers onstage, setting things on fire and throwing smoke bombs. The tabloid newspapers ate it all up. They signed one music-biz contract on the back of a topless model. But then Secunda went too far: the promo materials for one of their biggest hit singles, 'Flowers in the Rain', included a postcard featuring a satirical cartoon of a naked Prime Minister Wilson in bed with his secretary Marcia Williams, under the legend 'Disgusting, Depraved, Despicable'. The PM sued, and The Move were forced to donate all the single's royalties to charity.

The Crazy World of Arthur Brown became a sensation in the British underground in 1967 with a highly theatrical act and Brown's portentous, multi-octave singing. Wearing vaguely satanic-looking robes and a helmet that spouted flames, Brown sometimes made his entrance onstage from a mobile crane. Critics showered him and his band with plaudits: the *New Statesman*'s Charles Fox, for instance, hailed Brown as 'the first genuine artist to come out of our local underground', placing his 'disconcerting, even faintly perverse, but distinctly original' act in 'a very, very English tradition' that went back through the sadistic puppet shows of Punch

and Judy to the medieval mummers' plays. Produced by Who manager Kit Lambert, with input from Pete Townshend, *The Crazy
World of Arthur Brown* featured a cover of Screamin' Jay Hawkins's
'I Put a Spell on You' and a driving, guitar-less sound centred
around Vincent Crane's Gothick organ. Like 'Born to Be Wild' for
Steppenwolf, 'Fire' defined and fixed The Crazy World of Arthur
Brown for all time: in the summer of 1968, it reached #1 in the UK
and #2 in America. Looking at the clip of the group's *Top of the Pops*
appearance – Brown in witch-doctor greasepaint, gyrating perturb-
ingly in the midst of simulated flames, proclaiming himself 'the god
of hellfire' – it's easy to see how alarming it would have been to parents and the conventional-minded, both as a spectacle and through
its association with the 'burn, baby, burn' spirit of 1968's riots and
youth revolt.

The concept of shock was central to Brown's vision: 'Our act is
a shock-visual thing'; 'We like to . . . shock and attack the audience.' But it was shock for a higher purpose: to jolt 'audiences out of
their usual states of mind', with a view to changing perceptions and
raising consciousness. The emphasis on visual assault and insanity,
the use of props and stage machinery, the physical risks and ordeal
involved, such as robes catching fire and the updraft from the blazing helmet parching his throat – all make Arthur Brown the prime
precursor to Alice Cooper. Indeed, the latter did once support The
Crazy World at a Michigan pop concert, although Cooper insists
that he was already doing the scary black make-up around the eyes.

Talking to the *NME* in 1972, Cooper argued that while Britain
had produced 'hundreds of groups that had good images' – by which
he meant extreme or outrageous ones – 'America has never really
had a great rock and roll band with a wild image'. The only exception he could think of was The Doors, a generalisation that has the
ring of truth. Why did British rock, from the start, have a stronger
propensity for theatrics?

In his pop history *All You Need Is Love,* Tony Palmer attributed that to the British lack of an organic cultural connection to rock'n'roll, which arrived as an import and flourished despite being a shakily grafted transplant that bore barely any relation to 'the musical heritage of Europe'. Nor was there a natural circuit for the UK's fledgling rock'n'roll acts – no jukebox joints or dancehalls. So the new sounds reached the paying public largely through 'the old music hall circuit', with the booker treating it as just the latest fad. The rock'n'roll groups had to jostle alongside the other components of a given night's entertainment: 'stand-up comics, jugglers, animal acts, dancers, singers', as well as the pit band lurking beneath the lip of the stage, who were often hostile to the idea of a singer coming on with his own backing group. Through their exposure to professional all-round entertainers 'versed in the whole gamut of British stage skills', the young rockers absorbed ideas about 'presentation and stage discipline'. Hence the rise of acts that blurred the line between rock'n'roll and music hall, like Screaming Lord Sutch or Wee Willie Harris, 'Britain's wild man of rock'n'roll', who dressed like Tarzan and had long bright-orange hair.

While in America the managers, agents and promoters who handled rock'n'roll generally had no contact with theatre, Palmer notes that 'in Britain . . . theater was everything. The agents who sold the rock acts were almost exclusively theatrical agents.' Likewise, Jack Good, the pioneer of British pop TV, had a theatre background and applied his awareness of the dramatic potential of visual imagery to shows like *Six-Five Special, Wham!* and *Oh Boy!,* using meticulously rehearsed close-ups ('to catch all the carefully manufactured mean looks', writes Palmer) and hard white lighting techniques borrowed from the French National Theatre.

Legend has it that Good was disappointed when he first met Gene Vincent by the disparity between the sensual menace of records like 'Be-Bop-a-Lula' and the singer's polite demeanour and unthreatening appearance. So he remodelled Vincent's image, persuading him to dress entirely in black (including gloves) and exploiting his motorbike-accident injuries to create a limping, lurching Richard III-like presence. Such was Good's precocious grasp of pop's intrinsic audio-visual nature that in 1959 he prophesied music video, predicting that it would become 'standard practice for every artist to make a film of themselves performing their record. These short films will be sent to TV producers for their programmes.' This would indeed be the future of pop, and it would be one that the British pioneered.

As much as Alice Cooper could be mistaken for a British band, there was also a sense in which they were European, on the one hand renovating the French tradition of Grand Guignol, and on the other consciously aspiring to create a rock form of Dada and surrealism. Founded in 1894 and named after a traditional puppet character roughly equivalent to Punch and Judy, Le Théâtre du Grand-Guignol became popular for its extremely realistic and gorily graphic recreations of murder, rape and infanticide, as well as its dramatic explorations of states of insanity and psychosis. The Parisian public flocked to experience sensations and sights not available in banal everyday life, vicarious adrenalin-rushes that in some cases led to fainting or vomiting, and in others to sexual arousal and licentious acts. Similarly, Joyce Ciletti, a student conducting thesis research on the Alice Cooper phenomenon in the early seventies, found that some of her questionnaire respondents described the mock executions as the most thrilling moments in the concerts, sometimes using erotic language: 'It gave me such supreme satisfaction,' one female fan reported. Crowds left Alice Cooper concerts 'amazed . . . stunned', emotionally and libidinally drained.

'Dada rock' is what *Newsweek* actually dubbed Alice Cooper. Like so many teenagers with a gauche penchant for weirdness and portentously transgressive symbolism, Alice Cooper's true art crush was the surrealist Salvador Dalí. In one of the great publicity stunts of a career littered with them, a tête-à-tête between Cooper and Dalí – himself one of the great self-publicists and personality-as-performance hucksters of the twentieth century – was set up at the St Regis hotel in New York on 3 April 1973. Dalí was also paid $14,000 to create a holographic portrait of Alice for onstage display during that year's 'Billion Dollar Babies' tour: Cooper modelled for Dalí wearing a million bucks' worth of jewellery and clutching a brain designed by the artist and full of Dalí-esque symbols. At a presentation of the work in New York, Dalí hailed Cooper as 'the best exponent of total confusion', and the singer returned the compliment, dubbing Dalí 'the master of chaos'. Later on, Cooper admitted: 'To be quite honest I haven't ever understood one word he's said to me.'

The hook-up with Dalí served as both a photo op and an aspiration to highbrow credibility. It placed Alice Cooper in a lineage of *épater les bourgeois* that went back to the decadents of the late nineteenth century. This impulse to scandalise the middlebrow consensus about good taste and aesthetic decorum was the hallmark of every manifesto-brandishing 'ism' of the early twentieth century – the futurists, the Dadaists, the surrealists and many more – and it resumed after the Second World War with movements such as action painting and Aktionism. In these avant-gardes, the Shock of the New (the formal violence of abrasively anti-aesthetic or challenging forms) was typically combined with the Shock of the Real (the graphic depiction of content conventionally deemed too visceral or private or abject). The shocking realness side of this impulse is alive and well in today's culture in the form of television comedy's competition to show and speak of ever more gross things: vomiting, ejaculation, sitting on the toilet.

'Shocking the bourgeois is, alas, easier than overthrowing him,' the Marxist historian Eric Hobsbawm wrote in his 1969 essay 'Sex and Revolution', pointing out the tenuousness of the links between avant-garde insurrection and actual changes in political reality. But the truth is – as the TV-comedy example shows only too well – it isn't actually that easy to shock the bourgeois either any more. Even by the sixties, what Susan Sontag called 'the dialectic of outrage' was starting to look fairly fatigued. In 1962, art critic Leo Steinberg wrote about how the 'rapid domestication of the outrageous' had shrivelled the 'time lapse between shock received and thanks returned': *enfants terribles* became Establishment figures within just a few years. At the same time, because of the uneven development of sensibility across a society, what might seem clumsy and played-out to a minority of virtually unshockable sophisticates could still seem abhorrent to the less-advanced majority, some of whom would be enraged and others aroused. Alice Cooper's reputation at their height was similarly dependent on perspective. For the mainstream – mums and dads, the spiritually middle-aged and middle-class regardless of actual age or income – they were poisonous. For the kids, they were intoxicating. For the slightly older hipsters, they provoked mild titillation or a blasé shrug.

The meaning of *épater les bourgeois* has changed over time. When the French decadents first used the expression, it signified the shudder of outrage and scandal. But put the phrase into an online translation program and it comes out as 'wow the bourgeois' – as in 'impress' or 'amaze'. The French graphic artist and writer Sébastien Morlighem told me that '*épater*' today means 'to surprise someone', not in a negative way but 'with the aim of creating a positive feeling, to build some kind of *complicity*'. That word captures exactly how 'shock' nowadays works as a cultural mechanism: the consumer-spectator of outrageous art is almost always complicit, taking the side of the perpetrator against censorious authority, the priggish parents or shaken-up squares. As you experience the work or performance you engage in an odd mental process of imagining some less sophisticated person who *would* be shocked, *if* they just happened to be in range.

Often, conveniently, there are a few actual people who voice appalled objections, like the politicians and clean-up-the-airwaves campaigners who tried to ban Alice Cooper's records and concerts in the UK. And it can get more subtly complicated still, this internal process: to an extent you can get off on the frisson of shocking some residually staid part of your own personality still bearing the imprint of your upbringing, defying the finger-wagging parent or school principal, the priest or policeman, in your own head. There is a liberating thrill in crossing a boundary of taste or morals within yourself. Discussing A. Alvarez's concept of extremist art, Clive James warned of the dangers of this both for the artist and for his fans: the endpoint of the dialectic of shock is 'not so much in anarchy as in a kind of internal fascism by which the artist, to relieve his own boredom, becomes both torturer and tortured'. As we will see later on, too often this internal escalation – the pushing past one's own limits – culminates in a literal fascination with fascism.

Still, for all their art school-influenced Euro flirtations, Alice Cooper were at heart a supremely American band, steeped in pulp entertainment of every kind: television's cowboy and cop shows; the endless airings on the small screen of classic and not-so-classic black-and-white movies from the Hollywood vaults; and kiddie-hour cartoons in the Looney Tunes/*Tom and Jerry* vein of ultra-violence-without-consequences. Cooper told *Poppin* magazine that 'we weren't brought up under a blues influence. We were brought up under an electronics influence.' More than music it was 'television and movies and America' that shaped Cooper, who confessed that watching TV was 'the only thing I love to do . . . my favourite hobby . . . a vast vault of useless knowledge'.

Years before punk-era groups like The Dictators, The Ramones and The Cramps placed the trash aesthetic at their core, Cooper spoke about how 'there's not such a thing nowadays as bad taste . . . today most people are only interested in flagrant sex and violence . . . they just delight in witnessing a gory accident or sit glued to their television sets watching disaster, rape, war and murder'. Both the TV shows and the commercials in between were in the same business: stoking libido (and the darker drives), weakening impulse control. 'You just let your lower self go.'

Cooper had a gut sense of what J. G. Ballard would theorise about and enact in his fiction: the way TV's discontinuous barrage of highly charged imagery sensitised the eye into an erogenous zone, while desensitising moral and empathetic faculties. The distinction between reality and fantasy eroded. As Steve Turner, profiling Cooper for *Outloud* magazine, put it: 'The more Alice watched television, the more he wondered what is real and what is not.' Turner proposed the singer and his band as 'the Frankenstein of the cathode tube . . . a product of a sick society rather than a responsible human with the power to choose'.

Which makes Alice Cooper's work and the mass phenomenon of their success seem like a genuinely troubling development. But in another sense, they were just a giant joke, a refusal to take anything seriously. Comedy, after all, was another zone in which Sontag's 'dialectic of outrage' played out during the sixties. As much as rock'n'roll, or surrealism, or lowbrow mass entertainment, Alice Cooper were the by-product of the rise of sick humour: that impulse, driven both by an urge for liberation and a compulsion to offend, to push deeper into the indecorous, the grotesque, the raw real, as pursued by comedians and comic writers like Lenny Bruce, Joe Orton, Barry Humphries, Monty Python, Richard Pryor, National Lampoon and more.

N

The band was actually born in a spirit of lampoon. In 1964, they formed The Earwigs, a spoof on The Beatles, and wowed their fellow students in a talent show at Cortez High School in Phoenix, Arizona. Developing into a more serious proposition, The Spiders, they scored a local #1 single in 1966 with 'Don't Blow Your Mind'. Following a basically Anglophile trajectory, they evolved from Stones/Them-style garage punk to the psychedelic-sounding The Nazz – not to be confused with Todd Rundgren's early group of the same name, although both got it from The Yardbirds' 'The Nazz Are Blue'. Along the way the line-up settled as singer Vincent Furnier, bassist Dennis Dunaway, lead guitarist Glen Buxton, rhythm guitarist Michael Bruce and drummer Neal Smith.

Even in their early days, an element of absurdist theatre filtered into the performances: props, unsettling stage postures, the use of fog machines and ultraviolet light. 'Way back in '66, I had a bath tub on stage, with me in it,' Cooper recalled in 1972. Dunaway and Cooper felt the urge to 'incorporate a little bit of surrealism into what we were doing', he says now. 'To me a broom could be anything. Or it could be five different things. You found a bottle backstage or a light . . . At that time nobody'd ever done that in rock'n'roll – bring common things onstage and use them as other things.'

By 1967, the group had moved to Los Angeles and settled in Topanga Canyon, but for a long while they returned regularly to Phoenix – where they were an established live draw – to keep themselves solvent with paying gigs. On one of these trips, or so the legend goes, the band's new and lasting name came out of a seance that conjured the visitation of the spirit of a seventeenth-century girl called Alice Cooper. Her sister Christine had been burned at the stake as a witch. Overcome with grief, Alice had swallowed poison and, as a suicide exiled from heaven, she languished eternally as a wandering ghost. According to Dunaway, the name came first, out of nowhere, and the messing around on the Ouija board followed.

The creation myth, embellished with each retelling, stuck. Even with their unusual new name, though, Alice Cooper remained just one of a throng of bands in LA scrabbling around the edges of one of the country's hottest music scenes. That impelled them to make the act ever more garishly confrontational, to stand out but also to cover over their deficiencies as musicians and the derivativeness of the original material they were only now starting to write. Eventually they found the ideal milieu in LA: the freak scene surrounding Frank Zappa, so markedly at odds with the laidback country rock and singer-songwriter culture of Laurel Canyon, all those bands formed out of the debris of The Byrds and Buffalo Springfield.

A shrewd businessman and exacting band leader as much as he was a long-haired libertine and anarchic absurdist, Zappa had started his own twin record labels, Bizarre and Straight. In addition to his solo albums and work with The Mothers of Invention, these were the outlets for albums by a motley bunch of weirdos produced by Zappa. Among them was Wild Man Fischer, a schizophrenic street musician regarded by Zappa as a true American primitive. Then there was Captain Beefheart and the Magic Band, a mind-warping, body-dislocating merger of Dada and blues forged by Zappa's old friend Don Van Vliet, whose malign charisma and manipulative hold over his troupe of young players made him not too far off the Manson of music. And there was also The GTOs, which stood for Girls Together Outrageously: somewhere between a hippy Slits and a psychedelic Shangri-Las, this seven-strong girl gang included several of LA's most celebrated groupies, most notably Miss Pamela, later to become Pamela Des Barres, the wife of English glam rocker Michael Des Barres.

As with the Mothers of Invention albums, the Bizarre/Straight aesthetic involved the commingling of satire and spoken word with the sonic extremes of acid rock, free jazz, musique concrète and avant-garde classical. The comedy connection was crucial: among the first Bizarre and Straight releases were records by Lenny Bruce and the Beat-aligned stand-up comic and word-jazzer Lord Buckley. Some say Zappa initially saw Alice Cooper as a comedy act, a novelty rather than a serious musical proposition. Certainly the group lacked the virtuosity levels that Zappa prized. They were relatively conventional musically compared to Beefheart or The Mothers of Invention's own music. But Alice Cooper's sensibility gelled with Zappa's in many areas: the drive to talk about taboo and unseemly things; the cynicism vis-à-vis hippy ideals; a love of all-American pulp (Zappa and business partner Herb Cohen were looking for kindred-spirit artists who 'like monster movies'). Cooper and Zappa also shared a passion for parody: both their discographies are riddled with take-offs on styles of popular music.

It would be stretching it to claim that Zappa anticipated aspects of Cooper's act, but it is true that male members of the Mothers had worn dresses for photo sessions (as with the cover of *We're Only in It for the Money*) and that during the band's two-year stint in New York, when they played regularly at the Garrick Theatre, the dismemberment of a baby doll took place onstage. This, however, was a spontaneous event, and it served to make a political point: Zappa invited some US Marines in the audience to pretend the doll was a 'gook baby', i.e. a Vietnamese child. This impromptu anti-war statement was nothing like the ghoulish doll massacres that became fixtures of Alice Cooper concerts during the early seventies.

In 1969–70, Alice Cooper's showmanship was loose and spontaneous. 'A lot of it was improvised. We didn't have enough money really to buy props,' recalls Cooper. 'But we were innately theatrical.' What they inflicted on audiences was like a slapstick version of the free-form theatre experiments of the late sixties, with their nudity, confrontation and physical contact with the audience. Scholar Elizabeth Burns has described Julian Beck's Living Theatre as 'shock theatre' designed to 'drive the audience to reality'.

Alice Cooper's impulses weren't quite as high-minded or utopian: fundamentally they wanted to make a name for themselves. They would resort to anything to grab the audience's attention. 'We didn't have any money available, so our theatrics had to come totally from our environment,' recalls manager Shep Gordon of those early days. So Alice Cooper would fight onstage using laundry detergent they'd got hold of, or create visual chaos using feathers or a fire extinguisher. 'That kind of theatrics came from always staying in hotels. Hotels always have pillows and fire extinguishers are in every hall . . . We grabbed what we could get for nothing . . . just put our heads together to come up with cheap but effective ideas.'

Gordon had originally taken on Alice Cooper after witnessing their impact on a large audience at the Cheetah, a venue on Santa Monica pier in LA. He was impressed by how quickly they cleared the auditorium. This 'strong negative energy' proved Alice Cooper had 'an ability to motivate people . . . in the wrong way admittedly . . . But that's still a reaction. It's really what entertainment's about. Not many people can do that.'

Having some money to burn but zero music-industry experience, Gordon nonetheless had an instinctive grasp of the Andrew Loog Oldham principle: not only is there no such thing as bad publicity, but the manager's job is to *create* bad publicity. Just as the Stones' manager would go into audiences and start screaming to trigger hysteria among the band's female fans, or plant headlines like 'Would Your Mother Let You Go with a Rolling Stone?', or propagate scandalous stories of the band taking a piss against a petrol-station wall, Gordon was an inspired hatcher of grossly exaggerated rumours about Alice Cooper. He cites Loog Oldham as his prime role model, alongside the great nineteenth-century impresario P. T. Barnum, who used every conceivable sort of publicity stunt to generate buzz about his entertainment spectaculars. Gordon also used the classic self-fulfilling-prophecy technique of maintaining an illusion until reality caught up with the fiction: in this case, that Alice Cooper were rock stars. He got them a Cadillac limousine so that they'd always be seen getting out of it. Later on, he secured the group a rented mansion in Connecticut, where they lived communally and partially recorded their albums.

Soon becoming virtually the sixth member of the band, Gordon's instinctive flair for hustle and hype was accompanied with an intellectual detachment that anticipated punk-era managers like Malcolm McLaren. At college he'd studied sociology, which informed his conception of how to go about concocting a mass phenomenon that would polarise the general public. 'These mass movements are always driven by very basic dynamics – sex, violence or rebellion against parents,' Gordon says now. If you could figure out some fresh twist on these hardy perennials, or push them to a new lurid extreme . . . then the sweet music of cash registers would ring out. But Gordon was unlike McLaren in one key respect. The Sex Pistols' manager talked of punk rock as a giant con he'd perpetrated, a swindle to generate 'cash from chaos', but his real interest was the *chaos*: punk, for McLaren, was a social theatre of confrontation and controversy, a means to expose the giant soul-sucking machine of the record industry, siphoning off youthful energy that would otherwise threaten real change. 'The records, the music, those were never the point,' McLaren insisted. Whereas Gordon was driven by the twin motives of intense personal loyalty and money-making. His ultimate goal was to make Cooper into a long-term star – what we'd nowadays call 'a brand'. The 'anarchy' was just a means to an end.

Cooper found in Gordon a man after his own heart. He too was an enthusiastic fibber who filled his press conferences with tall tales, often capping the session with the confession that everything he'd said so far was made up. Disinformation and fantasy were 'a pure form of communication, because you don't have to make any sense . . .' Cooper told *Melody Maker*. 'Lying is a protection, because I don't want anybody to know if I'm really interesting or not. I rarely say anything that's true in an interview . . . It's one of my very favourite things in the world. A good lie is better than a dull truth.'

A lie – or, perhaps more accurately, a rumour that got out of hand – played a crucial role in Alice Cooper's rise to national infamy. In the autumn of 1969, Gordon wangled the band a premium spot in the line-up at the Toronto Rock Revival – a huge festival uniting contemporary bands and classic fifties performers. Gordon offered the band's services for free, so long as they got to play just before the headliner, John Lennon, who was performing with Yoko Ono and a pick-up band that included luminaries like Eric Clapton. For a virtually unknown band like Alice Cooper, this was a coup. During their set, a chicken somehow found its way onstage – probably Gordon's handiwork again. When Cooper grabbed the fowl and threw it into the audience, the bird got torn to shreds. The story that proliferated in newspapers and rock-world chatter was that Alice had bitten the head off the chicken and drunk its blood. When Zappa heard about the incident, he phoned the group and, discovering the less demonic truth, advised, 'Whatever you do, don't tell anyone you didn't do it.'

'It seemed to upset the whole world,' recalls Cooper. 'That's when I realised rock was looking for a villain, somebody that would have done that on purpose. That spurred me to create the Alice character to be darker.'

A big element in Alice Cooper's arsenal of shock in the early days was surprise: as a virtually unknown band, often playing support, they ambushed audiences who assumed that Alice Cooper was a Judy Collins-type female folk singer. Adding further confusion was the band's wearing of women's clothing and effeminate-looking garments: black leotards, pantyhose, flouncy wide-sleeved shirts. The GTOs took the group under their wing, foraging for things like outfits from ice-skating shows such as the Ice Capades that could be found dirt cheap in thrift stores and teaching them how to apply make-up. Alice's witchy, wonkily daubed eye make-up was inspired equally by Bette Davis in *Whatever Happened to Baby Jane?* and the character of the Black Queen in *Barbarella*.

In interviews, Cooper played up the ambisexuality, telling the *New York Times* that 'the typical male American thinks he is all male – 100 per cent, but what he has to realize is that he's got a feminine side'. In other pieces, he spoke of being into the idea of playing benefits for both Women's Lib and Gay Lib, imagined a near-future world of 'sex without any categorizations . . . no longer . . . homosexual, bi-sexual, or heterosexual – just sex'. He declared, 'I've never made it with a guy, but that doesn't mean I won't.' He fantasised publicly about owning his own men's cosmetics company, and eventually he would indeed market his own brand of mascara called Whiplash. The advertisements in the music magazines urged, 'Liberate your eyes with Alice's own unisex mascara . . . Alice says whip the one you love – get a tube for your best friend too.'

On the back of the group's 1969 debut album *Pretties for You* Cooper appeared in a green dress – an ugly sister to Bowie and actually pipping him to the post in the cross-dress race (*The Man Who Sold the World*, with Bowie on the front clad in a Mr Fish frock, came out 1970). *Easy Action*, the follow-up, displayed the whole band on the cover, their naked backs turned to the camera: with long tresses of hair hanging halfway down willowy torsos, it wasn't clear if you were looking at chicks or dudes. The *Easy Action* radio commercial pitched them as a freak act in the underground-sixties sense but expanded the concept to include a kinky ambiguity: against the screech of acid-rocky solos, an adman's voice intones, 'Alice Cooper, what a pretty child . . . pretty though she's so violent . . . Alice Cooper is unisex, raw, together and violent – just like you, fellow American. Because there's a little bit of Alice Cooper in us all . . . Now, look – you wouldn't really want to take a thing like Alice Cooper home to mother, would you?'

Easy Action's title came from the Broadway and Hollywood musical *West Side Story*, a boyhood favourite of Cooper's and Dunaway's. Snatches of Stephen Sondheim's lyrics – 'got a rocket in your pocket', 'when you're a Jet you're a Jet all the way' – appeared in the song 'Still No Air'. This was a clue to the future of Alice Cooper. Despite the success of *Hair*, musical theatre and rock were polar opposites at that time. But Cooper often talked in interviews of his love of *Guys and Dolls* and *Hellzapoppin'*, the 1941 movie adaptation of a hugely successful thirties stage musical that mixed slapstick, mischievous mockery of showbiz's own conventions, and songs with meta-gags that smashed through the fourth wall to involve the audience. Here was the first pointer to Alice Cooper's destiny: they would leave behind the hippy-era vibe and gradually embrace choreographed routines, stage sets and theatrical lighting – the discipline and precision of mainstream American showbiz.

One by-product of this shift from improvised happening to semi-scripted stage show was a switch of focus from Alice Cooper the band to Alice Cooper the singer. Instead of 'five people running all over the stage', Gordon told one reporter, it became a frontman in the spotlight. Cooper started to do the interviews on his own too. 'I learnt that to get public attention, you need that one identity, that one figure to concentrate on,' Gordon says. By this point Vincent Furnier had changed his own name to Alice Cooper – a shrewd but ultimately damaging move – 'so it was natural to use him as the frontman to get the attention'.

The image, the act and the rhetoric were moving in the right direction. What lagged behind still was the music. *Pretties for You* and *Easy Action* were hodgepodges of garbled psychedelia, a behind-the-time pastiche of British sounds (the pious-sounding high-register vocals of 'Magic Bus'-era The Who), with shreds of West Coast acid rock (Jefferson Airplane at their most highly strung and overwrought). Weakly produced and riddled with dated effects and shaky songwriting that spawned titles like 'No Longer Umpire' and 'Refrigerator Heaven', the albums sold poorly.

That all changed with the arrival of Canadian producer Bob Ezrin. Gordon had been courting Ezrin's boss, Jack Richardson, the producer behind hard-rock radio hits like The Guess Who's *Billboard* #1 'American Woman'. But it was the underling who was dispatched to check out the band live. Initially underwhelmed, Ezrin eventually met with them: he told the *NME* that he was 'shaking inside' with fear because the group's record covers led him to believe 'they were all faggots'.

Taking the reins for the third album, *Love It to Death*, Ezrin showed Alice Cooper how to de-clutter and simplify their sound. 'Dumb it down. Hit them on a basic level,' Cooper recalls Ezrin telling the group. Rhythm guitarist Mike Bruce responded to this new direction, becoming a mighty riff-generator. The very first track they worked on with Ezrin would be the group's breakthrough hit: 'I'm Eighteen'. Ezrin recalled that 'their original arrangement was eight minutes long and had a lot of excess bullshit. My job was first to transform stage arrangements into record arrangements, which was something they'd never bothered to consider.'

'I'm Eighteen' also showcased a new gutsy attack to Alice's vocal, something that rubbed off on him during a period at the start of the seventies, when the group moved to Detroit and assimilated the raw power of The Stooges and MC5. Gone were the pallid English-style vocals: Alice now rasped and snarled like a true American rock'n'roller. On 'I'm Eighteen', his vocal vaulted ahead of punk to grunge: that haggard Kurt Cobain–Eddie Vedder sound of an old man's voice coming from a young man's body.

That's the central idea of 'I'm Eighteen'. It's not a clear-cut celebration of youth by any means, but rather a cloudy yet defiant statement of not belonging, of knowing neither what you want nor how to get it: 'I've got a baby's brain and an old man's heart'; 'I'm in the

Sick things: Alice Cooper's third album, released in March 1971

middle without any plans.' Like Boston's 'More Than a Feeling',
'I'm Eighteen' is one of those timeless rock'n'roll cries that cuts
across all divides: apparently one of the first disc jockeys to play
it was the young Rush Limbaugh, later America's most polarising
conservative talk-radio host.

Self-consciously intended as a 'My Generation'-style youth
anthem, 'I'm Eighteen' was released in November 1970 and slowly
rose to become a *Billboard* Top 20 hit. Around this time Cooper
developed an interview riff about what he called 'third-generation
rock' – the first one being the original fifties rock'n'roll generation
and the second being the Beatles/Stones wave. Cooper often talked

about kids now being 'a lot heavier' than the preceding generation, his own demographic cohort. 'They're fourteen and fucking. I was eighteen before I fucked.' The third generation had never really known a world without rock; they had jettisoned the sixties illusions of a gentle revolution and brighter tomorrow, but kept the libertine attitude to sex and drugs. Jaded yet still wild, their repertoire of kicks and kinks now extended to gender-bending and decadence.

Hard-rock scholar Steve Waksman writes about the 'different, uneasy form of pleasure' offered by the sexually ambiguous imagery used by Alice Cooper and other third-generation rockers like the New York Dolls: the edgy titillation of 'the brush against homosexuality'. Cooper's patter about a new generation showed how he instinctively understood – like Bolan and Bowie – that the challenge for any band that wanted to define the seventies was how to surpass and in some sense defeat the sixties. In an interview with *Creem*, he talked about his suburban-housewife mother's horrified reaction to the Stones' appearance on *The Ed Sullivan Show* in February 1965. She told him that The Beatles were one thing, but 'don't ever come back here looking like those Rolling Stones'. Alice recalled, 'I knew right then and there that we had to make the Rolling Stones look like kindergarten.'

The bulk of *Love It to Death* showed Ezrin's success at training Alice Cooper to crank out arena-ready raunch: the rabble-rousing but vague 'Long Way to Go'; the unconvincingly studly postures of 'Is It My Body'. Other tracks displayed an opposite tendency in his production: a flair for cinematic arrangements. Wreathed with incense-swirling organ, 'Black Juju' found the doomy midpoint between The Doors and Uriah Heep. But it was 'The Ballad of Dwight Fry', a song that became a centrepiece of the stage act for a couple of tours, that really flexed Ezrin's talent for *over*production. This audio play about insanity runs through several acts in a little under seven minutes, decked out with piano trills, sound effects (an explosion simulated by slowing down the hiss of an Alka-Seltzer dropped into water), creep-crawly children's toy keyboards and gibbering guitar. The title comes from a real-life person called Dwight Frye, an actor typecast as a madman who appeared in thirties Hollywood horror movies. The live staging of 'The Ballad of Dwight Fry' involved a nurse coming on to escort Alice offstage for a while; when he returns he's strapped in a straightjacket and flails from one side of the stage to the other, pleading with the audience for freedom. But on record what cuts through is a less literal, life-can-drive-you-insane plaint: 'See my lonely life unfold . . . See my only mind explode.'

The partnership with Ezrin strengthened with *Killer*, usually considered Alice Cooper's best album and nominated by Johnny Rotten as the greatest hard-rock LP of all time. I wouldn't quite co-sign *that*. But opener 'Under My Wheels' tears out of the speakers, a macabre update of Chuck Berry automobile rock'n'roll, a boy's fantasy of running over his demanding girlfriend accidentally-on-purpose. 'Halo of Flies' is a multi-segmented song suite, intended to match King Crimson levels of complexity but coming out more like surf prog with its galloping rhythm and swashbuckling geetar twang. One section feels like an invisible fight scene from a movie, and indeed the storyline concerns a struggle against a spy organisation. There's another nod to Hollywood when Alice quotes the melody of *The Sound of Music*'s 'My Favourite Things' while singing about 'daggers and contracts and bright shiny limos'. Things stay cinematic with the string-swept mini-western 'Desperado'. While less impressive overall, *Killer*'s second side contains Alice Cooper's classic concert set piece 'Dead Babies'. Secretly a song of anguished compassion about child neglect, its enactment onstage played up the gloating-sounding chorus and emphasised lines like the parents' admission that 'we didn't want you anyway': Cooper dismembered and impaled baby dolls, using an axe, a sword and a large quantity of fake blood.

Going out with the grisly grind of the title track, *Killer* drew on another Alice Cooper stage routine for its famous cover image: the boa constrictor Kachina, one of a series of snakes who would join Alice onstage. They were originally just pets, but being on the road so much practically forced Cooper to bring the five-foot-long reptiles with him and incorporate them into the act. Draped with multiple dark associations – temptation in Eden, the fall from innocence, original sin; phallic symbolism; poison; the Lizard King Jim Morrison – the serpents incarnated the sinuously slimy decadence that Alice Cooper were coming to represent to the public.

School's Out, the group's fifth album but third with Ezrin in charge, wasn't as strong as *Killer*. But it was the one that broke them wide and huge. The title track, released as a single, reached #7 in America and topped the charts in Britain. A loose theme of the education system and its discontents ran through much of the album, with songs like 'Public Animal #9' ('I feel like a lifer in the state penitentiary'), although 'Alma Mater' was actually a sentimental adieu to the old schoolyard, with a namecheck for Cortez High back in Phoenix. But elsewhere there was a sense of padding and repetition. 'Gutter Cats vs the Jets' even re-ransacked *West Side Story*, interpolating parts of the 'When You're a Jet' song and shoving Leonard Bernstein and Stephen Sondheim alongside the band members in the credits.

Overall, *School's Out*'s contents paled next to the packaging, the best of their several great LP covers. Designed by Sound Packing Corp. and Wilkes & Braun, the sleeve was styled as a well-worn school desk, the old-fashioned kind with an inkwell, the stained and scratched lid marked with the deeply etched names of the band members. You could lift the sleeve's lid just like a real desk. Inside you found, albeit just depicted, the typical belongings of a major miscreant: a catapult and little rocks to pelt targets with; a pen knife with a dirty blade; marbles; chewing gum; a love note; a comic book. Flip the album over and there were pull-out legs (small ones, admittedly) to make the whole thing stand up like a proper desk and, in a nice touch, a wad of chewed gum stuck to the underside. But the *pièce de résistance* was the actual pair of panties wrapped around the vinyl platter itself – getting hold of a girl's knickers being a brag-worthy triumph and rite of passage for adolescent high-school boys. To drum up extra publicity, Gordon spread a fictitious news story about the album having to be recalled because of an error that had resulted in dangerously flammable panties being dispatched to record stores across the country.

School's Out's real problem as an album was simply that it started with Alice Cooper's single greatest song – an impossible act to follow. Intended like 'I'm Eighteen' as a third-generation anthem, 'School's Out' has proved to be timeless, harking back to Chuck Berry's 1957 hit 'School Days' and forward all the way to Ke$ha's 'TiK ToK' in 2009. Timeless, because these songs are *about* time: the dead, detained, gainfully invested time of education and employment versus the anticipatory ecstatic time of release and revelry. Cooper said the song is about 'the last three minutes of the last day of school when you're sitting there and it's like a slow fuse burning'. The music lived up to this incendiary scenario, kicking off with Glen Buxton's killer riff and screeching 'n' squealing like fingernails grating on a blackboard, right through to the explosive end: a phased swirl of guitar, pealing school bell and children's cheers.

But where Berry's 'School Days' was innocent, a mental fast-forward to dancing at the jukebox joint later that afternoon, 'School's Out' feels apocalyptic and vengeful: school is out 'for ever', 'completely', it's 'blown to pieces'. From the dark glee of the chanting children's voices, to the insolent pun 'We got no class and we got no principals' (neither a headmaster nor a guiding moral value system), to the evergreen Brechtian cheek of ending one verse with 'We can't even think of a word that rhymes', 'School's Out' is punk rock five years ahead of schedule.

'School's Out' had unexpected resonance in Britain because its release coincided with the rise of the Pupil Power movement. Encouraged by the militancy of the big unions, whose coordinated strikes in the early seventies repeatedly brought British industry to a standstill, the Schools Action Union formed to protest against the quality of school dinners, corporal punishment, the unnecessary regimentation of school uniforms and 'headmaster dictatorships'. In May 1972, there was a flurry of semi-spontaneous strikes and protests by schoolkids. One rally, on 9 May, involved sixty children from schools in the Marylebone area of London, then swelled to an 800-strong demonstration at Speaker's Corner, Hyde Park. There were a handful of arrests for obstruction and insulting behaviour, among them eighteen-year-old agitator and self-professed Marxist Steve 'Ginger' Finch. According to one participant, several of the marchers actually had tickets for *Top of the Pops* and proceeded to the BBC studio, where they mingled with the audience and gave Alice Cooper the clenched-fist power salute during 'School's Out'.

Pupil Power reached its climax eight days later, when a thousand kids marched to Trafalgar Square. According to the *Daily Telegraph*, scuffles with the police led to twenty-four arrests. Schoolgirls, some as young as eleven, dressed in their uniforms of short pleated skirts and dingy pullovers, brandished banners demanding 'Democracy in Schools' and chanted, 'We want a riot!' Others shouted, 'Fight the pigs!' and 'Seize the time now!' Then, just like that, the movement fizzled out, as quickly as it had frothed up. When quizzed about Pupil Power by the *NME*, Alice Cooper tentatively endorsed the movement, 'so long as it has some kind of constructive purpose'. He added: 'I'm not a real revolutionist . . . but in all honesty, I believe that schoolkids should be given a far better deal. I can remember getting kicked outta High School no less than eight times, because my hair was just one inch longer than the school regulations stipulated.'

Number 1 in the singles chart and with a huge arena concert lined up for the Empire Pool, Wembley, Alice Cooper had stormed the UK. Gordon kept the headlines coming, engineering yet another genius publicity stunt to make sure it was a sold-out show. A flat-bed truck carried a giant billboard advertising the 20 June concert through London: a Richard Avedon photograph of Alice, nude apart from the snake entwined around his body and nestled over his loins. The truck mysteriously broke down in Piccadilly Circus, where a bevy of reporters and photographers just happened to be waiting to document the ensuing traffic jam and police fracas. The driver, says Gordon, 'went to jail, I think, for about two weeks. We paid him. He drove off once, then he came back, and he broke it down again a second time and the police really went crazy. And then he drove it off and he came back again and broke it down a third time.' The publicity helped sell the remaining tickets for the show.

Further assistance in stoking Coopermania came from an unexpected quarter when Mary Whitehouse, a veteran campaigner for cleaner airwaves, demanded that the BBC stop giving any more exposure to 'School's Out'. Branding the song as 'violent', she wrote to Bill Cotton, the head of light entertainment, to get it banned from *Top of the Tops*, and to Douglas Muggeridge, the controller of Radio One, to have it pulled off the playlist. Speaking to *Melody Maker*, Whitehouse said she was particularly 'distressed' by the clip aired several times on *Top of the Pops*, in which Cooper brandished a fencing sword, pointing it at the audience and later drawing the blade across his own throat, and also pulled a girl's hair with flirtatious viciousness. 'The whole mood of it . . . was quite anarchic. We had the case of those boys who beat up a schoolmaster . . . Against such a background I am surprised they put on programmes like this.'

Paralleling Whitehouse's campaign was the one-man crusade of Leo Abse MP to get Alice Cooper's live performances banned. 'I would say he was one of the greatest things to ever happen to Alice's career,' says Gordon of the Labour Member of Parliament for Pontypool. 'Boy, we could not have bought that publicity,' laughs Cooper. 'They couldn't figure out why we were sending him cigars and her flowers. But every time they spent an extra hour trying to ban us in England, they helped us so much.'

Whitehouse and Abse formed an unlikely alliance. She was the driving force behind the National Viewers' and Listeners' Association, a media watchdog pressure group launched in 1965 for the purpose of curtailing smut and ungodly behaviour on TV and radio. Abse was actually the opposite of a prude. Famous for his dandy style, he had been a major architect of the permissive society, pushing for the legalisation of homosexuality and the liberalising of divorce laws, and strongly supporting birth control. In a certain sense, the private member's bill that Abse introduced in the House of Commons, which became the Sexual Offences Act 1967 and made sex between consenting male adults legal, paved the way for glam: a pop star could now talk openly about being gay without risk of prosecution (although such candour could still damage one's career, of course). It was a private member's bill because the Labour government of the day would not support it directly for fear of public hostility – an indication of Abse's courage, and something for which he paid in the form of the daily delivery of excrement through his mail flap.

Cooper's show, however, was too much even for the broad-minded Abse. Tipped off by his own daughter, Abse called a press conference, in which he fulminated that Alice was 'peddling the culture of the concentration camp. Pop is one thing – anthems of necrophilia are another . . . His incitement to infanticide and his commercial exploitation of masochism is evidently an attempt to teach our children to find their destiny in hate, not in love.' On 24 May 1973, Leo Abse stood up in the House of Commons and demanded that the secretary of state for the Home Department revoke the entry permit granted to Alice Cooper enabling him to perform concerts in

Britain. According to Cooper, on arrival at Heathrow he was indeed 'taken aside and kept for an hour while inquiries were being made'. His name was now on 'the list of undesirables. In the end they let me in, but that MP caused plenty of trouble.'

At a time of anxiety about rising levels of youth crime and vandalism, Cooper's disturbing image and gory theatrics easily connected in the popular imagination with A *Clockwork Orange* and the copycat ultra-violence that Kubrick's movie had allegedly inspired on its release in 1971. 'When I saw the film, I thought, "There's an awful lot of Alice in Alex,"' Cooper says of the delinquent anti-hero played by Malcolm McDowell. 'Like me, he's got a pet snake, he's wearing eye make-up. And later McDowell actually told me, "There's a few Alice references in there." So I totally related to A *Clockwork Orange* – not the mindless violence, but the fact that violence has its place in theatrics.'

By this point, Alice Cooper's act was a real show, with loosely choreographed routines and proper sets. 'Gutter Cats vs the Jets', for instance, was performed against a Hell's Kitchen backdrop of garbage cans and strewn trash. The band staged a highly realistic-looking fight between themselves, using switchblades, a broken bottle and bare fists. 'We don't hold any punches,' Cooper told one interviewer. 'I've been knocked-out cold a couple of times onstage, and so's Neal. I've got two ribs broken right now. The audience know when you're faking it.' After the entire band had been 'killed', Alice was then 'arrested' and, with the audience chanting 'hang him', led to the gallows by the band, now resurrected as masked executioners.

It wasn't just the older, pre-rock'n'roll generation and concerned mums and dads who found this kind of fare troubling. Cooper's act divided rock fans too. A July 1972 missive to the *NME* accused Cooper of polluting British music with his 'depraved act' and suggested 'he should see a doctor . . . he wants locking up'.

Others dismissed Alice Cooper as all spectacle and zero

substance, a sorry decline from the high levels of musicianship and artistic maturity of the late sixties. As if to confirm this notion of Alice Cooper as the rock equivalent of a carny freak-show barker or circus ringmaster, the rock papers carried a gossip item about a new stunt in which Alice would be fired out of a cannon. There was a third stance often voiced by the more thoughtful reviewers and columnists among the rock press, which asserted that Alice Cooper was fine as far as it went: good trashy fun, a sick and cynical cartoon just right for credulous kids, but not something that adults should take seriously.

As 1972 headed towards its close, Alice had those kids locked down on both sides of the Atlantic. On the brink of the super-fame they'd chased through years of hard-grind touring, Alice Cooper maintained the hectic pace and started work on their sixth album in just over four years. And they ended 1972 with their second-greatest single and most brilliantly opportunistic publicity stunt yet.

Timed for the US election campaign, 'Elected' offered a pretty convincing impersonation of unbridled megalomania: Alice's ego, swollen by the twin inflationary forces of infamy and fandom, exploding into a power-trip fantasy of himself as leader of youth. The video showed Alice and the band as a presidential candidate plus entourage, riding in limos and waving out of the windows, shaking hands with voters, revelling in the cash from donors, all the while accompanied by a monkey mascot.

Anticipating the disillusion-to-come of Watergate and promoting a cynical view of politics as winning for its own sake, the 'Elected' promo was probably influenced by the summer 1972 release of *The Candidate*. This unsettling satirical comedy starred Robert Redford as an idealistic politician gradually worn down during a campaign until he can only emit robotic inanities. In its day *The Candidate* offered a revelatory and unnerving behind-the-scenes glimpse of the mechanics of running for office, the kind of image manipulation that's wearyingly familiar to us, the inhabitants of a world where 'messaging', 'spin', 'narrative control', 'optics' are all sagely discussed as if they weren't actually euphemisms for lying. A world where we can read a mainstream political pundit (in this case *Slate*'s John Dickerson) casually comment that 'all campaigns and candidates require the manufacturing of authenticity. The best candidates manufacture it really well,' without immediately puking onto our iPads.

One of the few videos from the early seventies that still stands up as powerful, 'Elected' is really made by its music. A scalding intro riff, like the lash of a whip on fire, is followed swiftly by a soul-shattering scream from Alice, a dark whooshing sound like a kamikaze closing in exultantly on death. The song is a loose remake of 'Reflected' on *Pretties for You*, but the gulf between the fey, flaccid original and the blasting bombast of 'Elected' is vast. Ezrin decked out the song with portentous horns that create a sense of statesman-like weight and destiny. To get the demagogic vocal performance the song required, Ezrin 'had a full-length mirror placed in front of Alice on an angle. That way he could see his entire body in reflection.' Cooper rose to the imperious occasion, declaiming, 'The kids need a saviour, they don't want a fake,' and vowing that he and his following would make the whole country 'rock to the rules that I make'. During the fade Cooper addresses the fact that all across the nation, in every major city, 'everybody has problems', then mutters, 'and personally . . . I don't care'. It's a preview not just of punk's nihilism, but specifically of 'Pretty Vacant' by the Sex Pistols, in which Rotten jeers, 'and we don't care'.

Unlike his precursor Screaming Lord Sutch, Cooper was only pretending to be a presidential candidate. But he did achieve something of a coup for a rock singer, when in 1973 he and the band became the subject of a book by political journalist Bob Greene. He followed the band on tour, just like he'd covered the 1972 presidential campaigns of Richard Nixon and George McGovern in the widely read *Running*.

After Nixon's landslide victory (McGovern won just two states) some commentators directly linked the rise of Alice Cooper to this massive swing to the right. Pointing to the abject failure of the many pro-McGovern benefit concerts played by liberal-leaning rock stars in hope of swaying the youth vote, Michael Watts argued in a November 1972 *Melody Maker* essay that 'any illusions that [rock] could effect a new culture have been stripped away . . . pop can be seen for what it is at root: a way of making money . . .' Noting that since 1969 there had been 'a slide into grim resignation and dismay' – countercultural icons either snuffed out or in retreat – a new breed of star emerged espousing decadence-as-pose and 'vulgar amateur dramatics': glam, in other words. Picking up this theme the following year, the *NME*'s Charles Shaar Murray was blunter in connecting Alice Cooper and Richard Nixon: 'Who won the last American election? It sure wasn't Alice Cooper, but it might as well have been.' He found grim significance in the rise of Alice Cooper, arguing that the band had 'buried Woodstock'. But Murray claimed that this was a salutary disillusionment: Alice Cooper's very fakeness and commitment to showbiz artifice revealed 'the cold, hard, terrifying truth about his audience, his profession, and finally, his country'.

As if picking up on the Nixonian rock theme, Alice Cooper's next album was titled *Billion Dollar Babies*. The record was at once a celebration of rock as a money-making enterprise and an assertion of Alice Cooper as an all-American band: true patriot capitalists. Just like Bolan riding in a Rolls-Royce because 'it's good for my voice', Cooper invented bling, or parodied it decades in advance: he bought a Rolls and got the Gordon Gekko-like number plate 'GREED' to go with it. Shameless love of filthy lucre emblazoned itself across the packaging for *Billion Dollar Babies*. Designed by Pacific Eye & Ear, the cover was styled as a snakeskin wallet bearing a gold-coin logo. Inside the record was a giant billion-dollar bill, whose flipside depicted a nuclear missile being admired by a patriotic throng and was further embossed with images of money bags, naked chicks and knives held behind backs and ready to stab. There was also a David Bailey portrait of the group dressed in white satin suits and surrounded by cash. Each member clutched a white rabbit, evoking the idea of showbiz magicians, conjurors of illusions for the amazement of paying punters.

Inside the sleeve was a smorgasbord of typically foul fare, glossed up with a slickly cinematic production from Bob Ezrin. The contents ranged from 'Raped and Freezing', a jaunty ditty about a hitchhiking man who gets raped by an older woman and escapes naked into the desert, to 'Generation Landslide', an incoherent manifesto for the third wave of rock youth whose 'decadent brains' were 'at work to destroy'. A far better effort in this vein was 'Sick Things', a twisted tribute to Alice's audience – 'You things are heavenly / When you come worship me' – set against the group and Ezrin's most imaginative sonic backdrop yet: a thudding, torturous dirgescape of march beats and punctilious horns.

The first song on the album, 'Hello Hooray', was a cover version and was specifically chosen as the grand entrance number for the upcoming 'Billion Dollar Babies' tour. 'Bob Ezrin said, "We need an opening song,"' recalls Cooper. 'We had rock songs but we didn't have that "There's no business like show business" tune. We needed something BIG.' They found the candidate in an unlikely, and very unshowbiz, place: the Judy Collins album *Who Knows Where the Time Goes?* Originally written by Canadian singer-songwriter Rolf Kemp, Collins's version is wistful and gently yearning – nothing like the grandiose rendition by Cooper and the pomp of Ezrin's arrangement. 'Her version and ours bear almost no relationship to each other,' Ezrin has said. '[It] summed up the experience of this grand rock spectacle: the Billion Dollar Babies as they hit the stage with all their excess and . . . self-centeredness . . . all their posing and posturing.'

Probably the most compelling song on the album apart from 'Elected', 'Hello Hooray' vividly conveys the sense of an artist waiting in the wings, ready to seize the stage he and his bandmates have built after a long gruelling struggle, about to enter a pop career's 'imperial phase' (a term coined by the Pet Shop Boys' Neil Tennant to describe when a star's commercial dominance and creative daring reach a synchronised peak). 'I've been ready,' Alice croons haggardly, as the lights grow dim. 'Ready as this audience that's coming here to dream.' Now, in strutting command of the spotlit stage, Cooper roars, 'I feel so STRONG.' 'Elected' and 'Hello Hooray' suggest that Alice was developing a budding anti-messiah complex. As with 'Elected', the horn-draped arrangement on 'Hooray' creates an effect of doomy uplift, like a chorus line high-kicking in deep-sea diver boots.

'Alice Cooper meets *Cabaret*' was the band's stated goal with 'Hello Hooray', which was released as a single in February 1973 and reached #6 in the UK charts. One of 1972's smash-hit movies, *Cabaret* was a musical based on *Goodbye to Berlin,* Christopher Isherwood's *roman-à-clef* about the time he spent in Germany during the last few years of the Weimar Republic. Far more than the novel, the movie presents Berlin just before the Nazi takeover as a seductive demi-monde of erotic experimentation and gay despair. *Cabaret*'s central figure, Sally Bowles – played by Liza Minnelli – is a cabaret singer/aspiring film star and a pleasure-seeking, determinedly frivolous bohemian whose catchphrase is 'Divine decadence, darling!'

In the early seventies, decadence was what we'd nowadays call a 'meme'. The D-word tripped off lips all across the cultural spectrum, sometimes signifying a deplorable malaise that was rotting out Western civilisation from within, and sometimes as a pose to affect, a lifestyle suggestive of naughty fun, indulgence, excess. Talking to *Rolling Stone*, Alice described the group's 'Billion Dollar Babies' show as 'a Seventies stage thing on decadence. The cabaret was a period in German history when they were interested in decadence. And that's exactly what we're doing. Only we're doing it with rock music instead of the old beer-drinking music.' He added that the album was really about perversions: the fact that everybody has 'sick perversions'. But he stressed that these were 'American sexual perversions. It's got to be American – we're very nationalistic.' Cooper was so taken with *Cabaret*'s glamourisation of degeneration and decay that he recruited Liza Minnelli to sing backing vocals on 'Teenage Lament '74', a single off *Muscle of Love*, the follow-up to *Billion Dollar Babies*.

The D-word was frequently affixed to Alice Cooper, who were presented regularly as Exhibit A in the prosecution case against Modern Times. In a late-1971 *New York* cover story, 'The Rites of Fall: Driving the Demons Out, Letting the Good Times In', Albert Goldman argued that despite its late-sixties promise, rock had turned out to be 'the final paroxysm of pop culture, the twitch the corpse gives as the electric current shoots through it'. Its new stars, like 'kohl-eyed queen' Alice, were 'hideously decadent', offering sensation as a salve for 'universal ennui'. *Newsweek*, similarly, pointed to the band as 'repellent' proof that rock had devolved into 'a florid and self-conscious rococo period, which is also . . . often decadent'.

One of the best explications of 'decadence' came from a critic who intended to debunk its vogueish omnipresence in the seventies and expose it as a lazy, fundamentally ahistorical concept. Richard Gilman, author of the 1979 polemic *Decadence: The Strange Life of an Epithet*, wrote about how rebellion and the artistic imperative to break barrier after barrier tended to succumb to a fatal logic of 'rebellion for its own sake', condemning it to become 'a purely formal act, a pose'. His real complaint, though, was that 'decadence', as it entered the common parlance of informed chit-chat in the seventies, tended to compact together and caricature the received wisdom about three completely unrelated eras of history: Weimar Germany 1919–33; the late-nineteenth-century aestheticism of Baudelaire, Huysmans and Wilde; and the twilight centuries of the Roman Empire.

Still, given that epochs often understand themselves as echoes of earlier eras and draw on them as models of behaviour, 'decadence' seemed like fair game as a vague but effectively evocative term for much of what went down in the first half of the seventies. Rock *had* entered its 'bread and circuses' phase. And the 'Billion Dollar Babies' tour was a little like a nomadic version of the gladiatorial spectacles offered by the emperor to titillate the sated senses of Rome's citizens. It was the largest tour yet seen in rock: not just in reach and duration (sixty-four concerts, fifty-nine cities, ninety days across March, April, May and early June of 1973, with a total audience not far below a million), but also in the scale of the production.

Shep Gordon recruited Broadway stage director Joe Gannon, who had recently masterminded Neil Diamond's 'Hot August Night' series of concerts, the first time a pop star had worked with moving sets and theatrical lighting. Gannon devised a multi-level stage with Busby Berkeley-style staircases trimmed with lighting that flashed on and off as Cooper made his entrance, and a scaffold of metal tubes that seemed to cage each member of the band. In addition to Gannon, another showbiz professional, a magician whose stage name was the Amazing Randy, was hired to supervise the central illusion: the decapitation of Cooper by guillotine. As well as playing the role of executioner, Randy doubled as the sadistic dentist who plunged a giant-size drill into Alice's mouth during 'Unfinished Sweet'.

Another aspect of rock's decadent turn was the increasingly Nero-like lifestyle of the travelling superstars. Like Led Zeppelin, also touring America in 1973, Alice Cooper flew in their own private jet, which cocooned the band in an atmosphere that reporters likened to an airborne frat house, with beer cans rolling up and down the aisles and porn-mag centrefolds stuck to the inside of the fuselage. For their manager Gordon, the private jet wasn't just more convenient or a status symbol, it was 'important to our image . . . lends it more magic. We fly into a town in our *own* plane and it's like the circus is coming.' The tail of the jet bore the band's new symbol: a dollar sign made out of snakes.

At the time Alice Cooper often liked to say: 'We act as a mirror.' In other words, the group weren't actually decadent; they were a satirical exposé of decadence. 'It was a reflection of what we saw society becoming,' says Gordon today. Alice Cooper had seen the way things were going with rock – the emergence of a post-sixties generation addicted to sensation, the growth of an arena concert circuit that demanded visual spectacle on the same scale as its massive sound systems – and they sensed an opportunity for themselves.

As captured in the movie *Good to See You, Alice Cooper* – like Bolan's *Born to Boogie*, a hastily hashed together assemblage of exciting concert footage and lame, semi-improvised comedy sequences – the 'Billion Dollar Babies' tour was the most spectacular rockstravaganza yet staged. But film doesn't really convey the overwhelming impact it must have had on its contemporary audience. The staircase and scaffold look like a fairly standard backdrop from some BBC variety show or an ABC special on Anthony Newley in Las Vegas. Cooper, a seedy figure in his mismatch of thigh-level leopard-skin boots and stained undergarments, is not as commandingly demonic in his gestures as you'd expect, although that might be because of alcohol impairment. Some of the routines are risible: crouching over a headless female mannequin, Alice dribbles on her neck stump, then moves underneath the metal torso to catch the spittle in his mouth as it slowly runs down the cleavage. 'Unfinished Sweet', judged by this recorded outing, is just plain peculiar: a human-size tooth (played by the drummer's sister Cindy Smith) cavorts onstage, prompting Alice to grab a giant toothbrush with yellowing bristles and inflict rigorous dental hygiene on it.

'Dead Babies', though, is pretty twisted: impaling baby dolls on a sword, Alice changes the lyrics to 'Little Bettie ate a pound of Quaaludes', a nod to the tranquilliser popularly abused by rock audiences of the day, many pounds of which must have been swallowed by concert-goers that night. So big was the 'downs' phenomenon that in October 1972 *Creem* devoted a cover story to 'Sopors' – the pharmaceutical classification for these drugs – featuring a photo on the front of a girl with a pill on her tongue. Arena concerts were literally becoming zones of mass sedation. Yet the mood at concerts wasn't especially placid: Quaaludes and similar drugs (like Mandrax in the UK) released inhibitions, especially when combined with beer or cheap wine, but often rendered users groggy and aggressive. Indeed, at some of the concerts Alice Cooper played later in '73, the pelting of the band – with rocks, cigarette lighters, eggs, firecrackers, even bottles – became a regular occurrence.

During the summer '73 tour, though, the violence was all onstage. The climax to an evening's depravity-as-entertainment came with the grotesquely realistic execution. After placing a mannequin in the guillotine and testing the sharpness of the blade with his finger, Alice obeys the Amazing Randy's instruction and replaces the victim's head with his own. The blade plunges with sickening speed. Randy reaches into the basket, withdraws his hands dripping with blood, then reaches in again to pull out a convincing replica of Alice's head. In just moments, Alice returns for the encore of 'School's Out', dressed in white top hat and tails. The show ends with Alice unveiling the Stars and Stripes and the band saluting and brandishing 4 July sparklers, while Kay Smith's recording of 'The Star-Spangled Banner' blares out of the speakers. A Richard Nixon lookalike bounds out, waving to the audience, but the band beat him up and carry him offstage.

The 'Billion Dollar Babies' tour grossed so much money that Alice Cooper made the cover of *Forbes* as emblems of a new breed of rock tycoon. 'That just thrilled us. It was exactly the people we wanted to have tell their kids not to come to the concert,' recalls Gordon. But most of the $4.5 million in proceeds was swallowed by the costs of the stage production and the wages of the employees required to transport, assemble and operate it. Designed by theatre people who were thinking in terms of long-term residencies rather than the itinerant nature of rock touring, the set was monstrously heavy. One problem with the budgeting was that Alice Cooper's ticket prices were in the normal range for a rock band, despite the fact that their outlay was much larger than groups with minimal production costs.

If not the most lucrative tour of its era, 'Billion Dollar Babies' was nonetheless a landmark achievement, and a model for much that followed. In the immediate term it inspired imitations like Elton John's Hollywood Bowl spectacular, with its five baby-grand pianos, sixty-foot staircase and Elton's headdress made of white marabou feathers (an homage to between-the-wars Hollywood and stars like Marlene Dietrich). Elton had first been wowed by Alice Cooper at their own Hollywood Bowl show circa 'School's Out': a helicopter had dropped hundreds of spare panties on the audience, and Elton had found himself 'scrambling for a pair' like any other punter.

A triumph, then; the culmination of all they'd been working towards. But the 'Billion Dollar Babies' tour destroyed Alice Cooper as a band. As Michael Walker points out in his book about the excessive rock tours of 1973, *What You Want Is in the Limo*, the stage structure cut the band off from each other: they couldn't get into eye contact or transmit the band-as-gang, all-for-one/one-for-all vibe of camaraderie. At the same time, under the pounding glare of the Super Trouper spotlights, the singer was pushed further towards being the focal figure, with his bandmates relegated more and more into a backing group. This elevation of Cooper into a virtual solo star was exacerbated by the press conferences held in every city the band visited, conducted by the singer on his own.

Alice Cooper were 'destroyed' in another sense: obliterated by exhaustion. Alice in particular was drained to the point of becoming a ghost-like figure. 'I found myself out on stage doing this number to thousands of kids and thinking about something completely different,' he told the *NME* later in 1973. 'It got to be like a job . . . I was pretty brought down by it . . . I couldn't stand having flash photographs taken. Every time a bulb would pop off, it would feel like I'd been hit in the face . . . I was waking up in the morning with the shakes. It took me a full two months to come down off the tour.'

Cooper had always used alcohol to swaddle himself from the rigours of the road. He drank Budweiser from breakfast to bedtime, sustaining what he calls 'a golden buzz . . . I was the most functional alcoholic there ever was.' Interviews from that era invariably mention the can of Bud perpetually in his hand. So renowned were he and the band for their drinking that *Creem* did a cover story based around the concept of Alice Cooper's *Alcohol Cookbook*, hailing them as 'All-American lushes to a man' and a band that stood 'for booze almost as much as great music'. But when Alice graduated from beer to whiskey and 'started throwing up blood in the morning', he realised, 'I'm really killing myself.' Glen Buxton, too, was impaired thanks to drink and drugs. Onstage, his parts were covertly shadowed by a hired guitarist skulking in the wings.

After 'Billion Dollar Babies', the group were divided on where to go next. Alice, backed by Gordon, wanted to top the tour by conceiving and executing a production that would leave everybody else trailing far behind. But other members were keen to scale back the

All-American Lush: Alice Cooper brandishes *Creem*'s own-brand Boy Howdy! beer for the June 1973 issue

theatricality and shift attention to their musicality. They also chafed at the controlling role of Ezrin in the sound of their albums. During the recording of the next album, *Muscle of Love*, a rift between band and producer opened up, leading to his departure. But despite the avowed intention to return to a simpler, less-produced sound of raw bluesy energy, the product singularly lacked the 'balls' and 'guts' the band claimed for it in interviews. The concept was 'urban sex habits', but the packaging (a plain brown carton, of the kind that might conceal immoral periodicals or sex toys) was as dreary as the musical contents were enervated.

So Alice Cooper went solo, taking the name with him. The 1975 album/tour *Welcome to My Nightmare* was his most extravagant production yet, the consummation of his aspiration to be 'the Busby Berkeley of rock'. Broadway veteran David Winters handled the stage direction of Cooper's 'first real scripted show'. On the album and on the TV special *Alice Cooper: The Nightmare*, Vincent Price made a cameo appearance: a telling indication of Cooper's revised ambitions. No longer did he want to be the Rock Monster, the bogeyman whose corrupting powers worried parents across America; now he presented himself as a villain in a more vaudevillian sense, playing roles to the hammy hilt, but courteous and genteel offstage.

Interviews had already begun to establish the existence of a separation between the Alice Cooper character and the real-life Alice Cooper, a disarmingly pleasant, mild-mannered, easy-going fellow. A guy who was faithful to his long-term girlfriend, who didn't take advantage of the groupie scene. Surprisingly moral too, shaped by his Church of Jesus Christ background, in which his dad had been a lay preacher and his grandfather a missionary.

The singer started to describe Alice Cooper as a character, a costume he could put on and take off. He began to talk about 'Alice Cooper' in the third person: 'The way Alice thinks onstage is insanity,' he told the *NME*, adding: 'Alice will see somebody out front who's obviously on drugs . . . and Alice'll go out of his way to scare that person to death . . . Alice wants everybody to be insane.' He and Gordon both began to put out the idea that the shows, despite the voyeuristic pleasure in maniacal cruelty they seemed to encourage, were actually morality plays: 'Alice Cooper' did bad, bad things, but he always got his comeuppance. 'A despicable human being who does these despicable things to society – and gets executed for it,' says Gordon today. In interviews at the time, he also stressed that Alice Cooper concerts served as safety valves for negative energy: far from inciting violence, the shows were structured to leave the audience purged and spent.

Slowly but surely, Gordon craftily repositioned Cooper as a mainstream entertainer. At a 1975 music-biz awards ceremony, dressed in a tuxedo, Alice shared the stage with the dazzling Diana Ross, who observed, 'You're not what I expected – grotesque,' to which he replied, 'I'm trying to change my image.' And Cooper succeeded. He was a guest on the *Hollywood Squares* game show. Photos started popping up in the rock magazines of Alice in a clinch with showbiz legends like Jack Benny and George Burns. He became genuinely chummy with Groucho Marx and Bob Hope, both of whom, he claimed, appreciated the band's show as a new kind of vaudeville. Perhaps most mind-blowingly, he was the guest star of an episode of *The Muppet Show*.

There were charity works too, that staple of showbiz *noblesse oblige*: Alice recruited three hundred volunteers from among his fans to clear up Manhattan's garbage-strewn Riverside Park. He became a passionate and expert golfer – an older, squarer person's pastime, the sport of rich conservative men – playing in celebrity tournaments alongside the likes of President Gerald Ford. He grew an unfortunate moustache.

The culmination of this steady self-reinvention came in 2011, when Alice Cooper was incorporated into the Halloween season of entertainments offered by Universal City in LA. What had once been an anarchic rock band was now a sideshow at an amusement park. Songs like 'Cold Ethyl' – his second necrophilia anthem, off *Welcome to My Nightmare* – were turned into tableaux. In the late seventies, eclipsed by punk and a new breed of nasty metal, Alice had played the hipper-to-be-square card and claimed that he'd always seen Alice Cooper as 'all ages' entertainment, 'family stuff', 'Bambi meets Dracula'. Now the Disneyfication of Death Rock had become a reality.

4:

TEENAGE RAMPAGE: GLITTER STOMP AND DISCO ROCK

Slade – The Sweet – Mud – Suzi Quatro – Gary Glitter – Junkshop Glam – Hello

As 1973 rolled into '74, three singles by leading glam artists broke into the UK charts, all featuring the word 'teenage' in the title: Alice Cooper's 'Teenage Lament '74', Marc Bolan and T. Rex's 'Teenage Dream' and The Sweet's 'Teenage Rampage'.

The first two were strangely downbeat: 'Teenage Lament '74', Cooper explained, was sung from the point of view of 'a kid growing up today who doesn't want . . . glitter on his face or flashy clothes, but he has to conform because it's a social thing' – an idea expressive more of Cooper feeling trapped in his own role-play than anything going on out there in the minds of actual adolescents. The T. Rex tune was a mid-tempo, elegiac sway – 'Whatever happened to the teenage dream?' beseeched Bolan in a plaintive warble – that again seemed to reflect Bolan's sense of his own waning star power.

The Sweet's 'Teenage Rampage', though, was pure celebration. One of the hardest-rocking pop anthems ever made, 'Rampage' builds from its apocalyptic intro riff into a hysterical fantasy of adolescent insurrection: 'At thirteen they'll be learnin' / But at fourteen they'll be burnin'.' Underpinned by a stamping beat like marching feet, the song imagines the kids rising up, taking complete command, writing constitutions and starting revolutions. Dropping lyrical nods to Thunderclap Newman's counterculture anthem 'Something in the Air' and the 1968 riots, 'Teenage Rampage' climaxes with the sound of kids cheering in power-drunk glee: an echo of Cooper's 'School's Out' and the Pupil Power moment it inadvertently soundtracked a couple of years earlier.

The journalist's rule of thumb goes 'two's a coincidence, three's a *trend*'. Accordingly, in February 1974, as 'Rampage' stomped its way to #2 in the UK charts, *Melody Maker* pulled together a feature about this unexpected confluence of teen-themed singles. Performers, producers, pundits and some actual real-life adolescents were canvassed as to the significance of this spate of self-declared teenpop. Nicky Chinn – the co-writer, with Mike Chapman, of The Sweet's smashes – declared that 'now more than ever maybe since 1964/65 [the kids] are going *rampant* . . . they stopped for a while when heavy music came in but now screaming has come back'. He admitted that 'Rampage' was as much as anything a salute to the younger generation's spending power: 'the teenage contribution to commerce is amazing with all the records and clothes they're buying'.

Today, Chinn recalls the title's inspiration coming from when 'Mike and I were watching TV in my flat – the Osmonds were landing at London Airport, the place was crazy, and the reporter said, "This is like a teenage rampage." I just said immediately, "That's the next single." Teenagers in the seventies probably had more power than at any previous stage in society before . . . We certainly recognised they were buying our records.'

The surge of teenage consumer desire in the early seventies had revitalised the singles market. In 1970, it only took about 100,000 copies sold to get your single into the UK Top 5; a year or so later, it took half a million. Slade frontman Noddy Holder credited the switch to Marc Bolan, his monster success 'making us, and everybody else, strive to make a better single'.

But it wasn't just the manufacturers of black vinyl who were prospering. An entire economy organised around pandering to and exploiting teenage fancy awoke from the hibernation it had entered during the long hairy winter of album-based rock. It was boom time again for merchandising companies like Coffers Sports Limited, one of the UK's big producers of fan paraphernalia such as T-shirts, scarves, rosettes and badges. Existing teen-girl magazines with high music content such as *Jackie* and *Fabulous 208* enjoyed soaring circulations, and new pop-centric and heavily pictorial publications like *Popswop, Superstar, Popster Poster Magazine* and *Music Star* took off like rockets. (The latter, launched in January 1973, was selling 634,000 copies by September.) Resurgent fan clubs mailed out their own newsletters to tens of thousands, and there were new teen-focused TV shows too: London Weekend Television's *Saturday Scene* and *Lift Off with Ayshea*, while *Top of the Pops*, buoyed up by the new breed of hyper-visual artists and the shift of focus back to singles, entered its heyday, reaching viewing figures as high as 15 million.

Presenter Sally James is flanked by tweenybop idols on the cover of this spin-off LP for the kids' pop programme *Saturday Scene*

The three teen-themed hit singles by The Sweet, T. Rex and Alice Cooper symbolically capped a triumphant three-year reign of teenage taste – '71–'72–'73 – that had been an inevitable backlash to '68–'69–'70, when young-adult values and preoccupations dominated, the students took over and the college circuit ruled. The two big groups not served well by music during those years were working-class male teenagers, and teenage and tweenage girls. There was a relative dearth of music for dancing (black music saved the day, bubbling along with soul, ska, rocksteady) and a major deficit of faces with which to become remotely infatuated. Glam's edges blur into a wider revival of teenybop music that includes The Jackson 5 and their white replica The Osmonds, new heart-throbs like David Cassidy and, a little deeper into the seventies, boy bands like The Bay City Rollers and The Rubettes. But the sound of those performers was neither as dazzlingly produced nor as aggressively played as that of the glam groups. Nor did the likes of Cassidy and Donny Osmond go in for glitter's over-the-top stylings or overt gender confusion beyond the traditional kind of girlish pretty-boy appeal. When it came down to it, the pure teenybop fare was neither glam *nor* rock.

From a distance, though, glam and the teenybop resurgence looked like the same phenomenon: a drastic de-sophistication and re-excitation of pop that started in 1971. 'It's going back into the hands of the kids, the really young kids that buy singles,' declared Slade manager Chas Chandler in a *Record Mirror* special about the new pop explosion. In the same early-1972 feature Nicky Chinn stressed that melody and a danceable beat – things that teens and pre-teens 'can latch on to . . . can understand' – were crucial once again. Around the same time, the *NME*'s Nick Logan wrote of a new generation hungry for 'the sheer gut and crutch power of rock' – music that wasn't aimed at the head, or at 'heads' as a demographic.

The heads weren't happy about this power shift. The hollowing-out of sixties counterculture rhetoric in songs like 'Teenage Rampage' and T. Rex's 'Children of the Revolution' rubbed salt into the wound. Writing to *Melody Maker*, Brian Mordecai of Brighouse, Yorkshire, won a 'Letter of the Week' LP for his caustic take-down of The Sweet's pretty-vacant postures:

> It is encouraging to see that the revolutionary movement of the late 60s, which was closely connected with the rock music of that time, has not died away completely. For it is alive and well in the hands of those arch urban guerrillas, the Sweet. Their cries of 'change the constitution' and 'join the revolution' ring true in these times of crisis and bring a lump to the throat of even those hardened souls who remember the days when revolution was not just a dream . . . Yes, once more the feeling is in the air and if Donny Osmond re-released the Stones' 'Street Fighting Man' surely the structure of capitalist society in this country would be destroyed forever?

But as Noddy Holder put it, speaking not just for Slade but all the teen-stomp bands, 'We don't want no underground leftovers. We are after the kids.'

Slade were one of the hugest bands of the first half of the seventies. Between the winter of 1971 and the winter of '74, they had twelve Top 5 UK hits, half of which reached #1. As glitter-era hit-makers they eclipsed Bolan (whose imperial phase produced ten Top 5 hits, including 4 #1s) and wiped the floor with Bowie (who would score, during that same three-year span, just five Top 5 and *zero* #1s). Slade's success wasn't limited to the UK either: they were big all across Europe and massive in Australia.

Yet somehow Slade have virtually vanished from the official history of rock. *The Rolling Stone Album Guide* (1992 edition) doesn't contain an entry on them, even though it has ones for early-seventies hard-rock contemporaries as minor as Bloodrock and Nazareth. Even in Britain they rarely come up as a reference point, relegated to a vague fond memory, a mascot of quintessential seventies-ness.

In their heyday, though, Slade were taken very seriously. 'In a few years' time we may all be saying that Slade are the most important rock group to have emerged since the Beatles,' wrote their biographer George Tremlett shortly after the release of their film *Slade in Flame*. Comparisons with the Fab Four were routine in those days, given credence by the astounding string of #1 singles – 'Coz I Luv You', 'Tak Me Bak 'Ome', 'Mama Weer All Crazee Now', 'Cum on Feel the Noize', 'Skweeze Me Pleeze Me', culminating with that hardy perennial 'Merry Xmas Everybody'. There was a sonic resemblance, too, with the Lennon-as-foghorn blast of Holder's voice.

But Slade weren't just recognised for the statistical scale of their success; they were critically respected too. In Britain, *Melody Maker* and the *NME* praised them as a literally rejuvenating force for rock, while *Creem* hyped them to the heavens in America. Perhaps what's most surprising, when you consult the yellowing archives of the music press, is that two rock writers revered today as prophets of punk for their real-time mythologising of Iggy Pop, Lou Reed and the New York Dolls were barely less gushing about Slade.

Creem's Lester Bangs seized on the Midlands band as potential saviours of rock in the way that he'd earlier hailed The Stooges and would later garland The Clash. In an impassioned June 1973 feature, Bangs described witnessing the band's effect on their audience at a UK concert as the rebirth of his faded faith in rock'n'roll, bringing 'chills and then literal tears to my showbiz-jaded frame'. His reporter's eye zoomed in on a seventeen-year-old boy up in the balcony, hanging 'halfways off the rail in free flight, sweating and shuddering in ecstasy, wriggling his entire body and flinging his arms out in wild erratic arcs, eyes shut, gaping, blessed by total beautiful mindless transport'.

The praise of the *NME*'s Nick Kent took on a more sociopolitical slant, proclaiming that same heady summer of 1973 that 'Slade are easily the most important rock band to appear from these fair shores since the 1970s were ushered in'. Whereas Bowie and Roxy Music were 'little more than intriguing tangent offcuts' from the dominant bourgeois art-rock tradition, Slade were the real deal: 'the first great unashamedly working-class band to cross the boards in a dog's age'.

Bangs and Kent were rehearsing the rhetoric of punk rock when they celebrated Slade as – in Kent's words – 'a total reconstruction of the energies . . . of pure rock'n'roll' that returned the music to the kids on the street just when rock 'seemed to be going through its final death pangs'. That's exactly how Slade and manager Chas Chandler saw themselves too. 'For a period, there were no groups around that knew the same wage-packet type of background as the football fans: it was very much a students' thing,' Chandler told one interviewer. 'Now it is back to the people.'

Slade had immaculate working-class credentials. They came from the Black Country, a region of the West Midlands that acquired its name from the smog and soot caused by heavy industry. In the early days of the group, drummer Don Powell's day job was testing metals like brass, iron and steel to make sure the composition was right; he had studied metallurgy at college, dropped out when he got the music bug, but took a foundry job to pay off his hire-purchase drum kit.

The Black Country's connection to metalwork – locks, brasswork – actually predated the Industrial Revolution by centuries, owing to the proximity of the coal seam to the surface. But it was during the early nineteenth century that the area acquired its nickname, as the countryside became crisscrossed with canals carrying barges loaded with ore, and the skyline was riven by giant smokestacks. Aghast observers noted how nature's cycles had been inverted in the region, with smoke causing perpetual twilight by day and the infernal glow of furnaces disrupting night-time. The author of an 1841 guidebook to England fulminated not just about the foul-smelling, despoiled surroundings, but the Morlock-like 'savages' who lived there, 'coarsely clad in filthy garments', their conversation 'belarded with fearful and disgusting oaths, which can scarcely be recognised as the same as that of civilised England'. Some Tolkien buffs argue that the desolate, ash-blasted kingdom of Mordor – in Elvish, 'black land' – in *Lord of the Rings* was based on the Black Country.

Another Tolkien-like aspect to the region is its dialect, which preserves features of Middle English from a thousand years earlier, when it was part of the Anglo-Saxon kingdom of Mercia. You can hear the Black Country's distinctive 'sing-songy' accent in the between-song banter of Noddy Holder on Slade's biggest-selling album, *Slade Alive!* The stronger retention of Germanic words and unusual expressions like 'Ow bist?' ('How are you?' via 'How be-est you?') reflect the insularity of the locale, which includes towns like Dudley, Sandwell, Smethwick, Wolverhampton and Bilston, where Don Powell grew up. 'People always used to say that we came from Birmingham,' recalls Powell, 'and we had to explain that although Birmingham is only like ten miles away, it might as well be a totally different country.'

By the time Slade formed, 'thee' and 'thou' and 'thy' were fading from Black Country parlance, and heavy industry was starting to decline. But an industrial proletariat mindset lived on long after the mills and factories went away. *Melody Maker*'s Michael Watts, who championed Slade and came from the same area himself, described the band as 'true sons of this industrial soil' with 'a grip on normality' unusual 'in this unreal business of rock and roll'. The last colliery may have closed but it was still a harsh environment, from which hard-working locals sought release at the weekend, supporting a vibrant local scene of bands and dance venues. Two places Holder frequented as a youth were Willenhall Baths and Bloxwich Baths, where the swimming pools were boarded over for dance nights, the cold air off the water below making for a rather chilly ambience.

The members of Slade came up separately through a variety of local bands before coalescing as The 'N Betweens in 1965. They became one of countless 'Hard Up Heroes' (to borrow the title of a 1974 compilation of mid-sixties beat groups) shuttling around the country, playing working-men's clubs, dancehalls and the occasional wedding reception, and getting ripped off by promoters.

After stirring interest in various managers and A&R people, The 'N Betweens signed with Fontana, who insisted the group change their name. As Ambrose Slade, they released a debut LP, *Beginnings*, and single, 'Genesis'. Then, in the summer of 1969, they journeyed to the Bahamas for a short residency at a hotel and, owing to a mis-understanding, ran up a huge bill. To pay it off, the group were forced to perform at the hotel nightly for much longer than they'd agreed. 'We were living in a very basic staff apartment, with four camp beds in there – which was sort of fun – and we were there for three and a half months,' recalls Powell. 'It really did bring us closer together. It was us four against the rest of the world, basically.'

Until Chas Chandler came along and, as their manager and record producer, became the fifth member of Slade. Hailing from shipyard centre Newcastle-upon-Tyne, Chandler grew up in a similar hard-bitten industrial environment to the Black Country. As bassist in The Animals, he'd also experienced how years of toil in a band could leave you with scant financial reward, even after scoring a string of big hits. Moving into pop management, Chandler discovered Jimi Hendrix and brought him to England, where he built a band, The Experience, around the guitarist and stage-managed his conquest of first the UK scene and then his homeland, America. But halfway through the sessions for Hendrix's third album, *Electric Ladyland*, Chandler quit, exasperated with the protracted, increasingly expensive and – in his view – self-indulgent studio experimentation that his artist was pursuing. Slade, the next band he would take on as manager, couldn't have been more different in their approach. They recorded quickly, sticking with a 'live' sound whose core was all four members playing and singing simultaneously, with only minimal overdubs and additions.

Before Chandler came along, Slade had gone along with the trippy tropes of the time to a degree. Their May 1969 debut, *Beginnings*, released as Ambrose Slade, featured phased guitars and covers of 'Journey to the Center of the Mind' by The Amboy Dukes, along with tunes by Frank Zappa, The Moody Blues and Steppenwolf. On the front cover, naked from the waist up, Slade looked like any other bunch of longhairs running late for the Summer of Love. And, in fact, Slade could easily have carried on along the path to full-blown prog: Jim Lea, who co-wrote the songs with Holder, was a classically trained musician who played violin and keyboards as well as bass guitar. But instead Lea – influenced by Holder's preference for soul and the raucous Lennon side of The Beatles – veered towards the instant and impactful: shout-along hooks, driving riffs, brevity. 'I used to write quite complicated stuff for the group, with harmonies and arrangements,' Lea recalled in 1972. 'After listening to and playing classical music I've come to the conclusion that really "simplicity" is what it's all about . . . Beethoven was a pop writer – he wrote for the masses. You have to communicate.'

One of Chandler's first managerial decisions was to align Slade with the emerging skinhead subculture. Materialising during the football season of 1968–9, the skinheads had quickly become the focus of media and public alarm. Their belligerent aura and tendency to travel in menacing packs earned them the name 'bovver boys', in reference to their penchant for 'bother' and 'aggro'. In addition to their fanatical support of football teams, skinheads were also defined by their hostility to hippies. Their cropped hair and steel-capped Doc Martens boots, their obsession with looking clean and sharp, was a rejection of the sloppy, let-it-all-hang-out ambience of 'dirty 'ippies', who increasingly found themselves under brutal physical attack from skinhead gangs.

Bemused and repelled by the progressive sounds of the day, the skins liked danceable music: Motown and ska. Both of these were imported styles usually heard in the UK as records rather than as live performance by bands. The emergence of the skinheads as a large nationwide subculture without a native music with which to identify or bands to follow pointed to a huge gap in the market for an English group playing rock'n'roll that was both danceable and relatable. Chandler's plan was to latch Slade onto the skinhead movement in the same way The Who had been craftily targeted at the mods.

Step one was haircuts all round – severe ones. 'Chas brought us down to London and plied us with drinks, and we thought, "Something's up,"' recalls Powell. 'We had very long hair at the time, a bit hippy. But we thought, "Let's go along with it, because if we don't, Chas may actually lose interest."'

The image makeover got Slade a lot of attention, but ultimately it backfired – promoters started to avoid booking them for fear of bovver at the gigs. 'We weren't those kind of people . . . totally the opposite to how we were,' says Powell. The skinhead style was swiftly abandoned, although a residue remained in the form of Holder's working-man-style braces. Instead, Slade gradually assembled their own unique look.

Jim Lea and Don Powell looked smart but not particularly flashy; they were also the closest contenders to heart-throb material in the band. But Holder's get-up was as visually loud as his mighty roar: calf-length tartan trousers and sometimes a tartan waistcoat too, red and yellow platform boots with similarly hued striped socks, the ensemble often completed with a gaily coloured neckerchief. His curly cloud of ginger hair exploded out from under a mirrored top hat or a working men's flat cap, mingling with the jawline flames of his sideburns. The overall effect resembled an English archetype from the nineteenth century or earlier: a yeoman from a Thomas Hardy novel, perhaps, dandied up for a night out painting Dorchester red.

Guitarist Dave Hill was the Slade member who did most to align the band with the glitter trend started by Bolan. Hill would spray his hair with lacquer and scatter sparkly dust over it, daub circles of metallic gloss on his forehead, whose surface area was unusually large because of his unique self-invented hairstyle – cropped short at the fringe and hanging in long curtains at the side. Working closely with designers, Hill developed broad-shouldered silver or gold suits inspired by Emperor Ming from *Flash Gordon*, often covered with reflector patches like little mirrors. He sported silver knee-length boots (even developing a strange one-leg-in-the-air stage move to show them off and catch the spotlight). Yet the overall effect was less androgynous than fancy dress. 'I'm really not a pretty character because what I put over is more brutish,' Hill admitted, explaining that his image could only 'be a reflection of the music which has a hard masculine feel . . . I couldn't be camp if I tried, because my background is working class and I'm tough at heart.'

Although they dropped the skinhead affiliation like a hot potato, Slade aimed for a similar working-class gap in the British youth market. YOB 1 was the personalised licence-plate number Hill bought for his Rolls-Royce; later he had the word 'Superyob' emblazoned on a special custom-made ray-gun-shaped guitar and on a tunic he wore onstage. Slade invented their own unique laddish salute, a sideways 'thumbs-up' with the fist pointed outwards, as displayed on the cover of *Slayed?*, their 1972 breakthrough album. The deliberately

misspelt names of their singles also came across like a jovial gesture of delinquent solidarity with kids who left school at fifteen with
zero qualifications and a life of labour ahead of them. According to
Powell, though, titles like 'Tak Me Bak 'Ome' were really phonetic
renderings of how words were said in the Black Country. 'It started
with "Cuz I Luv You" – we changed the spelling because otherwise
the song seemed a bit namby-pamby, soppy . . . But we did get in
a lot of trouble with the educational authorities, who actually contacted our office saying we were misleading the kids, taking them in
the wrong direction.'

In reality, Slade weren't yobs at all. Belying the illiterate or even
dyslexic aura of titles like 'Gudbuy T' Jane' and 'Look Wot You Dun',
Holder's favourite book was *Catch-22*; Lea's was *Animal Farm*. The
son of a window cleaner, raised in a Walsall terraced house whose
outdoor toilet was shared with several families, Holder's background
was solidly working class. But he passed the 11-plus – the test that
sent the brighter working-class kids to grammar schools, then on
to higher education or white-collar work, while streaming the less
academically promising pupils for factory or service jobs. Holder
would probably have gone on to attend university or a teacher-
training college if he hadn't got the bug for music. 'Rock and roll
– when it appeared, that was *me*,' he once said. Lea applied to four
art colleges and received an offer from Hornsey College of Art, but
opted for a position in The 'N Betweens. He'd also studied violin
from the age of nine, played in the Staffordshire Youth Orchestra
and narrowly missed a spot in the string section of the National
Youth Orchestra. Hill described himself as a working-class hard nut
but had a passion for fashion: when the Slade money came through,
he bought a hair salon, talked about wanting to start his own design
and fashion business, and told one interviewer, 'I've got an idea in
my head for a revolutionary boot design.'

Musically, though, Slade were determinedly non-cerebral. 'When people say we're "mindless rock and roll" . . . that's a nice description,' Holder told the *NME*. 'We don't aim for the head anyway – we're a rock and guts band.' Slade took the heaviness of late-sixties rock – bruising bass, thudding drums – and squeezed it into three-minute pop. The texture of the sound was similar to a group like Ten Years After, but there was no bluesiness or guitar solos, just uproarious uplift.

Slade's albums and singles were recorded with incredible speed – and cheapness – in a deliberate reversion to how records were made before *Rubber Soul. Slayed?*, for instance, was completed in just ten days, during which time they also laid down two non-album singles, plus B-sides. Often the first take was the one they went with. 'We'd play everything together, and Nod would do a guide vocal track at the same time,' recalls Powell. 'And most of the time we'd keep everything, even the lead vocal. Chas would always be, "We've already got it."' The group's biggest album, 1972's *Slade Alive!*, would actually be recorded live in front of an audience of fan-club members at Command Studios in central London, a fully equipped theatre with a stage, seating and a balcony with a mixing board.

The Slade sound was not completely raw and unproduced, though. Holder's voice was put through automatic double-tracking, a process – originally invented by Abbey Road engineer Ken Townsend and particularly favoured by John Lennon – that doubled a voice or instrument while placing each identical recording slightly out of synch, which created a thicker and wider sound. 'Nod's voice was really an ADT sound. We used it nearly every time,' says Powell. 'But that was about it in terms of effects.'

Holder's voice was the dominant aural presence on Slade's records, occupying a huge swathe of the sound-space. His style starts where John Lennon on 'Twist and Shout' leaves off. An Isley Brothers cover and the last song of the session for The Beatles' debut album, 'Twist and Shout' was famously captured in a first take, with

Lennon blasting through vocal cords tattered after twelve hours of non-stop recording. Holder took this shredded rasp and blew it up into a wide wall of in-your-face blare. At his doctor's recommendation, Holder drank rum and blackcurrant for his throat and gargled with TCP antiseptic every day. Powell recalls the time Noddy had to go to a voice specialist. He couldn't believe the state of his throat. After asking Holder to sing, Powell says the doctor 'looked at Nod and said, "I'm sorry – can't do a thing for you." But Nod hardly ever lost his voice, which is unbelievable the way he murdered it night after night onstage.'

The other dominant force in Slade's records was rhythm – Powell's pounding drums in conjunction with bass, rhythm guitar and sometimes simple piano parts, all merged into an almighty chug. Add handclaps and stamping feet, and the sound just clicked. Slade recorded at Olympic Studios in Barnes, west London, a former theatre and cinema. 'There was a stairway down the side of the building, and we'd put a couple of mics in there and go into the stairway and start stomping and clapping,' says Powell. 'The first time was when we finished "Coz I Luv You" – we thought it was a bit soppy, so we tried to heavy it up a bit and added the stomping and the handclaps. It became our trademark.' It also became one of Holder's onstage exhortations to the audience – 'Everybody clap your hands! Stomp your feet!' – and, inverted, the title of a US-only album, *Stomp Your Hands, Clap Your Feet*.

'The beat is the main thing with us,' Holder told *Melody Maker* in 1972. 'We like to hit their guts with the beat and get some feeling going through their bloodstream into their hands. If you want to . . . sit down and delve into the music, it's no good coming to see us.' Where progressive music was designed for listening – in contemplative, stoned reverence, sprawled in the stereo hi-fi's sweet spot or encased in headphones – Slade-type music was music to move to, to feel ('Cum on Feel the Noize') and, above all, to feel together in a crowd. It was first-person-plural music: hence the 'we' of 'Mama Weer All Crazee Now'.

'There is the section of younger kids who aren't into sitting and listening, and are wanting to rave from the start,' Holder told the *NME*, describing Slade's following. 'They sweat their bollocks off . . . and when they pour out of the club they are shagged out . . . Sometimes you get a whole audience too shy but we just pummel their brains until they give in.'

Holder described their sound as 'a violent kind of music, but it provides a release in the form of an escape valve'. The aura of aggro was often noted by nervous reviewers, seeping out in references to *A Clockwork Orange* or a 'street fighting' quality in songs like 'Mama Weer All Crazee Now'. Music-press readers of a delicate persuasion, like Gavin Dunnett of Caithness, Scotland, complained of the reek of violence coming off the records: 'I've lost count of how often on hearing Slade, I've imagined someone's face under those stamping boots.' Other commentators likened the atmosphere at their shows to football matches, which in the early seventies were increasingly disrupted by armies of hooligans. Slade often performed the football-terrace favourite 'You'll Never Walk Alone', while audiences chanted the Tottenham Hotspur ditty 'Nice One, Cyril' but changed the line to 'Nice one, Noddy, let's have another one'.

Damage was rife at Slade's concerts, costing the group up to £500 per gig – broken seats, lights pulled off walls, handrails wrenched loose – and reaching £5,000 after their career-peak show at Earl's Court on 1 July 1973, when they played to nearly 20,000 fans. At the group's London Palladium shows earlier that same year, the balcony cracked: Powell recalls seeing it moving up and down like a trampoline from the kids stomping. Alex Harvey of The Sensational Alex Harvey Band marvelled at the memory of a Slade show at the Glasgow Apollo: 'Fifteen seats disappeared. I don't know whether they ate them, or what, they just disappeared.' But the high spirits were harmless, destructive only to property and fixtures rather than other members of the audience. In the aftermath of the Liverpool gig he witnessed, Lester Bangs found a near-religious significance to a 'mound almost six feet high' gathered in front of the empty stage: 'the remains of all the chairs in the first two rows. The audience had stomped and broken them into tiny pieces, then piled them up in a monument to Slade.'

Many Slade songs were monuments to the audience, inspired by their frenzy: 'Mama Weer All Crazee Now', 'We're Really Gonna Raise the Roof' and, above all, 'Cum on Feel the Noize', which stemmed from a gig, Lea told the *NME*, where 'the audience was shouting so much they drowned us out. Which is some feat . . . We were on stage and there was this rumbling . . . like a train . . . going through the stage . . . and we couldn't work out at first what it was.' A feedback loop of fervour passed from the band to the audience and back again, an escalating spiral of incitement and excitement.

Often dressed Slade-like in top hats, boots and braces, with glitter on their faces and hair, the crowds almost self-consciously performed their own hysteria. Nick Kent, reviewing the Earl's Court mega-concert, observed girls who seemed to be 'passing out overawed by their own frenzy', a pair who screamed themselves 'into a state of total collapse' and another girl in the front row so overcome 'she vomits over the barrier'.

What kept it all the right side of chaos was Slade's mixture of rowdy 'n' bawdy. 'We are fifty per cent humour and fifty per cent music,' Holder declared. His speciality was flirty-dirty banter with the audience. One stage favourite was his 'How many girls here with red knickers on? How many girls with black knickers on? How many girls here with NO knickers on?!!' routine, with the loudest barrage of yells in response to the last option. According to Powell, a lot of it came from Holder's love for the music-hall tradition of cheeky comedians like Max Miller. Holder for his part defended the band from accusations of vulgarity. 'What we indulge in is back street cracks – the kind of language that every kid of our age has heard before.' Slade's down-to-earthiness earned them huge devotion from their fans, who plied them with gifts like watches, rings and sweaters. Despite being one of the biggest record- and ticket-selling bands in Great Britain – indeed, much of Europe – they remained grounded, continuing to live in the Black Country and, following Chandler's guidance, generally avoiding rock-star extravagances.

Soon Slade had imitators. The best of the bunch was Geordie, whose raspy-voiced singer, Brian Johnson, would eventually front AC/DC, wearing a Noddy-esque flat cap. The Newcastle band had a couple of boisterous UK hit singles, but their best song was mystifyingly shunted to a B-side: 'Geordie Stomp' featured the boogie-down chant-hook 'Stomp on-on-on' and skirling guitar that anticipated Scottish new-wave group Big Country. Another Slade-influenced band was The Jook, whose football-hooligan image and boot-stamping anthems like 'Oo Oo Rudie' found the missing link between skinhead-era Slade and Oi!-punk bands like Cockney Rejects.

Nineteen seventy-three was Slade's peak. They sold 2.5 million singles. They played all over Europe and made it to Australia, where *Slade Alive!* was the biggest-selling album since *Sgt Pepper's*. Here they were embraced by an existing Aussie subculture called the sharpies, a Down Under mutant of skinheads. Sharpies had their own uniquely odd style of dancing and a look that merged skin with glitter, plus quirky local variations. High-waisted denim trousers, platform boots, a torso-hugging cardigan worn a couple of sizes too tight – the sharpie style was a harder, meaner version of the look that The Bay City Rollers would adopt in a year or two. But the hairstyle was something else: cropped at the front and on top, but mullet-like with rat-tail wisps straggling over the back collar. In addition to Slade, sharpies loved other stompy glitter performers like Suzi Quatro, but they also rallied to local acts purveying basic bluesy boogie, such as Lobby Loyde and the Coloured Balls.

Only one major territory held out against Slade's charms: America. In 1973, they toured the US a couple of times. The second visit, in the autumn, saw the band playing large halls and generally winning over audiences through sheer gumption; they were riding a wave of music-magazine attention and praise. The expectation was that Slade would break America – they seemed to possess the determination, the mettle, the tunes and the live showmanship to succeed where others had stumbled. But it never happened. Like T. Rex before them, Slade's sound fell in the cracks between AM and FM. 'We were too rowdy for the AM stations and not hip enough for FM stations,' says Powell.

But the real problem for Slade was that the gap they filled in the UK didn't exist in America. No-nonsense, get-down boogie was amply available on the arena circuit, supplied in many cases by Brit bands from the generation before, sixties survivors like Humble Pie and Foghat. There were also home-grown counterparts like Brownsville Station, who supported Slade on their spring 1973 tour. 'Smokin' in the Boys Room', Brownsville's *Billboard* Top 10 hit of that same year, offered a similar sort of harmlessly delinquent vibe and gutsy rock'n'roll as UK glam (indeed, they would later cover Gary Glitter's 'I'm the Leader of the Gang') but without the glitzy costumes.

The real Stateside rival for Slade, though, was Grand Funk Railroad, who hailed from the industrial zones of Michigan – America's equivalent to the Black Country. Paralleling *Slade Alive!*, Grand Funk's breakthrough record was *Live Album*. Both groups were about the community feeling their basic raunchy rock generated. In Grand Funk's case there was a 'People Have the Power' rallying tone to their anthems, recycling the 'brothers and sisters'/'come together' vibe of late-sixties groups like The MC5 and Sly and the Family Stone, but denuded of political content. Slade and Grand Funk share a couple of other things: comparisons with The Beatles (which Grand Funk deliberately played up by filling Shea Stadium), offset by the fact that, despite their contemporary hugeness, neither left much of a mark on rock history. In Grand Funk's case, only 'We're an American Band', their 1973 smash, is still on classic-rock radio. Perhaps Slade should have nicked the concept and written 'We're an English Band', filling it with references to football pools, steak-and-kidney pudding, Bass Pale Ale – perhaps even some Black Country-specific things like groaty pudding and battered chips – in hope of charming the American mass audience like The Beatles' 'Penny Lane' had done.

Beatles comparisons both elevated and dogged Slade. Chandler was determined to follow the Fab Four's path and make a Slade movie. But instead of doing what people would expect – a light-hearted caper, exploiting Holder's rascally humour and bunny-faced Hill's buffoonery – the band decided they wanted to make a serious film. The result was both a triumph and a disaster: *Slade in Flame* was praised by critics as a brave move, an unexpectedly gritty exposé of the music biz, but its bleak honesty deflated the band's momentum. It was too big a dose of reality for their core audience.

Flame was based on the anecdotes the band told scriptwriter Andrew Birkin about their own early struggles as an unknown band, leavened with stories they'd heard from other groups dealing with the same shit: rip-offs, dodgy promoters and booking agents. Set in 1967, the film has Slade playing Flame, a working-class group from the industrial north of England. Rather than go for what Powell calls a 'slapstick, speeded-up, running-around-and-jumping film', the approach was social realism: *Flame* was shot entirely on location, achieving a look and feel similar to *Get Carter*, the 1971 gangster film set in Newcastle. Flame claw their way to fame through an industry crawling with crooks and manipulators, including unscrupulous booking agent Harding (played by Johnny Shannon, previously known for his turn as an east London mobster in *Performance*) and smooth-talking, posh record executive Seymour. One of Seymour's exploits is engineering a publicity stunt in which Flame appear as guests on an offshore pirate-radio station, only to narrowly avoid getting hit by a volley of machine-gun fire from a rival pirate. In another key scene, the drummer Charlie (Don Powell) walks alongside a polluted canal with his former boss, confessing his disillusionment with an industry that is just 'a bunch of bleedin' gangsters in dinner jackets . . . But what can you do? The whole scene's run like it.'

Flame features creditable performances from all of Slade, especially Powell, who comes first in the credits – most likely as a tribute to how well he'd done considering he was recovering from a very serious car accident that damaged his ability to learn his lines. But what is really surprising about *Flame* is not just that it's so superior to the average pop-star exploitation movie, but that it's such an unrelentingly desolate view of the music biz.

'It's not a nice film,' admits Powell. 'We felt good when we were doing it – "this isn't fake". But I always remember at the premiere Robin Nash – the producer of *Top of the Pops* – telling me at the reception afterwards, "I really admire what you've done, but do you think you've done the right thing? Do you really think the kids, your following, want to see this kind of thing?" In hindsight, I think it did backfire on us.' According to Holder, *Flame* 'killed the myth of Slade as this jolly band – four mates who entertained, had a laugh. That's what the fans wanted to see in the film.'

The irony of *Flame* is that it didn't actually reflect Slade's own recent experience of the music industry: success had not destroyed or divided the band, nor had they been ripped off. Their manager,

Chas Chandler, was financially shrewd but ethical, protecting his charges by encouraging them to keep their outgoings low and maximise their earnings while they were hot.

But if Chandler made one error it was that he discouraged Slade from growing musically. 'He doesn't want us to step too far ahead too quickly,' Holder told *Melody Maker*. 'He doesn't want us to get complicated or introvert. He wants us to do what we are good at doing instead of experimenting with things we won't be good at.' Internalising Chandler's caution, Slade held back some songs 'because we feel they are too clever – too indulgent for our fans at the moment', admitted Dave Hill.

It's as if Slade were The Beatles but stuck in a permanent 1964. Or The Who, if they'd never progressed to rock opera ('We're doin' a cock opera,' Lea quipped to *Creem*). Slade sold a lot of albums, but they weren't an albums band; their approach was to record every song as if it was a single, resulting in albums without ups and downs, little sense of a journey across two sides.

In this light, Lester Bangs's remark that Slade will 'never get trapped by an inflated concept of themselves like the Beatles did' or Nick Kent's promise that 'you won't be hearing any primal scream albums from Noddy Holder, or Dave Hill playing the sitar' ultimately reveal the band's limitations. These might have been inherent or self-imposed, but we'll never really know. What made The Beatles The Beatles was their impulse to evolve, expand, absorb both other musical influences and extra-musical ideas from art and literature. Slade, in contrast, turned The Beatles' starting point into a destination. Development was arrested.

Bubble gum *adj*. Describes anything that appeals to young adolescents (teenyboppers), usually considered by older people to be of silly or shallow composition – e.g. *They like bubble gum music*. See TEENYBOPPER.

From *The Underground Dictionary*, by Eugene E. Landy, PhD, 1971

It's not easy to write plastic songs . . . It's ten times more difficult to write a number one pop song than it is to write a great album track.

Mike Chapman and Nicky Chinn, 1973

Although they benefited from having a strong manager, Slade were a real group, an autonomous creative unit that wrote its own songs, in the lineage of Beatles–Stones–Who. As the band's producer, Chandler's approach was minimal, oriented towards capturing their live power.

In contrast, The Sweet were closer to the classic mould of teenybop, with the emphasis on the word 'mould'. Their hit singles were written by Mike Chapman and Nicky Chinn. Their records were highly produced by Phil Wainman. Their career was steered by New Dawn Productions, the management/production/publishing company that Wainman and Chinn and Chapman formed, which in addition to controlling The Sweet as performers and recording artists also owned the publishing of any songs the group themselves got to write as B-sides or album tracks.

Demeaning as this arrangement was for The Sweet, the results testify to the potency of the pop manufacturing process, the electric effectiveness of the specialised division of labour. Yet it's also true that Wainman and Chinnichap (as they became known), who had each made attempts in the past at being performing and recording artists, couldn't have achieved anything without The Sweet. They needed the performers' raw talent, physical presence and ability to command a stage. It was a tense relationship on every side, fraught with mutual resentment. But for as long as it worked – late 1972 to early 1974, 'Wig-Wam Bam' to 'Teenage Rampage' – the three-way, if far from equal, partnership between Wainman, Chinnichap and The Sweet produced five of the most exciting singles of their era. Of any era. The machine made magic.

Like Slade in their early days, the future members of The Sweet did their mid-sixties apprenticeship with twenty-quid gigs at pubs and social clubs, while playing in combos with names like Wainright's Gentlemen and The Army, mostly in north London and Middlesex. In early 1968, singer Brian Connolly, drummer Mick Tucker and bassist Steve Priest coalesced as The Sweetshop, a name that attempted to hitch a ride on the fad for sugary-themed groups like Marmalade, Strawberry Jam and Tangerine Peel.

Dropping the 'shop', The Sweet released a bunch of indifferent singles, written by various professional songsmiths, the most notable being 'Lollipop Man', a brazen attempt to emulate 'Sugar, Sugar' by The Archies. A massive US hit in the summer of 1969, 'Sugar, Sugar' would do even better in the UK, where it held the #1 spot for eight weeks that autumn. 'Sugar, Sugar' was the most successful of a spate of catchy candypop by groups with names like 1910 Fruitgum Company. Together they formed the genre nicknamed 'bubblegum', a classic example of a derogatory term flipped into a positive identity. Bubblegum pop took the beat-group sound of the mid-sixties but removed the creative autonomy aspect, placing control entirely in the hands of the producer and the songwriter (sometimes the same person, but usually not).

The Monkees were the archetype of this process. But when Nesmith, Dolenz, Tork and Jones got ideas above their station – wanting to write their own material, play on their own records – The Monkees' pissed-off Svengali Don Kirschner went one step further with his next project, The Archies: creating not just a fabricated group but a non-existent one, a figment that existed only in the recording studio and as animated characters in a kids' cartoon show.

The word 'bubblegum' suggests audio cud for the distraction of vacant ears and empty heads; a substance plastic in texture, artificial in taste and devoid of nutritional worth. 'Its appeal lies in the fact that it's not complicated,' Brian Connolly declared in a 1971 *Melody Maker* feature on the bubblegum genre's peculiar sticking power. He further explained that its 'simple melody' appealed to kids who were 'not musically educated'.

To its detractors, bubblegum was merely the latest in a long line of mercenary hackwork from the pop industry: a cynical form of talking down to the kids. There was a grain of truth there: Mike Chapman would later say in an unguardedly arrogant moment that he and Chinn were 'the people responsible for telling the kids what they were going to buy. Not asking them what they wanted, but *telling* them.' This top-down dynamic was the opposite of the underground's belief that true music came from below. Two ideologies clashed here: pop as populist, music by and for the people, versus pop as a fizzy-soda-like product manufactured and marketed to the masses. As they evolved, The Sweet would be torn by this community versus commodity division. But in the early days, they were desperate enough to grab at any chance of success.

Producer Phil Wainman was impressed by The Sweet's Motown-style harmonies and talked about recording them, if he could find a suitable sure-fire hit. Around the same time, early 1970, Wainman met aspiring songwriter duo Nicky Chinn and Mike Chapman. Captivated by 'Sugar, Sugar' – the sound, the producer-in-total-control mode of its production and, most of all, its stupendous worldwide sales figures – Wainman suggested to Chinn and Chapman that they take a stab at writing something in that sickly vein.

The duo came back with 'Funny Funny' – complete with 'Sugar, Sugar' baby-talk-like repetition in the chorus/title – and The Sweet had their first hit single in spring 1971. How much it was actually

Chinnichap at work: Mike Chapman (left) and Nicky Chinn (right) are profiled in *Melody Maker*, 30 June 1973

theirs is debatable, since The Sweet did not actually play on 'Funny Funny' or, indeed, the next four hit singles they scored. Connolly sang, but the musical backing was supplied by session musicians. As a band The Sweet at this point primarily existed to front the records during TV appearances and to play the gig bookings that multiplied with each single's success.

Wainman's modus operandi was modelled on Tin Pan Alley. He'd caught the twilight of its British heyday in Denmark Street, when he was given a retainer as staff writer for the song publishers Mills Music. When he moved into production, Wainman became obsessed with keeping recording costs down. He preferred working with session musicians rather than bands because they were reliable and quick: a single could be completed in a couple of hours.

With Wainman cracking the whip and keeping an eye on the clock, the New Dawn Productions assembly line churned out hits for The Sweet. Chinn and Chapman penned sticky-to-the-ear tunes like 'Co-Co' and 'Poppa Joe'; Wainman and his hired-by-the-hour players gave them a lilting, Caribbean feel, complete with marimba and steel drum. A song 'about a little negro boy who loves to dance' – as Connolly told one music paper, which does not record whether the singer then buried his face in his hands – 'Co-Co' was #1 in several European countries and was only held off the top spot in the UK by the even more anodyne 'Chirpy Chirpy Cheep Cheep' by Middle of the Road. 'The deal with The Sweet was that if we made them a million pounds in the three years that we had them signed for, they had to re-sign for another three years,' recalls Wainman. 'Well, we made a million pounds in the first nine months.'

Money may have soothed their wounded pride to some degree but the arrangement that Wainman set up – The Sweet as pretty-boy puppets, their role limited to 'the vocal and visual face of the band' – was immensely frustrating for the group, who harboured cravings to be a credible hard-rock band. This was especially the case for their newest recruit, Andy Scott, a potent blues-rock guitarist with budding songwriting talent of his own. A chasm steadily grew between the lightweight froth The Sweet mimed to on TV and the hard-riffing material that made up most of their live sets. The tough stuff also slipped onto their B-sides, written by Scott or jointly by the band, then bashed out by The Sweet themselves only after the session players had polished up the A-side.

Tension between Wainman and The Sweet was not the only fault line in New Dawn Productions' three-way coalition of talent. The producer would increasingly come into friction with Chinn and Chapman, with the latter particularly eager to get his hand on the mixing board. Chinnichap itself was a peculiar partnership. When they met, both Chinn and Chapman were aspiring songwriters. But as time went by, the Australian-born Chapman became the musical driving force. Having grown up in a wealthy entrepreneurial family, Chinn's true forte was hustle, and he increasingly dedicated his energy to chasing industry contacts and to the management of The Sweet. Chinn continued to contribute lyrics, but tune-wise his role gradually became that of an editor, or 'quality control of the melody', as he puts it.

'Little Willy' was The Sweet's first genuinely exciting hit: nursery-rhyme silly, but a strong step in the direction of the group's live sound. On the record itself, though, what you hear is still session men rather than the band. It was only after The Sweet threatened to walk if Wainman didn't let them tackle the A-side of the next single, 'Wig-Wam Bam', that the producer relented. But he made an ungracious condition. 'I told them, "If you spend more time than I would have done with my session guys – a few hours – then I'm taking the extra recording costs off your royalties." So the boys went in the studio and they played their socks off,' Wainman laughs. 'Then they told me, "There you are – we can do it, so up yours!"'

'Wig-Wam Bam', Wainman concedes now, was 'a turning point'. Not just for The Sweet, but for the producer and the songwriters too, given that the previous singles had done nobody any favours. The lyric remained as daft as those of its predecessors: sexy doggerel about Hiawatha and Minnehaha, Running Bear and Little

White Dove getting it on in the Wild West, loosely based on Henry Longfellow's 1855 poem 'The Song of Hiawatha'. But the convergence of Mick Tucker's propulsive pounding, Steve Priest's agile grind, Connolly's blend of raw and honey, and Andy Scott's thick-toned menace showed how powerful The Sweet had become as a rock band.

Starting with 'Wig-Wam Bam', The Sweet hurtled through a hot streak of chart smashes that set standards for what could be called 'radio rock': guitar music that has all the brawn and internal combustion of a live rock group, but channels that force and friction through the structural precision of pop, using arrangement and space to construct three-minute mini-dramas that can withstand endless repetition on the airwaves. Raw power with a high-gloss finish, rock heat meets pop frosting. The Radio Rock pantheon holds lofty perches for Cheap Trick and Def Leppard . . . anoints moments from Van Halen, Boston, Billy Squier and The Scorpions . . . exalts *Nevermind*-era Nirvana for producer Butch Vig's blend of grunge and glisten. But The Sweet reign almost unrivalled in this roll call of honour. Their killer singles – 'Blockbuster!', 'Hellraiser', 'Ballroom Blitz', 'Teenage Rampage'– have nothing but sell in them: there's no superfluous soloing or bluesy ballast. Everything in those classic Sweet smashes is purely sensationalist: the Four Seasons/Beach Boys harmonies, often phased or flanged into a blow-dried sheen; the streamlined stainless-steel riffs; the cartoony lyric scenarios, concocted purely for hysteria; and last but not least, judiciously deployed audio gimmicks, like the police siren on 'Blockbuster!', which had to be removed from the American single release for fear it would confuse drivers listening on their car radios.

Booming kettle drums adding to the single's exhilarating emergency, 'Blockbuster!' tells of a villain on the rampage, the unstoppable Buster – he who must be blocked at all costs. The Sweet's first really monster-sized hit, reaching #1 in early 1973, 'Blockbuster!'

debuted what became a fixture of subsequent Sweet hits: the inter-
jection of a few lines of campy histrionics from Steve Priest, in this
case the flustered, eyelash-fluttering 'We just haven't got a clue
WHAT to do!'

'Steve's bit was something that came up in the studio,' says Chinn.
'And from that point on, he always had a vocal bit in the songs, and
he always sounded crazed.' The follow-up single 'Hellraiser', which
got to #2, was even more histrionic: Connolly, at once awestruck
and shit scared, warns of a voracious libertine, 'a natural-born raver'
whose 'ultra-sonic eyes' flash 'like hysterical danger signs', a sex-
crazed girl who'll drive you crazy.

The mid-sixties were The Sweet's foundation. 'Blockbuster!' was
based on a loping riff previously used by The Nashville Teens on
'Tobacco Road' and The Yardbirds on their version of Bo Diddley's
'I'm a Man'. The Sweet admired and emulated The Who's classic
run of singles from 'My Generation' (which they covered) to 'I Can
See for Miles' – that electrifying clash of amphetamine aggression
and saintly, soaring harmonies. But if a single song served as a template for The Sweet Sound, it's The Beatles' 1966 single 'Paperback
Writer', with its cross-meshed chorus harmonies and flashy, if
slightly empty euphoria. Andy Scott introduced 'Paperback Writer'
into The Sweet's live set because it was ideal for a four-voice group.
'Andy had the highest voice in the world,' says Wainman. 'He could
go into orbit with the high notes.'

Glam and glitter involved a return to the simpler musical structures of fifties rock'n'roll and the pre-psychedelic sixties beat group,
but sluiced through late-sixties/early-seventies sound-recording
techniques. Glam rejected the tripped-out shapelessness of late-
sixties music, but kept and built on the era's studio advances, in
particular multitracking and close miking of the drum kit. Similarly,
glam guitarists assimilated the preceding era's innovations in guitar
sound but applied them to punchier purposes.

When you listen to fifties rock'n'roll, and to most sixties rock up until about 1967, it's striking how low in the mix and physically unimposing the drums are compared to subsequent norms, and how thin-bodied the guitar parts are. Guitarists made up for it with speed and energy, a scrappy 'n' scratchy propulsiveness. It was only with the advent of guitar effects like distortion, fuzz-tone, wah-wah, etc., and with studio practices like multitracking the same guitar part to thicken the sound, that heavy riffs and power chords became effective. (In early rock'n'roll, the function of the riff was generally supplied by horns, whose 'wide' sound gave muscle and heft to the records.) As for drums, 'close miking of each individual drum in the kit was the big change from the sixties to the seventies', says John Hudson, sound engineer on the percussively potent Gary Glitter records. 'Before that, producers just used an overhead microphone and possibly a mic on the kick drum.'

Before he got into production, Phil Wainman had been a professional drummer from the age of fifteen, playing in a cabaret act that toured Royal Air Force bases in Europe and then joining The Paramounts – later to become Procol Harum – for a year. His dream was to make drum records, like his hero Sandy Nelson, and he made a single in that vein for EMI called 'Hear Me a Drummer Man'. The obsession with powerful and prominent drums carried on with The Sweet. 'You'll notice that on all the Sweet's singles, there's an emphasis on drums,' Wainman told *Melody Maker*. 'To me they're a trade secret because whenever I'm stuck – I just push the drum sound forward.'

'Ballroom Blitz' was the culminati   is process. 'All my ideas that I had kind of put in the back o.   d, I thought, "I can use every single one with this song,"' W.   alls. When Chinn and Chapman's demo for 'Ballroom Blitz   gh, The Sweet didn't really know what to do with it, accorc   an. 'So I sat behind Mick Tucker's kit and I played that s.   ounding,

Advert for 'Ballroom Blitz', September 1972: The Sweet in a clinch with showroom girls (apart from saucy Steve Priest, whose mannequin is a man)

Bo Biddley-goes-military beat that drives 'Blitz' – 'and I kept on playing it while the rest of the group ran through the song. Until Mick was itching, "Come on, come on, get off the stool, I want to play it.'"

But it wasn't just the drum pattern – so catchy it worked as one of 'Blitz''s primary hooks – it was the sheer size of percussive sound that Wainman achieved that was remarkable. This was created partly through altering the drum kit itself and partly through the microphone set-up. Through his session work Wainman had developed various drummer's tricks, like inserting newspaper and a sheet of polythene under a drum skin to make it thicker, which meant you could tune it lower and get a bigger sound. As a producer, he worked out ways to capture the room ambience as well as the individual elements of the kit, putting 'pressure zone' microphones on the wall to catch that tiny but vibe-creating gap between the stick hitting the drum skin and the ambient sound reflections bouncing off the wall. Juggling all these different inputs from the mics, Wainman built up a massive sound for 'Ballroom Blitz', whose recorded version sounded very different from the Chinnichap demo.

Lyrically inspired by the crazed crowd at a Sweet gig that Chapman attended, boosted by Wainman's bionic production and invigorated by the group's most off-the-leash playing so far, 'Ballroom Blitz' lived up to its title, attacking disco floors and rampaging across the radio. But The Sweet's supremely career-defining single was cheated from its righteous throne at #1 in the UK hit parade, first by Wizzard's 'Angel Fingers' and then by 'Eye Level', the theme song to a TV detective show. Consolation came later on with the American chart success of 'Blitz', giving The Sweet their second *Billboard* Top 5 hit ('Little Willy' had reached #3). One of the song's most beloved hooks is the inspired intro scripted by Chapman, which extended Steve Priest's campy cameo roles to the whole band: Connolly asks each member in turn if they're ready, receiving fey murmurs of assent, then kicks off the onslaught   'Okay, boys . . . let's go!'

Connolly argued in magazine in.   that The Sweet were no longer the bubblegum puppets th.   'een at the start: he claimed that the band played a big role   ng the tunes, that Chinn and Chapman were now writing   nd members' specific abilities in mind, that The Sweet   authors of

their own sound. Nonetheless, the fact that none of the A-sides had been composed yet by the group still rankled. In interviews The Sweet incessantly referenced Deep Purple – a band they'd known socially going back many years – as the model to which they aspired.

Where The Sweet had the greatest input into the direction of their career was, funnily enough, their image: clothes, showmanship, persona. 'All the camping, the make-up and outfits, that was Sweet being Sweet,' says Nicky Chinn. 'It didn't come from us. They were the founders of their own image.' In fact, at the time, Chinn confessed to the *NME* that the group's gender-bending larks were 'a total turn off' as far as he was concerned. 'I loathe it all . . . They embarrass me, but they know what they're doing.' The Sweet, he noted, 'want to become more outrageous . . . I think the loonier they get the bigger they'll become.'

The Sweet were picking up on moves made by Bolan and Slade, obviously. But they were also tuning into seventies style in general – a riot of voluminous flares, teetering platform boots, absurdly wide lapels and ties, unnecessary buttons and stitching, collars that jutted way out to the shoulders, clashing colours in intensely artificial shades, man-made fibres and glossy, plasticky fabrics.

Their dalliance with excess started as far back as 'Wig-Wam Bam', when The Sweet glammed it up for their *Top of the Pops* appearance, with Andy Scott flouncing about with a handbag and Steve Priest sporting a Native American headdress. Because singer Connolly consistently avoided gender-bending, choosing to lean on his natural good looks and long blond hair, bassist Priest became the instigator of androgynous mischief. Milky skin, wavy red hair, puckered lips . . . 'I looked like a twelve-year-old girl,' Priest later recalled.

After his fancy-dress Native American look, Priest escalated to wearing cat's-eye make-up and green hot pants over red tights. The climax came with the infamous Christmas 1973 appearance on *Top of the Pops*, in which Priest dressed up as 'a gay SS stormtrooper'.

The Sweet's 'Teenage Rampage' (Dutch version)

What the look lacked in historical authenticity – the helmet Priest wore was from the First World War – was made up for by cheap shock: less than thirty years after VE Day, the swastika arm band and Hitler moustache were still fearfully offensive to the generation that lived through the actual Blitz as opposed to just the 'Ballroom Blitz'.

'Here you go, it's the Nuremberg Rally' – so said Mike Chapman when he presented The Sweet with the demo for 'Teenage Rampage'. The single became the group's third #2 in a row, but it turned out to be the last act of the Wainman–Chinnichap–Sweet three-way partnership. Chinn and Chapman were distracted by their work with Suzi Quatro and Mud, for whom they produced as well as wrote.

Indeed, it was Mud's 'Tiger Feet' that kept 'Teenage Rampage' off the #1 spot, something that aggrieved The Sweet hugely. 'Tiger Feet' would go on to be the biggest-selling single of 1974. Now that they were producing for their new protégés, Chinnichap pushed to take over the whole process when it came to The Sweet's singles too. Forced to choose between their original producer and the songwriters, The Sweet opted for Chinnichap.

The Sweet's first post-Wainman single, 'The Six Teens', was their most sophisticated song yet. Like 'Teenage Rampage', the lyric contained oblique nods to late-sixties revolutionary dreams: 'Where were you in '68?' But somewhere between Chinnichap's writing and production and the band's playing, the result ended up more fussy and filigreed than before, lacking the pure pop attack of 'Blitz' and 'Blockbuster!' 'The Six Teens' placed lower in the chart than anything The Sweet had done since before 'Little Willy', the single just scraping into the Top 10 at #9.

But Chinnichap's plastic-punk instinct for simplicity hadn't deserted them at all; it was getting funnelled entirely into songs for Mud, such as their first big hit, 'Dyna-Mite'. Mud had originally been talent-spotted by Nicky Chinn's mentor, Mickie Most of RAK Records. A British music-industry legend for his success producing The Animals, Herman's Hermits, Lulu and Donovan, Most became a household name in the UK with his appearances on the TV talent show *New Faces*: handsome but unsmiling, he offered sometimes harsh but always constructive and perceptive advice to the hopeful acts. Chinn revered Most for his infallible knack of picking the future hit out of a bunch of demos, his flair for spotting the X-factor that distinguished a potential star from a definite nobody.

When Most first caught Mud playing live, he reckoned that sound-wise they'd found the sweet spot between Slade and Sweet, but lacked the right song. So he handed them over wholesale to Chinn and Chapman. Hard-slogging veterans of the working-men's

'Fancy a screw, darlin'?' Mud, still lewd, still crude, but past their proto-punk prime on *Use Your Imagination* (1975). Left to right: Rob Davis (guitar), Les Gray (throat), Dave Mount (drums), Ray Styles (bass)

club and cabaret circuit, Mud had once played as The Mourners, even getting black visiting cards printed with 'We're Dead With It' as a gimmick. Image-wise, they would have been a straightforward rock'n'roll revival troupe – leering, shades-sporting singer Les Gray clad himself in Teddy Boy drape jackets or Evel Knievel-style white leather jumpsuits trimmed with rhinestones – if not for guitarist Rob Davis, the only member who intersected with glam. Davis's big earrings and permed blond curls, his giant flared pantaloons and billowing sleeves created the effect of a secretary in a maxi-dress dancing at the Christmas office party.

There was nothing fey or delicate about Mud's sound, a boorishly effective pummel that makes you wonder why pub rock even needed to be invented by bands or championed by journalists in 1974. The breakdown in 'Tiger Feet' cuts down to a zigzagging riff worthy of some obscure, cult-fetishised sixties shindig band from deepest Illinois. But 'Dyna-Mite' was their killer, a greasy churn of sub-punk commotion. In the video, Mud perform a dance that's been dubbed the shoulder-jive: a macho manoeuvre that involves hooking your thumbs through your belt loops and jack-knifing your body at an angle, right elbow towards left knee and vice versa. Probably generated by Slade's following, although it may well date back to the mod-battling, bike-riding rockers of the early sixties, the shoulder-jive entered the folk memory of provincial British youth and could still be seen at Young Farmers' discos in the eighties, whenever the DJ whipped out a golden oldie from the glitter era.

Feeling both neglected by their hit-making masters yet stifled by them, The Sweet vacillated: they were desperate to record only their own material and produce it themselves, but nervous about breaking with the team whose winning streak continued with Mud and Quatro. Trying to toughen up their image, they stressed in interviews that 'We're a nasty group.' Their stage show had long contained uncouth elements: Connolly would exhort the audience to 'Give us a wank!' and rub his crotch bulge with the mic stand, or the band might sing a version of 'Chirpy Chirpy Cheep Cheep', with the chorus changed to 'Where's your titties gone? With the nipples on?' In Belgium, Priest and Connolly were arrested and held in jail for several days following onstage incidents in which fans were suggestively manhandled.

In early 1974, The Sweet embarked on a tour that amped up the provocation while also competing strongly in the post-Alice Cooper visual-theatrical stakes. The stage show included several costume changes, smoke bombs, smutty jokes and a full-size cinema screen on which were projected animations and short filmed clips, including spoof commercials, a car chase and a segment that allowed Mick Tucker to do a drum duel with himself on screen. *Melody Maker* reviewer Jeff Ward noted the 'blatant phallic symbolism' – rockets, banana peeling – running through The Sweet's 'hard 'n' horny, sexist-sadist road show'. He described 'a "rape" sequence' in which Steve Priest attempted to grope Andy Scott and fellate the tremolo arm on his guitar. In a follow-up feature, The Sweet told Ward about their plans for the next album, which they intended to title *We're Revolting*. 'Instead of being "sweet" we're going to try and put over an album sleeve with the group on the front but a grotesque cartoon on the back, warts and everything. "Revolting" can mean "we're horrible" or that we're revolting against "Funny, Funny", if you like.'

In the event, The Sweet's next album was titled *Desolation Boulevard*. Recorded in America, with Chapman at the controls, it featured a gritty, urban-wasteland cover and a strong mixture of Chinnichap tunes and band originals. But credibility continued to elude the band, despite their macho overcompensation on tour.

Finally, The Sweet broke loose from their songwriter-producers. Their first self-produced single, 'Fox on the Run', showed how well they'd learnt from their proximity to Wainman and Chapman: buffed and burnished to a dazzling sheen, it was a perfect merger of bubblegum and hard rock. The lyric continued a Sweet mini-tradition of put-down songs, usually aimed at women, like 'Heartbreak Today', 'Take a Look at Yourself' and 'No You Don't'. A massive hit on both sides of the Atlantic, 'Fox on the Run' was followed by their most punk statement yet, 'Action', an embittered biting of the hands that had fed them for so long. 'Action' is a massive 'F*@$ you!' to record-biz exploiters and manipulators, with the sound of cash registers chiming in the Sabbath-heavy breakdown. A solid-sized hit in the UK and US, 'Action' didn't buoy up the sales or cred of the accompanying album *Give Us a Wink*, though. The missing link between

The Archies and 'Anarchy in the UK', The Sweet could never quite shed the tangy taint of bubblegum.

Suzi Quatro was once hailed as 'the world's only female punk rocker' by the *NME*'s Charles Shaar Murray. Hailing from Detroit, Quatro had actually started out in The Pleasure Seekers, a garage band whose 1965 single 'What a Way to Die' is prized by sixties punk collectors for its raw sound and lyrics that unfavourably compare a boyfriend to various brands of beer.

The Pleasure Seekers weren't really punks, though: they were a pioneering all-girl band, comprised mostly of Quatro sisters, whose parents were in showbiz. They performed wearing skirts, sang Motown songs and played for wounded troops in Vietnam hospitals. A hard-working music professional from the age of fourteen, Suzi played bass and sang on some songs. The Pleasure Seekers put out a bunch of singles and eventually changed their name to Cradle, conforming to the late-sixties trend for names without a definite article.

When Mickie Most saw Cradle, he spotted the X-factor he was looking for not in the lead singer Nancy Quatro but in the petite bassist and occasional vocalist Suzi. Other labels were interested in Quatro as a solo artist, but, she says, Most had the winning pitch. 'Elektra's president Jac Holzman told me he would take me to New York, form a male band around me and turn me into the next Janis Joplin. Mickie Most told me he wanted to take me to England and make me the first Suzi Quatro.'

That's a story that flatters both the producer and the artist, of course, emphasising the non-manipulative integrity of the producer and the artist's unbending authenticity. In fact, the process of making Suzi Quatro into 'Suzi Quatro' was not instant or easy. There was an album, produced by Most himself, that was quietly shelved as 'not right'. In 1972, RAK and Quatro released a single, 'Rolling Stone' – a gently jaunty slice of country-tinged pop only marginally more gritty than The Partridge Family – that flopped everywhere in the world but Portugal, where it reached #1.

The first step in the right direction was forming a full-time band with Quatro as leader, its sound based on her love of raw rock'n'roll, which she often said had 'died' during the late sixties. 'It's a band with no egos, no intellects, which is the only way to have a rock'n'roll band,' Quatro told *Melody Maker*. They toured as the opening act for Slade, without much impact. Then came the decisive move: Most handed over production and songwriting to the men with the Midas touch, Chinn and Chapman. As Quatro describes it, they listened to the band's set – all original material – and then wrote 'Can the Can'. Crude but catchy bubblegum-boogie, it shot to #1 in the UK in the early summer of 1973.

The success of 'Can the Can' involved two further breakthroughs, the first sonic and the other visual. Quatro typically sang in a low, gutsy growl, rooted in the raspy, driving Detroit rock of Mitch Ryder and Bob Seger. During the 'Can the Can' session, Chapman kept asking her to sing it higher. 'He said, "Sing it in this key," and then he kept going up, up, up, up, up. He took me right up to where I was dying, the very top of my range, and he said, "That's it." I said, "Are you nuts?" And he said, "Nope, that's exciting."' Chapman was right: Quatro's shriek cut right through the band's boogie chug like the snarl of a feral cat – the perfect sound for lines like the spat-out pre-chorus 'scratch out her eyes'. The pint-sized Quatro suddenly sounded like someone you wouldn't want to mess with.

The image makeover transformed her into somebody you might want to mess with, or be messed around by – if your seething teenage hormones got the upper hand over your understandable trepidation. Quatro and Most conceived of the idea of the singer being clad in a black leather jumpsuit. Clinging tightly to her skinny,

'I'm the leader of the gang I am': Suzi Quatro's debut LP (1973). The boys: (left to right) Dave Neal (drums), Alastair McKenzie (keyboards), Len Tuckey (guitar)

androgynous frame, the leather outfit made Quatro into a different kind of sex symbol – 'unisexual', in her words. It stirred something in tweenage boys still likely to crush on tomboys rather than curvy uber-babes: 'Little boys write and say they wanna peel it off,' Quatro laughed in one early interview. But it also stirred something in teenage girls who weren't sure if they wanted to be her or be with her. In Los Angeles County, for instance, fourteen-year-old Joan Marie Larkin gaped open-mouthed at the pictures of Quatro in *Creem* and *Rock Scene*. Within a few years, she would become Joan Jett.

The cover of *Suzi Quatro*, her debut album, showed the singer in leather jacket and tight denim jeans, half turned to face the camera, her gaze impassive, with a hint of challenge. She's surrounded by her band, greasy-haired, unshaven, leering and surly. One of them – guitarist Len Tuckey – tips a bottle of beer down his gullet, his other hand shoved down inside the crotch of his jeans. The message was multiple: Suzi as one of the boys, as leader of the gang, as beauty among the beasts. Before concerts, the male members of the band smeared glycerine on their arms and other exposed flesh because it looked sweaty and caught the stage lights, adding to the men-at-hard-work grubbiness. Onstage and in TV appearances, Quatro screwed up her eyes when she screamed the chorus, looking mean but cute.

'Unladylike' was Quatro's image – like most pop personae a mixture of her true Detroit self and performance for public consumption. 'I ain't no lady,' she told *Melody Maker* in one of her first major interviews in June 1973. 'I'm just like the fellas, I guess I'm a bit of a yobbo.' Referencing the exquisite effeminates fronting glam groups, she added: 'The men are prettier than the women these days . . . Bowie makes me feel real ugly.' Interviews teemed with swearing and frank discussion of the gusset-level impact of rock'n'roll: Quatro loved playing bass, she often said, because the sound hit you 'right between the legs . . . it's so horny'. Her stance was intransigent and unapologetic: 'You could call me the Butch Bitch in your paper,' she told the *NME* that same summer. 'My character won't change – it won't budge an inch.' She explained that because she lacked 'physical strength . . . I have to use my mouth. And my mouth is like a bit of barbed wire.' Her 'fuck yous', she said on another occasion, 'have to be my weapons'.

Quatro walked a delicate line. So tough and independent she didn't care to join the Women's Liberation movement, having no need for sisterly support or solidarity; on the other hand, happy to be a role model to young girls, who, she told the *NME*, wrote in droves 'to say, "I'm just like you. I wear my hair like you and I swear too and I've got a tattoo.'" Not so uptight she'd turn down an invitation to pose for a *Penthouse* centrefold; on the other hand, self-possessed enough to say, 'No problem, but clothed' (she did the session in a white leather jumpsuit).

If there was a problem with the Quatro stance, it was that she tended to identify power and autonomy with traits conventionally identified as 'masculine': hardness, roughness, coarseness, being unemotional (or masking your emotions). 'If I didn't have a lot of guts, I'd have been as messed up as all the other females in this world,' she told the *NME*. 'You're supposed to be soft, you're supposed to be cute and you're supposed to be pretty.' In other interviews, she talked about how women were vulnerable because 'unfortunately they're very emotional' and were further conditioned to lean towards 'something lovey-dovey in a song'. Asked why she sang 'I Wanna Be Your Man' but kept the genders the same, Quatro says, 'Why didn't I change it? I was making an analogy . . . When you say, "I wanna be your man," what you're saying is I want to be your strength. So I kept the words the same because "I want to be your strength." There, you've got me in a nutshell.'

Perhaps my favourite Suzi Quatro song is the B-side to 'Devil Gate Drive', a loping, bluesy number titled 'In the Morning'. The scenario is the morning after a drunken one-night stand, the couple waking in a fug of bad breath and sour regrets. 'In the morning / You sure look ugly in the morning,' taunts Quatro, in a playground sing-song that doesn't disguise her bitterness. In the middle, a British male voice rouses itself and oafishly demands breakfast in bed; Suzi snarls back that he should get lost ASAP. The voice is that of Len Tuckey – by the time of the session, Suzi's lover, soon to be her husband. 'Oh my God, we were just newly together, we were very much in love,' laughs Quatro, when I bring up the song. 'I remember that whole session.' But what a curiously unsentimental way to commemorate the first flush of a lifetime's great love.

Quatro's body of work is modest: four or five fierce singles, barely more than a chanted vocal over a boogie-punk chug, Chapman's production detectable only in the terrifically thumping, sticks-of-lead drum sound; a few unusual originals, like 'In the Morning' or the jungly percussive 'Primitive Love'. But she's an important figure both in the history of rock and in the context of glam. Before Quatro, there had been virtually no tough frontwomen in rock who had also been successful. There'd been Grace Slick and Janis Joplin, but that was about it. All-female bands existed (Fanny, Birtha, Goldie and the Gingerbreads) but none had broken through. Virtually all the rock frontwomen who were both successful and taken seriously were either singer-songwriters or swathed in the glamour of a witchy or ethereal or folk-maiden-ish type (Nico, Sonja Kristina of Curved Air, Sandy Denny).

As for glam, the movement was all about feminised men, but it was not feminist: Quatro was alone as a significant female glitter-era star. As glam scholar Philip Auslander observes, women played vital roles in glam, but they were generally behind the scenes. June Bolan and Angie Bowie made huge contributions to the development of their husbands' images, operating as a combination of mentor, muse, adviser, stylist, networker and protective filter between the star and the outside world. There were other influential background figures, such as Chelita Secunda (who managed Bolan for a period) and costume designers like Jean Seel of Alkasura. But when it comes to the music, glam is pretty much an all-male zone. There's really just Suzi.

Quatro's androgynising move was not exactly equivalent to the dandy male's embrace of elegance and excess. To get tougher and rougher looking is to leave behind glamour as conventionally understood. But with her glistening black bodysuit, her studded leather choker and wristbands, her unfussy mid-length shag hair and just-a-touch make-up, her narrowed eyes and lip-curled sneer, and that raging glee with which she shook her bass guitar and stamped out the beat with her boots, Suzi Quatro created her own anti-glam glamour. *'Just 'cause I've got a couple of buns in front don't mean I can't play rock'n'roll.'*

⚡

Mickie Most's RAK Records – the home of Suzi Quatro and Mud – was located at 2 Charles Street, in Mayfair, the swanky heart of London. Right next door was Bell Records, the other big UK label for teenpop. 'Teen Avenue' is how Most once described Charles Street. Right round the corner from Rak and Bell, on Curzon Street, was RCA, The Sweet's record label, while Chinnichap's operational base – a luxurious flat, walls covered in gold and silver discs – was in Mayfair too. There was even a studio called Mayfair in South Molton Street, where many of the major glam records of the period were recorded, among them Gary Glitter's early hits. The area – like the era – was electric with excitement and what Nicky Chinn describes as 'very friendly rivalry'. Everyone was 'buzzing', recalled Most, 'because nobody was taking it seriously . . . and the records were selling in *millions*'.

RAK was named after 'rack jobbing', a method of selling records that had taken off in other parts of the world but, in the seventies, had yet to reach the UK: distributing them to non-record-store retailers like supermarkets, petrol stations, liquor stores and so on. Mickie Most tried to interest British retail chains like Tesco and Boots in the idea, but when they declined, he turned RAK into a conventional record label.

Most's commercial clairvoyance – unlike most record-company executives, he could sense what would shortly be selling rather than merely following what was already commercially proven – came, he said, from reducing his thinking to the level of a seventeen-year-old.

RAK quickly became one of the most chart-successful labels in the UK. In addition to Mud and Quatro, they scored with lesser lights of glitter like Kenny and The Arrows, with chart perennials like the brilliant Brit soul and funk group Hot Chocolate and with the unlikely pop star Cozy Powell, whose #3 smash 'Dance with the Devil' kicked off a string of drum-centric hits to make Phil Wainman weep with envy.

RAK was an independent, owned by Most but distributed through a deal with EMI. Bell also went through EMI, but was originally the British and European branch of a US division within the sprawling Columbia entertainment empire. Gradually it became more autonomous and developed its own character, under the direction of general manager Dick Leahy.

Rivalled only by RAK's yellow-sail yacht, Bell's metal-grey label and bell-shaped outline *is* the icon of seventies teenpop. All through the early seventies, that logo spun around millions of cheapo record players at forty-five revolutions per minute, thanks to the company's extraordinary success with artists like David Cassidy, Gary Glitter, The Bay City Rollers, Barry Blue, Showaddywaddy, Hello, Slik, The Glitter Band, The Partridge Family and more . . . not forgetting #1 one-offs like Terry Jacks's 'Seasons in the Sun' and Dawn featuring Tony Orlando's 'Tie a Yellow Ribbon'.

Leahy decided to focus on pure pop when he took over Bell UK in 1970, sensing that the market was wide open. 'I felt there was no glamour or fun,' he told *Melody Maker.* 'The music industry was grinding to a halt with needless guitar solos.' By 1973, one in three of the sixty-four singles Leahy put out made the charts; six of the year's top twenty best-selling singles bore the Bell logo. It was the UK's leading company for singles.

Bell achieved this by finding alternative routes to the eyes and ears of the teenage market that completely bypassed radio and the music press. Pop broadcasting until late 1973 was monopolised by the BBC's Radio One, which had a narrow playlist for new singles; the weekly music papers at the start of the seventies focused mainly on rock and other 'mature' genres like jazz and folk. So Bell looked to the only avenues where they could hope to break acts: the teen-oriented magazines and the discotheques. With David Cassidy, Leahy told *Melody Maker*, 'we offered the teenybop magazines' what they were famished for: 'a face . . . As a result, circulations doubled in six months.'

As for the disco scene, Bell's innovation was to develop a comprehensive list of discotheques across the country, with information about the size of the club, the type of audience that attended, the genres of music favoured, even the time when particular records got played during the night. Bell would then mail out new releases to as many as six hundred of the thousand or so discos in the UK. They maintained close relations with particularly influential DJs, who gave feedback about which songs received a positive response on the dancefloor. Another way to measure audience reaction – and detect the first stirrings of a hit – came from a sudden pick-up in orders of a specific record from local record shops, in response to kids asking for a song they'd heard at the town's discotheque. One advantage of this grass-roots monitoring was that singles could be put out as promos, and if they didn't catch on, they'd never get a proper pressing, thus saving the expense of a full-release promotion: radio pluggers, ads in the music papers, etc.

Bell wasn't the only record company to realise the importance of the disco market: Motown and Pye also serviced the clubs with new releases. But it was the most systematic about using that circuit as a marketing tool. 'It's the one medium where . . . you can actually judge reaction to a record,' Leahy told the *NME*. 'The only thing that means anything are kids at discos.'

Discos had only recently become a crucial component of the British pop infrastructure. Invented in France, they spread during

the sixties as chic metropolitan hang-outs for the in-crowd. But outside London or New York, the idea of dancing to records didn't
catch on instantly: people still preferred to see live bands playing
songs from the Top 40 rather than the original recorded hits. By
the early seventies, though, you could find a discotheque in every
decent-size town in the UK.

The first years of the new decade also saw the mushrooming of
the mobile-disco phenomenon, as pioneered by the company Roger
Squire's Mobile Discothèques. Soon Squire had so many imitators
that he realised the company's future lay with catering to the new
DJs rather than competing with them. Squire set up Disco Centre, a
company that sold and serviced sound and lighting systems. Events
that would once have involved the hiring of a band like The 'N
Betweens or The Sweetshop – office parties, college dances, wedding receptions, Masonic dos, football-club functions, birthdays and
anniversaries – increasingly involving the hiring of a mobile disc
jockey, who drove up with his own sound system, lights and a stack
of tried-and-true platters. Speaking to *Melody Maker* in 1974, Squire
estimated there were as many as 25,000 mobile discos across the UK
and perhaps 40,000 professional DJs, thanks to the increasing number of pubs who had resident DJs and sound systems.

The word 'disco' conjures up certain images and associations:
Saturday Night Fever and The Bee-Gees; cocaine-eyed celebs
at Studio 54 and gay New York underground clubs like Paradise
Garage. You think primarily of black music: Van McCoy's 'The
Hustle', Gloria Gaynor's 'I Will Survive', Chic's 'Le Freak'. But
here's a funny thing: all the music in this chapter was considered
disco music at the time. Before disco took on its mid-seventies-
onwards enduring meaning, pundits used terms like 'disco dance
records' to describe the singles of Mud, Slade, The Sweet, Quatro
and their ilk. Disco meant loud guitar music with a foot-stomping
beat and a yell-able chorus.

Reviewers even condescended to these groups in ways that anticipated the discophobia we're familiar with from the late seventies,
describing the Sweet/Chinnichap singles as 'the computerised
sound that enthralls the crowds . . . music for the feet rather than
ears', or talking of Quatro's 'bouncy discotheque singles'. In 1973, a
mobile-disco DJ who went by the remarkable name of E. A. Fresh-
Gibbon wrote to *Melody Maker* to praise Slade, Sweet et al. for
'restoring guts and energy' to pop: 'Thanks to artists such as these
the disco scene is in better health than for a long time.' Confessing
that the music was not to his own taste, Fresh-Gibbon nonetheless
gushed that whenever he dropped those records at his DJ gigs, 'the
response of these kids is a joy to witness'.

Bell's biggest triumph in reaching those kids – by reaching around
a radio blockade and directly impacting the disco floor – was 'Rock
and Roll, Part 2'.

'You know that record didn't get one single review?' Leahy would
recall of Gary Glitter's debut single, which peaked at #2 in the UK
charts in the summer of 1973. 'Rock and Roll' received just a handful of radio plays during its slow climb to the almost-top, making
the Radio One playlist of regularly rotated singles only after four
months of club play had pushed it into the chart. Originally the
B-side of the single 'Rock and Roll, Part 1', until Bell noticed that
the stripped-down, near-instrumental flip was getting all the disco
action, 'Rock and Roll, Part 2' was built around an astonishingly
punishing and dead-eyed drum sound, ominous swoops of treated
guitar, gang chants and empty space. The minimalism and the dub-
like use of space looked ahead to the synthetic disco of the late seventies and to electro and early rap in the eighties.

This prophetic quality was rooted in the record's advanced means
of production, which involved looping of drums, extreme processing
of sounds and dense layering of voices and instruments. Mechanistic
and emaciated, 'Rock and Roll' was a studio creation rather than the

document of a band playing live; instead of simply rocking the disco, like the Mud or Quatro singles did, this was a genuine rock–disco hybrid, but one invented before disco in the black American sense even really existed.

The trajectories that brought together the two men responsible for 'Rock and Roll' – Mike Leander and Paul Gadd, better known as Gary Glitter – are long and winding journeys through the British music industry of the sixties. Glitter's autobiography is titled *Leader*, after one of his biggest hits, 'I'm the Leader of the Gang (I Am)'. Just add an 'n' and you have the name of his producer, co-writer, manager, mentor and close personal friend. Leander and Glitter formed a symbiotic unit: Glitter, recording under earlier aliases like Paul Raven, toiled in vain for over a decade without finding the right sound, until Leander built it around him; Leander would never have had the balls or gall to front such monstrous records. A dashing and somewhat autocratic figure in professional life, good-looking in a strong-nosed, aristocratic sort of way, Leander didn't have the commanding presence required for showbiz. One appearance on *Top of the Pops* in a hastily assembled backing band for Glitter convinced him he had most to offer behind the scenes.

Educated at a minor Sussex public school, Leander was all set to become a lawyer, then stepped sideways into the music biz: he played guitar and drums in professional bands, did session work too, and had a job at song publisher Freddie Music. At the age of just twenty-one, he was hired by Decca as an arranger and musical director, working with singers like Marianne Faithfull and Billy Fury. Then MCA made him head of production, where he executive-produced Andrew Lloyd Webber and Tim Rice's *Jesus Christ Superstar* and worked on hits for many established stars. Along the way Leander produced The Drifters' 'Under the Boardwalk' and wrote the string arrangement for The Beatles' 'She's Leaving Home'. He made his own orchestral album, and formed the Mike Leander Orchestra to accompany The Bachelors on tour. In none of his diverse but conventional projects was there the slightest indication of what Leander would wreak with 'Rock and Roll, Part 2'.

Leander harboured ambitions to be a songwriter, recording demos for potential publishers and performers and drawing on a pool of session singers to do the guide vocals. Amazingly, he had three of Britain's biggest stars-to-be of the seventies at his disposal in the late sixties: Elton John (or Reg Dwight, as he was then) handled the lush ballads; David Essex did the bouncy pop numbers; and Gary Glitter (trading then as Paul Russell) was designated for the raunchy, R&B-flavoured material.

As we've seen, nearly all of the glam bands who defined the seventies were sixties veterans, toiling away for years and jumping on almost every fad and music phase as the decade unfurled. The successful pop singers and beat groups of the sixties had usually been the same age or a few years older than their fans; in contrast, the glam stars, by the time they made it, were significantly older than their primary audience. Gary Glitter was the most extreme example of this syndrome. His career actually started *before* The Beatles began theirs; he was twenty-eight when he finally achieved stardom in 1972.

Born in 1944, Glitter came from an unstable background: the identity of his father unknown, the parenting divided between a single mother and his grandmother, who ran a small bed-and-breakfast hotel in the Oxfordshire countryside. After a spell in foster care, a happier period ensued living with his mum and her new husband, Alan Prince Russell, in London and Sutton. Kindly and generous, the stepfather – whose surname Gary took on – indulged the boy's interest in music. By 1957, he had his first guitar.

At first most of his energy went into practising a Presley-style stance in the mirror: 'I'd try to get my hips and my shoulders, my lips and my eyes just like Elvis,' Glitter recalled decades later. But

September 8, 1973   NEW MUSICAL EXPRESS   Page 17

Twice the man he used to be

GARY GLITTER – the improbable past and preposterous present:

by JULIE WEBB

The *NME* mocked Glitter mercilessly, in this 8 September 1973 feature contrasting 1961's slim-line Paul Raven with '73's super-size Gary Glitter

soon he'd formed a skiffle group, Paul Russell and the Rebels, supplementing the guitar with a tea-chest bass and ersatz drums made out of tin cans with brown wrapping paper stretched over the top.

Aged only fourteen, in 1958 the future Gary Glitter started doing turns at clubs like The Two I's, and a year later he was a professional performer, earning up to £100 a week. By early 1960 – when The Beatles were still the unsigned skiffle band The Quarrymen – he had released his debut single, 'Alone in the Night', using the name Paul Raven.

Then came a contract with Parlophone. 'Paul Raven is our most exciting artist since Helen Shapiro,' declared an EMI spokesman in 1962. 'We regard him as a long-term prospect.' In the event, he released just a handful of singles for Parlophone. The first sold well and got him on the cover of *Disc*, which touted him as Britain's first true rhythm-and-blues singer. But subsequent efforts failed: a cover of Bacharach and David's 'Tower of Strength', done at George Martin's instigation, was cruelly eclipsed by Frankie Vaughan's version, a #1 smash.

Before he'd even reached twenty, Raven/Glitter found himself a has-been. The pop tide moved away from singers to beat groups, and to make a living he started working for the TV music show *Ready Steady Go!*: first as a scout trawling clubs like The Flamingo for cool-looking kids to join the studio audience as dancers; later as a warm-up act to get that same audience buzzing before the stars did their turns.

The *Ready Steady Go!* gig was fateful and fortuitous, though. Mike Leander went down to the TV studio regularly with his friend Andrew Loog Oldham and was impressed by Raven/Glitter's ability to work the crowd. 'I thought he was as good as half the acts on,' he later recalled. He recruited Raven to front the Mike Leander Orchestra Show during The Bachelors' summer 1965 tour.

Despite having a wife and kids by this point, Paul Raven spent most of the second half of the sixties in Germany, where the pop music broadcast by Radio Luxembourg stoked demand for any band with English or American accents. Like Slade in the Bahamas, but for a much longer and more arduous period, he performed in smoky, rowdy, often violent bars in Hamburg and Kiel, where he dealt with conniving promoters, punishing workloads and squalid living conditions. A typical residency might involve playing eight sets between 7 p.m. and three in the morning, each one forty minutes long, with twenty-minute breaks. At the Kaiserkeller in Hamburg, the eight-piece band slept four to a room in bunk beds, the cramped quarters reeking of sweat and the fumes from a Primus stove on which all the cooking was done. 'Like living on a ship,' is how the singer recalled it. As had the pre-fame Beatles half a decade before, he turned to amphetamines to survive: not just to cope with the eight hours of performing, but to avoid the fetid sleeping quarters. He'd pop pills and wander the streets all night, or pick up a girl just to have somewhere pleasant to kip.

Hamburg, Kiel and nightspots in other West German cities were where Glitter-to-be learnt how to read a crowd and drive an audience crazy. Rubbing shoulders with travelling rockers like Gene Vincent and Bill Haley, Raven was earning up to £500 a week. On his intermittent returns to the UK he would get together with Leander, who was still convinced that his friend was destined to become a big star, if only they could find the right song and the right sound. There was a long string of failed singles, in misguided directions and under various names, from the Traffic-like 'Musical Man' to covers of The Beatles' 'Here Comes the Sun' and 'Stand' by Sly and the Family Stone.

The sessions took place at a South Molton Street studio called Spot, later renamed and renowned as Mayfair Sound. It was here that Leander fell into a working method of playing all the instruments himself rather than getting session players in, with Raven laying down multiple vocals. Stitching a record together from a session inevitably involved juxtaposing different tracks of tape, moving jigsaw pieces around and, soon, the use of tape loops; Leander's control-freak tendency and perfectionism was pushing him further away from the naturalistic model of recording a live performance. But nothing that he and Raven came up with worked as yet.

By 1970, the singer had returned from Germany and was living in Marylebone, just north of Mayfair, where he hung out with a clique of showbiz pals that included Dusty Springfield and Michael Aldred, formerly a presenter on *Ready Steady Go!* At a party Aldred came up with the campy game of thinking up ludicrous names for the sort of fabricated British rock'n'roller that Svengalis like Larry Parnes foisted on the general public in the late fifties. Various candidates were tossed into the fray with much hilarity – Terry Tinsel, Stanley Sparkle, Horace Hydrogen – before Aldred came up with Gary Glitter, agreed by all as the winner. It soon became Paul Raven's nickname.

Social amusements aside, Paul/Gary was morose during 1970 and early '71, with little to show for the last decade of showbiz graft other than a divorce. He was piecing together a living with spo-radic work – session singing as a priest on the album *Jesus Christ Superstar*, north of England gigs with his old band from Germany – but contemplating giving up altogether. The attempts at recording a hit with Leander had ceased for a while, as the producer – who'd quit MCA – was occupied with other projects. Among them was an alliance with an organisation called GTO, which represented producers, hit writers and managers – initially in music but soon expanding to film and other entertainment areas. With Leander and others on the roster operating out of the company's offices, located on the edge of Mayfair, the atmosphere was not unlike a British Brill Building: a hive of creative activity.

Glitter happened to be hanging out at Leander's office one morn-ing in November 1971 when David Essex phoned to say he couldn't make a session. Rather than waste the booked studio hours, Leander suggested that he and Glitter go in and see what they could cook up.

Over the previous year, the two friends had spent quite a bit of time going to London clubs, where they noticed that the only music that seemed to get the kids moving was black music from America – funk in the mould of innovative records by James Brown and Sly Stone. But, as Glitter rationalised it in his memoir, 'What Mike and I were really looking for was . . . a white disco sound – something . . . made in the UK . . . that could compete with the Americans' – and win back the hearts and dancing feet of those British kids in the clubs.

This 'white disco sound' was what Leander groped his way towards during that accidental session with Glitter in the winter of 1971. The lyrical and vocal side of the song – Glitter's domain – came from a different place. The phrase 'Rock and Roll, Part 1' had lodged in Glitter's mind recently when flicking through *Melody Maker* and seeing it as the headline of a feature about fifties music. That reminded him also of the born-again epiphany he'd had not so long ago, when he'd witnessed Little Richard perform in Berlin. Glitter was transfixed, totally lost in the music. 'It's there that I decided to try and get back to the initial flash I'd received from the first rock'n'roll I'd heard . . .' Glitter told the *NME* in 1974. 'I tried to get back to being fifteen again . . . the very first rock'n'roll thrill.'

This double inspiration – memories of being enraptured by black rock'n'roll in the fifties meeting a desire to outflank the black dance sounds of the seventies – explains why 'Rock and Roll' harks back *and* points forward. Glitter's lyrics to 'Part 1' are rock-revival boilerplate – jukebox halls and high-school hops, little Queenie shaking her pony tail, blue-suede shoes – albeit delivered with foreboding intensity. Leander's music is atavistic-futuristic, the missing link between The Troggs and techno.

There were some very contemporary influences on 'Rock and Roll', however. Leander and Glitter had both been blown away by 'Neanderthal Man' by Hotlegs – three future members of 10cc – which became a #2 novelty hit in summer 1970. Starting out life as an experiment to test drum sounds on a new recording-studio set-up, 'Neanderthal Man' consisted of little more than very loud drums and a singalong playground chant set far back in the mix. Leander had also been listening to Afro-rock by Osibisa and what he called 'black voodoo rock' from New Orleans by Dr John and Exuma. His vague ambition to create discotheque-ready pop based around 'pure chanting, African rhythm, and drums' was focused further by the UK chart success of South African rocker John Kongos in 1971, with hits like 'He's Gonna Step on You' and 'Tokoloshe Man', which embedded boogie-guitar grind in a dense thicket of percussion. These tracks anticipated what Leander would do on 'Rock and Roll' because their producer, Gus Dudgeon, used tape loops of percussion 'lifted from an African tribal dance record', over which a real drummer played in the studio.

Leander had been using tape loops of his own drum patterns for a while when making demos. Now he placed this technique at the centre of the process. Spot Studios' in-house engineer John Hudson recalls Leander drumming for hours on a kit damped with tea towels to create 'a dead sound' that the engineer could then tweak with equalisation, with the tape running continuously. Leander stopped, dripping with sweat, when he finally felt he'd found the groove. This sequence was then looped and played through a speaker, while Leander improvised on a guitar until a song arrangement emerged. More drums – tom-toms and cymbals – were added. The rhythm track, already uncommonly heavy, was augmented with handclaps and, according to Glitter, the sound of two pieces of wood being smashed together. Track upon track of handclaps were superimposed on each other, the slight out-of-synchness creating a 'wide' sound. Glitter recalled their palms being red and raw after the session.

The other constituents of 'Rock and Roll' came about through a mixture of deliberate degradation of sound and serendipity. The ominous guitar originated partly from the 'dirty growl' of the nasty old five-watt amp Leander used, which created an effect like a saxophone underneath the guitar chords (something they would do with horns on later records). But it was also caused by Leander's lack of proficiency as a guitarist, which led him to select a tuning that allowed him to slide his fingers up and down on the same fret, creating a slide-guitar-like effect. On later records, he would use a lead jack or small round cigarette lighter as a slide. Finally, says Hudson, 'The main reason for the strange sound was that Mike would multitrack the guitar part about six or eight times' – on later Glitter records as many as fifteen times – which not only made the guitar sound huge, it concealed mistakes in his playing. The roaring chants, caveman grunts and threatening 'HEY!'s that dominated the 'Part 2' version were likewise multitracked as much as sixteen times to create a mob-like atmosphere out of the just one or two voices available in the studio.

The most exciting moment in 'Rock and Roll' is when everything drops away, leaving just drums, claps and chanted call-and-response – what Hudson calls the 'switch-out'. This would become part of the structural grammar of disco and all subsequent dance music, but

Glitzing the hits: Mike Leander, Gary Glitter's mentor and producer, profiled in *Melody Maker*, 26 January 1974

it was discovered accidentally. During the mixing stage, Leander wanted to isolate the drums to check if they were right; Hudson used a ruler to mute all the tracks manually, and happened to do so 'just on the down beat going into the chorus. Mike nearly wet himself' – recognising the impact this would have on a dancefloor.

After a sixteen-hour session, six bottles of wine and many beers, Leander, Glitter and Hudson ended up with a fifteen-minute-plus track. Playing it back was a revelation for its makers: groping in the dark for a direction, they'd created something they couldn't have planned, a 'brand-new sound' that simultaneously summoned back into existence a lost spirit. As Leander put it, 'We had produced something that was like all the songs we had heard before, and was yet different to all of them . . . the sort of record we had both loved to listen to when we were 14 or 15 years old . . . yet quite unlike anything that either of us had ever heard before.'

Unlike all the rock-revival garbage around in the early seventies, 'Rock and Roll' *deserved* to be called 'rock and roll'. Instead of a remake, a replica, a re-enactment, 'Rock and Roll' was a reinvention: resurrection through reduction. 'A castration op where you throw away the patient and keep the balls,' as one journalist put it.

After twelve years of hustle and graft, finally everything clicked for Gary Glitter. A few months shy of his twenty-eighth birthday when 'Rock and Roll' was released on 3 March 1972, at last he had a record to his name containing the indefinable X-factor. 'It was like unleashing a coiled spring,' Leander recalled. During the agonising sixteen weeks it took to break as a hit – it was rejected by every DJ and producer at the BBC – Glitter was calm, carrying 'this aura of inevitability', according to Leander.

When, driven by disco demand, 'Rock and Roll' reached #8 in the charts and *Top of the Pops* finally invited him to appear on its 21 June show, Glitter had to hastily pull together a fictitious backing group and give a slightly chaotic rendition of 'Part 2', miming the title chants and the 'HEY!'s, punching the air and doing an odd swaying dance, as if steadying himself after being jolted by the blows of his own music. He then hurriedly assembled a proper backing group, The Glitter Band, for the live shows that were now in heavy demand. The group was modelled on the Mike Leander Orchestra line-up for the 1964 tour with The Bachelors, which featured two saxes and two drummers. 'They needed two drummers on stage to get the same sound,' says Hudson, explaining that on the records the tom-toms are hit on the same beat as the snare, something no single drummer can physically do. 'It's pretty subtle but it made a huge difference to the sound.' Although The Glitter Band would record with Leander and score a series of hits based on the thuggish template of 'Rock and Roll', they would never play on Gary's own records, which remained studio constructions, with all the instruments played by Leander, apart from the horns.

Peaking at #2 in the UK – it was kept off the top only by Donny Osmond's abject 'Puppy Love' – 'Rock and Roll' became a huge hit across Europe and in Australia. It even penetrated the *Billboard* Top 10, thanks partly to early support on black radio stations in Chicago and Los Angeles. While this was going on, Glitter frantically applied himself to developing a look and a stage show. Determined to out-glitz Bolan, Slade and The Sweet, he set about matching the larger-than-life proposition of his stage name. He had recently seen the Jean Genet play *Le Balcon*, which was set in a whorehouse where the girls dressed the johns up as prestigious figures such as generals and bishops; the costume designer had created outfits with massive jutting-out shoulders for the male actors. With this vision of the male torso turned into an imposing triangle, Glitter headed down to Alkasura, the King's Road boutique where the likes of Bolan and Rod Stewart shopped, and commissioned them to make him huge-shouldered, metallic-looking garments and impossibly towering platform boots.

Glitter astutely realised that he could never pull off androgyny. He was just too manly: a beefy British Elvis, with thick sideburns and a complexion the colour of sirloin. His burly build required exaggerated machismo, a butch-fabulous look. The infamous welcome mat of chest hair poking through the cleavage-chasm between his jacket lapels was an accidental addition to Glitter's image: when he did a photo shoot and exposed his chest to show off a silver fishbone pendant, fans wrote in by the hundred pleading for more fur.

Glitter had been a fashion fiend since his early performing days in the late fifties, when most of his earnings went on clothes; like Slade's Dave Hill, he sometimes talked of how, if he'd not been a singer, he'd have liked to have been a fashion designer. When 'Rock and Roll' took off, he immediately spent £4,000 building a wardrobe, and clothing would remain a huge part of his expenditure, both for the stage and for everyday wear, since he had always remembered something British rock'n'roller Vince Taylor had said: 'image is everything', so you should never ever let the public see you as your real self. Glitter's most extreme outfits could only be worn for TV appearances or photo shoots, because they'd shred under the rigours of live performance. For concerts he developed a special line of suits made of silver paper held together with wire, which made him feel like 'a roasting chicken' when the spotlights hit him but were less likely to rip. Often he'd have to throw the suits away after just one performance, since they were uncleanable.

Just as the stage name dictated the clothes, the clothes now dictated the stage show. 'I'd look in the mirror before I went onstage, see all the glitter I was wearing, and know I had to summon up the same glitter, the same flash and showmanship, from within,' Glitter recalled. 'The Gary Glitter Rock'n'Roll Spectacular' was the name they came up with for the first tour; later ones usually followed the 'Glitter Over . . .' template, which when prefixing a city like Berlin or Hamburg (Glitter was huge in Germany) brought to mind one

of Bomber Harris's punitive RAF raids designed to break the Third
Reich's spirit.

Every prop and ploy, stunt and routine that Glitter and Leander
could dream up was used: motorbikes, smoke, fireworks. For a
1973 concert at the Rainbow Theatre, filmed for the documentary
Remember Me This Way, they approached the props department at
Pinewood Studios and rented a giant Busby Berkeley-style staircase,
not for a grand entrance but a grand exit: it was concealed until the
very end of the show, when Glitter sashayed up the steps, flanked
by about forty girls in Esther Williams-like silver swim-caps and art
deco glittery skirts. The concert's opening was no less impressive:
six Harley-Davidsons drove onto the stage, their deafening synchronised revving and blinding headlights preparing for the entrance of
Glitter himself on a silver chopper bike.

The Glitter performance persona mixed up the stylised, once-
removed moves of early Brit rockers like Duffy Power with the
regal schlock of Vegas-era Presley. Liberace was in there too, and a
touch of P. J. Proby, the Texas loudmouth who became a sensation
in mid-sixties Britain with his mixture of hammy melodrama and
coquettish prancing, culminating in a career-terminating concert
ban when his trousers repeatedly split onstage, accidentally on purpose. The same thing happened at one Glitter concert, unintention-
ally: 'After a couple of numbers I noticed all the birds in the front
row were smiling. I felt a bit loose and when I looked down my balls
were hanging out.'

Increasingly the stage show drove the direction of the music.
'We start off with the premise that the song will have to work in the
stage-act,' Glitter told the *NME*, so that singles like 'Do You Wanna
Touch Me? (Oh Yeah)' and 'Hello! Hello! I'm Back Again' had been
'constructed strategically for use onstage . . . God only knows how
we'd be able to write if I wasn't performing.' 'Hello! Hello! I'm Back
Again' was performed as an encore number, or on his return to the

stage after a costume change. 'Do You Wanna Touch Me?' was actually inspired by something that happened onstage and then became a
fixture of the act, Glitter explained to Sally James, presenter of kiddie
pop show *Saturday Scene*: 'I was onstage and shouting to the fans,
and then I extended my hand to some fans on the left-hand side of
the stage, and they held on to my hand, and there was a load of kids
on the other side of the stage . . . waving to me, so I said automatically,
"Do you want to touch me?" and they all shouted back, "Yeah" . . . In
the car on the way back, I thought, "That sounds like a good idea for
a song!"' The single, Glitter claimed, 'was written by the audience'.

The hits that swiftly followed 'Rock and Roll' – 'I Didn't Know
I Loved You (Till I Saw You Rock'n'Roll)', 'Do You Wanna Touch
Me?', 'Hello! Hello! I'm Back Again' and 'I'm the Leader of the
Gang (I Am)', his first #1, in the summer of 1973 – build on the template of the debut hit, sometimes adding honking horns for extra
levels of queasy-cheesy blare. Leander and his engineer Hudson
kept pushing the drums and guitar sound to ever more bullying levels of bombast. On 'Touch Me' the beat sounds sploshy, like a boot
splintering through a frozen puddle or slamming into soft, unprotected parts of the human body; the guitar riff lurches across the
mix like a seasick cloud of drone.

As the sound and visuals escalated in intensity, so too did the
mismatch between the two sides of Glitter as musician and showman. The whole ensemble worked on fundamentally opposed levels at once: minimalism and excess, coercion and comedy, savagery
and schlock, the primal and the parodic. The caveman crunch of
the beat cut through discernment and critical sensibility to impact
the body directly; the campy theatrics and costumes could only be
viewed without irony by very small children.

Glitter oscillated between these registers in his interviews. On
the one hand, he liked to make out that his music was 'purely physical. It's vulgar . . . crude . . . raw,' insisting that there was 'nothing

intellectual about me or my music'. Glitter described himself as 'basically an animal', and in one *NME* interview mentioned a scene in *Last Tango in Paris*, 'where Brando says to his lover, "I don't want to talk, I don't need to talk, but we can still communicate." And he grunts and groans . . . That's pretty similar to what I achieve.' On the other hand, he talked in candid and nuanced terms about the parody aspect of the Glitter persona and performance: 'You have to respect something before you can send it up in a way that is going to turn out at all amusing.'

In a bizarre self-referential ceremony that blended publicity stunt and a sincere desire to obliterate the past, in January 1973 Glitter staged the burial at sea of Paul Raven (and all his other unsuccessful pseudonyms), with his old flop records, his press photos and trade-publication clips encased in a coffin and lowered into the Thames Estuary. DJ Alan Freeman presided over the ceremony, Charlotte Rampling was guest of honour, and afterwards everyone repaired to a champagne wake on HMS *Belfast*.

Glitter's personal manner offstage was urbane, with a creamy thespian tinge to his conversation and humour. Quite a few people assumed, wrongly, that Glitter was gay. Regardless, he had gay fans who appreciated the preposterous splendour of the Glitter performance. In Sydney, Australia, the first ten rows of the concert were full of drag queens, Glitter liked to say. But on his first Australian tour, his Melbourne show was also picketed by the Gay Liberation Front, who felt that he was trivialising and travestying the movement. 'All this came as a complete surprise to me,' Glitter told *Melody Maker*. 'I told them I wasn't trying to harm their movement and whatever people do with their sex lives was up to them.'

Somehow the two elements coexisted: the brute physical reality of sex and stomping rhythm versus Glitter's tendency to 'over-act and over-emphasise everything'. Speaking to *Melody Maker*, Glitter reasoned that 'in spite of my clothes being very gay – for want of a better word – there's quite a strong butch thing in me as a person. Having a hairy chest, the aggressive way I perform . . .' Without those aspects of his physical bulk – and the intimidating might of the music – he might come across more like 'a downtown drag show'.

Gary Glitter's route to success had bypassed the rock press altogether, and the weekly papers were uncertain about how seriously to take him. His appearance and performances were a bonanza for reviewers with a flair for vicious description: the *NME* was particularly insulting, describing him as 'the Michelin-tyre man' of glam. Others found a compelling strangeness to the Glitter spectacle that set him apart from the rest of the lumpen glam pack. *Melody Maker's* Michael Watts and Rob Partridge included him in a round-up of the best of British rock, describing him as 'the Titan of Trash . . . so bad he's rotten beautiful'; the same paper's Richard Williams argued that his appeal was only denied by 'impossible snobs who lack any real feeling for rubbish'.

But some critics detected something gross and aberrant about the Glitter phenomenon. The disparity in age between Glitter – prone to weight gain, he looked more middle-aged than his twenty-nine years – and his audience did not go without comment. The *NME's* Bob Edmands observed that when you placed Glitter's second album, *Touch Me* – whose label featured a full-body photograph of the star – on your turntable, the record spindle jutted out 'from Gary's nether regions' like an erection, adding: 'Luckily, there's no law against aurally molesting young girls.'

There are laws against literally molesting young girls, and in 2015, Glitter was convicted of various counts of sexual assault, attempted rape and sexual intercourse with underage girls. The crimes dated back to as early as 1975 and involved girls ranging from ten to thirteen years of age. The latest in a series of cases against Glitter in the UK and Vietnam involving possession of child porn and the sexual abuse of minors, the conviction saw him sentenced to sixteen years in jail, most likely meaning that he will die in prison.

In one foul swoop, Glitter managed to wipe out his achievements and poison the substantial reservoir of public affection he'd earned as an entertainer and symbol of the British seventies. As with many other musicians, as well as actors, sportsmen and politicians, all the reasons he'd entered public life – the hope of achieving something glorious and astonishing, something that would be remembered – were now irreparably contaminated and cancelled out by his depravity. Glitter's fall has been steep: the compilers of a recent five-disc box set of glam decided to exclude his music from the tracklist, while some sports arenas in America have stopped using 'Rock and Roll' as the crowd-rousing jock jam it has been for decades. Glitter's 'historic crimes', to use the legal term that appeared in the newspaper reports, threaten to make him an unperson in pop history.

If you look through the archive of Glitter's early interviews, you can find hints of what was to come. Less than a year into his stardom, interviewed by *Melody Maker* in May 1973, Glitter almost seems to weigh up in public the pros and cons of ignoring the age of consent. Asked about the song 'Happy Birthday' on his second album *Touch Me*, he explains that it's about a young man waiting until his girlfriend turns sixteen: 'It's a bit tongue-in-cheek . . . He's staying on the right side of the law by waiting to give her her "present".' He then mused, unguardedly, about the 'loads and loads of letters from young kids of 13, 14, and 15. Some of them are very, very to the point . . . They say the most incredible things for their age. But, even if one wanted to pursue any of their suggestions, one couldn't, by law, of course . . . That's partly how the idea for "Happy Birthday" came up. They often say "When I'm making love with my boyfriend" . . . and it's signed "Christine So and So, from Scunthorpe, aged 13". It makes you sit up and think. Although I suppose, in days gone by, people were getting it on at 13 or 14, and, indeed, in the Middle East and so on, they still do.' In subsequent interviews, he often returned to this subject – the fan letters that started out innocent and polite but later got 'very horny . . . telling what they'd like me to do to them', the requests for nude photographs.

In the memoir *Leader* – written and published in the early nineties, long before scandal attached itself to his name – Glitter is also surprisingly candid. He fingers his carousing buddy Keith Moon as a corrupting influence. The Who drummer repeatedly turned up at Glitter's home, picking up girl fans who had been waiting outside, then knocking on the door and saying 'Can I borrow your bedroom?' Glitter grew annoyed with Moon's conduct ('I thought it was unfair to take advantage of the fans') and asked him to stop, only for Moon to retort that 'he didn't think it was right *he* [Moon] took advantage of them when I wasn't . . . that my wasting them should be a criminal offence'. The next time Moon came round, according to Glitter, 'He shoved a girl in my bedroom and just pushed me in after her! I think that was when my outlook on success altered.' Glitter also writes in *Leader* about his romance in the eighties with a fan called Alison, which started – chastely, he claims – when she was fifteen years old and was consummated only when she reached the age of nineteen.

Whether he was a born pervert or someone gradually corrupted, it does seem that Glitter's imperial phase of pop stardom gave way to a Nero-like stage, living off the proceeds of his earlier achievements and buffered from reality by enablers and sycophants. His career reached a plateau in 1974, and the following year he spent more and more time at his newly acquired mansion in Hampshire, on which he lavished a fortune on luxurious additions, such as an octagonal bath. His lifestyle was an anglicised version of Elvis in Graceland: acting the lord (he even started his own local cricket team), frittering his fortune on fine wines, lavish parties and cocaine, his social world became increasingly stocked with free-loaders and celebs with contagious vices.

In the wake of his glutinously sentimental ballad 'I Love You Love Me Love' – Glitter's biggest-selling hit, performed astride a silver crescent moon on *Top of the Pops* – his music sagged and split its skin. In the papers there was empty talk of him doing a lavish, Busby Berkeley-style West End musical called *Razzle Dazzle*. Leander claimed that Glitter would do serious movies that would 'out-Bond Bond'. In the event, there was only the documentary/ concert movie *Remember Me This Way*, featuring a ludicrous section intended as a foretaste of Glitter's Hollywood future, in which the tubby star defeats a gang of assassins with Bruce Lee-style kicks and chops.

By 1976, the hits had dried up and Glitter staged a 'Farewell Tour' – a ruse to shift tickets for concerts that weren't selling. He even concocted a story to justify his retirement: a fake marriage with the young woman who worked as The Glitter Band's hair stylist. There was a big engagement party, interviews with the 'lovestruck couple' on television, even a honeymoon. When the truth came out, Glitter left the country until the stink dissipated. If only this had been his life's nadir. But there was so much worse to come.

Gary Glitter may have tossed himself onto the trash heap of pop history, but recent years have seen many of his lesser-known contemporaries salvaged from it. 'Junkshop glam' is a term invented by record collectors and dealers to describe the tsunami of second-division glitterpop that was commercial in aspiration but commercially unsuccessful in cruel reality. It consists of seven-inch singles by Slades who never got paid, Sweets that went uneaten, Glitters that went down the shitter.

Most of the people pushing the fad have been collectors, dealers and music fiends who have assiduously mined earlier seams – sixties garage and freakbeat, seventies punk, the scrappier sort of do-it-yourself post-punk – to exhaustion point, and now desperately crave a new untapped mainline for basic hard rock. Which is precisely what most glam and glitter is underneath the sugar-frosted production. Most of these groups were doing something else before opportunistically restyling their sound and songs with Steve Priest edge-of-hysteria vocals and stompy drums, while raiding their girlfriends' dressing tables for lipstick and eye make-up. They also came up with visual gimmicks: the lead singer of Iron Virgin, for instance, wore a chastity belt.

Most of these bandwagon-jumping bands went on to do something else after the glitter moment passed, repackaging themselves as pub rock or metal or new wave. Part of the buzz about junkshop glam overlaps with an interest in 'punk before punk': figures like Jesse Hector, who, after starting out as a nine-year-old skiffle performer in the late fifties, worked his way through every stage of British music, from mod through heavy rock, until he formed the glam-era proto-punk combo The Hammersmith Gorillas – cult renowned for their hairy-palmed assault on 'You Really Got Me' – all the while making only minor adjustments to how he sang or played.

Junkshop glam has produced a handful of solid compilations – *Velvet Tinmine* and *Boobs* are the best – and excavated perhaps a couple of dozen genuine nuggets, including Jimmy Jukebox's 'Motorboat', Iron Virgin's 'Rebels Rule', Screemer's 'Interplanetary Twist', Daddy Maxfield's 'Rave 'n' Rock'. Probably the greatest junkshop-glam anthem is a single you can find on *Velvet Tinmine* by a group that actually had several hits, but in this case flopped: 'Another School Day' by Hello.

Signed to Mike Leander's newly formed Rock Artists Management company and Bell Records, Hello were that rare thing in glitter pop: actual teenagers. They'd started out as a mime group: not in the Lindsay Kemp sense, but competing in and often winning competitions in which they strummed mock guitars to the accompaniment of the latest pop records. Much of their material, and all their hits, consisted either of sixties oldies redone or tunes written by their mentor, Russ Ballard of Argent.

But 'Another School Day' was all their own work, from the feedback squeal at the start, through the thrilling jolts in the groove at each chorus, to the jubilant dismay of the 'Oh no!' chant. Unlike Alice Cooper or The Sweet, Hello didn't have to strain to recall what it felt like to count the clock in class; for them it was barely yesterday that they were itching to break loose. A flashback to Chuck Berry as much as a glimpse ahead to The Undertones, 'Another School Day' is that rare thing: a truly teenage rampage.

5:

HARD TO BE REAL: DAVID BOWIE AND FRIENDS CONQUER THE WORLD

David Bowie – Lou Reed – Mott the Hoople – Iggy and the Stooges – Jobriath

On Sunday afternoon, 16 July 1972, David Bowie held a tea-time press conference at the Dorchester, a deluxe five-star hotel on London's Park Lane. Mostly for the benefit of American journalists flown in to watch him and his new backing band, The Spiders from Mars, in action, the event was also a chance to show off Bowie's new 'protégés', Iggy Pop and Lou Reed. They had – separately – made their UK live debuts on the two preceding nights, at the exact same venue, King's Cross Cinema.

Glammed up in maroon-polished nails and rock-star shades, Reed sashayed across the second-floor suite and kissed Bowie full on the mouth. Sitting in the corner, Iggy also displayed a recent glitter makeover, with silver-dyed hair, eye make-up and T. Rex T-shirt. Reed, Iggy and Bowie would later pose for the only known photograph of the threesome together, Bowie looking resplendent in a flared-cuff Peter Pan tunic made from a crinkly, light-catching fabric. That was just one of three outfits he wore that afternoon – surely the first time in history a rock'n'roll press conference involved costume changes.

During a wide-ranging and somewhat grandiloquent audience with the assembled journalists, Bowie declared: 'People like Lou and I are probably predicting the end of an era . . . I mean that catastrophically. Any society that allows people like Lou and me to become rampant is pretty well lost. We're both pretty mixed-up, paranoid people, absolute walking messes. If we're the spearhead of anything, we're not necessarily the spearhead of anything good.'

What a strange thing to announce – that you're the herald of Western civilisation's terminal decline, the decadent symptom that precedes a collapse into barbarism or perhaps a fascist dictatorship. But would an 'absolute walking mess' really be capable of such a crisply articulated mission statement? There's a curious unreality to Bowie's claims, especially made in such swanky surroundings. Yet the reporters nodded and scribbled them down in their notepads. Suddenly Bowie seemed to have the power to make people take his make-believe seriously . . . to make *them* believe it too. Something that in the previous eight strenuous years of striving he'd never managed before, apart from a smatter of fanatical supporters within the UK entertainment industry.

When last we met David Bowie, some eighteen months before the Dorchester summit, the singer looked washed-up. Deserted by his primary collaborators Tony Visconti and Mick Ronson, he put out the career-nadir single 'Holy Holy'. (Can you hum it? Did you even know it existed?)

Yet a little over a year later, Bowie had everybody's ears, everyone's eyes. His fortunes had transformed absolutely: if not the biggest star in Britain, he was the buzziest, the focus of serious analysis in a way that far better-selling contemporaries like Marc Bolan and Slade never achieved. No longer a loser, he had somehow become the Midas man, a pop miracle-worker resurrecting the stalled careers of his heroes, from long-standing admirations like Lou Reed to recent infatuations like Iggy Pop and Mott the Hoople. Sprinkling them with his stardust, Bowie even got them to change their appearance in his image. There was talk of movies and stage musicals, the sort of diversification that's tediously commonplace in today's pop business, but back then was unusual and exciting.

'People look to me to see what the spirit of the Seventies is,' Bowie said to William S. Burroughs in a famous 1974 dialogue convened by *Rolling Stone*. This was not boasting, just the simple truth. How did Bowie manage to manoeuvre himself into place as weathervane of the zeitgeist? The battle was not won on the radio airwaves or at record-store cash registers. There are bands from the early seventies who sold millions more records than Bowie ever did, but they never came near to having the high profile he had at the time and are barely remembered today. Bowie's theatre of war was the media, where victory is measured in think pieces and columns, controversy and the circulation of carefully chosen, eye-arresting photographs. To wage and win this war of words and images, Bowie needed a supreme strategist, a dark magus of optics and frame-setting.

Enter Tony Defries, master illusionist.

There are perhaps two kinds of entrepreneurs, executives, politicians. The first inspires confidence with managerial competence, through expertise and command of the facts. The second seduces using techniques that bypass the rational: charisma, word-magic, a sense of theatre. Tony Defries had a little bit of the first mode going for him, but a whole lot more of the second. In some ways he resembled a seventies music-biz version of Donald Trump. In *The Art of the Deal*, Trump wrote that 'the final key to the way I promote is bravado. I play to people's fantasies.' These P. T. Barnum types seem like throwbacks to the credulous nineteenth century of snake-oil salesmen and carnival barkers. But their understanding of how business works may actually be more in touch with (un)reality than that of conventional economists, who believe that the market is driven by rational actors making decisions based on the sober calculation of their interests. The showmen-businessmen understand the power of wild promises, impulsive investments, irrational exuberance.

Hooking himself up with Defries, Bowie finally acquired the hype-man he'd always needed, as opposed to the quietly honourable, gentleman manager Kenneth Pitt. 'That's why a little hyperbole never hurts,' Trump wrote of deal-making, which always involves a fictive element: you're selling a possibility, something yet to be fulfilled. Exaggeration, distortion, if not always outright deception – these make up the essence of hype, salesmanship and public relations, but also permeate many other forms of public life, from politics to punditry to pop itself. In Bowie's career there would be a constant tension between his awareness of the power of putting on an act and his personal existential yearning for authentic truth. A tussle, in many ways, between the seventies he would symbolise and the sixties that shaped him.

Tony Defries was himself a performer: someone who knew how to make a powerful impression, or rather, an impression of power. One person who fell under Defries's sway almost instantly was Iggy Pop. Defries had built the management and production company MainMan as a vehicle for Bowie's diverse ambitions, which included producing records by artists he admired. Iggy's career was one of the first lined up for resurrection.

In 1972, Iggy seemed way more star-struck by his new manager Defries than the other way around. 'Tony is an artist, not a businessman,' Iggy declared. 'His art is in handling money, not for money's sake but in a purely artistic way.' Even two decades later, the business relationship having long before ended sourly, Iggy spoke with fond awe of their first meeting, which took place at Max's Kansas City, New York, in the autumn of 1971. 'Defries I thought was a character. I thought people will go for this guy. He had a big cigar and a big pointed nose and a great big Afro and a smug look on his face and an English accent and a big fur coat and a belly! And to the people who were running the American industry, it just spelt "Hot Manager". He had an image and it would work, it would sell . . .' Defries and Bowie, who was also present at the Max's meeting, worked like a double act: 'British music hall, pure vaudeville,' Iggy recalled. 'I've always had a good sense of who's going somewhere and a good sense of circus, and I could just tell there was a circus in town – "Join!" That was my immediate instinct.'

Before she took a job at MainMan, Bowie publicist Cherry Vanilla worked in advertising for the Madison Avenue super-agency McCann Erickson, and conceivably had more experience of the corporate world than Defries. Yet, Vanilla recalls, 'Although Tony was younger than me, he came on as older. He always had an innate authority about him. A great calm – nothing seemed to fluster him. I'm not even sure he really knew the business all that well, but he came off like he did to the people at RCA. Tony actually kind of tricked RCA into spending a lot more money on Bowie than they normally did on artists.'

In fact, Defries had propelled himself forward and upward through chutzpah and sheer will at every stage of his career. Although a mere solicitor's clerk, his commanding presence at a business meeting with the record-company executive Olav Wyper made such an impression that Wyper passed his name on to Bowie, then looking to dispense with Kenneth Pitt. At that point Defries had not yet managed anyone, although he had advised Mickie Most in various capacities and helped sort out the financial affairs of a few fashion models and photographers.

At their first meeting, Defries sized Bowie up instantly as both a potential star and someone malleable. 'They were like a couple of children,' is how he described David and Angela Bowie in a 1974 interview with *Melody Maker*, which may well be the only one Defries ever gave. 'The three-year-old bringing its closest friend to see you. I've never been able to think of either of them as anything but a couple of children.'

Defries extricated Bowie from his existing tangle of management, publishing and record-company arrangements, even buying back the rights to his previous albums from Mercury. 'I felt sorry for Bowie . . . I thought "Poor little chap. He's got himself in a terrible mess,'" Defries told his interviewer Michael Watts, betraying a degree of patronising disdain for his business-unsavvy charge. He would assume a father-figure role in all his dealings with Bowie: calming and coddling, encouraging and advising, always supernaturally assured about the singer's superstar destiny. Less paternally, the ten-year management contract Defries drew up for Bowie to sign designated the singer as 'Employee' rather than client.

'To be honest with you the way I think about David is as a building,' Defries told Watts in that same 1974 interview. 'I told him at a very early stage in our relationship . . . he has the potential – in my hands, anyway – to create the income to make a building on Sixth Avenue. In other words he is the beginning, potentially, of an empire syndrome.' The allusion to New York's Sixth Avenue, home to entertainment giants like RCA, CBS, Warners and NBC (as opposed to an equivalent London district like, say, Mayfair), was not coincidental. Defries and Bowie were both obsessed with New York, but for different reasons. The manager and would-be mogul aspired to the midtown Manhattan of money, media power and skyscraping ambition; the singer admired the downtown underground of artistic deviants like Warhol and The Velvet Underground.

Following the showbiz logic of 'If you can make it here, you can make it anywhere', Defries would attempt to break Bowie in America using New York as the launch pad. Even before his star was fully established in Britain, Defries moved his base of operations to New York, setting up the MainMan office in a duplex apartment on 58th Street in the Upper East Side, and staffing it with colourful weirdos recruited from the Warhol scene. Most had been involved in producing or acting in *Pork*, the Warhol play that had outraged and thrilled audiences in equal measure during its London run in August 1971. Apart from Cherry Vanilla, none had any real business experience but they supplied that crucial intangible known as 'vibe', which made MainMan seem like a happening place.

'Tony let us be outrageous,' remembers Vanilla. 'We acted like crazy people when we were up at RCA – I think he almost used us as a distraction, so that he could talk them into things. It was kind of a fabulous thing to have this daddy figure who took care of you. I mean, we were working for nothing. A hundred dollars a week, plus our rent being paid. But we had a charge account at Max's Kansas City and a charge account with the limo company. And that made us feel even more like he was a daddy, because he was taking care of us. We were like his kids. And we adored him.'

Not long after David and Angela Bowie had first befriended the *Pork* crew during their London stay, the singer and his manager travelled to New York in September 1971 to meet with RCA. Defries had deliberately singled out RCA for the historical connection of Elvis and Colonel Tom Parker (one of his role models). But he also knew how to target the venerable but rudderless record-biz giant's vulnerabilities, telling them they'd had no artist of any stature since Presley and had effectively missed out on the entire sixties. They could 'own the Seventies' if they signed Bowie, who was all set 'to remake the decade'.

Before that happened, though, Bowie had to remake himself – sonically, visually and in terms of his public profile, which had waned to nearly nothing in the three years since 'Space Oddity' was a hit. There had to be a total relaunch of the 'product' (a word Defries tended to use in place of 'artist'). A new look, a new musical direction, an attention-grabbing gesture.

'I'm just an image person. I'm terribly conscious of images and I live in them,' Bowie told the *NME* in 1972 – a catch-all confession that covered his interest in style and his song lyrics, which were like compressed screenplays that turned your imagination into a silver screen. Bowie started developing a series of startling new looks, urged on by Angie and assisted by the new gay and ambisexual friends they'd acquired through frequenting gay clubs like The

Sombrero. One new pal, the androgynous Freddie Buretti, became his exclusive clothes designer.

The defining style move came when Bowie cut off his long wavy hair: a symbolic break with the sixties. At first, his new coiffure looked vaguely mod, but then, with further sculpting and the application of virulently artificial-looking dye, Bowie achieved a hairstyle that screamed, 'It's the seventies!' – a sort of electrocuted mullet, goldfish orange in hue.

This angular, inorganic hairstyle was matched with equally stark and lurid make-up. Cosmetics had already been introduced into pop by Bolan (tentatively), Alice Cooper (grotesquely) and The Sweet (clumsily). But Bowie's use of theatrical make-up, informed by his dalliances with mime, was both more extreme and more exquisite. Coached by master cosmetologist Pierre LaRoche, Bowie became an expert on the subject and an eloquent defender of male self-beautification: 'Normally before a battle the men would make themselves up to look as beautiful as possible,' he observed. 'And look at all the old kings and dandies . . . And if you look to the animal world, so often the male is more beautiful than the female – look at peacocks and lions. Really, makeup and beautiful clothes are fundamental to me . . .'

At the height of glittermania, *Creem* magazine started a style column called Eleganza, and one month it was partly devoted to 'David Bowie's Makeup Dos and Don'ts'. Nestled amid full-page ads for Peavey monitor speakers and a piece on bottleneck guitar techniques, you found Bowie recommending 'a very light liquid base, usually white, pink, or yellow, but for stage, sometimes iridescent, applied with a damp sponge', suggesting Elizabeth Arden eight-hour cream for a nice shine for lips and eyelids, and kohl 'smudged right along the lash line'. It also gave away the recipe for the 'now iconic gold circle on his forehead' – tiny gold rhinestones stuck on with eyelash glue. But actual glitter was a no-no on account of its tendency to fall into his eyes during performance – a problem made worse, no doubt, by his intermittent penchant for shaving off his eyebrows, to increase the weirdness quotient.

As for a new musical direction, things had begun to shift during the course of 1971, when Bowie took up writing songs on a piano. The result was *Hunky Dory*: a clean, bright, prettily arranged sound that had almost nothing to do with rock. Instead, it resembled an existentialist Elton John: lovely, extended melodies that delivered questioning and questing lyrics that turned over quandaries to do with time, death, doubt and spiritual confusion, in an incongruous mood of bouncy gaiety. 'Changes' combines philosophical musing about impermanence with third-generation plaints ('these children that you spit on', 'don't tell us to grow up and out of it'). Over time the song has acquired a retroactive status as a mission statement, as if foretelling his career's succession of 'strange changes' and the 'fascination' these persona shifts would induce in his fans-to-come. Multiple 'best of's titled *Changes* solidified this interpretation. 'Oh! You Pretty Things' likewise addresses a potential constituency, flattering his yet-to-arrive followers with Nietzschean allusions to the new breed of 'homo superior' they represent.

'Life on Mars' is *Hunky Dory*'s jewel. A study in contradictions, it's a song about ennui, emptiness and inertia that is dramatic, overflowing with lavish detail and melodically mobile, with lyrics that project a mind-screen of brilliant images, from workers striking for fame to the 'saddening bore' of a film watched by a mousy-haired girl. 'Life on Mars' captures the superiority complex of the over-bright teenager who views everything from a distance with the absolute clarity of adolescent contempt: rowdy sailors become apemen, commuters are like milling hordes of rodents (perhaps lemmings). 'I think she finds herself disappointed with reality,' Bowie has said. 'She's living in the doldrums of reality [but] she's being told that there's a far greater life somewhere . . . that she doesn't have access to.'

Less impressive is 'Quicksand': a rambling collage of fragments from philosophy, religion and esoteric thought, with namechecks for twentieth-century icons like Churchill, Himmler, Garbo (although what sounds like 'Bardot' is actually the Bardo of Tibetan Buddhism: a transitional state, a stage in the afterlife) and another nod to Nietzsche's superman. The song is a testament of spiritual and intellectual paralysis brought on by . . . reading too widely and indiscriminately? Rifling through systems of belief for bandages to apply to some deep wound of self? Its (in)conclusion is hopelessly wishy-washy: 'Don't believe in yourself, don't deceive with belief.' Elsewhere on *Hunky Dory*, three heroes are paid homage in a row, with the songs 'Andy Warhol', 'Song for Bob Dylan' and the zippy Lou Reed/*Loaded* pastiche 'Queen Bitch'.

Although *Hunky Dory* was Bowie's most attractive album to date and has since become one of his most beloved records, it came out to a quiet, politely appreciative reception in December 1971, making the need for a dramatic publicity stunt all the more urgent. So, in early 1972, David Bowie decided to be gay. Very publicly gay.

Tentative moves towards 'coming out' had been made earlier. There'd been an interview with gay magazine *Jeremy* in 1970, which presented the singer as very much on 'our side', without printing anything like a definitive declaration of his orientation. An April 1971 profile in *Rolling Stone* edged nearer: the piece ended with Bowie flirtatiously instructing his interviewer John Mendelsohn to 'tell your readers that they can make up their minds about me when I begin getting adverse publicity: when I'm found in bed with Raquel Welch's husband'. In the piece, Mendelsohn also reported that when Bowie turned up for a guest spot on San Francisco's progressive radio station KSAN-FM, he told the 'incredulous DJ that his last album was . . . a collection of reminiscences about his experiences as a shaven-headed transvestite'. But these were flippant, jesting remarks, and hardly anyone had noticed. So Bowie turned to the media outlet in which his announcement could make the biggest splash: *Melody Maker*.

From the late sixties through to the end of 1973, *Melody Maker* was Britain's leading music magazine. By 1972, it was also the best selling, having outstripped the pop-oriented *New Musical Express* and achieving a weekly circulation that hovered just above 200,000. 'You'd go to work on a Thursday morning on the Tube on the Central Line, and any male under twenty-five would be reading the *Maker* the morning it came out,' recalls *Melody Maker* staff writer Richard Williams. Thanks to a phenomenal pass-on rate, it was read by maybe five, perhaps as many as ten times the number who bought it.

Melody Maker had more substance than its rivals (*NME*, *Disc and Music Echo* and *Sounds*, which was originally started as a left-wing offshoot of *Melody Maker*). Not only did it beat its competition in the quality, depth and range of the writing, but it was literally more substantial: at sixty or seventy pages, often three times the size of a typical *NME* issue. Read internationally – and for a time actually printed in the US, sold on news-stands there and operating a New York bureau, with correspondents in other major US music towns – *Melody Maker* could legitimately bill itself as the 'World's biggest selling music weekly'. Pop and rock's paper of record, it was even based on Fleet Street, like a proper newspaper, directly opposite the hacks' watering hole, El Vino's. Unlike the *NME*, which eventually took over as the cool rock weekly by recruiting writers from the underground press, *Melody Maker*'s staff came almost entirely from local newspapers around the UK. The ethos was very much 'if it moves, cover it': teenybop phenomena like Osmonds-mania received judicious coverage alongside longhair prog bands like Atomic Rooster and Hatfield and the North, folk rock, jazz and the other serious-minded genres. On the front cover, the news story might be David Cassidy arriving at Hearthrow but inside you'd find a double-page spread on Stockhausen or Sun Ra. Along with the in-depth reporting, *Melody Maker* in the early seventies had the most intelligent critics, and it was to one of the paper's star writers, Michael Watts, that Bowie decided to give the big scoop.

A photo of Bowie looking willowy and gorgeous graced the front cover of the 22 January 1972 issue of *Melody Maker*, with a caption describing him as 'rock's swishiest outrage: a self-confessed lover of effeminate clothes'. Inside, the interview story featured another photo and the headline 'Oh You Pretty Thing'. Watts's introductory paragraph was written as a playful parody of drooling same-sex lust:

> Even though he wasn't wearing silken gowns right out of Liberty's, and his long blond hair no longer fell wavily past his shoulders David Bowie was looking yummy.
>
> He'd slipped into an elegant, patterned type of combat suit, very tight around the legs, with the shirt unbuttoned to reveal a full expanse of white torso. The trousers were turned up at the calves to allow a better glimpse of a huge pair of red plastic boots with at least three-inch rubber soles; and the hair was Vidal Sassooned into such impeccable shape that one held one's breath in case the slight breeze from the open window dared to ruffle it. I wish you could have been there to varda him; he was so super.

Such a tone of frank male-on-male delectation had never been seen in the pages of the serious but very straight music papers, in which critics focused on musicianship or social issues rather than physical appearance or style. Watts's use of words like 'varda' was a delicious in-the-know touch: it came from the slang idiom palare (sometimes spelt 'polari' and various other ways), favoured by gay men in the era when homosexual acts were illegal and code was a necessity. Traceable back to nineteenth-century itinerant theatrical companies and used by criminals, prostitutes and showbiz folk as well as gay men, palare would have been incomprehensible to most readers. 'David's present

'I'm gay. And always have been': the 22 January 1972 *Melody Maker* cover story that lit the blue touchpaper of Bowie's career

image is to come on like a swishy queen, a gorgeously effeminate boy,' Watts noted, implying that this was a gambit, a pose likely to be abandoned as abruptly as it had been adopted.

Then came the quote that reverberated around the world and instantly ignited Bowie's career: 'I'm gay. And always have been, even when I was David Jones.'

The feature's galvanising effect on Bowie's career came not just from the shock statement, but from the pictures that illustrated it. It is hard to reconstruct the drabness, the visual depletion of Britain in 1972, which filtered into the music papers to form the grey and grubby backdrop to Bowie's physical and sartorial splendour. Even in black and white, the elegance of the images leapt out of the pages, surrounded as they were – in that particular issue of *Melody Maker* – by thickly bearded minstrel Cat Stevens, sideburned ex-Spooky Tooth singer Gary Wright and his new band Wonderwheel, and the startling ugliness of a full-page ad for Grunt, Jefferson Airplane's label. 'He was a fantastically glamorous figure. I remember being quite dazzled by him when I first met him,' recalls Watts. 'It was like being with Marilyn Monroe. There was nobody else around like that. He was such a break with that sixties past.'

On *Melody Maker*'s front cover, the portrait by Barrie Wentzell showed the new shorter-locked Bowie, wearing a delicate bracelet and an open patterned zip jacket showing a bare, hairless chest. Inside, a close-up of Bowie's face, cradled delicately in one hand, features doe-like eyes cast to one side as if demurely avoiding the viewer's gaze. The framing was studiedly unmasculine, almost as if informed by reading John Berger's *Ways of Seeing* (published that same year), in which the critic suggests that judging by the history of Western art, 'men act and women appear . . . men look at women; women watch themselves being looked at . . . The surveyor of woman in herself is male . . . Thus she turns herself into an object – and most particularly an object of vision: a sight.' Watts's write-up likewise broke ground by encouraging the (mostly male) readers to look at another man as an aesthetic object, a treat for the eyes.

'It was *Melody Maker* that made me . . . that piece by Mick Watts,'

Bowie recalled in the middle of 1973. 'It all exploded.' Yet the funny thing about the Shock Revelation is that the quote was immediately followed by a hint of doubt: 'There's a sly jollity about how he says it, a secret smile at the corners of his mouth,' Watts observed. The idea that it was all a game was made clear right at the outset.

'I was a bit sceptical,' says Watts today. 'He was pretty certainly bisexual, as far as one can deconstruct what bisexuality is. But I think it's inescapable that most of Bowie's sexual encounters have been much more heterosexual than gay. I interviewed him quite often after that, and he was always very keen to make the point that he wasn't going to be flag-waving for Gay Lib. And Gay Lib got very cross with him because he wouldn't throw in his lot with them and proselytise for homosexuality. Now, how do you interpret that? It may have been a form of commercial self-protection, or it could be his genuine belief . . .'

While some gay men regarded Bowie as a tourist, others saw him as a pop-culture pathbreaker, making it easier for others to come out. The gay American critic Andrew Kopkind, for instance, hailed Bowie in an October 1972 piece for the *Boston Phoenix* as 'an authentic gay superstar, authentically a superstar and authentically gay at the same time – for the first time in our culture since Oscar Wilde'. He zoomed in on the 'lyricism' of his stage movements and the way he and Mick Ronson 'exchange erotic glances, gestures and dance steps hitherto only acceptable between man and woman in a band'.

Over the ensuing years, Bowie oscillated wildly, sustaining a miasma of sexual undecideability that enabled him to be all things to all people. In one single year, 1976, he told a British journalist that his professed bisexuality 'was just a lie . . . I've never done a bisexual action in my life, on stage, on record, or anywhere else', but also recounted his same-sex history to *Playboy*, which started with 'some very pretty boy in class in some school or other that I took home and neatly fucked on my bed upstairs' and continued intermittently.

Cherry Vanilla, who knew him intimately as well as professionally, says, 'You can tell when men really love women or don't really love women, and as far as I'm concerned, he really loved women . . . I would consider him heterosexual, but who fooled around, experimented a bit. And in those days, didn't we all?' Her MainMan colleague Tony Zanetta believed Bowie '*was* bisexual, but what he was really was a narcissist – boys or girls, it was all the same. He was attracted to the gay culture because he loved its flamboyance.'

Bowie's interest in gayness seems more cultural than sexual – a classic case of 'love and theft'. That's the title of Eric Lott's classic study of nineteenth-century blackface minstrels, his term for the simultaneous admiration and appropriation directed by whites towards black music and black style. In the same way, Bowie looked to gay culture as a vanguard of sensibility. If the sixties had been about the White Negro (mostly British groups, like the Stones, playing tough rhythm and blues), Bowie was guessing – gambling – that the defining crossover of seventies might be the Straight Gay. There was one important difference, though: unlike with the white sixties groups co-opting blues and R&B, there wasn't an exclusively gay-identified style of music for Bowie to appropriate. Opera and show tunes, while associated with gay taste, had plenty of straight (and, indeed, square) fans. So what Bowie did was to layer gayness over the existing post-sixties British tradition of pop and rock.

Along with his encounters with the Lindsay Kemp milieu, clubs like The Sombrero and, most recently, the polysexual *Pork* Warholites, Bowie had also been inspired by reading John Rechy's novel *City of Night*, which chronicles the journey of a young man from his small-town background to the homosexual underground of New York (and later Los Angeles), where he turns tricks to survive. 'A stunning piece of writing,' Bowie recalled in 1993. 'I found out later that it was a bible among gay America . . . There was something in the book akin to my feelings of loneliness. I thought – this is a lifestyle I really have to explore because I recognize things in this book that are really how I feel. And that led me a merry dance in the early Seventies, when gay clubs really became my lifestyle and all my friends were gay. I really opted to drown in the euphoria of this new experience which was a real taboo with society. And I must admit I loved that aspect of it.' But Bowie also admitted that 'as the years went on it became a thing where, sexually, I was pretty much with women the majority of the time. But I still had a lot of the trappings of the gay society about me. In terms of the way I would parade or costume myself or my attitudes in some of the interviews I did . . . It seemed to be the one taboo that everyone was too afraid to break. I thought – well, if there's one thing that's going to put me on the edge, this is it. Long hair didn't mean much anymore.'

City of Night is the perfect title for Rechy's gay odyssey. In *Mother Camp*, her groundbreaking 1972 study of drag-queen culture, social anthropologist Esther Newton points out how important the concept of 'urban' was to the subculture: many queens who came from small towns in the rural south or Midwest spoke of feeling uncomfortable in the country. 'It is the country that represents to us "nature" and, ultimately, what is real,' Newton wrote. Cities, especially nocturnal, after-hours cities, offered the rootless freedom and dark spaces in which you could be your non-normative self. Female impersonators, she observed, 'would say of themselves "we are city people; we are night people".'

For Bowie and other 'straight gays' in the early seventies, male homosexuality was the New Edge in two different ways. A new frontier of gritty and graphic realness: sex acts, sex customs, sex attitudes, sex locations that were all bracingly unfamiliar. But also a new frontier of campy unrealness. One thread in Rechy's novel that might have intrigued or influenced Bowie is the theatricality of sex. The hustlers in *City of Night* are actors as much as they're sex workers: they quickly learn not to say or do anything that might disrupt the john's particular 'sexdream'. One regular's special kink is dressing up a boy in biker gear of leather and heavy boots, then promenading around the city for an hour or two in his company. No sex takes place. The customer maintains a wardrobe of costumes in different sizes, what one character calls his 'drag', even though it's the opposite of what that usually refers to – the garb of female impersonation.

The buried idea here extends forward to RuPaul's 'We're born naked, everything else is drag' and as far back as Shakespeare's 'All the world's a stage'. Even when we're not overtly in costume, we're all 'players' acting out a social self. As W. H. Auden put it in 'Masque', 'Human beings are, necessarily, actors who cannot become something before they have first pretended to be it; and they can be divided, not into the hypocritical and the sincere, but into the sane who know they are acting and the mad who do not.' This poetic insight was given solid sociological credence in 1959 with the publication of Erving Goffman's famous study *The Presentation of Self in Everyday Life*, in which he formulated concepts like 'impression management' and the 'personal front'. Depending on your perspective, the conclusion to be drawn is either melancholy (we can never be really real, in any interpersonal situation – and perhaps even on the stage of our conscious mind we act out an ideal or prettified version of our self) or liberating (since there's no core to identity, we can reinvent ourselves, change the roles we play and the self we present, over and over again).

Camp is hard to pin down, but one core strand to the sensibility is what Susan Sontag called 'the metaphor of life as theater'. The origins of the word are much disputed, but some point to the French *se camper*, which means to posture boldly, to strike a provocative pose. For some gay men, being camp was a way of flaunting one's difference from the hetero-norm, a cultural separateness as much as a sexually determined one. Yet that made camp detachable as a sensibility; if you could be gay but not the least bit camp, that opened the possibility of acting camp without ever engaging in homosexual acts. Bowie's coming out was itself a camp gesture: a form of public theatre, the striking of a provocative pose, not necessarily backed up by anything he did in his private life.

Hunky Dory's back cover features the handwritten credit 'This album was Produced by . . . KEN SCOTT (assisted by the actor).' Kemp's camp, Rechy's novel, the Warhol crew – all these influences had intensified Bowie's existing tendency to view himself as an all-round entertainer, a variety artist, skipping between different mediums and swapping out roles constantly. Rock, at the turn of the sixties into the seventies, demanded commitment and consistency; songs and singing were about revealing one's inner truth or speaking truth to power. Bowie had tried to go along with rock's anti-showbiz values for a moment at the end of the sixties, but now, liberated by his immersion in gay culture, he could goad rock orthodoxy. 'What the music says may be serious, but as a medium it should not be questioned, analysed, or taken so seriously,' he declared in the 1971 *Rolling Stone* interview. 'I think it should be tarted up, made into a prostitute, a parody of itself. It should be the clown, the Pierrot medium.'

Unwittingly or not, here Bowie tapped into a set of negative associations surrounding the theatre that conflate acting, prostitution, homosexuality, cross-dressing and insincerity. 'The antitheatrical prejudice', as the historian Jonas Barish called it in his 1982 book of the same title, goes back as far as Plato, who distrusted and disapproved of mutability and mimesis. But it was at its most pronounced and hysterical during the sixteenth and seventeenth centuries, when Puritans published countless tracts with titles like *A Mirrour of Monsters* that decried playhouses as ungodly and ultimately closed down the theatres during Cromwell's rule. Plays were accused of arousing base passions with their depictions of sex and violence, as well as their effeminising emotional extremes. Actors were seen as analogous to prostitutes, feigning unfelt emotions for money. Some Puritans equated acting's pretence with the sin of hypocrisy (which actually comes from *hypokrite*, an Ancient Greek word for 'actor'). Others even saw it as a usurpation of God's role as Creator.

Highest among the concerns of many Puritan tract writers was the reigning practice in sixteenth- and early-seventeenth-century England of women's roles being played by men, or rather by pretty, androgynous boys. In his thousand-plus-page diatribe *Histriomastix* (1632), William Prynne rails against 'our artificial stage-players' who 'emasculate, metamorphose, and debase their noble sex', in the process becoming 'neither men nor women, but monsters'. Cross-dressing offends God because 'it perverts one principal use of garments, to difference men from women'.

Anti-theatricality still had a half-life even in the twentieth century, cropping up in fictional contexts like *The Catcher in the Rye*, where Holden Caulfield voices his contempt for the theatre and all actors because they're 'phoney'. While rock can hardly be characterised as puritanical, it does contain a long-running vein, stretching from the late-sixties underground through to indie and alternative rock, of antipathy to showiness and spectacle. As if to deflect such prejudices among *Melody Maker*'s readers, Michael Watts's feature concluded: 'Don't dismiss David Bowie as a serious musician just because he likes to put us all on a little.' There's a double sense in which 'put on' can be taken: a playful trick, but also a mask or role that can be put on and then taken off once its purpose has been served. So it would be with Bowie's gayness.

Bowie's stagey exit from the closet was perfectly timed. All things gay, bi, trans and ambiguous were 'in'. David Percival's 1970 West End play *Girlfriend* became the 1971 movie *Girl Stroke Boy*, in which a young man called Laurie brings home Jo to meet his parents, who find it impossible to determine whether their son's sweetheart is his girlfriend or boyfriend. Michael Apted's 1972 directorial debut *Triple/Echo* (retitled *Soldier in Skirts* for America) concerns a Second World War deserter who hides on a farm, starts dressing as a woman, then rashly goes for a date with a brute of an army sergeant from a nearby base. Bowie actually auditioned for the cross-dressing soldier's role. He also auditioned to play the beautiful bisexual youth embroiled in a love triangle with an older man and an older woman in 1971's *Sunday Bloody Sunday*. Meanwhile, in America, *Myra Breckinridge* – the 1970 film version of Gore Vidal's best-selling satirical novel – featured a transgender protagonist, S&M and anal sex with a strap-on dildo, while Russ Meyer's *Beyond the Valley of the Dolls* (1970) included a trans character, the record-biz Svengali Z-Man. As scriptwriter Roger Ebert explained, Z-Man 'seems to be a gay man for most of the movie, but is finally revealed to be a woman in drag'. The is-she-or-isn't-she-(a-he)? theme infil-trated pop, too, with The Kinks' 'Lola', a huge, career-resurrecting international hit for the group in 1970.

While he remained a divisive, uncertain figure for the gay com-munity, for his hetero audience Bowie became a symbol of possibil-ity: his songs and his image spoke to forbidden frissons, an expanded sense of latent erotic potential, a flexibility and flux that might never be realised beyond the realm of imagination but felt liberating. It spoke above all to boys alienated from straight-and-narrow manli-ness, and to girls looking for objects of desire outside those confines.

'I seem to draw a lot of fantasies out of people,' Bowie admitted, appearing on Russell Harty's TV chat show in 1973. Harty had asked about the kind of fan mail he received; Bowie would not be drawn on the details, except to say that some of the letters were 'heavy duty' and 'very sexy'. It was really with the singer's next move after *Hunky Dory* that this kind of obsessive projection took off, with the creation of the Ziggy Stardust persona. The combination of Bowie's unusual beauty and the Ziggy look – the glossy wrestling boots and tight-fitting two-piece outfits made of quilt in oriental or retro-futuristic patterns, influenced equally by *Clockwork Orange* and *2001: A Space Odyssey* – inspired strange reveries. The dreaming surely got weirder still with Bowie's next image-phase, the *Aladdin Sane* era, with the lightning bolt slash across the face, the mystic gold circle on the brow and Kansai Yamamoto's astonishing body-suits, vinyl geometric constructions that wore the person inserted into them rather than the other way round.

Drawing on fan letters sent c/o record companies, as well as interviews with fans looking back on their fevered past, Fred and Judy Vermorel's book *Starlust* explores in detail the kind of fantasy narratives Bowie triggered. At the extreme, the erotic scenarios stray into hallucinatory and mystical zones, verging on self-invented forms of sex-magic, phantasmic projection and even imagined tele-pathic communion.

'I thought he was so extraordinary that he couldn't possibly be human,' confessed Julie, one of the *Starlust* interviewees. 'He was paranormal almost . . . I began to think he was a new kind of Messiah . . . He had the qualities of a type of ruler . . . He was science fiction personified. To me he represented the most bizarre things which were evil and not of this world and completely beyond the imagina-tion . . . the most peculiarly advanced stages of sexuality.'

The Beatles were the first to create a fictional group, Sgt Pepper's Lonely Hearts Club Band. There was also Zappa and The Mothers of Invention's doo-wop homage alter ego Ruben and the Jets, while The Turtles released a concept album, *The Turtles Present the Battle of the Bands*, in which they pretended to be eleven different groups, parodying styles from psychedelia to surf band to country rock. They were photographed as each group for the gatefold inner sleeve. So Bowie wasn't really breaking new ground when he con-ceived the concept of Ziggy Stardust and the Spiders from Mars.

But the idea of playing a rock star, rather than simply attempting to become one, went to the core of Bowie as an artist in a much deeper way than it had with The Beatles or Zappa. It extended his sense of himself as an actor. Paradoxically, by seeing it as just one role out of the many he could take on, Bowie could commit to rocking out and to rock-star postures, despite having no great attachment to rock. As late as 1970, interviewed by *Jeremy*, Bowie located his heroes in English music hall (George Formby, Gracie Fields, Nat Jackley, Albert Modley), with *chansonniers* like Jacques Brel and oddballs like Tiny Tim thrown in. Bowie saw this as something that differentiated him from Bolan. 'Marc only has his music . . .' Bowie mused to the *NME* in 1972. 'He knows that my areas stretch out, and so my conviction for music probably isn't as strong as his . . . I can't see myself always being a rock and roll singer.' In other interviews, Bowie talked about feeling 'like an actor when I'm on stage, rather than a rock artist', and how 'if anything, maybe I've helped establish that rock'n'roll is a pose'.

The persona also served as a mask, giving him confidence on stage (he had barely appeared in public in the UK since late 1969) but also shielding him from the audience. Through Ziggy, he could enter into the rock-star trip while simultaneously keeping a distance from it – protecting himself, or so he hoped, from the psychological pressures of stardom (a source of anxiety, given that his family background was littered with suicides and mental illness, and that his half-brother was schizophrenic).

Bowie could play with rock'n'roll madness without succumbing to it. He would refer to Ziggy in the third person – 'that dear creature. I loved him' – and describe himself as a Dr Frankenstein, assembling the monster out of fragments of existing and should-be stars. Iggy Pop was part of the assemblage, echoed in the name Ziggy. So was Bolan (at one gig, a picture of Marc was projected behind the band during the song 'Lady Stardust'). But the largest chunk of stolen myth-flesh was the story of Vince Taylor, one of Britain's first rockers. Although born in Britain, Taylor grew up mostly in America, which gave his ersatz Elvis act added authenticity. Bowie had got to know the singer a bit in his has-been days, when Taylor had spiralled into cosmic paranoia. 'One day, on Tottenham Court Road, he took out a map of the world and put it on the pavement. All these people were walking past us and he was showing me where the aliens were keeping their arms and encampments.' Playing a gig in France, where he was a cult figure, Taylor 'went out on stage in white robes . . . and proclaimed himself the son of God'.

Others believed that a science-fiction novel by Robert Heinlein contributed a hefty amount to the loose, quasi-concept album narrative of *The Rise and Fall of Ziggy Stardust and the Spiders from Mars*. Looking back at the LP years later, rock writer Mick Farren said that he'd always thought of it as a mélange of Heinlein's 1961 classic *A Stranger in a Strange Land* – a big book for counterculture heads – with a little H. P. Lovecraft: 'I was certain someone would call him out for plagiarism. Nobody did.' Bowie did talk in the press about either being lined up to play the lead character in a movie version of *Stranger* or that he and MainMan had acquired the rights to adapt the novel for a movie. Heinlein's convoluted plot resists summary, but its gist is that the child survivor of a manned expedition to Mars is raised by Martians; returning to Earth, he becomes a star and ultimately founds his own syncretic Church of All Worlds, whose telekinetically enhanced initiates are destined to become the homo superior that ultimately supplants homo sapiens.

There is certainly some resemblance to the Ziggy Stardust scenario of a messianic rock star who comes from another planet bearing prophecies of hope for the doom-laden inhabitants of planet Earth. But then, lyrically and musically, the whole album is really a postmodern tissue of borrowings, allusions and echoes, from the Morse code guitar figure in 'Starman' (a replica of The Supremes' 'You Keep Me Hanging On') to the traces that some Bowieologists detect of William S. Burroughs, Michael Moorcock's Jerry Cornelius and Nik Cohn's *I Am Still the Greatest Says Johnny Angelo*, a mytho-manic tale of a psychopathic rock star.

The Rise and Fall of Ziggy Stardust was also a product of the era's ecological anxieties and general post-sixties gloom. The album's scenario, established in the opening cut 'Five Years', is that the planet is 'really dying', with just five years of resources left. The lyric – and the sighing, sagging feel of the melody and vocal – captures the feeling of apprehension and future-fear abroad in the culture. Worries about resource depletion, pollution and environmental collapse riddled the popular fiction and non-fiction of the day, along with anxieties about media overload and technology running amok. Alvin Toffler's *Future Shock* was a best-seller in 1970; The Club of Rome's report *The Limits of Growth* came out in 1972. Movies like *THX 1138*, *Silent Running* and *Soylent Green* imagined the near future as – respectively – a dehumanised surveillance society, a despoiled Earth stripped of all greenery, and an overpopulated America where people unknowingly eat food made from recycled human beings.

In the UK specifically, there was a boom in dystopian and cataclysmic fiction, such as Christopher Priest's 1972 novel *Fugue for a Darkening Island*, in which British society collapses under the weight of mass immigration from Africa, along with TV series like the BBC's *Doomwatch*, which was set in the present and concerned a government scientific agency responsible for dealing with ecological and technological emergencies. Released in 1971, Stanley Kubrick's controversial movie *A Clockwork Orange* took Anthony Burgess's 1962 novel about feral youth gangs of the near-future and situated it in a recognisably seventies urban landscape of brutalist architecture. Pundits across the political spectrum bemoaned the disintegration of the social fabric and the ugliness of the modern world.

Speaking to the *NME* in early 1972, Bowie talked of wanting to face 'the inevitability of the apocalypse' yet also 'promote some

feeling of optimism in the future'. That seemingly flat-out contradictory impulse came across convincingly in songs like 'Starman',
with its up-up-and-away melody (indebted to 'Somewhere Over the
Rainbow') and chorus image of the extraterrestrial saviour who shies
away from visiting Earth because 'he thinks he'd blow our minds'.
But the overall implication of the Ziggy Stardust scenario is what
was once called *Kulturpessimismus*: fatalistic resignation and make-
merry-while-we-may in these the Last Days of Man.

As with so much of Bowie's work, *The Rise and Fall of Ziggy
Stardust* works by being essentially writeable by the listener: the
images are vivid yet disjointed, inviting you to project your own
pictures onto your mind's movie screen. Bowie's own attempts to
explain the storyline were garbled. 'The time is five years to go
before the end of the earth,' Bowie told William S. Burroughs in
their 1974 *Rolling Stone* dialogue. 'It has been announced that the
world will end because of lack of natural resources . . . The older
people have lost all touch with reality and the kids are left on their
own to plunder anything. Ziggy was in a rock-and-roll band and the
kids no longer want rock-and-roll. There's no electricity to play it.'

Seemingly undeterred by the presence of Burroughs, a writer
whose own work is classified by some as avant-garde science fiction,
Bowie rambled on with his synopsis, talking about how the End
comes 'when the infinites arrive. They really are a black hole, but
I've made them people because it would be very hard to explain a
black hole onstage.' The song 'Starman' is about these infinites, or
'black-hole jumpers', who 'will be coming down to save the earth'
and in fact land 'somewhere in Greenwich Village'. Yet the infinites
turn out not 'to have a care in the world' and prove to be 'of no possible use' to humanity. 'They just happened to stumble into our universe by black-hole jumping.' Ziggy starts to believe he is 'a prophet
of the future starman'. But when the infinites arrive, 'they take bits
of Ziggy to make themselves real because in their original state they

are anti-matter and cannot exist in our world. And they tear him to pieces during the song "Rock'n'Roll Suicide".'

This far-out and far-fetched fare was layered on top of music that was not particularly cosmic or futuristic but firmly in the tradition of post-Beatles pop: a sound that moved around between cleanly produced rock and show tunes, just as its stage performance, as the *NME*'s Nick Kent observed, existed in an uneasy limbo between full-blown theatre and a live band rocking out.

The Spiders from Mars were both the fantasy band in the album's storyline and a real band of musicians that Bowie pulled together to flesh out the fantasy onstage: down-to-earth musicians from Hull who took some persuading to get togged up in Bowie and Buretti's outfits. Only after taking the group to see Alice Cooper (Look, chaps, you can wear costumes and still rock hard!) were drummer Woody Woodmansey and bassist Trevor Bolder brought on board. Mick Ronson was particularly resistant and, according to Woodmansey, actually 'packed his bags and left'. At Bowie's bidding, Woody ran after the guitarist and, after an hour of hard persuasion standing on the platform at Beckenham station, talked him round.

Musically and visually, Ronson was yang to Bowie's yin, something dramatised with the famous stage stunt of the singer kneeling to fake-fellate Ronson's guitar at Oxford Town Hall. 'Bowie had that incredible face, but he was not rock'n'roll, whereas every note played by Mick was masculine,' recalled Morrissey, who saw the Ziggy tour in September 1972. 'Mick's toughness saved Bowie . . .'

Yet listening to *The Rise and Fall* now, what becomes clear is that it is not a guitar-dominated record at all: if anything, voice, strings and perhaps even the drums (superb throughout) prevail. Rock is the theme that governs the album, but it's not really the sound here – which is lean and clean, light and almost unbodied in its swaying motion, as on 'Five Years', or the soaring, balladic, piano-centred 'Lady Stardust', or the overwrought Scott Walker/Brel dramatics

Bowie thanks the fans, using a photo of him going down on Mick
Ronson's guitar at an Oxford Town Hall concert on 17 June 1972

of 'Rock'n'Roll Suicide'. With its jabbering Sha Na Na-ish backing
vocals, 'Star' is 'rock'n'roll' in the same way that Elton John's fifties
pastiches of the same period are. 'Suffragette City' is tougher and

more modern but still retro-tinged. Only 'It Ain't Easy' approaches hardness or heaviness, with perhaps 'Hang on to Yourself' qualifying on account of its Skynyrd-like slide fills. This is not a record attempting to spar with Led Zeppelin.

When rock does rear up on *The Rise and Fall of Ziggy Stardust*, it almost feels like a cameo appearance, Ronson strutting out to take a turn in the spotlight, unfurling a solo or some flourishes at the song's end. A genius arranger, Ronson fits like a glove with Bowie because they're both Apollonian in sensibility, all about clarity and control. From his much-praised guitar tone – poised perfectly between clean and distorted – to his contoured riffs, Ronson's playing has a sculptural quality. A sense of stylised distance is also evident in the way the guitarist moved onstage: striding between legs-splayed poses that act out 'guitar hero', a Kabuki-like abstraction of rock-performance codes. Despite his discomfort with having to wear the theatrical costumes, Ronson instinctively grasped what Bowie's vision required.

Bowie and Ronson's gifts come together most perfectly on the title track 'Ziggy Stardust'. It's a Rock Classic that doesn't sound like anything before it, neither rocking nor rolling but proceeding at a stately, pageant-like pace. Nothing like the terse, punchy, horizontal melody-riffs of blues-based rock, 'Ziggy Stardust' extends itself as a winding, elegantly epic melody line, whose entirety is repeated only twice in the song. There's no chorus, just a clarion-like Ronson-riff that intros the song and recurs at intervals. The lyric never repeats once. Whereas most rock songs freeze-frame a moment of intense emotion and stay within that loop of feeling, 'Ziggy' is a saga being unfolded, a heroic myth: the rise and fall of a superhuman being.

You can see why David Bowie might want to take on a persona for artistic or personal reasons. But what is the added value for the listener? Why not simply identify with and worship an actual rock star rather than an imaginary one? Simon Frith argued in *Creem* that 'the Ziggy Stardust album is not really about being a rock star, it's about being a rock *fan*'. The fact that Bowie was performing his own fantasy did seem to exacerbate the fantasy-generation process in his fans. He had been just like his fans; indeed, still was the biggest fan, constantly enthusing about old heroes and new discoveries, like Lou Reed and Iggy and Mott the Hoople. The superstar success of this fan-turned-idol suggested that all fans could dream their way to becoming idols in their own right some day.

T. Rextasy had pioneered the glam syndrome of fans dressing like their idol. But, as Peter York noted, Bowie 'had this extraordinary effect in Britain . . . of producing more *clones* than anyone else'.

'I had the second-best Ziggy cut at my school,' says Hugo Burnham. Sixteen years old when the album came out, Burnham would six years later be the drummer in the now legendary post-punk outfit Gang of Four. 'I went up to Vidal Sassoon in London – because I read that's where Bowie got his hair done – to have mine cut. Showed them the picture. I tried to get my mum to let me wear her big lace-up thigh-length boots too.'

Burnham says that seeing 'Starman' on *Top of the Pops* was the turning point for him and his peers. This was the famous 6 July 1972 appearance, when the song was just outside the Top 40, during which Bowie draped his arm around Ronson's shoulder – a seemingly tiny gesture of homosocial intimacy that felt subversively feminine. Burnham and his contemporaries at Cranbook Grammar School, in Kent, had only been vaguely aware of David Bowie as a name. 'Starman' on *Top of the Pops* was 'like someone had thrown open these huge doors. Literally within a matter of weeks, we were wearing different shoes and doing different things with our hair.' He and his fellow glam converts travelled up to London for gigs by Bowie, Mott, Roxy and others. 'I'd get the train up from Kent in my regular clothes and would change into my glam gear and put my make-up on in the men's toilets at Charing Cross station. Fucking mad!' Soon he and his glitter gang would be travelling up and down the country for shows.

So dedicated was Burnham that he mailed off a desperate dispatch to Bowie via *Melody Maker*'s letters page:

> A personal plea to David Bowie: Please please don't do your gig at the Manchester Hardrock before we finish school! Spare a thought for us poor school kids who will come up from Kent to see you, but only break up a few days before Christmas. Please! – HUGO BURNHAM

Scratch the veneer off a punk or new-wave musician in Great Britain and nine times out of ten you'll find a glam fan underneath. Siouxsie Sioux, Ian McCulloch, David Sylvian, Gary Numan, Duran Duran, Kevin Rowland, Ian Curtis . . . the formative effect of Bowie is the common denominator that connects an otherwise hugely diverse spectrum of post-punk performers.

By September 1972, Bowie had eclipsed his frenemy Bolan in every category except sales. He was the most talked about, the most looked at, the most imitated rock star, yet 'Starman' only reached #10 in the charts, while its follow-up, the bisexual anthem and non-album single 'John, I'm Only Dancing', fell just shy of the Top 10. Meanwhile, Bolan, Slade, The Sweet and Gary Glitter were topping the charts.

Bowie was still more of an album-oriented artist, indicating that his core constituency was older and more sophisticated – those in their late teens and early twenties. During their early-seventies research into what they dubbed the 'Glamrock cult', sociologists Ian Taylor and Dave Wall surveyed Sheffield schoolkids between the ages of twelve and eighteen and found that Bowie enjoyed appeal across all age groups, but his true base was 'the older children' who read the rock weeklies rather than teenybop mags, and who 'tended to interpret his music as an extension of the underground music of the 1960s, a music to be listened to for its intellectual content'. Like Roxy Music, Bowie belonged to a category that's been called 'high glam': artists whose albums stayed in the charts a long time, selling steadily, and whose music-paper interviews – witty, intelligent, full of esoteric references, an education in aesthetics for their fans – were as important as their image.

Some managers might have opted to push Bowie further towards full-spectrum dominance in his homeland before attempting an American invasion, but Tony Defries was a double-or-nothing, high-stakes gambler. In early September 1972, on the eve of The Spiders from Mars's assault on the US, Defries gathered his MainMan troops in Manchester, where Bowie was playing a new venue called Hardrock. He told them that RCA was confident that Bowie would be the biggest thing to come out of Britain since The Beatles. Defries was depending on them all, and part of their responsibility was to 'learn to look and act like a million dollars'. They had to project megastardom in order to bring it into existence.

Defries's technique is interesting: selling his MainMan minions on the idea that RCA is sold on the idea of Bowie – an idea that he sold RCA in the first place. Now the MainMan soldiers must sell the idea to the American media and public. There's a circularity to the hype here, a spiral that becomes self-propelling.

'Listen, we peddled David's ass like Nathan's peddles hot dogs,' Cherry Vanilla would recall of that 1972 US campaign, when interviewed for the 1975 *Village Voice* article 'Selling Gay to the Masses'. But in her account, three years on from the US tour and press blitz, it was she and the *Pork* gang who convinced Defries that 'David could be the biggest star in the world', not the other way around. 'Of course, we didn't know if we were right. We were just bullshitting.

But bullshit works. I used to be in advertising. McCann Erickson. Coca Cola . . . Well, Defries is a shit – I mean, I really love him – but he's a shit . . . but he did a number on RCA, told them David was this big fag star in England, and at that time all American record companies believed that the New Beatles would be coming out of England at any moment.' She told *Village Voice* that RCA embarked on 'a huge publicity push' – with the tab for just one tour's first-class travel, accommodation and sundry expenses totalling $400,000.

Part of looking and acting 'like a million dollars' was spending heedlessly, just for the effect it created. For the US tour that meant not just limousines everywhere, but 'two karate-uniformed body-guards', Vanilla says today. 'It all created the illusion that he was more important than he was already.'

Interviews were similarly tightly restricted, to create a sense of exclusivity and mystique. 'Tony was keeping the press away from David as a ploy to make him seem that much more important,' says Vanilla. 'We would only let the *New York Times* and *LA Times*, just a few select people talk to him.' A colourful personality with the gift of the gab from her days in advertising, Vanilla ended up conducting the lion's share of interviews herself. She'd travel ahead to the next stop on the tour and do local newspaper and radio interviews to drum up sales for concert tickets that were often lacklustre.

'I would be as outrageous as possible on the radio, tell these wild stories, and they'd play clips from his songs, which helped, because a lot of kids weren't familiar with his music yet,' Vanilla recalls. 'I did all this talking for him, and things had happened so fast that I didn't even really research a lot about him from before we met him. So sometimes I gave probably stupid or outlandish answers to the press's questions because I didn't really know. Everything was going so fast, I didn't really have time to go back and find out what albums he had done before, and what this song meant or that song meant. But it worked.' The issue of Bowie's undefined sexuality was something that Vanilla worked hard. 'We kept it a mystery, just to keep that "Is he or isn't he?" thing going. They'd ask, "So is it true he's gay or bisexual?" Sometimes I'd say, "I don't know – he's a pretty good fuck." This maybe even before I had even had sex with him!'

Along with the wholly superfluous bodyguards, another image-enhancer was Bowie's 17 September arrival in America on-board the *QE2* ocean liner. Later, during the 'Ziggy' world tour, Bowie left Japan by boat, boarded the Trans-Siberian Express at Vladivostock, travelled across the USSR, then took another train to Paris. Although the surface-level travel was dictated by his fear of flying, it imparted an Old World retro-tinge of aristocratic elegance. 'We never knew if that was another Defries ploy or not, just to make things more glamorous and garner more press and stuff,' laughs Vanilla.

Breaking Bowie in America was a challenge: the vast hinterland of the US was sluggish and cautious in its tastes. Still, Vanilla and her MainMan colleagues were totally dedicated to the task at hand. 'I had been writing about rock stars and bands for *Creem* and *Circus*, and from the moment I first saw him, I thought, "This is the one that I can be an integral part of making a star." I was on a mission to prove to the world that he was someone like Andy Warhol – really special, unique, different and deeply talented. I believed it with all my heart. And we were all a bit in love with him.'

New York was already sold on Bowie thanks to advance reports and word-of-mouth. *Melody Maker*'s New York correspondent Roy Hollingworth reported that the Carnegie Hall concert drew a swarm of people 'who resembled Christmas trees on legs. There was much glitter, and several men dressed as ladies.' Despite rumours that RCA had been forced to 'paper the house' (give away unsold tick-ets), Bowie received a standing ovation. New York was his home from home. Dense with hipsters and homosexuals, plus a large swathe of the nation's rock critics, it was also a fount of obvious inspiration to the singer – Warhol and The Velvet Underground,

Dylan. New York periodical *Rock Scene*, the creation of Richard and Lisa Robinson, was pretty much a glitter-zine, with backstage pics of Bowie in his dressing room, gossipy items about Lou Reed and the New York Dolls, and an advice column by the outrageous trans-rocker Wayne County, who'd signed with MainMan.

Cleveland and Detroit also gave Bowie a warm welcome. Cleveland had one of the most adventurous FM stations in the country, WWMS, which gave Bowie's records heavy support; Detroit was home to *Creem*, which, unlike *Rolling Stone*, put its weight behind the glitter bands. The local scene had produced Iggy Pop and the Stooges and had sheltered Alice Cooper for a period. Elsewhere in the heartland, Bowie faced half-empty halls: the concert in St Louis, for instance, made him 'feel very underground', he confessed. In huge swathes of the US, glitter fans were an isolated breed of virtual outcasts. One *Creem* reader wrote to bemoan his predicament, complaining of being surrounded on all sides by 'blinkin' hippies' and beseeching the magazine: 'You're my last resort before I buy a ticket to England. Please, will somebody tell me where all the flash rock and roll boys and bands are? I'm a lead singer into Faces, Slade, Stones, T. Rex, Etc . . . Isn't there anybody out there with a little class and flash? Let's show the British where glitter and camp is at!'

San Francisco's rock scene was still hung up on its waning status at the capital of the counterculture, and it treated Bowie with snooty suspicion. Looking back over Bowie's career to date while reviewing his 1979 album *Lodger*, Greil Marcus mordantly recalled the Ziggy concert at Winterland: 'a San Francisco hall that holds a good 5000, when a lonely 400 of the faithful and the curious huddled in front of the stage – for warmth – as Bowie Ziggy struggled through his act, gamely crying: "You're not alone! Give me your hands! Give me your hands!"'

But Los Angeles, immediately prior, had been a triumph. Anglophilia ran deep in LA. As with New York, there was already a fledgling glitter scene, which was soon to find its focus at the dive club The English Disco, which launched in October 1972. That same month, when Bowie made his debut at Santa Monica Civic Auditorium, 'Three thousand people came and the difference was very visible,' recalls John Mendelsohn. 'The way people were dressed was lurid and "look at me".'

If New York and LA were the most welcoming and glam-attuned cities for Bowie, it was because decadence held sway there as both an ideal and an actual sociocultural phenomenon in process. Manhattan, in particular, seemed simultaneously the realest and unrealest place on Earth. New York, edging closer to its mid-seventies collapse with every year, offered a dose of urban existence at its most abrasively raw and intense. But it was a paradise of urbanity taken to the limit: a place where sensibility and sensuality were refined to baroque degrees of artificiality, where libertines could create lives free from the small town's watchful communal superego. Bowie was enthralled by this combination of civilisation and savagery, represented above all by the Warhol Factory scene and The Velvet Underground.

Bowie had first met Andy Warhol and Lou Reed – separately – during a September 1971 trip to New York with Defries to secure the RCA deal. The Warhol hang-out was awkward, the ice breaking only when the artist spied Bowie's bright-yellow shoes and gushed admiration. In the various accounts Bowie subsequently gave of this meeting of legends, the common themes are Warhol's vacancy ('he has nothing to say at all, absolutely nothing'), his pallor ('this white, pudding face', 'living dead yellow in complexion') and his near-autistic lack of affect ('slightly out of this world, really inhuman', 'emotionless, indifferent, just like a dead fish'). Bowie often recycled a joke of Lou Reed's about how you could manufacture an Andy Warhol doll that you wound up and it *didn't* do anything.

Despite this non-encounter – 'I left knowing as little about him as a person as when I went in' – Bowie would often sound Warholian notes during the next several years, describing himself in terms of the very attributes he found so unsettling in Warhol. In a 1972 *Rolling Stone* interview, for instance, he characterised himself as 'a pretty cold person . . . I get so numb . . . I'm a bit of an iceman.' Warhol talked about wanting to be a machine and described the 'Pop person' as 'a vacuum that eats up everything, he's made up from what he's seen'. Bowie confessed to being 'just a Photostat machine. I pour out what has already been fed in.' Warhol and Bowie both pioneered what is now the reigning ideology of creativity, which is really *re*creativity: the 'everything is a remix' notion that originality and innovation are outmoded and increasingly unhelpful myths, that artistically you are what you eat.

Bowie's get-together with Lou Reed was vastly warmer and more productive than the Warhol meet-up. Dinner at a fancy restaurant, followed by drinks at Max's Kansas City, this was a destiny date: the beginning of a mutual-admiration pact, a virtual love affair of artistic like-minds. 'He's the only interesting person around,' gushed Reed to *Melody Maker* not long after. 'Everything has been tedious, rock'n'roll has been tedious, except for what David has been doing. There's a mutual empathy between us . . . That tedious thing about what's been happening . . . we're gonna take care of all that . . . They can't suppress us anymore.' Bowie, meanwhile, took every opportunity to hail Reed as 'the most important writer in modern rock . . . New York City *is* Lou Reed.' The meeting had been enabled – and attended – by scenester/journalist Lisa Robinson and her husband Richard, who was just about to produce Reed's debut solo album. By the end of the night, Bowie had smoothly positioned himself to produce the follow-up LP, while MainMan would soon take on the management of Reed's career in Europe.

'New York's present is our future . . . Reed is reality as Bowie is fantasy,' wrote *Melody Maker* reader Robert Hardy, a fan of both artists. Bowie himself grasped that there was a crucial gulf between their sensibilities: 'Lou writes in the street-gut level and the English tend to intellectualize more.' He venerated Reed as 'the real thing' – authentic in a way that was inaccessible to him, capable of a directness of expression that didn't come naturally to him.

The Velvet Underground are traditionally regarded as prime ancestors for glam rock, but when you look closely at what the band actually did, it's hard to see why. Dressed down and clad in black, they weren't glamorous-looking; Warhol added Nico to 'the act' precisely because the Velvets 'themselves were not very charismatic onstage', said Factory superstar Gerard Malanga, who would dance onstage with the group at the *Exploding Plastic Inevitable* shows, sometimes wielding a giant syringe to accompany 'Heroin'. Nor did the Velvets' sound anticipate any of the signature aspects of glam rock, like its stompy beat or the glossy sound with its cleanly articulated riffs. Quite the opposite: The Velvet Underground's spectrum ranged from abrasively indistinct walls of rolling noise to fragile, folkadelic ballads; the rhythmic pulse underneath was subdued and trance-inducingly monotonous; and the overall sound aesthetic was lo-fi and murky.

The Velvet Underground weren't particularly theatrical, either. In the first, most publicised but short-lived phase of their career, Warhol inserted the group amid a mixed-media sensory overload of projected films, dancers miming S&M with bullwhips and other decadent props, and dazzling lights. But the effect was very much akin to the psychedelic happenings going on at the exact same time in San Francisco and London, and nothing like the showbiz-spectacle direction pursued by Bowie, Alice Cooper and other glam groups.

So why, then, are the Velvets commonly considered proto-glam? Partly it's because the most creative and respected figures in glam – Bowie and Roxy Music – enthused about the group. But while the Velvets' debut LP is audible here and there in Roxy's work, there's really not much evidence of a musical influence in Bowie's records. His imagistic lyrics display barely a trace of Reed's pared simplicity. The truth is that Bowie had far more influence on Reed than the other way round.

Because of the association with Warhol's Factory scene, because they were so extreme, The Velvet Underground are considered pioneers of art rock. But their extremism was actually sourced in literature and avant-garde music. None of the Velvets attended art school. Reed's background was in English literature: he was mentored by the poet Delmore Schwartz. John Cale studied music at Goldsmiths College, before plunging into New York's experimental underground, where he participated in renegade composer La Monte Young's Theatre of Eternal Music.

Really, the only thing that connected The Velvet Underground and glam rock was disillusion. Glam's disillusionment came after the death of the sixties dream, whereas the Velvets had never been illusioned in the first place. They were non-believers in real time, shrugging off sixties hopes and sixties pieties. 'We were a little bit sarcastic about the love thing,' Reed recalled in 1975. 'Which we were right about, because look what happened. We knew that in the first place. They thought acid was going to solve everything . . . And we just said bullshit, you people are fucked. That's not the way it is and you're kidding yourselves. And they hated us.'

This cynical stance made The Velvet Underground seem, in hindsight, a premonition of the seventies, punk prophets. But in other respects, they were still very sixties, creating a version of psychedelia oriented around heroin's oblivion and amphetamine's solipsistic-nihilistic rush, rather than the ego-melting transcendence and dream-like surreality of acid and pot. Live especially, the goal was a painfully overwhelming abstraction, what the group nicknamed 'the Cloud'. As Reed put it, 'On certain songs, we used to consciously enter the Cloud, and you just hear all these funny things.'

Reed admired a few of his contemporaries: The Byrds (particularly Roger McGuinn's guitar on 'Eight Miles High'), the violence of The Who, Ray Davies's storytelling. But what set Reed's writing apart was its unsparing and unflinching commitment to reality. This pained humanism and painful honesty seems at odds with Warhol's celebrations of superficiality and plasticity, as with his paean to Los Angeles: 'I love Hollywood . . . Everybody's plastic – but I love plastic. I want to be plastic.' Seeing clearly, without illusions – that was what Reed and The Velvet Underground were about.

Looking back on his output to date in the liner note to 1975's *Metal Machine Music*, Reed recalled that 'When I started the Velvet Underground . . . my concern was not, as was assumed, abidingly lyrical, verbally oriented at heart, "head" rock, the exploration of various "taboo" subjects, drugs, sex, violence. Passion – REALISM – realism was the key. The records were letters. Real letters from me to certain other people.'

This became the leitmotif of his long career and its attendant, notoriously surly interviews. 'They're really *about* something . . . that *really* happened, that has some bearing in *real* life,' Reed said in 1986, surveying his body of work. 'I was really trying to give you a shot of the street.' His lyrical style seemed unstyled: a carefully crafted plainness, colloquial rather than poetic. It was often compared to that of *Last Exit to Brooklyn* author Hubert Selby Jnr (who Reed praised for his 'straight line between two points . . . no fucking around . . . no polysyllabic anything' approach), although Reed said that the hard-boiled fiction of Raymond Chandler was his true model. The delivery, falling somewhere between song and speech, conjured the faltering rhythm of thoughts taking shape in real time.

'I don't think I'm a singer, with or without a guitar,' Reed said. 'I give dramatic readings that are almost my tunes.' Although to a large extent a case of Reed making the most of his limitations, this refusal of vocal theatrics suited the content: it contributed to the effect of naturalism, of his lyrics as a clear window onto reality.

This was how the group's handful of critical supporters at the time celebrated The Velvet Underground. *ZigZag*'s Geoffrey Cannon, for instance, praised Reed for his 'journalist's ability to mirror what there was – and is – to see in New York': the songs literally emerged like reportage from the edge zones, via a notebook Reed carried around with him 'on his transit through the city'.

If there was glamour here, it was the decadent romanticism of sickness and nihilism. In a 1974 *NME* interview, Reed explained why he put a verse from 'Heroin' on the cover of the live album *Rock 'n' Roll Animal*: it summed up exactly the kind of character he'd always been obsessed with, he said, the person able to make 'a big decision' and stake everything – in this case on the Nothing of the orgasmic, life-nullifying heroin rush. From a bohemian perspective, this kind of absolute commitment is more alluring than political commitment (sacrificing yourself for something: a cause, ideology, utopian dream, the Revolution), let alone the more mundane pledges and self-sacrifices involved in marriage and parenting.

Addiction is about sacrificing yourself for nothing. Junk gets its name from the idea of waste; the worthlessness of addiction achieves its own kind of purity. Decadence in the late-nineteenth-century sense was all about exquisite sterility, an elaborate squandering of the self, the refusal of productivity. Reaching back for antecedents, journalists writing about The Velvet Underground made *fin de siècle* allusions to 'the flowers of evil' being 'in full bloom' or the 'sickly sweet, rotten smell' of cultural morbidity wafting off the group's music like heady incense, along with the inevitable references to Weimar Berlin.

The name Velvet Underground came from the title of Michael Leigh's 1963 book about 'the sexual corruption of our age', which (as was the norm in the 'shock exposé' genre) offered an outwardly stern, secretly prurient glimpse into the underworld of specialist erotic taste – practices like sado-masochism and fetishism. This fed into songs like 'Venus in Furs', which was named after Leopold von Sacher-Masoch's classic novel about bondage and domination, and teemed with darkly sensual imagery of whips and leather. 'Sister Ray' depicted a 'scene of total debauchery and decay', explained Reed. Poking through the group's obliterating noise overdrive, the storyline concerned 'a bunch of drag queens taking some sailors home with them and shooting-up on smack and having this orgy when the police appear'.

Along with decadence, the other proto-glam aspect of The Velvet Underground was Lou Reed's uncertain sexuality. As a college freshman, he underwent electroconvulsive therapy. Reed always insisted this treatment was to 'discourage homosexual feelings', and he wrote bitterly about the experience in the song 'Kill Your Sons'. After his death, though, Reed's sister Merrill spoke up to defend their parents, claiming they were 'blazing liberals' rather than homophobes and had resorted to ECT in desperation, after doctors' advice that it was their only hope for dealing with their son's mental breakdown.

Although Reed would marry three times, for much of the seventies his live-in lover was Rachel Humphries, an exquisite half-Mexican drag queen whose birth name was Tommy and who inspired most of the songs on the album *Coney Island Baby*. Lou and Rachel met in a Greenwich Village club; Reed took her home and, already several days into a no-sleep methamphetamine run, 'rapped for hours and hours' while Rachel sat in silence. This must be love, Reed decided – the perfect acoustic mirror for his speed-freak soliloquys! The only catch was that he was still married to his first wife. 'I kind of wanted us all three to live together but somehow it was too heavy for her. Rachel just stayed on and the girl moved out. Rachel was completely disinterested in who I was or what I did. Nothing could impress her. He'd hardly heard my music and didn't like it all that much when he did. Rachel knows how to do it for me. No one else ever did before.' The slippage between 'she' and 'he' in that recollection adds credence to the argument of some Reed experts that the singer was fundamentally gay. Reed's own self-description was 'bi-sexual chauvinist pig'.

Hovering in a third-sex interzone – make-up and stubble, delicate features but substantially taller than the five foot ten inch Reed – Rachel was glambiguity given strapping, stunning bodily form. Decadence's core impulse was to go 'against nature', which is why the city was its anti-natural habitat. The Velvets mocked the hippy cult of the countryside in the song 'Train Round the Bend', a piss-take-by-inversion of Creedence Clearwater Revival's 'Up Around the Bend': instead of hitching a ride to the end of the highway, 'where the neon turns to wood', the Velvets bitched about being 'sick of the trees' and missing 'city streets' and 'neon lights'. Guitarist Sterling Morrison joked that Coney Island was back-to-nature enough for his taste. The Velvets could only have come from New York, the world's ultimate city – so much so that it had pushed urban existence to breaking point by the end of the sixties, with crime, drugs, flight to the suburbs and looming bankruptcy.

Bowie had managed to hear *The Velvet Underground and Nico* before almost anyone else in Britain because Kenneth Pitt had been given a promo of the LP while in Manhattan. Blown away by its contents, he covered 'Waiting for My Man' and wrote 'Little Toy Soldier', a song lyrically indebted to 'Venus in Furs'. Despite the flagrant lifting of lines like 'taste the whip and bleed for me', 'Little Toy Soldier' bounces along in the jaunty Newley-esque music-hall mode of his debut album. The supposedly profound influence of the Velvets on Bowie is similarly nowhere to be found on the self-titled second album, on *The Man Who Sold the World*, or on *Hunky Dory*, apart from 'Queen Bitch', a straight-up parody. Neither The Spiders from Mars's live versions of 'White Light/White Heat' nor the studio take that eventually came out on Mick Ronson's second solo album, *Play Don't Worry*, show much understanding of what was really revolutionary about the Velvets' approach.

Bowie and Ronson were too neat-freak to risk real chaos. The upside of their orderly approach to sound was that when they co-produced Lou Reed's second solo album, *Transformer*, the result was immaculately arranged pop that gave the ex-Velvet the only hit single of his life with 'Walk on the Wild Side'. But the gulf in sensibility was yawning. For instance, during the sessions Ronson was repeatedly vexed by Reed's guitar being 'way out of tune'. Ronno would attempt to fix it, while Reed scowled, impatient to get on with recording. Reed – Ronson remembered, still bemused a couple of decades on – 'didn't really care whether it was in tune or whether it was out of tune'.

Recorded in London in August 1972, *Transformer* sounded far more like a David Bowie record than any of the four Velvet Underground albums or the Richard Robinson-produced (and disappointingly flat) solo debut, *Lou Reed*, that came out earlier in '72. *Transformer* was Lou Reed songs fed through the pristinely produced, semi-orchestrated *Hunky Dory/Ziggy Stardust* sound. That had everything to do with Ronson, who was effectively the musical director (while Bowie's primary job was emotional management, coddling and coaxing a singer in a drug-addled state of mental disarray). Ronson contributed a hefty amount to the arrangements, worked closely with the session musicians and played gorgeous piano on songs like 'Perfect Day', as well as contributing guitar and even a spot of recorder-playing elsewhere on the record.

The songs on *Transformer* were different to Reed's previous work: a case of 'Lou Reed' with quotation marks around it, almost.

It was as though the singer was reflecting back Bowie's distant fantasy of the Warhol–Velvets demi-monde.

'Make Up' is a drag-queen (wo)manifesto, a campy, vaudeville-style run-through of the cosmetic artifice involved in switching genders, climaxing with the rallying cry: 'We're coming out / Out of our closets.' 'New York Telephone Conversation' fondly sends up the bitchy, gossipy phone chats of the kind that Warhol routinely taped and got transcribed by a long-suffering assistant. 'Andy's Chest' is a bagatelle of sweet childish nonsense written as a gift for Warhol and named after the scars left behind when Valerie Solanas's bullets pierced Warhol's body. Elsewhere, 'Vicious' was a rabbit-punch reprise of the fourth Velvets album, *Loaded*; 'Hangin' Round' a marginally tougher take on the same; while the carefree kite dance of 'Satellite of Love' could have come straight off *Hunky Dory*.

The drag-queen- and Warhol-themed songs on *Transformer* amounted to a New York mini-concept album whose centrepiece, of course, was 'Walk on the Wild Side'. It became a big hit on both sides of the Atlantic and smuggled the words 'giving head' onto the radio. The title originally came from a 1956 novel by Nelson Algren, whose stories generally involved lowlifes, criminals and drug addicts (as with *The Man with the Golden Arm*). Reed was approached about turning it into a musical, but after reading the book purloined the title for a completely unrelated song: a fond tribute to the Factory's three most famous drag queens – Holly Woodlawn, Jackie Curtis and Candy Darling – along with Warhol-movie leading man Joe Dallessandro and Joe Campbell, who played Sugar Plum Fairy in *My Hustler*.

'Walk on the Wild Side' lilts along on a shuffling jazz-lite swinging rhythm and Herbie Flowers's immortal bassline (actually a meld of acoustic double bass and electric bass guitar). There's a languid smoke wisp of a saxophone solo and doop-de-doop backing vocals, whose entrance is preceded by Reed's arch introduction 'And the coloured girls go . . .' – even in 1972, dated and borderline offensive. In fact, the singers weren't black at all but a trio of very white and very British girls called Thunderthighs, who would later sing on Mott the Hoople's 'Roll Away the Stone' and score a minor hit with 'Central Park Arrest'.

Transformer was a semi-concept album about transgender as much as it was about New York. The two themes entwined: Manhattan was the city of cities, a place where you could jettison your born-and-raised provincial identity and reinvent yourself. 'Walk on the Wild Side' touched on this idea with the lines about Holly Woodlawn hitch-hiking from Miami, shaving legs and plucking eyebrows en route, and arriving in New York as a she. *Transformer*'s striking cover sealed the conceptual deal. The photo of Reed didn't resemble his previous image in the least: thick eyeshadow and the bleaching-out of the image created a Pierrot effect that again threw Reed into a Bowie/Lindsay Kemp world of mime and *commedia dell'arte*. This makeover extended to the live performances around the album, which saw Reed glitzed up in a rhinestone-studded black suit, gold shoes and maroon nail polish. *Transformer*'s back cover was even more startling: Reed's friend Ernie Thormahlen appeared twice as if in a kind of mirror – except that each image was a totally different pose/guise. On the right, an absurdly butch muscle-boy, with cigarette pack rolled up in tight white T-shirt sleeve, leather cap pulled down over the brow and a huge erection slanting visibly beneath the blue-jean crotch; on the left, an absurdly femme vamp, in high heels, lipstick, wig and what looked like a black leather negligee, with a coy hand covering the crotch and the truth of sexual identity.

In 1972, *Transformer* was asserting flamboyantly through its images and lyrics what academics would later theorise more drily: the idea that sexual identity was constructed and performative, rather than innate. Esther Newton actually made this point as early as '72 with *Mother Camp*, which argued that drag queens – by

Lou Reed glitters at the peak of his brief but intense dalliance with glam on the back cover of the live album *Rock 'n' Roll Animal* (1974)

achieving femininity despite being 'the "wrong" sex' – showed that all gender is learnt rather than instinctive. 'The gay world, via drag, says that sex-role behavior is an appearance,' she wrote. 'It can be manipulated at will.' Gender wasn't about the body you were born with; it was a code that could be learnt and unlearnt.

Reed was typically evasive about what *Transformer* meant as a statement. He downplayed glam's cultural significance, telling *Creem* in July 1973 that the vogue for gender-bending and male make-up was just that – a vogue, a fad, 'a style thing . . . like platform shoes . . . The notion that everybody's bisexual is a very popular line right now, but I think its validity is limited. I could say something like if in any way my album helps people decide who or what they are, then I will feel I have accomplished something in my life. But I don't feel that way at all. I don't think an album's gonna do anything. You can't listen to a record and say, "Oh that really turned me onto gay life, I'm gonna be gay." A lot of people will have one or two experiences, and that'll be it. Things may not change one iota.' He even joked that for the follow-up to *Transformer*, 'I may come out with a hardhat album. Come out with an anti-gay song, saying "Get back in your closets, you fuckin' queers!" That'll really do it!'

In fact, Reed's next album was neither *Transformer 2* nor a complete departure. *Berlin* simultaneously reverted to the harsh realism of 'Heroin' and plunged deeper into self-conscious decadence with a sordid song-narrative about the doomed love affair between Jim and the speed-freak Caroline, a couple who lived among fellow exiles in contemporary West Berlin. Breaking with Bowie and Ronson, Reed perversely went even further into lush, orchestrated rock, hiring Bob Ezrin – one of the hottest producers of the moment through his work with Alice Cooper. Ezrin recruited what he liked to call a 'company' of top session musicians in order to realise what he envisioned as a 'film for the ear'. The *Berlin* cast included Jack Bruce, Michael and Randy Brecker, Steve Winwood and Dick Wagner. Ezrin contemptuously dismissed Reed's previous producers for mangling his gift: they had treated Reed 'like a rock'n'roll performer, which is wrong. I mean if you put Louis in a studio with a rock'n'roll band he'll automatically sing loud, which is disastrous because his voice isn't suited for that . . . He's not a rock'n'roller or really even a songwriter as much as he is a dramatic poet . . . In one line Lou Reed can convey a whole space, a flavour, an attitude.'

Reed had never been to the divided German city when he wrote the songs, so why did he call the album *Berlin*? The received image of Weimar-era Berlin as a paradise of chic depravity had been made *au courant* thanks to the movie *Cabaret*. The myth of the Weimar Republic is that the licentiousness and the cynical spirit of gallows humour that flourished in the *Kabarett* clubs led directly to the Third Reich. Nazism is presented as a reaction against 'degenerate art' and the pleasure-enfeebled unmanliness of a demilitarised democracy. *Cabaret* plays along with this idea by juxtaposing jaded decadence and fresh-faced fanaticism in a scene where Prussian playboy aristocrat Maxmilian and his American and English companions Sally and Brian stop off in a Bavarian beer garden. Here, a bright-eyed blond-haired Hitler youth sings 'Tomorrow Belongs to Me' to an audience of villagers, who gradually join in. The pleasure-seeking threesome, carelessly living like there's no tomorrow, don't know it yet but they have no future in this country.

Goodbye to Berlin, the Christopher Isherwood novel on which *Cabaret* is loosely based, actually features a surprisingly slim amount of debauchery. The nightclubs, with their salacious acts and indulgence of sexual kinks, are presented with a tinge of irony: they've become tourist traps, a performance of 'decadence' for the titillation of provincial Germans on a trip to the big bad city and goggle-eyed Americans, who, like visitors from elsewhere in Europe, benefited from the collapse of the German currency and could indulge their appetites for sex and drugs, as well as fine dining and wine, at cut-price rates. In one club scene, Isherwood's narrator observes the stage lesbians, drag queens and pretty-boy exquisites dancing in same-sex pairs, drily noting how every so often a theatrical peal of 'the laughter of the damned' would issue from one clutch of decadents. The novel spends almost as much time on ordinary Berliners and with an idealistic troop of Communist youth scouts as it does on the divinely decadent Sally Bowles, with her tasteless jokes about expensive abortions ('There goes my fur coat'). But even the frivolous Sally of Isherwood's tale is a caricature of the historical figure the character is based on: Jean Ross, a libertine but also a radical who, after leaving

Berlin, became a newspaper correspondent and anti-fascist activist.

By the time Lou Reed wielded it as an album title, then, 'Berlin' as an evocation consisted of compounded layers of exaggeration and myth. It had virtually nothing to do with West Berlin bohemia in the early seventies, which – while certainly druggy – was also a hotbed of countercultural activism. Reacting against the country's recent past, West Germany had probably the most idealistic youth in the world, its student protestors voicing militant opposition to the Vietnam War and neo-imperialism. Since 1949, West Berlin had been a free city affiliated to the Federal Republic of Germany but separated by a hundred miles of Communist-controlled East German territory. Because West Germany's military-service call-up did not apply there, radicals and bohemians flocked to West Berlin. Many formed squat communes in empty buildings left by the steady exodus of residents as a result of the Soviet blockade of 1948–9 and the erection of the Wall in 1961. The political spectrum ran from Greens, pacifists, feminists and autonomists through every conceivable sect of the New Left, right across to paramilitary outfits like the Red Army Faction. There was radical rock, too, most notably Ton Steine Scherben, who formed in 1970, pioneered do-it-yourself by starting their own record label and won a large following for their tough rock and anti-capitalist, pro-liberation lyrics. Although their singer Rio Reiser had been involved in radical theatre and was gay, Ton Steine Scherben could not have been further from Reed and Bowie: the Berlin youth culture they represented was the opposite of decadent. Instead of individual transformation, they were fighting for collective change – a better tomorrow.

When *Transformer* first came out, it received a mixed response. Most of the big-name critics who had built a cult reputation for Reed felt like the album's glam makeover tarnished and trivialised the legacy of the Velvets. Ellen Willis and Lester Bangs both used the put-down 'pseudo-decadence' – a simulation spun for the vicarious titillation of voyeurs, like the tourist-trap cabaret clubs of early-thirties Berlin, in other words. Others, such as Richard Williams, said that it was an album for 'Bowie fans . . . who heard about Lou Reed this year', accusing Reed of self-parody and Bowie of using Reed to enhance his 'status as a kind of cultural vortex around whom the whole rock world spins'.

But these mixed reactions were nothing compared to the slating that *Berlin* received. Critics seemed genuinely repelled by the album's aura of dank malevolence: the gloating, taunting way Reed-as-Jim sang about how Caroline – hooked on speed, a hooker to pay for it – has her kids taken into care by the authorities; the callous ecstasy of his crooned 'Oh, oh, oh, oh, oh, oh, what a feeling', as he contemplates the bed in which their children were conceived and in which she slit her wrists. *Rolling Stone*'s Stephen Davis described it as 'a disaster', filing it under those 'certain records . . . so patently offensive that one wishes to take some kind of physical vengeance on the artists that perpetrate them'. The incongruity of such lavish, cabaret-like orchestration wrapping the decadent package seemed to add salt to the wounds of these embittered Reed believers. Ezrin had entertained expansive plans for a stage version of the album, but, following the poor reception for *Berlin*, quietly shelved them.

Berlin's reputation has recovered over the years – some regard it as a morose masterpiece – but as Reed told the *NME* a few years after its release, 'It was insanity coming off after a hit single ['Walk on the Wild Side']. If I hadn't got it out of my head I would have exploded . . . *Transformer* is a fun album and *Berlin* isn't.'

In 1974, Reed went through a series of visual shifts, leaving behind the campy *Transformer* look for progressively more unsettling images. The cover of *Rock 'n' Roll Animal* – a live album consisting of stocky-stodgy, conventional hard-rock run-throughs of selected Reed classics, with hired guitar gunslinger Dick Wagner backing – showed him looking confrontationally queer in black lipstick, short-cropped hair, diamante choker and similarly glittered wristbands. Then, as if following the Weimar/Nazi logic, he started shaving an Iron Cross into his already skinhead-short hair. Journalists who profiled Reed during this period were aghast at his grey-skinned emaciation and zombie-glazed eyes, the product of a worsening speed addiction.

The culmination of this trajectory was the double album *Metal Machine Music*, four sides of seething, ear-splitting noise, surpassing anything Reed had done with John Cale, jousting with La Monte Young's drones and the abrasive electronics of the European avant-garde. Yet still rock in some remote but real way: rhythm-less, riff-less, but nonetheless electric-guitar music, created from feedback that was then twisted and ravaged even further using tremolo effects, ring modulators and other treatments. In a way, it was the ultimate extension or quintessence of 'shock rock' – a full-body jolt of electrocution. Or abstract punk that sonically surpassed anything that would be produced in 1977, vaulting ahead to industrial music, power electronics and The Jesus and Mary Chain's *Psychocandy* (minus the tunes). Most reviewers dismissed it as unlistenable garbage, a fuck-you to the fans or the record label. But Reed talked it up as a serious bid for composer status, insisting that RCA release it through their classical imprint Red Seal.

The key to *Metal Machine Music* is the second part of its subtitle, 'An Electronic Instrumental Composition *The Amine ß Ring'. That enigmatic, chemistry-evoking phrase led in turn to a footnote at the bottom of the sleeve: 'dextrorotory components synthesis of sympathomimetic musics'. 'Sympathomimetic' is the class of drugs that stimulate the nervous system by mimicking the effects of neurotransmitters like adrenaline and dopamine. *Metal Machine Music* was a methamphetamine symphony, an attempt to convey and hymn the intensities of intravenously injected speed, turn that annihilating rush into an enveloping environment. The album completed a circle begun with 'Heroin' on the first Velvet Underground album: different drug, same pharmacological machismo.

A firm believer in 'Better Living Through Chemistry', Reed was a true connoisseur, contemptuous of those who didn't know the difference between methedrine and methamphetamine, a total snob when it came to purity, provenance and method of administration. Inside the gatefold, an increasingly disjointed sleeve note rambled on about 'those for whom the needle is no more than a toothbrush. Professionals, no sniffers please, don't confuse superiority (no competition) with violence, power or the justifications.' Opaquely referring to 'The Tacit speed agreement with Self', Reed warned of the 'possible negative contraindications' – 'epilepsy (petite mal), psychic motor disorders' – that might be induced by exposure to *MMM*, and then climaxed with the ultimate bohemian bid to out-hip and one-up everybody: 'My week beats your year.'

On *Metal Machine Music*, Reed passed right through decadence and into a sort of private fascism, an impregnable superiority complex glazed into a black mirror of noise.

Mott the Hoople, the next group to be fed through the MainMan career-saviour machine and emerge as pop stars, also represented the Real Thing to Bowie. A 'heavy biker gang' is how Bowie originally imagined the group, recalled singer Ian Hunter, with a hint of bemusement. Nothing could be further from the truth – neither macho nor especially hell-raising, they were a mild-mannered, lower-middle-class bunch from Herefordshire and Shropshire in the provincial west of England.

'I never asked Bowie why he took such an interest in us, but I was told by numerous sources that his image of us was that of

Mott being the only true punk band ever in England,' Hunter told the *NME*. Aged thirty-three in 1972, married and with two kids, Hunter was a little too old to pull off the Kid on the Street persona. But, like Springsteen, he drew on his stockpile of teen memories of small-town life, recalling the way its claustrophobia and boredom had been shattered by the lightning bolt of rock'n'roll arriving from another world to zap England back to life. Mott's music and stage presentation, though, was nothing like 'punk' in the Stooges sense but a thickly swirling, keyboard-laced blues boogie that was fairly par for the course on the mid-level concert-hall circuit of early-seventies Britain.

Bowie's strange projections – 'David falls in love with ideas and he just had to have us,' Hunter told *Melody Maker* – were based on a surprisingly brief infatuation with the group: he'd heard Mott's fourth album, *Brain Capers*, released on Island Records in late 1971, and caught them live just the once. 'I couldn't believe that a band so full of integrity and a really naive exuberance could command such an enormous following and not be talked about,' he enthused. In truth, the following, while loyal, wasn't big enough to sustain the group: none of their albums had penetrated the UK Top 40, and the demoralised, road-weary group – facing the prospect of a 50 per cent wage cut and the loss of their stage-lighting rig – were contemplating packing it in when Bowie saw their show.

Nor were Mott quite the 'naive', integrity-exuding entity Bowie imagined. At the start, they were almost as moulded as The Sweet, the construction of charismatic manager Guy Stevens, who had an obsessive vision of the Ultimate Band and looked around to create it with the raw materials available. 'It's true that Guy did manipulate us into something that was almost purely his idea,' Hunter admitted to the *NME*. Drummer Dale Griffin – better known as Buffin – pegged Stevens as 'the total motivating force behind Mott the Hoople at that time. He *was* Mott the Hoople.' Stevens's concept was simple but strong: 'a band with the balls of The Rolling Stones and the lyrical quality of Dylan', says keyboardist Morgan Fisher, not an original member of Mott but involved during the Bowie era.

Stevens came up with the group's name, and many of the song and album titles too. In one case, 'When My Mind's Gone' was written in real time by Ian Hunter while he was under hypnosis by Stevens – surely a first, even in the extensive annals of rock Svengali-hood! 'It was as if he was singing through me,' Hunter told *ZigZag*. 'Guy stood in front of me with his eyes wild and screaming "you can do it, you can do it" . . . I played and sang these words and then I listened to the playback; it didn't sound like me, it hadn't come from me . . . It was totally Guy. It frightened me to death . . . It all came from him.' 'When My Mind's Gone' appeared on the third Mott album, *Mad Shadows*, on which Stevens is credited for 'spiritual percussion and psychic piano'.

Stevens described his role in the bands he managed as 'a volcano operator . . . I'm like their motor.' His talent was being able to 'recognise talent' and then create the turbulent, electrifyingly unstable vibe in which they could come up with the goods.

A highly strung, pill-gobbling, goblin-like figure with a receding hairline, huge brow and curly side-tufts, Stevens could never have fronted a band himself. But he had a better idea of how rock'n'roll should be put over than most rockers who looked right for the part. An expert on black music, Stevens looked after Island's R&B sub-label Sue. He also worked with Island acts like Spooky Tooth (whose guitarist Luther Grosvenor, later to join Mott using the alias Ariel Bender, remembered Stevens as 'a nightmare genius') and was involved with Procol Harum (another name he came up with). It was while serving a spell in Wormwood Scrubs prison for a drug-fuelled escapade that Stevens read the Willard Manus novel *Mott the Hoople* and decided that it would make a great name for a pipe-dream band that would blend *Let It Bleed* and *Blonde on Blonde*.

He initially tried his ideas out on a group called Silence, who showed promise but lacked an inspiring frontman. So Stevens placed an ad in *Melody Maker*: 'Wanted: Dylan-style singer/pianist. Must be image-conscious and hungry'. Hunter auditioned, even though he was a bassist rather than a pianist. Vocally, he fitted the Dylan-esque bill because 'I didn't know how to sing properly. I had to get it across with my phrasing.' His own role model was Sonny Bono, who vocally made a little go a long way. As for 'hungry', Hunter had been scrabbling for years on the outskirts of the British music biz.

The 'image-conscious' element was a complete bust, however: Hunter, by his own admission, was at that point an overweight slob, with unfashionable short hair and prone to wearing three-piece suits. 'For Guy to see anything in me was quite incredible, because there was nothing there to see,' he recalled. 'There was something about three layers under which he saw but which nobody else has ever seen.' Stevens chose him in part because of the shades he wore – actually a ploy to conceal his pudgy face and weak eyes. These perpetual shades would become Mott's signature, their clichéd 'rock star' quality coming to express the way that Hunter and his band were a commentary on rock'n'roll as much as an enactment of it. Under the guidance of Stevens and the one Mott member who took an interest in clothes, bassist Overend Watts, Hunter became a rock-star cartoon: the shades, the frizz of curly reddish hair, the chalky-white face with its leonine prong of a nose. Even his voice, a nasal, slightly unsteady drawl poised exactly midway between Jagger and Dylan, came across like 'rock'n'roll' in air quotes.

Three of Mott's four Island albums were produced by Stevens, but as a non-musician he was more a catalyst than someone able to offer helpful hints about structure or arrangement. All four records – including the self-produced country-rock effort *Wildlife* – flopped commercially, with sales plateauing for the band at around 20,000.

But Mott had a formidable reputation as a live band. Gigging incessantly (just two days off a month) they shuttled from one end of the UK to the other, packing mid-size concert halls. Guitarist Mick Ralphs told the *NME*, 'People would say Mott the Hoople are okay for a rave-up. They're not much good, but they get everyone going.' Critics warmed to the band because their high-energy rock seemed like a populist alternative to the cerebral convolutions of the progressive sound. Hunter railed against Soft Machine-type groups 'who try to bring jazz into rock . . . Jazz in Britain was middle and upper class-type music. It wasn't balls music.'

Mott also had a down-to-earth approachability that wasn't at all glam but looked ahead to pub rock and the Clash/Sham 69 side of punk. 'All we ever had, at least in the beginning, was our ability to relate to audiences,' Hunter told *Creem*. Roughly equivalent sixties bands like The Who and the Stones were so big they were out of reach. 'Mott translated the Stones into something we could touch,' recalled Kris Needs, president of Mott's fan club The Sea Divers and later a leading punk-era journalist. Future Clash guitarist Mick Jones recalled following Mott all over the UK with other diehard fans, bunking rides on trains and hiding in the toilet to avoid the ticket inspector. 'I'd jump off just before the train got to the station and climb over the fence.' After the gig, they'd sleep on town-hall steps or station platforms. The Clash would eventually recruit Guy Stevens to produce 1979's *London Calling*.

After one last blast with Stevens for *Brain Capers* – the producer hurled chairs at the wall and let off fire extinguishers in a desperate attempt to ignite edgy excitement – Mott were utterly demoralised. None of their records had managed to bottle their live power. Stevens quit Island and spiralled into self-destruction, smashing his entire record collection and drowning in booze: 'I tried pretty hard to kill myself.' The final straw for Mott came when on tour in Europe: they arrived at a venue in Zurich only to discover it was a gas tank.

Bowie had already phoned to offer the as-yet-unrecorded

'Suffragette City' as a potential single. When Overend Watts called him to say 'thanks but no thanks . . . the band is splitting up', Bowie was devastated. 'They were breaking up, I mean, they broke up for three days and I caught them just in time and put them together again,' he told the *NME*. Defries was not keen to take them on – preferring to work with individuals rather than groups – but went along with Bowie's enthusiasm. The manager hooked them up with a new and bigger label, CBS.

'How David Bowie Became Hoople's Fairy Godfather' ran the headline for *Melody Maker*'s 26 August 1972 cover story on Mott's changed fortunes. The turning point was the second song Bowie offered Mott: 'All the Young Dudes' was both a sure-fire hit and a tune that Mott could make their own. The stately trudge of the groove, the autumnal organ swirls, the swaying hymn-like chorus all added up to an archetypal Majestic Rock Anthem, perhaps even a stereotype of one. It found the sweet singalong patch between 'A Whiter Shade of Pale' and 'Hey Jude'. Imitating the steadily ascending melody struc-ture, 'Dudes' rose to #3 in August 1972 (higher than any Bowie single to date) and would go on to crack the Top 40 in America.

'All the Young Dudes' was understood at the time – and has been ever since – as an anthem for the third generation of rock fans. There was the reference to being 'too young for all that revolution jive' of the sixties bands like the Stones and Beatles; the cast list of disaffected, ambisexual youths like Freddy (who scars his cheeks when he pulls off the glitter stars) and Lucy (who dresses like a queen); even an echo of The Who's 'My Generation' declaration 'Hope I die before I get old' in the bit about Billy and his plan to top himself aged twenty-five. Ironically, Hunter himself had overshot that *Logan's Run*-like cut-off point by a good eight years. In fact, he was actually old enough to count as first generation, able to remem-ber rock'n'roll when it first hit.

There's also a recruitment-drive air to 'Dudes', marshalling youth into an undefined but potentially potent movement. In the song's long fade, Hunter shouts out to the audience with beseeching rally cries of 'I wanna see you, hear you, talk to you – all of you'. Mott talked up their anthem in these terms, too: Ralphs claimed 'our audiences are really young. They are like a new generation' and predicted that sixties hangover bands like Black Sabbath were done for because 'the kids will want bands of the Seventies'. (In reality, Mott's Stones plus Dylan formula was utterly sixties, while Sabbath – all under twenty-five in 1972 – actually co-invented one of the seventies' true new music movements in heavy metal.)

Actually, 'Dudes' had never been intended to speak to or for a new generation. It was a *Ziggy Stardust* off-cut, as Bowie later explained to William Burroughs in *Rolling Stone*. The line about the dudes who 'carry the news', he said, related to the doomsday scenario of Earth in entropic decline. Ziggy's adviser tells him to collect and sing the news, in the absence of newspapers. But the news is all terrible. 'All the Young Dudes', Bowie insisted, is 'about this news. It is no hymn to the youth as people thought. It is completely the opposite.'

But in pop music, reception is reality: the meaning of a pop lyric is partially created by what listeners make of it, as opposed to the artist's intent. The capacity of fans and critics to project and misread generally served Bowie's lyrical opacities very well, as it had for Dylan.

In the US, 'Dudes' was taken as a song of gay or bisexual liberation: according to *Creem*, it 'practically became the national anthem of the newly gay' in 1972. Critic Mark Dery has tracked the etymology of 'dude' back to the Oscar Wilde era, where it meant 'a fop or exquisite', a dandy excessively refined in their dress, speech and manners. Fascinating as this is, by the seventies 'dude' was more likely to be the parlance of surfers, skateboarders, stoners and other slacker-y, scruffy young straights, for whom it served the same function as 'man' or a contemporary term like 'bro'.

Truth is, Mott were as hetero as they come, and weren't shy about letting folks know, using lingo of the era that would ignite a Twitterstorm today. 'We ain't fairies – not one guy in the band is,' Hunter insisted to the *NME* in 1972. 'The last thing we want to be called is camp. There's only one person who can do that well and that is David. And he's not a fairy.' Although Mick Ralphs tried to fend off the view that Mott were Bowie's puppets, claiming they always 'used to love dressing up . . . Victorian clothes . . . all sorts of props . . . We were into the theatre of rock thing even then,' in truth the guitarist was deeply uncomfortable with the 'Dudes' direction. His gut impulses lay with bluesy raunch and eventually he split to form the arena-conquering Bad Company with Free frontman Paul Rodgers.

Most of the *All the Young Dudes* album stayed within that gritty-but-groovy mould (indeed, 'Ready for Love' would be repurposed by Bad Company in a few years as a hit single). Guy Stevens's original Stones-meets-Dylan conception of Mott could still be detected in songs like 'Sucker', sidewinding along on a cowbell pulse and sinuously woozy horns. Bowie's input as producer came through mainly in the 'cleaner and clearer' sound and in the choice of 'Sweet Jane' from *Loaded* as the opening cut. This was clearly Bowie implanting his own obsessions: he even got Lou Reed, in town for the recording of *Transformer*, to lay down a guide vocal so that Hunter could get the phrasing right.

Oddly, the mentoring influence of Bowie is way more evident as a sort of delayed effect on the next album, *Mott*, which the band produced themselves. After 'Dudes' was a hit, Bowie had urged Hunter 'to write more songs like this', recalls Morgan Fisher. 'You've got to write more pop-oriented material. And Ian took him seriously and really tried, and succeeded.' A string of big hit singles followed – 'All the Way from Memphis', 'Honaloochie Boogie', 'Roll Away the Stone' – all of which owed more to the *Hunky Dory/Ziggy* template of well-structured, nostalgia-tinged rock'n'roll than to what Mott had been doing for the four albums before Bowie showed up.

On *Mott*, Ian Hunter was credited as arranger, something he'd never been before. This power shift was also down to Bowie's influence: he'd been whispering in Hunter's ear that he really needed to push himself forward as the leader of the band, hitherto a directionless democracy. Bowie also encouraged Hunter to abandon the existing stage set-up (two keyboard players flanking either side of the stage, Hunter being one of them) and seize the foreground. Eventually Hunter gave up playing piano altogether and took up rhythm guitar for the more classic rock-frontman role. 'He soon became a riff-meister,' recalls Fisher. 'It was a bit like working with Keith Richards.' These shifts in the inter-band balance of power contributed to Ralphs's departure shortly after *Mott* was completed.

Still, it is undeniable that the Bowie-fied Mott the Hoople were a vastly improved group: there's no earthly reason why anyone today would listen to *Mad Shadows* or *Brain Capers*, but *Mott* is a seventies classic. Partly that's because few records sound more quintessentially first-half-of-the-seventies. Yet, paradoxically, what makes the songs so reflective of their era is the way their gaze is often turned back to the past: the fifties and sixties, the first and second generations of rock rather than the third. A gift for writing rock-about-rock songs had reared its head previously ('Rock and Roll Queen' on the debut declared – presumptuously, prematurely – 'I'm just a rock and roll star'). There was something in the air too: over the next few years, emerging artists like Bruce Springsteen and Patti Smith would make subject matter out of rock mythology, rock's lost promise, rock as salvation and liberation theology. Mott songs, likewise, increasingly addressed the trials and tribulations of being a struggling band chasing stardom but gradually losing touch with the spark that ignited their quest in the first place.

Hence, *Mott* songs like 'Ballad of Mott the Hoople (March 26,

1972 – Zurich)'. As the subtitle indicated, it told the tale of that crisis in confidence when the group almost gave up the ghost. Hunter tots up the toll taken on each member of the group – the lines on the face of organ player Verden Allen, drummer Buffin losing his child-like sheen of innocence – before turning to his own story: how he changed his name in hope of winning fame (actually he'd just dropped the surname Patterson in favour of his middle name, Hunter), crossed the sea to tour America, grew disillusioned ('behind these shades the visions fade') but never stopped aching for the prize. 'Rock 'n' roll's a loser's game / It mesmerises and I can't explain.' Mining the same seam of jadedness, 'All the Way from Memphis' is an oblique road yarn about a misplaced guitar, loosely based on something that happened to Ralphs. Shamed for his negligence by another musician, the narrator muses about how 'as your name gets hot so your heart grows cold' and 'you look like a star but you're still on the dole'.

By the early seventies, there were plenty of bands whose subject matter shrank to rock'n'roll itself and the lifestyle of touring: it's an occupational hazard. Hunter went further than anybody else at that time, though, by publishing his road journal as a book, *Diary of a Rock Star*. Jotted down in real time during a five-week tour of the US in the winter of 1972, the book documented what it was like to be a band 'neither big nor small in America' ('Dudes' had perforated the lowest reaches of the Top 40, and the album peaked at #89 in *Billboard*). Hunter described *Diary* as 'like a letter to a fan in the front row at the Rainbow, a diary to keep in touch. It's meant as a buzz for the people who dig us and will never be able to go to the places we travel.' In one passage, he explains in detail what it's like to take a long-distance airplane flight, for the benefit of 'those of you who have never flown' – a reminder that the horizons of an average young person, particularly in the UK, were decidedly narrow in the seventies.

Yet *Diary* was no glimpse of rock-star glamour. Hunter's down-to-earth nature and bullshit-proof scepticism inclined him to demystify, almost compulsively highlighting the humdrum aspects of the touring lifestyle: the soundchecks, the patches of dead time punctuated by visits to instrument shops or jet-lagged vegging out by the hotel pool. There wasn't much in the way of sleaze either: Mott weren't into drugs much, and groupies, he claimed, were an annoyance: 'lousy lays as a rule and you can never get rid of them once you've let them in', plus 'you run a big risk in the dose stakes if you decide to dabble'.

Hunter once told *Melody Maker* that the reason he was in a rock'n'roll band was 'because you never know what's gonna happen next'. But *Diary* really showed the opposite: random excitements occurred, for sure, but pretty soon it became a grind, the same types – promoters, sound engineers, liggers, groupies – recurring in town after town. 'I just wanted to give the readers an insight on what it's really like being in a rock 'n' roll band and how incredibly boring it is travelling around,' Hunter told the *NME*.

America lapped up Mott's shtick. The music was just right, perfectly pitched between the new Brit thing (Bowie et al.) and the old Brit thing (Stones, Faces, Humble Pie); between the stuff that wasn't selling in America yet and the stuff that had never stopped selling. *Creem*'s readership voted 'All the Young Dudes' the #2 single of 1972. *Rolling Stone*, named in double homage to the Stones and Dylan, could not fail to love a band that fused the two. American critics who revered Rod Stewart as rock's most lyrical storyteller loved the tender side of Hunter's songwriting, plaintive slowies like 'I Wish I Was Your Mother' and 'Sea Diver'. The fact that Hunter clearly worshipped the US ('I kissed the ground when I got there,' he recalled of landing in the country for the first time) and littered his lyrics with American place names also went down well.

Another part of Mott's appeal to American critics was the

incorrect image of them as punks, a gang of everykids mooching disaffected and surly along Main Street. Although too old and too mild
to fit that role really, Mott did have a line of street-ruckus songs:
'Violence', 'One of the Boys', 'Crash Street Kidds'. The standout
tune on *Mott*, 'Violence' was the perfect merger of old Mott and
new Mott: Ralphs's low-slung riff grind and Hunter's lurching snarl
collided with a camp simper of a backing vocal (Hunter himself,
doubling as a sort of fey devil-on-his-own-shoulder, inciting him to
aggro) and the unexpected entrance of a flamboyant violin solo (a
cute pun – violins, violence). This last element was a pure chance
inclusion: an eccentric, dishevelled session musician called Graham
Preskett happened to be hanging around the studio and was roped
into the session.

Bitterly bitching about teachers and preachers, complaining
about having nothing to do and nowhere to go, and ending with the
sounds of a simulated street fight, 'Violence' seemed to be Hunter
writing about – and perhaps writing to – a younger version of himself. 'That was me, that street kid image,' Hunter told the *NME* in
1974, talking more generally about the retrospective gaze of many
of his songs. 'I've never lost it. And as I get further and further away
from it in some ways, it's easier for me to write about that situation,
and easier for me to see it all more clearly.' In his case, that 'situation' was growing up repressed and oppressed, feeling like he might
be 'mental' but bottling up all the doubt and rage. Hunter's background was 'tight-reined': his father, a policeman, was 'a very bitter
man'. Leaving the Shrewsbury grammar school that bored him to
death, he became a miscreant, hanging out in billiard halls, keeping
the company of minor criminals and working his way through something like twenty dead-end jobs.

Then Hunter decided that rock'n'roll could be his escape route
from the 'heart attack machine' of the factory. 'Honaloochie
Boogie', he said, was 'about being on the streets of Northampton

with no money about, and then a kid turns you onto rock and roll'. Seeing the rock'n'roll nostalgia movie *That'll Be the Day*, set in fifties England, 'reminded me of my days as a kid at the Town Hall dance. All the kids know is rock and roll.' A strange circularity – a cycle of illusionment and disillusionment – started to characterise Hunter's songwriting. The experience of rock'n'roll package tours and concerts made Hunter want to be a rocker: to experience that excitement from the inside. But what seems like supreme glory to kids in Nowheresville turns out to be a different drudgery. An Event for the audience is routine for the band.

The encroaching fear of becoming a cog in the rock machine inspired songs on *The Hoople*, the album that followed *Mott*. On 'Marionette', Hunter snarls defiance as he struggles to avoid being turned into a puppet ('I ain't one yet') but ultimately loses his 'will to fight' and goes out moaning, 'Oh God, these wires are so tight.' In 'Through the Looking Glass', the dressing-room mirror shows the wear and tear exacted by the touring grind, the lines and 'dark accusing eyes' poking through the greasepaint; in the end the star smashes the mirror. Looking back on Mott's 1972–4 peak decades later, Hunter said, 'When you finally get it, there's nothing there.'

MainMan and Bowie propelled their ascent. But Mott soon broke with Defries, finding the manager too preoccupied with Bowie's career. (He in turn did not like dealing with a group where five individuals had to be consulted on every decision.) The group also moved to distance themselves from Bowie and glam. The result was some pretty ungracious and undignified backsliding. Talking to *Creem* about the self-produced and entirely self-written *Mott*, Hunter stressed that 'I psyched up against Bowie for the album. I mean, I even told him about it.' He ludicrously asserted that while 'David helped us . . . I think we gave him as much as he gave us, for reasons I won't go into now . . .'

The protestations grew shriller and less convincing: 'It has been said that David created Mott's image. That is totally untrue . . . We had our own image beforehand. And I would say our involvement did damage us.' The ingratitude – 'I never learned a thing from Bowie, not one iota . . . it's completely wrong to say Mott were influenced in any way' – must surely have stung their erstwhile patron. Even Ralphs, now strutting his bluesy stuff in Bad Company, got in on the Bowie-bashing: 'One good thing about this tour, there aren't all those poseurs about . . . all these manicurists and hairdressers and all. We got REAL KIDS coming to see us.'

Yet despite Mott's efforts to put distance between themselves and 'the fag rock craze', as they charmingly put it, their whole direction had been turned around by Bowie, who was really their second Guy Stevens. Nowhere was this more evident than in their sense of style and approach to stage performance. Photographs of Mott in 1973–4 show them to have been one of the glam era's most garishly attired groups. Overend Watts, in particular, seemed to be competing with Gary Glitter, favouring thigh-high boots in silver or cherry and open-torso tunics in glitzy fabric, and once even spraying a silver cross over his hairy chest. Morgan Fisher anticipated late-glam fops like Sailor and Cockney Rebel with his debonair look: white beret, twirled moustache, 'Mr Piano'-style jacket with ivory keys, and even a Liberace-style candelabra on top of his instrument.

Another sign of Bowie's influence – and proof that Mott gladly embraced glam's showbiz drift – was their week-long run of performances at New York's Uris Theatre in May 1974. This prestige-boosting manoeuvre (no rock band had previously done a Broadway residency) was the bright idea of their new US manager, Fred Heller. Theatrical accompaniments were devised to enhance the songs. For 'Marionette', recalls Morgan Fisher, 'we had puppets onstage. They were quite large, almost life-size, and they needed operators dressed in black so they couldn't be seen.' Fisher says they also had a moving figure made by Roger Ruskin Spear, from

The Bonzo Dog Doo-Dah Band: 'a feather-brained soldier where you pressed a button and feathers fall out over his head. Ridiculous, now I think of it . . . but it sort of seemed to fit. The Uris shows were the peak of our flashy-dressing period as well.' The rock'n'roll circus continued during the intermission: the punters milling in the foyer were entertained by clowns, a juggler, a glass swallower, a magician and a balancing-dog act.

If Mott really wanted to distance themselves from glam, it is surprising that they teamed up with Mick Ronson, whose post-Spiders from Mars solo career was sputtering. In 1974, a Ronson-enhanced Mott seemed like a world-conquering proposition; Angie Bowie sent a telegram saying it was the wedding of the year. While Hunter was ecstatic, other members of Mott were uneasy about incorporating a superstar.

On the eve of a major tour, their first with Ronson, the weight of worry induced a nervous collapse in Hunter. After a stay in hospital, he left the group on medical advice. 'Maybe we could have worked it out, if Ian had sat down with us and said, "I'm not feeling well,"' muses Fisher, attributing the failure to do this to the classic English inability to talk about emotions. The remainder of the group dropped the second part of their name and continued, fruitlessly, as Mott. Hunter, restored after a rest, launched a solo career focused on breaking America, for much of which he reunited with Ronson as collaborator and co-producer. He also recorded with members of Springsteen's E Street Band and had one album produced by his former fan Mick Jones.

The only recorded relic of Ronson's brief stint in Mott was '(Do You Remember the) Saturday Gigs', a valedictory song that ran through Mott's entire career verse by verse: playing at the Roundhouse in 1969, nearly quitting in '72, getting duded-up in glitz and platform boots in '73, but by '74 'we didn't much like dressing up no more'. The price of admission to concerts went up

– from the pre-decimal currency twelve shillings and six pence to two pounds. But what was on sale – 'a fairy tale' – remained the same. The kids needed the fantasy, so they kept on buying. The last words of the song were 'So long'. Mott's inspiration had exhausted itself. And they'd exhausted the public's interest: 'Saturday Gigs' stalled just outside the Top 40.

Bowie had succeeded in turning around the careers of Lou Reed and Mott the Hoople. In both cases, he influenced their sound and image more than either cared to admit, giving them the modish makeovers that propelled them into the pop charts. But Bowie's other salvage project of 1972 – transforming Iggy Pop into a star – did not work out so well. The very quality that made Iggy so attractive to him – his rampaging realness – also made him intractable. At the Dorchester hotel press conference where Bowie showed off his hero-protégés Lou and Iggy, he had raved about The Stooges' frontman's sense of 'natural theatre. It's very interesting because it doesn't conform to any standards or rules or structures of theatre. It's his own . . . just a Detroit theatre that he's brought with him. It's straight from the street.' But this same wildness was what would prove so challenging to tame or tidy up for mass consumption.

Bowie had first heard The Stooges through the American rock writer John Mendelsohn. Now regarded as classic rock albums, the band's self-titled 1969 debut and 1970 follow-up *Fun House* had been ignored or actively abhorred by nearly all critics and discerning rock fans. 'They were very obscure,' recalls Mendelsohn. But he remembers Bowie reacting 'with delight' on first exposure to songs like 'I Wanna Be Your Dog'. The obsession deepened after Bowie's return to the UK, where he played *The Stooges* and *Fun House* over and over again. A line from *Fun House*'s blazing 'TV Eye' would seep, mangled, into his new song 'Moonage Daydream' – 'She's got her TV eye on me' became 'Put your electric eye on me, babe.'

Ultimately, Bowie would score one of his biggest UK hits of the glam era with a song partly inspired by Iggy, 'The Jean Genie'. At a press conference shortly after the single hit #2 in winter 1972, Bowie was asked if the title was a reference to Jean Genet. He replied that it would have been 'marvellous' if that was the case, but it was in fact inspired by Iggy, as well as the street-punk characters you might run into in the more ragged parts of downtown New York. Very soon – not wanting to squander this cool-enhancing misinterpretation – Bowie would incorporate the Jean Genet/Jean Genie connection into his official account of the song's genesis, linking it to Lindsay Kemp's 'fantastic production' of *Our Lady of the Flowers*. 'It was very, very sub-conscious, but I think it's probably there . . . [*Flowers* has] always been in the back of my mind.'

More than the actual music of The Stooges, it was Iggy as a personality who so impressed Bowie: Iggyism as a way of walking through the world – although strutting, prowling, marauding through the world was more like it. That and 'natural theatre' – the kinetic grace of the contortions and torsions he put his body through, the splits and back-bends that made you flinch and gasp, even seeing them decades later in photographs. The self-inflicted harm and self-degrading humiliation: smearing his torso with peanut butter, slashing his chest with a broken drumstick, writhing on shards of smashed glass. Iggy would crawl on all fours like some feral half-human. On one occasion the Ig even bit guitarist Ron Asheton 'on the balls – bad', recalled his victim.

Then there was the famous incident in the summer of 1970 at the Cincinnati Pop Festival, which took place at a gigantic baseball stadium and was filmed for a TV show: Iggy striding into the crowd on top of their upstretched hands, a Dionysian Christ walking on human water. The photo of that moment – Iggy frozen in a triumphant pose, defying gravity, in complete command of his audience – circulated widely and must have impacted Bowie as an unreachable ideal of performance taken to the limit.

The opposition between Iggy as chaos in human form and Bowie as contrived and calculated is a familiar one. It maps onto the long established Dionysian versus Apollonian distinction that Nietzsche laid out in *The Birth of Tragedy from the Spirit of Music*, an 1872 work that could be taken as the first major contribution to rock criticism, even though written eighty years before rock'n'roll came into being. (Bowie and Iggy were both enthusiastic readers of Nietzsche; there's a 1980 clip of Iggy on the Tom Snyder show, where he discusses his work in terms of the Dionysian/Apollonian divide.) Summarised crudely, Apollonian art is orderly, structural and creates pictures in your mind; it tends towards serenity, sanity and clarity. The Dionysian current in art, poetry and, above all, music stirs the unruly mob of emotion and sensuality; it intoxicates and maddens, clouds vision and, at the ultimate degree, approaches the blackout of oblivion or frenzy. The greatest art, for Nietzsche, involves some kind of fusion or balance between the Apollonian and the Dionysian. Still, there remains a fundamental conflict between the image-making faculty, which tends towards pose and poise, and the abstract turbulence of sound, which tends towards self-loss. This tension is especially evident in pop, a hybrid of the visual and the sonic, but also of the verbal – lyrics, interviews, hype and publicity.

Allies and critical champions of Iggy have often translated this Dionysian versus Apollonian divide into stereotypes about national character: American looseness versus British uptightness. Leee Black Childers, one of the MainMan staff, once described Bowie as a 'wimpy little South London art student' unable to 'achieve the reality that Iggy was born into'. Actually, Bowie never went to art school or college of any kind (having left school aged sixteen), and it was Iggy who went into higher education, albeit briefly, studying anthropology at the University of Michigan. The truth is that Iggy, in his own way, was just as arty and intellectual as the Englishman. Furthermore, 'Iggy Pop' was a character, a persona invented by James Osterberg.

Where Iggy differed from Bowie was that he was far more fearless and committed about his total immersion in the persona. Fuelled by drugs, it verged on a kind of catastrophic method-acting that spilled off the stage and into everyday life. *NME* journalist Nick Kent, who spent a good amount of time in Iggy's company, discovered that the Osterberg/Iggy split was like Jekyll and Hyde. Rather than triggered by taking a serum, it all depended on how you addressed him: 'Jim' was affable and lucid, but call him 'Iggy' and the feral-puerile punk was unleashed. Eventually, though, as the drugs took over, the Iggy self was 'on' all the time.

The Stooges also started out in 1967 as a surprisingly arty proposition, a free-form noise outfit inspired by the hobo composer Harry Partch, who built his own unique instruments, such as the Cloud Chamber Bowls and the Gourd Tree, based around highly unorthodox tuning systems and scales. The Psychedelic Stooges, as they were originally known, struck fifty-gallon oil drums with mallets, attached microphones to vacuum cleaners and kitchen blenders, and built a feedback-funnelling device called the Jim-A-Phone. In addition to Partch, they listened to avant-garde composers like John Cage and Robert Ashley, and ethnological recordings from Africa and Indonesia (Iggy was a member of the university's Gamelan Society). All this while the supposedly arty Bowie was still besotted with Anthony Newley and dreaming of writing a West End musical.

The Psychedelic Stooges' rare performances had a chaotic theatricality not so far from the early Alice Cooper or The Crazy World of Arthur Brown: Iggy plucked out his eyebrows and painted his face white; he might wear a maternity dress or dance 'on an amplified washboard wearing . . . spiked golf shoes', in critic Ben Edmonds's description, 'his head a Medusa tangle of tinfoil snakes'. Seeing The Doors was a major inspiration. Morrison's goading of the audience, the creation, through unpredictability and impropriety, of a real Event rather than just a show, pointed Iggy in the direction of the 'natural theatre' that Bowie admired so much: high-stakes drama that didn't have anything to do with props, sets or routines, but was all about how far you could push the audience and push yourself.

Musically, the breakthrough for The Stooges was the realisation that stupidity could be smarter, that 'sophistication' (in the sense of eclecticism and versatility) was actually for the unsophisticated middlebrow. 'I realised that if we played at a university, people who were highly intelligent and creative like the professors might get it, but the students wouldn't get it because they're herd mentality or they wouldn't be in college in the first place,' Iggy recalled. The decision to shift from art-noise to lumpen-puerile aggression was an attempt to reach 'high school drop-outs, troubled drug kids, kids who were so totally into music that it wasn't just a part of a life-style'. The fact that The Stooges couldn't play that well gave them an advantage. 'I thought that gave us a good "in" for disaffected youth.' For his lyrics, Iggy deliberately simplified the language, a brilliant impersonation of an inarticulate, substance-impaired teen-ager, resulting in timeless haikus of restlessness and rage, lust and boredom: 'Real Cool Time', 'No Fun', 'Little Doll' . . .

Thanks to far-sighted A&R man Danny Fields, The Stooges and their Michigan allies The MC5 were signed to Elektra in 1968, even though that label's roster was for the most part oriented towards the same college-educated audience that *Rolling Stone* and progressive FM radio catered to and Iggy disdained. The 1969 self-titled debut was produced by John Cale and greeted with the same puzzled contempt as The Velvet Underground's first album. *Rolling Stone* described it as 'loud, boring, tasteless, unimaginative and childish', the work of 'stoned sloths making . . . repressed music', and a feature in the magazine the following year even came with a disclaimer: 'Warning: The following article does not constitute an endorsement of current phonographic products.'

The second Stooges album *Fun House* got an even poorer reception. That seems so odd and wrong today, when it clearly stands out as the most powerful hard-rock album of all time. *Fun House* was fatally out of synch with 1970, the downbeat year it came out, a year of singer-songwriters and tasty, bluesy licks. Only a few people then had any time for the sound of absolute abandon that The Stooges were making, or unleashing. Iggy and the band used to talk about the O-Mind: a paradoxical state of hyper-alert oblivion where 'reckless' and 'wrecked' merge, fuelled by the full pharmacopeia of stimulants and psychedelics. More than drugs, though, it was amplified sound itself that seemed to alter consciousness through physical vibration: an obliterating roar. 'It is the proximity of the electric hum in the background and just the tremendous feeling of buoyancy and power . . .' Iggy testified. Recalling his compulsion 'to use the noises on myself, as if I were a scientist experimenting on himself, like Dr Jekyll or the Hulk', Iggy described how he became 'a human electronic tool creating this sort of buzzing, throbbing music'.

Elektra hated *Fun House*, all but a few far-sighted critics loathed it, and radio wouldn't go near the band. Their masterpiece universally spurned and scorned, The Stooges disbanded. Iggy made a desultory attempt to get a new thing going with his old Detroit guitarist pal James Williamson, but hard drugs had him in their grip. By late 1971, Iggy seemed thoroughly washed up. Then, while crashing out at Danny Fields's apartment in New York for a spell, he received a phone call from his host, who urged Iggy to come down to Max's Kansas City to meet some people who were interested in jump-starting his career.

'I was sittin' around Danny Fields' one night watching *Mr Smith Goes to Washington* and I was deep into it,' recalled Iggy three

years later (during a 1974 interview with *Creem* magazine). That
fateful late-'71 night, Fields kept calling and calling, saying, 'Listen,
man, do yourself a favour,' and pointing out that one of them was
Bowie, the guy who'd said in *Melody Maker* recently that Iggy was
his favourite singer. At last, Iggy pulled himself away from Jimmy
Stewart on the TV and made it to Max's Kansas City. 'I finally stroll
in, y'know, and there's Bowie and Tony Defries and a couple of the
company freaks. So I hit it off with David and Tony . . . They said,
"Are you hungry?" . . . I hadn't eaten in about four days, so they took
me out and I ordered two dinners.' Bowled over by Bowie's enthusiasm, but most of all by Defries's big talk, Iggy effectively signed to
MainMan by the night's end.

Soon his new manager secured an audience with Clive Davis, the
president of Columbia Records. After regaling the bigwig with a
rendition of the showbiz standard 'The Shadow of Your Smile', Iggy
was signed to Columbia in a $100,000 deal. He told *Melody Maker*
that one minute he was 'on the bum with no plans and no food', the
next he had a record deal and was on the plane to England to record
an album.

Iggy had been signed as a solo artist, and Bowie's initial proposal
was that he and Defries would hook him up with a British backing band. Among the names suggested were Third World War. This
would actually have been a decent English approximation of the
Detroit street-rock vibe, for Third World War had been conceived
as the UK's first real working-class 'aggro' band, singing hard-left
political songs like 'Get Out of Bed You Dirty Red' and 'I'd Rather
Cut Cane for Castro'. Another name mentioned was hairy Ladbroke
Grove staples The Edgar Broughton Band.

But the very idea of inserting Iggy into existing bands (both of
whom already had lead singers) showed how Bowie and Defries
'had a very pop mentality in the way they did things', as Iggy put
it. Neither understood that band-as-bloodbrothers mentality that

was such a huge part of the Stooges spirit. They saw musicians as interchangeable components, employees to be hired and fired. But then for Defries, the star was an employee too: Iggy was on the same demeaning contract as Bowie. The $100,000 from CBS went to MainMan as the production company; Iggy never got to touch it. With some bitterness, Iggy would later talk about how 'I signed my soul. He talked me into it.'

In the event, Iggy asked to bring James Williamson over with him to England. Once they were there they fended off the various candidates presented to them for the rhythm section, on the grounds that they were insufficiently aggressive. Eventually, Ron Asheton and his drummer brother Scott were flown over and The Stooges were effectively reconstituted, albeit with Williamson now the lead guitarist and Asheton relegated to bass. According to Iggy, making a third album with The Stooges had always been his game plan.

Bowie had talked of producing Iggy's comeback album, like he had *Transformer* and *All the Young Dudes*. But when Iggy politely demurred, he backed away. 'That was the beginning and end of that conversation,' recalled Iggy. 'There was never any pressure or anything like that.' The Stooges were left pretty much to their own devices during the recording of *Raw Power*, with nobody from MainMan even checking in on their progress.

Iggy often wrote songs in Kensington Gardens, in the south-west corner of Hyde Park, directly opposite the Royal Garden Hotel, where they were stationed in typical MainMan swank. 'Search and Destroy', the album's opening salvo, came from reading a *Time* magazine article on the Vietnam War, while snorting heroin 'under those grand English oak trees . . . on a summer day in civilized Merrie Olde'. The recorded version featured a simulated sword fight buried deep in the mix. 'We got some old sabres from an antique store . . . I wanted sword-fighting and boot-stomping.'

When The Stooges sent demos for Defries to inspect, the

Svengali was horrified by the muddy production and the flagrant anti-commercialism, and, one senses, there was an instinctive revulsion from the music's kamikaze realness, which went way beyond anything that could be presented to the public as entertainment. Defries 'just went completely apeshit', recalled Iggy. 'Like "I would *never* allow you to put out anything like this! This is not music!" . . . Just out and out flat refused to put it out.' With hindsight, Iggy conceded that the mix was too abrasive: everything was maxed out in the red, an effect that today's recording engineers actively seek out and achieve through compression (flattening out the dynamics in the music so that the loudness levels never dip). But in the seventies, such levels of blare were aberrant in the extreme.

MainMan dispatched The Stooges to Los Angeles, ostensibly to rehearse for a huge tour. Once they were out of the way, the band were told by phone that *Raw Power* would not be released in its present state. Bowie would remix it and save the day. The session took place at Western Studios, Hollywood – 'a very poorly lit, cheap old studio', Iggy recalled – and lasted only a few days (Defries clearly keen not to sink any more money into what he regarded as a lost cause). The result – credited to both Bowie and Iggy – launched one of rock history's most enduring controversies. To those who had never heard Iggy and his band before, who had only ever heard of them at all thanks to the Bowie connection, *Raw Power* was a sort of initiation riot: punk's first blast, a full three years ahead of schedule. But anybody who had heard the debut or, especially, *Fun House* found the mix lopsided: in critic Joe Carducci's words, Bowie seems almost wilfully to 'frustrate the rock sense' of the band. Instead of a seething murk of smelted sound, the lead guitar and voice leap out with undue prominence, while the drums and bass feel suppressed.

The songs and the ferocity of their performance cut through anyway. But most fans concur with Iggy's misgivings: 'It's always sounded fragile and rickety . . . The sound of the thing is *weedy*. It's

a beautiful weedy little record.' Iggy would remix the album himself in 1997 to bring out the latent monstrousness, only to produce
something much worse: a compression-addled, red-zone blare that
hurts the ear and even gets you sympathising with the way Tony
Defries recoiled when he heard the demos in 1972.

In his sleeve note for the remixed *Raw Power*, Iggy tried his best
to be diplomatic towards his benefactor's efforts. But in the immediate aftermath of the album's original release, Iggy railed to *Creem*
that 'half the time the good parts were mixed out by that fuckin'
carrot-top . . . sabotaged'. Ron Asheton complained, 'It got artsy-
fartsied up too much.'

This approach to The Stooges calls into question the extent to
which Bowie ever really viscerally understood rock. In interviews,
praising his heroes turned reclamation project, he would always
describe Iggy (as he did with Lou Reed) as a great 'writer': as if
these compositions could become standards, have any kind of life
separate from their embodied enactment by Iggy. Iggy had a spectacular physical presence, but his essence was always too kinetic to
be reduced to a pose. In the end, the blinding black storm of the
music was what it was all about.

That's why The Stooges could never really coexist with glam.
They flirted with the imagery for a moment. A photo of Iggy in
silver lamé jeans, black lipstick and thick black eyeliner, taken at
the King's Cross Cinema show in July 1972, appeared on the cover
of *Raw Power*. MainMan tried to channel the group along their
standard 'superstar' trajectory, which meant making Iggy the absolute focus: the credit reads 'Iggy and the Stooges', yet both sides of
the cover were plastered with images of the singer, with the band
nowhere to be seen.

But there is nothing androgynous or fey about The Stooges. *Raw
Power* is riddled with hyper-phallic masculinity in the form of militaristic imagery ('Search and Destroy', with its references to 'a heart

full of napalm') or slam-bam sexual aggression ('Penetration'). As a drama of energy, Stooges songs are about ignition, blast-off and explosive impact. Or they're a steady-state pummel of intransitive aggression, as with the title track 'Raw Power', 'Shake Appeal' and the closing 'Death Trip'. The latter, Iggy claims, was written when he realised that the relationship with MainMan was going off the rails, that the band was doomed. But he didn't care because this music was the mission he had to complete.

After *Raw Power* came out – to plaudits but modest sales – The Stooges were maintained by MainMan in an LA limbo. They holed up in a house in the Hollywood Hills that had recently been acquired by Defries, running up bills on drugs and having sex with groupies from the Sunset Strip glitter scene. Like soldiers kept out of action – in their case, a tour that MainMan refused to set up on the grounds that there's 'no demand for you' – the band sank into decadence. MainMan 'kept us happy and dumb, just stupid, in that luxury', spat Asheton. There were rumours that Defries still entertained notions of separating Iggy from Williamson and the other Stooges and making good on his investment by turning him into a solo act. There was even talk of Iggy as a film star, playing the part of Peter Pan: the Wild Boy who never grew up.

'The Jean Genie', Bowie's song about 'an Iggy-type character', was written during the US leg of the 'Ziggy Stardust' tour and recorded in New York in October 1972. The single was Bowie's first really huge hit, reaching #2 in the UK that winter of '72 into '73, although it was swiftly overtaken by The Sweet's 'Blockbuster', which reached #1 with a very different take on the same primordial Yardbirds/Bo Diddley riff. Where the Sweet song's production was ultra-modern, 1972 pop rock at its most state-of-art studio-processed, 'The Jean

308 SHOCK AND AWE

Genie' was a deliberate throwback to the bluesy, harmonica-laced sound of British beat music in the mid-sixties. Bowie said that he was aiming for the sound of The Rolling Stones' 1964 debut album: 'I didn't get that near to it, but it had a feel that I wanted – that '60s thing.'

Almost as if re-rooting himself after the disorientation of the US tour, Bowie's next album pivoted back to British reference points. *Aladdin Sane*'s primary template was the Stones. Opening track 'Watch That Man' was like a cleaned-up, less muddy offcut from *Exile on Main Street*; 'Drive-In Saturday' didn't sound that Stonesy but namechecked the band's singer with the line 'when people stared in Jagger's eyes and scored'; there was even a cover of 'Let's Spend the Night Together'. Bowie had deliberately selected Olympic, where the Stones used to record, as his studio. The fetish for the Stones and their ilk continued for the next year, with *Pinups*, an album of mid-sixties Brit-beat covers, and the 'Satisfaction'-like anthem 'Rebel Rebel', the big hit single off 1974's *Diamond Dogs*.

Bowie was obsessed with Mick Jagger. Just as Alice Cooper in his early days had decided that the Stones were the group to beat in terms of scaring parents, Bowie yearned to knock the band off their pedestal. Yet he knew that the Stones were unassailable. They were, in fact, the ungodly godfathers of glam, pioneers of aggressive androgyny and elegantly wasted decadence. The Velvet Underground may have been the first group to write songs about hard drugs with studied dispassion, but hardly anyone noticed because hardly anyone bought their records. On *Let It Bleed*, and even more so with 1971's *Sticky Fingers*, the Stones referenced heroin and cocaine in songs that got onto the radio and into millions of households.

Bowie and Jagger socialised but there was always a jostling, jousting subtext to their relationship, and sometimes this spilled out publicly. 'I wonder how long he's going to last,' Jagger mused in a

1974 *NME* interview, adding quickly: 'I really shouldn't talk about [Bowie] because I know him too well and know his fears and his hauntings.' That same year, in the *Rolling Stone* Burroughs colloquy, Bowie described Jagger in a contrived tone of emasculating condescension: 'Jagger is most certainly a mother figure and he's a mother hen to the whole thing. He's not a cockadoodledoo; he's much more like a brothel keeper or a madame.'

In that same interview, Bowie made an observation that gets to the roots of his Jagger fixation: he describes the Stones singer as a 'white boy from Dagenham trying his damnedest to be ethnic'. The tone, again, seemingly aims to belittle. But Bowie knows full well that such imposture – a white English boy trying to sound like a black American man – is the essence of the sixties British rock adventure. He knows, moreover, that by any measure, Jagger not only tried 'his damnedest', he succeeded mightily, with world-historical repercussions. Despite clearly being imposters, the Stones – and the rest of their generation: Animals, Kinks, Yardbirds et al. – created the model of intensity and impact against which subsequent British rock would necessarily be judged. The question for Bowie was, if Jagger could 'fake it so real' he was 'beyond fake' (to borrow a line off Courtney Love), then why couldn't he, also a well-brought-up middle-class boy from the English suburbs? As with Iggy, what counted was total immersion in the persona, such that the transparently inauthentic magically became the new benchmark of authenticity. Playing the role of the decadent rock star Turner in 1970's *Performance*, Jagger proclaimed that 'the only performance that makes it – that really makes it – is the one that achieves madness'. Bowie at once aspired to and held back from the madness of total commitment to a role.

Aladdin Sane's title alluded obliquely to Bowie's anxieties about mental fragility and to his schizophrenic half-brother Terry. The title track is the 1973 album's least Stonesy song, vaguely evoking

Cabaret with the poisoned luxuriance of Mike Garson's astonishing piano part. Rather than the Weimar Republic, though, it's the British version of twenties decadence that inspired Bowie: the 'Bright Young Things', those gay (in both senses) upper-class aesthetes who shirked their Oxford studies for frivolous revels, and chic socialites who danced frenziedly to Dixieland in between sniffs of cocaine. There were definite parallels between the Bright Young Things of the twenties and glam's Pretty Things. As Martin Green shows in *Children of the Sun*, his history of between-the-wars British cultural life, the male aesthetes rejected the world of their fathers (Isherwood spoke of being motivated by 'ancestor-hatred'), organised as it was around ideals of service to the British Empire. Refusing to grow up and become men, they became *noblesse sans oblige* – aristocrats unrestrained by duty. Androgyny was the look of the age: the boy-men shunned the Edwardian bearded ideal, while posh girls bobbed their hair short and aspired to a non-curvy figure. Bowie had recently read *Vile Bodies*, one of Evelyn Waugh's satires of this post-First World War generation, alongside *Decline and Fall* and the more elegiac *Brideshead Revisited*. The song's full title is 'Aladdin Sane (1913/1939/197?)', suggesting – in tandem with the line 'passionate bright young things take him away to war' – the familiar narrative arc of decadence followed by authoritarian barbarism.

Most of *Aladdin Sane* drew on Bowie's recent American experiences. Although clearly projecting his own frayed mental state onto the landscape – the stress and anomie of a tour that had been only half successful – Bowie talked in the end-of-tour press conference about his sense that 'the American is the loneliest person in the world. There's a general feeling of a lack of security and a need for warmth in people that's so sad.' Talking to the LA rock critic Robert Hillburn, Bowie described the whole album as 'a result of my paranoia with America . . . I ran into a very strange type of paranoid person . . . very mixed up people, and I got very upset.'

'*Aladdin* was really Ziggy in America,' Bowie said in the same interview. But the sound had a much fiercer attack and sting to it than *The Rise and Fall of Ziggy Stardust* ever approached, especially on 'Panic in Detroit', an impressionistic sketch of social breakdown and urban warfare, and 'Cracked Actor', a sordid vignette of a fading Hollywood star picking up a drug-addicted teenager. A lighter by-product of his trans-American travelogue, 'Drive-In Saturday' was a miniature science-fiction yarn conceived on a train travelling through the Arizona desert, which prompted Bowie to imagine a post-nuclear wasteland and the whimsical, if still apocalyptic, notion of teenagers having to learn the lost art of sexual intercourse ('a crash course for the ravers') from old blue movies from before the bombs dropped. Released as the next single after 'The Jean Genie', 'Drive-In Saturday' was another huge UK hit.

'I know I didn't have very much more to say about rock'n'roll,' Bowie told Hillburn, with regard to *Aladdin Sane*. 'Ziggy really said as much as I meant to say all along.' It was time to move on. After touring the US for a second time in early 1973 and bringing the *Ziggy/Aladdin* set, with its stage routines and increasingly outlandish costumes, to other territories in the world, Bowie was ready to kill off the Ziggy Stardust persona. Announced from the stage of the Hammersmith Odeon on 3 July, this auto-destruct would bookend the eighteen-month surge of frenetic activity and super-intense attention that had been kicked off with the 'coming out' in the pages of *Melody Maker*.

Like that publicity putsch, the termination of Ziggy was instant myth; like 'I'm gay', the rock'n'roll suicide was premeditated and carefully calculated. There were a number of humdrum, non-artistic reasons to jettison the alter ego. It would give an exhausted Bowie time to regroup, by eliminating a lined-up forty-date tour of the UK. It solved a problem for MainMan too: a financially risky third tour of America, which unlike the previous two would not be supported by RCA, could also be shelved. Ending Ziggy would also deal with problems that had emerged with his band: The Spiders from Mars wanted more pay, and mutiny had been forestalled only by the divide-and-rule stratagem of buying off Mick Ronson with the promise of a solo career.

None of the fans who came to the two Hammersmith Odeon shows knew about these grubby background wranglings. Rumours of Ziggy's demise had circulated, though, and an army of lookalikes congregated outside the venue, kids with orange shocks of hair and the lightning-strike Ziggy logo daubed across their cheeks. Inside, the zigzag lightning-bolt insignia on the stage backdrops created a cult-like and vaguely fascistic atmosphere, as Walter Carlos's electronic music from Kubrick's *A Clockwork Orange* set a tone of futuristic bombast.

Looking more gaunt than ever, Bowie hit the stage in a golden tunic with exaggerated dolman sleeves and a hem that cut off just below the crotch. Combined with his knee-length boots, this created a thighs-exposed effect that coded 'feminine'. This was the first of several costumes worn that night. The style parade included a jester-meets-leprechaun outfit of gold, green and red stripes; a skin-tight suit and giant cape, not unlike a wrestler's costume but with one shoulder bare, accessorised with a feathery boa; and a fairly hideous leotard, with a snap crotch, in which Bowie, one diamante earring dangling, did the corny old Marcel Marceau routine of a glass pane between himself and the audience.

There was a pause between songs and Bowie addressed the audience. 'Of all the shows . . . this particular show will remain with us.' Another pregnant pause. 'Not only is it the last show of the tour . . . it's the last show we'll ever do.' Bowie was being cruelly unclear here: was it just Ziggy and the Spiders being retired, or was he announcing that he would never perform onstage again? Howls of dismay and disbelief erupted from the audience, as the band launched into 'Rock 'n' Roll Suicide'. They left the stage to the stately sound of 'Land of Hope and Glory', also known as Elgar's 'Pomp and Circumstance'.

'When he killed off Ziggy . . . that really, really disturbed me because I really had a hang-up about these characters he had created,' recalled Julie, the Bowie ultra-fan interviewed in the Vermorels' *Starlust*. 'I was crying a lot and everyone was crying because he was killing off Ziggy . . . There was hysteria, particularly on the left-hand aisle because people were going wild when he reached down to the audience.'

There is a folk myth about what happened at the last Ziggy show: tales of fans driven delirious with grief, engaging in public sex acts, frenziedly masturbating, even fucking. Julie claimed to have witnessed this with her own eyes, if not actually participated: 'A lot of men were throwing off their underwear and showing their cocks all over the place. A lot of fluid was flying about. One girl was actually sucking someone off at the same time as trying to listen to what was going on. I thought it was so extraordinary because nobody had any inhibitions . . . Wanking was nothing. There was a guy next to me who was wanking in time to one track.' Yet nobody there in an official capacity – as music journalists, venue staff, MainMan personnel or, indeed, as part of D. A. Pennebaker's film crew documenting the night for the concert movie *Rock'n'Roll Suicide* – appears to have seen anything orgiastic or indecent going on. Was this all just another Ziggy-triggered fevered fan fantasy?

The band were shell-shocked too: apart from Ronson, who'd been tipped off, they learnt the news onstage, at the same time as the fans. As a sop to them, and a stop-gap measure for himself, Bowie would record one more record with the ex-Spiders, the sixties-covers album *Pinups*. In public, though, he made it all seem as dramatically final as possible. 'That's it. Period. I don't want to do any more gigs,' Bowie announced to the *NME* the following week.

'From now on, I'll be concentrating on various activities that have very little to do with rock and pop.'

'It was just a magical coming together of energies,' says Cherry Vanilla of Bowie's golden MainMan period of 1972–4. 'I think we all believed in magic too. We just believed so hard that I think we created it. For sure, if Bowie wasn't so talented, it wouldn't have worked. But a lot of it was just magic, and that's all I can say. When a lot of people come together around one thing, it does create a certain energy of "everything's possible".'

'Magic' is a word often used in connection with both Bowie and Defries. For instance, Hugh Attwool, head of the English office of MainMan, told Bowie biographer Paul Trynka that the Svengali 'spun a web of magic, which no one had ever done before, and persuaded RCA to spend huge amounts of money, both in the UK and US'. Although not overtly sorcerous in tone, business-advice manuals and self-help books do often promote what are essentially magical techniques – positive visualisation, projecting a hypnotic aura of certainty. In *Secrets of a Corporate Headhunter*, for instance, author John Wareham argues that confidence and authority are self-sustaining illusions dependent on tricks that bypass rationality; tricks played on *oneself* as much as on others. 'Success in almost everything . . . is largely based on nonverbal transmission of powerful abstract messages,' he writes. Wareham verges on advocating fantasy – even a kind of madness – when he suggests that 'keeping a hold on reality is a luxury you can rarely afford when you set out to become a tycoon'. In business, 'appearance is the only reality'.

Such was Defries's brilliance at projecting an image that he convinced almost everybody he met in those days that he was an unstoppable force on an endless upward path. That said, there was a fair amount of reality to substantiate the appearance: by the autumn of 1973, MainMan's 'instant empire' comprised power bases in London, New York (the Upper East Side duplex penthouse had been joined by a Lower West Side loft and various other Manhattan apartments, along with a compound outside the city in Greenwich, Connecticut), Los Angeles and Tokyo (where Defries would be representing avant-garde fashion designer Kansai Yamamoto). Although Lou Reed and Mott had departed the roster of clients, they had left it as rock stars, their careers turned around. Still on the books were Iggy Pop (admittedly in limbo), Dana Gillespie (a bluesy singer in the Elkie Brooks mould who was an old friend of Bowie's), the avant-garde singer and synth player Annette Peacock (who some thought potentially a 'female Bowie'), the cross-dressing shock-rocker Wayne County, and several others in development. Mick Ronson's solo stardom was considered inevitable.

But Defries did not even see himself as primarily a music manager. His 'international entertainment conglomerate' MainMan was really 'in the business of stars'. That's what Bowie was, Defries insisted: not someone in the same bracket as Rod Stewart, but 'a Marlon Brando or James Dean-type star', he informed *Melody Maker*. 'I see him more in that category of large scale untouchable.'

'His ambition has no end,' said Barry Bethell, former head of MainMan's London office. In Michael Watts's *Melody Maker* feature, which was titled 'Portrait of a Mogul', Bethell recalled Defries talking sometimes of trying to buy a whole record company, Decca, or maybe even RCA itself. The piece alludes darkly to Defries having moved into banking (the registering of Main Bank in New York, Switzerland and London), with precious metals purported to be another interest. But it was common knowledge that his 'ultimate ambitions lie in politics'. John Brewer, boss of a rival management company, confessed that 'the only thing that's worried me about Tony is that one day he might be representing a country in which

I happen to live. And I might find myself at war, with no control whatsoever!'

Bowie and Defries even inspired American imitators in the form of singer Jobriath and star-maker Jerry Brandt. Jobriath was actually gay, while Brandt, who'd clearly studied what MainMan had been doing, gamely endeavoured to out-hype Defries, proclaiming that Jobriath was 'composer, arranger, singer, dancer, painter, mime artist, ballerina, woman, man'. He boasted of having spent $200,000 of his own money on an ad campaign in high-end fashion magazines. Echoing Defries's patter about Bowie being destined to become a single-name glamour brand like Dietrich or Sinatra, Brandt said that Jobriath (note the single name) was a Garbo-level star in waiting: 'The world needs a new silhouette to admire. It's Crosby, Sinatra, Presley, the Beatles and Jobriath. There's no question, no doubt about that.' While conceding that Bowie had pointed the way ahead by putting elegance and spectacle back on the agenda, Brandt claimed that he'd already been surpassed: 'David Bowie has taken his best shot. He's tacky and he can't pirouette and he can't move and he's rigid and he's scared to death.' He boasted that Jobriath wouldn't be seen dead in rock venues: 'He's starting out at the Paris Opera House . . . Fuck all that other shit.'

The self-titled Jobriath debut had a fabulous cover: a gatefold with the blond singer as a fallen statue with shattered lower half. Opening track 'Take Me I'm Yours' was a deliciously over-ripe melodrama of romantic surrender: 'Use me abuse me amuse me / Chained to your insanity, your perversity.' But overall the music was less like Bowie and closer to the missing link between Bette Midler and Elton John if he'd ever gone fully 'out'. The roots were musical theatre (Jobriath had been in the original cast of *Hair*) far more than the Beatles/Stones lineage. On the second album, *Creatures of the Street* – like the debut, a flop – the standout track 'Dietrich/Fondyke (A Brief History of Movie Music)' was lyrically a checklist of gay

Fallen idol: the gatefold sleeve of Jobriath's 1973 debut album was also
turned into a Times Square billboard by the singer's hype-man Jerry Brandt

silver-screen icons: Dietrich, Garbo, Swanson, Harlow, Crawford,
Monroe . . .

Jobriath and Brandt were no threat to Bowie and Defries's joint
throne. But internal weaknesses at MainMan were becoming apparent. The company was dangerously overstretched, with a staff of
twenty-five but not enough success to keep the show on the road.
Cash-flow problems and unpaid bills caused recording studios like
Olympic and Château d'Hérouville to close their doors to the company's artists. Lou Reed and Mott, the only unqualified successes,
had moved on. Iggy and the Stooges were an expensive bust. Mick
Ronson, it turned out, was one of nature's sidemen, unable to front
his own albums compellingly. Dana Gillespie's two albums got the full
music-paper ad-spread treatment, but to no avail, despite her lovely
cover of Bowie's 'Andy Warhol'. Other potential stars like Simon
Fisher, Man Parrish and Annette Peacock slipped into development
limbo. 'He bought me an awful lot of equipment and took care of my
expenses for a year,' Peacock recalled of Defries. 'He was just like a
patron . . . That's his style – to pull acts off the market for about a year.'

The bigger problem for MainMan was that despite a tremendous investment of energy and cash, Bowie had not conquered America yet. RCA had sunk nearly $1 million into his promotion and tour support, but without achieving a radio hit ('Starman' had done best, reaching #65 in *Billboard*) or a truly successful album (*Ziggy Stardust* reached #75, *Aladdin Sane* peaked at #17). The British artists who achieved sales success in America between 1972 and 1974 were almost all sixties performers: Moody Blues, Rolling Stones, Jethro Tull, Cat Stevens, Pink Floyd, Eric Clapton, Rod Stewart, Humble Pie and, above all, the solo ex-Beatles. With the exception of Alice Cooper, glam did not exist in America as an album-based form as far as the *Billboard* Top 20 was concerned.

Even among the younger audience who followed rock with fanatical seriousness, glam had not been taken up as the third-generation sound like it had in Britain. *Creem* was far and away the most glitter-championing magazine in America but Bowie divided its readership. In the June 1973 Readers Poll, *Ziggy Stardust* was the #5 album and Bowie placed at #4 as punk of the year (a term of appreciation). But Bowie was also voted #3 in both the Crumb Bumb and Rip Off of the Year categories. Glam itself was voted #1 Fad of 1973, an ambivalent trophy at best, especially when it was identified as 'Glam-Glitter-Anal Rock'. Then again, homophobic language was actually used by some *Creem* writers when celebrating glam: for instance, the August 1973 'Androgyny' issue, which was headlined 'MEET ROCK'S DECA-SEXUAL ELITE!', described Gary Glitter as 'the first Anglo-anal cash-in'.

In America, rock fans and critics alike were suspicious of Bowie for his open disregard for rock as a genre. 'I don't think that's much of a vocation, being a rock-and-roller itself,' Bowie told *Rolling Stone* in 1972. In another interview, he mused aloud, 'Maybe I'm not into rock 'n roll. Maybe I just use rock 'n roll. This is what I do. I'm not into rock 'n roll at all.' This idea of rock as a pose, a vehicle, didn't sit well with those who viewed it as a belief system. Nor did

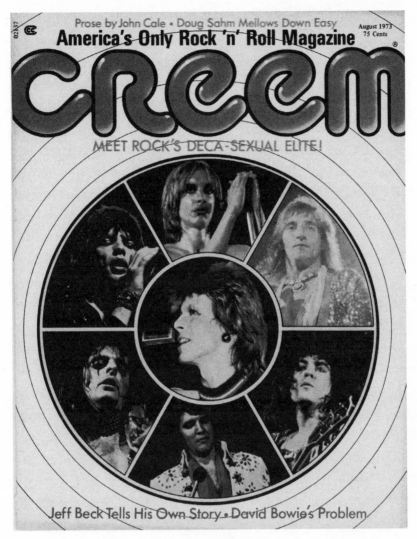

Creem's August 1973 cover tells the story of androgyny in rock

they warm to Bowie's scorn for the notion of a rock community: 'The coming together of people I find obscene as a principle,' he told Burroughs in *Rolling Stone*.

Looking back, it can be startling just how many tepid, unconvinced reviews *The Rise and Fall of Ziggy Stardust* and *Aladdin Sane* – now accredited monuments in the rock pantheon – garnered at the time.

Particularly in America, the most famous and influential arbiters of the day responded to Bowie with scepticism. *Creem*'s Dave Marsh enthused about *Ziggy Stardust* but in faint-praise terms, arguing that Bowie's knack was executing 'relatively exciting readymades . . . competently, interestingly, intricately', while also complaining that his work lacked the 'uniquely naïve' quality of truly great rock'n'roll. Lester Bangs, looking back at Bowie's entire 1972–3 output when reviewing a later album, sniffed at him for being 'as accomplished an eclectician (aka thief) as Elton John' with 'a façade as brittle as it was icy'.

Most revealing of the responses was Ellen Willis's *New Yorker* essay of October 1972, which bore the title 'Bowie's Limitations'. She basically dismissed him as a sexless faker (while celebrating Mick Ronson as the real sexy deal). As one of the journalists flown in for the Dorchester hotel press conference and the Spiders from Mars gig at Aylesbury Friars, she found herself wandering through Hyde Park in the company of Iggy Pop and Dave Marsh the following day. '"This country is weird, man," said Iggy. "It's *unreal.*"' Willis and Marsh discussed what was missing: Marsh reprised his *Creem* misgivings (a lack of innocence), but Willis thought that 'unlike Lou Reed . . . or Iggy . . . Bowie doesn't seem quite real. Real to me, that is – which in rock-and-roll is the only fantasy that counts.'

British critics obviously did not share the crypto-Anglophobic leanings of some of their American peers. But some of the major pundits in the UK rock press did have reservations about Bowie, essentially agreeing with the Marsh and Bangs view of him as a pasticheur. In a 1974 review, the *NME*'s Mick Farren saw the magpie eclecticism at work not just in the lyrics and music, but the visual presentation: 'He's almost like an animated flick-book, moving fluidly from one pose to the next. The creativity lies in the outrageous juxtapositioning. One moment he'll hit a bent knee, guitar slung across his back, pointing finger, total reproduction of a classic Elvis

Presley photograph – the next he's instantly switched to the brave little girl, à la Judy Garland.'

But then Bowie often talked about himself in the same terms: as a synthesist, a reprocessor, a cool-hunter. Sometimes he would flippantly say that it didn't matter who did something first, what counted was who did it *second*. At other times Bowie sounded less confident in the value of this role of popularising other artists' innovations. He disparaged himself as a human Xerox machine: 'When I heard someone say something intelligent, I used it later as if it were my own. When I saw a quality in someone that I liked, I used it later as if it were my own.' He admitted to worrying that 'sometimes I don't feel I'm a person at all. I'm just a collection of other people's ideas . . . I honestly feel that there is something incredibly lacking in my life, and I'm not quite sure what it is.' It seemed to be this 'continuing, returning feeling of inadequacy over what I've done', as much as artistic hunger or artful career management, that propelled the restless remaking of self and style.

Yet when he was feeling proud – and not wracked with hollow-inside anxiety – Bowie talked up these same qualities as what made him different. When *Rolling Stone*'s Cameron Crowe asked him if he thought he was original, he said, 'Not by any means. More like a tasteful thief. The only art I'll ever study is stuff I can steal from.' In a 1973 TV interview with chat-show host Russell Harty, Bowie talked with disarming candour about his impressionability: 'I take on the guises of different people I meet. I can switch accents in seconds of meeting someone. I've always found that I *collect* – I'm a collector. I've just always seemed to collect personalities – ideas. I have a hotchpotch philosophy.'

It is surprising, though, how often Bowie beats himself up in public, mood-swinging in the early interviews in almost bipolar fashion on the issue of his ultimate worth as artist and human being. 'I feel that I may be a very cold and unemotional person,' he once said.

'And at times I wish that I wasn't so mentally vulnerable.' His phrasing is intriguing, making me think of the psychoanalytic disorder known as 'the influencing machine': the paranoid belief that you're being controlled by a remote power. At the risk of misusing the term, you could characterise Bowie himself as an 'influence machine'. He is simultaneously one of the most influential artists of all time and one of the most *influenced* artists of all time. You could see his work as a switching centre for the retransmission of ideas and images. Looking back on his early career, Bowie said his ambition was that 'I wanted to be well-known and turn people onto new things.' And he has indeed been the consummate pop-star-as-portal, directing his fans to esoteric music but also to things well outside the traditional domain of rock culture: books, films, philosophies. This in turn has invited the reigning approach to Bowie's work: breaking it down into its constituents, meticulously mapping every last construable reference and allusion.

'If I wasn't a fan, I'd probably be far more individual,' Bowie admitted in 1973. 'The kind of individuality where it's very, very ingrained in the self . . . All I can do is assemble information that I've received.' This sense of the self as a super-absorbent sponge is totally adolescent. Most people by their late twenties, if not earlier, have undergone a degree of hardening of the character armour; they've likely come to provisional conclusions about values; avenues have been closed off; most have settled into a life-defining fandom, an ideology, or at least an occupation. Artists and art rockers are able to avoid that closure and stay within that unfinished state of openness. 'I'm still very much a teenager. I go through all sorts of fads,' Bowie admitted in early 1972 – when he was actually twenty-five. That same year he described himself as 'a grasshopper. I really want to move on all the time.' This adolescent skittishness carried on into his thirties and forties, although by a certain point it had become his signature, his shtick, his selling point: what you expected him to do was the unexpected. His inconsistency became his consistency.

Bowie's masterstroke was to reframe what until then was generally considered a defect in other artists (trend-chasing, dilettantism) and turn it into a virtue. The exact same chopping and changing that had seemed desperate in the first seven years of his career became the mark of someone in command, ahead of the pack. More than that, it became his method of outrunning the fickleness of the public's taste: he turned himself into the New Thing again and again.

Bowie didn't destroy the late-sixties model of the artist as someone who grew organically. The preponderance of acclaimed artists in the seventies still evolved in that fashion: Joni Mitchell, Neil Young, Roy Harper, Robert Wyatt, John Martyn. But Bowie did almost singlehandedly install a different value scheme that put what he did in a favourable light: he taught fans and critics to see contradicting oneself as agile and flexible rather than random and opportunistic. This then became the norm with many post-punk and early-eighties artists, who came of age in Bowie's wake.

Bowie made not standing for anything stand for something. But what, exactly? Simply mobility as a value in itself. (A 'stand' is a stopping point: 'Here I make my stand.') Politically, in the context of the early seventies, Bowie's career represents a shift in which the cult of individual mobility starts to supersede the idea of collective movement. Instead of Change . . . ch-ch-changes.

6:

WHAT'S THE DATE AGAIN? THE FUTURE-RETRO VISIONS OF ROXY MUSIC

Roxy Music – David Bowie's *Pinups* – Bryan Ferry

'Something that's very futuristic, something very weird, kinky . . . A kind of new world . . . really bright buildings . . . gadgets . . . the women really fantastic, perfection itself . . . everything's a kind of peak of excellence . . . the ultimate image of man's creation, a sort of Space City . . . Really fantastic architectures everywhere . . .' These were the mental pictures of 'the lifestyle, the whole Roxy/Bowie image' that reeled through the brain of seventeen-year-old Chris in 1975, when the commercial-design student was interviewed for a *Let It Rock* feature on the fans of Roxy Music and David Bowie.

Science-fiction images came up a lot when Roxy Music arrived on the scene. But so did images of bygone glamour. Roxy, it was observed in reviews, smashed together past and future, old and new, in a way that itself felt new – and breathtakingly original. Richard Williams, the writer who gave Roxy their first coverage with an August 1971 piece in *Melody Maker*, took delight in their deliciously deliberate echoes of Jan and Dean, Duane Eddy and The Shangri-Las. But he simultaneously thrilled to the way Roxy were 'forging ahead' by using bracingly avant-garde techniques involving pre-recorded tapes, sound-processing effects and electronic noise.

The futurism had a retro tinge, though. 'Late Fifties rockers who'd got mixed up with *Star Trek*,' is how one journalist described Roxy's image. The group's electronics man, Brian Eno, described some of their costumes as looking like the kind of garb that the president of the Galactic Parliament might have worn in some science-fiction

B-movie from the fifties. Even the synth splutters and burbles sometimes sounded a bit like the electronic score to the 1956 science-
fiction movie *Forbidden Planet*. Decades later, Eno remembered
Roxy as 'looking to the past in a kitsch way, and imagining the future
as it might be . . . but perhaps in an equally kitsch way'.

The band's presentation also wove together yesterday and tomorrow. Their early logo, featured on flyers and also on the reel-to-reel
tape demo that Roxy frontman and leader Bryan Ferry dropped
off at Richard Williams's home, featured an old-fashioned airplane
skywriting the word 'Roxy' against a stylised Manhattan skyline:
the whole image evoked art deco, a style that in its own era was
modernist, an early-twentieth-century celebration of streamlined
technology and chrome sheen. The cover of Roxy's 1972 self-titled
debut album, meanwhile, caused a stir with its forties-style cheese-
cake pin-up of a model in a swimsuit and a suggestive pose midway
between 'Come hither' and 'Be gentle'.

Nowadays, we'd use terms like 'retro' and 'postmodernist' to
describe this kind of temporal mishmash. But neither of those words
belonged to seventies parlance. Critics recognised and appreciated
the disorientating jumble of eras and styles in Roxy's music and image,
but they didn't have a pat concept for it. You might say that Roxy were
ahead of their time in being behind of their time: that their pastiche
and quotations anticipated the pomo pop of the eighties.

'I don't think a group so much into advanced music has ever used
these old sources so obviously before,' Ferry told the *NME* in 1972,
with evident pride. In his disjointed, impressionistic sleeve note for
the debut album, Simon Puxley – Roxy's publicist and Ferry's aesthetic adviser – pinpointed the slipperiness: 'What's the date again?
(it's so dark in here) 1962 . . . or twenty years on?'

It wasn't just future and past that Roxy played havoc with. They
were also a crush-collision of progressive 'head' music and danceable
pop, experimentalism and showbiz, abstraction and cliché, Europe

and America, anti-commercial and commercial, irony and passion, effeminacy and misogyny, virtuosity and non-musicianship . . .

You could almost argue that Roxy Music were two different groups coexisting uneasily within the same band. So perhaps the best way to get to grips with Roxy is to write about them *twice*: the same individuals, even the exact same songs, seen from different angles . . .

'The Perfect Guitarist'
for Avant Rock Group
Original, creative, adaptable,
melodic, fast, slow, elegant, witty
scary, stable, tricky . . .
QUALITY MUSICIANS ONLY
'Roxy' 223 0296

Musician-wanted advert, *Melody Maker*, 1971

Just as their sound and image squashed together elements of avant-garde and pop, as personnel Roxy Music were a hodgepodge of incongruities and affinities. Four of the core five (the bassist being a fluctuating position for most of the group's existence) were working class. But Bryan Ferry, Brian Eno and Andy Mackay (who played oboe and sax) had each reacted against their backgrounds in slightly different ways.

Bryan Ferry grew up in County Durham, in the north-east of England, the son of a farm worker who had later become a handler of pit ponies, working in the dark depths of the coal mines. Ferry attended the Fine Art department of Newcastle University (this was a deliberate choice to avoid the unserious slackness of art colleges, a more common destination for working-class aesthetes). Dedicating himself to elegance and taste, Ferry distanced himself from his humble background, erasing almost all traces of his Geordie accent, which would resurface only in rare moments of rage.

Raised in the rural quiet of Essex, on England's eastern coast, postman's son Brian Eno had gone to the kind of free-form art school that Ferry sniffed at – two of them, in fact: Ipswich and Winchester. At the former, he was fed through the process-oriented, question-all-assumptions training of Roy Ascott, emerging the other side with radically expanded notions of what art could be and how to go about getting results. While working out his ideas, Eno had also been in a couple of experimental bands, Maxwell Demon and Merchant Taylor's Simultaneous Cabinet; his interest in sound manipulation dated back to boyhood, when he had experimented with tape recorders and discovered phonetic poetry.

Andy Mackay's sensibility seemed totally art school, but in fact he'd studied English and music at Reading University. On arrival, he soon gravitated towards the students hanging out at Reading's Fine Art department, which was similar to Newcastle's and was linked in various ways, with staff moving from one to the other. The son of a south London gas man, Mackay was something of a dandy, with esoteric interests in avant-garde and aesthetic provocations of every kind, including Swinging Sixties ones. He participated in the arty intellectual magazine *Sunshine Group*, organised happenings at Reading and other colleges, and performed at the Drury Lane Arts Lab, with a piece that involved wrapping a piano in polythene and amplifying the squeaking, rustling sounds through microphones. Eno witnessed one such Fluxus-like performance at Winchester and struck up a friendship with Mackay.

Like Ferry, both Eno and Mackay developed well-spoken middle-class accents that bore no trace of their social or regional origins. Drummer Paul Thompson was alone among the working-class majority of Roxy to retain his Geordie speech patterns, which can be heard on the B-side track 'Your Application's in the Mail'. Unlike the others, he never made it into higher education, instead working in Newcastle's shipyard while playing in various club bands. Nicknamed 'Blooter Blatter' by the rest of Roxy for his drum-skin smacking, heavy-rock style of playing, Thompson provided a vital solidity that kept the group from drifting off into disparate weirdness. 'If we'd had an avant-garde-type drummer who just flopped around the place or played every other three beats or something really complicated, it just wouldn't have worked,' says guitarist Phil Manzanera. 'But the fact that we had someone who idolised Jon Bonham and who just laid it down behind all the other elements, that pulled it all together.' Despite his lack of affectation – he was the only member in Roxy who could have related to Slade – Thompson was a fan of progressive and heavy rock, which is why he answered Ferry's *Melody Maker* advert announcing 'Wonder Drummer Wanted For Avant-Garde Group'.

Phil Manzanera was the only posh member of Roxy. His mother was Colombian and his English father worked for the airline BOAC (and earlier, his son speculated, could well have been a spy operating in Latin America). Manzanera had enjoyed a cosmopolitan youth flitting between various South American countries and his boarding school in London. During his later years at Dulwich College, he formed the psychedelic school band Pooh and the Ostrich Feathers, which evolved into the more serious proposition Quiet Sun. Influenced by Zappa, Pink Floyd and Soft Machine, the group's music – played insanely fast at strange time signatures – earned them a reputation as 'just about the most listener-unfriendly band in London' (according to King Crimson's Pete Sinfield).

Ferry moved to London after university. He earned a living as a schoolteacher while nursing his vision for a rock group and starting to recruit the other members. Nearly all the songs on the first two albums, *Roxy Music* and *For Your Pleasure*, were written during this period or during the early formative days of the band, when they were hatching a sound and going through personnel fluctuations. Roxy Music were Ferry's brainchild and baby, no doubt. But it is also inconceivable that the songs as we know them on the debut and *For Your Pleasure* would sound anything like they do without the contributions of the band. For proof you need to search no further than the 1975 remakes of certain Roxy songs on Ferry's third solo album – and first since Roxy's break-up – the doubtless ironically titled *Let's Stick Together*. The de-Roxyfied versions of tunes like 'Remake/ Remodel' are flat, enervated and pointless, undermining the very point Ferry was striving to make: that he was the sole auteur of Roxy Music and his songs were standalone 'standards' of the modern era.

Ferry's bandmates' contributions to the original, definitive versions of the songs blur the already fuzzy line between arrangement and co-writing. But then this is more often than not the case with rock, where the overall sound, the energy, the distinct feel and motion of the band as rhythmic engine are as much the selling point – and the pleasure point for listeners – as the tunes or words. Any really great group has a band-voice, a sound-signature that's often recognisable within a few seconds of hearing them on the radio, before you've even heard the melody unfurl.

The most sensible and equitable arrangement for rock bands is a four- (or five-, or six-) way split of credits and composition royalties: bands that operate with that kind of collective division from the start, like R.E.M., tend to last longer and have much warmer and closer relationships. Song publishing, however, is based around ideas that date back to the sheet-music era: it traditionally assigns copyright to whoever writes the top-line melody and the lyrics. So it was with Roxy. *For Your Pleasure* even bears the pointed assertion 'Words and Music by Bryan Ferry' on its sleeve, adding insult to the injury of zero publishing income for the other members of the band.

'It goes back to Tin Pan Alley and the thirties,' says Manzanera. 'But Eno's synth part on "Ladytron" or Andy's oboe parts – that came from them. Each member was contributing to the music and to all the arrangements. We produced the musical context for Bryan to put his vision into. But that's not reflected in the publishing.' For a band as sonically radical – and radically sonic as Roxy – to be hidebound by such an old-fashioned conception of musical creativity was to shore up tensions and resentments that would haunt the group later on.

Although Ferry played keyboards, in purely musical terms his greatest invention was his voice: a rattling, reptilian vibrato that bridged the gap between Roger Chapman of UK heavy-psych band Family and neurotic new-wave mandroids like Devo's Mark Mothersbaugh and Gary Numan. Ferry's combination of jolting imbalance and crooner poise, the jarring stresses on particular words or phrases, made his vocals sometimes feel like a series of stills or the paused poses of vogue dancing. Indeed, vibrato is a little bit like a stop-motion camera for the voice.

Adding to the strangeness of Roxy's songs was the fact that Ferry was a self-taught musician. He wrote most of his early songs on the piano but didn't know the correct way to play the instrument, so he used mostly black notes and chords of only two notes, missing out the middle one. As Roxy biographer David Buckley points out, this third-finger middle note is what decides whether a song is in a major or minor key. The combination of melodies that hovered in a harmonic no-man's-land and Ferry's corrugated vocal timbre and phrasing made for a quality of wrongness-become-rightness that had far more in common with Captain Beefheart or Van Der Graaf Generator than the songwriters and singers that Ferry usually talked of admiring, such as Cole Porter or Smokey Robinson.

There is a viewpoint on Roxy Music that likes to make out that they really don't have anything much to do with rock. One adherent is Peter York, the style-culture maven. In a 2008 tribute for art journal *Frieze*, York writes about Roxy as if the group was Ferry's creation alone and brushes past the involvement of such lowly rock fixtures as guitar, bass and drums. A self-confessed art-student hanger-on who picked up the patter, if not the paintbrush, York waxes nostalgic about how Roxy were a blessed reprieve from all those horrid underground bands with their appalling dress sense and endless solos: 'I'd stopped reading the *NME* or *Melody Maker* because they featured this person called King Crimson.'

That's York being arch – he knows perfectly well King Crimson was a band. Being such a Roxy aficionado, he also surely knows that Ferry actually auditioned to be the singer with King Crimson (after Greg Lake quit to form Emerson, Lake and Palmer). And that Roxy signed to management company E.G., whose other clients included King Crimson and ELP, while the first Roxy album was produced by Crimson's lyricist Pete Sinfield.

Roxy Music's route to success could hardly have been more proggy, more rock-in-1971. E.G. hitched the group to Island Records. The group's first publicity came through *Melody Maker*, when Richard Williams put them in the paper's 'Horizon – New Names That Could Break the Sound Barrier' section. Roxy then secured a John Peel radio session, after the DJ saw them play as support group to Genesis at a Wimbledon venue called . . . wait for it, wait for it . . . The Hobbit's Garden!

The truth is that at the start Roxy were a progressive band as much as glam. Before Manzanera took the job, the group's original guitarist was David O'List, already a big name from playing in The Nice – one of the first late-sixties groups to rework classical-music themes. The first in a *Spinal Tap*-like sequence of bassists was Graham Simpson, whom Ferry knew from a Newcastle R&B group they'd both been in. Jazz-freak Simpson grew progressively more spaced out during his Roxy tenure, thanks to LSD and Nepalese hashish oil, along with his spiritual odysseys into Sufi and Buddhist mysticism. Eventually he had a breakdown and, virtually catatonic, left the group shortly after the recording of the debut LP.

Andy Mackay and Brian Eno supplied a different sort of avant-garde sensibility, rooted not in freak-out rock but in sound art and experimental music. Both shared a passion for American composers like John Cage, Morton Feldman and Steve Reich – that whole field of 'New Music' based around aleatory techniques and conceptual scores (where instead of a musical score the composer provided loose guidelines – closer to a blueprint, a recipe or even a haiku – for the creation of a unique and unrepeatable sonic event). Mackay's interest in this area would result in the 1980 book *Electronic Music*, while Eno would explore Reich-style tape-delay systems in projects with King Crimson's Robert Fripp, like 1973's *No Pussyfooting*, and on his post-Roxy solo albums. Within Roxy, Eno's initial role was sound technician (he was a whiz with gizmos and cobbled-together electronic devices). Early on, he made his contributions from off-stage, processing the group members' playing through effects. 'I'm mostly interested in modifying the sound of the other instruments,' Eno said in 1972. 'You get a nice quality – the skill of the performer, transformed by the electronics. Neither the player nor I know what each other is going to do – which means you get some nice accidents.'

Eno actually hated prog rock for its maximalist bombast and cult of virtuosity – he liked to describe himself as a non-musician – but that didn't mean that he was particularly pop oriented. At Roxy's out-set, Eno recalled, none of the group felt like they were competing in the same field as, say, Marc Bolan. 'We always thought of him as pop music, and we thought that what we were doing wasn't pop music.'

Even Bryan Ferry – the person in Roxy closest to the pop aes-thetic – initially thought of the group as uncommercial. 'We're not a singles band, really,' he told the *NME*. 'I certainly don't want to find myself sliding down the Slade/T. Rex corridor of horror.' Years later,

Ferry recalled that 'when we started . . . we thought we'd be a kind of art student band, and that's as far as it would go . . . King Crimson were one polar extreme, and Bowie was the other, and we were in the middle . . . I was astounded when we had a hit record.'

'Virginia Plain', the group's first single – and first hit, reaching #4 in autumn 1972 – was not your typical pop tune. By the standards of hit factories like the Brill Building and Motown, it would be considered unfinished – there's no chorus, just a single-verse melody repeated. 'Pyjamarama', the second single – which reached #10 in April 1973 – was equally eccentric. Instead of writing it on the piano, Ferry decided to use a guitar – an instrument he had even less proficiency with. According to Manzanera, Ferry fancied having a go more for the look of it than its musical potential. 'Bryan had this fantastic green guitar – you can see it on the cover of the second album. So I open-tuned the guitar for him so he could play it using just one chord. And he wrote a song based on one chord all the way through, just one finger moving down four frets. There's nothing else to "Pyjamarama".' According to Manzanera, the challenge for the other Roxy members then became, 'How can we make this interesting?' So they 'dressed it up' with tumultuous Thompson drums, outbursts of near-dissonant sax, guitar discords and a little firework display of soloing from Manzanera.

On the debut album itself, the rules of pop and rock were broken even more extensively. Both 'If There Is Something' and 'The Bob' are multi-segmented song suites. 'If There Is Something' starts like The Band in Southern boogie mode (think 'Up on Cripple Creek'). Then it morphs into a romantic melodrama that slips from Valentine's card triteness to pratfalls of bathos: Ferry's amorous pledges of devotion climax with the promise to 'grow potatoes by the score'! The third segment features a keening, ruminative sax soliloquy over weary piano chords, then 'Something' glides into a soulful coda wracked apart by Ferry's most blood-curdling vocal

Roxy in 1972. Left to right: Bryan Ferry, Brian Eno, Phil Manzanera, Andy Mackay. Front: bassist Graham Simpson holds a picture of Paul Thompson, who couldn't make the shoot

theatrics ever – stricken histrionics wrenched from deep within, at once harrowingly visceral yet somehow utterly beyond human. Like some monstrously unwholesome caricature of the love song, 'If There Is Something' makes no sense structurally or emotionally, yet it's shatteringly moving. As Ferry told the *NME*, 'What interests me, far more than ambiguity, is juxtaposing things so they shock. I like surprise.'

Kicking off the album's second side, 'The Bob (Medley)' contains seven separate segments and eight tempo shifts in a little under six minutes: synth-drone doomscape intro; Sabbath-meets-Crimson bombast; a *Spinal Tap/*'Stonehenge' interlude of dancing-dwarf pan pipes; a musique concrète simulated battlefield with the sounds of artillery and exploding bombs; a West Coast hippy-rock singalong; an oboe-accompanied pastoral poem; a reprise of Sabbath–Crimson; then a finale of tympani, grand piano and epic power chords. 'It's a mini-film,' explains Manzanera, intended to recreate in sound the Battle of Britain ('Bob' = 'B.O.B.' – get it?). The booming kettle drums at the end are an homage to the Rank movies of the era.

Other songs on *Roxy Music* aren't disjointed horizontally (structural extension through time) but vertically (the layering together of jarring textures and incongruent emotions). Opener 'Remake/ Remodel' is raw, blasting rock'n'roll literally spaced out by Eno's synth squibbles. For 'Ladytron', Ferry asked Eno to supply sounds like lunar landscapes, while Mackay's oboe played what Ferry called 'The Haunted Landscape Theme'. The guitar figure is so queerly processed it sounds like the wobbling of a spangled jellyfish, and Ferry, in his own words, comes in 'singing like a cowboy with castanets'. 'If There Is Something' follows and then, concluding one of the most stunning first sides of a debut album in rock history, comes '2HB': a smoky-ballad homage to silver-screen idols that drifts off into a vaporous sequence of tape-delayed sax. These superimposed but out-of-synch layers of repeating signals create an effect somewhere between epiphany and disorientation: like dawn rising on a planet with three separate suns. 'It's an Eno effect on a Ferry song with a Mackay saxophone – one of those collaborative things that just wouldn't have happened in any other situation,' recalls Mackay.

These post-psychedelic/proto-ambient experiments were taken further on 1973's *For Your Pleasure*, one of the greatest albums of all time. 'In Every Dream Home a Heartache' proceeds in a glassy trance, slow steps towards a scene of horror – the dreadful tension exploding finally in an uproar of maximalist majesty, with Manzanera's gaseous billow of a guitar solo ('That was my chance to vent my inner psychedelia,' he laughs), Thompson's phased and stereo-panning drums, and a 1967-style false ending, the track fading and then returning for a final flare-up. A true group composition, whatever the credits may say, 'The Bogus Man' is a wheezing, lurching hypno-groove that sidles somewhere sinister midway between *There's a Riot Going On* Sly and *Tago Mago* Can.

Finally, the title track, which is like nothing else in rock before or after. Rock purged of its soil-clad American roots and replanted in the Europe of Bergman's *The Seventh Seal*, Lotte Lenya and Resnais's *Last Year in Marienbad*. The song is built around Thompson's broken drum beat, which seems to roam around the serrated edges of a crater rim. 'I try to create my own licks,' Thompson said. 'For instance – when drummers go right round the kit, they almost always do it clockwise. It seems to be the natural way. So I sometimes try it anti-clockwise – and it sounds really interesting.' This stop–start ungroove, combined with misty piano hazed with reverb, conjures a Gothic tableau of macabre elegance: I picture a Bavarian mansion's frozen lawns, animals striking curious poses, heraldic and eldritch. Ferry's hieroglyph-like images and stilted, stately phrasing create a halting effect, again like a series of stills. After the impossible gravitas of Ferry's adieu ('Old man / Through every step I change / You watch me walk away / Ta-ra'), the song morphs into a mind-blowing extended coda: one-note riffs and upper-octave trills on the piano paint a skyscape mad with stars. Finally the song expires like a galaxy swirling down a black hole's funnel.

The product of the strong bond that Manzanera formed with

Eno, 'For Your Pleasure' is comparable with Hendrix's '1983 . . . (A Merman I Should Turn to Be)' or Tim Buckley's 'Starsailor' in its use of the studio mixing board and recording tape as a canvas for painting with sound. 'It was built around the Eno treatment of the piano, using butterfly echo,' recalls Manzanera, referring to an effect Eno developed that involved putting sticky tape on the tape recorder's capstan, which caused the tape's tone to flutter like the rapid shimmer of a butterfly's wings.

In hindsight, Bryan Ferry described *For Your Pleasure* – the record on which Eno's abilities and techniques are most integrated – as Roxy Music's best album. That makes it all the more puzzling why Eno was ejected from the band by Ferry four months after its release in March 1973. The conflict was anything but the proverbial 'musical differences' scenario, for in that department things were going swimmingly. Rather, Ferry resented the way that Roxy had become bipolar in terms of its public profile. A scintillating interviewee with a host of colourful theories about music, Eno became increasingly prominent and vocal in features about the band; he was also getting interviewed separately from Roxy. 'I just got very pissed off with reading articles supposedly pertaining to Roxy Music, but in fact talking about Eno tape-recording earth-worms,' Ferry recalled peevishly, half a year on from the July 1973 split.

Journalists adored Eno – and so did a substantial faction within Roxy's following. Ferry felt severely put out by the raucous chants of 'Eno! Eno!' that kept breaking out at gigs. His flamboyant, feather-clad appearance was pulling attention away from Ferry onstage and in photographs too – not to mention being a rival draw when it came to the young ladies that flocked to the band. 'I've never seen anything like it,' grumbled Ferry about Eno's success with – and appetite for – women.

The final straw came when the group were performing at the York Festival in June 1973. Ferry's rendition of 'Beauty Queen', a dreamy mid-tempo ballad, was disrupted by boorish 'Eno! Eno!' chants. Mortified by this – and aware of the build-up of tension between the singer and himself over the preceding months – Eno left the stage to allow the song to be finished. Afterwards a seething Ferry announced to the band that he would never appear onstage with Eno again.

Explaining the schism to the *NME* in early 1974, Ferry said that it had reached the point where he felt 'either Roxy doesn't exist anymore or else it redefines itself in my terms, more strongly than I'd originally thought . . . I'd started out very easygoing on the out-side, but still diplomatically controlling the thing. I just put my foot down, otherwise I would have stopped the band existing com-pletely.' For Mackay and Manzanera, the shock assertion of control by Ferry – forcing out someone they valued as a friend as well as a vital component of the band's sound – shattered the amiable illu-sion of near democracy that they'd laboured under from the start. Ferry's diktat sent a chilling message: no one is indispensable; I'm the boss.

After Eno's replacement by Eddie Jobson – a classically trained young prodigy who'd played electric violin for proggers Curved Air – Roxy Music soldiered on, with Manzanera manfully con-tinuing the Eno-esque side of the band as much as he could. 'Amazona' – one of the highlights of the third album, *Stranded*, and Manzanera's first co-writing credit on a Roxy record – starts as slinky loping funk, but halfway through is split asunder by an indescribably strange guitar solo midway between a fire storm and a gigantic bubble machine. It sounds like the work of several gui-tarists, but it's Manzanera playing through a complex of distortion, repeat echoes and vari-pitch.

'Brian had been working on treatments of my guitar for the live shows, feeding it through his VCS3 synthesizer and then into a Revox tape recorder, which we'd customised in this very British,

Top left: Marc Bolan in his Ladbroke Grove flat, 1972 – with household god Poon on the mantelpiece
Top right: Erectile warrior: Bolan electrifies the fans at the Boston Gliderdrome, Lincolnshire, 1972
Bottom: Barry Langford, producer of pop show *Gadzooks, It's All Happening*, ruffles David Jones's hair as The Manish Boys watch, March 1965

Top: Axe hero: Alice Cooper dismembers a baby at the Empire
Pool, Wembley, June 1972
Bottom: Bawdy 'n' rowdy: Slade's Noddy Holder at Wembley, 1973

Suzi Quatro bosses her band: (left to right) Dave Neal, Len Tuckey, Alastair McKenzie

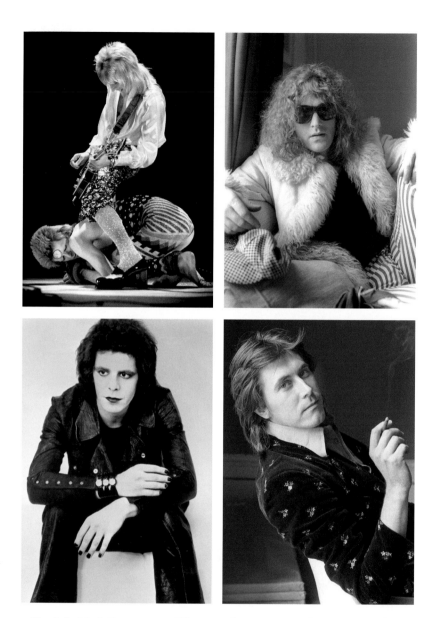

Top left: Mick Ronson straddles David Bowie at Earl's Court, London, 1973

Top right: Ian Hunter, Rock Star, in a working men's caff on Fulham Broadway, London, 1973

Bottom left: RCA publicity shot of Lou Reed, New York, *c.*1973

Bottom right: Blithe spirit: Bryan Ferry at the EG management office in Chelsea, London, 1972

Top: New York Dolls perform on Dutch TV, 6 December 1973
Bottom left: Wreck 'n' roll: drag-rock shocker Wayne County, *c.*1973
Bottom right: *The Rocky Horror Picture Show*'s star Tim Curry (seated)
and its creator Richard O'Brien

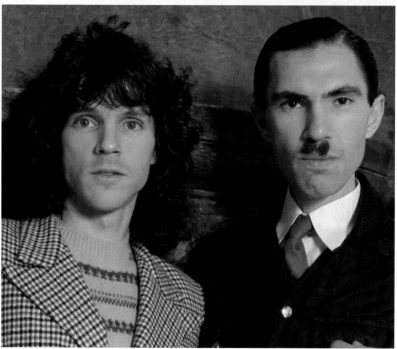

Top: Making a right Spector of himself: Roy Wood, 1973
Bottom: A couple of bright Sparks: Russell and Ron Mael, 1975

Top: Rodney Bingenheimer (centre front) surrounded by Les Petites Bonbons and other LA glitter scenesters
Bottom: The Tubes, fronted by 'Quay Lewd', in concert in New York City, 1975

Top: Iggy Pop lashed by Ron Asheton during the 'Murder of the Virgin' performance at The English Disco, Los Angeles, 11 August 1974
Bottom: David Bowie's infamous 'Nazi salute' – or was it just a friendly wave? – at Victoria Station, London, on 2 May 1976

mad-inventor fashion,' says Manzanera. 'So live we'd have the clean sound of the guitar and the treated sound at the same time. After he left, I asked the guy who built the synth to make me a guitar version of it that I could control using foot pedals. He made this contraption – and it worked, once. That's what you hear on "Amazona". It was done in a single take, and afterwards everybody in the studio control room just clapped. Everyone just laughed – "What the hell was that?" I've never been able to recreate it.'

Like 'In Every Dream Home a Heartache', 'Amazona' translates psychedelic techniques into a seventies gestalt: it has all the adventurism of Hendrix, but the sound isn't cosmic, it's worldly and glitzy. 'Mother of Pearl', the other *Stranded* highlight, similarly updates the Velvets' 'All Tomorrow's Parties', replacing Nico's junkie ennui with a jittery extroversion that corresponds to cocaine. Over a wiggling, jumpy, almost insubordinate bassline, guitar jangles and tingles on the edge of dissonance, a swirly shimmer that *sounds* like mother-of-pearl and may even have suggested the title. That's because the band laid down the instrumental first, then Ferry came up with the top-line melody and lyric. Going forward, this became Roxy's modus operandi: increasingly Ferry fronted the group more than the group backed the singer.

Sonically, *Roxy Music*, *For Your Pleasure* and *Stranded* express Roxy Music's drive to push forward into unknown sound-worlds – an extension of the sixties rock spirit of discovery and expansion. But on those same records, Ferry's words, delivery and song personae are preoccupied with pre-rock ideals of elegance and glamour. More and more, Ferry's utopia is located in the past, not the future: the very *ancien régime* that the fifties–sixties youthquake sought to abolish.

N

'The Roxy was the last splash of light before Stradhoughton
petered out and the moors took over.'
   Keith Waterhouse, *Billy Liar*

The Roxy is the place where the young people of Billy Fisher's
northern home town go to escape the dreary routine of their lives,
lured by a neon 'Come Dancing' sign to jive under a 'revolving ball
of mirrors' in Keith Waterhouse's 1959 novel *Billy Liar*. The book's
original title was *Saturday Night at the Roxy*, in fact. The dance-
hall is also where Fisher achieves a sole moment of triumph: a song
he co-wrote with his funeral-parlour workmate is performed by the
house band. His other aspirations – which include scriptwriter for
a top TV comic and world-famous novelist – look likely to remain
idle dreams.

Billy Fisher and Bryan Ferry share more than just initials. Both
grew up in the hard-bitten industrial north of England; both were
determined to escape the lowly intellectual horizons and aesthetic
deprivation of their backgrounds. Fisher did it through daydreams
in which his humble, humdrum family – small-businessman dad,
housewife mam – morph into frightfully posh people out of some
Noël Coward drawing-room drama, brandishing cigarette holders
and sipping cocktails. Fisher also imagined himself as the benign
dictator of a fantasy country called Ambrosia: the book starts with
the lines 'Lying in bed, I abandoned the facts again and was back
in Ambrosia.'

The facts of Ferry's early existence included living in a house with
an outside toilet shared by other families and using cut-up newspaper as toilet tissue. Streamed for state-run grammar school like
other bright working-class boys, Ferry – like Fisher – gradually
'rejected my parents in my mind', the singer recalled. In an unusually revealing 1975 interview with *Melody Maker*'s Caroline Coon,
Ferry confessed, 'I went through a period of resenting my parents

because I wasn't born rich and I felt . . . that my lot wasn't all that it should be. My parents are the nicest people you could possibly meet, but they're not the least bit intellectual. And I really resented that, too, at one time.'

There's a reason why Roxy Music's most fervent fan bases were in industrial cities in the north of England – Sheffield, Liverpool, Manchester, Newcastle itself. Especially in the seventies, when industry was still relatively strong but brutalist housing estates and shopping schemes had replaced the old terraced communities and corner shops, these cities were the parts of the UK where the hunger for that 'splash of light' ached fiercest. Curiously, it was in the cities where trade unions were strongest – and which to this day remain bastions of socialism – that working-class youths were most enthralled by a fantasy of aristocracy. As Ferry marvelled in a 1975 interview, Roxy fans in those northern towns sometimes came to the concerts in full black tie. Others costumed themselves in clothes that evoked a pre-rock, even pre-Second World War ritz and razzle. In America, too, Roxy's few inroads into popularity occurred in Cleveland and Detroit – 'places like where I come from, a very hard area', Ferry told *Creem*. 'They see [Roxy] as a means of escaping all that.'

'Roxy' was not inspired by the nightclub in *Billy Liar*, though, but by its more common use as a movie-theatre name. Speaking to *Rock Scene* in 1973, Ferry recalled the process of christening the group: 'I wrote out a long list of cinema names – Roxy, Ritz, Granada, Odeon, Regal, Astoria.' Rialto was another candidate. 'They all had a kind of nice flavour. I've always been star-struck, basically. Hollywood has always been Mecca.'

The original Roxy Theatre, which opened in New York in 1927, was the largest movie house in the world, with seating for 6,200. The creation of Samuel Lionel 'Roxy' Rothafel, it cost a then astronomical $10 million and represented the pinnacle of the 'picture palace' boom. Replacing the seedy Nickelodeons, picture palaces were designed to make 'the average citizen feel like royalty', according to cinema historian Mary Halnon; they ensconced the moviegoer in opulence and luxury, the decor of velvet, marble and gilt incorporating exotic flourishes from the ancient Orient's pleasure domes and from ocean-going cruise ships. As much as the pictures on the silver screen, the movie-theatre environment offered pure escape from dingy and dimly lit domestic conditions. Sinking into plush upholstered seats, the viewer drifted into a narcotic reverie.

By the fifties, thanks to the rival attraction of television, the picture palaces were fading; by the early seventies, the huge balconied auditoriums were being subdivided into multi-screen cinemas or becoming derelict. The word 'Roxy' was a potent evocation of Bygone Hollywood. It's symbolically apt that Roxy's audition for E.G. took place in a disused cinema, the Granada, on Wandsworth Road, south London. 'Cinema has always been the most magical thing to me,' Ferry told the *NME*. The movies directly inspired several Roxy songs: 'Chance Meeting', on the debut, drew on the classic British romance *Brief Encounter*; 'Three and Nine', on 1974's *Country Life*, got its name from the old-money price (three shillings and nine pence) of a ticket at the flicks when Ferry was a kid in the fifties; '2HB' was a luminous homage to Humphrey Bogart and his breed.

Glamour, in the modern sense of the word, pre-dated motion pictures. But with the advent of Hollywood, the movies became the primary source of role models for ordinary people in how to dress, carry yourself, hold a cigarette and kiss. '2HB' is about this kind of watch-and-learn relationship with screen idols; Ferry said it could have been any male movie star of that era, Cary Grant as easily as Bogart. These men offered models of masculine elegance and composed strength. Glamour became a secular religion, the image of a terrestrial transcendence that was attainable, if only momentarily for most people, on a Saturday night dancing at a club like the Roxy, or vicariously on screen. But you could dream of grasping it permanently, living full-time inside the dream, by becoming a star. '2HB' also alludes to the dream beyond that, the idea of fame as immortality: by becoming an image, there's the possibility at least that you might 'fade away never'.

Just as the word 'Roxy' evoked something bygone, the concept of glamour itself had an inherent retro quality, harking back to the way things used to be done: fur coats and diamante, tuxedos and bow ties. Glamour had largely gone out of style in the sixties, a decade when Hollywood struggled to redefine itself, its output often seeming staid next to what youth culture was producing. As fashion historian Carol Dyhouse observes, during the sixties the natural look came in: straight hair and minimal make-up (pale opalescent lipstick), smocks and frocks, denim and earth-toned fabrics. The feminine ideal promoted in fashion photography was child-like and twig-limbed, rather than sophisticated and full-figured curvy. Furs, jewellery, wigs all took on the aura of matronly or 'tacky' (how a mistress would dress). The very word 'glamour' was used less frequently, connoting as it did fakeness. But this was exactly the point when it became the property of drag queens, and thus began its circuitous route back to hipness.

When Eno wore feathers or Ferry put on garments made of leopard-skin fabric they were echoing (albeit with an absurdist edge) the feather-adorned and fur-draped movie goddesses of the early twentieth century: Theda Bara, Hedy Lamarr, Mae West, Marlene Dietrich. Adopting the same imagery in the first years of the seventies was pure camp, especially if you were a man.

In their earliest days, the group were identified on flyers and in similar contexts simply as Roxy; there was no 'Music' originally (that was added only after they discovered there was an American group called Roxy). But significantly the word came with quotation marks around it: 'Roxy'. These air quotes – a rare and recent mannerism in those days – placed upfront the self-conscious irony at work: 'Roxy' involved a wry, distanced commentary on glamour as much as a yearning re-enactment of it. Sophisticates are too clever to fall for the illusion any more, but secretly wish they still could be fooled. What tantalises is the remembrance of a long-gone possibility of absolute enchantment and entrancement.

'Whenever I saw a movie I'd really live it, and if it was sad I'd cry,' Ferry told *Melody Maker*'s Caroline Coon, who noted the framed photos in the singer's flat of Marilyn Monroe and Kay Kendall, the Yorkshire-born film star who – like Monroe – died tragically young.

Irony is the hallmark of advanced and rarefied sensibility. 'That was the period when pop music became slightly self-conscious, and started to look at its own history as material that could be used,' Eno recalled in a 2001 interview with *Rock's Back Pages*. 'And one of the things we didn't like about the bands who'd preceded us was that they were so un-ironic. They were so serious about what they were doing. We were serious, but in a different way.'

UK art schools were spawning grounds for this *different* seriousness, the non-earnest sort. Traditionally they were places for those who failed (or who were temperamentally unsuited for) the traditional metrics of seriousness: academic qualifications, leading on to higher education, then to careers that one way or another administered the world through business, industry, public service or the professions. At art school, other hierarchies were cultivated, involving aesthetics and sensibility and cool. Camp, irony, a detached but genuine appreciation for the products of mass culture – these were things that Ferry learnt in Newcastle University's Fine Art department.

One of Ferry's tutors was Pop Art pioneer Richard Hamilton, the British counterpart to Warhol. Hamilton would describe Ferry as 'my greatest creation', playfully rating him above his pioneering Pop Art collages and other works such as *Hommage à Chrysler Corp.*, *Pin-Up* and *$he* (the latter inspired by the use of female sexuality in advertising). Before 'launching' Ferry, Hamilton's first direct intervention in pop culture came with his famous cover design for *The Beatles*, also known as *The White Album*.

What Pop Art bred was a blithe superficiality, in the literal sense of being happy to stay at the level of surfaces: the modernist's angst-wracked concern with psychological depth suddenly became middlebrow, adolescent, as passé as existentialism. 'Virginia Plain' is about the allure of the flat world of advertising: logos, billboards, pin-ups, packaging. The song is based on a painting made by Ferry in 1964. Virginia Plain sounds like a girl's name, or possibly a place, but it is actually a type of tobacco, used in many brands of cigarette and typically referenced prominently on the packet.

Ferry's lyric for 'Virginia Plain' is a dizzy composite of icons and brand names, including Studebaker (a car that he bought as a youth for just £60, attracted purely by its design rather than its roadworthiness), Warhol Factory star Baby Jane Holzer, Acapulco (a Mexican beach resort and cruise destination once favoured by Hollywood stars), Las Vegas and Route 66. All these 'little images and throw-away lines', as Ferry put it, weave together to form an airbrushed fantasy landscape of post-Second World War Americana. 'At least fifty percent of the things that influenced me were American . . .' Ferry told *Disc*. 'The best films were American films, the best stars were American stars . . . and the best music was American, until the Beatles came along.'

'Virginia Plain' ends with the declaration that 'me and you' have 'got to search for something new'. That's an ironic end to a song that comprises a smorgasbord of clichés and received images. Perhaps the idea is to embark on a quest for something that gives us the thrill of newness that Hollywood movies, Googie diners, Elvis Presley, Coca-Cola and all the other gifts of American mass culture bestowed when they landed in Britain.

In a 1976 *Harpers & Queen* piece, Peter York described Ferry as 'the most important pasticheur in Britain today'. That seems like a backhanded compliment (although he did add that 'Ferry should hang in the Tate, with David Bowie') given that the dictionary definition of 'pasticheur' is one who mimics the style of another, and secondarily, blends together selections from different works into a new composition. Postmodernism, in other words, although that term was still an obscure one in '76. The *Harpers* piece pinpoints Roxy as the house band for a London-based milieu of design-conscious, fashion-forward aesthetes who were culturally if not always sexually 'gay'. This loose scene of creatives, which York dubbed 'Them', was united by a sensibility in which camp, the trash aesthetic, Pop Art and what we'd today call 'retro' but which York identified as 'art necro' converged.

Roxy Music's other Brian was not quite one of 'Them' but shared many of the same traits and aversions. Eno was still half in love with modernism, all those experimentalist process-not-product approaches of the sixties, like Fluxus or the John Cage school of composition. In interviews, he often spoke in terms of creating new sounds, exploring unknown territory. But like Ferry, Eno displayed a snobbery towards concepts like 'sincerity' and 'roots'. Sincerity was dull and worthy, it stripped away mischief and wit with its straight-from-the-heart bluntness. Roots implied building on an honoured and stable tradition. What replaced the rooted relationship with the past was pick-and-mix – reference rather than reverence.

'Anything out there was for the taking – it's just a palette,' is how Eno has characterised the approach. 'The whole history of music . . . you can take what you want from it, stick it with whatever else you like.' Much of the musical activity of the early seventies – blues rock, folk rock, jazz rock, country rock – was based around an organic model of evolution through hybridisation and fusion. Roxy proposed something different: a fissile, fickle, flighty mode of archival pillage and collage.

Eno famously said of the 1972 Roxy debut that it contained a dozen different futures for rock. But it also contained a dozen different pasts. Ferry agreed that their most progressive-sounding album was paradoxically also their most regressive. 'It was the most backward-looking, lots of clichés and things like that,' he told *Melody Maker*, adding: 'It's very smart.' The linearity of modernist time, surging forward in both high culture and the rock mainstream, had become scrambled. 'Lennon describes his music as seventies rock,' Andy Mackay told *Disc*. 'Ours is fifties, seventies, and eighties.' He could equally have added twenties, thirties, forties *and* sixties. 'It's inevitable that we're going to be influenced by lots of things, people, and ideas. The combinations are endless.'

This idea is inscribed into the final stretch of 'Remake/Remodel', the song that launches the debut. The other instruments cut away repeatedly to allow each player a moment in the spotlight – and each unfurls a highly recognisable musical quote: Graham Simpson does the bass riff from The Beatles' 'Day Tripper'; Manzanera parrots Eddie Cochran's 'C'mon Everybody'. Mackay's riff is the driving refrain from Wagner's 'Ride of the Valkyries', but rendered as King Curtis-style sax honk – making for a sort of double cover, someone else's song done in yet another artist's style.

The lyric involves 'found text' (the group-shouted 'CPL 593H' is the registration of a car owned by a girl Ferry had met at the 1971 Reading Festival), while the title itself nods to Pop Artist Derek Boshier's 1962 painting *Re-Think/Re-Entry*. This playful quoting from pop history filtered into Roxy's live performances too: Mackay did a Chuck Berry-style duck walk during the solo in 'Editions of You'. 'It was just a dare the first time,' he laughs now. 'But then I got rather stuck with it and it got to the point where I slightly dreaded getting to the "Edition" solo!'

'Do the Strand', the opener on *For Your Pleasure*, is also a kind of mission statement, disguised as a fictitious dance craze. The key line is 'all styles served here'. There's a rejection of the idea of . . . rejection itself: the notion that aesthetic choices represent stances and world views that you have to buy into and believe in. Being a rock fan doesn't require spurning the earlier mass-cult phase of Hollywood and Broadway musicals, nor the European high culture of the early twentieth century or the centuries before (*Guernica* and *Mona Lisa* both get namechecks in the song). 'Do the Strand' is a meta-dance-craze song that name-drops other dance crazes (tango, fandango, samba, beguine, waltz, mashed potato) and celebrated dancers like Nijinsky and La Goulue of can-can fame.

The word 'Strand' has classy associations. It's the London thoroughfare known for its palaces, townhouses, grand theatres and luxury hotels like the Savoy. But Ferry stresses that you can dance the Strand 'in furs or blue jeans' – which means to say that the aesthetics of the upper and lower classes appeal equally to Ferry. 'I like tacky things and low life as much as high life,' he professed in one interview. Another layer of meaning is the once popular cigarette brand, whose slogan – 'You're never alone with a Strand' – played off the word's other connotation of being stranded on a desert isle.

Ultimately 'Do the Strand' seems to evoke the elusive 'It' that twenties Hollywood screenwriter and novelist Elinor Glyn coined to describe the X-factor possessed by a star – and by extension any other brand or icon, sensation or fad. As Simon Puxley, Roxy's publicist, put it, the Strand represents 'where it's at, whatever turns you on. The buzz, the action, the centre, the quintessence, the energy. The all-embracing focus, past, present and future, the ineffable. The indefinable.' The unattainable too, perhaps: the impossible perfection of a Moment or an Image – it could be a lover, or the tableau of the in-crowd scene – that is the ever-receding quarry of the glamour chase.

Another key line in the song is the description of the Strand as 'a danceable solution to teenage revolution'. Instead of the sixties meaning of revolution – momentous, irreversible change, the consigning of the Old World to the dumpster of history – here it means the relentlessly revolving turnover of fashion, which constantly issues new style diktats. 'Do the Strand' is both invitation and instruction – an order.

But if all styles are served here, all styles are ultimately meaningless, once severed from the social struggles that brought them into being. *Revolt into Style*, George Melly's brilliant book about British pop in the fifties and sixties, is named after this very process: 'What starts as revolt finishes as style – as mannerism.' The title comes from a line in Thom Gunn's poem about Presley: 'He turns revolt into a style.' In time each new insurrection of youth energy and libido (Sinatra despised Elvis and his music as 'deplorable, a rancid smelling aphrodisiac') becomes 'classic', its threat defused. Elvis's quiff, his twitching hips and up-curled lip, are now part of the archive of timeless cool, right next to Frank's fedora and croon. Bryan Ferry loved – and borrowed from – both.

'A certain kind of flippancy, or at least a lighter touch in how you access the past,' is how Andy Mackay now characterises the sensibility of 'high glam', what we think of today as postmodernism. 'In some ways, that might be the weakness of it, that it can be slightly lightweight, whereas a true modernist statement is solid and concrete.'

A lot of the time Roxy were about affectionately sending up styles that were dated. Manzanera has talked about how there was 'a lot of humour . . . a lot of piss-taking' of genres such as heavy rock in Roxy's music. Eno admired rock parodists The Bonzo Dog Doo-Dah Band ('they're great heroes of mine') and participated in the Portsmouth Sinfonia, an orchestra in which everybody played an instrument at which they weren't fully proficient, resulting in hilariously wonky versions of well-known classical pieces.

Parody offers a 'legitimate' form of what would otherwise be redundant, derivative, an uninspired act of plagiarism, as literary theorist Linda Hutcheon points out. Laughter, along with a smidgeon of appreciation for the sheer craft involved, excuses what would otherwise be empty imitation. Take *All You Need Is Cash*, the Beatles-inspired 1978 mockumentary about The Rutles, with songs composed by ex-Bonzo Neil Innes. It's not so much that the satiric intent inoculates against the nostalgia, more that we enjoy The Rutles on several levels simultaneously: a trip down memory lane, a witty piss-take, a skilful reproduction.

Mackay prefers to think of Roxy's recycling of past style less as parody but more 'an affectionate acknowledgement of things that perhaps you admire but don't really want to get totally involved in. There are touches of modern jazz on the early Roxy albums – my solo on "Re-Make/Re-Model" is a sort of modern jazz solo. Which is not something that I'm deeply in love with. But I could hear there was something about the way Coltrane or Charlie Parker played that was very compelling. So I suppose I wanted to refer to it, but I didn't want people to criticise me for not doing it very well, because I didn't really feel that I could play proper jazz.'

Roxy rarely went in for wholesale genre-parody exercises. One exception is 'Bitters End', between-the-wars light music, with Ferry imitating the blithe tone and prissy-precise enunciation of Noël Coward, whose 1929 operetta *Bitter Sweet* is probably one reference point for the title, alongside the cocktail flavouring. For Eno, the cocktail-party evocations were saying something about decadence and the coming apocalypse: 'At least enjoy the luxury before it's too late.'

More often, Roxy merged styles through superimposition or jump cut. 'Would You Believe?' lurches from stately Otis Redding soul back in time to fifties rock'n'roll, complete with 'Duke of Earl' backing vocals and wheezy sax. The second half of 'In Every Dream Home a Heartache' is both genuinely psychedelic and 'psychedelic', redeploying circa-1967 clichés like phasing on the drums and guitar, and the trick fade/surprise return as heard on albums by Hendrix and others. But again, Mackay doesn't see it as send-up. 'We loved psychedelia. We weren't a psychedelic band, but we wanted to say, "Yeah, we like this," as well.'

Echoing Peter York's 'art necro' concept, the scholar Andrew Ross argues that camp sensibility is essentially a 'necrophiliac economy', in large part based around the 'resurrection of deceased cultural forms'. Necrophilia may be a little over the top as a description for what could more benignly be considered cultural recycling: Warhol's 'I always like to work on leftovers . . . Things that were discarded.'

From his earliest music-paper interviews Ferry talked openly of his love of things that belonged to a world that rock music seemed to have historically eclipsed. He spoke of his fondness for musicals ('If I became very rich tomorrow, I'd go out and buy all the records of musicals I could get my hands on') and his admiration for the chutzpah of Ethel Merman, whom he compared to Dylan: 'She doesn't have a great voice, but she's got a terrific personality.' When he praised Sinatra's *Songs for Swinging Lovers*, it was done in the campest of ways, revelling in all the received visual associations: 'I love that mohair suit in the spotlight business . . . Pour a couple of martinis, sling it on the phonogram, kick off your shoes, put your feet up, and survey your G-Plan furnished apartment.'

This knowing irony had become Ferry's natural way of looking at the world, of processing cultural input. He'd first imbibed it at art school, through proximity to Richard Hamilton. But it was reinforced and intensified by the circle of gay pals that the very straight Ferry surrounded himself with soon after arriving in London in the late sixties. 'Bryan had a lot of gay friends who were designers and photographers,' Mackay recalls. In contrast, Eno – despite the effeminate clothing, which he'd worn for some years prior to joining Roxy

– was 'the least camp person you could meet', according to Mackay.

This milieu of mostly gay aesthetes served as a kind of brain trust for Ferry – or more accurately, eye trust. In addition to Newcastle associates like Nicolas De Ville (who did much of the group's artwork) and Simon Puxley (originally part of Mackay's circle at Reading but soon Ferry's *consigliere*) there was the photographer Eric Boman and the fashion designer Antony Price – both products of the Royal College of Art, and both gay. Like Ferry, Price came from the north of England, just sixty miles or so from Newcastle but a world apart: the Yorkshire Dales, all hills and heather, stone walls and babbling brooks.

Price was known to remark that he felt Ferry was essentially gay in every respect – sensibility, style, taste, humour – except for between the sheets. 'I found them more simpatico,' is how Ferry spoke of his gay friends in a 1974 interview with Gordon Burn. 'A year ahead of everybody else. Being so close for so long to the art world, my friends have nearly always been gay. Most of the people I really know or see at all now are in fact in fashion because they're attractive, personality-wise, and therefore not incredibly deep. They are not really interested in what I do, mostly they're only interested in themselves – which really, I suppose, is fair . . . It's your fashion-society type scene, who I happen to get on with very well . . . because they're interested in style . . .' Addressing the same topic in *Melody Maker*, Ferry explained that 'gay people usually have very good taste, and I tend to be fairly camp onstage, anyway. Maybe it's rubbed off on me with lots of my friends being gay.'

Through this circle and its wider network of contacts, the nucleus of Roxy's fandom coalesced from the earliest gigs, garbed in a retro-chic look – fake leopard skin, mesh veils, pillbox hats – that drew a sharp line between the new elite and the hairy denim types still everywhere in London. As 'Virginia Plain' on *Top of the Pops* and the group's appearance on *The Old Grey Whistle Test* made Roxy a national phenomenon, little tribes of glamorously attired fans began to congregate at gigs, especially in the northern cities. The *NME* dubbed it the 'nouvelle eleganza'. In a report headlined 'Chic to Chic', Roy Carr and Charles Shaar Murray described Roxy's four consecutive shows at London's Rainbow Theatre in 1974 as an 'amateur couture catwalk' teeming with 'flat-chested femme fatales', 'heavy-boobed waterfront B-girls with scarlet slashes for mouths' and 'fresh-faced fops in white tie and tails'.

Even though most of the music on *Roxy Music* and *For Your Pleasure* was a more melodically focused and concise form of progressive rock, all the ancillary aspects of the group's image, packaging and attitude signalled loudly to an audience looking for something different, something *a cut above*. The interviews were full of little clues: Ferry spoke of how Roxy were 'determined to make it in as civilised a way as possible' – rejecting the standard notion of slogging up and down the country in a van, paying your dues. He would quip that where other bands 'wanted to wreck hotel rooms, Roxy Music wanted to redecorate them'. Journalists followed their lead, making much of the fact that the group always stayed in the finest suites of four-star hotels, quaffing champagne. The care taken with clothes and photography, record design and typography was obvious to the eye, but Roxy pointedly signalled their separateness from the rock hoi polloi by placing credits on the album sleeves for their hair stylist, make-up artist and clothes designer.

Roxy's perceived emphasis on visuals over sound provoked suspicion among the old guard. *Whistle Test* presenter Bob Harris subtly indicated his disapproval of the band through his thicket of brownish beard when introducing them on the 20 July 1972 show. 'There was clearly a sense that we'd been hyped,' recalls Mackay of the gist of Harris's animus. Harris elaborated later in 1972 during an *NME* interview, in which he lamented the rise of image-bands deficient in musical substance. 'People say these days – about bands like Sparks and Roxy Music – well, they're not much musically, but they're great visually. I've been in music for a long time and I think it's a sad state of affairs when the best you can say about a band is they're great visually . . . What an indictment.'

Yet for the new breed of Roxy believers *The Old Grey Whistle Test* was a weekly showcase of all that had gone wrong with rock. 'Everything went flat,' recalls Manzanera of 1969–71. 'A lot of musicians were getting strung out on heavy drugs. They were out of it, so they weren't even bothering to wear kaftans or other hippy stuff, which had been stylish in their own way.' With Roxy and their ilk, 'suddenly there was colour and exoticism and the spirit of rock'n'roll again'. Manzanera points to the June 1972 gig at the Croydon Greyhound, where Roxy supported Bowie, as the flash-point. 'It was a tiny stage but it had theatrical lighting, so you had to wear make-up, because that's what theatre people do, otherwise you look washed out. Bowie was in his full Ziggy Stardust gear and us in all our regalia, performing to just 150 people in this little upstairs room.'

The 'regalia' was Roxy's mash-up of classic rock'n'roll, twenty-third century and pre-rock glamour tinged with tackiness. Ferry favoured fake leopard and tiger fabric, combined with an Elvis-in-outer-space quiff, but his persona was generally described as that of a lounge lizard ('a very slimy Dirk Bogarde–Laurence Harvey type', is how he put it). The bearded Manzanera came across as a snazzed-up, tidier version of a late-sixties freak, wearing Antony Price-designed sun-glasses that looked like fly's eyes. Eno combined bolero jackets with feather boa plumes, referencing thirties glamour while travestying it.

Eno had experimented with androgynous clothing and make-up for years before Roxy. Thanks to his lover Carol McNicoll, a sculp-tor and clothes-maker, he started to wear stage costumes not unlike the preposterous constructions into which Gary Glitter inserted him-self. 'It was impossible to do anything normal, like making a cup of coffee, in them,' Eno told *Rock's Back Pages* in 2001. The choice of such architectural garments was deliberate, to magnify the otherwise minuscule gestures involved in twiddling the tiny knobs of a synth. Because his stage presence involved 'standing still a lot of the time', he and McNicoll 'were really thinking in terms of sculpture rather than clothing. They were clothes that you could only really wear onstage.'

Despite Ferry's 'gay' sensibility and circle, despite Eno's flaunted effeminacy, both were rampantly heterosexual. Like so many sixties rock androgynes, Eno found that dressing like a girl was attractive to girls. Very attractive. In 1974, Eno – now a solo artist – cancelled a gig because of a collapsed lung. He later boasted to the *NME* that this was the result of 'a night of extreme activity. I don't think I've ever been that active in such pursuits . . . six girls in thirty hours, mate – and that's when it started, I suppose.'

Ferry was not a sex maniac, to use the seventies term, to the same degree; if anything he was a romantic, chronically pursuing a femi-nine ideal. But he did date most of the female models who appeared on the Roxy album front covers: *For Your Pleasure's* Amanda Lear, *Stranded's* Marilyn Cole, then doubling back to bed Kari-Ann Muller from the debut album's cover, and finally seducing *Siren's* Jerry Hall, then nineteen years old, to whom he would become engaged, only for her to ditch him for Mick Jagger.

On the *Roxy Music* cover Muller (later, bizarrely, to marry Jagger's brother Chris) featured as a forties pin-up in halter-neck swimsuit, blue eye make-up and silver platform-heel sandals. This was a sly, cheeky subversion of rock-iconography norms. As Roxy biographer Paul Stump points out, rock albums at that time rarely featured a woman on the cover, preferring abstract, trippy or sur-real imagery, or photos of the band. Having a beautiful girl on the front of the record was something associated with easy listening or light jazz – like the white-goo-covered nude on Herb Alpert and the Tijuana Brass's 1965 LP *Whipped Cream & Other Delights*. The sexual politics of the Roxy cover were deliberately retrogressive, from the wedding-cake colour palette of pink, cream and pale blue, to the sash tied in a bow around Kari's waist like she's a present waiting to be unwrapped, to her stricken look of parted-lips desire and thrown-down, about-to-be-ravished posture. As well as referencing the Hollywood tradition of Rita Hayworth and Jayne Mansfield, the *Roxy Music* cover alludes to the illustrator Alberto Vargas's pinups for *Esquire* that were often copied and daubed on the fuselage of B-17 bombers. The retro-cheesecake was designed to be both titillating and amusing, the two modes undercutting each other in the same way that vintage porn incites the viewer to have a 'wistful wank'. In yet more exquisite attention to detail, the posed photographs of each group member inside the gatefold sleeve are framed like fifties postcards, with serrated edges.

For Your Pleasure's tableau of ultra-glamour is less overtly retro. Against the nocturnal backdrop of a neon skyline, a pathologically elegant woman – Amanda Lear – is glossily sheathed in haute couture: a darkly glistening blue dress, offset with diamond wrist cuff and gloves to her elbow. The pose catches her in mid-catwalk strut, teetering on absurdly high heels, torso twisting as she holds back the straining leash of a black panther; her eyes are closed in a grimace of smiling self-pleasure. The image is a visual pun – model on a catwalk, walking a big cat – that contains the subliminal equation of woman with a beautiful beast. Open out the gatefold and the back cover continues the same image, with Ferry, playing her chauffeur, leaning on the open door of a crimson limousine and grinning in delight: a modern update of the admiration-from-a-distance and vassal's fealty that the courtly lover offers the *belle dame sans merci*.

The *For Your Pleasure* image is a delirious concoction, a photo retouched to the point where it looks like an airbrushed portrait. The panther appears to have been painted onto the photograph's surface. Amanda Lear recalls that the shoot took place in an empty south London street and the panther had been drugged too heavily. 'They overdid the Valium . . . and the poor animal couldn't get up . . . It was lying flat on its stomach . . . When it came to it, they had to paint the eyes open on the sleeve.'

Another layer of artifice relates to Lear's enigmatic gender. She was rumoured to be a transsexual. Lear's line today is that this story was always just 'a phoney publicity stunt', but others maintain that her birth name was Alain Tapp, later known as the drag artiste Peki d'Oslo. Ferry had first seen Lear modelling during an Ossie Clark show. He and Price thought her commanding height suited their concept for *For Your Pleasure*. 'They wanted a girl who looked like a Hitchcock movie, a little bit dangerous but arrogant at the same time,' Lear has said. 'I had to be able to carry off that ridiculous shiny dress look.' Lear would go on to have a disco career whose glammy and kinky overtones made her something like the white Euro Grace Jones. The title of Lear's first disco album: *I Am a Photograph*.

Writing about the Roxy covers in their book *Art into Pop*, Simon Frith and Howard Horne note how the models were 'photographed to draw attention to the discomfort of their pose'. But this is just high fashion: the jutting angles and broken-looking contortions show off

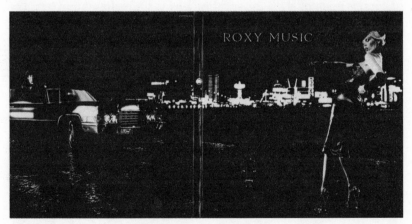

Amanda Lear and feline friend on the gatefold sleeve of Roxy Music's *For Your Pleasure*; limo driver Bryan Ferry admires from a distance

the clothes to advantage and accentuate the model's bony physique. Fashion demands mortification of the flesh: self-starvation, constant cigarettes or stimulants to suppress appetite. Beauty achieved through cruelty.

When *Melody Maker*'s Caroline Coon observed that the Roxy Girls, as they came to be known, were generally as close to men in drag as possible, Ferry admitted that 'there's something removed from reality about the girls on the covers, which I also like'. After *For Your Pleasure*, the album covers moved into an erotica zone midway between Helmut Newton art-porn and Pirelli Calendar cheese. *Stranded* featured Marilyn Cole, the first British Playmate of the Year, as Amazonian beauty, seemingly washed up on a tropical island, drenched chiffon clinging to her figure, a mass of golden curls strewn across rocks and foliage. *Country Life* had Constanze Karoli and Eveline Grunwald brazenly facing the viewer in semi-see-through lingerie, pubic hair discernible: one girl covers her crotch with her hand and the other, bra-less, squishes her breasts behind red-nailed fingers. Along with making a lewd pun, the title *Country Life* references the weekly magazine of the landed gentry, a publication famous for its full-colour ads for real estate. Chasing women is equated with the sporting life, genteel masculine pursuits like hunting and fishing. *Siren* – the fifth and final studio LP before Roxy (temporarily) split – shows Jerry Hall as a mermaid-like seductress, an aquatic femme fatale luring man to heart-wreck.

Clever, multi-layered and visually arresting, the Roxy covers reflected Ferry's frank anti-feminism. Talking to Coon for *Melody Maker*, he mused that 'if you buy a woman you can control her without commitment. Prostitution has always seemed quite a sensible thing to me, really.' Asked about the Women's Lib movement, he confessed in an earlier *Melody Maker* interview that 'I don't think I'd really get on very well with them at all. I'm probably more interested in domination . . . I do hate all these characters who detest beauty competitions and [the *Stranded* cover] will be dreadful for them. I think it's marvellous, and the girls love it, don't they? They love to show off, and basically you've got to do what you can do best . . . If you aren't really very intelligent or intellectual or whatever, but can look fantastic, then it's great that you should promote that as much as possible.'

The word 'model' has multiple meanings: the perfect Platonic form; the subject or muse for an artist or writer; someone whose job is to wear or pose with a product for display or advertising; a design of a product. 'Model', then, exists exactly at the intersection of desire and consumerism, the very place where Ferry did much of his songwriting. So it's hardly surprising that a number of Roxy songs relate to these various meanings of 'model' and its close relative, the mannequin.

One of *For Your Pleasure*'s high points, the shimmering 'Beauty Queen' is loosely inspired by an actual model called Valerie whom Ferry had known in Newcastle. A revealing anatomy of Ferry's ideas about love and desire, the song describes what appears to have been a brief, perhaps unrequited ardour between a man and a woman who share 'an ideal of beauty'. There's a suggestion that the two went their separate ways to preserve their illusions of each other as much as to pursue different career paths. She makes his 'starry eyes shiver', but their 'soul-ships' pass in the night 'plying very strange cargo'.

Although in classic chauvinist style Ferry professed that 'no one admires women more than me', often it came across as a peculiarly narrow appreciation, the way someone might feel about a sports car or some other prized possession. In Ferry's retro-sexual politics, woman lies somewhere between *objet d'art* and sex object. The song 'Ladytron' casts the woman as a love machine, intimidatingly perfect. The chase is thrilling but exasperating ('You got me, girl, on the runaround'), which explains the vengeful twist at the end as Ferry vows, 'I'll use you . . . confuse you . . . then lose you.'

'Editions of You', the track that follows 'Ladytron' on the debut, seems to preview two future Roxy album covers, referencing both the 'country air' and 'slinky sirens' who lure sailors with their crazy-making music. 'Editions of You' is also about how men pursue iterations of the same romantic ideal over and over again. There's a fatalism to the chauvinism – 'boys will be boys will be boys', forever tramping along a treadmill of fixated desire, reflected in imagery of the roulette wheel and love/life as a gamble. Losing is the only guaranteed outcome.

Ferry's conflation of the language of romantic love with consumerist desire climaxes with 'In Every Dream Home a Heartache' and 'Mother of Pearl', the centrepieces of *For Your Pleasure* and *Stranded* respectively. 'Every Dream Home' is a kind of answer record to Richard Hamilton's most famous painting, *Just What Is It That Makes Today's Homes So Different, So Appealing?* Created in 1956 for the catalogue of 'This Is Tomorrow', the exhibition that launched the British branch of Pop Art, Hamilton's piece is a collage of mostly American advertising and mass-entertainment images: furnishings, appliances, logos, brand names. There's a vacuum cleaner, a bodybuilder, a nudie pin-up, a canned ham, a reel-to-reel tape recorder (state-of-the-art domestic leisure technology in '56), a framed image on the wall from a teenage-romance comic and, visible through a window, a movie theatre.

The painting was a renegade gesture at a time when most British intellectuals and members of the cultural elite deplored the influence of Americanisation, from the arrival of supermarkets to the new TV channels featuring advertising. At the same time, the Conservative government was proclaiming that economically the British public had 'never had it so good'. Ferry's lyric for 'Every Dream Home' refers to standards of living rising on a daily basis. It sets the scene for a twisted tale about love that's literally for sale. Ferry's wealthy man sends off for a mail-order inflatable woman.

Slowly he descends into madness as he becomes obsessed with the unresponsive blow-up bimbo.

The scenario is slightly gauche – like The Doors' 'The End', it's the kind of thing that impresses you hugely when you're seventeen. Still, it's Ferry's writing at its most vivid, conveying the aridity of the perfect penthouse existence ('What goes on there? What to do there? Better pray there!') and glimpsing ahead to the decadent suburban interiors of painter Eric Fischl. The religious aspect of the song is what's most striking: 'Every step I take / Takes me further from heaven,' intones Ferry's protagonist. Consumerism is devil's advocacy, its stoking of insatiable desire pushing its victims into a living hell.

'In Every Dream Home a Heartache' was a fan favourite. 'The audiences used to love it,' recalls Manzanera. 'There'd be an inflatable doll that some joker would buy and bring to the gigs. You'd see this thing bobbing towards you from the back of the hall, coming over people's heads!' Yet it's a deeply chilling song. The dynamic – numb, faltering recitation that explodes into freak-out – mirrors the narrative of Ian McEwan's 1977 short story 'Dead as They Come', in which a rich businessman falls for a mannequin in a shop window, buys her, pampers his 'mistress' and then descends into paranoia that she's having an affair with his chauffeur. The story climaxes with ecstatic rape/murder and the moneyman smashing his deluxe apartment and art treasures to smithereens.

In 'Mother of Pearl', Ferry's other retro-sexual masterpiece, the singer plays a socialite, a jaded roué scanning the party for his next conquest, still hopeful of finding a pristine edition of his feminine ideal. In this 'looking-glass world', appearances are deceptive; those who live by them, lose by them. 'Mother of Pearl' uses imagery of the gem trade to describe the romantic arc of illusionment and disappointment. Ferry soon realises that his 'lustrous lady' is not a blue-blooded *belle dame* but a 'so-so semi-precious' social climber with a rough-cut past (just like himself). When Ferry's character declares that he wouldn't exchange her for any other girl, the sarcasm behind the word 'trade' is acrid.

Just as 'Every Dream Home' has a religious undertow, 'Mother of Pearl' references goddesses and the Holy Grail. But the most significant aspect of the song is the choice of mother-of-pearl as the trope of perfection (as opposed to diamonds or gold). The subliminal association is with the Virgin Mother: the whole song revolves around the Madonna/whore dichotomy. Mother-of-pearl, also known as nacre, is an iridescent substance generated by particular species of oyster and other slimy molluscs. Nacre is found on the inside of the shell, or on the outer surface of pearls. This pearlescent shimmer-stuff is a real-world analogue for glamour: an optically dazzling patina produced by an abject, formless biological interior. Virtually imperishable, nacre exists right on the edge between the organic and inorganic, the mortal and the deathless. It suggests that there is something life-denying, or at least life-freezing, about glamour. Reversing William Blake's dictum that 'exuberance is beauty', glamour replaces liveliness with a cold, still perfection: the pose, the photograph.

'Mother of Pearl' would be a fabulously beautiful and inventive piece of music on its own, but it would be empty without Ferry's words and his incredible vocal performance (which apparently was laid down in a single take). Every line is delivered with a deranged archness of emphasis, suffusing the entire song with a kind of poisoned camp.

Camp involves a doubling of the self. It stages a split within utterance itself, as if the camp performer is hovering above or standing to one side of the emotion that's being emoted. Most entertainers proceed as if their vocal mannerisms and facial expressions are 'natural', but the camp performer is aware that it's just a style – and that one day it will go out of style. Talking about this camp consciousness at work in Roxy, Andy Mackay described it as 'a kind of cynicism and a replacement of emotion with style – very much Bryan's way of approaching things, in that he couples direct feeling with a stylistic thing . . . Which in turn means [Roxy] miss out a little bit on the whole range of human emotions which are equally important, like sentimentality.'

The ultimate destination for this sensibility is performance that addresses the fact of performance itself (which may explain why showbiz is so full of songs like 'There's No Business Like Show Business' (from *Annie Get Your Gun*) and 'Make 'Em Laugh' (from *Singin' in the Rain*, a movie musical about the early days of movie musicals)). Roxy reached this point with the title track of *For Your Pleasure*, which in part addresses the strangeness of putting on a show: 'For your pleasure in our present state / Part false part true like anything / We present ourselves.'

We have become used to this kind of meta from mainstream pop in the last few decades (Robbie Williams rolling his eyes while singing as if to undercut the otherwise earnest rendition, or seeking to entertain us with a song called 'Let Me Entertain You'). But when Roxy Music did it in the context of rock in the early seventies, it was new and startling; unnerving to some, even decadent.

Camp, as Susan Sontag argued, expresses the idea of social life itself as a form of theatre. That can open onto a despairing fatalism about the possibility of truth, of any real kind of encounter or exchange. In *Billy Liar*, Fisher deals with his alienation from his allotted roles in life (son, employee, fiancé) by viewing everything in terms of scenes and comic routines. He is 'trying on expressions, as though I carried a mirror about with me and was pulling faces in it. I tried to look stunned, because after all there was the material for it, and I tried to assemble some kind of definite emotion that I wasn't putting on or concocting out of the ingredients [of the situation].'

Fisher is forever donning vocal 'masks' – 'the hearty voice', 'the bluff, appeasing voice', 'the explanatory voice'. Even the realest, most profound experience – the death of his grandmother at the hospital – can't be experienced without role play: 'I had been trying on various expressions and by now I was searching feverishly for one that really belonged to me . . . I felt disgust at myself but, when I shopped around for some deeper emotion, there was none. I had a nervous urge to laugh, and I found myself concentrating entirely on keeping my face adult and sad.'

Ferry often spoke of the theatricality involved in singing onstage. 'With every song you play a character a bit. You take an aspect of yourself and either simplify or ham it up. To some extent it's like method acting . . . you get into a role for it and leave that role when the song ends.' Where rock culture imagined an authentic, integral correspondence between the singer and the truth of the song being sung, Ferry was thinking in much more showbiz terms. This naturally led him to the cover version, or the standard. Indeed, before rock, the actorly approach to singing was the norm, whether it was British music hall with its character songs, or vaudeville, cabaret and musical theatre, where singers hardly ever sang songs they had written themselves.

Conversely, prog-rock bands almost always wrote original material; cover versions were virtually unheard of. Likewise, the singer-songwriters: for a song to be performed meaningfully, you had to have written the words yourself, ideally drawing on your own life experience. So Bryan Ferry's decision to fill his first solo album – *These Foolish Things*, released in the autumn of 1973 – entirely with cover versions was a striking gesture. It tilted Roxy Music nearer the postmodern (albeit by association: first-phase Roxy Music did not record any cover versions themselves). The decision to do a solo album was not unrelated to the recent power struggle within Roxy Music and Eno's departure: Ferry was asserting himself as both the leader within Roxy and as someone who could, and would, prosper independently of the group.

These Foolish Things came out on 5 October 1973. By freakish synchrony, it entered the UK album chart the same week as David Bowie's own covers album, *Pinups*, a collection of mid-sixties mod, psych and beat-group tunes. Ferry was aggrieved that Bowie had stolen the thunder of what he felt was his own highly original idea – to break with the cult of originality! Salt was rubbed in the wound when *Pinups* (#1 for five weeks) eclipsed *These Foolish Things* (peaking at #5). Still, the simultaneous release of such similar projects doubled their impact, coming from artists hitherto seen as cutting-edge and science-fiction futuristic in their sound and imagery.

This switch from innovation to renovation was well timed. The UK's autumn 1973 album chart was overrun with compilations of fifties and sixties pop, as well as *Quadrophenia*, The Who's concept album about mod. That same October had also seen the release of The Band's *Moondog Matinee*, a collection of R&B and blues covers. Amazingly, The Sweet had also been pursuing a similar nostalgia-oriented project, albeit not based around covers but the writing of original songs in the style of other artists and earlier eras. 'A concept album relating to rock'n'roll over a 20-year period with the songs possibly joined together with monologue,' is how Andy Scott described it to the *NME*. In Brian Connolly's account, the journey would start with Elvis circa 1956 and end with 'a futuristic number from 1976'. The Sweet had got halfway into the project when they learnt of *Pinups* and *These Foolish Things*, and abandoned it for fear of seeming like bandwagon-jumpers.

These Foolish Things was not a celebration of rock but a subversion of it. By covering 'Sympathy for the Devil' by the Stones and Dylan's 'A Hard Rain's a-Gonna Fall', alongside sixties pop like Leslie Gore's 'It's My Party' and the pre-rock title track (which dated

from 1936 and whose most famous version out of countless is Billie
Holiday's), Ferry proposed these rock anthems as showbiz standards, separable from the original performer's voices. The avowed
intention was to showcase Ferry's skills as an interpretive singer and
to resituate 'originality' in style as opposed to content. But with the
most recent song coming from 1968, and the bulk from the early
sixties and fifties, the slant was overtly nostalgic.

The title *These Foolish Things* calls to mind the much-quoted
line 'Extraordinary how potent cheap music is' from Noël Coward's
1930 comedy *Private Lives*: the notion that it's the commercial pop
trifles of any era that lodge themselves in our heart and later unlock
precious memories, à la Proust's madeleine. Conversely, *These
Foolish Things* also argues for the timeless quality of the professionally written song.

'The people who did the best songs were, for me, pre-Beatles,'
Ferry argued in *Melody Maker*. *These Foolish Things*, then, struck a
stance of forthright aesthetic conservatism: it's time to roll back the
rock revolution, the band revolution, and restore slipped standards
by . . . writing some new standards. But the treatments sometimes
had the opposite effect: 'Hard Rain' survived the 'standard-isation'
rather well, but 'Sympathy' became a hammy farce, as if Jagger had
been ousted in favour of Vincent Price.

Bowie's *Pinups* was a peculiar undertaking. Critics were bemused
that Bowie dissipated his energy on what clearly seemed like a place-
holder project: mannered remakes of songs at once dated yet too
recent to feel nostalgic for, all wrapped up in a sleeve with Bowie
posed next to Swinging Sixties It girl Twiggy. (A nice joke – Twiggy
plus Ziggy, especially as she was clad in 1973 Bowie style rather than
her 1965 look.)

On one level, it seemed like an ahead-of-the-pack move: with
fifties nostalgia rampant, Bowie gets a jump-start on the next big
wave of revivalism, the sixties. But there were personal motivations

for Bowie to revisit tunes by The Pretty Things, Yardbirds, Them, Pink Floyd and other more obscure groups of the middle sixties. Pausing for breath between retiring Ziggy Stardust and launching into his next self-reinvention, Bowie cast back fondly to the days when he was a mod wannabe: Davie Jones, 'Wardour Street pill-head' and frontman of undistinguished groups with generic names like The Manish Boys. 'These are all bands which I used to go and hear play down the Marquee between 1964 and 1967,' Bowie told one interviewer of his cover choices. 'Each one meant something to me at the time. It's my London of the time.' Originally he intended to redo his ambivalent 1966 song about mod 'The London Boys' for inclusion on *Pinups*.

The covers project was also a reorientation for a disoriented star, reconnecting him to his Britishness after an extended period in which he'd looked to America both for inspiration and for the success that would seal his superstardom. It also allowed him to keep his name out there and put product in the record stores without having to write new material at a time when he was exhausted and emptied. Finally, like Ziggy and the trio of homage songs (Warhol, Dylan, Velvets) on *Hunky Dory*, this was another case of Bowie highlighting his own fandom – and presumably why he chose the odd title *Pinups*, evoking the teenager who cuts out pictures of idols and sticks them on the bedroom wall.

Alongside the idea of the photographic image of the star, *Pinups* also contains a subliminal hint of the butterfly collector, who takes living things, wild and free, and pins them in perpetuity. Something of this process seems to be going on with Bowie's cover versions. With just a few exceptions, some of the most insurrectionary songs of the sixties are rendered as caught-in-aspic replicas. The glossy seventies stereo production ought to be a bionic enhancement of these riffs and big beats, but the results are clinically contoured, losing the smudged roar of the mono originals, which were mixed for seven-inch 45 rpm singles heard through transistor radios or Dansettes. Reviewing *Pinups* for *Rolling Stone*, Greg Shaw recalled how 'the vocals in this genre would scream for attention from the very center of the tracks' blast of pure noise. But Bowie's vocals float carelessly above the music.' Beyond production, some inner drive seemed absent: the volcanic release that made this music the soundtrack of what people called the youthquake.

The remakes of 'See Emily Play' by Pink Floyd and The Yardbirds' 'Shapes of Things' were hopelessly mannered, almost comic, but the album's nadir is surely the ridiculously florid and campy take on The Easybeats' 'Friday on My Mind': Bowie's smarmy, over-enunciated diction is a travesty of the original's glad–mad blend of euphoria and desperation ('working for the rich man', the crucial line of this wage slave's roar of defiance, is virtually yodelled), while the production coats the song in a sickly glacé sheen.

The urgency in these mid-sixties songs is history itself: the *need* for this sound to exist right at that point. Groups like Them, Pretty Things, Who, Kinks were already the second generation of rock, but so caught up were they in the hurtle of the sixties, so fanatically committed to their second-hand sound, that they blast right through the inauthenticity and imposture. By the seventies and the third generation, a fatal layer of distance and detachment intervenes. Perhaps in *Pinups* there is a submerged undercurrent of aggression towards ancestors who were somehow able to overcome their unrealness.

Writing about Warhol and the postmodern painters and appropriation artists who followed, Donald Kuspit argues that the celebration of the copy is linked to a 'disbelief in primordiality and its transmutative power' – which for him is fundamentally therapeutic, healing, cathartic. Art that remakes, quotes, pastiches is 'informed by the decadence syndrome: the sense of the decline and impending death of art. This is expressed as a feeling of déjà vu and a sense of art's loss of significant human purpose.' Such (re)creativity has a vampiric relationship with earlier forms, 'as though to suck the dregs of that faded vitality and ambition from it'. They imitate 'the shell' while discarding 'the spirit'.

Bowie originally intended *Pinups* as instalment #1 of a two-part series (the second to consist of American songs from the same time frame) but he abandoned the idea. Ferry, however, swiftly followed *These Foolish Things* in the spring of 1974 with *Another Time, Another Place*, which turned to soul and country – both realms where the songwriter/singer split prevailed – for its source material. More significant than the song choices, though, was the photograph of Ferry on the front: an image change that would come to define Ferry – and ultimately trap him. *These Foolish Things* had him styled in 'a motorbike look' of black T-shirt – vaguely fifties, compatible with rock'n'roll. *Another Time* cast back before the rock era for an image of timeless elegance: white sharkskin dinner jacket, black bow tie, gold watch, cigarette. The backdrop was a Los Angeles swimming pool; shoe designer Manolo Blahnik lurks in the background, a private joke that surely bypassed even the aspiring sophisticates of Roxy's audience.

Another Time, Another Place's cover says, 'I've made it.' It further exposes the politically reactionary subtext of Ferry's nostalgia: the link between elegance and elitism. The white tux is a gesture of affiliation to the *ancien régime*. There is a time-honoured, 'correct' way of doing things, the image seems to say. The solo albums are about 'standards' in both the showbiz and politically conservative sense: things that need to be maintained, kept high or restored.

Dinner jacket and bow tie would be Ferry's look on the *Stranded* tour. Going forward, his image left behind the campy eclecticism of the first two Roxy albums for archetypes of strong masculinity, like the gaucho look and the GI with sleeves-rolled-up khaki shirt. There was even a brief flirtation with fascist aesthetics on a 1974 tour: Ferry wore jackboots, padded shoulders and riding breeches, with a hint of a Hitler parting in the hair; the stage decor involved a gold eagle with a thirty-foot wingspan.

Ferry spoke admiringly and unguardedly of the Nazis' 'great sense of visuals'. Ever the aesthete capable of separating style and content, Ferry repeated the sentiment at intervals over the years, most tactlessly in a 2007 interview with the German magazine *Welt am Sonntag*. He gushed about 'the way in which the Nazis staged themselves and presented themselves. My lord! I'm talking about the films of Leni Riefenstahl and the buildings of Albert Speer and the mass marches and the flags. Just fantastic – really beautiful.'

As much as it appears to say something unwholesome about Ferry and his relationship to ideas of authority, this fascination for fascism also has much to do with fashion logic. The design-minded fashionista company that Ferry kept in those days rubbed off on him, or further brought out something that already existed within him: the ultra-aesthete's ability to separate style and content. Fashion, as an industry, is a remorseless machine for detaching signifiers from their historical signifieds. That process can be seen at work in, say, the eighties fad for Soviet chic – Lenin badges, record covers and Swatch designs that drew on suprematist and constructivist graphics. More recently, you can see it in the craze for T-shirts bearing the face of Che Guevara. Images and styles that really *represented* something – revolutionary or reactionary, threatening or abhorrent – are emptied of meaning.

One of Ferry's most successful solo singles, taken off *Another Time, Another Place*, was 'The In-Crowd' – a ferocious hard-rock remake of the song made famous by Dobie Gray, a favourite of sixties mods. 'The In-Crowd' celebrates membership of an elite of taste and knowledge: those who have the sharpest clothes and latest dance moves, those whom others imitate. The line about 'the originals' still being 'the greatest' is a nice little joke for a single that flags an album of cover versions.

Ferry told the *NME* that he did the song as 'a kind of gift' to his core fans, that aristocracy of stylists who coalesced around the group. This was the in-crowd that he had sought from the start: 'Bitters End' ends Roxy's debut LP with the listener-flattering line 'should make the cognoscenti think', while in features Ferry often buttered up his following, describing them as 'the "crème de la crème"', smarter and sharper than the fans of other groups.

'The look was . . . all to do with superiority. We felt that we were so clued up about the scene . . .' Janet Street-Porter told Roxy scholar Michael Bracewell, in reference to a shared working-class-gone-to-art-school ethos of a 'ruthless sense of self-improvement', involving drawing up endless lists of books and films to be read and watched. Such autodidactic discipline seems commendable. But there was a nasty, proto-Thatcherite edge as well. Chris, the seventeen-year-old Roxy/Bowie-loving design student at the start of this chapter, was candidly anti-egalitarian: 'I'd like to live somewhere where there was a lot of money, where there were a lot of really smart people . . .' he told *Let It Rock*. 'I don't like ugly people so I'd like to live in a place where I could always go around with attractive people, say in modelling.' Peter York revealed a slightly different kind of snobbery, sneering at the middlebrow, middle-class prog-rock fans as 'hideous, half-educated . . . the downside of the Butler Education Act' – a reference to the legislation that expanded higher education in Britain beyond the traditional upper classes, through the creation of red-brick universities and polytechnics.

Roxy fans often celebrate the band in terms of an invented aristocracy, based around cutting-edge taste rather than inherited wealth and expensive private education. But Ferry was very interested in the actual upper crust. A huge fan of F. Scott Fitzgerald's novels, his attraction to E.G. as a management company was partly down to David Enthoven and John Gaydon being Old Harrovians. Their approach to business was 'gentlemen at play'. Even early on, 'all of Bryan's friends were rich', Roxy's first bassist Graham Simpson noted mordantly.

Ferry's penchant for the posh was acknowledged in the throwaway line in 'Editions of You' about old money being better than new. But it became increasingly evident in his lifestyle: hanging out at Annabel's and Tramp (favoured drinking-and-dancing spots for scions of the nobility), attending dinner parties at country estates. 'Street cred' was a potent concept in the UK music press during the seventies. As the gossip items about Ferry's social activities accumulated and his snooty attitudes snuck out in interviews, many of the writers who had once celebrated Roxy Music started to turn against the singer. The *NME* was merciless in its campaign of mockery, generating an endless string of nicknames along the lines of Byron Ferrari and Biryani Ferret.

But the real sign of changing times came in November 1974, when the designers Malcolm McLaren and Vivienne Westwood started selling a T-shirt they'd made in collaboration with future Clash manager Bernie Rhodes. It bore the slogan 'You're gonna wake up one morning and know what side of the bed you've been lying on.' On the right side of the T-shirt (as you wore it) was a large block of text listing 'hates' – often former heroes considered sold out and co-opted – a roll call that included Mick Jagger, Andy Warhol, Rod Stewart, June Bolan. On the left side, as worn, unfurled a much smaller collection of 'loves': true rebels, living and dead, among them Valerie Solanas, John Coltrane and the fledgling band 'Kutie Jones and his SEX PISTOLS'.

Bryan Ferry, of course, was on the wrong side of the divide: right near the top of the T-shirt's list of counter-revolutionaries.

7:

TRASH CITY: NEW YORK DOLLS AND WAYNE COUNTY

Wayne County – Theatre of the Ridiculous – The Cockettes – John Waters and Divine – Andy Warhol and Paul Morrissey – New York Dolls

In mid-summer 1973, New York's Channel 2 – the CBS local news station – ran an item on the weird rock energy bubbling up in down-town Manhattan. 'The music is rough, not polished . . . the lyrics are shouted, not sung . . . the sound is belligerent, hostile and defi-nitely loud,' intoned reporter Joel Siegel, over live footage of a band whose performance collided camp and chaos. 'They call themselves the New York Dolls,' Siegel continued, adding that they were just one of a number of young New York bands with names like Street Punk and Queen Elizabeth. 'The Dolls are a social phenomenon . . . They sell out every show. They're in their late teens and early twenties, and so is their audience. This is a new generation, and a new music.'

Interviewed for the news clip, the Dolls' big-lipped, gangling singer David Johansen came across as surprisingly thoughtful. He co-signed Siegel's third-generation framing, arguing that the last wave of rebellious music had come 'from San Francisco. It had a definite purpose, the enfranchisement of certain people. This is the next wave of music, for the under-twenty-ones. The basic dif-ference is that a lot of the liberation was already done. We had a lot less trouble to go through – a lot of change the people went through to liberate themselves has been done. We just picked up where they left off.'

Channel 2's report had a twist in the tail. For all their louche assault on eyeballs and eardrums, the Dolls were actually 'one of the tamest groups' on the scene, Siegel claimed – there were others who were even more shocking and destructive. 'The way things are going, it will probably end up with some kind of extreme violence onstage,' Siegel predicted, mentioning Iggy Pop's recent performance at Max's Kansas City, during which the singer cut up his chest on broken glass and needed sixteen stitches. But he probably also had in mind Queen Elizabeth, the band mentioned earlier in the news story. Fronted by cross-dressing shock-rocker Wayne County, Queen Elizabeth's act involved simulated sex and the defecation of realistic-looking excrement.

The roots of County's act went back to the drag subculture of Atlanta, Georgia, where she lived for some years in the sixties. 'Wrecking' was basically the drag-queen equivalent to *épater les bourgeois*. 'Screaming at cars, screaming at people, just being outrageous. Literally stopping traffic,' recalls County, who nowadays goes by the name of Jayne County. 'We were performing for people. We were wrecking them, but we were performing. We loved to perform. The streets were our stage.' All that Queen Elizabeth added to wrecking was rocking – electric guitars, played hard and fast.

Before moving to Atlanta in the late sixties, County had grown up in a small town in Georgia. She became obsessed from an early age with Hollywood glamour, above all the vamps of the twenties and thirties. 'I studied all the old movies.' From watching stars like Jean Harlow, County learnt how to shave off eyebrows and draw them in again with pencil, and tricks for accentuating cheekbones. For a while, she had a theatre erected in front of the family tool shed and put on productions involving neighbourhood children. County also became obsessed with ancient history, 'the amazing outfits and hairdos' of Rome, Greece, Persia. Her Queen Elizabeth stage look involved huge wigs and gold metallic outfits that invoked the regal

origins of glamour as political theatre, the grandiose staging of hierarchical power.

After a few years in Atlanta, County moved to New York. Her
roommates there included Leee Black Childers, who became the
court photographer to the Warhol scene ('take a camera out in front
of a bunch of drag queens and they start posing automatically'), and
Factory superstar Jackie Curtis. Then County became involved in
the Theatre of the Ridiculous, a genre of absurdist-parodic fringe
drama spawned out of New York's drag scene.

The first Ridiculous play County saw was *The Life of Lady Godiva*,
starring Jackie Curtis and Ruby Lynn Reyner, whose role involved
sex with a wooden horse. Then there was *Heaven Grand in Amber
Orbit*, again starring Curtis, which started in the theatre lobby and
featured a song called 'Thalidomide Baby'. 'During "Cock Strong"
a huge cock came out of the wall and it was coming glitter,' recalls
County with a giggle. 'People were singing under umbrellas as glitter piled out of this huge cock.'

Even more than the eye-popping outrage, County was entranced
by the clothes worn by the cast. 'Thrift-shop clothes that were
meant to look like movie-star clothes, and they used sequins and
glitter everywhere. Glitter on their eyes, lips, their whole bodies.
Everything just shone. They'd leave the stage and you could shovel
the glitter off the stage.'

County's first role in a Ridiculous play was in *World: Birth of a
Nation*, which she describes as 'about the castration of man, the
castration of the human race. All the characters were androgynous,
the genders were blended. The men wore high heels and glitter and
ribbons in their hair, and some of the women had beards.' The characters were all from history: County played Florence Nightingale
and her twin sister Ethel 'in this prom dress, with a beard'. Cherry
Vanilla was in it too, playing 'a necrophiliac. Anytime anybody would
die in the play, she would go have sex with them. She carried her

dead puppy around with her in a shoebox, because when she was a little girl it got run over. Anytime anyone would die in the play, she would crawl over to them and dry hump them and go, "Please don't die, little Spot, please, please, little Spot. Don't die."' John Wayne was a character in the play, says County. 'He gave birth to a baby out his asshole while doing poppers.'

County wrote a play of her own – *Wanker: Fascist Rhapsody* – but it was too outrageous even for Ridiculous producer Tony Ingrassia to take on. 'It made *World: Birth of a Nation* look like *The Singing Nun.*' According to County, *Wanker* opened with 'a Christmas nativity scene, baby Jesus being born in a manger, but when you took the swaddling clothes off, baby Jesus had a Hitler moustache and swastikas around his arm.'

Theatre of the Ridiculous is a term people use nowadays to encompass two estranged companies: the original outfit, John Vaccaro's Play-House of the Ridiculous, and Charles Ludlam's breakaway Ridiculous Theatrical Company. Things got so rivalrous that Vaccaro and Ludlam both put on different versions of Ludlam's script *Conquest of the Universe.*

These two squabbling Ridiculous factions flourished in New York as part of the larger gay underworld of outrage and excess that included Warhol's films and stage play *Pork*, and Jack Smith's movies, like *Flaming Creatures*, along with the free performances staged at his apartment. Elsewhere in America, Baltimore film-maker John Waters mashed together camp and shock, with Divine as his leading lady, while San Francisco troupe The Cockettes fused drag's retro-fabulous artifice with Living Theatre spontaneity.

If these new forms of gay underground performance shared one thing, it was the collision of spectacle and scatology, glitz and shit. The shows revelled in the anti-natural – wigs, make-up, costumes – but entwined it with the abject and animalistic: biological functions like excretion, childbirth, sex, death. What was going on in these plays seemed like a celebration-cum-exorcism of two opposed forms of woman power: feminine versus female, culture versus nature, the seduction of glamour versus the might of procreation. This came directly out of the drag subculture, where slang terms like 'cunty' and 'fishy' betrayed ambivalence about the physical facts of born-female life. In her book about female impersonators, *Mother Camp*, Esther Newton writes about one drag performer whose act involved throwing a ketchup-covered sanitary pad into the audience.

Perhaps this queasy alienation from biology explains the fetish for glitter. Generally made of plastic or aluminium foil ground up into tiny reflective particles, it's the sparkly inorganic quintessence of glamour as a victory over nature. Micro-sequins that catch the light, glitter seems very twentieth century. There are ancient pre-cursors to glitter, made from mica, beetle shells, even ground glass. But its modern mass-produced form is a cut-price gesture towards the regal. Shimmering somewhere between class and trash, glit-ter harks back to Hollywood (sequins and lamé showed up well in black-and-white movies, notes glamour historian Carol Dyhouse). 'It was the desire for that sort of Hollywood illusion that we all grew up on,' says Cherry Vanilla of the New York scene penchant for put-ting 'glitter on everything. It was cheap and if you saw the sparkle on drugs – LSD, mushrooms, pot – it looked glamorous and beautiful at night in the lights.'

In *Popism*, Andy Warhol reminisces about 'The Glitter Festivals': parties frequented by Factory members that took place in an apart-ment with mirror-lined walls, where host Stanley Amos would reach into a bureau drawer completely filled with bags of multicoloured glitter and hand them out to the guests, many tripping on acid. They would 'shower sparkles in the air till the whole house was covered in them'. The original Factory location was nicknamed The Silver Factory because Warhol hired Billy Name to cover virtually every surface with tinfoil, silver paint and fractured mirrors. Warhol often procured silver balloons to bob around the room and, of course, his own wig was dyed a lustrous inorganic silver.

Warhol attributed some of the appeal of the metallic-glimmer environment to the amphetamines that tingled through the nervous systems of just about everybody at the Factory, but he also believed that 'it was the perfect time to think silver. Silver was the future, it was spacey – the astronauts wore silver suits,' as he wrote in *Popism*. 'And silver was also the past – the Silver Screen – Hollywood actresses photographed in silver sets. And maybe more than anything, silver was narcissism – mirrors were backed with silver.'

The glitter obsession cropped up independently in other cities where gay men defined the vibe. In San Francisco, The Cockettes centred around a figure who called himself Hibiscus, who wove glittering beads into his hippy beard and wore eye make-up thickly encrusted with tiny sequins. Often wearing ceremonial headdresses and robes, Hibiscus's stage persona seemed like a recreation of the primal scene of the boy child secretly dressing in his mother's clothes, smearing on make-up and preening in front of the mirror. Cockettes performances started out improvised and trippy, but gradually moved into Theatre of the Ridiculous territory: parodic celebrations of bygone showbiz, like the musicals mash-up extravaganza *Gone with the Showboat to Oklahoma*. Paralleling the Ridiculous Theatre schism, The Cockettes split into the utopian free-form company The Angels of Light and the remainder of the original faction, who became more rehearsed and choreographed.

The San Francisco scene formed an alliance with John Waters when Cockettes manager Sebastian started showing the Divine films at the Palace Theatre as part of his midnight-movie series 'Nocturnal Dream Show'. The Waters/Divine approach was much closer to the Ridiculous Theatre's New York proto-punk shock than San Francisco's psychedelic frolics. Taste and decorum were violated. *Eat Your Makeup*, made in 1965, was a simulation of

Abraham Zapruder's hand-held film of JFK's assassination, Divine as Jackie splattered with brains and blood; 1969's *Mondo Trasho* climaxed with Divine being raped by a lobster. But it was 1972's *Pink Flamingos* that catapulted Waters and Divine to worldwide notoriety, with the scene of the drag queen eating a still-warm dog turd off the sidewalk.

Pork, the Warhol play whose cast included Wayne County and Cherry Vanilla, came from a similar place as the Waters/Divine films. It even featured a shit-eating scene. 'There's a scene where my character is describing a plate job,' recalls Vanilla. 'That's where a hooker holds a clear glass plate under her behind, a man lays down under it, looking up, and she shits in the plate. We depicted that onstage. I would mix up instant chocolate pudding onstage and do it with the chocolate pudding, and then I would lick the spoon, of course, and the audience would be totally disgusted.' Bowie was blown away when he saw the play during its 1971 London run. Even three years later he could still be heard rhapsodising about its potential as a TV series, telling William Burroughs that '*Pork* could become the next *I Love Lucy*, the great American domestic comedy. It's about people hustling to survive. A smashing of the spectacle.'

A sharp, somewhat vindictive lampoon of the Factory itself, *Pork* was based on tapes that Warhol had made of his conversations with Brigid Polk, also known as Brigid Berlin. Anticipating today's self-archiving mania of Facebook and selfies, Warhol was obsessed with documenting and preserving everything – phone and dinner conversations, but also personal detritus like receipts and wrapping, which all got boxed up for posterity. After Factory secretary Pat Hackett laboriously transcribed the hours and hours of phone recordings, Tony Ingrassia edited them into a script in which key Warhol-scene figures appeared thinly disguised. Brigid Polk became 'Amanda Pork', played by Cherry Vanilla; Viva became 'Vulva Lips', played by County; Warhol himself became 'B. Marlowe', played by Tony Zanetta.

'Vulva was a piss-take of Viva, which infuriated her,' recalls County. 'Andy did *Pork* to make everybody crazy – that was his favourite thing in the world. He tried his very best to torture people any chance he got.' Vanilla enjoyed playing the Brigid Polk-based lead character 'because she was a speed freak and kind of an aristocrat too'. But the role was challenging because, she says, '*Pork* didn't follow any kind of sensible storyline. Being a speed freak, she would jump from talking about her abortions to talking about her mother's society dinner parties and back to the abortions, and then on to something else about animal faeces.'

Like *Pork*, Warhol's films were a strange mixture of low-budget *vérité* and high unreality, grit and glitz. Take *Trash*, the 1970 movie produced by Warhol but written and directed by Paul Morrissey. Many of the scenes involve the collision – and mutual fascination – between low-rent and high-society characters. The heart of *Trash* is the relationship between the sexually inert, emotionally unresponsive Joe (played by Joe Dallesandro) and the amorously needy Holly (played by Holly Woodlawn). They live together in squalor. Joe can't get it up and suggests they use 'the beer bottle'. While Joe nods out, Woodlawn holds his limp hand while moaning, 'Oh, that beer bottle hurts . . . Tomorrow it's gonna be with you, Joe, promise . . . No more beer bottles.' In another scene, Joe and Holly become a parody of a heterosexual married couple, as she feigns pregnancy using a pillow in order to claim welfare. When the visiting welfare official takes a shine to Holly's silver shoes, which she found in the trash, and offers to expedite the process in return for the footwear, Holly perversely declines, even though this condemns the couple to continued destitution. For Holly, the shoes are a totem of the high life that she adamantly refuses to relinquish, even as the departing welfare officer shrieks, 'You're garbage, you're lowlife, you're not getting a dime.'

In Warhol's universe, glamour and trash weren't so much opposites as a conceptual couple. His proposition that 'in the future everybody will be world famous for fifteen minutes' effectively trashes the concept of stardom as a time-defying eminence, pointing with cynical clarity to how the star-making industries of Hollywood and pop music are built around disposability and planned obsolescence, just like washing machines and motor cars. This is the subtext of *Heat*, a later Warhol-produced movie starring Dallesandro as a former child star hustling in LA and, in a parody of *Sunset Boulevard*, seducing an older, failing actress.

Despite his involvement with Warhol's world, director Paul Morrissey was critical of liberalism and the permissive society. ('I'm with Rome 100 percent,' is how he has described his views on sexual morality.) But he nonetheless insisted that he always had the utmost sympathy and respect for drag queens, claiming that he was the first and only director 'to use transvestites' to play proper female roles. 'I think the artifice of using a man as a woman makes it more of a movie. And movies are great because they create artificial situations, and only through artificial situations does the real truth sneak out.'

Warhol, likewise, was an admirer of the sacrifice and commitment that went into drag's performance of femininity, observing that 'being sexed is hard work . . . Getting rid of all the tell-tale male signs and drawing in all the female signs . . . It's hard work to look like the complete opposite of what nature made you and then to be an imitation woman of what was only a fantasy woman in the first place.' In *The Philosophy of Andy Warhol*, he describes drag queens as 'ambulatory archives of ideal moviestar womanhood' who are 'consecrating their lives to keeping the glittering alternative alive'. This sterling 'documentary service' preserves 'the way women used to want to be, the way some people still want them to be, and the way some women still actually want to be'.

That these ideas have an uneasy relationship with feminism can be seen by the Morrissey-directed, Warhol-produced *Women in Revolt* (1972), whose three main characters are played by Warhol's most illustrious female impersonators, as celebrated in 'Walk on the Wild Side': Holly Woodlawn, as a model; Jackie Curtis, playing a school teacher; and Candy Darling, in the role of an heiress social-ite turned aspiring actress. The Women's Liberation movement is presented as fuelled by hysterical petulance and man-hatred, with characters making statements not unlike those of Warhol's would-be assassin Valerie Solanas: 'You know that males are inferior to the females, don't you!', 'I can't stand the sight of men – I'll make it with women!', 'Men suck!', and so forth. There are parodies of consciousness-raising meetings (during which Jackie Curtis's char-acter finds 'very little difference between rape and sexual inter-course') and a scene where the rad-fem group P.I.G. (Politically Involved Girls) randomly attack a labourer who's digging a hole in the road, inflicting an enema upon him.

The women's movement – and implicitly all attempts to change society – are ridiculed as a passing pose: Jackie's teacher ends up a suburban mom, Holly's model becomes a Bowery bum pissing in the street, while Candy's rich girl does become a movie starlet of sorts. Promoting her new picture *Blonde on a Bum Trip*, she is pat-ronised by an interviewer who sneers that 'Women's Lib, it sounds so dated now, just another phase, like the Hoola Hoop,' and then makes fun of her various non-speaking roles in European art-porn films: 'Underneath all that veneer and polish, if we looked close enough, we would find a very sick, tired, afraid little girl who pushed her way to the top, who slept with every man who got in her way, including her own brother . . . A girl who stopped at nothing to get to the top – not a blonde on a bum trip but a bum on a blonde trip.'

Queer theorists find liberation in the idea that sex roles are con-structed and performed, regardless of whether the outward symbols match the genital reality beneath the costuming. But some fem-inist theorists and gay critics have found a fatalistic conservatism lurking beneath drag, which is based on role reversal rather than androgyny's dissolution of binary divisions. To cross-dress means to cross over a defined line, rather than wipe the line away. Film critic Andrew Britton's 'Notes Against Camp', published in *Gay Left* journal in 1978, sternly argued that 'camp behavior is only recognizable as a deviation from an implied norm, and without that norm it would cease to exist . . . It does not, and cannot, propose for a moment a radical critique of the norm itself . . . Camp simply replaces the signs of "masculinity" with a parody of the signs of femininity.'

County says she named her band Queen Elizabeth in homage to an 'outrageous queen in Atlanta' who achieved the ultimate drag feat of fooling everybody. 'She called herself Queen Elizabeth and she got a job at Rich's Department Store, modelling women's clothes. They had no idea. She wasn't even a trans person, she was just a drag queen who was passing. Then one day, in the dressing room, changing, a co-worker saw her "little friend" down there and freaked out! "You're a man!" And Elizabeth said, "Well, my birth certificate says male, but the subject is quite debatable." She was promptly fired. So I had to name the band in tribute to her.'

One of the main venues Queen Elizabeth and similar glammy-but-punky bands played was Club 82. Located at 82 East 4th Street, in the then very sketchy Lower East Side, Club 82 had been a female-impersonation club since the forties – 'one of the most glamorous drag theatres in New York', says County. By the early seventies, 'rock groups started playing there. 82 became this after-hours, glam glitter place.' County debuted her song '(If You Don't Wanna Fuck Me, Baby) Fuck Off!!' there, she says. 'It brought the house down.'

The venue's cabaret history created an atmosphere of faded old-timey glitz. 'All the old posters with all the old girls that worked there were still up,' County remembers. 'The stage was like a circle, with lights around the bottom of it, just like old vaudeville or burlesque. Chic gold curtains in the back, with the dressing room behind the curtain. And there was a dance space in front of the stage, and then tables and chairs going up in tiers, so people could see.' In addition, Club 82 'had fabulous lighting, which is very important for a really good theatrical drag show'.

Not that County's act was drag exactly: the scales were tipped decidedly away from glamour and into grotesquerie. For a warm-up, 'just to get people going', County would whip out a dildo gun full of milk and spray the people at the front of the club. Then there might be a song like 'Dead Hot Mamma', about incestuous necro-philia, whose staging involved Wayne going down on a mannequin. 'It Takes a Man Like Me to Fuck a Woman Like Me' boggled eyes with a self-fucking routine that involved a strap-on dildo and an arti-ficial vagina. 'The fake pussy had a David Cassidy mask, with faces from *16* magazine stuck on the box. I'd put the dildo into the little fake pussy and fuck myself, and the box would turn around and be different faces. It was very bizarre, very out there. Pornographic, but it wasn't real porno – it was satire.'

The final number – left until last, because it drove most of the audience out the door – was 'Shit': *Pink Flamingos* goes punk. 'I pretended to poop onstage, using Alpo dog food. Then I would reach down and pull out the dog food out of the toilet. People thought it was real shit. And I would start to eat it and people would scream and jump out of the seats. Chairs would go flying through the air.' According to County, there was a serious point underneath the gag-reflex triggering. 'It's about how no matter what you think of yourself, how high-minded you may think you are, everyone's equal when you go into a toilet, because we all have to take a shit. Whether you're a rich person or a junkie, royalty or lowlife, everybody's got to poop.' Glamour and grossness collided in the ultimate trash gesture.

On 6 October 1973, a photograph of Wayne County onstage – huge platinum blonde fright wig, white panstick face darkly gouged with mascara and lurid lipstick, mouth scrunched in a grimace as she groped her own falsies – appeared on the front cover of *Melody*

Trans-fixing sight: Wayne County makes the cover of *Melody Maker*, 6
October 1973, as MainMan's next shock-rock sensation

Maker. The caption announced the signing of New York's 'latest
rock outrage' to MainMan. Later that same month, County popped
up again in a *Melody Maker* piece on a new project of Bowie's: the
filming at the Marquee club in central London of a TV special, *The*

1980 Floor Show, for American broadcast. 'I'm here to record an album which will be coming out in March, but it's very hard to get musicians who are drag queens,' County told the reporter, adding: 'The only instrument I play is the mouth harp, but I refuse to play it – because it messes up my lipstick.'

The original plan was for Bowie to produce the debut Wayne County album, just like he'd done with Lou Reed and Mott. But MainMan seemed in no hurry to get started on the project. They did, however, put their full resources behind *Wayne County at the Trucks*, an April 1974 showbiz spectacular staged at the Video Exchange Theatre on Bank Street, on the west side of Manhattan near the Hudson River. Midway between the gay landmarks Christopher Street and the Meatpacking District, this area was known for cruising, drag queens, leather and bondage clubs like Keller's . . . and for its promise of anonymous, near-instantaneous sexual encounters inside the huge Mack rigs that were left open all night after unloading their freight of animal carcasses. *At the Trucks*, for those who knew, was a sly reference to hardcore gay action in a semi-public place thronged with other thrill-seekers.

The show was directed by Tony Ingrassia, who'd previously done *Pork*, and it was produced by MainMan's Tony Zanetta, who'd played the Warhol character in *Pork* and had recently managed the Ziggy Stardust tours. Zanetta came up with most of the staging concepts for *Wayne County at the Trucks*.

'We did this incredible show with all this amazing staging and lights,' recalls County, including swinging white doors through which the star made her grand entrance, wearing a dress made out of dozens of green condoms. County's new backing group, The Backstreet Boys – no connection to the nineties boy band – 'were on the left side of the stage', like in a showbiz revue. 'I had costume changes galore. Every song had a prop and a costume.'

'You've Got to Get Laid to Be Healthy (And I'm the Healthiest

Girl in Town)', a bluesy shuffle that advised 'a good fuck is worth more than one hundred doctors', was performed with a gynaecological table. There was a cover of garage band The Barbarians' 1965 mini-hit 'Are You a Boy or Are You a Girl' and a rendition of County's own ambisexual anthem, 'Queenage Baby'. Another song written to stroke the scene's collective ego, 'Max's Kansas City' – it featured namechecks for the Dolls, Lou Reed and Iggy – was staged with garbage cans, a plastic rat and dancers garbed as whores. The grand finale was 'Shit', now augmented, for reasons unclear, with Nazi accoutrements: County goose-stepped across the stage, wearing a swastika armband and swastikas in her wig. Then she went into the usual toilet routine, except that instead of dog food she scooped out hamburgers, fried chicken and cheap jewellery, which she hurled into the audience.

Wayne County at the Trucks was filmed by MainMan, the idea being that it would be turned into a concert film for the midnight-movie circuit. But then nothing happened. No movie – and no album either. County claims that Trident Studios in London was booked to record the album, with Mick Ronson lined up to produce as surrogate for a busy Bowie. The plane tickets were bought, but then the trip was abruptly cancelled. Not long after this, Zanetta worked on the staging of Bowie's *Diamond Dogs* tour and – in County's opinion – recycled some of the same ideas from *Trucks*, much to her surprise and upset. She became convinced that her career was being deliberately stifled by her own management, because Bowie had been 'infuriated when I appeared on the cover of *Melody Maker*'. MainMan insider Leee Black Childers told County that Bowie felt threatened. 'David wanted to be top freak,' claims County. 'And here I was, somebody freakier than him . . . David was playing a part. I'm not playing a part. David was just pretending. That's what I *am*; that's what I was born as . . . I am a real gender-fuck.'

It's an intriguingly Machiavellian theory, the idea that Defries deliberately put County into development limbo. But it seems more likely that a badly overstretched MainMan, with too many shaky projects already in motion, backed away from what would have been a difficult act to mass-market – something that wouldn't translate to vinyl. And as a cold-hearted business calculation, the hunch that the world in 1974 was not quite ready for a trans rock star might have been a shrewd one. Although crushed in *Trucks'* immediate wake, County picked herself up and ultimately made it on her own terms as a late-seventies cult figure, fronting a new backing band, The Electric Chairs, and sporting a peroxide punk look not a million miles from Nancy Spungen.

New York Dolls were yet another band who aroused talk about Bowie possibly producing their debut album. He was a big fan – raving at the time about how the Dolls had 'the energy of six English bands', and decades later fondly recalling the 'intoxicating' knock-out impact of their 'humour and drunk "don't give a shit" attitude'. Ultimately Bowie passed, while stressing that he 'adored' David Johansen and thought the Dolls' singer should be a movie star. But the two hung out in New York and even had a girlfriend in common: retro-glam Marilyn Monroe lookalike Cyrinda Foxe, who briefly worked at MainMan as a publicist, appeared in the 'Jean Genie' promo video and ultimately became Mrs Johansen.

One of the other things Bowie and Johansen had in common was an easy comfort with – and considerable debt to – gay culture. Johansen had been involved with the Ridiculous theatre company as a teenager. 'When I was about sixteen, I joined up,' he recalled in an interview with gay magazine *Chicago Pride*. 'I would help make costumes after school. I used to work in the basement a lot, and I started noticing that there were these really garish costumes down there, made with sequins and sparkles.' Johansen ended up playing small roles in Ridiculous productions. 'I never really acted . . . but I would be a spear carrier or had a bit part. But I would do lights, I would do sound . . . I was with them for a couple of years, and I just kind of, by osmosis, learned a lot about show biz presentation.'

During this apprenticeship in glitz and provocation, Johansen was also involved with various bands, including Fast Eddie and the Electric Japs, where he initially served as choreographer but eventually took on the role of singer. Meanwhile, the other future Dolls were playing in a variety of groups based on the Brit Invasion model, outfits like The London Fogg and The Pox. All of the Dolls – bassist Arthur Kane, rhythm guitarist Sylvain Sylvain, lead guitarist Johnny Thunders and the band's original drummer Billy Murcia – came from the outer boroughs of New York, from Queens, the Bronx and, in Johansen's case, Staten Island. They also amounted to a mixture of nearly all the great New York ethnicities: Italian, Irish, Jewish, Latino.

Before Johansen joined, the group was briefly called Actress. It would have been the perfect name for a cross-dressing group. Indeed, *The Male Actress* was the original title of Roger Baker's pioneering 1968 study *Drag: A History of Female Impersonation on the Stage*. Drag takes what is already artifice – a set of gender mannerisms that evolved in the theatre world and Hollywood movies – and makes it even more performative, a caricature of a caricature.

Mind you, the name they switched to, New York Dolls, is itself rich in camp associations. Although the name was actually inspired by a toy hospital in Manhattan, 'doll' was by 1971 already a quaint term for 'cute girl' or 'broad' (as in the musical *Guys and Dolls* or the Swinging Sixties term 'dolly birds'). But it also evoked *Valley of the Dolls*, Jacqueline Susann's 1966 pulp best-seller about show-biz starlets in Hollywood, which then became a hugely successful movie melodrama. In the book and movie, 'dolls' is the nickname for pills: the uppers and downers to which one of the actresses becomes addicted. By 1970, the already absurd film had a parody sequel in the form of Russ Meyer's glorious camp fantasia *Beyond the Valley of the Dolls*, in which an all-female rock band arrive in LA and become embroiled in druggy, polysexual decadence. So the name New York Dolls neatly compacted the city of their birth and source of their spirit with a campy, outmoded ideal of feminine beauty, plus a hint of chemical excess.

'Low camp' was Johansen's term for the visual style that the Dolls adopted. Raised in Cairo, Sylvain Sylvain was born Sylvain Mizrahi and came from a Jewish family of tailors, from whom he picked up a knowledge of fabrics and needle-and-thread technique. He and drummer Murcia even started a knitwear brand called Truth and Soul. This passion for clothes fed into the group's image, albeit twisted by a trashy spirit of burlesque and parody. Sylvain favoured leopard-pattern fabrics and backcombed hair, and sometimes wore leather chaps open at the back to expose a butt clad in frilly knickers. Scarves tied around his wrists, Arthur Kane sported micro hot pants or crotch-hugging Batman and Robin-style leotards, matched with glossy-coloured thigh-high boots. Johansen had a range of looks: sometimes a chiffon top that showed off his stomach, or what looked like the top half of a Wilma Flintstone dress, with a single shoulder strap and a rip to reveal chest and belly, or a Fred Astaire-like top hat and tails mismatched with a marabou stole, or just a dickey without the rest of the shirt or a tuxedo, leaving his side and shoulders bare. Johnny Thunders similarly would sometimes arrive onstage naked above the waist apart from a stick-on bow tie. Several times the guitarist sported a swastika armband.

Over the course of 1971, rehearsing by night in Rusty's bike shop in the Upper West Side of Manhattan, the Dolls developed their sound. The Brit Invasion orientation of the members' previous groups remained at the core, augmented with elements from sixties girl groups like The Shangri-Las and The Angels, Chuck Berry's rhythm-guitar chug and raspy blues of the Willie Dixon sort (a particular passion of Johansen's).

Chuck Berry and Chicago blues are both components of The Rolling Stones, of course, and most people, on first exposure to the New York Dolls, took them as Stones copyists. 'My first impressions were that they were the early Stones in strippers' clothes,' Bowie recalled. 'Fabulous early R&B sound, but much sloppier and more vital.' Writing in *Melody Maker*, Richard Williams pinpointed it more precisely as the Stones between *Aftermath* and *Between the Buttons*, especially songs like 'Stupid Girl', in which Jagger sang somewhere between sneer and snarl. The Dolls' groove likewise found the place between swagger and stagger: if the Stones were a car, then the Dolls had one wheel missing and veered constantly on the edge of careening off the road completely.

The stage chemistry between Johansen and Thunders was pure Jagger/Richards. Johansen even had the same huge mouth and rubbery lips. But while the Stones had pioneered glam androgyny, they were sporadic about it: dragging up for 'Have You Seen Your Mother, Baby, Standing in the Shadow?', Jagger wearing a mandress at the Hyde Park free concert . . . The Dolls *lived* it, on and off stage.

The first public performance by the New York Dolls was at the Christmas 1971 party of a seedy welfare hotel directly opposite their rehearsal space. Some of their other early shows took place in gay bathhouses like the Continental Baths and Man's Country. Located in the basement of the Upper West Side hotel the Ansonia, the Continental Baths was where Bette Midler made her name, with music director Barry Manilow sometimes sat at the piano wearing nothing but a towel – just like the patrons. 'It was like there was no audience because all the guys stayed in their cubicles having sex,' recalled Kane of the Dolls' gigs there. Man's Country was out in

Brooklyn Heights. 'The decor was like Marlboro Country, cowboys, saddles . . . all leather and real butch,' recalled Johansen in an early-seventies video interview. 'We ripped the saddles off the wall and put the cowboy hats on and took our pants off . . . The queens were freaking out.'

The band really started to make a name for themselves when they were given a weekly residency at the Mercer Arts Center, a complex of performance spaces in Greenwich Village, not far from New York University. Starting on 13 June 1972, they played there every Tuesday – usually in the smaller Oscar Wilde Room, but sometimes in the larger Sean O'Casey Theatre – until October. The Dolls' ravaged-glamour look and Johansen's coquettish camping – playing with his hair, posing with hands on hips, daintily wiggling his bottom, crooning into the mic with hands clasped in front of him and swaying – drew a loyal following of gay men and downtown bohemians. It made for an audience tableau described by visiting Brit journalist Miles as 'a welter of day-glo, Lurex, tinsel, glitter dust on flesh and clothes, studs, satin, silk and leather'.

One Dolls diehard was Kristian Hoffman, recently transplanted to New York from southern California in the company of school friend Lance Loud. A nationally known figure as the overtly gay son in the pioneering reality-TV show *An American Family*, Lance Loud (amazingly, his real name) was obsessed with the Factory scene and somehow even established a phone-pal friendship with Warhol. Hoffman and Loud infiltrated the Max's Kansas City crowd. Then, after Hoffman read about the Dolls in *Melody Maker*, they caught one of the very early Mercer shows. 'After that, we went to every single show they played,' he recalls. 'At the Mercer but also at the Diplomat hotel and other places.'

A Dolls gig was a dress-up occasion. 'You'd go to thrift stores in advance to buy wild clothes,' says Hoffman, who would later form the proto-punk band The Mumps, with Lance Loud as singer. 'You wanted to out-outlandish everybody else in the room. Whatever was outrageous, you would do it.' Garish forties-style Hawaiian shirts were one popular look. 'Or you might put on a total nineteen-forties Cary Grant outfit. Everyone at that point was watching thirties movies, repeats that were only shown on TV after 11 p.m. until about 3 a.m. That's how everyone started wearing Bakelite bracelets.'

For Hoffman, the Dolls were 'everything that The Rolling Stones pretended to be but never were. They were legitimately outrageous. They were legitimately sexually playful. They would do crazy songs like "Vietnamese Baby" that you didn't know how to respond to: a hilarious take on what America was about at the moment, a button to push that was very uncomfortable for every single person in the room – but they did it and were laughing the entire time.' Hoffman acknowledges the group's limitations as players and the monotony of their melodies. 'I'm not saying they're the best songwriters. I would say they're the best live band I ever saw. I've never seen anything to compare with them. It was like a Saturday-morning cartoon. Every single member of the band had a specific character. They all were incredibly charismatic. You were invested in them from the moment they came onstage. They were all in the greatest outfits and dancing around. You were dying to see what they would do next, and you never could guess it.' And Johansen was the star, 'making fun of everyone in the band, making fun of everyone in the audience. He would ad-lib constantly.'

Johansen, for his part, often talked about the energy and inspiration he drew from the Mercer crowd – how he was their mirror, not vice versa. 'From the stage, I'd watch people on that dance floor and just reflect them . . . I would become whatever I was looking at . . . I would do all their little [gestures], whoever I saw.'

Amid the gay and bohemian followers, a substantial segment of the Dolls' audience consisted of rock critics. The band became a cause célèbre for a certain breed of writer on-board with the punk rhetoric issuing forth from magazines like *Creem* and *Who Put the Bomp*. The Dolls were among the first Manhattan-identified exponents of that kind of raw, high-energy sound that rock critics based in New York could rally behind. The first band that justified an upsurge of local patriotism since the Velvets.

That said, the first piece on the New York Dolls was written by a Brit: *Melody Maker*'s New York correspondent Roy Hollingworth. In his July 1972 report, he wasted no time in hailing the Dolls as possibly 'the best rock and roll band in the world'. A gonzo-style writer who in many ways did 'Nick Kent' before Nick Kent did, Hollingworth celebrated the band in punk terms: 'Musically, they hurt, because they don't have any manners. They can't play very well . . . Their singer, a lovely young replica of Mick Jagger, shouts as though each word were a swear word.' There was a pre-emptive, or proleptic, defence against the doubters: 'Their music may sound like drivel, but whatever it is, it is indeed alive.' The kiss-off was classic Brit rock-paper oversell: 'There's no hype – they're just the best new, young band I've ever seen.' So blown away was Hollingworth that within the year he quit *Melody Maker* and formed his own NY-based trash-rock outfit, Roy and the Rams.

Despite all the hype from leading rock critics on both sides of the Atlantic, the Dolls struggled to get signed by a record company. Major labels were wary of a band whose sloppy, brutish sound was the opposite of what was getting airplay, whose anarchic aura suggested imminent self-destruction. During the band's first trip to the UK, in November 1972, Billy Murcia died as a result of a bad combo of champagne and downers. This hardly inspired confidence in record labels about the New York Dolls as a long-term investment.

Murcia was quickly replaced by Jerry Nolan, a much more solid drummer with experience from playing in Suzi Quatro's old band Cradle, as well as an outfit called Kicks that contained future hard-rock star Billy Squier. Most recently he'd drummed in

Queen Elizabeth. But even this tighter, Nolan-enhanced Dolls did not sway the A&R people at the major labels. At a showcase for interested record-company parties, Atlantic mogul Ahmet Ertegun and Rolling Stones guitarist Mick Taylor thought the Dolls 'were the worst high school band they'd ever heard', recalled Johansen. Presumably there representing Rolling Stones Records, which went through Atlantic, Taylor told the Dolls, 'You guys got just six months to polish it up,' Johansen claimed. 'I told him to go screw.'

Ultimately the band signed with Mercury, but only after a long campaign of persuasion mounted internally by A&R man Paul Nelson, who was himself a leading rock critic. Todd Rundgren was hired to produce the debut. An incongruous choice, perhaps, given that his own albums, like *Something/Anything* and *A Wizard, a True Star*, showcased dazzling multi-instrumental virtuosity and oozed a decidedly un-punk cosmic utopianism of the late-sixties kind (Todd had gotten into psychedelics belatedly in the early seventies). Still, Rundgren could tell there was something happening with the Dolls, something uniquely New York. 'I live here, and I recognize all the things about New York . . . in their music,' Rundgren told *Creem*. 'The main reason that I did the Dolls album was because it was a New York City Record.'

Released in July 1973, *New York Dolls* has one of the most arresting album covers of all time. Caked in make-up, wearing what look like wigs but could also be their own hair permed and lacquered, the Dolls sprawl on a sofa, their expressions ranging from wasted to sullen to coquettish. A garishly rouged Sylvain looks like a Pierrot prostitute crossed with Dustin Hoffman in *Tootsie*. Johansen, head tilted downwards, gazes into a make-up compact cradled in his limp palm, like a shopping-mall Narcissus. The picture is black and white, with the group's logo scrawled like pink lipstick on a mirror; the silver lipstick tube hovers magically above Sylvain's frizzed-out hairdo. On the back, the group are pictured in their more typical stage outfits

Lipstick killers: New York Dolls' self-titled debut. Left to right: Arthur
Kane, Sylvain Sylvain, David Johansen, Johnny Thunders, Jerry Nolan

of tight lamé jeans and silvery platform boots, while an album insert
features a raunchy graphic drawn by Kristian Hoffman: a rear view
of a girl bending over and clutching her ankles in readiness.

Unfortunately, the music didn't quite match the shock impact of
the cover. Like Iggy and the Stooges' *Raw Power*, the Dolls' debut
suffered from a quickly done mix and a clash of sensibilities between
band and producer, who did not appreciate the shambolic vibe,
the drunken randomness, the hangers-on in the studio. Rundgren
couldn't bottle the wild energy of their live shows. 'He fucked up
the mix really bad,' Thunders railed to the *NME*.

Rundgren would later gripe back that the band 'were only barely capable of a half-decent effort anyway . . . I always had to keep the first take that wasn't literally offensive to the ears.' He did concede, though, that 'punk rock heavy-metal downer Velvet Underground New York consciousness' was not really where his head was at.

Rundgren perceptively described the Dolls as the first real critics' band: it took a certain refined sensibility to hear the sophistication within the shambles. But for most people who had read the hype, *New York Dolls* just sounded like a less tight, less tuneful Stones. Hearing it for the first time almost a decade after it came out, I can remember the 'Is that it?' chasm between what I'd read about the band as a live force and what I was hearing – rock history's ultimate example of 'You really had to be there, to be *then*.' The titles are great – 'Personality Crisis', 'Lonely Planet Boy', 'Looking for a Kiss', 'Jet Boy' and the mighty, aesthetic-defining 'Trash', their most glorious racket. But hardly any lines stick in my mind, even after a score or more plays.

Fans always go on about 'Frankenstein', which ends with the question 'Do you think that you could make it with Frankenstein?' Johansen's explanation of the song's meaning is that it's about 'how kids come to Manhattan from all over, they're kind of like whipped dogs, they're very repressed. Their bodies and brains are disoriented from each other . . . it's a love song.' That garbled precis captures the semi-coherent, unfocused quality of the lyrics: blurts of adolescent lust and unrest, pills 'n' thrills 'n' heartaches.

The buzz about the Dolls was loud enough to catch the ear of rock's ruling class at the time, earning mild disparagement from Mick Jagger and stirring what seemed like genuinely rattled offence from The Eagles. In interviews, the LA country-rockers had started making pointed jibes at image-bands who relied on costumes and theatrics, aimed as much at Jethro Tull as Alice Cooper. At one point, The Eagles even had T-shirts specially printed that bore the substance-not-spectacle slogan 'SONG POWER'. Onstage at a concert in New York, they made a point of dissing from the stage those local heroes, the Dolls. Speaking to *Melody Maker*, Don Henley claimed they weren't necessarily 'opposed to theatrics, but when you can't play and you have to rely on weird clothes, make-up and stuff then that's not valid to me . . . At the moment there's an awful lot of bands who need the freakiness to get by . . . The music is secondary to the theatre trip . . . That's burlesque.' Henley and crew understood that what the Laurel Canyon scene stood for – musicianship, melody, mellifluous multi-part harmonies – was being trampled on by songs like 'Trash', whose own 'harmony' vocals were wonderfully wonky and raucous.

But if the Dolls' hype peeved the mega-groups of the seventies, the group never came close to being a threat. *New York Dolls* sold nearly 100,000 – a decent amount for a regular band's debut but a huge shortfall for a group that had enjoyed such a build-up.

In spring 1974, *Creem* ran a one-page piece as part of the magazine's 'CREEM'S PROFILES' series, with the band dressed as gangsters playing cards. In the jokey checklist, under 'Last Accomplishment', the Dolls were credited with having 'Divided a continent; managed to work the "You either love 'em or hate 'em" dichotomy better than anybody since the Stones.' The comparison was sort of true, but ultimately misleading: the Stones had conquered the US, whereas in the Dolls' case the divide among rock fans nationally was more like 98 per cent 'hate 'em' versus 2 per cent 'love 'em'. Even in *Creem*, the magazine that pushed glitter more than any other US publication, the readership voted the New York Dolls as both Best New Group and Worst New Group of 1973.

In a post-mortem assessment a year later, Lester Bangs – a Dolls believer – ran through the various theories for the band's 'zip-zap rapid ascent and declension', which included their constant drunkenness and drugging, the group's rudimentary instrumental skills, the fact that 'all (or a great many) of their songs sounded almost exactly the same', while 'the lead singer had one note' and 'so did their compositions'. Overhype led to overkill and, ultimately, 'Who cares about a who-cares stance?'

The very New Yorkness of the Dolls was a problem. As Lou Reed said, 'New York has nothing to do with the rest of the States at all.' But in the UK – much closer in sensibility to the city state of NYC – the Dolls had a bigger impact. They didn't become stars or sell many records, but they had a catalytic effect on young musicians-to-be, many of whom would in a few years be the front-line troops of punk rock.

On their first trip to the UK in October 1972, the Dolls played support to a variety of mismatched headliners, including Kevin Ayers and Status Quo. Lou Reed decided at the last minute not to let them play at a Liverpool University concert, and the only other simpatico gig lined up – with Roxy Music at Manchester Hardrock – was cancelled when Billy Murcia died.

But when the Dolls returned to tour the UK (and Europe) in the winter of 1973, they were the headline act and riding a wave of enthused press coverage. The legendary gig that people always talk about is their 26 November 1973 show at the department store Big Biba, the hubris-tinged expansion of Barbara Hulanicki's fashion boutique Biba. Described by *Vogue* as 'a palace of apricot marble, coloured counters and fake leopard-skin walls', Big Biba was thir-ties retro-fantasia as total environment. Like other music perform-ers, the Dolls played in the Rainbow Room restaurant, located on the fourth floor, below the roof garden. The £2.50 ticket included a meal, transporting you back to an era when show bands performed to diners at seated tables. 'The most glamorous venue I've ever been to,' is how Michael Watts describes the space. Unconvinced by the Dolls' album, Watts suddenly became a convert: 'Somehow the band clicked with the venue.'

That same trip, the Dolls appeared on *The Old Grey Whistle*

Test, the BBC's serious rock show. Presenter Bob Harris couldn't stop himself smirking and murmuring a mild put-down as 'Jet Boy' clanged to a halt: 'Mock rock'. Harris wasn't wrong exactly: this was parody rock, as Johansen himself said, 'a camp on pop', sending up its ego-swagger and preening.

The Dolls' appearance was polarising – a hairline fissure in the prog versus punk schism to come. *Melody Maker*'s letters page filled with anti-Dolls indignation. 'I pen this epistle only seconds after the end of *The Old Grey Whistle Test . . .*' snorted Peter Moxon of Rotherham, Yorkshire. '. . . I have never, at any level, seen such an amateurish performance or heard such an unmoving, meaningless row.' E. A. Burrows of Harrington Gardens, London, castigated *Melody Maker* for putting the Dolls on the front cover and thus capitulating to the deluge of 'gimmickry and tripe' threatening 'true music', as bands jumped on 'the "Pouff Rock" bandwagon'.

Among the electrified viewers were such stars-to-be as Sex Pistol Steve Jones, John Foxx of Ultravox, most of Duran Duran, and David and Steve Batt, the future singer and drummer of Japan, who renamed themselves David Sylvian and Steve Jansen in mangled homage to Sylvain and Johansen. Then there was Morrissey, who as a teen wrote a now impossibly hard to find fan history of the New York Dolls and as an adult recalled his televisual rapture aged thirteen as 'my first real emotional experience'. In his memoir, Morrissey also described 'Jerry Nolan on the front of the Dolls debut album' as 'the first woman' he ever fell in love with. And he marvelled at the subversiveness of the headline to a *Disc* magazine story about the band, '*Lock up your sons, it's the New York Dolls!*' – a gender twist on traditional warnings to parents about daughters at risk from rock'n'rollers.

In 1974, the band released a second album, *Too Much Too Soon*, recorded with Shangri-Las producer Shadow Morton. A marginally cleaned-up and pop-tidy version of the Dolls' ruckus, the record did no better than the debut, although the critics continued to rave. The title *Too Much Too Soon* was stolen from the 1957 tell-all memoir by movie star Diana Barrymore: she had been '1942's Most Sensational New Screen Personality' but went off the rails through drugs and drink, dying of an overdose in 1960.

The album's front cover reads, 'The New York Dolls in TOO MUCH TOO SOON', like a film poster or a picture palace's glittering marquee sign. 'We were living this movie: everybody wants to see it, and we were giving it to them,' is how Sylvain Sylvain described the Dolls' grip on their fans' imagination to punk historian Jon Savage.

Even more than the live footage that survives, it's the interviews and the hand-held backstage and offstage footage in DVDs like *All Dolled Up* (shot by their rock photographer friend Bob Gruen and Nadya Beck) that capture the spirit of the Dolls. Scenes like the band, on their way to LA, straggling through JFK airport – Sylvain in hot pants and knee-length boots, Johansen in open-chest chemise and bowler hat – and eliciting open-mouthed stares from old ladies and businessmen who look like they could be from the Eisenhower era.

Morgan Fisher from Mott the Hoople, who toured America with the Dolls as support, recalls Johnny Thunders looking 'like a kabuki puppet' and Arthur 'Killer' Kane 'staggering everywhere in these ten-inch-high platform boots. He had to be carried through the airport check-in, a roadie on each side of him, this blond giant in a semi-coma.' For a good chunk of the Dolls' late-summer 1973 tour, Kane just stood onstage nursing a heavily bandaged hand, unable to play: his girlfriend had attempted to cut off his thumb to stop him going on tour.

The Dolls got into plenty of trouble on the road – the kind of havoc that recalled Jim Morrison in Miami, 1969, or anticipated the Sex Pistols in Dallas, 1978. Playing Memphis in September 1973, the band had been warned not to impersonate women on stage (reading the advance press, or perhaps just seeing the album cover, the authorities had got the idea that they were full-blown drag queens). There was heavy police attendance at the Ellis Auditorium Music Hall, and when a young man leapt onstage and kissed Johansen full on the lips, the cops beat up the boy. Johansen stopped 'Jet Boy' in mid-song and shouted to the audience, 'Are we going to take this?' These words and further taunts of defiance were taken by the police as an incitement to riot. Johansen and a number of unruly audience members were taken in handcuffs to jail, where they spent the night.

While the New York Dolls zigzagged across America in an increasingly ragged state, a whole trash-rock scene formed in downtown New York more or less in their image. True, some figures had been around before the Dolls, like The Magic Tramps, whose bisexual singer Eric Emerson had been in Warhol's *Chelsea Girls*. 'Eric's thing was he had a bag of glitter, and he would throw glitter at people in the audience,' remembers Kristian Hoffman. But other groups had clearly been inspired by, or opportunistically remodelled themselves, according to the Dolls template.

One band, The Harlots of 42nd Street, had songs with titles like 'Cool Dude and Foxy Lady' and 'Spray Paint Bandit'. *Creem* described them as 'a great parody of a parody of a parody'. Johansen remembered them, possibly generously, as the Dolls' main competition and 'my favorite band . . . a group of guys who looked like truck drivers but dressed like the Dolls and wore fishnet stockings over these big muscular hairy legs'. In a similar trashy vein were Teenage Lust, Luger (the stage act involved bullwhips), actress turned rocker Ruby Lynn Reyner and her vampy-campy band Ruby and the Rednecks, The Miamis, Street Punk, The Fast, The Brats, and Another Pretty Face (who had some sort of connection to Gay Lib). Some of the bands on the scene contained future stars of New York punk: The Stilettos and Sniper featured Debbie Harry and Joey Ramone respectively.

The Dolls and their fellow travellers were prominent enough to inspire a sour swipe from Lou Reed in the form of 'N.Y. Stars' on *Sally Can't Dance*, which sneered at a scene 'too crowded' with 'fourth-rate imitations', 'so-called "stars"' churned out by 'the faggot mimic machine' and ogled by an audience of 'night ghouls'. The song's kiss-off is Reed saying he can't wait for them to die – presumably from overdoses. Still, for all the bitterness, Reed had a point: this two-year period in the life of New York rock – between *New York Dolls* and the twin debuts of The Ramones and The Patti Smith Group – is historically fascinating and importantly transitional, but decidedly thin in terms of actual musical achievement.

Hardly any of the post-Dolls outfits got to record anything. One exception was Elliott Murphy, whose major label debut, *Aquashow*, prompted some leading rock writers to propose him as the best thing out of New York since Johansen and co. Murphy's connection to glitter was fairly slight, although onstage he did sometimes sport a green fur coat and mirror shades. His thing was far more literary (he was obsessed with F. Scott Fitzgerald) and self-consciously clever, with songs like 'White Middle-Class Blues', 'Last of the Rock Stars' (the 'best where-are-we-now anthem since "All the Young Dudes"', declared Ellen Willis), 'The Love Song of Eva Braun' and 'Marilyn'. The latter proclaimed that 'Marilyn Monroe died for our sins' and 'Our thoughts were dirty, though she was clean.'

New York's trash scene would, however, spawn one of the biggest rock bands of the seventies: Kiss. They started out 'copying the Dolls, playing the same sort of places like the Diplomat hotel', says Hoffman. Then they decided to go full-blown rock'n'roll circus and came up with the horror-clown make-up and tongue-extended grimaces that slayed the arena audiences of middle America. Kiss drummer Peter Criss had once auditioned to be Billy Murcia's replacement, but the Dolls had the sense to pick someone who could actually swing.

N

Given their aggressive sound and irrepressible anarchy, the big question about the New York Dolls is why they were merely a premonition of punk rather than the full-blown revolution. So many of their antics and attributes are flash-forwards to the Sex Pistols, from Thunders puking at airports, press conferences and onstage mid-concert, to the fact that during the band's swansong phase they were managed by Malcolm McLaren. He momentarily gave them a Communist image makeover – red patent leather, a hammer and sickle stage backdrop – in the hope of upsetting an America smarting from its defeat at the hands of the Vietcong.

But that sort of seriousness just did not suit the Dolls: capitalism versus communism was too large a dose of geopolitical reality, involving actual world-historical stakes. Smart and articulate, Johansen could occasionally be lured into a semi-serious discussion of what the Dolls stood for. He might talk about the next stage of liberation beyond feminism and gay activism, which involved 'a kind of "third sex" [where] everybody has male and female characteristics'. But for the most part Johansen's impulse was to play everything for laughs: 'We're trisexual. We'll try anything once.'

Melody Maker's Roy Hollingworth pinpointed the Dolls' delinquency as a form of truancy from meaning: 'No messages. No instructions through song! Nothing to think about. Nothing to admire.' The Dolls were Utterly Without Redeeming Social Value, to borrow the title of a 1967 low-budget movie. Their flip attitude to anything to do with causes or consciousness can be seen in a concert clip of the band in LA. Johansen mentions the tour's next stop is San Francisco, where, he notes mockingly, 'people are into social reform'. When the Dolls arrive in 'Frisco and play their gig at The Matrix, he introduces 'Private World' and describes it as influenced by Cuban rumba. Recalling reading about Castro's takeover of Cuba in newspapers as a child, Johansen jests about how 'before those horrible Communists took over, they used to gamble and swing. Now all they do is build hospitals and work on the farm – and how boring is that.'

In her essay 'Notes on "Camp"', Susan Sontag said that camp is about dethroning the serious. To twist Wilde, the essence of camp is the Importance of *Not* Being Earnest. In another famous passage about camp – from Christopher Isherwood's *The World in the Evening* – one of the characters expresses his vexation with Quakers: their dogged dedication to simplicity and sincerity, plain dress and plain speech. 'I respect them . . . They've got the courage of their convictions, and they mean exactly what they say . . . What I do hate about the Quakers, though, is their lack of style. They don't know how to do things with an air . . . They've no notion of elegance . . .' (Isherwood lived for a while with a Quaker community in California, so knew about this first hand.) Another version of the puritan versus cavalier divide is Willa Cather's dichotomy between Presbyteria and Bohemia. In her short story 'Paul's Case', a highly strung, dandy youth in turn-of-the-century Pittsburgh, Pennsylvania – a state founded by Quakers – flouts his father's desire for him to go into business, moves to New York and fritters all his potential in the pursuit of exquisiteness.

The big difference between Paul's early-twentieth-century brand of foppery and its late-twentieth-century version was, as Sontag observed, that 'the old-style dandy hated vulgarity. The new-style dandy, the lover of Camp, appreciates vulgarity.' This was the Dolls and their audience to a T: they found amusement, even a sort of sublimity, in after-midnight B-movies, comic books and other mass-culture pabulum.

The trash aesthetic emerged towards the end of the sixties. Its earliest manifestation was in movie connoisseurship, shaped partly by a new availability of older films. In the classic era of Hollywood, movies disappeared from circulation: there were obviously no video stores, no television repeats (because TV either didn't exist yet or was largely a live-broadcast medium). By the sixties, though, old movies were being shown heavily on TV. At the same time, a growing hip taste emerged for exploitation and genre movies – horror, science fiction, action – as well as an ironic appreciation of failed or bad movies.

In 'Trash, Art, and the Movies', a February 1969 *Harpers* essay, Pauline Kael contrasted 'honestly crummy' movies (low ambition, low budget, formulaic, made with purely mercenary intent) from the arty, modish, reviewer-approved fare that for her was the *true* trash because it was so phoney, pretentious and ponderously paced. Examples of the latter for Kael included *2001: A Space Odyssey* and the entire genre of Oscar-winning, socially conscious 'message movies'. Worthy was worthless, because it didn't even offer the simple consumer value-for-money escapist entertainment. Kael celebrated the truant thrill of escaping didactic films and used words like 'pedagogic' as a prime insult.

Meanwhile, in the nascent field of rock criticism, figures like Nik Cohn and Lester Bangs were formulating their own version of the trash aesthetic. In 1969's *Awopbopaloobop Alopbamboom*, Cohn described *Revolver* as 'a big step forward in ingenuity' but a 'big step back in guts', blaming the influence of The Beatles' new artiness for 'why there's no more good fierce rock'n'roll music, no more honest trash'. Cohn directly compared his beloved 'Superpop' (rock'n'roll's cartoon flash of image, noise and hype) with Hollywood's heroic pulp. Both possessed 'the same power to turn cliché into myth', generating 'images' that are 'giant caricatures of lust, violence, romance and revolt'. But his tone was elegiac: rock's destiny was to become like 'art movies . . . sensitive, brilliant and meaningful', with polite, discerning audiences. But Cohn would still be found 'in the back row of the Roxy . . . gawking at Hollywood'. And playing his old rock'n'roll 45s.

As for Lester Bangs, alongside his classic manifestos in favour of adolescent blurt 'n' blare (garage bands like Count Five, The Troggs) he also wrote the B-movie celebration 'The Incredibly Strange Creatures Who Stopped Living and Became Mixed-Up Zombies, or, The Day the Airwaves Erupted'. This March 1973 *Creem* essay defended 'unreconstituted trash' and dismissed the concept of 'Good Taste' as just a mechanism 'to keep people from having a good time'.

By the time the New York Dolls released 'Trash' as their debut single in July 1973, then, a proto-punk anti-aesthetic was already well established, at least in bohemian and rock-critic circles. In gay culture, it had existed for a decade at least, probably much longer.

'Trash' is overloaded with evocations. It suggests disposability, the thrown-away, but also the low-class: white trash, trailer trash. 'Trashy' means badly made, but also bad manners and loose morals. As a verb, 'to trash' is to vandalise or destroy (a room or a reputation). 'Trash talk' is foul or abusive language; 'getting trashed' involves getting drunk and losing dignity. All these meanings relate to a core idea of waste: squandered energy, dearth of worth. Trash is the lumpen version of decadence.

So the Dolls couldn't have picked a richer word, a more suitable signifier, for the title of their greatest anthem. But the word also speaks to their limitations as a band, the reason they didn't spark the punk revolution three years ahead of schedule. The Dolls' trash aesthetic makes them ancestors to a lineage of punk and new-wave bands – The Dictators, The Ramones, The Cramps, The B-52s and many others – who are great fun, but no threat. The flipness of the Dolls – their camp and cavalier refusal to take anything seriously – is what held them back from being the Sex Pistols. The Dolls *didn't* mean it, man. Johansen didn't have Johnny Rotten's puritan streak of righteous wrath. Rotten could do sarcasm, but there was nothing ironic about the Sex Pistols. When Rotten sang about being society's 'flowers in the dustbin', he wasn't saying, 'We're trash and proud of it'; he was railing against the wasting of youth's precious potential.

8:

LET'S DO THE TIME WARP AGAIN: FIFTIES FLASHBACKS AND ROCK'N'ROLL REPLAYS

Rock Dreams – Wizzard – The Moodies – David Essex – *Rock Follies* – *The Rocky Horror Picture Show*

'The country of "Now".' That's what George Melly called pop music in *Revolt into Style*. He argued that the worldwide nation of youth 'denies having any history. The words "Do you remember" are the filthiest in its language.' Melly persuasively explained apparent discrepancies in his thesis – like the craze for Victoriana and Edwardiana pervading psychedelia's record covers, posters and clothing – by arguing that in spirit all this was actually *anti*-nostalgic, 'a subtle method of rejecting the past'. The unavoidably omnipresent history surrounding British kids as they grew up was being mischievously wrenched out of its context and turned into a plaything for a present-minded generation. Sifting through the antique shops and street markets for bric-a-brac, hipsters reduced history to 'a vast boutique full of military uniforms, grannie shoes and spectacles, 30s suits and George Formby records'.

Revolt into Style was written in 1968–9, but by the time the book came out in 1970, cracks had already appeared in Melly's thesis. Pop had plunged into nostalgia mode. A full-blown rock'n'roll revival was under way. Far from denying it had any history, youth culture was flicking through its own back pages, wistful for lost innocence. While not identical with the rock'n'roll revival, glam overlapped with it significantly. Fifties echoes flickered through particular songs by T. Rex, Bowie, Roxy Music, Gary Glitter, Mott the Hoople and others. And there were certain artists whose whole shtick was heavily based around either replicating or invoking early rock'n'roll: Roy Wood and his band Wizzard, Alvin Stardust, the songs and movies of singer/actor David Essex.

The fifties were the prime focus for revisiting and re-enactment, but soon other decades got a look in too: the twenties, thirties, forties and even – with *Pinups* leading the way in late 1973 – the sixties. The first half of the seventies was, in fact, the first great age of retro (although that word was not in common parlance in those days).

Articles and newspaper columns expressed bemusement and dismay about the plethora of revivalist crazes. Reporting on Roxy Music's fancy-dress-wearing fans, the *NME*'s Charles Shaar Murray complained that 'the '70s have become the most nostalgia-obsessed decade of the century . . . Everyone's getting so heavily into nostalgia that if the '70s don't get into gear there ain't gonna be anything for people to get nostalgic about in the '80s and '90s.' Others diagnosed the wider cultural mood of retrospection as rooted in a fear of the future and a loss of faith in the very idea of progress. Christopher Booker pinpointed the prevailing mood in Britain in the early years of the seventies as 'weary, increasingly conservative, increasingly apprehensive disenchantment', bringing with it a hankering for 'the charms of almost every time except our own'.

The critical year – regarded by some cultural historians as when the sixties really ended – was 1973. In rock, the mood shift was captured as much by a book – Guy Peellaert and Nik Cohn's *Rock Dreams* – as by nostalgic covers albums like *Pinups* or The Band's *Moondog Matinee*. Belgian Pop Artist Peellaert painted imagined scenes from rock history that were based on magazine photographs but set in semi-fictional tableaux and locations. The effect was at once hyper-realistic and radiantly dream-like. Inventing his own method of photo-surrealism, Peellaert montaged the faces of stars onto Polaroid photos of himself or friends striking poses to establish the imagined tableau. Then he added backdrops that were either painted or similarly photo-montaged. Finally, he airbrushed over the composited images until the painting was seamlessly integrated. Cohn supplied mythopoeic captions, like this one about Mick Jagger: 'Immured in his palace of mirrors, he never grew any older and, even though his stock of games had long since run out, he went right on playing them, over and over and over.' The book received huge attention when it came out in '73, and it helped launch Peellaert's career as an album designer, with commissions to paint the sleeves of Bowie's *Diamond Dogs* and The Rolling Stones' *It's Only Rock'n'Roll*.

Rock Dreams originally came about because Peellaert had attempted to make an animated TV series based on Cohn's 1969 book *Awopbopaloobop Alopbamboom*, also published under the title *Pop from the Beginning*. That book's elegiac tone – Superpop as a period that had passed as absolutely as Golden Age Hollywood – infused *Rock Dreams*, whose final sombre images were of Alice Cooper, Lou Reed and David Bowie. 'Left to my own devices the book would have been the death of rock,' recalled Cohn. 'But although Guy had his dark side and was attracted to these themes, he infused them with love. He was the fan weeping at the foot of the coffin. I was the fan laughing at the foot of the coffin.'

For *Rock Dreams'* 1982 reissue, Michael Herr's introduction developed this theme, pinpointing 1973 as the moment when 'rock and roll . . . had all but passed over into the shadow form . . . Many people were . . . pining for the old tribal jukebox jive and the days of common climax. It was a time of unparalleled bitterness in the culture,' a large swathe of which 'stoned itself blind with nostalgia'.

Nineteen seventy-three was also the year of Wizzard, the most overtly revivalist of all the UK glam groups, whose frontman and leader Roy Wood declared of early rock'n'roll that 'I feel that in those days there was a lot more magic in the pop scene.' Wizzard scored two UK #1 singles in the first half of '73 with 'See My Baby

Jive' and 'Angel Fingers', and ended the year with the Top 5 seasonal smash 'I Wish It Could Be Christmas Everyday'. All were based around Spector's Wall of Sound and were performed by the band in retro Teddy Boy-style jackets (although Wood's own image – lurid face paint and hippy hair-frizz – harked more recently to 1968 and Crazy Arthur Brown).

Wood rationalised his retreads with the argument that 'there was an awful lot of good sounds around which are still usable today – and which, with a bit of thought, can be improved on . . . We are exposing younger audiences to things they didn't hear the first time around.' He rebuffed the accusations of plagiarism levelled at him in letters sent by readers to the music papers, telling the *NME* that 'if someone says any of our records sound a bit like Phil Spector's that's O.K. by me, 'cause Phil Spector is the greatest producer of them all'. His goal was to beat Spector at his own game, using seventies multitracking as well as four drummers, four pianists, eight tracks of acoustic guitars, four cellos and four saxes to build a denser and wider Wall of Sound. The music-paper ads for 'See My Baby Jive' proclaimed, 'The sound Phil Spector was always searching for!'

Roy Wood's project was half humorous and half homage. The full title of Wizzard's second UK #1 hit was 'Angel Fingers (A Teen Ballad)' and the credits included vocal backing from The Suedettes and The Bleach Boys. Rather than push forward into unknown soundworlds (the modernist impulse), Wood was an innovator in the art of renovation. Like pop's very own Dr Frankenstein, he pulled off new stunts of scission and suture. His solo single 'Forever', for instance, was a jump-cut composite that leapt from The Beach Boys to Neil Sedaka. 'I'm a big fan of both artists and I thought, "Now wouldn't it be great if they were both on one record?"' Wood told the *NME*. 'I know that could never happen so I went in the studio and emulated the way I thought it would sound.' To pull this off involved the precise forging of vocal signatures and method acting: 'I had to visualize that, for the moment, I was those people – otherwise I'd never have been able to come anywhere near the sound I wanted.'

Unlike Ferry and Bowie, Wood never did covers: instead, he wrote original, all-new songs in another artist's style. As *Performing Glam Rock* author Philip Auslander notes in a penetrating study of Wood's work, the Wizzard leader was breaking with the sixties rock tenets of authenticity and artistic growth. (The alternative: show-biz, where entertainers have an act and stick with it – a dread fate that befell the less artistic sixties acts, who moved on to the cabaret circuit and played the hits over and over.) Like a human jukebox, Wood jumped around from style to style, anticipating the digital era's logic of shuffle and cut-and-paste.

On the Wizzard albums (and Wood's solo LPs, like *Boulders* and *Mustard*) you found a smorgasbord of pastiche: immaculate replicas of Chuck Berry, Duane Eddy, Carl Perkins, Del Shannon, Gene Vincent. The second Wizzard album, *Introducing Eddy and the Falcons*, adopted the imaginary-rock-band ruse invented by The Beatles and reintroduced by Bowie with The Spiders from Mars. *Introducing*'s witty packaging features a business card declaring that the group are available for weddings and social functions. Yet as Auslander notes, The Falcons possess no signature sound of their own; *Introducing* is even more diversely derivative than its prede-cessor, *Wizzard Brew*.

A real group called The Falcons had been Wood's first band in the Birmingham scene of the early sixties. He then became the primary songwriter in The Move, those gimmicky hit-makers notorious for their publicity stunts. The Move exhibited a precocious habit of musical quotation, albeit mostly from classical music, including Tchaikovsky's *1812 Overture*, *The Sorcerer's Apprentice*, Bach and others. 'Fire Brigade', released in early 1968, is considered one of the first rock'n'roll revival songs, on account of its twangy Duane Eddy lick. The Move can also claim to have started a sixties revival

Roy Wood on the cover of the US version of Wizzard's 1973 debut album
– titled *Wizzard's Brew* rather than *Wizzard Brew*, as in the UK

way ahead of schedule, right in the middle of the sixties, in fact! On
the flip of their 1967 psychedelic hit 'I Can Hear the Grass Grow',
'Wave Your Flag and Stop the Train' is a Beatles-circa-1964 pastiche, its bass riff a dead ringer for 'Day Tripper'.

Just before forming Wizzard, Wood was involved in the launching
of The Move offshoot Electric Light Orchestra, but ultimately left
that project in the hands of Jeff Lynne. ELO remained Wizzard's
sister band at least in spirit. Its primary debt, though, was to a single
predecessor: The Beatles, and specifically that band's orchestrated
side. Lynne said he had wanted to start a group that began where
'I Am the Walrus' left off – that cello sound. In the eighties, Lynne

penned the song 'Beatles Forever', a mixture of elegy, epigone's lament and exorcism: he sings about writing a song and feeling quite proud of it, until 'I hear one of *theirs*'.

Wood, though, seemed to lack the anxiety of influence that haunted Jeff Lynne and in other cases spurs artists to break new ground. He was pop's equivalent to Mike Yarwood, the famous British TV impressionist of the seventies. Except that unlike Yarwood, there was no 'And this is me' song at the show's end. Wood remained permanently in character(s). Not content with vocal impersonation, he even resorted to technological trickery to transgenderise his voice and pull off the Andrew Sisters pastiche 'You Sure Got It Now'. Despite his forgeries and masques, Wood was a pioneer in a certain sense, blazing a trail for new-wave pasticheurs like Nick Lowe (who appears on the 'split-screen' cover of 1978's *Pure Pop for Now People* dressed in the style of six distinct types of rock performer), MTV magpies like Lenny Kravitz and the sonic reproduction antiques made by lo-fi cult figures like R. Stevie Moore and Ariel Pink.

In this rock counter-tradition, creativity is redefined in artisanal rather than artistic terms: achievement is measured in how meticulously exact the replica is. 'A craftsman knows what he's going to make and an artist doesn't know what he's going to make, or what the finished product is going to look like,' said ceramics sculptor Ken Price, a man who turned a craft into art. Innovative artists sometimes take a break and 'vacation' in the low-intensity, hobbyist activity of pastiche. The attraction is that it liberates the fun aspects of art-making (the technical challenges) from the more difficult part: the en*vision*ing of something new, something that didn't exist before.

That's certainly the modernist's view of pastiche, at any rate – looking down on it disparagingly! But quite a few serious artists in the early to mid-seventies were starting to explore the possibilities of appropriation and simulation. Friends with Roxy Music – but much more like Roy Wood's lost sisters – The Moodies were an almost entirely female band that emerged from the Fine Art department of Reading University and whose shows lay somewhere between performance art and cabaret. Going one step further than Wood, a Moodies concert involved no original material at all, just absurdist cover versions of songs like Presley's 'Return to Sender' or The Shangri-Las' 'Remember (Walking in the Sand)'.

Originally named Moody and the Menstruators, the group's warped yet celebratory renditions anticipated things like the New York drag festival Wigstock and the drag-king phenomenon. At one performance, lead singer Anne Bean appeared in an Elvis-style leather jacket, with slicked-back hair and a leather cap, while for 'Lonesome Cowboy' Polly Eltes dragged up as a cowboy and rode a hobby horse.

The Moodies became a cult phenomenon. They received a double-page spread in the *Sunday Times* in 1974 and endorsements from publications ranging from *Time Out* to the feminist magazine *Spare Rib*, which described routines like 'Smoke Gets in Your Eyes' – involving a huge cigarette hanging from Mae West-style lips made of satin – as 'simultaneously glorifying and ridiculing glamour'. In Germany, where the spirit of cabaret lived strongest, The Moodies were actually big: *Westdeutsche Allgemeine* said they 'vamp the music so affectionately that the parody ends up better than the original'; *Hamburger Morgenpost* raved that they were 'the greatest sensation since the BEATLES'; and there was even a one-hour Moodies TV special.

Back in Britain, management overtures were made by figures like Malcolm McLaren (this before he hooked up with the New York Dolls, let alone the Sex Pistols). Tipped off by Roxy, Island Records expressed an interest in signing The Moodies: there was an attempt to record a live album in November 1973, at west London's Bush Theatre. But their live magic couldn't be captured on record and Island abandoned the idea.

The Moodies arrived too early for video, alas. Later a successful installation artist, Anne Bean described their collective project as an exploration of 'the ambivalent edges between entertainment and sending up entertainment . . . between style and sending up style'. Influenced by the esoteric philosopher George Gurdjieff's notions about the flux and mutability of identity, about how everything was artificial and fictitious, Bean has talked about how 'who one is is not a stable place. This idea affected me very deeply; that I could do Moodies but something very different the next day . . .' *Sudetendeutsche Zeitung*, another admiring German newspaper, pinpointed Bean's ability 'to change so dramatically, not only visually, but in what I can only describe as "essence" that I began to question if there was not more people in the group'.

Like Roy Wood, The Moodies took to the limit that tendency within glam of treating pop history as a wardrobe of costumes to be put on and taken off at will. This is fashion logic, in the sense that fashion was the first area of popular culture to treat its own archive as an auto-cannibalistic resource. Quentin Crisp – himself a living *objet d'art*, a perpetual performance – took a starkly different stance: he defined true style as singularity, the removal of options. 'Fashion is never having to decide who you are. Style is deciding who you are and being able to perpetuate it.'

Crisp's maxim points to a contradiction within postmodernism. Parody and pastiche both depend on the prior existence of defined styles, at either the level of the individually distinctive artist or the genre. You can't have recreativity without creativity in the first place. To dedicate yourself to parody and pastiche is thus to go against the creative force of history itself. It's a detour up a dead end.

N

The rise of pastiche and parody in rock from the early seventies fits the concept of 'the descent into pattern work', a syndrome identified by Oswald Spengler in his writings about decadence and the decline of the West. When civilisations pass their peak, they no longer generate new forms but content themselves with repeating and embellishing the achievements of their past. 'Pictures and fabrics, verses and vessels, furniture, dramas and musical compositions – all is pattern work. We cease to be able to date anything within centuries, let alone decades, by the language of its ornamentation. So it has been in the Last Act of all Cultures.' The 'last' here is probably a nod to Nietzsche's concept of the Last Men – a species burdened by its sense of history, its surfeit of self-consciousness. As rock theorist Phil Knight argues, irony is what smooths over the transition from art to craft, from passion to pastiche. You still want to rock but you can't quite muster the belief that it matters any more. So you rock with a sense of distanced humour.

Pattern work with a wink was all over pop music in 1973–4. 10cc reached #1 with 'Rubber Bullets' – 'Jailhouse Rock' transposed to Belfast – while their self-titled debut album contained loving parodies of the motorbike-death song ('Johnny, Don't Do It') and fifties teen ballad ('Donna'). Massive with songs like 'My Coo Ca Choo', Alvin Stardust based an entire career on impersonating Gene Vincent, right down to the black leather gloves. Elton John's 'Crocodile Rock' whipped The Diamonds' 'Little Darlin', Chuck Berry's 'Oh Carol' and Pat Boone's 'Speedy Gonzales' into irresistible but sickly mousse. 'I wanted it to be a record about all the things I grew up with,' said Elton, known for owning one of the largest collections of pop records in the world. 'Of course it's a rip-off.' The lyrics ran through a checklist of fifties clichés: Chevys, jukeboxes, blue jeans, girls called Suzie and 'hopping and bopping to the crocodile rock'. The combination of elegy ('Do you remember when rock was young?') and buoyancy was revisited with Elton's later hit 'Your Sister Can't Twist (But She Can Rock'n'Roll)'.

Mott the Hoople had veered into outright revivalism by the time they reached their third glam-era album, *The Hoople*, replicating The Ronettes on 'Foxy Foxy' and sliding down the *Grease*-y pole into the Sha Na Na mire with 'The Golden Age of Rock'n'Roll'. In live concerts, they'd play Don McLean's rock'n'roll elegy 'American Pie' right up until the line 'the day the music died', then cut to abrupt silence. 'Or did it?' Hunter would ask archly, and the band would then launch into 'Golden Age'.

One of the ironies of a song like 'The Golden Age of Rock'n'Roll' is that it is based on a bygone period that was unaware of its own status as a golden age (because busy living it) and furthermore had no interest in or consciousness of any previous golden age (because fully inhabiting Melly's 'country of "Now"'). Retro is dependent on the existence of the *un*-retro: moments of nowness and newness that get trapped for ever in the amber of the archives. Revivals *never* revive earlier revivals; they must always re-enact what was new in its own time, the truly nourishing and vigorous stuff.

Yet, equally, the melancholy truth is that everything that is new and vital will inevitably return again as retro and undead. The NOW!-ness of sixties pop that Melly rightly identified *ensured* its later half-lives in the form of revivals. Culture succumbs to nostalgia in much the same way that an individual in middle age looks back wistfully to adolescence or childhood: the nostalgia is partly for a time when he or she *wasn't* nostalgic, just lived purely in the now.

Yet sometimes what is intended as a resurrection somehow ends up producing new things. The titles of David Essex's massive pop hits, like 'Rock On' and 'Good Ol' Rock and Roll', suggest fairly straightforward revivalism. Add to that Essex's parallel career as an actor: he starred as the rock'n'roll-loving youth Jim MacLaine in the movie *That'll Be the Day*, set in late-fifties Britain, and its sequel *Stardust*, which followed the rise of MacLaine and his band The

Stray Cats to stardom in the sixties. As a musician and actor, Essex would surely seem to be entirely locked in the past.

But just as those gritty films were far from rose-tinted nostalgia, likewise the David Essex sound wasn't any kind of straightforward fifties replica. Hypnotic, stripped-down, teeming with studio-warped sounds created by Essex's producer Jeff Wayne, 'Rock On' and similar songs like 'America' were closer to the cinemascopic funk of 'Papa Was a Rollin' Stone' by The Temptations or Dr John's humid junglescapes, like 'Craney Crow'. (Dr John was one of Essex's heroes and influences, in fact.)

A working-class East End boy, Essex started his career drumming in a combo called The Everons, which became The China Plates Blues Band. Somewhere along the way, his bandmates prevailed upon Essex to sing. The husky rasp that made him a smokin' seventies sex symbol for teenage girls and middle-aged housewives alike came literally from heavy smoking: because he wanted to project a 'hard and tough' image, Essex constantly smoked Player's Weights, a filterless cigarette that, he said, 'wrecked' his voice. The other elements of Essex's magnetism – the eyes, the rogueish smile, the Gypsy-like curls of hair – were spotted by manager Derek Bowman, a journalist for the *Sunday Telegraph*, at a pub gig when Essex was still just the drummer. 'The first thing that struck me was his eyes and his great sort of charisma,' Bowman recalled. 'It was the way he played the drums in a cool, arrogant way . . . a throw-away technique.'

During a stint in the rock musical *Godspell*, Essex met Jeff Wayne through the latter's girlfriend, also in the cast. Originally from an American showbiz family, Wayne was busy applying his classical training and facility with music technology to a career as one of Britain's leading composers for commercials. Operating an all-electronic studio from an apartment above the Strand Theatre, Wayne had already written over a thousand jingles by the time he met Essex – raking in the equivalent of £1.5 million a year in today's money. All this experience of writing indelible hooks, finding ear-catching sounds and audio gimmicks, and working at speed with session musicians gave Wayne the makings of a genius pop producer.

'Rock On' was born, indirectly, out of a session for a Johnson's Pledge commercial. Wayne called Essex in to do the vocal, but instead of a paean to a floor polish, they ended up creating a trans-atlantic smash. When he walked into the studio, Essex asked if he could first play the producer a song he'd come up with. 'I thought David was going to sit down at the piano and start playing the tune and singing,' recalls Wayne. 'But he walked straight past the piano, picked up a trash can, turned it over and emptied its contents on the floor, and started banging away like a conga, playing rhythmi-cally. And by avoiding the piano, I guess it just gave me a different impression of how it could sound as a record.'

When it came to recording 'Rock On' as a potential single, Wayne explained the minimalist concept to his squad of session players: 'It's all built around hollows, and we're going to add repeat echoes, sort of fifties-style' – an idea triggered by the lyrics, with their references to Jimmy Dean. Bassist Herbie Flowers immediately responded to Wayne's concept and came up with the song's twin basslines, which the producer swathed in dub-like echo. Starkness was the key to the striking sound of 'Rock On'. 'We didn't have any instrument that played a chord,' says Wayne. 'Chords of any kind fill the space of the sound – you hear harmonies, tonality. But if the bass guitar is the only thing that's playing notes, that changes the whole perception of the sound and the *size* of the track.'

Wayne extricated Essex from his pre-existing tangle of contracts and they signed to CBS. The label initially wanted to turn the B-side, the more conventionally poppy ballad 'On and On', into the debut single's A-side: they saw Essex as a potential British David Cassidy. But Wayne and Essex stuck to their guns, insisting that 'Rock On' be the debut single. In the autumn of 1973, it reached #2 in the UK and #5 in America. Just as importantly, with 'Rock On' Essex and Wayne had invented a personal micro-genre, a sound template they returned to repeatedly with songs like 'Rollin' Stone', 'America', 'Window', 'Streetfight', 'Good Ol' Rock'n'Roll' and the uproariously percussive 'We All Insane'. The partnership was a fifty–fifty symbiosis: Essex wrote most of the songs, and all the hits; Wayne was the music director, marshalling the session musicians and his bag of studio tricks to create the spacy, cinematic sound.

Although Essex insisted that he was primarily a rocker, his acting roles directly shaped several of his biggest hit singles. 'Rock On' came from working on *That'll Be the Day* and researching the fifties, which got him thinking about James Dean's 'effect upon a generation'. Ironically, he'd never actually seen a James Dean film himself. Without *That'll Be the Day*, Essex said, 'I probably wouldn't have written the song . . . I love the fifties, though they were before my time . . . I found the directness and naïveté of the period really refreshing.'

'Gonna Make You a Star', his first #1, and 'Stardust', the Top 10 hit that followed it, both stemmed from *Stardust*, the sequel to *That'll Be the Day*. The first was a delightfully buoyant mini-satire of the rock business, a Svengali fallen on hard times trying to sell his faded services to a potential star he half despises as not 'too much more than a pretty face'; 'Stardust' was a portentous ballad about a rock'n'roll king who 'crashed out the sky'.

Stardust director Michael Apted said the film was about the sixties as a period comparable to Hollywood in the twenties and thirties, when 'people from unspectacular backgrounds could become very rich and very powerful very quickly . . . We wanted to tell the story of how someone deals with the financial and media pressures.'

Essex, for his part, spoke of the strangeness of playing a movie rock star, even as 'Rock On' and sold-out concert tours made him one of the biggest pop idols of 1973–4. 'At one concert in the film there are 6,000 David Essex fans there all shouting out "We want Jim MacLaine" . . . I'd walk on the set and do a scene, walk off the set and do the same scene in real life.' He added that the movie was just as 'peculiar' to make for his co-stars, Adam Faith and Ringo Starr, both of whom had been the focus of fandemonium in the past. A surprisingly heavy movie with a harrowing end, *Stardust* was 'a hundred times more difficult to make than *That'll Be the Day*', admitted Essex. It took him 'months to get over it'.

Movies about rock, rock about rock – there was a lot of it about in the first half of the seventies. Brian De Palma's *Phantom of the Paradise* from 1974 could be seen as a 'glam movie', what with its Jobriath-like star Beef and the Alice Cooper parody The Undeads. Combining rock satire and campy horror movie, *Phantom of the Paradise* is the tale of a Spector-like Svengali called Swan and his diabolical schemes. De Palma also lampoons the nostalgia craze along the way: Swan declares that 'the future of rock'n'roll is its past', and one of his bands is the Sha Na Na-like revival troupe The Juicy Fruits.

That same year of 1974, The Kinks created a British TV special called *Starmaker*, about a rock star who feels so empty of inspiration he swaps places with an ordinary man just to have something to write about for his next album. *Starmaker* was just one of a string of projects – including the albums *Lola Versus Powerman and the Moneygoround, Part One*, *Everybody's in Show-Biz* and *The Kinks Present a Soap Opera* – in which Ray Davies mused wryly and self-reflexively on aspects of rock-star life, touring and the music business.

A far more entertaining and provocative televisual delve into the sordidness and occasional glory of struggling through the music biz

arrived on British TV screens a few years after *Starmaker*. Across
two series aired in the UK in 1976 and 1977, and later shown on PBS
in America, *Rock Follies* was an innovative genre-blend of comedy,
musical and drama that followed the tortuous route to fame of The
Little Ladies, a band fronted by three women. Roxy's Andy Mackay
wrote the songs, but the real force behind the series was playwright
Howard Schuman, who, in addition to writing the lyrics, scripted
the series and devised the original idea.

Combining shabby seventies realism influenced by fringe theatre
and radical drama – scenes in communal squats, in grotty recording studios and rock clubs – with fantasy sequences harking back
to Busby Berkeley and sideways to TV's middle-of-the-road variety
shows, *Rock Follies* was shot entirely in the studio, with no exterior location filming. Schuman's guiding concept was to create a
heightened sense of artifice. The satire, which encompassed every
aspect of the music biz, from high-handed record companies and
manipulative managers to fast-talking PRs and earnest music journalists, was well informed but deliberately over the top, an absurdist
lampoon. Before moving to the UK, Schuman had worked at New
York's Brill Building pop factory penning what he calls 'hamburger
songs'. He was a disillusioned rock fan who felt that 'all the meaning
that rock had had for us began to disappear' with the rise of 'manufactured groups . . . Rock seemed to be decadent.'

Rock Follies was overtly feminist, tracking the tribulations of
three women – Dee, Q and Anna – in a male-dominated record
industry where everyone from their musical director, Derek 'Hyper'
Huggins, to a series of managers and label bosses reckon they know
best when it comes to moulding the group and steering it towards
fame and fortune.

One of the most fascinating threads running through *Follies* concerns nostalgia and revivalism. Alongside the implication that rock
itself just turned out to be a new branch of showbiz, the word 'Follies'

harks back to the theatrical revues and variety shows of Broadway in the early twentieth century, like the Ziegfeld Follies and Earl Carroll's Vanities. Schuman was also a fan of Stephen Sondheim's recent and ground-breaking *Follies*, itself a kind of meta-musical. 'It's about a reunion of Follies girls that disintegrates into a surreal Follies show as the central characters try to work out their demons,' he says. 'There's a ghostly chorus line of what these women looked like forty years before, when they were glamorous.'

The Little Ladies form themselves out of the cast of a doomed attempt to revive a Depression-era musical in order to ride 'the nostalgia wave'. Schuman says he got the idea from the fact that 1971's 'biggest hit on Broadway was a revival of a famous old musical called *No, No, Nanette*, whose hit song was "I Want to Be Happy".' For *Follies*, Schuman invented his own imaginary thirties musical, *Broadway Annie*, satirising the widespread seventies yen to go back to supposedly 'happier times' – nostalgia that kept the jolly songs and razzle-dazzle and conveniently forgot the soup kitchens and homeless hobos. The songs from *Broadway Annie* were so convincing that Schuman's writer friend Michael Frayn was momentarily convinced it was a real thirties musical. One of the Little Ladies, Q – played by Rula Lenska – is a time-warp figure who wishes she had lived in the era of George Gershwin and seriously doubts she'll fit in a rock band: 'I like rock not when it's deep but fun . . . camp . . . I like Sha Na Na.'

After many misadventures The Little Ladies fall into the clutches of aspiring record-biz mogul Stavros, who completely remakes their image. They perform the song 'Biba Nova' – a nod to retro-fashion boutique Biba – at the nostalgia restaurant Idols. But the waiter hips them to the fact that 'the heyday of the elegance, Bryan Ferry and his white dinner jacket' has passed. So Stavros decides that with the economy in crisis, 'Austerity Rock' will be the next big thing. Schuman recalls that with the UK seemingly in perpetual crisis in 1973–5 (strikes, the three-day week instituted by the government to conserve energy, an IRA bombing campaign), he imagined 'a return to that Blitz spirit' of Keep Calm and Carry On. So Stavros remodels The Little Ladies as forties nostalgia act The Victory Girls, singing songs like 'Where's My Gasmask?', 'I'll Be a War Bride' and 'Glenn Miller Is Missing'. He builds the Blitz Club, which is styled as a London Tube station turned bomb shelter: attendees purchase deliberately grotty grub using ration cards and experience a simulated air raid. But on the opening night it's blown up for real by a terrorist bomb.

Pulled together at the last minute, an album of the best tunes Andy Mackay wrote for the first series of *Rock Follies* startled everyone by going straight in at #1. (Among the surprised was Bryan Ferry: his own solo albums had failed to place that high; indeed, the *Rock Follies* LP outdid the last two Roxy albums, *Country Life* and *Siren*.) The LP of the second series didn't do nearly as well (#13) but did spawn the Top 10 hit single 'O.K.'. That song and others, like 'The Road', featured long-held-note choruses that exploited the strident power of Julie Covington (who played the punky, cropheaded tough girl Dee). Mackay was writing in a style midway between rock'n'roll and musical theatre – roughly the same region in which *The Rocky Horror Picture Show* situated itself.

Distributed by 20th Century Fox, the 1975 film was based on the hugely successful stage play *The Rocky Horror Show*, which opened on 19 June 1973 and ran for years at various theatres on London's King's Road, as well as enjoying runs at the Roxy Theatre in LA and the off-Broadway Belasco Theatre. In both the play and the movie, Tim Curry starred as Dr Frank N. Furter, a transvestite alien who is also a Frankenstein-like mad scientist, and at whose castle two clean-cut Eisenhower-era kids, Brad and Janet, are forced to spend the night.

Rocky Horror is a convergence point for all the glam-aligned trends of the early seventies: the rock'n'roll revival, the trash aesthetic, decadence, camp, gender-bending and drag. Although some say that its vampy horror-show look presaged punk and goth – Siouxsie Sioux, Dave Vanian of The Damned, Jordan and Soo Catwoman probably borrowed a bit from the make-up – in truth the movie is better understood as a gaudy tombstone for an entire era.

For Richard O'Brien, who conceived and wrote *Rocky Horror*, glam was a background influence, the context that allowed his creation to come into being, and also helped him feel more comfortable in his trans skin. 'When I was six, I said I wanted to be a fairy princess when I grew up,' O'Brien remembers. But his older brother made fun of him, precipitating years of hiding his true self. 'Glam rock allowed me to be out but not "out", if you know what I mean. Allowed me to be myself more. I could dress a little more flamboyantly, without anybody pointing fingers or being disparaging.'

Although O'Brien appeared in the play and the film as the grotesque butler Riff Raff – in which role he resembles a cross between Eno and Quasimodo – he says Dr Frank N. Furter is his real alter ego: the cross-dressing bisexual from the planet Transylvania represented for him an ideal self, 'this very, very liberated human being from way out there . . . throwing off the cloak and singing "I'm just a sweet transvestite" with his hands on his hips and looking smug about it . . . *claiming* his right to be so'.

Taking on the part, Tim Curry originally essayed different versions, including one with a German accent and Aryan peroxide-blonde hair. After overhearing an Englishwoman asking someone, 'Do you have a house in town or a house in the country?' Curry decided that Furter shouldn't just be a queen, he should speak like the Queen of England – extravagantly, ringingly posh. All the while wearing nothing but a corset, suspenders and stockings.

'Don't dream it, be it' – Furter's catchphrase – would alone make *Rocky Horror* part of glam, even if the movie wasn't riddled with kinky and retro elements. O'Brien spotted the slogan in a magazine advert for the lingerie store Frederick's of Hollywood. 'It appealed to me instantly. Especially being a transgendered person and seeing this page full of drawn pictures of girls who look very like transsexuals rather than women. The strapline at the top was "Don't dream it, be it" – and I just thought, "Oh, yes. That's the way."'

Warhol was another background influence, specifically the epochal Hayward Gallery 1969 exhibition 'Pop Art Revisited'. 'That blew me away. I walked out of there about three feet off the ground. I felt so moved. Somebody once said about *Rocky* that we put Pop Art onstage, which was a nice thought.'

O'Brien had acted in the UK productions of *Hair* and *Jesus Christ Superstar*. During a spell without work, he conceived *Rocky's* innovative hybrid of horror, comedy and musical, and started writing a script woven out of motifs from every kind of B-movie, from science fiction to Hammer House of Horror. The title was originally going to be *They Came from Denton High*. In its finished form as *The Rocky Horror Show*, the play was not only inspired by pulp movies, it was styled as a double feature: spectators were escorted to plush red velvet seats just like in a picture palace, and then the night's entertainment was announced by a singing usherette. The song 'Science Fiction/Double Feature' ran through a checklist of obscure B-movie actors – Michael Rennie, George Pal, Leo G. Carroll – and the films in which they starred.

Nostalgia for fifties music was an equally strong element in *Rocky Horror*. Partly spurred by his dissatisfaction with what passed for rock in musicals like *Jesus Christ Superstar*, O'Brien wrote a bunch of jiving-and-twisting tunes, like the fan favourite 'Time Warp'. The monster created by Frank N. Furter is a rock'n'roller called Eddie (played in the movie by Meatloaf) whose brain has been partially removed.

But amid all the campy celebration of bad taste and bygone teen thrills, there's also a tinge of darkness and decadence. The full speech surrounding the oft-quoted 'don't dream it' bit is Furter's exhortation to 'give yourself over to absolute pleasure. Swim the warm waters of sins of the flesh – erotic nightmares beyond any measure, and sensual daydreams to treasure for ever. Can't you just see it? Don't dream it, be it.' O'Brien describes the plot as 'your basic Garden of Eden scenario': wholesome naifs Brad and Janet are Adam and Eve; Furter is the serpent. You could also see Furter as representing the late-sixties excess of 'nothing is forbidden, everything is permitted', the essentially Lucifer-an philosophy of Aleister Crowley's 'Do what thou wilt shall be the whole of the law'. Brad and Janet are the fifties – innocence about to be despoiled. Near the end of *Rocky Horror*, there's a strange scene of a polysexual orgy in a swimming pool: Furter bobs around in a *Titanic* life ring. The ending is downbeat: the narrator, aka the Criminologist, rambles ominously about insects called the human race, lost in time and lost in space.

Although the play had been wildly popular (2,690 showings in London alone), *The Rocky Horror Picture Show* flopped initially – something hard to process given its monstrous success over subsequent decades as a midnight movie (grossing over $360 million). What happened to the film in the years after its underwhelming first release represents an unfurling of glam logic to its utmost extension: audiences responding to the 'Don't dream it, be it' incitement, but in a curiously literal way.

Starting at New York's Waverly Theatre in 1976 as a weekly event, *Rocky Horror Picture Show* screenings became the focus of a cult phenomenon: audience members addressing the characters on screen with ribald responses (what came to be known as 'callbacks') and an increasingly complicated and ritualised commentary on the storyline, with rice being thrown during the wedding scene, squirt guns and newspapers coming out for the rain scene, and so forth. Soon *Rocky Horror* fans were turning up to screenings dressed as characters from the movie and forming a 'Shadow Cast' that stood immediately below the screen, mimicking gestures and lip-synching to dialogue or songs during key scenes. Creating an atmosphere that mixed fancy-dress party, performance art and a Gay Pride float, it's as though The Moodies became an entire subculture, but with the parody restricted to a single pop-cult text. Callbacks and Shadow Casts anticipated subsequent phenomena like karaoke, vogueing, YouTube spoofs, fan fiction and other manifestations of interactive para-culture.

The message taken from *Rocky Horror* by the fans was 'be true to thine own inner freak'. Some were drawn to the Shadow Cast community as a home for misfits, loners and the gender queer. People go hundreds of times, ritually re-enacting, to the point where it's almost a church for godless postmoderns.

You could read what happened to *Rocky Horror* as the audience asserting themselves as the stars. Shadowing is like breaking the fourth wall, but from the other direction. It's competing with the stars for attention, perhaps even analogous to stalking (invading the performer's space). Nineteen seventy-six, the year it all started at the Waverley, was also the year of punk and do-it-yourself. O'Brien recalls the first time he witnessed the phenomenon, at a *Rocky* convention in Long Island in the late seventies: 'It was like people had stepped out of the screen.'

But you could also, less sanguinely, read *Rocky Horror* as the terminus of glam logic. An audience parodying what was already a parody. A hall of mirrors of ever more empty reflections, quotations of quotations. Postmodernism reaching its dead end, before it had even really started its public life as a concept and practice.

9:

BAROQUE 'N' ROLL: LATE GLAM

Steve Harley and Cockney Rebel – Sparks – Jet – Queen – Be-Bop Deluxe

'GLAM ROCK IS DEAD! SAYS MARC,' shrieked *Melody Maker*'s front cover of 16 June 1973. Inside the paper, Bolan spoke dismissively of 'the dying embers of Glam-Rock' and how uninvolved he felt in the party he'd started. 'Personally I find it very embarrassing,' he professed – at once a transparently self-serving attempt to pull down the house behind him and a publicity gimmick to flag up his uninspired new T. Rex single 'The Groover'.

Bolan's verdict was presumptuous and premature. Nineteen seventy-four would see a second wave of glam come through. With Bowie, Roxy, Slade, The Sweet et al. still riding high and new glam-aligned outfits like Cockney Rebel, Sparks, Queen and others emerging, the only thing on the verge of extinction was T. Rex.

'Mirror Freak', a song on Cockney Rebel's 1973 debut album *The Human Menagerie*, was partly inspired by Bolan. Singer and band leader Steve Harley professed admiration for Marc and all his great little 'boogies'. But the tone of the song seemed – not untypically for Harley – sneery: a mordant dissection of the aspiring-star syndrome as a narcissistic personality disorder. Rhyming 'lies' with 'flimsy disguise', the song paints an unpretty picture of someone in thrall to 'the image fatale' – hip-shimmying and Mae West pouting in front of the looking glass, rehearsing for a big time that may or may never come.

It's also possible that 'Mirror Freak' was meant as a self-mocking self-portrait. Harley understood intimately the mentality he was satirising because he shared it: the circularity of being inspired to be a star by stars who themselves were inspired by earlier stars. Initially besotted with Dylan, he was jolted out of folk-singer mode by Bowie, who showed the possibilities for a new rock theatre, one that took place not just on the stage, but in the pages of the pop press. Harley had observed the successful unfolding of the MainMan masterplan – 'Talk like you're already a star, act like you're already a star, and you'll become a star.' Launching Cockney Rebel, he followed the Bowie/Defries playbook page for page (while also taking style notes from Bryan Ferry). When the band played at Biba's Rainbow Room, Harley introduced himself as 'Muhammad 'Arley' – funny, but also spot on. His brazen boasting and put-downs of the contemporary scene really did recall the former Cassius Clay's pugilistic patter of self-hype and goading of his adversaries.

For Cockney Rebel's first major feature in November 1973, Harley came out swinging, telling *Melody Maker* that 'we're rehearsing music now which is so hard and tough it knocks me through the roof. There's a buzz in Cockney Rebel saying we're on the brink of being big, being leaders not followers, a musical force that others will follow.' Muhammad Ali is sometimes mentioned as a pioneer of rap; like rising hip hop MCs aiming diss rhymes against established rappers, Harley launched his career by squaring up against the biggest name in the biz, as if they were already on a par. 'I hope that when Bowie hears Cockney Rebel it'll knock him sideways and he'll say ". . . I've got to step on it to stay at the top". I'll chase him until I either fall flat on my face or make him run. He needs someone like Cockney Rebel . . . There's no one around to kick him up the arse.'

The music papers ate up this kind of thing. Harley knew how to give good quote partly because, says Cockney Rebel keyboardist Milton Reame-James, 'He read every single line of every single music paper every week. He was really good at following the trends, and he knew the journalists, what to feed the press so that they hadn't really got to think about writing an item – Steve had written it for them.' It was also because Harley had himself been a journalist before he'd picked up a guitar: not a rock writer, but an experienced reporter on local newspapers like the *Braintree and Witham Times* and *Colchester Evening Gazette*. Working his way up from tea boy to sports editor, he eventually got a brief taste of Fleet Street – including six weeks on the *Daily Express*, Harley claimed in an early feature – but then gave it up, he said, because he was becoming cynical and ruthless in his pursuit of a story.

Harley definitely already possessed the ego of a pop star, the will to power. 'To be on stage is to be a Messiah,' he told *Melody Maker*. 'Our job is to take a thousand people up to cloud nine, that's all we're there for.' Sometimes he invoked the Almighty as the reason for both his unshakeable self-belief and his ability to hold an audience's attention. Recalling his early pronouncements about Cockney Rebel's destiny, Harley insisted in 1974 that 'it wasn't bragging, it wasn't bigheadedness. I was purely saying, Look, I feel like God's touched me and said "Here's a mission and someone's gotta do it" . . .' A year later, coming off his first UK #1 single, Harley told *Trouser Press*, 'I'm not Goebbels, it's just this knack I've got where somehow, up there, He gave me something that's hypnotic. Maybe it's the shape of me nose . . . Maybe it's because I've got blue eyes. I don't know . . . It's a funny thing – it's very strange, like a spell.'

The spell – that magnetic influence that certain people radiate – was the strange glow that seems to come above all from damaged narcissism. When life gives the nascent ego a big knock, sometimes the ego fights back even fiercer. Born in a tough part of south London in 1951, the boy whose real name was (ironically, some would say) Steve Nice contracted polio at the age of three. Paralysed in his right leg from the hip down, he spent a total of four years in hospital during his childhood, undergoing corrective surgery to make sure his legs were the same length, and using crutches until the age of sixteen. But in an indication of Harley's mettle, he overcame

Messiah for hire: Steve Harley onstage at Victoria Palace
Theatre, London, 1974

these challenges and played in his school cricket team, competed in
table tennis, won swimming medals. Onstage, although short and
restricted in his movements by the limp, Harley used his strong features – a large mouth and piercing blue eyes – along with expressive
hand gestures to create a commanding presence.

Harley learnt determination and ruthlessness from his 'tough as
nails' working-class father, who put him through private school for
some of his childhood. The education gave him a love of literature
and language, which fed into his somewhat verbose Cockney Rebel
lyrics. Learning first from Dylan and then from Bowie, he developed the knack of writing floridly imagistic lyrics – teeming with
bitches crucified, suicide streets, painted faces, lips like morgues –
that conjured a sense of hidden depths and cutting angles.

Anticipating post-punk bards like Howard Devoto, Elvis Costello and Kevin Rowland, the tone was often see-through-you scornful, jousting with unidentified enemies or passing panoramic judgement. 'Unreality' rhymed with 'vanity', 'Schemeland' with 'Dreamland', 'ego' with 'Quasimodo', and Nero got a namecheck too. The title of the debut Cockney Rebel album, *The Human Menagerie*, gives a sense of how Harley viewed the world – a stew of corruption, fak-ery, self-deception, bravado and betrayal. Underneath it all bubbled bitterness about the hand – or, rather, leg – the world had dealt him. Yet the prettiness of the melodies and the quirky, playful arrange-ments concocted by Harley and his bandmates made the whole package attractive.

Harley's naturally embattled stance and immodest proclamations divided the readers and writers of the music press. While *Melody Maker* embraced him, the *NME* took against him big time, dismiss-ing *The Human Menagerie* as vacuous 'clap-trap . . . a hype and a rather effete one at that'. Reviewer Roy Carr's kiss-off was brutal: 'By the way, Steve; when you're finished with it, David Bowie would like his voice back and Bryan Ferry his vibrato. You can keep the clothes.' An *NME* interview with Harley – also by Carr – concluded that the singer was 'certifiable'. Taking the press so seriously and reading it so attentively, Harley was incensed; his brittle egotism redoubled the claims of greatness, but with an increasing tinge of 'They're against me!' paranoia.

The single most divisive thing about Steve Harley was not his gran-diosity but his voice. Like his right leg, it lacked strength and stability, yet by sheer force of will he fashioned its weak 'r' and wobbly vow-els into a mesmerisingly quirky instrument – all fey chirrups, gob-lin sneers and shaky soars of would-be operatic emotion. The effect was vaguely repellent . . . yet gripping. 'You'd never have said Steve was a good, conventional singer,' says Reame-James. 'But he did, by using mannerisms – by acting – get across. And we had a very quirky sound, so that he could be animated and use his voice in a different way.' Harley had learnt from Dylan about how you could use phrasing to make something out of a voice that lacked range and power.

'I was overawed, enraptured,' Harley said of his first encounter with Dylan's work, which propelled him into a pre-Rebel career as a Dylan casualty playing for free in folk clubs and busking, doing the whole 'harmonica holder and the nasal bit'. It was during this phase that Harley hooked up with violinist Jean-Paul Crocker, the first of the components that made up Cockney Rebel's unusual sound. At the age of seventeen Crocker picked up a fiddle for the first time. Applying five years of studying classical guitar to a completely different instrument, he came up with a style that blended elements of rock'n'roll and bluegrass, heard to captivating effect on tunes like 'Hideaway' and 'Crazy Raver'. Crocker 'was able to create this enormous sound that moved and rocked', says Reame-James. The keyboard player's own background took in training as a concert pianist, playing for a youth orchestra and writing music for theatre. Like Crocker, Reame-James 'approached the keyboard from the perspective of the classical tradition. I was also very influenced by the jazz players who were using electric piano. That's why I chose the Fender Rhodes – I really admired what Herbie Hancock and Chick Corea were doing at that time. Writing my parts I borrowed from classical music a lot, in a disguised way, changing the notes a bit. Quite often in Cockney Rebel, I'd be playing the left hand from one piece and the right hand from a different composer, a completely different piece!'

Although the rhythm section – bassist Paul Jeffreys and drummer Stuart Elliott – corresponded to the rock-pop norm, the kind of rhythmic structures Harley's songs followed often seemed more like European vaudeville or folk-meets-cabaret. Factor in the presence of violin and the classical-infused piano, and the absence of electric guitar, and the Cockney Rebel sound amounted to one of the real curios of the British seventies.

Harley made a huge rhetorical deal about having a guitar-less sound. In interviews, he railed against the cult of the guitar hero that had ruined rock from 1968 onwards, saying that the kids 'must be tired of screaming guitar licks that say nothing'. He wrote a song, 'Tumbling Down', whose long fade features the singalong chorus 'Oh dear! Look what they've done to the blues, blues, blues.' Guitarists had no place in Cockney Rebel, with their 'rude noises' that 'couldn't do anything for my songs'.

But knowing Harley, it seems like the decision not to have a lead guitarist was as much to do with not wanting to share the limelight with a Ronson-type figure. 'I wasn't going to take on anyone who was likely to upstage me,' he recalled of the group's formation. This only-room-for-one-star-here stance carried through to the songwriting, which was his province entirely. 'They had to be guys who didn't think they could write better songs than me . . . I laid it on the line . . . I'm the guv'nor and everyone knows it. Five heads are never better than one.' Harley added that it was tricky at first because, not having any money to pay for their acquiescent participation in the project, 'I had to find guys I could brainwash into joining me on the strength of my songs. They had to have total faith in me and the belief I could make them stars.'

Having no guitarist became Harley's way of upping the ante on glam's first wave. He picked up on Bryan Ferry's patter about the lost art of songcraft and talked loudly of being 'basically old-fashioned. For me the greatest works of contemporary song writing were by Gershwin, Irving Berlin, Jerome Kern and Cole Porter.' He took the 'carry yourself like a star' classiness further too. He boasted about how Cockney Rebel would 'spend all our earnings on a good hotel to look fresh' on tour. He claimed that at a time when rock bands came onstage looking like roadies, Cockney Rebel's roadies looked as smart as the band. 'We have the cleanest roadies in the business. They come in, shower or wash and change like us. They're special, they're not the average roadies,' Harley solemnly informed the *NME*. At some early gigs, chief roadie Terry Pinnell wore top hat and tails and carried drinks onstage on a silver tray, like he was Cockney Rebel's butler.

According to Harley, the group's own look was 'very much show-business'. Early on, there were plans for the whole group to adopt a *commedia dell'arte* look of clown outfits and make-up. But they saw sense and contented themselves with having a mime support act at their Biba Rainbow Room concert. Instead, Cockney Rebel dressed for photo shoots and concerts in a cabaret-circuit style of silk outfits, high boots and toreador jackets. Reame-James recalls the flouncy outfits coming from boutiques like Essence on the King's Road and the famous Granny Takes a Trip. 'There was one that I wore on *Top of the Pops* that was made of Queen Victoria's own lace.'

Reame-James was a vital element of the visual chemistry when Cockney Rebel played live – dancing around the piano, pirouetting and twirling, a foil to Harley's central presence. 'I'd had this theatre career, and it was this wonderful, liberating time when the band first started. I just thought, "Well, yeah, this is part of me, how I'm going to make myself an important part of Cockney Rebel."'

Their debut single, 'Sebastian', looks like a conscious attempt to situate the band as 'glam', but only in terms of the lyrics, not the music. A symphonic epic, drawing on a forty-piece orchestra, a choir and the full largesse of EMI's budget, the song feels like a throwback to the progressive late sixties, when groups first started integrating quasi-classical elements into the music. The heavy phasing effects that make Harley's wobbly vocal even more wavering hark back even further to psychedelia. Harley has spoken of the song being influenced indirectly by his LSD experiences, a period when he 'blew a lot of brain-cells' with acid and speed.

'Sebastian' doesn't sound anything like a hit single in 1973's context. But what did make the single timely and glammy were the elliptical hints of bisexual passion in the lyric (a passing reference to a paramour who's 'oh so gay', images of a pallid, angel-faced seducer with green eyeshadow), combined with the swooning languor of Harley's vocals. The title itself is a name so overloaded with layered gay associations that it's become a self-perpetuating tradition: St Sebastian, icon of homoerotic passion; Sebastian Melmoth, the alias adopted by a disgraced Oscar Wilde after his release from gaol; Lord Sebastian Flyte, the decadent aristocratic heir and wastrel of *Brideshead Revisited*; Sebastian Venable, the aesthete torn apart by rent boys in Tennessee Williams's *Suddenly Last Summer* . . . Yet, according to Harley, 'Sebastian' means whatever you want it to mean: its 'six minutes of Gothic poetry' dated back well before glam, to his busking days at the start of the seventies.

Sonically at odds with the times, 'Sebastian' flopped totally in Britain. But it became a #2 hit in both Belgium and the Netherlands, and did well in Germany. This success convinced EMI that Cockney Rebel really were potential second-wave glam superstars. Alan Parsons, who had trained under The Beatles' engineer Geoff Emerick, was lined up to produce the group's second album, *The Psychomodo*. Before the LP was finished, though, Cockney Rebel scored a #5 hit in March 1974 with the non-album single 'Judy Teen'. A rare moment of pure gaiety in the Harley songbook, this reminiscence of adolescent sex rides an odd pizzicato rhythm, at once lilting and stilted. The herky-jerky un-rock feel is matched by Harley's scansion ('all hanky-panky' is rhymed with 'seldom she bored me') and the singer's gelatinous warble, a cross between Fagin from *Oliver!* and Noël Coward.

The Human Menagerie had contained one or two really eccentric tracks, most notably 'Death Trip': a ten minute, tempo-shifting piece that suggested an alternate world where all music had followed the direction pointed by 'A Day in the Life'. *Psychomodo* plunged deeper still into grandiose experimentalism. Reame-James recalls the sessions as crazily creative, with himself playing atonal stuff on

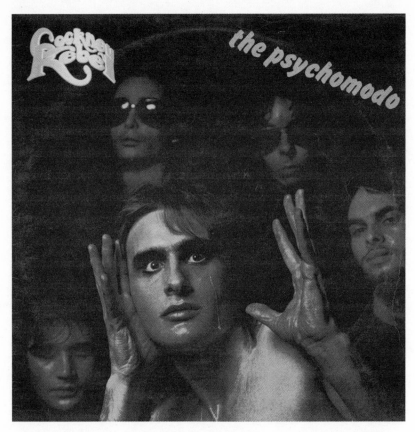

Cockney Rebel Is A Band: (clockwise from top) Milton Reame-James, Jean-Paul Crocker, Paul Jeffreys, Stuart Elliott. Centre: Steve Harley

the keyboards and violinist Crocker off on 'a wacky trip . . . doing all sorts of weird things with his bowing . . . and getting into gizmos – anything with a foot pedal, anything he could do to modulate the sound. We called him the Gizmo King.' Stuart Elliott, meanwhile, laid down super-syncopated breakbeats on 'Singular Band', a song that flipped back and forth between solo drums and sung verses.

The heart of *Psychomodo* is a challenging stretch that starts with the last track of side one (the droning seven minutes of 'Ritz') and recommences with the first track on side two (the droning nearly nine minutes of 'Cavaliers'). *NME* reviewer Charles Shaar Murray grudgingly praised 'Ritz', comparing it to *Last Year at Marienbad*, Alain Resnais's spatially and temporally disjointed dream-drift through the corridors and gardens of a central European chateau, which is described, in Alain Robbe-Grillet's incantatory script, as 'this sprawling, sumptuous, baroque, lugubrious hotel . . . salons heavy with ornamentation of a bygone era'. 'I think "Ritz" is literally to do with "putting on the ritz",' says Reame-James. 'It's about glamour.' The sound itself is like a sepia-tinted mist of Old World elegance, a haze through which Harley intones heady lines about the eyeless gaze of 'clowns in drag' and 'the twisted tale of man'.

The sense of decay and corruption intensifies with 'Cavaliers', an uncharacteristically heavy song for Rebel (featuring electric guitar for once, distorted with pedal effects, as were Reame-James's keyboards) that rolls out like an endlessly cycling portent of doom. Suicide, masturbation, blow jobs, absinthe and crucifixion all figure in one of Harley's most garish lyrics – a jaundiced panorama of modern times in the vein of 'Desolation Row'. What the concept of the cavalier signified to Harley is unclear: a history buff, he may well have seen the parallel between the dandy Royalists and glam's decadents. The song's choruses proposed Cockney Rebel's following as cavaliers, invited them to testify, but the tone was vaguely taunting, with the Dylan-esque 'How does it feel now you've testified?'

Cockney Rebel now had a fervent following, after the Top 5 success of 'Judy Teen' and another oddball hit taken from *Psychomodo*, 'Mr Soft' – a sort of Brecht–Weill polka. Their new disciples copied the singer's penchant for wearing a bowler hat; some threw them onstage. As the group embarked on a forty-date tour in the early summer of 1974, a real Rebel-mania was brewing; an increasingly paranoid Harley, jittery about the crowds, hired extra security. But then it all came tumbling down.

Harley's bandmates had grown unhappy with the meagre money they were receiving for their contributions, which felt increasingly disproportionate given the band's runaway success. 'We really were paid £5 a night,' Reame-James says of the tour dates. In the early days of the band – all camaraderie and shared struggle – this had been fine. The keyboard player had supplemented his income by picking up duty-free cigarettes and booze on the band's frequent jaunts to play gigs and TV shows on the Continent, then reselling them to friends. Now they were playing the large concert halls, they ought to have been raking in more money, but – claims Reame-James – the proceeds were being eaten away because of Harley's insistence on everyone (himself, band and crew) staying in the best hotels.

More problematic was the creative hierarchy within the band. Early on, it was established that Harley was the sole songwriter. This assured him of a much larger revenue stream than his band-mates. Now, the other members of Cockney Rebel wanted their input to be acknowledged and rewarded. 'We had a meeting, the four of us, and we just decided, "What the hell is this about? We're going to get nothing out of this. We're educated guys; this is our career,"' Reame-James recalls. What they told Harley, he says, was, 'Look, our contributions really are arrangements. We should have an arranger's fee.' In Harley's own account of the dispute, the band demanded to write songs for the third album, while he wanted to continue the existing set-up of himself as sole songwriter for at least one more album after *Psychomodo*. Crocker, Reame-James and Jeffreys refused and announced they would quit after the completion of the forty-date tour.

Harley understood how crucial it was to control the narrative and went straight to the music press, which accepted his framing of the schism – making him both the injured party and the victor. The 27 July 1974 issue of *Melody Maker* reported that 'it was entirely Harley's decision to disband' Cockney Rebel, that he'd been aware of undercurrents of insubordination within the group and had called a meeting to confront them.

'Steve made out it was him who'd split up the band,' recalls Reame-James. 'But *we* left *him*. In that *Melody Maker* piece, he actually repeats the same things he said to us: "I don't need you guys. I could stand there with four cardboard cut-outs and I'll still be a star." And we said, "If you don't need us, we're going. That's it. Bye." I think Steve genuinely believed that he didn't need us, that he'd be able to get some session guys and it would carry on exactly the same as it was before.'

But even amid the bluster – 'I've got plans for a new project which will probably wipe the floor with anything you've ever heard the present Cockney Rebel do . . . I've got another master plan' – it was clear how deeply Harley had been shaken by what he saw as a great betrayal. 'There can only ever be one Cockney Rebel, the definitive Cockney Rebel. Those five people you saw tonight are, were and always will be Cockney Rebel.' As he ranted, like a dictator in his last days, about how he'd carried the other guys 'on my back' and how 'they owe me everything', Harley's diagnosis of their treachery came across like self-analysis projected outwards: 'It's difficult for a young man to cope with that kind of speed . . . of success . . . He tends to get confused, bewildered. Suddenly his ego takes over . . . A few egos took over from the personalities of the musicians.' He added, absurdly, 'I'm not an egomaniac, but I understand egomania in other people.'

Possibly smarting from the fact that Reame-James and bassist Paul Jeffreys had joined the rising post-glam band Be-Bop Deluxe, Harley was still ranting in November, when he did a big interview with the *NME*, that perpetual thorn in his side. The piece was tied to his first solo single, 'Big Big Deal', on which he played all the instruments except the drums (handled by Stuart Elliott, the only Rebel who'd opted to stay). 'It was a vicious, nasty split due to hatred for each other,' Harley spat. 'An inside job . . . There was a ringleader . . . who thought he could take over the band . . . They were ganging up on me, talking behind my back for two weeks on that tour.' While interviewer Nick Kent made merciless notes about the singer's mannerisms (the frenetic chewing of gum, the dismissive gestures), Harley rambled on in increasingly soul-baring manner: 'I *am* ruthless – sometimes I revel in it . . . They used to call 'em grudges . . . chips on shoulders. Now they call 'em "raison d'êtres" . . . I've got a lot of anger . . . I'm stripping it down to the real me . . . Y'see, I just don't want to lose. I just want to win. That's all.'

When 'Big Big Deal' left no impression on the charts, Harley funnelled all the unattractive emotions displayed in that *NME* feature into a supremely appealing song – 'Make Me Smile (Come Up and See Me)' – that became a career-saving smash: #1 in the UK for five weeks, a million-plus copies sold worldwide and to date around 120 different cover versions.

Most people took 'Make Me Smile' as a sweet, sexy tune – an impression created by the beguiling chorus title phrase, with its suggestions of assignations and afternoon delight. In fact, the song is 'a finger-pointing piece of vengeful poetry', in Harley's words – an acrid and very public (if somewhat veiled) kiss-off to the group who 'betrayed' the singer's trust. It was written within days of the split, with the first verse, Harley has said, probably emerging from a swamp of brandy-soaked self-pity. The lyric indicated just how fearfully Harley had contemplated the abyss of going back to being a nobody again.

Rallying his resources of spite, Harley retaliated with the song that would ensure his pop immortality and (as he put it) pay him a handsome pension. 'Make Me Smile' is basically 'The Ballad of Cockney Rebel', a self-reflexive anthem. Harley accuses his erstwhile bandmates of bringing the Rebel 'to the floor', taking everything away from him. And all for the lowest of motives: 'metal, what a bore', meaning money (as if the other Rebels were a trade union striking for a pay rise). The cooing chorus refrain about coming up to see him and making him smile was – Reame-James believes – a private message to the band, referring with a sort of soured fondness to the lost camaraderie of the band's early days. 'Steve lived in an upstairs flat in Chelsea, with an entry phone, and we'd always turn up at his place before going off to gigs.' Before buzzing them in, Harley would always answer with a Mae West-like 'Come up and see me some time.' 'It was his little joke, and we'd hurl abuse into the entry phone. It'd make him laugh.' Harley himself has said the chorus was simply a taunting anticipation of future triumph: one day you'll know you blew it, one day I'll laugh in your faces.

Credited to Steve Harley and Cockney Rebel, 'Make Me Smile' previewed a Top 5 album, *The Best Years of Our Lives*, recorded with an all-new (apart from drummer Elliott) line-up of session-level skilled musicians. Just check guitarist Jim Cregan's lyrical solo in 'Make Me Smile' and the delicious way the groove halts teasingly after each chorus before swaying into motion again. The new recruits all knew their place.

Muhammad 'Arley reigned supreme as champion: 'Make Me Smile' was a bigger hit than his role models Bowie and Ferry had achieved up to that point, while his enemies were in disarray (Reame-James and Crocker did not last long in Be-Bop Deluxe), cut off from the success he'd promised and predicted if only they'd follow his leadership.

But in a strange twist, it turned out to be a pyrrhic victory. Nothing Harley would ever release would come close to the same heights; soon, punk would consign him to the old wave, and he would prove unable to adapt as Bowie and Roxy did. 'Make Me Smile' trapped him. How must it feel when your greatest song – or, at least, most *beloved* song – the one you're always obliged to sing at public performances, the one that gets the warmest response, is really a beautifully crafted memento of your lowest point? A wound reopened every time you sing it? 'It is starting to bother me a little bit these days that people only know me for "Make Me Smile",' Harley confessed to *Acoustic* magazine in 2010. 'I realised half the world and its grandmother think I wrote just that song.' Deep down he must also know that the most inventive music he made in his life was on the two albums with the original Cockney Rebel.

'Make Me Smile' and Harley's whole journey through the rock media is a case study of glam as pop about pop. In a 1976 *Melody Maker* interview – conducted during a limousine ride to Stonehenge, because just doing it in a room would be too commonplace for the singer – Steve Harley held forth on his favourite subject: Steve Harley. 'I'm a great self-preservationist . . . To be a survivor you've got to be,' he insisted, continuing: 'If it really is a rat race then the winner has got to be a rat. I'm not a particularly evil human being. But there's a whole love/hate thing in everything I write . . . My personality is aggressive and yet very sensitive.' By the end, Harley was setting some kind of world record by squeezing eight first-person pronouns into three sentences of empty bluster: 'I've proved that I believe in myself. I'm not pretending that I believe in myself any more. I know I believe.'

'SPARKS FLY FOR REBEL,' frothed the 29 June 1974 cover of *Melody Maker*. The news item identified Harley's original Cockney Rebel and the band Sparks as 'the two major new phenomena of British rock. They've both begun their first British tours, and are both going down a storm!'

Two American brothers living in London, Sparks had their first and biggest hits in the early summer of 1974: 'This Town Ain't Big Enough for Both of Us' and 'Amateur Hour'. Teenyboppers adored the falsetto histrionics and frantic pace of the singles and the group's kooky image, as seen on their indelible *Top of the Pops* appearances:

Ron Mael, looking like a cross between Groucho, Adolf and Chaplin, played keyboards and stared into the camera with a cryptic, horribly suggestive half-smile under his toothbrush moustache, while his younger, prettier brother Russell pranced and stamped and shook his curls.

At the height of Sparksmania in 1974, there were riots at gigs: Russell had his clothes ripped off and a chunk of his hair torn out at a Newcastle concert, while their poor bass player was knocked over in the melee and had to be taken to hospital for suspected concussion.

Brainy critics, meanwhile, raved about the originality of Sparks' hectic and histrionic pop, as heard on *Kimono My House*, their first album for Island Records. They were never more thrilling than on the swashbuckling #2 smash 'This Town Ain't Big Enough for Both of Us': a stand-off between rivals in love, perhaps, recast as a gunfighter duel from a western. From the opening 'heartbeat, increasing heartbeat' to the gunshot taken from a BBC library of sound effects and the tossed gauntlet of 'and it ain't me who's gonna leave', the song's sense of drama never relents, propelled by a sharp beat with the feel of flamenco foot-stamping and a guitar figure that seems to catch the light like a flashing blade.

Sparks shared a couple of things with Cockney Rebel besides the timing of their breakthrough. One was tensions and power struggles between the creative core of the group – the Mael brothers, from Los Angeles – and their English backing band, some of whom didn't see themselves as mere employees but wanted to get in on the creative action. Another thing in common was a classical-music influence – or, to be more exact, a mishmash of ideas and flavours borrowed from popular classical music, operetta and cabaret. Unlike prog-rock bands, whose emulation of the classical tradition entailed swelling to symphony scale and in some cases working with symphony orchestras, Sparks injected an un-rock'n'roll precision and formality into pop's concision. Their songs stayed within the three-to-five-minute range and were melodic and usually danceable, in a slightly hyper sort of way. But at a time when most guitar bands – including most glam and glitter bands – were still loosely based around blues-derived rhythm and chords, Sparks invented a form of rock that was about as white and un-American as imaginable, supremely distant from early-seventies values of 'rootsy' or 'feel'. Half a decade before Devo came up with the slogan as the title of a single, Sparks decided to 'Be Stiff'. Indeed, Sparks anticipated new wave: the shrill singing and herky-jerky anti-grooves looked ahead to XTC and Wire.

The highly strung, slightly strained feel of the music came from the particular way that Ron Mael liked to write songs. 'I tend to write on the piano using my right hand,' he explained to Sally James, the presenter of kids' pop TV show *Saturday Scene*. 'Which obviously is on the higher end of the scale. And we just leave it there, and Russell sings it, and it comes out really high.' Russell added, 'It's a painful experience, but I put up with it, because I like how it sounds in the end.' In another interview, Russell dryly noted that when Ron wrote 'Equator' – Sparks at their most helium-shrill – 'he never took into account that it mightn't be possible to sing'.

The Sparks sound was essentially operatic rock, as opposed to rock opera in the *Tommy* sense. More precisely, it was operetta rock – there was a discernible Gilbert and Sullivan influence in Russell's phrasing on some Sparks songs. The Maels grew up in the well-heeled suburbs of Los Angeles, a city that has long looked to Great Britain when it comes to pop. But Sparks' words and music took Anglophilia to unprecedented levels of whimsy and formality.

Growing up in Pacific Palisades, the Maels initially loved LA bands like The Beach Boys, Jan and Dean, and The Seeds, then fell big-time for the British Invasion sounds of The Who, The Move and The Kinks. Their mother had ambitions for the boys and got them into child modelling for the Sears Roebuck and Montgomery Ward catalogues. At UCLA, Ron – five years senior to Russell – studied graphic design and cinema; Russell majored in theatre. While at college, they formed the group Halfnelson in 1968. Initially, it was more a studio-recording entity, involving the technical wizardry and tape-recording skills of their friend Earle Mankey, who would later go on to be a sound engineer at The Beach Boys' studio and a cult producer in the power-pop genre.

'Very thin and reedy, totally unheavy and very naïve,' is how the Maels described their early sound. With Earle's brother Jim Mankey joining on bass and Harley Feinstein drumming, Halfnelson did play live sporadically, at unusual venues like a Hollywood delicatessen and a Mormon dance, as well as more conventional outlets like the Whisky a Go Go on Sunset Strip. It was here that Russell injured himself badly during a routine for the song 'No More Mr Nice Guy' that involved him brandishing a sledgehammer; the head wound required twenty-five stitches. For another song, 'Slowboat', Russell would be pushed by a roadie across the stage in a little ocean liner made of papier mâché, from which the singer tossed candy and flowers into an audience usually comprising a handful of people. These literally theatrical theatrics would get phased out gradually in favour of a heightened sense of musical drama. 'We really do like exaggeration in sound,' said Ron.

Halfnelson signed to Bearsville, the label founded by Bob Dylan's manager Albert Grossman, and recorded their self-titled debut with Todd Rundgren producing. Sharing their Anglophilia and love of the studio, Rundgren was simpatico to the Sparks way of doing things. 'He could see that the recording process was . . . part of what we were,' recalled Russell in a *Sound on Sound* interview. 'It wasn't that we needed to be changed into a traditional band.' *Halfnelson's* opening track – and debut Sparks single – 'Wonder Girl' was exemplary: 'It's not like a live band sound at all. The guitar parts are really deliberate.' At once stark and elaborate, the song is a strange clock-work contraption, Russell's trilling voice weaving around Ron's two-note Wurlitzer tinkle, the clucking guitar riff and a rhythm section that refuses to keep a low profile – the bass moody and mobile, the hi-hats obtrusively splashy and processed to catch the ear's attention. The song sounds like it would fit right in with the contents of Talking Heads' 1977 debut, yet it was recorded six years earlier. 'Biology 2', another *Halfnelson* highlight, is even more advanced, harking forward to The Residents of *Commercial Album*, to John Peel post-punk eccentrics like The Native Hipsters and Family Fodder. Sped-up, studio-warped vocals drape languidly like folds of fluorescent Play-Doh over a lurching, deconstructed rhythm that sidles disconcertingly like a seven-legged animal.

Doing what comes unnaturally: this was the Mael brothers' impulse. 'I like the idea of writing songs which in their demo form do not sound like rock songs – it's kinda forcing the mating of songs that shouldn't be performed by a rock band but yet having it with a rock band instrumentation,' Ron told *Melody Maker* in 1974. Russell elaborated: 'We'll have an electric guitar playing what the clarinet or the banjo should be playing.' Another thing that made their songs sound uptight and awry was their extreme slant towards the whitest side of pop: The Beach Boys, the music-hall side of The Kinks. In another *Melody Maker* interview, Ron recalled a tragi-comical Halfnelson show at a recreation centre in Watts, where the predominantly black audience was expecting a soul band. 'The things we were playing were, well, really lightweight in the beat way. It was impossible to dance to except jigging or polking or something like that.' Added Russell, 'And the one thing you don't play in Watts is a polka.'

Halfnelson didn't make much impact on the music scene in 1971. But when the group switched their name to Sparks and re-debuted with the same album, re-self-titled *Sparks*, the single 'Wonder Girl' took off unexpectedly, getting strong radio play in some parts of America. It peaked at #112, which would be their highest *Billboard* ranking until the eighties. It might have done even better if Sparks had not decided to go to England at that exact point. In 1973, they played a handful of UK gigs and appeared on *The Old Grey Whistle Test*, where they joined the select company of glam-era groups – including the New York Dolls and Roxy Music – that presenter Bob Harris disparaged on air. 'He said something to the effect that we were a cross between Bobby Vee and The Mothers of Invention,' recalled Ron. That year also saw the release of a second album, *A Woofer in Tweeter's Clothing*, featuring Brecht and Weill influences and a cover of 'Do-Re-Mi' from *The Sound of Music*. There was a song called 'The Louvre' and another called 'Girl from Germany'. The latter concerned a young man who brings home his German sweetheart, but the folks won't accept her because all they can think of is stormtroopers on the front lawn. It could be taken as an allegory-cum-prophecy of the difficulties Sparks would face in their future attempts to turn their homeland on to their Europeanised (per)version of an American music form.

When Sparks visited the UK and Europe in 1973, the tour was managed by a character called John Hewlett, formerly of John's Children. Instantly recognising the unique properties – and potential – of the Sparks sound, Hewlett encouraged the Mael brothers to move to England but leave their band behind. He would help them assemble a new group of English musicians more in sympathy with the Mael vision.

What happened next echoed the story of Jimi Hendrix, a musician who in other respects could not have been further from Sparks. Just as ex-Animal Chas Chandler persuaded Hendrix to move to the UK and take up with an English rhythm section, similarly Hewlett – like Chandler, the bassist of a British beat band who had turned to rock management – transplanted the Mael brothers to London and assembled a ferocious backing band of local musicians. He also hooked them up with Island Records. The Jimi Hendrix Experience and Sparks both shot to pop-sensation status and critical acclaim in the UK. But that's where the parallel ends: Jimi was able to return and conquer his native land, but Sparks would always remain cult figures in America, utterly at odds with taste there until the new-wave eighties, when they scored a couple of near-hits.

The Maels' new backing group – bassist Martin Gordon, drummer Dinky Diamond, guitarist Adrian Fisher – gave the Sparks sound muscle. Particularly prominent were Gordon's plunging basslines, aggressively played on a Rickenbacker 4001. Muff Winwood, the producer of *Kimono My House*, had been the bassist in The Spencer Davis Group, and he accentuated the punch and presence of the bass on the record. Sparks' music now sounded dynamic and rhythmically imposing like never before, but still shunned funkiness or raunch or any of the other properties that rock was supposed to possess in the early seventies. 'Falling in Love with Myself Again', for instance, has a uniquely bombastic, fussy-sounding rhythm, like Black Sabbath in waltz-time. 'Amateur Hour' even uses a classical-music metaphor to counsel the sexually inexperienced and inept male, advising, 'It's a lot like playing the violin / You can't start off and be Yehudi Menuhin.'

Ron Mael's lyrics were all about this kind of wit, which some find a bit too flip and clever. But Ron insisted that this sensibility was just how he and his brother naturally were. What would really be fake would be to pretend to be more inarticulate and uneducated than you really were, in order to seem more rock'n'roll. 'For a long time in pop music the lyrics didn't matter,' Ron told the *NME*. 'A lot of groaning and sweating was enough because pop music was prim-itive anyway. These days, though, nobody's primitive and I don't think you set out and pretend you are. That would seem really false. I know I can't do it.'

The same be-true-to-your-well-schooled-self approach applied to the group's image. Ron had tried looking 'rock'n'roll' but just felt 'really out of place in blue jeans or neon suits. I feel most natural . . . in these kind of clothes,' he explained, referring to his so-square-it's-cool clothing. 'This is in keeping with what I am. Something that isn't anything to do with what is traditionally rock.' He talked about really liking 'being civilized', saying that he and Russell were 'both fans of civilization'.

Like Steve Harley and Bryan Ferry, Ron's role models in song craft and lyrical wit were pre-rock or un-rock: Cole Porter, Noël Coward and Brian Wilson's erstwhile collaborator Van Dyke Parks. 'I often tend to think of the title first, then work on it until there's a song without one dull moment. I feel craftsmanship in songs is something you don't see too much of.' Ron talked of his dislike of 'the tortured artist syndrome . . . A good lyric . . . can make the trivial become important.' Not that there wasn't angst or emotional turmoil lurking under some of the songs, but they were always veiled protectively in dark humour. Morrissey, a huge Sparks fan, probably picked up a trick or two. He has praised Mael's songwriting, saying that Ron's 'lyrical take on sex cries out like prison cell carvings. It is only the laughing that stops the crying.'

Sometimes it seemed like what may have been real-life aches and pains were being projected into absurdist scenarios. 'Equator' is about a romantic rendezvous at the hottest latitude on the planet, for which the girl is distressingly late, such that all of the lover's gifts 'are now melted or dead'. 'Here in Heaven' concerns a suicide pact between lovers, in which the man follows through but the girl baulks: he wonders, as he waits in the afterlife, if it was all a trick and he's just 'that sucker in the sky'. 'Tits' is the lament of a husband who's been displaced from his favourite source of comfort and fun by the arrival of a tiny rival: a suckling baby whose nourishment needs take precedence. 'Don't Leave Me Alone with Her' is twitchy with fear-of-female, flinching from 'a Hitler wearing heels . . . De Sade who makes good tea'.

Like Morrissey, the Maels littered their interviews with quips as witty as their songs' lyrics. Russell imagined Sparks getting so huge that they'd 'have all the little ten-year-old boys in England slicking back their hair and growing tiny moustaches. And the ones that can't grow them will have to pencil them in before they come to the concerts.' He also spoke of how they'd hoped that their first tour of the UK as pop stars would leave them in the position of being 'the big Romeos' after each show, only 'it's turned out we're . . . big Romeos for tiny, 12-year-old Juliets'.

Moving swiftly to consolidate their UK stardom, Sparks recorded *Propaganda*, their second Island LP, and released it in November 1974. Everything was intensified a notch or two beyond *Kimono*: the classical-infused primness, the absurdist wit. The opening title track featured a Vienna Boys' Choir of stacked Russells (overdubbed thirty times!) twittering dementedly. 'Reinforcements' is *Pirates of Penzance* meets *Tommy*, a mad march of punctilious paranoia: 'You can't tell me why the shrubbery moves / Or why there always has to be a subterfuge.' 'Bon Voyage' imagined the sadness of the animals that didn't get to board the Ark. 'Achoo' turns the sound of sneezing into a contagiously catchy chorus.

By 1975's Tony Visconti-produced *Indiscreet*, Sparks had broadened their range to include all kinds of non-rock styles from up and down the twentieth century, from vaudeville jazz ('Looks, Looks, Looks') to palm-court tea-dance music ('Under the Table with Her'). 'It Ain't 1918' sounded like it actually was. The single 'Get in the Swing' was some kind of pinnacle of mischievous invention, shifting from a Sousa-like march of romping brass and whistles to a Three Musketeers all-for-one, one-for-all surge and then into a cello-laced calm, during which God calls down to Russell with a questionnaire he'd like filled, but Russell politely declines. But despite a hilarious

Top of the Pops performance for which Russell wore hot pants with bare thighs, legs and feet, 'Get in the Swing' was only a modest hit.

The trajectory from *Kimono* to *Propaganda* to *Indiscreet* had propelled Sparks along what I call the Arc of Fruitless Intensification. This is when artists almost irresistibly find themselves increasing the dosage of whatever it is in their music, lyrics and presentation that makes them unique and stand out from the pack. The thing that starts out as an attraction swiftly becomes an irritant, even a repulsion. Russell's mannered, high-pitched vocals, the choppy rhythms, the scraps of classical and showbiz music quilted together, the preposterous lyric scenarios – it all became a teensy bit wearing. But toning it down, which is what Sparks tried to do on their next few albums, didn't work either – they just sounded bland, depleted of their individuality. It wasn't until they transplanted that (un)natural state of hysteria into a completely different sound (Giorgio Moroder's all-electronic Eurodisco) that Sparks would enjoy UK chart success again, with 1979's astonishing hits 'Number One Song in Heaven' and 'Beat the Clock'.

The *NME*'s Ian Macdonald identified Sparks' secret theme as decadence. By this he meant not the oversubscribed Weimar kind that Lou Reed, Bowie, Alice Cooper and others had dabbled with, but the decadence of the in-bred elite – which, in American terms, meant the preppy East Coast old-money dynasties. The Maels had talked in interviews of a family connection to the Kennedys, how as children they 'used to play at their place about once a year . . . We can relate – I hate to use that word – to them better than musicians or even most Americans. There was something about them more aristocratic – less brash in an obnoxious sort of way.' True or not, for the B-side of the US single release of 'Looks, Looks, Looks' Sparks recorded a whimsical ditty, 'The Wedding of Jacqueline Kennedy to Russell Mael', whose lyric consisted entirely of the betrothal vows of these imaginary nuptials. This Wes Anderson-anticipating fascination for upper-class mores and preppy aesthetics fed into *Kimono* songs like 'In My Family', with its references to Rockefeller and Getty.

Rather than decadent – given that Sparks were about as unde-bauched as a rock band got in the seventies – the word I'd use to describe their aesthetic is baroque. Not in the narrow histori-cal sense of eighteenth-century architecture, art and music, but a looser continuum that celebrates ornamentation, grandeur, hier-archy and the intertwining of formality and exuberance. One of the precepts of the baroque aesthetic is that one can never be too civilised. Baroque culture celebrates the great indoors of manners and urbanity, rather than the great outdoors of rough-hewn and rugged simplicity. The natural world exists to be cultivated and tamed, like fancy breeds of dogs or the gardens of stately homes with their terraced flower beds, manicured topiary, landscaped slopes and complex fountains. That spirit surfaced in Sparks with the single 'Never Turn Your Back on Mother Earth', which featured a harpsichord – that baroque-era instrument – and was described by Russell as 'an anti-nature, anti-ecology song . . . It says how nature can sometimes be up to no good.'

With Sparks racing ahead of Cockney Rebel as the hottest band of 1974, the record-company hunt was on for soundalikes. CBS grabbed one for itself when they signed Jet towards the end of that year. The resemblance was uncanny, but explicable, given that Jet was partly composed of musicians who'd either backed Sparks on *Kimono My House* or played in the touring line-up.

Martin Gordon, the bassist whose strident playing contributed much to the forceful sound of *Kimono*, had been fired abruptly after the album sessions and a single *Top of the Pops* performance of

'This Town Ain't Big Enough'. The Maels were discomfited with his showmanship and desire to contribute songs. When Sparks then poached a new bassist and guitarist off Slade-like hooligans The Jook, the bereft parties pooled their grievances. Gordon hooked up with The Jook's furious drummer Chris Townson; the latter pulled in his former John's Children bandmate Andy Ellison as singer. Another ex-Sparks employee – live keyboard player Sir Peter Oxendale – was also recruited. To complete the line-up, Jet approached David O'List, formerly of the first incarnation of Roxy Music and whose blazing guitar had more recently been heard on Bryan Ferry's hit single 'The In-Crowd'.

Roy Thomas Baker, the producer assigned to Jet's self-titled debut, was 'told by CBS to make it sound like Sparks', Andy Ellison frankly admits. To promote the album, Jet were then packed off to tour as support to another glam supergroup, Hunter–Ronson, the partnership of the ex-Mott singer and the ex-Spiders from Mars guitarist.

Despite all their credentials and the muscle behind them – in addition to CBS, Jet were managed by Mike Leander's RAM company – the album was a complete flop. The press either ignored or derided them as glam bandwagon-jumpers; their poorly chosen singles died; the kids had moved on to pure teenybop like The Bay City Rollers and The Rubettes. It's a shame, because *Jet*, while not quite a lost masterpiece, is a lovely little curio of the era, taking glam traits to the limit while also leaping ahead to new wave.

'Fax 'n' Info' merges fey and ferocious with thrilling preposterousness. Gordon's growling, echo-delayed bass anticipates Jean-Jacques Burnel from The Stranglers; his lyrics recall Gilbert and Sullivan, referencing cricket ('sticky wicket') and bad etiquette ('manners like a gannet') as if in a bid to show Sparks how Anglophilia should really be done. Ellison's prissy-posh enunciation draws a line between Syd Barrett in '67 and debonair all-too-English outfits of the eighties like The Monochrome Set and The Cleaners from Venus. 'I was doing that towards the end of John's Children, using a voice without any Americanisation,' recalls Ellison. 'So I thought I'd take it to the extra limit . . . We were really coming from a very English heritage – boarding school, and humour like Monty Python and the Goons.'

Anglo-surrealist comedy fed into the group's image, courtesy of costumes by Jean Seel, the designer who worked with Leander acts like Glitter. 'We had people dressed up as anteaters. Davy O'List played in a dinosaur costume. I wore these jackets with a hood with "Jet" on the back, a cape with "Jet" on it, and designer, knee-length white boots that zipped up the side. And Martin was done out in riding gear, like he was playing in a polo match. Peter Oxendale was dressed up as Sir Peter Oxendale – an aristocrat.'

After a failed album, a chaotic tour and a perversely counterproductive showcase to the record company of potential material for a second album, Jet abruptly found themselves label-less. But then punk happened. The group barely had to change the sound of the tougher and more frantic Jet numbers like 'It Would Be Good' and 'Nothing to Do with Us'. All they had to do was drop the daft stage clothes and change the name, which they did. As Radio Stars, they became a successful pop-punk group, earning press support and scoring a couple of minor hits. The biggest alteration in their sound was Ellison's voice: he dropped the exaggeratedly aristocratic accent several rungs down the class ladder to guttural guttersnipe.

While Jet were recording their doomed debut during all-night studio sessions, their producer Roy Thomas Baker was burning the candle at both ends and working by day on Queen's *Sheer Heart Attack* as well. If Sparks invented baroque 'n' roll – and Jet cloned it with the rock operetta of 'Fax 'n' Info' – then it was Queen who would take the style much further, both in terms of conquering the global rock market but also the sheer scale and excess with which they executed the concept. Sparks and Queen intersected early on: the latter supported Sparks on a tour, and at one point, around the time of *Propaganda* (Sparks at their peak, Queen's career yet to take off), the Mael brothers attempted to poach guitarist Brian May.

When they arrived on the British scene, Queen were bracketed as glam, as opposed to metal or stadium rock. Critics called them out for copying Sparks as well as The Sweet's studio-processed four-part harmonies. (The Sweet were *incensed* when Queen broke through with 'Killer Queen' and 'Bohemian Rhapsody', feeling that they'd been ripped off, yet somehow the imitators had garnered more cred than they ever had.) Queen toured with Mott the Hoople, support-ing them during their theatrical Broadway run at the Uris. Their stage costumes were glammy too, mingling the effeminate and the exotic, and their frontman was as camp as could be. His stage name, Mercury, had a quicksilver glisten that fitted perfectly alongside pop names like Glitter and Stardust, while also expressing his drive to become a godstar. Queen's guitar hero Brian May picked up on the pageantry of Mick Ronson's motifs as much as Jimmy Page's flash and Jimi Hendrix's fantasia of tone-colours.

In their earliest interviews, Queen expressed anxiety about the possibility that they might just have missed the boat: May told *Melody Maker* in 1973 that Queen 'were into glam-rock before groups like the Sweet and Bowie and we're worried now, because we might have come too late'. Their big glam anthem actually arrived very late indeed, in 1977: 'We Will Rock You' was a monumentally tardy but undeniably monumental-sounding reply to 'Rock and Roll, Part 2'. The wide crunch of its bass-drum thud and the shouted threat of the chorus would in decades to come rival Glitter's anthem as a 'jock jam' chanted by sports fans at American arenas.

Queen may have been accused of clinging to glam's coat-tails, but early on the band's sound was more like a clinical copy of Led Zeppelin. Freddie Mercury picked up on a willowy feyness in Robert Plant's stage posture; he took Plant's stratospheric high-pitched scream and pushed even further from blues and into opera. Rock theorist Nick Katranis was a teenage fan of the group in their 1973–4 phase. He recalls seeing the band play in Detroit: 'It was long hair, white/black robes . . . The hybrid of glam ballads with Zeppelin fairy-tale myth and Mott the Hoople was like nothing else at the time. Their androgyny was from the past, more Beardsley than Bowie. Mercury's occult name, his strange dark beauty and serpentine bracelets . . . alien! And they rocked *hard*!! . . . I still love those first three LPs, *Queen*, *Queen II* and *Sheer Heart Attack*: kitsch and camp confused, and real feeling too in there . . . *for something*.'

Mercury actually was gay, but he kept it concealed, involving himself in various relationships with women, including a long-term one that was close to a marriage. Like showbiz figures such as Liberace and Danny La Rue, publicly Mercury kept his sexuality under wraps right to the end.

Yet Mercury's gayness seeped out all over the place: in the band's lyrics and presentation, and above all in the name Queen. This had been chosen at Mercury's insistence. 'It's ever so regal,' he declared at the time. 'It was a strong name, very universal and very immediate,' Mercury recalled many years later. 'It had a lot of visual potential and was open to all sorts of interpretations, but that was just one facet of it.' His diva-like persona onstage, and his campy manner in everyday life and interviews, along with his black-painted fingernails and eyeliner, now seem like they give the game away fairly blatantly, but at the time – with straight rock musicians feminised in their clothing and hair – the clues weren't picked up. Even when, later in the seventies, Mercury adopted a moustache in the reigning 'gay clone' look of the time, most Queen fans remained oblivious.

He was one of those performers – like Elton John and Rob Halford from Judas Priest – that the straight rock audience clutched to its breast: an embrace that hovered somewhere between acceptance and ignorance, the flamboyance and kinkiness of their stage personae seen purely as rock excess.

During the glam era, just a few journalists seem to have cottoned on, transcribing every single one of Mercury's 'my dears' and 'darlings'. Some say these flourishes stemmed from his great love of *Cabaret* (Liza Minnelli was one of Mercury's favourite singers). But others claim that young Freddie talked like this at school, even addressing his teachers as 'dahling'.

The outrageous camp of his 1974 remark to the *NME* – 'My dear I'm the vainest creature going . . . I'd like to be carried on stage by six nubile slaves with palms and all' – seems totally legible today. So does titling a song on *Queen II* 'The Fairy Feller's Master-Stroke'. The title comes from the name of a painting by nineteenth-century artist Richard Dadd. Mercury visited the Tate museum repeatedly to view it and insisted that the other members of Queen and producer Roy Thomas Baker accompany him. Created over a period of six to nine years, the fairy-tale landscape draws the eye into its intricate tangle of detail, while also disorienting the gaze with what one art critic called its 'strange disruptions of scale and lack of perspective'. Dadd had written an accompanying poem from which Mercury borrowed archaic words and phrases – ostler, tatterdemalion, apothecary-man – for the song's lyric.

In the painting and poem, 'feller' means someone who wields an axe to chop down a tree or, in this case, break open a large chestnut that will be fashioned into a carriage for the fairy Queen Mabs. But in colloquial seventies language, 'feller' would suggest 'fellow' and 'fairy feller' would be the equivalent of 'gay man'. If that feels like reading too much into a lyric, there is also the repeated phrase 'what a quaere fellow' – not from Dadd's poem, but of Mercury's own devising, and probably his attempt at an archaic and semi-disguised spelling of 'queer'. There are several other suggestive phrases – 'dirty laddio', references to fancies being tickled by 'fairy dandies' – that would support an interpretation of the song as an allegory of a sex life kept hidden from the public.

The painting, the poem and the song also plug into a very English obsession with fairies that goes back to Edmund Spenser's *The Fairie Queene*, a dense allegory in praise of aristocratic rank and hierarchical order, with Gloriana, the Fairie Queene, symbolising Elizabeth I. Titania, the Queen of the Fairies in Shakespeare's *A Midsummer Night's Dream* (who also appears in Spenser's poem), is mentioned in Mercury's lyric. Did he see himself as the figure his song invokes: 'the arch-magician' who 'presides' over a spellbound following? And in *Midsummer Night's Dream*, the haughty, over-weening Titania fights with Oberon, the King of the Fairies, over the keeping of an Indian changeling boy. Although Mercury rarely mentioned the fact, he was Indian, the son of Parsee parents who'd emigrated to Zanzibar, off the east coast of Africa.

He was born Farrokh Bulsara in 1946, back when Zanzibar was still a protectorate of the British Empire. Although his family were Parsees practising Zoroastrianism, Mercury's father worked as a high-court cashier for the British government. The Bulsaras were upper middle class, comfortably off, with servants and enough money to send Freddie to a Church of England boarding school back in India at the age of eight. This traditional English-style private education continued when the family emigrated to the London suburb of Feltham in 1964, after British colonial rule ended in Zanzibar. Mercury's cultural diet was high European too: he was exposed to opera at an early age. Then, in 1966, he enrolled at Ealing Technical College and School of Art, where he took classes in fashion and graphic design.

Mercury was the only member of Queen with any grounding in

the humanities. Curiously for a band that indulged so heavily in myth, legend and supernatural fancy, Queen was almost entirely composed of scientists. Brian May was a student of maths, physics and astronomy at Imperial College, engaged in apparently brilliant research that he resumed in later life. Bassist John Deacon had a master's degree in acoustics and vibration technology. Drummer Roger Taylor (full name Meaddows-Taylor) had pursued dentistry.

The group coalesced in 1970, when Mercury joined Smile, a band started by Brian May that included Taylor on drums. Mercury had been a fan of the group and – although bursting with desire to be a star – bided his time until the original singer left. He then persuaded May and Taylor to change the name to Queen. Going forward, Queen approached their career with a methodical organisation rare in rock music at that time. They supposedly drew up a ten-year plan for success. They hitched up with the powerful management/production company Trident Audio Productions, who poured a ton of money into the group, ensuring that Queen's PA system and lighting set-up was on the level of an established big-selling band rather than a group just starting out. They signed to EMI, the most major of the British major labels.

The same combination of force and finesse was applied to their music-making. 'We are the most meticulous band going,' Mercury admitted to *Melody Maker*. 'Sometimes this can go to the point of distraction. But we believe in perfection.' To quote 'Killer Queen', the group was 'fastidious and precise' in the studio. Complicated structures of vocal harmonies and guitar parts were plotted out in advance like architectural blueprints by May, whom Taylor described as 'very dots-on-paper minded'. Enlisting the expertise of his electrical-engineer father, May even built his own edition-of-one guitar, nicknamed the Red Special, using mahogany from an eighteenth-century fireplace, valve springs from an old motorbike, an old bicycle saddle-bag carrier, the end of a knitting needle and other repurposed scrap. The sound was unique, unavailable to any other guitarist in the world.

In Queen's albums, two traditions rooted in the British sixties converged to maximum effect: the heaviness of the Yardbirds/Cream/Jeff Beck/Jimmy Page lineage, which stunned audiences in the live arena with volume, fluency and focused power; and the more studio-bound school of super-production that came out of *Sgt Pepper's* and the Paul McCartney/George Martin side of The Beatles, as carried on by seventies outfits like 10cc and Electric Light Orchestra. Somewhere in between the two lineages was Jimi Hendrix, whose work spanned incandescent improvised noise and obsessively studio-sculpted soundscapes, as on *Electric Ladyland*. Hendrix was a common reference point for all the members of Queen, but was particularly beloved by May and Mercury. For May, Jimi was *the* guitarist ('On hearing Hendrix my immediate reaction was, he's done it all,' he gushed), while Mercury had actually written his Ealing Art College thesis about Hendrix.

After a 1973 self-titled debut that largely sounds like a cleaner Led Zep, Queen really started to develop their own maximalist style on *Queen II* (indeed, the album's working title was 'Over the Top'). Around the time of its 1974 release, May talked about loving The Who and Led Zep, 'but what we are trying to do differently from either of those groups is this sort of layered sound . . . I wanted to build up textures behind the main melody lines. We were trying to push studio techniques to a new limit for rock groups.'

The whole of *Queen II*'s second side was given over to what Mercury called 'little fairy stories', with titles like 'Ogre Battle'. And it was here, with 'The Fairy Feller's Master-Stroke', that Queen's compulsion to embroider and ornament their sound became demented, a preview of the rococo overload of 'Bohemian Rhapsody'. Riddled with panning effects, this was Queen's 'biggest stereo experiment', according to Roger Taylor, an attempt to 'break the boundaries of what people thought you could do in a recording studio'.

But it was the stacked vocals on 'Fairy Feller' that would become Queen's true and florid signature going forward: Freddie's already superhuman lungs, bionically boosted with studio effects and layered like a gateau. Yet this push for elaborately interlocking Mercury-upon-Mercury harmonies actually came more from Brian May than the singer himself. Like the overdubbing and interlacing of guitar lines, it appealed to May's technical-minded nature. Phasing – a sixties effect originally associated with psychedelia – sounded impossibly creamy and sweet when applied to Queen's vocals: a diabetic delirium. Another trick that Queen would use to the point of overkill was backing vocals that lunge out of nowhere and abruptly cut off. The effect is akin to the 'terracing' dynamics in baroque styles like concerto grosso: sharp transitions from loud to soft, or fast to slow.

Bach and other baroque-era composers believed music was a science, subject to laws that could be divined (and were Divinely instituted). This view of music as 'sounding mathematics' had an obvious affinity with May's scientific mind. In Queen's music, as in baroque art of all kinds, there's a combination of rationality and excess, simple elements building up through what eighteenth-century composers called *elaboratio* into majestic edifices.

The term 'pomp rock' that was slung at Queen by hostile reviewers brings to mind ceremonial splendour, from the Elizabethan court of Spenser's day to seventeenth-century Versailles. W. H. Auden described baroque as 'a visible hymn to earthly pomp and power'. The antithesis of Puritanism, baroque was Royalist art, essentially. 'Procession', the opening track on *Queen II*, is a march in the stately and grave vein of Purcell's *Music for the Funeral of Queen Mary*, played with a crisp flourish by May on his electric guitar.

Why call your band Queen, as opposed to King? Apart from the gay resonance, the appeal of queenliness is that it involves – with a few exceptions, like Elizabeth I – majesty without responsibility. Kings actually had to administer the nation, do tedious things like attend councils and sign endless documents. But, because usually a king's consort, the queen is about pure regality: as with Marie Antoinette, it's a life devoted to vanity and luxury, splendour and caprice.

Queen's other connection to the baroque era is that this was when opera was invented. In the eighteenth century, the majority of Italian opera singers were castrati; the most successful were the period's equivalent to rock stars, wealthy and idolised by women, even though they wouldn't have been much use to them in the boudoir. But the castrato sound divided listeners, with many critics complaining there was something unmanly and morally corrupting about the 'farcical trilling and warbling'. One early nineteenth-century newspaper complained about singers emitting sounds akin to 'the discordance of a peacock's scream', neatly conflating dandy conceit and emasculation. The high-pitched, self-preening falsetto voices of pop and rock have been similarly polarising. Some rock fans, preferring a bluesy, guttural rasp, would probably concur with classical-music snob Anthony Burgess, who – through the mouthpiece of droog leader Alex in *A Clockwork Orange* – complains about the shrill histrionics of 'yarbleless' pop singers – 'yarble' being slang for testicle in this near-future novel. Freddie Mercury was just one in a lineage of falsetto pop singers running from doo-wop and The Four Seasons through Sylvester and Michael Jackson to Prince, Jimmy Somerville and Antony Hegarty. But more than anyone before or since, he pushed rock singing into the stratospheric zones of opera.

'We have hid inside music,' Wayne Koestenbaum wrote in *The Queen's Throat*, his book about opera and its allure to gay men. 'In music we can come out without coming out, we can reveal without saying a word.' Koestenbaum notes the proximity of the words 'queen' and 'queer' and describes falsetto as a form of vocal drag. If the appeal of the girlishly high male voice to female listeners is the fantasy of a male lover as tender and sensitive as a woman, for male listeners the pleasure is perhaps to do with accessing their own inner gender-flux, a latent potential for angelic gentleness and ethereality: an escape from the heaviness of masculinity. The scholar Ken McLeod points out that where the castrato is a chest voice (and thus 'naturally' unnatural), the falsetto is a head voice: less visceral, heading towards being an out-of-body sound altogether, already in the next world (as with Sparks' soprano disco classic 'Number One Song in Heaven').

Koestenbaum describes operatic singing as a style that 'forbids flaw' and 'sings its training'. Queen were often denigrated by populist rock critics for their ostentatious virtuosity, with insults like 'flash-rock' or 'techno-flash' being used. Mercury certainly shows off his command over his vocal cords at every opportunity. Whether it's opera or Mongolian throat-singing or even yodelling, any highly developed vocal technique is, in a sense, a technology: a discipline imposed and implanted within lungs and throat, as coercive and constraining as a corset. It's the triumph of human will and ingenuity over the body's limits. There is a perfectly logical drift from these extreme forms of cultivation of the voice to using technological artifice in the recording studio: thickening the voice by layering, speeding up or slowing down the tape, application of reverb or more extreme effects. The studio sorcery explored by Queen anticipated the even more drastic transubstantiation and morphing of the digital era, with the use and abuse of pitch-altering devices like Auto-Tune and Melodyne.

From Mercury's operatic voice to May's doilies of guitar, there had never been a band with such a lacquered sound before Queen. Their early albums bore legends like 'This album was created with

absolutely no synthesizers.' But rather than being synthphobic rock-
ists, I think Queen simply wanted the listener to know that they
hadn't taken any easy routes: all these astonishing sounds, as on 'In
the Lap of the Gods', had been extracted – extorted, even – at tremendous trouble from electric guitar, bass, drums and the band's
vocal cords.

The fruition of Queen's operatic leanings and studio-concocted
illusionism came with their two biggest hits, 'Killer Queen' and
'Bohemian Rhapsody'. Frosted with phased vocals, 'Killer Queen'
was as sumptuous as a wedding cake; lyrically, it sketched an affectionate portrait of a high-class call girl, according to Mercury. But
his further comment – that the song is him trying to say 'that classy
people can be whores as well' – makes you wonder whether 'Killer
Queen' is really a displaced self-portrait. Mercury sometimes talked
of his stage persona as 'sluttish': he loved to perform 'Big Spender'
from *Sweet Charity*, a musical about hookers; and he described
'Killer Queen' in Liza Minnelli terms as 'one of those bowler-hat,
black suspender belt numbers'.

'Bohemian Rhapsody', it's said, was inspired by seeing Mott the
Hoople perform 'Marionette' when Queen supported them in
America, although whether it was the musical melodrama of the
song or the lyrical theme of feeling trapped and controlled that
was the catalyst is unclear. Mercury described 'Rhapsody' as 'mock
opera', but you might also call it hyper-opera: it vaults far beyond
what could be achieved live in the theatre by the undoctored human
voice, exploiting the capacities of the studio to the utmost with 180
vocal overdubs.

The 'Rhapsody' of the title references the classical-music form,
a single-movement work that encompasses structural shifts and
mood contrasts. This certainly fits the way 'Bohemian Rhapsody'
leaps from piano ballad into comic-opera recitative, then to a choral
representation of a jury trial, then into the much-loved hard-rocking

sequence immortalised in *Wayne's World*, then into a grandiosely swaying section with guitar-playing that sounds crenellated, before returning to the melancholy ballad.

But what about the 'Bohemian' in the title? It suggests alternative lifestyles, an existence on the edge of society, transgressively dedicated to forbidden pleasures. Queen, if anything, were politically conservative: hard-working, ultra-professional, unashamedly interested in making money. Could it be, then, that 'Bohemian' alludes enigmatically to Mercury's secret sexuality? Nothing in the lyric really supports this analysis, except for a sense of being an outcast, a criminal being punished. Is the jury shrieking, 'No, we will not let you go!' really Mercury's superego, internalised family values holding him back and racking him with guilt? Why is the song initially addressed to a mama? The song, so exuberant in its middle sections, begins and ends with despair: 'nothing really matters . . . to me'.

'Bohemian Rhapsody' was the centrepiece of *A Night at the Opera*, released a few weeks before Christmas 1975. Alongside the baroque and operetta influences, this album plunged wholesale into campy retro-zones similar to those indulged by Sparks on *Indiscreet* earlier in '75. 'Lazing on a Sunday Afternoon' was a straw-hat-waving vaudeville number; Mercury's voice was filtered through headphones placed inside a metal can to create a vintage lo-fidelity effect redolent of the scratchy sound of shellac 78 rpm discs coming through a gramophone horn. 'Seaside Rendezvous' hailed from a similar sort of undefined 'good old days', chucking in ragtime piano, kazoos, braying New Orleans horns, a spoons solo, barbershop quartet harmonies and Mercury camping it up with '*très charmant*, my dear' and a valedictory 'give us a kiss'. 'Good Company' was the most peculiar retro-exercise on the LP: a ukulele-jangling number for which Brian May painstakingly made his guitar sound like a trombone, piccolo and other instruments you'd expect from an early jazz band.

A *Night at the Opera* ends with an electric-guitar version of 'God Save the Queen'. Right from the start, in their earliest interviews, Mercury had stressed that 'the concept of Queen is to be regal and majestic. Glamour is a part of us and we want to be dandy . . . We want to be a good British regal rock band.' Why was this so important to Freddie?

Until Queen, rock bands had generally aligned themselves with the people. With the possible prior exception of Led Zeppelin, Queen were the first group overtly to break with rock's cult of the underdog and actively identify instead with the overlord. For rock critics in America – a country founded on the ejection of the British monarchy – this made Queen uniquely offensive: it rubbed against their liberal-populist politics, which at that time made them invest hopes for rock's renewal in street punks like the New York Dolls and Springsteen. Reviewing Queen's 1977 album *News of the World*, *Rolling Stone* described the band as making 'elaborate music from shards of nostalgia for the British Empire' and said 'We Will Rock You' had 'the atmosphere of a political rally in a Leni Riefenstahl movie'. Queen's later album *Jazz* prompted Dave Marsh to suggest that the British quartet 'may be the first truly fascist rock band'.

While Marsh's verdict is a tad harsh and hyperbolic, there's no denying that songs like 'We Are the Champions' (with its taunting refrain 'no time for losers') and 'One Vision' do have an unsettling triumphalist and totalitarian vibe to them. Some of Mercury's grandiose onstage gestures more than slightly resembled the strutting of a Mussolini or Latin American dictator. It is tempting to read a certain sympathy for authoritarianism into things like Queen playing huge stadium concerts in Argentina in 1981 – the era of the military dictatorship, when dissidents were 'disappeared' by being dropped, drugged, from a helicopter into the Rio de la Plata estuary. (To be fair, they also played in Brazil, where the junta were gradually re-democratising the country, and in the fully democratic Venezuela.)

Queen liked to make out they were apolitical, 'just entertainers', but for many they took this stance way too far when they played concerts at Sun City in 1984, breaking the anti-apartheid movement's cultural boycott of South Africa.

A group like Queen were never going to have a lot of sympathy for punk rock, a movement that stuck a safety pin through the nose of Elizabeth II. And in 1977 – the year of the Sex Pistols' 'God Save the Queen' – Queen did in fact record not one but two ripostes to punk: 'Sheer Heart Attack' and 'Fight from the Inside'. Both were written by Roger Taylor, who also sang on 'Fight'. Where 'Sheer Heart Attack' mocked the punks for their inarticulacy and vacancy, 'Fight from the Inside' was a semi-veiled assault on the reigning music-press ideology of street credibility: it proposed that the only way to change the status quo was to infiltrate the Establishment yourself.

Part of the backdrop was that *News of the World*, the album on which the songs appeared, was recorded in a studio adjacent to where the Sex Pistols were making *Never Mind the Bollocks*. Freddie Mercury and Sid Vicious had a contretemps, or at least a mildly abrasive exchange.

'So you're this Freddie Platinum bloke that's supposed to be bringing ballet to the masses?' Vicious jeered. This was a dig at the leotards Mercury had lately taken to wearing onstage; in a couple of years, he would actually dance and sing with the Royal Ballet. 'Ah, Mr Ferocious,' Mercury tartly counter-quipped. 'We're doing our best, dear. We're doing our best.'

Be-Bop Deluxe had two things in common with Queen: they were on EMI – more precisely, on its progressive imprint Harvest – and their second album *Futurama* was produced by Roy Thomas Baker.

Perhaps three things: Be-Bop leader Bill Nelson's guitar-playing came from an exquisitely controlled and serenely non-Dionysian region not so far from Brian May's. Unfortunately, Nelson's singing was as nondescript as May's own infrequent turns at the mic. The characterless vocals hampered Be-Bop's advances into the charts (they had a couple of small hits), but it didn't stop the band from being one of the more arresting anomalies of the mid-seventies – impossible to classify as prog or glam, and mutating across their 1972–8 career into arty new wave before expiring.

For a couple of years between glam's ebb and punk's explosion, Nelson was a bona fide guitar hero: dazzling on his instrument, fusing the sculpted grace of Mick Ronson with the cascading lyricism of Hendrix, while also texturally prophesying the clean, clear sounds of post-punk groups like The Skids. In terms of his personality and interests, he came over like a cross between Robert Fripp and Brian Eno. A musician's musician, dedicated to instrumental mastery . . . yet also a product of Wakefield College of Art, and someone whose esoteric leanings included making environmental soundscapes.

Image-wise, Nelson was far more Ferry than Eno, though: he favoured suits and ties and short, combed hair. With his clean-cut good looks and soft, high, Yorkshire-accented voice, Nelson was the kind of presentable young man that made grannies and older folks coo, 'What a nice boy.' Sometimes Bill would go so far as wearing a white tux and bow tie onstage. He said that he liked playing image games, creating a disparity between the guitar-heavy sound and the well-groomed non-rock'n'roll appearance. 'We play music you wouldn't associate that image with. That's the fun of it for me . . . We can confuse people and make them think a bit.'

Ultimately, despite the flash get-up, Be-Bop Deluxe's appeal didn't really lie with the Bowie/Roxy audience; it was with the 'serious music' crowd. Three of their albums had guitar-related titles: *Axe Victim*, *Sunburst Finish* and *Futurama* (the latter being a make of guitar). The covers gave off mixed messages, ranging from the prog-rock visual pun of *Axe Victim* (a guitar that looks like a skull) to *Sunburst Finish*, which fell somewhere between Roxy's hip erotica and Hipgnosis: a naked, model-emaciated girl holding a flaming guitar aloft.

Lyric-wise, Be-Bop's sci-fi songs hovered somewhere between Bowie and Blue Öyster Cult: 'Dance of the Uncle Sam Humanoids', 'Lost in the Neon World', 'Quest for the Harvest of the Stars'. There was a cute nod to Ziggy Stardust and the Spiders from Mars with 'Jet Silver and the Dolls of Venus'. 'Rocket Cathedrals' – written and sung by bassman Rob Bryan – seemed like the son of 'Space Oddity', with a little bit of Elton's 'Rocket Man' in the DNA too. It's the blues of a working astronaut (or 'whizz man') heading off into space again because 'I need the money'.

The future cropped up a lot, and in stark contrast to Bowie's fetish for doomsday and entropy scenarios, Nelson looked to tomorrow with wide-eyed optimism. 'Jets at Dawn' imagined rebirth in the aftermath of a war: 'I saw the future age had risen / Time to make a brand-new start.' On the cover of 1976's *Modern Music*, the group look very snazzy: Nelson sports an art deco-ish silver-jet brooch on his lapel, while adjusting a television-watch with tiny aerials on his wrist. Be-Bop Deluxe also wrote a non-album track called 'Futurist Manifesto'. When the actual rock future arrived, Nelson adapted quickly, forming the new-wave-aligned Red Noise and releasing the very moderne-sounding single 'Furniture Music', which was named after Satie's proto-ambient concept of tranquil background sounds to settle one's equilibrium. Soon he moved on to a solo career making electro-pop and ambient.

In 1976, perhaps sensing something in the wind, Bill Nelson distanced himself from glam, telling *Melody Maker* that 'the last few years in rock music . . . has been lots of falsehoods and lots of lies, false images, people who aren't what they say they are'.

10:

RUN TO THE SHADOWS: BOWIE VERSUS LOS ANGELES

David Bowie – The English Disco – Silverhead – Zolar X – Les Petites Bonbons – *The Man Who Fell to Earth*

September 1974: David Bowie rides in the back seat of a limousine through the desert outskirts of Los Angeles. The sunlight streaming through the side window makes his skin look even more ashen than usual. Eyes hidden under his wide-brim fedora, Bowie is shockingly thin, but he chatters with a brittle vivaciousness in between sips from a giant half-gallon carton of milk. 'America supplied a need in me,' he proclaims. 'It became a myth land.'

Probably set up for the purposes of the BBC documentary crew filming Bowie, the car journey is presented as if the star is heading towards LA, where he's set to play seven nights at Hollywood's Universal Amphitheatre – the victory lap in his conquest of America. The *Diamond Dogs* tour has been Bowie's – and rock music's – most visually and theatrically extravagant performance spectacle to date. The album itself has become Bowie's first real American smash, cracking the *Billboard* Top 5.

Hollywood is Bowie's destination, and his destiny – or so the documentary makes out. Directed by Alan Yentob and broadcast by the BBC in January 1975, *Cracked Actor* frames Bowie's tryst with America's dream factory – the world capital of illusion and delusion – as the logical culmination of his quest for stardom.

The car cruises past the Movieland Wax Museum, and Bowie quips, 'Bleedin' wax museum in the middle of the desert – you'd think it would melt!' In the documentary, superstar effigies from

474

the museum (Shirley Temple and Marilyn Monroe, Fred Astaire and Clark Gable, Judy Garland and Humphrey Bogart) are juxtaposed with Bowie singing 'Cracked Actor', his *Aladdin Sane* song about a decrepit Hollywood star. Bowie performs it as a modern-day Hamlet, in a Prince of Denmark cape and superstar sunglasses, all the while cradling an 'Alas, poor Yorick' skull in his palm. Yorick was a performer too: the court jester, 'a fellow of infinite jest, of most excellent fancy'. But, Hamlet muses morbidly, 'Where be your gibes now? Your gambols? Your songs? Your flashes of merriment, that were wont to set the table on a roar?' The juxtaposition of the embalmed-looking wax idols and the clown's skull is a memento mori cautioning against the vanity of chasing stardom in hope of immortality: *sic transit gloria mundi*.

Cracked Actor is a fascinating snapshot of a moment in Bowie's journey. Containing some of the only footage of the *Diamond Dogs* tour, it shows him in musical transition: shifting from rock to the funk/R&B-influenced sound of his next album, *Young Americans*. In fact, when the tour resumed for its second leg in October 1974, Bowie stripped away the theatrical excess and renamed it 'The Soul Tour'. In *Cracked Actor*'s car scene, Bowie lip-synchs passionately to Aretha Franklin's 'Natural Woman'. Later, we observe him working out a vocal arrangement with his black backing singers and performing a disco-funk reworking of 'John, I'm Only Dancing'.

The documentary gives a foretaste of Bowie's future in another sense. In just a few months, Los Angeles will become his home. But what's interesting is that Bowie seems aware already that he will not *feel at home* there. A chain-smoking mannequin, he pontificates about LA's 'underlying unease' as landmarks and iconic boulevards roll past. 'You can feel it in every avenue. It's a kind of superficial calmness that they have developed to underplay the fact that there's a lot of high pressure here.' Bowie recalls how the very first time he visited LA, an earthquake hit as his train glided into the station.

There were aftershock tremors – 'a revolting feeling' – for much of his stay. 'Since then I've been aware of how dubious a position it is to stay here for any length of time.' This comment suggests that Bowie semi-consciously *chose* the city as the place to embark upon the next phase of his life and career precisely because of its tectonic and existential instability.

Legend maintains that *Cracked Actor* is the portrait of a rock star in meltdown. Bowie himself would claim to be unable to remember much about this period, when he was in the grip of cocaine-induced grandiosity and paranoia, and would describe his *Cracked Actor* self as 'so blocked . . . so stoned . . . it's quite a casualty case, isn't it?' Yet his conversation in *Cracked Actor* is not fractured: it's lucid, articulate, razor-sharp. The documentary's title was originally going to be *The Collector*, after Bowie's comments in the Russell Harty TV interview about collecting personalities and accents. 'Collected' is how Bowie sounds in *Cracked Actor*: he talks calmly and clearly about how Ziggy became 'a monster' that took him over, about how 'I got lost at one point . . . I couldn't decide whether I was writing characters or whether the characters were writing me.' A fan in the documentary gushes about Bowie's preservation of his own mystery, but what comes over is the contrary: the singer compulsively and incessantly explaining what he's doing, what he's about.

It's like Bowie is following a script that he's written but keeps breaking the fourth wall to comment on it. Moving to LA seems like a deliberate escalation of the plot, a third act of willed estrangement. Whatever the case, Los Angeles became the stage for Bowie's next psychodrama.

There is a music-biz maxim that if a band simply repeats the same album over and over, by about the third version they'll make it.

Diamond Dogs was not exactly a repeat of *Aladdin Sane* and *The Rise and Fall of Ziggy Stardust*, but like its precursors it largely continued the straightforward rock direction and apocalyptic pessimism that fed into earlier songs like 'Five Years' and 'Drive-In Saturday'.

Diamond Dogs emerged from the ashes of a thwarted attempt to create a stage musical of *1984*, which was blocked by George Orwell's widow. Some of the song material went into a TV special for NBC filmed in London, *The 1980 Floor Show*. Bowie then decided to come up with his own dystopia: *Diamond Dogs*. The MainMan press release promised a 'vision of a future world with images of urban decadence and collapse', and that's what Bowie delivered: over-the-top lyrics about genocide, decomposing bodies and 'defecating ecstasy', plus *Clockwork Orange*-influenced scene-setting involving a subculture of roller-skating thugs with luridly coloured hair, clad in fur and brandishing knives, which Bowie later claimed was a clairvoyant vision of 'the punk thing . . . [they were] all little Johnny Rottens and Sid Viciouses'.

This was draped over songs that mostly continued the Stones obsession of *Aladdin Sane*. The title track was a raunchy rip-off of 'Honky Tonk Women', and the session for 'Rebel Rebel' – the album's big hit – kicked off with Bowie simply instructing his minions to 'play Stones'. But everything was produced with a new gloss and grandeur, matching the staging of the tour, with its elaborate set pieces involving boxing rings and the use of a cherry-picker that lifted Bowie out above the audience's heads, all set to the magnificent backdrop of 'Hunger City', a Fritz Lang-inspired metropolis for a dark future.

Diamond Dogs also contained glimpses of where Bowie was headed next. '1984' is blatantly indebted to the jolting funk drama of Isaac Hayes's 1972 hit 'Theme from *Shaft*', with some of Fifth Dimension's 'Aquarius' woven in there too. Onstage and in its original recording, '1984' segued into 'Dodo', a brilliant track mystifyingly left off *Diamond Dogs*. Eventually materialising decades later on the *Diamond Dogs* expanded reissue, 'Dodo' was even more in tune with the black American state of the art, its sinuous, horn-massaged groove modelled on the Al Green/Willie Mitchell sound that ruled America's R&B radio stations between 1971 and 1975.

Back in '72, Bowie had been quizzed by the *NME* about his relationship with three fashionable buzz concepts of the day: camp, punk and funk. 'I've never considered myself funky,' Bowie candidly declared, vowing that 'I'm never gonna try and play black music because I'm white. Singularly white!' Now he reversed on this stance, and how. He was once again in synch with his old mod pal Marc Bolan. While touring America both had heard the new wave of black seventies pop, which ranged from luxuriant, cinematic productions like 'Papa Was a Rolling Stone' by The Tempations, to James Brown's gritty minimalist funk, to silky-soft ballads by The Chi-Lites and The Spinners. Both men had recently become involved with black American women who were also singers: Gloria Jones in Bolan's case, Ava Cherry in Bowie's.

Genuinely excited by the new black sounds – their cutting-edge production and arrangements, their sophisticated but supremely physical grooves – Bowie and Bolan were also shrewdly picking up on shifts in the pop market. Sensual soul was displacing stompy glitter rock as the teenagers' choice in British discotheques. The UK pop chart overflowed with orchestrated lushness pumped out by the Philadelphia International label; Barry White sold almost a million singles in the UK during the course of 1974; the similarly titled 'Rock Your Baby' by George McCrae and 'Rock the Boat' by The Hues Corporation were smashes on both sides of the Atlantic and are generally considered to be among the first disco hits. Nineteen seventy-four was the year when disco as a *genre* rather than a location took hold.

If anything, Bolan was quicker off the mark than Bowie. Released
in February '74, *Zinc Alloy and the Hidden Riders of Tomorrow* featured songs like 'Interstellar Soul' and 'The Avengers (Superbad)'
that melded Bolan-boogie with the new black grooves. In interviews
Bolan raved about how 'black producers are just rediscovering the
use of sound'. In one feature, he even discussed how he and Bowie
were on the same wavelength: 'When David and I got together a
few weeks ago . . . we sat down and played records for each other.
Amazingly we had all the same records – black soul records.'

So it must have been galling in the extreme for Bolan when Bowie
made such a splash with *Young Americans*, forging a stronger statement out of his conversion to soul. Meanwhile, Bolan's career went
into a vertiginous slide: he was reduced to putting out the 1975 single 'Dreamy Lady', credited to the T. Rex Disco Party, in the vain
hope of scoring a dancefloor hit. He wasn't alone: Gary Glitter also
attempted a desperate soul makeover with 1975's *G.G.*, recorded
during three no-sleep, cocaine-wired weeks in a Manhattan studio
with a black session squad.

It was Bowie's *Young Americans* modus operandi that Glitter was
copying: recording in America (in Bowie's case, at Sigma Studios in
Philadelphia), drawing on black musicians (Glitter and Bowie even
had a backing singer in common – future star Luther Vandross)
and maintaining a feverish pace of work with the help of the white
powder. Bowie's band was mixed race and all American. Guitarist
Carlos Alomar was the most crucial of his new sidemen. He would
form, with bassist George Murray and drummer Dennis Davis, the
bedrock not just of *Young Americans* but of Bowie's five subsequent
studio albums, as well as of various tours. It was the most stable and
band-like musical situation Bowie would ever enjoy, and (probably
no coincidence) the ensemble with whom he would do his greatest work. But Alomar in particular would also be a writing foil for
Bowie – his new, funkier Mick Ronson. He secured a writing credit

on *Young Americans'* big hit 'Fame' – Bowie's most successful single in America ever, rivalled only by 1983's 'Let's Dance' – and he would contribute significantly (sometimes credited, sometimes not) to songs on the next five albums.

When he first met Bowie, Alomar had never heard of the singer and later described him as 'the whitest man I'd ever seen – translucent white'. So alarmingly thin was Bowie – weighing in at less than a hundred pounds – that Alomar suggested he come around to be fattened up with chicken, rice and beans made by his wife. 'Next thing I know, a limousine rolls up to my house in Queens.' With a pedigree that included a stint with James Brown and playing with the R&B group The Main Ingredient, Alomar combined shit-hot musicianship with an affable flexibility that would come in handy when dealing with an employer prone to experimental caprices who for much of their collaboration was unmoored from reality.

Young Americans was an immaculate facsimile of black US pop circa 1974–5. Bowie made strenuous attempts to do it right. But as if to pre-emptively deflect accusations of inauthenticity, Bowie called the sound 'plastic soul'. It was a kind of judo move, turning his own weakness (or self-doubt) into a rhetorical strength. Just as he had gently mocked Jagger as the Dagenham boy striving to be black, Bowie informed *Playboy* that *Young Americans* was 'the squashed remains of ethnic music as it survives in the age of Muzak rock, written and sung by a white limey'. 'Plastic' as a pejorative dated as far back as the twenties – there'd been a book and film called *The Plastic Age*, about modern youth gone bad – but it was really in the sixties that people started using the word to mean fake and superficial. Warhol, though, had used 'plastic' as an ironic praise-word. Bowie was probably echoing him when he talked on other occasions about Ziggy as 'a totally credible plastic rock star'. 'Plastic''s other meaning is 'mouldable', hinting that soul would ultimately be just another phase for the endlessly morphing Bowie.

The title *Young Americans* also refers to British fantasies about the US: the idea that Americans live in a consumer paradise. Based on imported American popular culture (songs, films, TV), these projections are doubly divorced from reality. The title track – another big hit single off the album – is about the shortfall between romance and mundanity, telling the story of 'a newly-wed couple who don't know if they really like each other', Bowie explained. He had assimilated some influences from the then largely unknown Bruce Springsteen, whose songs were similarly situated in the gap between American dreams and American realities. During the sessions, Bowie and the band would attempt a cover of Springsteen's 'It's Hard to Be a Saint in the City'. The sax draped all over 'Young Americans' and most of the album, played by David Sanborn, splits the difference between the E Street Band's Clarence Clemons and the slickly exuberant jazz-lite style associated with *Saturday Night Live* and American late-night chat shows.

Just as American radio DJs could not help but respond warmly to a song titled 'Young Americans', likewise many US rock critics felt *Young Americans* was the most emotionally open and 'warm' album Bowie had yet recorded – as if simply by singing 'black' he was dropping the concepts and personae. Listeners seemed to agree: 'Young Americans' was his first Top 30 hit in the States and the album sold steadily, going gold like *Diamond Dogs* had done.

Then came 'Fame'. Bowie's first US #1, this fierce, stabbing funk track was his first serious attempt at addressing a recurrent theme in his work to come: the topic of 'fame as injury', as Bowieologist Nick Stevenson put it. ('I wouldn't inflict fame on my worst enemy,' the singer declared in 2002.) America's mass audience, then and now, loves realness above all else: 'Fame' was simply the realest, most heart-splayed-open song he'd recorded at that point. Paradoxically, it was a starkly honest portrait of a world in which honesty, self-knowledge and true relations are rendered impossible. Harrowing dispatches from inside the paranoid bubble of superstardom, the lyrics describe fame as a place where souls freeze and 'things are hollow', where egos jostle ('Is it any wonder I reject you first?') and confidence requires a chemical crutch ('What you need you have to borrow').

In 'The Price of Fame', a 1982 essay for the *NME*, Barney Hoskyns examined how this most sought-after state 'only opens the floodgates of loss and bewilderment', stranding the famous 'in the schizoid domain of stardom, duplicated by the countless mirrors of television and magazines'. The genius of 'Fame' as a song is that it *sounds* like that schizophrenic hall of mirrors, where self-image distorts and ego balloons grotesquely – an effect captured with the echo trail of 'what's your name what's your name what's your name' and, above all, with that disorientating sequence where Bowie's pitch-shifted vocal chant of 'fame' plummets by stages from soprano squeak to basso profundissimo.

Alfred North Whitehead declared that 'Fame is a cold, hard notion.' That's what the song sounds like: cold, hard, but also scalding, like the sting of mucous membranes attacked by a line of cocaine. Like a pop translation of Miles Davis's *On the Corner*, the rhythm guitars etch livid weals in your frontal lobes. The crunching groove of interlocking guitar riffs was developed between Carlos Alomar, Bowie and John Lennon, whom Bowie had befriended and whose Buddhist lullaby 'Across the Universe' he covered, gruesomely, on *Young Americans*.

As Bowie lyrics go, 'Fame' is unusually clear to the layperson, but there is at least one private reference. *Fame* was the name of a play staged on Broadway by MainMan, written and directed by Anthony J. Ingrassia. Its main character, Diane Cook, is a Marilyn Monroe-like sexpot, and the storyline follows Monroe's life arc from illegitimate birth to suicide. On 18 November 1973, *Fame* ran, infamously, for just a single night, losing MainMan a quarter of a million dollars.

As one Broadway history records, the 'critics were astonished that a play stealing such juicy material could be so dull'.

Bowie's relationship with Tony Defries had already pretty much disintegrated by that point, following the singer's discovery that, far from being the co-owner of MainMan, as he'd imagined, he was simply its prime piece of human real estate. The expensive Broadway flop added injury to ignominy, since the play had effectively been funded by his record sales. But when Bowie moved to extricate himself from his manager's clutches, he discovered that Defries was set to keep on earning a huge cut from all his future releases up until 1982, a decade after the original contract had been signed.

Empires have to keep on expanding, but risk becomes exponential. MainMan had become dangerously overstretched and overstaffed. Glam chronicler Dave Thompson reports that 'a film division had been launched and then closed after just three high profile ventures went belly-up. A magazine was planned and abandoned'. After Bowie flew the coop, Defries's rock-management career dwindled. He discovered John Mellencamp and renamed him Johnny Cougar but wouldn't reap the fruits of his eventual stardom in the eighties. In subsequent decades, Defries has remained busy with a host of financial and business ventures (including a company that is developing a battery powered by biophotons – light emitted by humans!) but has generally kept a low profile.

Betrayed by his second father figure Defries, feeling orphaned and unprotected, Bowie followed through the logic of his conquest of America and moved to LA. His new manager, Michael Lippman – initially the lawyer representing him in an ongoing struggle with Defries – was based in the city. Los Angeles was also the location of the US's biggest and most rabidly Anglophile glam scene.

N

The hub of LA's glitter scene was a club on Sunset Boulevard with the rather apt name of The English Disco. It was launched in October 1972 by twenty-six-year-old Anglophile Rodney Bingenheimer, supposedly at the suggestion of Bowie, whom Bingenheimer had first met on a trip to the UK in 1971. 'He sort of gave me the idea for the club,' said Bingenheimer. 'It was basically a David Bowie cathedral.'

This direct connection to the stars was the source of Bingenheimer's somewhat inexplicable charisma, which was seemingly not based on charm, sex appeal, bright ideas, sparkling conversation or any of the other traditional components of personal magnetism. He is often compared to Zelig, the character in the Woody Allen film of the same name: someone who somehow always manages to be present in the background of important historical events alongside important historical personages. Bingenheimer endeared himself to British rock stars by being star-struck, but not offensively or annoyingly so; he was a great listener yet completely discreet and eager to be of service.

Bingenheimer had done some work as a music journalist and for record companies, but his cult status began when he got a gig as stand-in for Davy Jones of The Monkees. Spill-over magnetism from Davy, the cute and very small English member of the group, cloaked the equally diminutive Rodney B. Soon he had his own mini-following of local teen females. It became self-perpetuating: Anglorockers wanted to know him because of the access he afforded them to young women; the girls wanted to know him because he had access to the British rock musicians.

'If you were given the blessing of Rodney Bingenheimer, then your week at the Whisky a Go Go was like a pussy parade of girls wearing three sequins at most,' recalls Michael Des Barres of the English raunch 'n' roll outfit Silverhead. 'He was the guy. He met us at LAX airport, when we first arrived in '72, with a cavalcade of rich girls from Pacific Palisades. Then he followed us back to the Holiday Inn and the madness commenced.'

The English Disco was a natural outgrowth of Bingenheimer's role on the LA scene. The hanger-on became the host. He made sure that Rodney's – as The English Disco was also known – was a home from home for the English bands, providing pub fare to ease their triple malady of jet lag, hangover and homesickness: sausage rolls, Cornish pasties, steak-and-kidney pudding and British ales like Bass, Newcastle Brown and Watney's Red Barrel. The Watney's symbol – a little red keg – hovered over the venue's tavern-style counter.

Just like your typical UK red-brick pub, the venue was tatty and poky. But it had one feature that made it singularly perfect for glam: the compact dancefloor was flanked by three mirrored walls, which allowed the glitzed-up teens to admire themselves as they sashayed and shimmied to the non-stop soundtrack of The Sweet and Suzi Quatro served up by Rodney and The English Disco's other DJ, Chuck E. Starr.

'The dancefloor looked much bigger than what it was because it was completely covered with mirrors,' recalls Kari Krome, a teenage regular who would be instrumental in the formation of local all-female glitter-punk group The Runaways. 'So people would just dance in front of the mirror, in a very sexual way, and it was like they were making out with themselves. There were boys dancing with boys, and girls dancing with girls, and people who were saying they were gay or bisexual.'

Kim Fowley, the notorious LA-based Svengali and future manager of The Runaways, remembered The English Disco fondly for its 'teenage stench . . . Everybody had great hair and great make-up, and there were Lolita girls everywhere.' It was no secret that many of the girls were underage – fifteen, fourteen, even thirteen. A visiting reporter from *Melody Maker* described Bingenheimer as 'the prince of puberty', his wink perceptible even through newsprint.

The club was the go-to place for groupie-groping and Quaalude-lubricated lewdness.

Those were different times and nobody blinked an eye at behaviour that nowadays would terminate careers and result in prosecutions. In the music magazines, journalists referred casually – with seeming admiration even – to Johnny Thunders having a fifteen-year-old sweetheart, or Iggy Pop, in a downward career spiral, spending time 'at home with his parents and his 14-year-old girl-friend'. Not publicised at the time, but later controversially revealed, was Bowie's dalliance with fifteen-year-old Lori Mattix: she was 'de-virginized' – her term – by the singer, and subsequently became Jimmy Page's underage lover.

Since jaded decadence was the era's chic attitude to adopt, girls only a few years out of childhood pretended to be blasé. 'When you're a young girl, you want to appear more sophisticated than you are,' recalls Krome. 'I can remember them all smoking one cigarette after the other and just being like, "Oh, it's just so divine. Oh, it's so fabulous." A lot of men got away with stuff because these girls went along with wanting what everyone else was doing. They were just like, "Oh my God, I must be the luckiest girl in the world. Jimmy Page or David Bowie's paying attention to me . . ." Most of them were from the suburbs. They were really, really bored. There was nothing going on the radio that really excited them. There was no real movement happening for youth culture.'

The English Disco's mascot group was Silverhead: a bunch of Brits who looked like rock stars and comported themselves like rock stars, but for whom rock stardom had so far proved elusive. The covers of their self-titled debut and its follow-up, *16 and Savaged*, were plastered over the walls of Rodney's. Salacious things were scrawled about Silverhead in the toilets.

'Any great rock'n'roll fan likes to pick a band that nobody knows about,' reasons frontman Michael Des Barres with regard to the

Toast of The English Disco, the Most Honourable Michael Des Barres, loons it up on the cover of Silverhead's 1972 self-titled debut

strange LA cult for his band. Golden of hair and chiselled of cheekbones, Des Barres was an Anglophile's wet dream. Even better, he was a bona fide aristocrat – a marquis (the title had been in the family for eight centuries). After a spell at boarding school, Des Barres enrolled at the Corona Academy of Stage Training in west London and had some success as a child actor, with a role in the hit movie *To Sir, with Love*. Later, he played the sexually indeterminate love interest in David Percival's stage play *Girlfriend* – 'because I looked like Julie Christie' – and then landed the role of an androgynous rock star in a nude musical, *The Dirtiest Show in Town*. Andrew

Lloyd Webber spotted his star quality and took the singer under his wing, ultimately leading to a major-label deal for Silverhead.

Although he benefited from the LA scene's Anglophile ardour, Des Barres declared himself in love with 'the whole American thing'. In interviews, he waxed eloquent, displaying wide-ranging cultural references, but in Silverhead songs he shunned verbose lyricism because 'an American can tell you in one line what an Englishman would take a book to say'. Attitude-wise he felt closest to the New York Dolls – debauched, but with a wink of irony. Sonically, Silverhead had more in common with a band like Humble Pie than Bowie: their sound was raspy, ballsy, with some bluesy slide guitar in there. 'We're the dirtiest band in this country,' Des Barres liked to boast.

Concerning the sexual transaction that took place between LA's groupies and Anglo androgyne rockers, Des Barres speculates that 'they wanted to fuck us because they wanted to fuck themselves'. Disappointed with the hulking jocks that American high schools had to offer, Des Barres says the LA girls 'turned to little poofters like us. And we'd swap clothes, and it would be almost like a girls' party, except it was the wildest sex they ever had.'

Silverhead had everything going for them – the image, the raunch, the pretty 'n' witty dandy singer – except for that one killer song to make them rock stars. In the meantime, though, they *acted* like rock stars. Acting was a big part of Silverhead, and not just because of Des Barres's drama-school background. The song 'This Ain't a Parody' was a riposte to criticisms that they were playing at being rock stars. It's an almost Wildean statement about the honour of the poseur. 'When I sang that song, I was saying, "This is real, this is me" – it's about whoever you choose to be on whatever day. Nothing is immutable. We're all moving and shifting constantly. So who are you to tell me this is fake? How could you possibly judge – how could you possibly fill my platform boots?'

Des Barres's intellect gave him a distance from the hedonism even as he plunged balls-deep into it. 'I had a journalistic view of it – an objectivity,' he says. At one point Des Barres, in league with Frank Zappa, was going to form a spoof band – a 'parody of the heavy-metal trip' called XS. Another meta-rock scheme got him into big trouble. In partnership with Nick Lowe he planned to release a concept single about the final ten minutes in the life of Bernadette Whelan, a David Cassidy fan who died at the teen idol's White City Stadium concert in May 1974. The first line, he recalls, was going to go something like 'Crushed in the front / No publicity stunt.' But as word seeped out, the outcry was so instant and huge that Des Barres's management 'put the stops on it', despite his declared intention to give the royalties to charity. Today, although he regrets the upset caused, Des Barres doesn't recant the idea itself: 'Those kids, when they bought a poster of David Cassidy or whoever, it's a religious significance.' Whelan's death, he felt, 'was a cultural moment, and I was shocked by it, and I wanted to write a song about it'. The furore encouraged him to go into exile in LA, where, as consolation prize for Silverhead's failure, he won the heart of the all-time greatest groupie, Miss Pamela of the GTOs – soon Pamela Des Barres.

Groupies from the GTOs' generation were considered has-beens by the teenage upstarts of the Rodney's scene. 'God they're *real* old . . . As soon as we walk in, they might as well jump out the window,' sneered Sable Starr, who, in 1973, was the scene's fifteen-year-old queen. Alongside Shray Mecham, Lori Mattix and Queenie Glam, Starr's name and photo featured prominently in every article on the English Disco scene.

The glitter-era groupies were such a phenomenon that a teen-girl magazine was created to cater to them: *Star*. Founded by the major magazine group Petersen Publishing as a racy alternative to its existing, rather anodyne publication *Teen*, the monthly *Star* featured one of Rodney's dancefloor goddesses on its cover every issue. In keeping with its advertising slogan 'Should a Nice Girl Like You Read a BAD Magazine Like *Star*?', the mag was oriented around the concept of the fox: an underage libertine who uses her wiles to get close to rock stars and outwit parents, straight teachers and dodgy dudes. The series of articles by famous female performers on their memories of being fifteen made clear that *Star*'s target age group was situated precisely on the cusp between girlhood and womanhood.

Starting in February 1973, *Star* ran for just five issues before getting closed down, supposedly because of a complaint from the disapproving wife of the publisher. The contents were reasonably innocuous at the start, largely consisting of make-up tips, advice columns, romantic astrology, features on potential idols such as The Raspberries and Rick Springfield, and DIY fashion (how to customise your platform shoes with sequins).

But there was also a cartoon spread called 'Groupies', about the misadventures of two leggy chicks. (In the first episode they scheme to get backstage to meet Marc Bolan.) As the magazine developed, there were articles about chasing foxy dudes and managing them once captured. A recurrent theme was competition between girls, with articles like 'Be the Girl Who Wins Everytime' and 'You First Always'. Particularly alarming to parents was the fourth issue's 'Do Anything You Want (and Get Away with It)', which offered lessons on how to project the 'Wonderful Girl image' to parents and teachers in order to keep your foxy 'n' free secret life under wraps. 'Is image-making deceit?' the article wondered. 'The sad truth is that a foxy lady just has to lead a double life most of the time.'

Most likely the final straw for parents of *Star*'s teen readership was the June 1973 feature that gave the lowdown on groupie life. Below pictures of the girls hanging with the stars, Sable Starr and Queenie Glam spilled the beans. 'If you're the aggressive type, the flashy type, you make it,' declared Starr. 'You have to be very flashy, sometimes even sleazy-looking. In a way, sort of cheap-looking. You just have to be noticed . . . because you just can't stand in the crowd hoping that one of the guys in the band will notice you.' Queenie recounted a charming tale of how she stole Mick Ronson off another groupie by throwing a gin gimlet in her face, leaving her 'ugly' rival abandoned in her 'runny' make-up. Another story reflected even less well on Starr: she spoke of accidentally on purpose spilling a drink over that 'brat' Bolan, seemingly because he'd been ignoring her and her friends in favour of talking to 'all these black people'.

On the subject of parental concerns and parental control, Starr shrugged: 'I just say "Hi" and "Good-bye".' On the rewards of making a big-name score, Starr admitted it was 'more like an ego thing. Just to be able to call up my girlfriends the next day and say who I was with last night.' By her account, her tally included Iggy Pop, Alice Cooper, Bowie, Bolan, Rod Stewart, Robert Plant and Mick Jagger (whose amazing lips, up close, were horribly chapped – he was 'deformed looking'). Queenie offered an anecdote about Bowie painting her toenails blue that brings to mind the controversial scene in Kubrick's *Lolita*.

Where Queenie Glam's ambition was to marry a rock star, Starr aimed a little higher: 'I want to be an Andy Warhol star and do bizarre movies.' Starr actually achieved Queenie's dream when she got 'serious' with Johnny Thunders. The New York Doll took his little doll to New York – getting into some trouble because she was still underage, which meant he'd transported a minor across state lines – and they set up home together in Manhattan. But Thunders turned out be a controlling and psychologically abusive paramour, and she soon returned to LA.

There was a definite look that the English Disco girls rocked, which involved mixing up vintage forties and fifties elements with the 'hot tramp' seventies repertoire of fishnet stockings, Lurex tops and satin hot pants. 'Nobody in LA really sold glam clothes off the rack, so I would just be stitching sequins onto things and trying to

Partners in crime: Iggy Pop and Sable Starr backstage at the Santa Monica Civic Auditorium, 1973

find satin,' recalls Lisa Fancher, a local glitter fan. 'The teeny tiny shorts and the glittery tops – I just made a lot of that stuff myself. I drove myself crazy going to thrift stores and flea markets, trying to find things I could turn into outfits. Just 'cuz Bryan Ferry did it, I had to have old Hollywood clothes.' Platform shoes and jeans were de rigueur. 'Brittania or UFO jeans,' recalls Kari Krome. 'Really skin-tight around the waist and kind of high-waisted. They'd start to flare out and get bigger and bigger at the bottom. And we'd all wear these skin-tight little T-shirts, almost children's sizes, and you might iron on lettering. Like, I'd do big black block lettering saying "New York Dolls". A lot of times, we wore suspenders, or a bandana around the neck, or little-old-lady rayon scarves around the neck and knotted in the front.'

Focused on the Sunset Strip – but with outposts like the Valley club Sugar Shack and regular TV exposure on the pop programme *The Real Don Steele Show*, where the English Disco teen foxes danced every week – LA's glitter scene constituted a homegrown army that had risen up to resist the music that the city was identified with worldwide: the laidback country-rock/singer-songwriter sound of Laurel Canyon, groups like Crosby, Stills, Nash and Young or The Eagles. 'The thing I hated about Laurel Canyon was everybody just smoking pot and being like, "Yeah, man",' says Fancher. 'And that look! Fringe jackets, bell-bottoms, beards.'

Yet apart from attitude and cooler clothes, the glitterati of Hollywood didn't have a lot to fight back with. The scene was built around British groups. As regards solid rock achievement, there was even less going on in terms of local glitter action than at the Club 82 scene in Manhattan. Glam LA didn't have one band as good as the New York Dolls – which is why, breaking with the traditional LA versus NYC rivalry, it welcomed Johansen, Thunders and company with open arms. Wannabes were in plentiful supply, though inspiration rarely extended much beyond the name: Berlin Brats, Imperial Dogs. David Cassidy's brother Shaun fronted an outfit called Longfellow, an outlet for his irrepressible desire to be Iggy. 'Skin-tight white flares, this white halter-top shirt, and a dog collar,' is how Krome remembers Shaun Cassidy's image. 'And then full tin-grin braces on his teeth!'

Shady Lady were the great lost LA glitter group, or so claims rock writer John Mendelsohn. But he admits they were 'one of those groups that formed out of admiration for each other's wardrobes, completely oblivious to whether any of them could play'. There was also Queen (not to be confused with the British group), fronted by ex-Steppenwolf bassist Nick St Nicholas. His beauty had been immortalised by The GTOs in the song 'I'm in Love with the Ooh-Ooh Man'. Queen, says Mendelsohn, 'looked like Charlie's Angels but even better – suspender belts, stockings, huge platform heels. They made Bowie look like Tom Jones.' Krome fondly remembers LA's Jobriath equivalent, Smokey. Fronted by 'this absolutely beautiful leather boy' – John Condon – 'with long brunette hair all the way down to his butt, studded rhinestone collar and skin-tight black chaps that laced up in the back', Smokey wrote songs like the golden-showers anthem 'Piss Slave' and started their own label, S&M Records.

Probably the most striking-looking – if not sounding – band on the LA scene was Zolar X. They dressed like fifties B-movie aliens with 'space bubble heads, really stupid hair and pointy ears', says Fancher. Giving themselves names like Ygarr Ygarrist, Zory Zenith and Zany Zatovian, Zolar X didn't speak Earthling but communicated in a beebling 'n' fribbling alien language. They never broke character, which must have made doing a soundcheck challenging. Strangely, though, their actual songs were in English, such as the synth-laced 'Space Age Love'.

The ultimate LA glam statement – perhaps the ultimate glam gesture of all – came from Les Petites Bonbons. Just as The Moodies went beyond Wizzard by only doing covers, Les Petites Bonbons took a step further into pure conceptualism by dispensing with the playing-music part altogether. They had the image, the lifestyle, the publicity of rock stars. They just didn't bother with writing, recording, performing.

Les Petites Bonbons' central figure was the art polymath Jerry

Dreva, whose other claim to fame is having been a pioneer of mail art: a practice in which strange or elaborate or sometimes plain gross things (like dead animals) would be mailed between correspondents. Iggy Pop and David Bowie would be among the recipients of Dreva's work; Bowie later copied one of Dreva's ideas with the stamp-sheet inserts for the 1980 single 'Ashes to Ashes'. Another intriguing Dreva project was the book *Wanks for the Memories*, a literally seminal work . . . (I'll just let you work out the rest for yourself, okay?)

At the core of Dreva's thinking was the concept of life/art. Abolishing the boundary between life and art led to 'a continual performance' that was also a non-stop display of narcissistic self-celebration. Looking back on the conception of Les Petites Bonbons, Dreva recalled realising that 'for a person with the proper con-sciousness and attitude, everything we do is art. I began to take Will Shakespeare quite seriously and realize that all the world *is* a stage.' The English Disco was one important stage for Les Petites Bonbons, but they popped up at just about every gig or party of note during the period and appeared in the pages of *Newsweek* and *People*. In a 1980 career retrospective in the gay magazine *High Performance*, Dreva recalled: 'I found energy, excitement, and enthusiasm in the music scene that was not readily available in the art scene . . . The Bonbons worked within the rock and roll context as artists-in-residence to the glitter scene . . . court jesters to the rock and roll royalty.'

In terms of making a lasting contribution to rock, you'd have to say Les Petites Bonbons' achievement falls short even of such unglam journeymen as Foghat, who produced the immortal boo-gie of 'Slowride'. But Les Petites Bonbons didn't set out to create that kind of liberation-through-energy artifact. They simply laid claim to what they imagined was the point of rock'n'roll: the strut-ting and posing. The Bonbons' primary activities in LA were being photographed and attending parties, but they did create a clutch of entertaining and thought-provoking ephemera, including the parodic Iggy Pop School of Teenage Rebellion Certificate (it ratified achievement in areas like 'unbridled sickness and perversion') and the publication *Egozine*. The brainchild of core Bonbon member Robert Lambert, this magazine featured the group's press clips plus theory fragments like 'Mirror/Mirror' and 'The Death of Culture'. Art scholar Kirsten Olds argues that *Egozine* was like a Les Petites Bonbons fanzine made by the group themselves. You could also see it as the catalogue to an art exhibition that was otherwise dispersed across the media of the era, as photographs and gossip items.

Les Petites Bonbons came out of the involvement of Dreva, Lambert and the other members in gay liberation and radical sixties culture. They drew on Sontag essays like 'On Style', John Cage's writing, Norman O. Brown's visionary revision of Freud, the ideas of Artaud and Duchamp. 'We began to feel that a new synthesis of art, politics and sex was needed,' Dreva recalled. 'We aimed to be a walking exhibition of our beliefs' – human billboards promoting 'the unrepressed life'.

The project was launched with an 'Anti-Manifesto' published in *Gay Sunshine* in 1972. 'We are the playful remnant of Milwaukee Gay Liberation Front, Radical Queens, and our former ideological and rhetorical selves,' the collective announced. 'We seek thru rejoicing and personal creative mythology to rejoin the Whole World at Play.' What followed was a lattice of quotes – 'Bonbon mots', they called them – that ranged from Bowie and Ray Davies lyrics (they particularly adored 'Celluloid Heroes' from *Everybody's in Show-Biz*) to Ridiculous Theatre impresario Charles Ludlam ('gay people have a responsibility to sabotage seriousness'). The overall vibe was very sixties, mashing together radical psychiatry, play power, pandrogyny and Romantic vitalism: 'By having fun we are fighting the straightman's inebriation with death. Our lives are our art. Our art is our politics. Our politics is the way we make love. Our job is the erotic science of connections.'

The big difference from sixties radicalism was the total lack of hostility to the mainstream spectacle of stardom and showbiz. Les Petites Bonbons went beyond Warhol by achieving their goal of being 'famous for being famous rather than for doing anything in particular'. Dreva recalled the project as an education in 'the power of the media to create, define and distort reality. The media had a field day with the Bonbons. They used us and we used them.' Lambert says they were 'surprised by how *easy*' it was to penetrate the mass media. 'It took *nothing*. We didn't try that hard. It was easy to stand out, just by stepping a little out of line. There was so much conformity then.'

Usually ubiquitous on the scene, Les Petites Bonbons were conspicuously absent from The Hollywood Street Revival and Trash Dance, an 11 October 1974 event also known as 'The Death of Glitter'. Timed almost exactly two years after the launch of The English Disco, it was a self-conscious end-of-era gesture, probably inspired by the Death of Hippie march that took place in Haight-Ashbury at the end of 1967. Chuck E. Starr was carried through the Hollywood Palladium inside a glitter-encrusted coffin. Bingenheimer DJed. Kim Fowley, the scene's eminence sleaze, was the MC and was showered with abuse and detritus by the audience. Most of the entertainment line-up was either British (Michael Des Barres singing a medley of Presley songs) or from other parts of the US (Iggy Pop, from Detroit, and the Dolls, from New York).

Half a year later, Bowie arrived. He only lived there in a continuous stretch for a matter of months, but LA would set the tone of his 1975 – which he would remember as a long, dark, insomniac night of the soul, a cocaine-induced vacation from reality that took him to the brink of psychotic breakdown. Bowie talked of having 'got into a lot of emotional and spiritual trouble there'. In years to come he would scathingly describe Los Angeles as 'the most repulsive wart on the backside of humanity' and 'the most vile piss-pot in the world'. In Bowie's opinion, 'the fucking place should be wiped off the face of the earth'.

There is actually nothing that intrinsically makes LA 'the least suitable place on earth for a person to go in search of identity and stability' (Bowie's description). Los Angeles could make for a fine environment for someone in frail physical and mental health, if they were of a mind to get their shit together. There are beaches and canyons; wilderness is integrated with built-up areas; the warm weather creates a beatific atmosphere. The city of LA is home to a couple of million regular folk who live relatively grounded existences organised around work, family and community. For sure, much of the city's economy comes from the entertainment industry, but there is a profusion of businesses that have nothing to do with showbiz.

It's true that visitors who come from cities where public transport and pedestrian life dominate do find LA disorienting. Freeways seem to 'beam' you to locales that feel unconnected to the other parts of the city. The lack of defined seasons can cause time to become unmoored. If you are already in a state of flux, exacerbated by drugs, you could well start to feel malevolence lurking amid the jacaranda and palm trees, a demonic undertone within the whisper of the lawn sprinklers at night.

Such creeping paranoia might also be exacerbated if you'd had any acquaintance with movies like *Sunset Boulevard* and *Chinatown*, or an LA reading list featuring Nathaniel West's *The Day of the Locust*, Joan Didion's essay 'The White Album' (starring Jim Morrison and Charlie Manson) or that scabrous stockpile of local lore gathered by Kenneth Anger for *Hollywood Babylon* (published in 1975, the year Bowie arrived).

When looking back on his time in the city a few years later and complaining about having 'been exposed to a general LA-ism which

. . . I can't cope with', Bowie was offering a rather conventional critique. He was describing the same city as The Eagles' 'Hotel California': a cul-de-sac of spiritually empty pleasure.

But when Bowie further described LA as 'a movie that is so corrupt with a script that is so devious and insidious. It's the scariest movie ever written,' you start to get the sense that he unconsciously moved there with the intent to live out that movie: that whole set-the-controls-for-the-black-void-at-stardom's-heart trip. Because, when it comes down to it, there is literally nothing about moving to LA that *forces* you to live a recluse's life, shovelling mounds of cocaine up your nostrils for days and sleepless nights on end, interrupted only by the occasional Mercedes night ride or daytime visit to one of the city's many occult book stores.

In a 1979 Thames Television interview, Bowie revealed – or perhaps post-rationalised – that the move to LA had been motivated by a desire to 'put myself in dangerous situations . . . any situation I feel I can't cope with'. That's why he moved to 'a city I really detest' and lived 'among people I didn't like very much' – in order to 'see what would happen to my writing'. Living there, he discovered that he detested the city 'twice as much . . . everything it represented!' Curiously for one who set such store in artifice and fantasy, Los Angeles represented above all *unreality* – 'it's fabricated', Bowie complained – which he compared unfavourably with the gritty truth of tougher cities like Detroit and Chicago.

Dependent on coke, feeling abandoned after the break with MainMan and increasingly estranged from his wife back in England, Bowie plunged into an unwholesome lifestyle immediately upon arrival. Holed up in various Beverly Hills homes (first chez English rock-musician buddy Glenn Hughes, then at the house of new manager Lippman), Bowie endlessly watched sinister movies (often about Germany immediately before and during the Third Reich). An untidy guest, he'd leave rooms strewn with magical texts as well as his own esoteric scribblings. Unsavoury visitors called by occasionally – fellow coke fiends from the movie or music business, dealers.

It was only recently that cocaine had become a rock drug. Its original heyday was the twenties, when it was in vogue with the Hollywood elite and also associated with jazz-crazed flapper girls. Between 1930 and the late sixties, though, cocaine faded from view, in part due to declining supply and criminalisation, and partly owing to the fashion cycle. As the social historian of drug use Lester Grinspoon records, 'To the extent that it was available at all, cocaine became a plaything of the more adventurous . . . among the wealthy.' Youth culture had no interest in coke. Amphetamines did the same job, far more cheaply, and they were legal all through the sixties.

Round about 1970, though, cocaine filtered into the rock world. Jefferson Airplane's *Bark*, recorded in 1970, was made under the influence. The Rolling Stones' casual mentions of the drug on 1971's *Sticky Fingers* ('head full of snow' in 'Moonlight Mile', 'you've got cocaine eyes' in 'Can't You Hear Me Knocking') were criticised by some as self-consciously decadent. 'I think it was legitimised by the mythological photograph of Keith Richards with the cola slogan "Things Go Better with Coke",' suggests Michael Des Barres. As a rock aristocracy emerged, the posh powder appealed precisely for its aura of elitism and exclusivity. Some of the nicknames cocaine had at the time were very glam: 'stardust', 'gold dust'.

Unlike the more disruptive, time-consuming psychedelics or slow-things-down drugs like pot and Quaaludes, cocaine fitted with Bowie's personality – his workaholic, perfectionist streak. 'One attacks every problem with perfect confidence,' Aleister Crowley enthused in *Diary of a Drug Fiend*. Cocaine supplied Bowie – someone who by his own profession had low self-esteem, as hard as that is to believe – with a feeling of being in command. As Crowley put it, 'I felt myself any man's master.' The magician, whose life and work fascinated Bowie, compared the sensation to being a member of the British aristocracy (again, how glam is that?), all those feelings of insouciance and superiority instilled by breeding and public school. Cocaine gave the user the 'feeling that it was impossible to fail', that 'the very idea of coarseness or commonness is abolished'.

When cocaine euphoria shifts to dysphoria, symptoms include strung-out jitteriness and jumpy perceptions ('seeing shadows flitting by in the corner of my vision', according to one fiend). There's a notoriously twitchy Bowie appearance on *The Dick Cavett Show* in November 1974, where – looking like a broken animatronic figure – he restlessly taps and repositions a cane in his bony hands, stroking and rubbing the handle. Magazine interviews with Bowie in this period – late '74 to mid-'76 – present a picture of a man who is scintillating but unfocused. Conversation vaults from brilliant perceptions to proposed projects of a clearly phantasmal nature, ranging from film scripts (one would star Iggy as a character called Catastrophe) to a multi-volume autobiography. In a 1976 *Playboy* interview, Bowie confessed that 'my thought forms are fragmented a lot . . . I often think of six things at one time. They all sort of interrupt one another.'

Increasing the intake and going without sleep for days on end, the cocaine fiend starts to be afflicted by 'hypersensitivity to noises, flight of ideas, graphomania (compulsive scribbling), memory disturbances, mood swings', writes Grinspoon. Then come 'optical and auditory hallucinations, delusions of persecution and grandeur'. But the user may continue taking cocaine despite the paranoia because 'the accompanying self-magnification is too enjoyable'. The word 'magnification' is key. Cocaine doesn't just inflate the ego; it seems to magnify the sense of meaningfulness on both the micro and macro levels. The fiend becomes obsessed with details, but also constructs elaborate overarching scaffolds of interconnected ideas, what one pharmacological researcher calls 'paranoid delusional systems'.

Fuelled by cocaine and nicotine (he favoured the strongest, harshest brands – unfiltered Gitanes and Gauloises – and smoked up to four packs a day), Bowie pored through occult texts that were themselves delusional systems. Los Angeles has a cultic undertow, with figures like the rocket scientist and black magician Jack Parsons, L. Ron Hubbard and the film-maker Kenneth Anger. Whether Bowie ever met Anger is unclear but the singer would have been familiar with his work, if only through mutual friends like Mick Jagger. Anger described his movies as 'magickal spells': his Crowley-influenced films like *Inauguration of the Pleasure Dome* and *Invocation of My Demon Brother* collided glamour and pagan-hermetic ritual in kaleidoscopic montages of swastikas, cabbalistic symbols, occult ceremony and vampily made-up actresses. Manson family member Bobby Beausoleil recorded one Anger soundtrack; Jagger did another.

'There was something horrible permeating the air in LA in those days,' Bowie remembered. 'The stench of Manson and the Sharon Tate murders.' (They were committed five years before.) But instead of hightailing it to more wholesome places in Southern California – mellow Ojai or the Danish-styled town of Solvang – Bowie became a habitué of the city's many occult book stores, like Gilbert's on Hollywood Boulevard.

The Devil finds things for idle minds to dwell on. With too much time (now that he rarely slept) on his racing mind, Bowie's long-standing but dormant interest in the mystical and paranormal erupted. 'I never had any conversations with him about any of that stuff until 1974–5, when I was no longer working for him, and when he was heavily doing coke,' recalls Cherry Vanilla. 'Aleister Crowley, Merlin the magician – that's all he talked about. I think the drugs must have brought all that out in him.'

Bowie was in some ways simply in tune with the zeitgeist, following a path that other sixties survivors had followed into what

Theodore Roszak called 'the Aquarian Frontier': a panoply of spiritual and para-scientific adventures in evolved consciousness. That sixties push to re-enchant the world had sprouted a new profusion of cults and sects. The phenomenon predated the sixties. 'Second Religiousness' was Spengler's term, a syndrome that first stirred in the nineteenth century as a reaction against industrialism: 'archaic beliefs from earlier in humanity's history are rediscovered and combined in the guise of the popular syncretism that is to be found in every Culture at this phase'. But the sixties did spur a fresh surge of anti-rationalism: napalm and nuclear bombs, smog and sprawl eroded trust in technological progress. There was a publishing boom for spiritual and magical texts. The mystical lore of 'every society in history' was made available for 'mass consumption', wrote Daniel O'Keefe. 'Every successive revival feeds on past revivals.'

Like many sixties types, Bowie had, in parallel with his more dedicated exploration of Tibetan Buddhism, dallied with astrology and ufology. (He told a *Creem* interviewer that he'd once worked for 'two guys who put out a UFO magazine' and had himself made 'sightings six, seven times a night for about a year'.) Long a fan of Colin Wilson's existentialist lit-crit best-seller *The Outsider*, Bowie devoured Wilson's 1971 book *The Occult – A History*. In a way, Bowie was the Colin Wilson of pop – an 'independent scholar' roaming across a vast field of extremist beliefs, behaviours and psychologies, marvelling at it all.

Synapses crackling from the snowstorm of high-grade pharmaceutical cocaine, Bowie plunged into syncretic excess, cross-referencing and weaving together belief systems. There was barely a superstition, a lost lore, a mystic world view that he didn't sample: Kabbala, Gnosticism, Enochian magic, astral clairvoyance, Crowley's sex magick, Blavatsky's theosophy, tarot, Kirlian photography, Egyptology, Ouija boards, Gurdjieff, Arthurian legends of the Holy Grail, Atlantis. Most of the hermetic scholars that Bowie consulted were themselves syncretising diverse earlier bodies of renegade belief.

What drives adepts like Bowie and the authors whose books he devoured? First and foremost is the desire for answers and powers. They crave access to secret knowledge of a truth supposedly lurking beneath the surface of everyday life, including the dark forces that allegedly run the world. But they also hanker for knowledge about the future, and they want the power to make things happen. The seductive, regressive idea at the root of belief in magic is that willing something – visualising it, or just speaking it – can make it happen, if properly focused.

Overlaid on top of this is the need to be special. Common to Gnosticism, theosophy, Gurdjieff and many other belief systems is the ego-flattering conviction that you belong to an elite minority who are hip to the cosmic score. You alone, or almost alone, are aware and awake – unlike the sleeping sheep who make up the benighted majority of mankind.

Another impulse relates to alienation and boredom – the desire to make the world more exciting, to irradiate it with a sense of mystery glowing from beneath the drab skin of mundanity. As Gary Lachman, a historian of the links between the occult and rock music, writes, by using rituals and ceremonies 'the magician can escape . . . Reality is malleable, something our postmodern sensibilities feel instinctively.'

Bowie later talked about his search during this period for guidance in books like Israel Regardie's *The Tree of Life*, S. L. McGregor Mathers's *The Kabbalah Unveiled* and A. E. Waite's books on ceremonial magic. Key among the texts Bowie consulted that crazy summer of 1975 was Dion Fortune's *Psychic Self-Defense*. This 1930 manual of magical protection begins with Fortune's own experience of suffering a nervous collapse induced by the hypnotic suggestion of a vengeful employer.

In *Psychic Self-Defense*, Fortune describes how to ward off every kind of magical attack, from thought-forms to the malicious deployment of electrical magnetic energy. You might also find yourself persecuted by 'artificial elements': entities formed out of ectoplasm and 'ensouled' in order to serve as semi-autonomous instruments of remote revenge.

Interviewed decades later, Bowie laughed uneasily as he recalled how he followed Fortune's instructions: 'You had to run around the room getting bits of string and old crayons and draw funny things on the wall, and I took it all most seriously, ha ha ha! I drew gateways into different dimensions, and I'm quite sure that, for myself, I really walked into other worlds. I drew things on walls and just walked through them, and saw what was on the other side!' But Bowie didn't resort only to magic: in his paranoid distress, he also gave the world's most venerable monotheisms a go too, wearing a crucifix and wielding a mezuzah to chase away the dark forces.

Bowie took to heart Fortune's warnings about not letting things 'impregnated with the intended victim's magnetism' – hair, nail clippings, 'night-soil' (excrement), cast-off clothes, dirty handkerchiefs and, above all, semen-stained bed linen – fall into the hands of sorcerous enemies. So he started storing his bodily by-products and fluids in the fridge. He conducted banishing rituals, drew protective symbols like pentagrams all over his hosts' houses, and lit black candles constantly.

Then there was the swimming-pool exorcism. In some accounts, a visiting Peter Sellers warned him about the occult significance of black markings on the bottom of swimming pools. Bowie enlisted New York's white witch Walli Elmlark, a rock fan who hung out with Robert Fripp and other performers she considered 'cosmic children'. (She also penned a gossip column for American rock magazine *Circus*.) Elmlark conducted an exorcism by phone and provided Bowie with incantations to deal with his other anxieties.

According to Cherry Vanilla, who first put Bowie in contact with Elmlark, the witch was really hired to deal with the singer's belief that some girls (witches, he believed) were trying to get hold of his sperm in order to conceive a devil child: an idea surely spawned while watching *Rosemary's Baby*.

Daniel O'Keefe argues that our sense of reality is surprisingly fragile; it really doesn't take much to make it wobble: sleep deprivation or sensory deprivation, hunger, a hypnotic trance caused by repetition or music, fever, dance frenzy, even just falling under the spell of a charismatic speaker. Cults use these techniques to get outside 'the normal social frame of orientation', and the experiences, visions, 'truths' thus accessed become the basis of a renegade world view. The dizzying array of mystical creeds and fringe political sects in the world shows how variable perception is, as well as how suggestible human beings are when exposed to the magnetic effect of a commanding and manipulative personality. Sometimes a 'cognitive minority' – a sect or radical fringe group – can turn itself into a majority, enforcing a belief system that from a rational perspective amounts to superstition. An entire society becomes delusional, succumbing to the contagious and intoxicating madness of a leader – the largest and most terrible example from recent history being Nazism.

One of Bowie's passions during this period was books that purported to reveal the links between the Nazis and the occult. There was a publishing mini-boom of these titles in the early seventies, and Bowie was particularly engrossed by Trevor Ravenscroft's *The Spear of Destiny* and J. H. Brennan's *Occult Reich*. He bought multiple copies of the latter – whose main claim is that Hitler had precognitive powers that worked perfectly, at least until they stopped working at all – and distributed them to friends.

Ravenscroft's book is titled after the spear with which the Roman centurion Longinus pierced the body of Christ on the cross, to hasten his death. Supposedly, the inner circle of the Third Reich was obsessed with gaining possession of this sacred relic, for whoever held the spear controlled the course of human history. *The Spear of Destiny* does not limit itself just to that one fable, though. Good lord, no: it roams widely, scooping up a host of unsubstantiated, unprovable tales. There's the story of young Hitler taking peyote to penetrate the secrets of the Holy Grail, and the Thule lodge seance in which 'ectoplasmic heads and shrouds' emanate from a woman's vagina like 'ghostly birth from the nether world'. Dietrich Eckart, Hitler's early mentor, is said to have initiated the future Führer in a 'monstrous sadistic magic ritual'. That opened up the 'occult centres' of Adolf's astral body, enabling him to communicate with 'the powers of darkness' but also access memories of a past incarnation as the ninth-century count and black magician Landulf II, the historical source of a sinister character in Richard Wagner's opera *Parsifal*.

Recalling this fervid phase of his life in 1993, Bowie said that what fascinated him above all was 'this theory that [the Nazis] had come to England at some point before the war to Glastonbury Tor to try to find the Holy Grail. It was this Arthurian need, this search for a mythological link with God.' Certainly there were figures in the upper echelons of the Third Reich – Himmler and Rosenberg, mainly – who had more than a passing interest in 'blood and soil' paganism and regarded Christianity as an enfeebling and fundamentally un-Germanic faith. The SS insignia – so similar to the Ziggy Stardust zigzag symbol – derived from Norse runes. But while Hitler had fraternised with some esoteric scholars in his youth, he and other principal Nazi leaders like Speer, Goebbels and Göring were fundamentally godless. They put their trust in science and technocratic materialism. The Führer scorned Himmler's 'nonsense' and declared that 'nothing would be more foolish than to reestablish the worship of Wotan' (the old Norse god Odin). 'We have at last reached an age that has left all mysticism behind it.'

What's bizarre about the *Occult Reich* genre of pseudo-history is that the simple facts of Nazism – what they actually believed and implemented – are surely insane and bad-trip hallucinatory enough for anybody's taste. It's hardly necessary to imagine some deeper, darker magic behind it. But then the craving for 'more . . . always more' is the dynamic that drives occult scholars and their readership. As Lachman observes, Aleister Crowley is the archetype of this compulsive-addictive personality voraciously pursuing 'strong' things in mounting doses: intensities of sex, drugs, ceremonial magic, or combinations of all three.

Bowie exhibited a tendency not to focus on one spiritual path but rather to believe in all of them, simultaneously or successively. The rush of revelation eventually requires abandoning the historical facts altogether: many occultists, like A. E. Waite and Dion Fortune, had sidelines in allegorical fantasy novels and science fiction. The step beyond that is madness itself. Bowie recalled that after six or seven days without sleep, 'by the end of the week my whole life would be transformed into this bizarre nihilistic fantasy world of impending doom, mythological characters and imminent totalitarianism'.

In the nadir of his cocaine dysphoria, Bowie made a total identification between his fractured ego and 'World Collapse'. That's Daniel O'Keefe's term for narcissism turned apocalyptic: a state of mind that is the inverse of being in love. Where romantic ardour reaches out for ecstatic fusion with the Other, paranoia withdraws from an external reality that's become all Ominous Otherness.

'I had never been so near an abyss of total abandonment,' Bowie has said of these darkest LA days. 'When they say that one felt like a shell, an empty shell, I can really understand that. I felt that any of life's intrusions would crush that shell very easily. I felt totally, absolutely alone.'

N

Bowie had long desired to break into other areas of showbiz – acting in stage plays or movies, above all – and prove that he transcended the category of rock. He landed his first major film role in an interesting way.

Actors trained in the Method are renowned for the lengths they'll go to in order to achieve the mind-frame for the role. Sometimes that involves drastically changing their physical appearance through weight gain or weight loss (the famous example being Robert De Niro piling on sixty pounds to play the older Jake LaMotta in *Raging Bull* and training until he coulda been a contender in professional middleweight boxing). The rigours of cocaine addiction became an inadvertent Method-style preparation process for Bowie. His rail-thin and wraith-like presence in *Cracked Actor* served as a kind of unofficial screen test/audition for *The Man Who Fell to Earth*. Director Nicolas Roeg became convinced that Bowie's aura of absolute aloneness made him perfect for the movie's lead role of the stranded alien who calls himself Thomas Jerome Newton, and who becomes a kind of Howard Hughes figure, wasting away in alcoholic despair.

An agent named Maggie Abbott spotted Bowie's potential while watching *Cracked Actor* and procured a tape for Roeg. He abandoned his existing plan of casting Peter O'Toole, captivated by Bowie's pallor and 'curiously artificial voice' – its lack of definability by class or place. Roeg turned up at Bowie's house for a meeting, but the singer completely forgot about the appointment. Returning home eight hours late, Bowie was astonished to find Roeg waiting patiently.

It's possible Roeg might have dimly remembered 'Space Oddity', Bowie's hit from six years previously. The plot of *The Man Who Fell to Earth* is 'Space Oddity' turned inside out: instead of the human spaceman floating off into the void, a humanoid astronaut from another solar system crash-lands his tin can in the desert of the American south-west. Ironically, he's on a mission from his own desert planet, hoping – in some unexplained way – to bring back moisture to save his family and his world. Still, the predicament of Major Tom and Thomas Newton is the same: they've been separated from their wives, children, home.

Newton builds a huge business empire based around innovative products using technologies from his vastly more advanced civilisation. The reclusive mogul attracts the suspicion of the authorities, and when Newton attempts to launch the first privately owned spacecraft as the first step in a rescue mission for his home planet, he's imprisoned and subjected to scientific experiments. Ultimately, he's set free, but only on condition that he remains on Earth. He's last seen living a twilight existence, whiling away his exile making music: he releases an LP (which we never get to hear, sadly) under the name The Visitor that seemingly perplexes its few human listeners with its alien conception of melody.

Bowie's presence as Newton goes beyond glamdrogyny: when he strips off his humanoid disguise to satisfy the curiosity of his girlfriend Mary-Lou, his alien body has no genitals. Even those who felt the movie meandered recognised Bowie's brilliant performance – although in a sense, as Bowie himself admitted, he was more or less manifesting his coked-out and barely-there self.

Pauline Kael described Bowie-as-Newton as 'The Little Prince for young adults . . . purity made erotic,' praising Roeg's 'eerily easy, soft, ambiguous' sex scenes between Newton and Mary-Lou for bringing out 'the sexiness of passivity'. This 'wilted, solitary stranger', Kael wrote, speaks to 'everyone who feels misunderstood, everyone who feels sexually immature or "different", everyone who has lost his way' – a description that captures much of the appeal of Bowie, not just the alien character he played.

The Man Who Fell to Earth teems with iconic scenes – Roeg started his career as a cinematographer – but one tableau stands out particularly: Newton holed up watching a dozen TV sets piled on top of each other. His advanced alien brain would probably be bored stiff watching just one channel. The wall of televisions suggests psychologist Kenneth J. Gergen's concepts of 'multiphrenia' and 'the saturated self' – a new kind of flexible and super-absorbent identity emerging in the era of media overload.

The Roeg–Bowie collaboration deserves its reputation for having resulted in one of the most artistically successful rock-star-as-movie-actor turns to date. Probably its only real rival is the earlier Roeg movie *Performance*, which he co-directed with its writer Donald Cammell. *Performance* and *The Man Who Fell to Earth* go together, and not just because Bowie's frenemy Mick Jagger starred in the former. The two films form a conceptual pair, bookending the glam era. Filmed in 1968, *Performance* is absolutely sixties, but it rehearses the themes of the pop era that followed swiftly upon the film's delayed release in 1970. Decadence, sexual indeterminacy, the theatricality of performance are all in there, along with a persistent motif to do with mirrors (used for doubling and gender-blurring effects). There's magic too: upper-class bohemian Cammell was fascinated by Crowley and friends with Kenneth Anger, whose movies are a clear influence on *Performance*.

The plot of *Performance* involves the flight of an East End criminal, Chas Devlin, who has incurred the wrath of his Kray twins-like gang boss. Posing as a juggler, Devlin takes refuge in the Ladbroke Grove house of Turner, a burned-out, reclusive rock star (modelled largely on Brian Jones, but played by Jagger). Druggy, polysexual cavorts ensue, as Turner and his lover Pherber (Anita Pallenberg) try to dismantle their sociopathic guest's character armour and poke around inside his psyche.

The script was originally titled *The Liars*. Both rock star and gangster project a front as part of their trade. Devlin uses intimidation, a psychopathic aura, far more than actual violence. In the movie's critical exchange, Turner lectures the 'juggler' Devlin about theatre: 'I know a thing or two about performing, my boy . . . The only performance that makes it, that really makes it, that makes it all the way, is the one that achieves madness. Am I right?' But Turner also knows that he's lost his mojo: precisely, the ability to believe the illusion he's projecting. Devlin, whose name is close to 'devil', still possesses his 'daemon', as Pherber calls it. She says that the criminal provides a 'dark little mirror' that will perhaps help the fading rock star escape the hole in which 'he's stuck. Stuck!'

The second half of *The Man Who Fell to Earth* – Newton under house arrest, passing time with kinky but listless sex, drinking gin by the gallon – virtually repeats the atmosphere of cloistered decadence that pervades Turner's west London townhouse. Roeg spoke of how Jagger and Bowie both possessed a charisma and physical presence that couldn't be learnt at acting school. 'They're not just a singer with a band. Their whole magnetism comes out in acting.'

Bowie enjoyed making the movie. There was a father/son-like relationship between the director and his inexperienced actor: one magazine feature on the film shoot observes Roeg kissing his exhausted star on the head.

Around this period Bowie started to talk about how his albums to date had really been 'accompaniment for films' that hadn't been made, so that listeners needed to 'supply your own images'. He also claimed that 'a renaissance in film making is going to come from rock', asserting that Iggy Pop and David Johansen would be better off as actors rather than singers. He saw his own future in terms of movies – either acting in them or directing them. 'I've got nothing to do with music,' he liked to say.

Bowie also enjoyed being in New Mexico for the shoot. He

described the unpopulous and arid state as 'so clean and pure – and puritanical, too . . . Not just the people but the land too.' That off-hand remark reveals Bowie's feelings about Los Angeles as a toxic environment. Very soon he would take steps to extricate himself from its destructive influences, but in the meantime, he embarked on the recording of a new album – the only record he would make in LA – and with it the construction of a new performance persona.

During the filming in New Mexico, Bowie started jotting down a book that has been described variously as a fragmented autobiography or a collection of short stories. His next (and final, it turned out) character emerged somewhere in between the coke-addled scribblings and his assuming the personality of Thomas Jerome Newton. In the movie, Newton identifies himself as a different kind of resident alien, saying, 'I'm from England' or 'I'm British' – sufficient explanation for his icy reserve, as far as the American characters in *Man Who Fell* are concerned. Newton's lack of affect and vaguely aristocratic aloofness seem, then, to have suggested the title of Bowie's unfinished, never-published book: *The Return of the Thin White Duke*.

On 27 November 1975, Bowie entered a TV studio in Burbank, California, to record a long-distance interview with Russell Harty for his London Weekend Television chat show. Broadcast in the UK the following day, this would be the first public sighting of Bowie's new image: short swept-back hair, dyed golden blond, that harked back vaguely to the early twentieth century, and clothes that were smart but plain. The new look had a timeless formality compared with the swanky black American style that Bowie had favoured during *Young Americans*.

The conversation between Bowie and the chat-show host contrasted starkly with his first Russell Harty interview back in 1973. Looking at his most girlishly androgynous, Bowie had then been playful, almost coquettish, turning his body sideways in his chair

Elegantly wasted: David Bowie as the Thin White Duke (1976)

and leaning into Harty's personal space. Two years later, beamed remotely from Burbank, Bowie was rigid and erect in his posture, his gaze supercilious, his tone haughty. He replied to the questions courteously, sometimes candidly, but even when flattering Harty, there was a total absence of warmth.

When Harty asked what his new persona would be when he next toured the UK, Bowie replied: 'I'm sort of inventing me at the moment.' In fact, the process of self-construction was virtually complete: Harty was speaking to the Thin White Duke, a persona Bowie would later describe as 'a very Aryan, Fascist type' and 'a nasty character'.

Elegant but not effete, the Thin White Duke was Bowie's attempt to create his own impenetrable shell: an imperious solipsist 'with absolutely no emotion at all'. Accounting for the glacial remoteness of the Duke, Bowie would later talk about how 'cocaine severs any link you have with another human being'. This steely self, forged in the pale fire of line after line of snorted snow, involved a retreat to a hard kernel of pure will.

'Thin' almost seems redundant: Bowie had always been bony, and never more so than during the skeletal coke years. But 'White' and 'Duke' leap out as significant: for one so immersed in black American soul music, these words signalled a shift back to European culture, the Old World. There are no 'Dukes' in the US, a democratic republic: immigrants applying for citizenship must renounce any hereditary titles.

The unfinished book's title, *The Return of the Thin White Duke*, provided the first line of the first song – and title track – of *Station to Station*. Recording started in the autumn of 1975, shortly after the movie wrapped. That this character is 'returning' from somewhere or somewhen – like a long-lost archetype or legendary person – is just one of a number of impenetrable mysteries about 'Station to Station'.

Many fans regard the song as one of his most intense pieces of music. Musically, it's a multi-segmented, ten-minute track that shifts awkwardly from a stilted if compelling guitar figure to a disconcertingly blithe disco sashay. Lyrically, it's a cat's cradle of hermetic references, ranging from Kabbala and Crowley to Shakespeare's *The Tempest*.

I confess that my issues with 'Station to Station' are similar to the problems I had with T. S. Eliot's *The Waste Land* as a schoolboy: that gut-level feeling that a poem that requires footnotes to be understood is not much cop as a poem. Using a search engine or consulting Bowie-analysis fan sites, a listener today can find out that the song's references to Kether and Malkuth stem from Kabbalah's Tree of Life; that 'white stains' is taken from a book of Crowley's pornographic poetry, while the – admittedly striking – line about darts thrown into lovers' eyes may well allude to a murderous occult ritual said to have been conducted by Crowley and his acolytes. But in 1976, anyone listening to 'Station to Station' was dealing with a song utterly closed off in solipsistic opacity. Even today, Bowie's most dedicated interpreters, after decoding the song, still seem to be at a loss when it comes to identifying an emotion or mind state that it's meant to be conveying.

Bowie later described the song – and the whole album – as 'the nearest . . . to a magick treatise that I've written. I've never read a review that really sussed it.' He also admitted that he could barely remember anything about the recording of *Station to Station* and had come to feel like the record was the creation of 'an entirely different person'. That suggested the album's disjointed encryptions were no longer penetrable, even by its maker. 'My thought forms are already fragmented to say the least,' Bowie told Cameron Crowe in 1976, explaining that he resorted to Burroughs's cut-up techniques to put back coherence *into* his writing rather than fragment it further. In another interview, Bowie confessed, 'I don't necessarily know what I'm talking about in my writing. All I do is assemble points that interest me and puzzle through it.' Listeners were perfectly free to reassemble the constituent elements into new shapes meaningful to them. Bowie's songs were meant to be re-visioned, as opposed to being taken as completed visions.

The obtuseness of 'Station to Station' is, for me, highlighted by the focused brilliance of the song that immediately follows: 'Golden Years', which became another of his big hits on both sides of the Atlantic. This lustrous shiver-and-quiver of funk, with its exquisitely dovetailed clusters of vocal harmony, seems to be a sort of motivational anthem. It is saying, 'Get up and don't look back'; it holds out the promise of a paradise in which love and limelight (references to riding 'a dream car twenty foot long') are conflated. Supposedly, 'Golden Years' is a love offering to one or other of Bowie's partners, but to my mind it feels as much like a song addressed to himself. The mood is easy to grasp: euphoria and boundless confidence, but with cracks appearing during the course of the song. There's invulnerability ('nothing's gonna touch you') but it's as shaky as a castle built of sand. In the midst of a sound and a vocal performance of such radiant elation, what to make of the line 'run for the shadows'? It could be the onset of paranoia again, or just cautionary advice: this peak experience cannot possibly sustain.

On 'Golden Years' and on much of the rest of *Station to Station*, the sound of *Young Americans* is etherealised and subtly Europeanised. The album's overall message-to-self is: 'Go back east, young man.' The title track starts with locomotive sounds (a recording of the Orient Express departing from Vienna's train station) and ends with oblique references to 'the European canon'.

Station to Station's grand finale is the epic romantic ballad 'Wild Is the Wind', a cover of a song co-written by Dimitri Tiomkin, the Hollywood composer who trained in pre-revolutionary Russia and is best known for his western soundtracks like *High Noon*. Like Bowie an émigré to America's West Coast, Tiomkin often drew on Russian folk melodies and memories of the steppes for inspiration.

Bowie felt that the 'European feel' of his version of 'Wild Is the Wind' was 'a bridge to the future'. It literally pointed to where he would go next, artistically and geographically. He would quit Los Angeles for Berlin, a city that was in many ways its inverse: wintry, sombre, laden with history. Here he would make music – the greatest of his life – that broke radically with American idioms and leave rock'n'roll and R&B far behind.

11:

ULTRAVIOLENCE: PUNK BEFORE PUNK

Heavy Metal Kids – The Sensational Alex Harvey Band – The Tubes – The Runaways – Doctors of Madness – Ultravox

In November 1974, the BBC's current-affairs programme *Panorama* ran a report about a teenage crime wave that had swept the UK – 'serious offences, committed by children'. Titled 'Younger Every Day' and presented by Julian Pettifer, the programme claimed that between 50 and 60 per cent of crimes were now being 'committed by youngsters'. The list of prosecutions for a juvenile court in north London scrolled down the screen, showing a tally 'for one average day' that included burglary, robbery, threatening behaviour and handling drugs, with perpetrators as young as twelve.

Then the camera cuts to a band onstage, whose uncouth singer derisively dedicates the next number to the police. He starts to give the title as 'The Pigs Are Coming', before correcting it to 'The Cops Are Coming'. As the camera pans over a packed crowd of rapt 'n' rowdy youth, Pettifer quotes what the singer had told him earlier about the band's appeal to contemporary kids: 'In the sixties it was all beads and peace and pot . . . now it's boots, bovver and booze.'

As it happens, 'The Cops Are Coming' isn't particularly scary or subversive. Mid-song, the singer goes into a spoken-word section, relating – in his exaggeratedly Cockney accent – a tall tale about throwing something out of a car window that causes a scooter rider to get decapitated and then seeing the head bounce down the tarmac. Nonetheless, Pettifer solemnly informs the viewers that 'these songs, which are anti-authoritarian and violent, do seem to strike a chord with the young audience'.

The singer was Gary Holton and it's said that this alarmist *Panorama* programme got his band, Heavy Metal Kids, banned from many venues across the nation. In some accounts, the slant of Pettifer's story was affected by him coming into the band's dressing room just as a bottle was being smashed, and then, later at the concert, getting head-butted by a pair of Heavy Metal Kids fans dressed in top hats and *Clockwork Orange* outfits.

Although they signed to a major label and had a few UK hits, Heavy Metal Kids are a mostly forgotten outfit today; Gary Holton is remembered far more for his acting (playing the rogueish Wayne in much-loved eighties TV comedy drama *Auf Wiedersehen, Pet*), along with his death in 1985 from drink and drugs. But the band's story – and the *Panorama* youth-crime exposé – does reveal something about the UK in the mid-seventies. Something was stirring in the culture. As much as the authorities and the parent generation might have been deeply concerned and jittery with dread, among the youth there was a growing appetite for violence.

Pub rock satisfied some of the demand for rock that was street-level, but apart from the jagged amphetamine pummel of Dr Feelgood, it was tame stuff, completely harmless really. What people seemed to crave was some proper aggro in their rock'n'roll. Not staged gore like Alice Cooper, but something that oozed real threat.

There were a couple of British bands, at their most active and popular in 1974 and '75, who offered a taste of that kind of menace, and who paved the way for punk, if not sonically, then in terms of attitude and atmosphere. Heavy Metal Kids was one; the other was The Sensational Alex Harvey Band.

There's actually a small connection between the two groups. Around the turn of the seventies, Gary Holton spent a few months in the lead role of the musical *Hair*; Alex Harvey, formerly a Scottish

R&B performer, played rhythm guitar in the *Hair* pit band. In an *NME* interview, Holton recalled how he and Harvey rapped about music and its relationship to theatre. Each man would take the concept in radically different-sounding and different-looking directions, but the idea was more or less identical: a theatre of the streets (not to be confused with street theatre – plays performed in the street).

Holton told *Sounds* in 1975, 'I've 'ad this idea of 'ooliganism on stage in my brain fer abaht four years now.' Music journalists often spelt out Holton's quotes with the aitches dropped and the words spelt phonetically, because being a Cockney ruffian was Gary's shtick. Three years before the Sex Pistols' debut album, the Heavy Metal Kids' press release proclaimed that their intent was to 'put back some bollocks in rock n' roll'. The group didn't actually sound like punk, or indeed like heavy metal – they were more or less The Faces – but as Holton said, their name was chosen to evoke the mental image of 'a bunch of yobbos' onstage.

That image was really concentrated entirely in the physical form of Holton, whose East End urchin look crossed the Artful Dodger with Alex the Droog from *A Clockwork Orange*. Framed with black curls, his crow-like face bulged out between a black top hat and a white tasselled scarf. A red gypsy necktie bobbed on his bare chest, while a rakish rose peeped from the lapel of his black frock coat. Eyes ringed with smudged eyeliner leered insolently. Brandishing a black rolled-up brolly as a vaguely malevolent prop, Holton made V-signs at the audience, swore like a docker and generally put across what *Melody Maker*'s Chris Welch tagged as 'an outrageously exaggerated impression of the punk rock kid of fiction'.

There was an element of fiction to the Holton persona. Yes, his dad was an ex-boxer who owned multiple pubs. And yes, he was born in the East End. But Holton hadn't grown up there and he'd actually been educated for a spell at the top private school Westminster.

From there he went on to drama school and stints at Sadler's Wells Opera Company, the Old Vic Theatre Company and the Royal Shakespeare Company in Stratford-upon-Avon. Despite the cockney lingo, Holton was well read: the name Heavy Metal Kids came direct from William S. Burroughs, rather than via Steppenwolf's 'heavy metal thunder'.

Before he got involved in music, Holton had run with a gang who modelled themselves on Alex in *Clockwork Orange*. 'We all used to go around as a gang and listen to classical music. It was a little cult, dressed in bowlers and brollies – more refined skinheads 'cept we used to fight . . . Could get well violent . . . I was really into it, though if there was a fight I'd be running down the street.' The black rolled-up umbrella in his Heavy Metal Kids stage act, he said, was a survival from this 'perverted skinhead phase'.

Undercutting his street cred a bit, though, was the fact that before Heavy Metal Kids, Holton had been in a prog-rock group called Biggles. Overall, Heavy Metal Kids had the whiff of contrivance about them, but that didn't stop them getting signed to a major label and being promoted as a bunch of right little wrong 'uns, the genuine street-rock article. But the sharper elements in the music press treated the group with scepticism.

For instance, in July 1974, the *NME* ran a piece on the vogue among UK record-company A&R men for 'punk rock' – a phenomenon happening here two years ahead of historical schedule. Gary Holton and gang were singled out as the first of these ''74 model punks' to get scooped up by major-label scouts, who had been 'hightailing towards the East End of London' to sign up 'the leading aggro action makers'. While snidely observing that Holton hailed not from 'the switchblade jungle' but 'the West End Stage' (where he played the Artful Dodger in *Oliver!*), the *NME* conceded that Heavy Metal Kids were slightly closer to the Real Thing than a band from Liverpool called Nutz.

The July 1974 article also mentioned The Sensational Alex Harvey Band. They weren't a new band, though. They'd been signed for a couple of years by that point and the group's members were all music-biz veterans with roots in progressive rock and, in Alex Harvey's case, in showbiz going back to before rock'n'roll. SAHB were also way more theatrical in their presentation than Heavy Metal Kids or the punk bands of '77, putting on spectaculars involving costumes, props and semi-choreographed stage routines. Still, hailing from the tougher precincts of Glasgow, Alex Harvey and his band had an aura of authentic menace about them.

'I went to Southend to see Sensational Alex Harvey Band at the Kursaal Ballroom,' recalls Hugo Burnham, later of Gang of Four. 'And I have never felt such potential violence in the air at a concert. Boy, I really thought I was going to get killed that night.' Such tension was a tonic in the flaccid context of British rock music in the mid-seventies. A lot of future punks were in the audience at SAHB concerts, listening and learning about how to project threat. 'You'll find a lot of the punk-era musicians were big SAHB fans,' says Burnham. 'Paul Raven, the bassist in Killing Joke – he and I bonded through our love of Alex Harvey.'

The threat and the promise of violence seemed to be a turn-on for journalists. *Melody Maker*'s Allan Jones described Glasgow at 4 a.m. resembling 'the aftermath of a holocaust. Glasgow's reputation for violence has an awesome credibility.' Jones wrote of the SAHB sound as 'switchblade rock'n'roll with a cut so deep it'll carve you up and leave you half dead in an alley off Main Street'.

In interviews, Harvey played his part, pointing out landmarks such as George Square to visiting journos – 'There was a time when you'd be very lucky to be able to wait for a bus there without getting your face slashed by somebody with a razor.' He reminisced about running with gangs as a youth, when the accolade you craved was to be acknowledged as 'a hard citizen'. By Harvey's own account, he was a self-reformed wrong 'un from the Gorbals who'd witnessed two people being killed in front of him, and been in a few scraps himself. In one interview, he darkly alluded to the fact that 'if you go and stick-up some place when you're sixteen or seventeen, then you'll never be impressed by anybody ever again'.

His family background was as deprived as it came: mother, father, brother and Alex lived in a single room and shared a communal bathroom with a hundred residents. As a young man, Harvey had done dozens of hard-graft jobs, including whisky bottler, tombstone cutter, fruit porter and working the dodgems at a circus. But he'd turned his life around by finding an expressive outlet in music: he learnt guitar a few years before rock'n'roll arrived in Britain, and sang and led his own successful R&B band. Then, in the sixties, he'd gone through the whole peace-and-love adventure, spending time in a commune and becoming a confirmed pacifist. One of his most recycled catchphrases was 'Don't buy any bullets, don't make any bullets, don't shoot any bullets.' He would wax philosophical about how violence was 'a waste of energy which could be used in a lot of other ways'.

Yet violence was in large part The Sensational Alex Harvey Band's core of allure. There were songs like 'Framed' – for which Harvey would often pull a pair of stockings over his head, like a bank robber – and 'There Ain't Nothing Like a Gang Bang'. Like Holton (and also Ziggy Stardust), Harvey's look might touch on *Clockwork Orange* as he hit the stage in a frock coat and jockstrap, brandishing a cane. One music-paper ad for the album *Framed* depicted the band posing in a rubble-strewn, derelict lot like modern-day Dead End Kids. In an interview LP recorded to promote SAHB in America, Harvey addressed the band's attraction frankly: 'When we're on stage, we are not so much violent as an act of violence. We go close to the edge. I am the director and we're making a movie every night we're on stage and we're playing the sound track at the same time and the sound track's got to be good.'

Harvey was a mesmerising performer who'd learnt early on how to establish his authority over an audience, using his eyes and his phrasing: those pauses that make you hang onto someone's words whether you want to or not. His voice was quite high and fluting, but it had a bluesy rasp and was thickly accented. His physical presence was imposing: a huge head on a small, runty body, something he accentuated deliberately and effectively with a stage routine of reading from a giant tome – *The Book of Vambo* – propped between his hip and the mic stand. His face was craggy – a deep crevice of gauntness fissured each cheek – and surrounded by a halo of black curls. The gaps in his teeth were visible from quite deep into the audience. Harvey's trademark look was a black-and-pink striped T-shirt, which SAHB's large cult following soon adopted as concert wear.

'Alex was small but he was huge at the same time, if you know what I mean,' recalls SAHB guitarist Zal Cleminson. 'He had this monumental-looking face that was almost like hacked-up stone. A lot of presence. Didn't suffer fools gladly, either. He knew what he wanted.'

Zal was Alex's visual foil in SAHB, competing for the audience's eye as he sidled up and around the singer. 'I became somebody looking over his shoulder all the time.' Cleminson wore a peculiar green-and-yellow bodysuit and clown greasepaint (a couple of years before Kiss adopted that look). The make-up came about as a means of exaggerating his 'guitar-face' grimaces. 'I used to do a lot of parodying of guitar angst. But our manager Bill Fehilly said, "Nobody can see what you're doing beyond the front two rows." So we looked at what Marcel Marceau was doing, and came up with the idea of a semi-mime, semi-clown face that just projected right out into the hall. I could almost hide behind that mask and become a lot more outgoing onstage, a lot more theatrical.'

Cleminson and the other musicians had been in a Zappa-influenced prog band called Gas Mask. When Harvey saw them, they were

Alex Harvey and Zal Cleminson of The Sensational Alex Harvey
Band at Green's Playhouse, 31 May 1973

brilliantly accomplished players but not offering much in the way
of visual *divertissement*. A decade or more older than anyone in Gas
Mask, Harvey sold them the vision of theatrical rock he had tossed
around in the company of Gary Holton. They bought into his idea of
a rock band as a travelling revue. They happily eliminated solos and
applied their virtuosity towards versatility, coming up with a diverse
array of musical backdrops to Harvey's lyrics, ranging from blues to
cabaret to retro-tinged pastiches of all kinds. Formerly introverted
onstage, they got into doing dance routines, a throwback to bands
they'd all loved like The Drifters and The Temptations.

'SAHB got to be a West End production,' recalls Cleminson. 'We
did these Christmas shows in Glasgow and London – five nights in
Glasgow, four nights in London. We had dancers, girls with no backs
on their dresses. All these props. There was a wall with scaffolding
around it to climb up. A bookcase and ladder, like a study onstage.
We had this lamp-post set for Alex to do "Man in the Jar", his detective hat and trench-coat routine.'

Probably the most famous SAHB stage number – and the one that
most prefigures punk imagery, if not punk sound – is 'Vambo Marble

Eye', which featured a backdrop of a brick tenement wall, across which Harvey would aerosol-spray 'Vambo Rools OK'. The song's character is a cross between a street kid and a superhero. 'When Alex sprayed the graffiti, he wasn't Vambo, he was a kid who *believed* in Vambo,' explains Cleminson. 'Vambo was never really seen. Nobody really knows what he looks like.' The idea came from Harvey's love of comic books like *Sgt Fury and His Howling Commandos*, as well as movies like *King Kong* and pulp genres like science fiction.

'Vambo is based on my growing up in the street,' Harvey explained in the promotional interview LP. 'Vambo is not a vandal, 'cos Vambo knows the streets belong to him and you. Therefore, he must look after it.' The song actually inspired a socially conscious organisation in Sussex and London's East End: the Vambo Liberation Front, a group of squatters and working-class kids who started their own social programmes, helping the homeless.

SAHB's combo of musicianship, 'cartoon violence' and Harvey's charisma made the group one of the major concert draws of the British mid-seventies. They stole the show at the Reading Festival in 1974, performing 'Anthem', one of their crowd-pleasing numbers, with a troupe of bagpipers coming onstage. 'Framed' was staged as a crucifixion, Cleminson recalls, with Alex 'pinned up somehow on a cross we'd dragged onstage'. When they played 'The Faith Healer' – their greatest, hardest-rocking song – the sun was going down. 'Alex just stood there, singing, "Let me put my hands on you," and you could feel the atmosphere going electric. Just one of the most magic moments I've ever experienced in my life.'

In some ways the missing link between Alice Cooper and the Sex Pistols, The Sensational Alex Harvey Band sold out large concert halls across the UK. But although they had a couple of hit singles – a cover of Tom Jones's 'Delilah' that brought out its sexual violence, and 'The Boston Tea Party' – SAHB's album sales lagged far behind their live reputation. As with so many theatrical-rock bands, the challenge was capturing their atmosphere on record. Phil Wainman, producer of The Sweet, got closest with 1973's *Next*, by setting up the band in the studio like they were on stage.

Named after the Jacques Brel song covered on side two, *Next*'s high point is 'The Faith Healer' – one of seventies rock's supreme examples of controlled power, sustaining a pregnant tension that hovers malevolently for over seven minutes. The elongation of the track came about because the album's running time was short, so Wainman decided to stretch out what was essentially a three-minute tune into a 'Papa Was a Rollin' Stone' epic, using electronic production tricks to create a throbbing pulse that looped beneath the cross-hatched riffs.

'The Faith Healer' is a song about the nature of performance itself: the tricks of the trade learnt by all showmen, how to seize attention and get an audience to believe. The intimidating aura generated by Harvey onstage – the sense of the potential for trouble – strayed into an unnerving zone when Alex added 'Tomorrow Belongs to Me' from *Cabaret* to SAHB's set. During 1976 (around the same time as the first punks flirted with Nazi symbols, a year or so before the Sex Pistols wrote 'Belsen Was a Gas'), Harvey sported a swastika armband during live renditions of 'Framed'. Cleminson recalls a gig in Hamburg, of all places, where Harvey strutted onstage with a Hitler moustache, hair parted to one side, wearing jackboots. The album *Tomorrow Belongs to Me* contains 'Give My Compliments to the Chef', which kicks off with the line 'Mother dear, did you hear about how they're teaching me to do the goose-step?' Reviewers observed how Harvey onstage could come across as 'a malevolent dictator figure' and puzzled over the irony of a professed pacifist who was obsessed with war. Cleminson, for his part, insists that the whole thing was a send-up of Nazism, not a flirtation. Harvey 'despised Hitler and all he stood for'.

In America, despite the loud advocacy of Elton John – who told the *Detroit Free Press* that SAHB were 'bizarre and crazy . . . When America gets a taste they will flip' – Harvey and his band made little headway. One exception was Cleveland, where they drew large crowds and got airplay on the local progressive FM station. But one by-product of their not-so-successful visits to the US was the formation of a close alliance with some kindred spirits: they befriended and toured with The Tubes, another theatrical ensemble with one foot in the old wave and the other in the new wave. Says Tubes guitarist Bill Spooner, 'The thing to me that was amazing was that what Alex and his band were doing was pretty much the same crazy shit we were doing – unbeknownst to us, three thousand miles away.'

Originally from Phoenix, Arizona, The Tubes formed through the merger of two separate bands, The Red, White and Blues Band (a Zappa-influenced outfit not unlike Gas Mask) and The Beans, who had already developed theatrical performances spoofing science fiction and other B-movies in a way that paralleled Richard O'Brien's *Rocky Horror Show*.

As with fellow Phoenix native Alice Cooper, the inspiration came from the indoors lifestyle of watching TV to stay out of the baking Arizona heat. The group's name came from the cathode-ray tube; later on, they would do a whole concept album about TV called *Remote Control*. 'I would have been lost without TV during my childhood,' Spooner told *Melody Maker* in 1974. 'It kept me from losing my mind in Phoenix.' Today, he points specifically to a local children's TV programme: *The Wallace and Ladmo Show*. 'They showed cartoons, but mostly they'd just sit around and do silly things – vignettes, with costumes and characters and stuff. And I went on there when I was six or seven, because they'd have a little gallery of kids.' Years later, as an eighteen-year-old, Spooner and his band of the time appeared on *Wallace and Ladmo* as The Vegetables: 'I played lettuce, smashing it, and another guy rubbed two sticks of celery together.' He recalls it as 'the first of the kids' shows that was really for adults. They had a lot of in-jokes for the intelligent.'

As well as absurdist sixties kids TV, another influence was school theatre. 'There was a little theatre in downtown Phoenix for kids.' It was here that Spooner first spotted the future frontman of The Tubes, Fee Waybill. 'He was playing a character in "Bye Bye Birdie" – not the star, but I thought he stole the show.' When Spooner next ran into him, Waybill was roadie-ing for The Red, White and Blues Band. After the latter had merged with The Beans, Spooner convinced everybody that the roadie should be on the stage. 'The first time he went on as Carmen Miranda, a bunch of fruit on his head, and we did "Brazil". It was a huge hit with the crowd.'

That gig was at an art school in San Francisco, where the two bands had separately moved at the end of the sixties and then merged into The Tubes. It was the competitive environment of San Francisco – so many bands compared to Phoenix – that encouraged The Tubes to amplify the theatrics and keep pushing things to extremes.

Waybill wasn't the world's greatest singer but he had the true showman's willingness to go the extra mile. At a 1974 Streakers' Ball in San Francisco, during a song called 'Ode to the Vegetarians', Waybill materialised amid a table laden with fruit and veg – emerging from the aubergine, in fact – and submitted to having his nose and ears stuffed with squishy produce by the frenzied audience. Another facet of his performance flair was his ability to 'throw up on cue', says Spooner. 'I thought that was the ultimate in show business. People can cry on cue. That's one thing. But vomiting on cue without sticking your fingers down your throat? Amazing.'

The puke-at-will skill came in useful for the persona of Quay Lewd that Waybill developed as a concert fixture – a parody of a British rock star, clad in silver lamé pants and twelve-inch platform boots, who'd shake a bottle of champagne and ejaculate froth in the faces of front-row fans. 'The audience learnt "Don't sit in the front row." There was a lot of blood spray and vomit.' The blood came with 'Rock and Roll Hospital', a song-sketch in which a doctor operated on a guitar, for which The Tubes would buy pig offal and guts that flew out into the audience. The song climaxed with the doctor pulling out 'the baby' – a ukulele – and spanking its little butt.

As the performances grew more elaborate and ambitious, a huge amount of energy went into making their own props and costumes. 'We'd stay up all night making weird outfits and giant shoes. You know that urethane foam that they pour in boats? We would make saxophones out of that. We'd just put a kazoo in the mouthpiece and then we'd paint them to look like brass with a big, red tongue hanging out of them, and we'd call them "fleshophones". They looked like mutated, bubbling flesh. We would stay up all night making that stuff, inhaling these toxic fumes.'

Soon The Tubes recruited a choreographer, Kenny Ortega, and at their peak were travelling with about thirty people: the core band, stage extras, and roadies who also doubled as dancers onstage. The scale of the operation was one reason they preferred to do residencies – a month-long one at San Francisco's Bimbo's club or the highly successful week of performances at the Hammersmith Odeon, London, in 1977.

Among The Tubes' famous routines were a game-show spoof accompanying the song 'What Do You Want from Life?' and 'Smoke', in which a gigantic cigarette bashes Waybill around onstage. Not everything was successful, however. 'Mutated'/'The Dinosaur Blues' involved laboriously constructed dinosaur costumes (oil cans flattened to make the back plates of a stegosaurus) and 'horrible masks' that accompanied a part of the song about mutation, with 'bulbous growths coming up the side of our faces'. But when The Tubes played it to a large crowd in North Beach, San Francisco, the entire audience left, except for one girl who stayed until the end of the song. 'It turned out the only reason she'd stayed was that she was in a wheelchair and no one had come to get her.'

The Tubes can almost certainly claim to be the first rock band to secure a record deal on the basis of a video demo, thanks to A&M. Their vote of faith was repaid almost immediately with the success of 'White Punks on Dope', a single off the 1975 debut album that got a lot of attention. The title came from reading an interview with a musician who'd worked with Jefferson Starship and, alluding to their druggy habits, had described them as 'a bunch of white punks on dope'. But for The Tubes, it became a phrase they applied to some of the San Francisco people they knew. 'They were teenagers at the time – younger than us by maybe three or four years. And they just liked to get high and wreck their cars. Rich kids with no future.' The song was essentially a Zappa-esque satire of decadence, 'an absurd anthem of wretched excess'.

In 1975, the song got a lot of airplay and buzz but failed to chart. But two years later, 'White Punks on Dope' was re-released and became a Top 30 hit in the UK. The title's reference to punk had nothing to do with the revolution of 1977, but The Tubes were mistakenly lumped in with the new wave. Their cynical edge intersected slightly with Devo and UK outfits like Alberto y Lost Trios Paranoias, whose punk-parody EP *Snuff Rock* was garnering attention around the same time. Musically, though, The Tubes really couldn't have had less in common with punk. Spooner and lead guitarist Roger Steen had both studied at a conservatory of music. The group's songbook ranged across a spectrum as broad as that of The Sensational Alex Harvey Band, but slanted more to Zappa and Steely Dan-style slick and tricksy licksmanship.

The shock-rock aspects of their show also encouraged the confusion of The Tubes with punk. Performances were banned in a few places in Britain. In the American Midwest an outfit called Mothers Against Lewd Rock Music marched outside venues. One of the offending numbers was 'Mondo Bondage', which would see Waybill infiltrating the crowd dressed in an overcoat and hat, accompanied by the group's female dancer Re Styles. 'They'd have a special table out there reserved for them. Then they'd start arguing right in the middle of a song. We'd stop playing. They'd be screaming at each other and then Re grabs a bottle – a sugar bottle – and smashes Fee with it. He grabs her and throws her over his shoulder. People in the audience are trying to restrain him – they think he's really beating the shit out of this girl. He'd just push them out of the way and carry her up onstage. Whip off his raincoat – and he'd have his bondage gear on. And Re would whip off her dress and have her bondage gear on.'

In addition to 'White Punks on Dope', their not-really-punk anthem, The Tubes soon developed their own punk spoof, 'I Was a Punk Before You Were a Punk'. A parody punk called Johnny Bugger would be planted in the audience. 'He had all these razor blades glued to his cheeks. He'd start gobbing on Fee from the audience, and Fee would jump in the audience and beat up Johnny Bugger.'

The dissolute youth satirised in The Tubes' 'White Punks on Dope' could be found even more plentifully in Los Angeles than in San Francisco. Some were rich and spoiled, some rich and neglected, some less well off but from fractured or unstable backgrounds. They formed the core of glam's constituency. And this crowd segued pretty seamlessly from LA glitter to LA punk.

'All the punk kids from The Masque club, like Helen Killer and Trudie Plunger, they all used to hang out at Rodney's originally,' recalls scenester Kari Krome. Darby Crash from the legendary LA punk group The Germs, she says, 'could have crawled right out of scenes from *Diamond Dogs*'. The Screamers – LA's most convulsively compelling live punk act, fronted by the hyper-theatrical

Tomata Du Plenty – came out of Ze Whiz Kids, a Seattle troupe who had been the missing link between glam and The Cockettes. So obsessed with the visual side of things were The Screamers that they never made a record: they wanted to make movies and were holding out for a Videodisc Revolution they wrongly thought imminent. As for Rodney Bingenheimer, he resurfaced as the leading new-wave DJ on local radio station KROQ.

But in the gap between the 'Death of Glitter' party at the Hollywood Palladium in late 1974 and the opening of The Masque in August 1977, the LA scene was dormant; just about the only action came from The Runaways, an all-girl group whose sound and attitude fell exactly midway between glam and punk. According to their (mis)manager Kim Fowley, the concept was 'America's sweethearts mutated'. Later on, Fowley would say, apropos the pop success of the all-female new-wave outfit The Go-Go's, that 'They got it right . . . The Runaways got it wrong – they were too threatening.'

The Runaways' concept was originally devised by Kari Krome, who began jotting down concepts and lyrics for an all-girl group with a bad-reputation image when she was in her early teens. Fowley recalled meeting Krome in the summer of 1975, when she accompanied Rodney Bingenheimer to Alice Cooper's birthday party at the Palladium: the thirteen-year-old 'had 10,000 words and lyrics written since age ten'. In Fowley's account, this discovery retriggered a concept he had already come up with in the past but had mentally filed away: 'a power rock and roll group with female members'. Fowley signed Krome as a songwriter in August 1975, put her on salary and charged her with finding band members. But Krome was gradually edged out of the project, and ultimately only around four of the songs she co-wrote were ever recorded by The Runaways. She'd wanted to be the 'Phil Spector' moulding her own punked-up Ronettes. But there was only room for one domineering Svengali when Fowley was around.

When she was still involved, Krome did find the first component of The Runaways: Joan Jett. Although the rhythm guitarist, Jett defined the group's image with her sullen glower and tomboy style. Singer Cherie Currie's image – blonde hair, stockings and bustier – was more sexed up, but still tough: a trailer-park Brigitte Bardot, said Fowley. She had been discovered at the Sugar Shack, a glitter kids' hang-out in the Valley.

The glitter connection was so strong with The Runaways partly because Jett – Joanie Larkin originally – was pretty much the world's biggest Suzi Quatro fan. According to Krome, 'Joanie used to camp out in the Hyatt House hotel, the lobby downstairs,' just waiting for Quatro to come down when on tour in LA. 'She copped her whole deal from Suzi.' Ultimately, Jett would get her very own black leather jumpsuit.

Sound-wise The Runaways found the exact intersection between Quatro and The Ramones. Neither conquered America, of course, and nor did The Runaways. Probably this had something to do with the state of American radio in 1976, the year of their self-titled debut album and single 'Cherry Bomb'. This was the year of *Frampton Comes Alive!* and *Hotel California*. Juvenile kicks were in short supply, with only Kiss really contending in that department. But The Runaways' record – apart from the immortal 'Cherry Bomb' – was also not that strong. Neither a glam glitz-blitz nor a punk assault, it was just a bit middling.

After a few more albums, including 1977's *Queens of Noise*, The Runaways disintegrated. But the group's glam roots resurfaced with Joan Jett's solo career: the stark and crunching #1 hit 'I Love Rock 'n' Roll' was a cover of a 1975 tune by RAK act The Arrows. Jett also made the Top 20 in 1982 with her version of Gary Glitter's 'Do You Wanna Touch Me'.

Just as Glitter's sex crimes have almost obliterated his pop achievements, Kim Fowley has cast a heavy backwards shadow over The

Runaways, along with his own bizarrely varied career as a manager, producer and solo performer, because of the 2015 revelation that he raped Runaways bassist Jackie Fox at an after-party, when she was semi-comatose after being plied with Quaaludes. Worse, Fox asserts that certain other members of the band witnessed the incident, but did nothing. Whatever the precise truth, it's clear from multiple testimonies that Fowley used psychological and sexual abuse, in tandem with his intimidating six-foot-five height and brutal flair with language, to humiliate and control his young charges.

Fowley's own statements over the years are self-damning. 'The reason I'm in the record business is to fuck young cunt,' he declared early on. Blunt honesty of this sort was once considered bracing, even 'liberated', coming out of the sixties. Now it sounds creepy and disturbing: pathology hiding in plain sight.

Yet Fowley undeniably had charisma, something that even those who suffered his depredations find hard to shake off after all these years. Those who never had his darkness inflicted upon them, who were free to appreciate his intellect and find his super-hustler persona entertaining, have struggled to process the revelations. One such person is Lisa Fancher, who wrote some of the earliest pieces on The Runaways for magazines like *Bomp* while still a teenager, and who 'really, really thought that they were going to be the female band that changes everything'. She counted Fowley as a friend, despite the decades separating them in terms of age. 'He had a very specific type of girl that he liked, which was completely *crazy*. I like to think that's why he never even hit on me. If you had any home-life stability or parents, like I had, he was, "Hell, no."'

That's not necessarily a flattering account: it suggests the wiliness of a predator, instinctively drawn to the vulnerable. One of the background factors behind this whole era of glitter transitioning to punk – captured in the 1980 film *Foxes*, in which Cherie Currie plays an actual teen runaway – is that the parents simply weren't around. They were caught up in their own post-sixties trips of sex 'n' drugs hedonism or spiritual self-absorption. This was also the first big era for divorce. Krome recalls that the glitter/punk scene involved a mix of kids from 'busted-up homes' (like herself) or wealthy backgrounds where they were left 'to run amok, do whatever they wanted'.

The Runaways – as a name – was meant to signify going the next step beyond *Star* magazine's concept of the fox. Instead of using image maintenance to keep parents in the dark, these girls just broke loose from domestication altogether. The idea of youth gone feral is thrilling . . . but there are always bigger beasts and more dangerous predators out where the wild things are.

Over in Britain, another group that debuted in 1976 also suffered from being too late for glam and too early for punk. Doctors of Madness actually released two albums that year, *Late Night Movies, All Night Brainstorms* and *Figments of Emancipation*, but despite heavyweight management, a major label deal and some critical support, they fell between the historical cracks. As with The Sensational Alex Harvey Band, though, the punks of 1977 were in the audience, watching and learning.

Doctors of Madness frontman Richard Strange looked the glam-into-punk part: six foot four, starved and angular, with a raptor's beak of a nose. Blue hair and green sideburns completed the visual shock; white Levi's with zips running up the length of each leg made him seem even more towering. A poet before he launched himself into rock'n'roll, he sometimes started a Doctors of Madness set with a tape of himself reading from Burroughs's *The Naked Lunch*.

The Strange vision owed a lot to *Diamond Dogs* (Doctors of Madness titled one of their 1976 tours 'The End of the World'), while also looking ahead to the black-hearted misanthropy of The Stranglers. The sound was harsh, mostly frantic, and desolate, thanks to the electric violin and Violectra supplied by Urban Blitz, whose name sounds like a second-wave, second-division punk group. (The bassist and drummer also had cartoon punkoid names: Stoner and Peter DiLemma respectively). Blitz's violin could exfoliate the inner ear in the John Cale style; 'I'm Waiting for the Man' was a song the group covered live. You couldn't say Doctors of Madness were super-strong when it came to melody, but they churned up a thrilling pell-mell clamour on 'Mainlines', 'The Noises of the Evening' and 'Out', which pre-empted the Pistols by a year by featuring the word 'fuck', something you almost never heard on rock records at that time.

Despite the lack of obvious hits in their repertoire, Doctors of Madness drew the attention of flush-with-money managers Brian Morrison (who'd played a role in the careers of T. Rex and Pink Floyd) and Justin de Villeneuve (who'd once managed Twiggy). These canny hype-men somehow persuaded NBC to send a crew to the UK and make a twenty-five-minute documentary about the unknown Doctors of Madness. The idea was that when aired it would snag the attention of American record companies. This didn't happen, but in the meantime Villeneuve and Morrison secured Doctors of Madness a deal with Polydor in the UK.

All three of Doctors of Madness's albums bypassed the public. By 1978 and *Sons of Survival*, the group was falling apart, but Strange had an idea for a solo concept album, which he would ultimately record for Virgin. *The Phenomenal Rise of Richard Strange* centres on an archetype of the glam era, incarnated variously by such men as Shep Gordon, Tony Defries and, in a small way, perhaps Morrison and De Villeneuve too: the pop Svengali who talks dreams into existence.

'A glamorous figure, a little bit like a rock'n'roll Ronald Reagan,' explained Strange. 'Using techniques from show business but applying them to the acquisition of political power, in the same way that the Nazis did.' As related through songs like 'On Top of the World', 'Magic Man', 'Gutter Press' and 'Premonition', the storyline followed the trajectory of an impresario who'd 'learned the tricks of Rock 'n' Roll, self-promotion and advertising' and then deployed them in game-theory fashion just to see 'how far he could take it'.

Ultravox had two things in common with Doctors of Madness: the prominent presence of violin in their sound, and the curse of being too tardy for the glam explosion. Hiring Brian Eno to produce their debut album for Island didn't help to deflect the Johnny-come-lately jibes thrown by the music papers. Ultimately they would have the last laugh, launching not one but two careers in the eighties as electronic pop stars: singer John Foxx as a solo performer, plus a reformulated Ultravox. But for their three albums as the original line-up, they seemed stranded between eras.

Foxx had an almost impossibly perfect Anglo-pop trajectory. During the sixties, as a young fan, he passed through mod, psychedelia and hippiedom; in the seventies, as a musician, he progressed from glam, to punk, to post-punk and then synth pop. His path could not have been closer to Bryan Ferry's: he left his father's world of coal mining in north-west England for art school and London.

Ultravox actually began as 'an art project', says Foxx. After awarding him the first-year drawing prize, the Royal College of Art's head of design asked Foxx about the projects he planned to pursue next. 'There'd been an interesting discussion of "design for the real world" at the college a few days before. So I said, "I'd like to design a rock band."' Foxx set about trying 'to reimagine what British/ European popular music might have sounded like if America had never happened – if we hadn't been overcome by a tidal wave from such a powerful and energetic culture'.

With this 'brief' in mind, Foxx created songs drawing on the electronic and hypnotic-rock sounds coming out of Germany (Kraftwerk and Neu!), as well as French *chansonniers* like Jacques Brel and film music, from *The Third Man* to Italian cinema. The presence of viola in Ultravox's sound seems like a deliberate gesture to European classical traditions, but it was a product of happenstance: after Billy Curry joined as keyboardist, Foxx discovered his real instrument was viola and liked the idea of a ragged, John Cale-like texture in the sound. Roxy Music's 'A Song for Europe' on *Stranded* encouraged Ultravox to head in this un-American direction. But, says Foxx, even before that 'we'd already decided that we weren't going down Route 66. It was to be Route nationale 1 and the M6.'

Ultravox's sound incubated in the Doll Factory – a perfect name for their rehearsal space, given its echoes of Warhol and the New York Dolls. It was literally the premises of mannequin manufacturer Modreno, located in an old warehouse in a seedy area behind London's King's Cross station. (Foxx had met the guy who ran it when they both worked painting the faces of showroom dummies at another company.) Ultravox rehearsed in the big room, surrounded by 'dismembered plastic humanoids': an ideal environment for hatching songs influenced by dystopian science-fiction writers like J. G. Ballard and a sound that would ultimately evolve into robotic synth rock.

On their February 1977 debut *Ultravox!*, the group wielded an aggressive, thrashy guitar sound poised somewhere between glam and punk. Released later in '77, *Ha!-Ha!-Ha!* pushed a little closer to punk, but not enough for Ultravox to shed their behind-the-time aura. They were felt to be too cold, mannered and art school in that year of *The Clash* and *Never Mind the Bollocks*. Songs like 'Hiroshima Mon Amour' displayed Bryan Ferry-like cinephilia, but it was slanted less towards classic Hollywood and more towards the foreign fare shown at London's all-night movie houses. 'I wanted the songs to be like small, strange art movies,' recalls Foxx.

Other tunes, like 'I Want to Be a Machine' and 'The Frozen Ones', tapped into the social landscape of anomie and disconnection that fed 1977 novels like Margaret Drabble's *The Ice Age* and 1977 TV series such as *1990*, a near-future dystopia of surveillance and state control. 'The country was cold and grey, we were all going nowhere and didn't seem to care. England seemed a very numb, dead place in 1976–7,' remembers Foxx.

Moving beyond punk's fury even as it still raged through UK pop culture, Foxx developed the stance of a cold observer, an almost ghostly onlooker of the decay – a persona he captured in the song 'The Quiet Men'. 'You can't act out Mr Angry for ever, like some on-the-nose ham. I was looking for an effective sort of detached tranquillity.'

Foxx felt that Ultravox arrived at this cool, remote style with their third album, *Systems of Romance*, recorded in 1978 in a studio near Cologne with the Krautrock producer Conny Plank, and released later that year. 'To us, it was a clear indication of the future.'

Ultravox and Foxx were not alone. In their attraction to Germany, in their emotionless detachment, in their impulse to bypass punk and move forward into a frigid future they had famous company. Bowie had been thinking along similar lines. In fact, he was already there.

12:

JUST ANOTHER HERO: BOWIE'S BERLIN

David Bowie – Iggy Pop – Kraftwerk – Brian Eno

For some British émigrés, the attraction of Southern California is its newness – no aged buildings burdened with the past like in the old country they've left behind. Everything feels fresh and bright. (Think of the Cali-utopian swimming-pool paintings of David Hockney, an on-and-off LA resident for decades.) Other Brit visitors, though, find these same qualities – the space and light, the newly built landscape and lack of weather – unnerving, as if the whole place is *unreal*.

Christopher Isherwood was one of those English expats who arrived in Los Angeles and never went back. On 11 February 1976, the seventy-year-old Santa Monica resident and his friend Hockney went to the after-party for David Bowie's concert at the LA Forum. A fan of Isherwood's *Goodbye to Berlin*, Bowie was thrilled. He bombarded the writer with questions about Weimar life. Tiring eventually, Isherwood tartly declared Berlin to have actually been 'rather boring' when he lived there. He added, with a trace of tetchiness, 'Young Bowie, people forget that I'm a very good fiction writer.'

Bowie filtered out this unwelcome data. He had already been planning to move to Europe, but meeting Isherwood planted in his head the idea of settling in Berlin. For months now his brain had been on fire with visions of Germany in the early twentieth century. The stark lighting adopted on the *Station to Station* tour came from his passion for the silent black-and-white films of Lang and Pabst, which he'd watched repeatedly in his Beverly Hills bunker. Overdosed on America, Bowie's plan now was to 'throw myself back into Europe' – a willed act of cultural immersion and physical transplantation.

Renouncing the New World was also an act of throwing himself back in time. It was the Berlin of the past that attracted him, far more than the city as it was in the mid-seventies. 'Berlin appealed to me because of German Expressionism,' Bowie recalled a few decades after he moved there. 'It was the artistic and cultural gateway of Europe in the Twenties and virtually anything important that happened in the arts happened there. And I wanted to plug into that instead of LA and their seedy magic shops.' He could have added, 'and LA's creepily accommodating coke dealers', since his plan was also to clean up while in Berlin.

Picking one of the heroin capitals of the world, a city teeming with counterculture and bohemian temptations of every kind, as a place to straighten out seems misguided. But in Bowie's head, Berlin represented decadence of a superior sort: not bell-bottoms, soft rock and stoned entropy, but rather an aristocratic decline entwined with century upon century of European high culture.

Bowie's companion on his self-salvaging mission was Iggy Pop, a man in dire need of rescue himself. Iggy had succumbed to 'LA-ism' (Bowie's term) even more than his English friend. 'He was in bad shape,' says Kari Krome, who recalls seeing Iggy 'rolling around in the gutter' in front of Rodney Bingenheimer's English Disco. Wasted on whatever drugs were going, prominent among them heroin, Iggy indulged in the teenage groupie scene too – experiences that inspired a song he wrote with James Williamson titled 'She-Creatures of the Hollywood Hills'. There was a dalliance with Sable Starr and a more prolonged involvement with her younger sister, Corel Shields (who inspired another new song, 'Rich Bitch'). A couple of decades later, Iggy revisited this grim phase in 1996's 'Look Away', a bleak confessional that chronicled his sleeping with Starr when she was just thirteen and her ill-starred romance with Johnny Thunders.

Separated from The Stooges, Iggy made sporadic attempts during 1974–5 to play live and record. With Williamson, he recorded the material that a couple of years later was released as *Kill City*. The title track is an anti-love song to LA, described as 'a playground for the rich' but 'a loaded gun to me'. There was a bizarre performance at The English Disco in August '74 entitled 'Murder of the Virgin', in which a whip-wielding Ron Asheton wore a Nazi uniform, while Iggy pulled out a butcher's knife and slashed up his own chest. (It was an anticlimax for those led to believe that the show would end with Iggy killing himself onstage.) Iggy's behaviour got so erratic that he submitted to an enforced period of observation and treatment in the Neuropsychiatric Institute at UCLA. For a while he lived in an abandoned garage, shoplifting for food.

'I was pretty untogether at the time,' Iggy recalled. 'This was my lowest ebb. No one wanted to work with me.' Then Iggy 'ran into Bowie again, literally, in the street'. Bowie generously invited his ailing friend to come with him to Europe. There, they would both kick drugs and Bowie would produce a solo album to relaunch Iggy's career.

It seems likely that the association of Europe in general, and Germany in particular, with 'cleanliness', renewal, a fresh start, owed a good deal to the music Bowie was listening to at that time: Krautrock. 'I was a big fan of Kraftwerk, Cluster and Harmonia,' Bowie recalled in 1997, mentioning also Neu!, Can and Tangerine Dream man Edgar Froese's solo album *Epsilon in Malaysian Pale* as his favoured listening. By comparison, punk rock – in late '75 and early '76 emerging with things like the first Ramones album – seemed to Bowie like a blast from rock's past. 'I had absolutely no doubt where the future of music was going . . . for me it was coming out of Germany.' For Bowie, Krautrock offered pointers to a post-glam sound (and possibly a post-fame career). Indeed, the German approach could hardly have been less glam: mostly making instrumental music and leaning towards longer tracks, the Krautrock bands were un-pop, imageless and non-theatrical in their stage presentation.

Bowie was particularly taken with Neu!, enthusing about their self-titled debut album as 'just gigantically wonderful'. The group's sound was as bright and awake as the name Neu! – a euphoric surge through glistening vistas of wide-open possibility. Bowie was 'completely seduced by the setting [of Michael Rother's] aggressive guitar-drone against the almost-but-not-quite robotic/machine drumming of [Klaus] Dinger'.

But while Neu! still retained rock's electric guitar and human drumming, Kraftwerk ventured even further into a post-rock future, their serene electronic landscapes propelled forward by steady drum-machine rhythms and synth pulses. 'What I was passionate about in relation to Kraftwerk was their singular determination to stand apart from stereotypical American chord sequences and their wholehearted embrace of a European sensibility,' Bowie recalled. He was such a fan of *Autobahn*, Kraftwerk's 1974 breakthrough album – whose title track became an unexpected hit single in mid-1975 – that he asked the group to join the *Station to Station* tour of North America and Europe.

That never happened. But Kraftwerk would later slip a name-check into 'Trans-Europe Express': 'From station to station back to Düsseldorf city / Meet Iggy Pop and David Bowie.' The song, even the entire *Trans-Europe Express* album, could be imagined as a gift to their famous fan, since he'd told them about listening to their music while travelling across America by train. In the black-and-white promo film for the single, Schneider, Hütter and the other Kraftwerk members resemble a time capsule from out of Bowie's fantasies of the German twenties: debonair in their hats and leather gloves, the quartet travel in a train compartment past a cityscape that finds the sweet spot between *Metropolis* and art deco. The

Thin White Duke would fit right next to these gentlemen travelling in style.

One of the mysteries of glam is the relative lack of a European response artistically (as opposed to European pop fans, who lapped it up). Bowie-indebted performers cropped up here and there; there was a fair amount of stompy Slade/Sweet emulation in northern Europe. But there is a case to be made that the one significant European contribution to glam was Kraftwerk. Their trajectory parallels Bowie and Roxy. Fans of The Velvet Underground, The Stooges and the New York minimalist avant-garde, Florian Schneider and Ralf Hütter initially started in the progressive underground, composing extended instrumentals dominated by Schneider's flute. But from *Autobahn* onwards the group focused their music around songs and dance rhythms, becoming a smash in discotheques worldwide and intermittently infiltrating the pop charts. Especially after they acquired an image consultant in the form of artist Emil Schult, Kraftwerk were stylish and stylised, dropping their early longhair look for a between-the-wars formality.

Like Roxy, their futurism had a retro quality. Even as their mechano-disko beats and synth melodies invented the future – Kraftwerk sired eighties synth pop and electro, nineties techno and trance – the group's song themes and album covers harked back to the early twentieth century, invoking everything from Soviet modernist graphics to the days when radio was a new medium. There was a homoerotic tinge, too, to the restrained elegance of Kraftwerk's image: clean-shaven, short hair, suits and ties. This was especially so on the sleeve of *The Man-Machine*, where they wore lipstick, while *Trans-Europe Express*'s front cover resembled a touched-up thirties publicity shot for a vocal-harmony group. Kraftwerk's bachelor-machine, robot-musician image could be seen as a glam strategy: a mask they hid behind, protecting their privacy. One press conference was conducted by mannequin-like dummies that bore their likenesses.

Mirror image: Kraftwerk's Florian Schneider and Ralf Hütter confront their mannequin doppelgängers at a 1 January 1978 promotional event for *The Man-Machine* in New York

Kraftwerk also recorded one of pop's greatest songs about glamour, 'The Hall of Mirrors'. It appears on the same album as the Iggy-and-Bowie salute 'Trans-Europe Express', and like that song could be construed as a gift to their famous friend. Or a discreet piece of advice, since the song is about the distortions of personality induced by fame. Based around a reverberating synth pattern that spirals endlessly over a trudging rhythm, the song is a twentieth-century retelling of the Narcissus myth. 'Even the greatest stars / Discover themselves in the looking glass,' Hütter intones portentously. But when the star falls in love with his own image, the picture – and the personality – gets warped.

Kraftwerk's line about the star making up 'the person he wanted to be' and changing 'into a new personality' seems inspired by Bowie. But the song is also about Kraftwerk's discomfort with the attention that came with pop success. Although the song's title suggests the funfair house of mirrors, it's also probably a reference to the Hall of

Mirrors at the Palace of Versailles. This gallery was the setting for costume balls and weddings, processions and pageants of every kind. If Kraftwerk intended the resonance with Versailles (and German counterparts like Munich's baroque Nymphenburg Palace), 'Hall of Mirrors' is about fame as the twentieth century's replacement for royalty: splendour that those of lowly birth can attain.

The next song on *Trans-Europe Express* extends the theme of vanity and voyeurism. 'Showroom Dummies' is about mannequins who tire of being looked at, smash through the department store window and go out clubbing, losing themselves in the dancefloor crowd. 'In the disco, the spotlight is on everybody,' Hütter told *Melody Maker*. 'Unlike concerts where you see only the star of the show and everyone else is in the dark.' The third panel of Kraftwerk's glam triptych arrived on the next album, *The Man-Machine*, in the form of 'The Model': this beauty-for-hire feigns weariness with being photographed, but 'it only takes a camera to change her mind'.

In the end, Kraftwerk were not so much glam as an intermittent commentary on glamour and its commodification. They used their android image as a shield against stardom, a way of navigating pop while staying separate from it. 'The whole ego aspect of music is boring,' Hütter declared. 'In Germany in the thirties we had a system of superstardom with Mr Adolf from Austria and so there is no interest for me in this "cult of personality".' Perhaps Bowie saw in Kraftwerk – and the even more imageless Neu!– a way out of the mirrored maze of his own stardom.

Considering how much he admired the new German music – and the old German culture of the twenties that was terminated by the Third Reich with its crackdown on 'degenerate art' and its book burnings – Bowie paved the way for his arrival in Berlin in a strange way. Over the course of a dozen or so interviews, he made a series of deliriously unguarded, deeply questionable public statements about Hitler, Nazism and the urgent necessity of strong, dictatorial leadership in the UK and the West generally. Although in later years he would present cocaine's effect on his mental state as an extenuating circumstance, or plead artistic licence, Bowie's remarks don't read as addled provocations. They are so frequent, so articulately argued, so consistently *excited* in tone, it's hard to avoid concluding that Bowie had developed a morbid fascination with fascism.

The interest in totalitarian dystopias and the supposed occult leanings of the Third Reich went back many years. But it all started to take on a fixated quality somewhere between *Diamond Dogs* (with its 'This ain't rock'n'roll . . . this is genocide' opening cry) and *Young Americans*. The latter's 'Somebody Up There Likes Me' was a warning about hero worship. 'What I've said for years under various guises is that "Watch Out, the West is going to have a Hitler!"' Bowie told an interviewer in late 1974, before alluding to how at certain moments in his own recent stardom, 'I could see how easy it was to get a whole rally thing going. There were times . . . when I could have told the audience to do anything.'

Over the course of subsequent interviews, however, Bowie's twin concern about a new Hitler and his own slippage into the role of charismatic cult leader seemed to slide into outright admiration for the Führer as a showman. He even compared Hitler to Jagger. 'Boy, when he hit that stage, he worked an audience. Good God! He was no politician. He was a media artist himself. He used politics and theatrics and created this thing that governed and controlled the show for those 12 years. The world will never see his like. He staged a country.'

This idea of Hitler as the first rock star – framed in Speer's cathedral of light, whipping his audience into a frenzy with oratory and gesture – wasn't a new one among Bowie's circle. Former Mott producer Guy Stevens had recently told the music press about his plans for a band called Raw Glory ('the Final, Total, Heavy Metal Assault . . . unless it's Blitzkrieg, forget it!'), hailing Hitler as 'the first rock'n'roll operator'.

Bowie, however, personally experienced the rock star–Führer affinity. 'Everybody was convincing me that I was a Messiah,' he told Cameron Crowe in 1975, for a *Rolling Stone* profile published the following year. 'I got hopelessly lost in the fantasy. I could have been Hitler in England . . . Concerts alone got so enormously frightening that even the papers were saying, "This ain't rock music, this is bloody Hitler!"' As he rambled on, he got lost in another thicket of fantasy, imagining how 'I might have been a bloody good Hitler . . . an excellent dictator. Very eccentric and quite mad . . . I wouldn't mind being the first English president of the United States either. I'm certainly right wing enough . . . I'll bloody lead this country, make it a great fucking nation.' Later in the same conversation, he upped the ante from the US to the entire globe: 'I do want to rule the world.'

A year later, in a separate interview with Crowe, this time for *Playboy*, Bowie was still harping on about his desire to enter politics but had modified the ambition to establishing 'my own country first . . . create the state that I wish to live in'. Not mincing words, Bowie declared he believed 'very strongly in fascism': in his view, 'a rightwing, totally dictatorial tyranny' was the only way to blast away the fog of 'liberalism that's hanging foul in the air at the moment'.

This was a running theme of his interviews in 1975–6: dictatorship as the next big thing, 'a political figure in the not too distant future who'll sweep this part of the world like early rock and roll did'. But unlike the alarmism of 'Somebody Up There Likes Me, Bowie now welcomed the 'extreme right front' that would come along to 'sweep everything off its feet and tidy everything up'.

In the earlier Crowe feature for *Rolling Stone*, Bowie characterised pop culture itself as the Weimar decadence that would bring upon itself its own comeuppance. He called for 'a very medieval, firm-handed masculine God awareness where we go out and make the world right again', a short sharp shock of discipline dispatching the permissive society and its soundtrack: that 'musical soma' disco and the 'devil's music' that was rock, with its incitement of 'lower elements and shadows'. Echoing the 1972 Dorchester hotel press conference in which he presented himself and Lou Reed as decadence personified, Bowie said that 'with our makeup and funny clothes . . . we're only heralding something even darker than ourselves'. In August 1975, he talked enigmatically about his plan 'to do something that's actively concerned with trying to clear up the mess', saying that 'the morals should be straightened up for a start'. In another interview from this period, Bowie spoke with apparent admiration of 'two bands now who come close to a neo-Nazi kind of thing – Roxy Music and Kraftwerk'.

Despite this string of inflammatory utterances, it was a Swedish newspaper interview in the spring of 1976 that finally blew the flirting-with-fascism story wide open. Offering himself as the only alternative candidate for prime minister, Bowie announced that 'I believe Britain could benefit from a fascist leader.' He paused to clarify, explaining that he meant fascism 'in its true sense', rather than Nazism. 'Fascism is really nationalism. In a sense, it's a very pure form of communism.' Perhaps even these statements would have passed without major repercussions, if it wasn't for the 2 May incident at Victoria station.

Arriving on the Orient Express, looking at his most Thin White Duke-like, Bowie then boarded his favourite mode of transport: a black Mercedes with an open-top back seat – the same car used by Hitler. When Bowie stood up to greet the throng from the back of the car, the tableau was uncomfortably redolent of the Führer's mode of addressing his troops. One widely seen photo appeared to capture a hand-wave that in frozen form could be construed as a *Sieg Heil*.

Immediately following the media furore inflamed by this (probably unintended) gesture and the circulation of damning quotes from
the Swedish newspaper piece, Bowie attempted damage control
and image repair. 'What I'm doing is Theatre, and only Theatre,' he
wheedled to *Daily Express* columnist Jean Rook. 'I'm using myself
as a canvas and trying to paint the truth of our time on it. The white
face, the baggy pants – they're Pierrot, the eternal clown putting
over the great sadness of 1976.' He affected hurt astonishment that
anyone could have taken his comments seriously: 'I'm not sinister.
I'm not a great force . . . I don't stand up in cars waving to people
because I think I'm Hitler.'

Bowie made out that he barely remembered having made the
comments to the Swedish journalist, who'd been probing him
relentlessly for political opinions. Yet the obsession with strong
leadership actually went back years. In December 1969, he had
informed *Music Now!* that Britain was 'crying out for a leader' and
pinpointed as the only likely candidate Enoch Powell, the renegade
Conservative politician whose apocalyptic speeches about the dangers of immigration had made him the darling of the racist right.

By 1976, Powell's anti-multicultural views were back at the forefront of British politics, with the rise of the National Front both as
an electoral force and in terms of their street presence (demonstra-
tions and marches provocatively organised to pass through urban
areas with large numbers of ethnic minorities). That summer, Eric
Clapton's drunken onstage rant about the country being overrun by
dark-skinned foreigners (during which he said that Enoch was right
all along) catalysed the formation of Rock Against Racism. Bowie's
statements were timely in the oddest way, tuning into vibrations in
the culture, as he so often did. In a country beset by strikes, power
cuts, terrorist attacks, shortages in supermarkets and unprecedented
levels of inflation, some worried whether British democracy could
survive. Others believed it might have to be dispensed with, to save

the nation. Bowie's calls for a strong leader were uncomfortably in synch with the chatter about emergency measures – military coups, private armies – to restore order, standards and security.

Pundits often made an analogy between this no-longer-Great Britain and the Weimar Republic, with its hyper-inflation, collapsing morals and hard-left and hard-right militias sparring in the streets. Bowie seemed to be equally stimulated by both sides of the historical struggle: Weimar decadence and the crackdown that followed. Both strains of sympathy ran through his work concurrently.

The Nazi chic had popped up in songs like 1970's 'The Supermen' and 'Quicksand', with its reference to 'Himmler's sacred realm'. There was an unreleased early version of 'Candidate' from *Diamond Dogs* on which he referred to himself as 'the Führerling', while his verbal mood board of stage-set ideas for the *Dogs* tour encompassed 'tanks, turbines, smokestacks . . . watchtowers, girders, beams, Albert Speer'.

Most bizarrely, there was the little matter of the Goebbels musical. When he was travelling around Europe, with Iggy as sidekick, during the spring of 1976, Bowie paid a brief visit to Moscow. At the Polish–Russian border, he and Iggy were detained by the KGB and their luggage searched. Biographies of Albert Speer and Josef Goebbels were confiscated. Bowie explained he was doing research for a musical about the life of the Nazi minister for propaganda. Although the concept inevitably summons up the memory of *Springtime for Hitler*, the musical deliberately designed to lose money in Mel Brooks's *The Producers*, Bowie was serious about the idea – and who knows, if he'd pulled it off, he might have beaten *Evita* to the punch.

Bowie was genuinely drawn to Goebbels, describing him as 'an extraordinary guy. He used the media the way nobody used it.' Goebbels certainly did sound like a modern political consultant and spin doctor when he talked, in his famous 'total war' speech of 1943

– which rallied the German people to make fresh sacrifices after the setback of Stalingrad – of how it was vital to take account of 'the war's optics'. Bars, nightclubs, fancy restaurants, luxury boutiques – all must be closed because 'they disturb the image of the war'.

Iggy Pop had his own affinities with that cloudy region of Romanticism that lurks midway between Nietzsche and Nazism. His expression of these tendencies took a militaristic rather than magical cast, though, oriented towards heroic physical tests like putting his body on the line onstage rather than the cerebral symbol-play that Bowie indulged. In the late seventies, Iggy would describe himself as 'a leader who does not want to be followed' and 'exactly the man who Friedrich Nietzsche could only write about' – that's to say, the superman. Around the same time, he put out albums with titles like *Soldier* and *New Values* (a concept taken from *Thus Spake Zarathustra*: new values are what the *übermensch* will create to fill the nihilistic vacuum left by the death of God). But in the mid-seventies, Iggy had a hell of a lot of what Nietzsche called 'self-overcoming' to do before he achieved his ideal state of laser-focused will. As he noted of his wasted LA daze, 'I was trying to be a hero without heroic qualities. My heart was in the right place, but the rest of me was out to lunch.'

Iggy and Bowie were very much on the same wavelength in 1976, indicated by the lyrics 'I stumble into town just like a sacred cow / Visions of swastikas in my head, plans for everyone' from 'China Girl' off *The Idiot* – Iggy's debut solo album, produced by Bowie, in Europe.

How you feel about *The Idiot* probably depends on the sequence in which you encountered Iggy's work. If, like me, you're neuro-logically wedded to the unleashed Iggy of *The Stooges* and *Fun*

House – the sound of Dionysian oblivion merged with the military-industrial complex – you'll never be entirely comfortable with the poise and control that Bowie encouraged Iggy to adopt for *The Idiot*. 'I was working on the lyrics to "Funtime" and David said, "Yeah, the words are good. But don't sing it like a rock guy,"' Iggy recalled. '"Sing it like Mae West." Which made it informed of other genres, like cinema. Also, it was a little bit gay. The vocals there became more menacing as a result of that suggestion.'

For my money, the one unqualified success of the un-rocked Iggy on *Idiot* is 'Nightclubbing'. Brecht-y and bluesy, dirge-like but swinging, it's one of a number of tunes on *The Idiot* that assimilate the mechanistic feel of Kraftwerk and the other German groups Bowie was so into. But overall, Stooges fans keep waiting for Iggy to cut loose. There had been moments on Stooges records where Iggy crooned sonorously – the stoned Sinatra of 'Ann' on the first album, the lustrous lassitude of 'Dirt' on *Fun House*. But too often on *The Idiot* it feels like he's been forced to wear a tux and bow tie, and the effect is haggard and enervated, or like he's crooning through a belch. The only trace of Detroit is 'Dum Dum Boys', where at Bowie's suggestion Iggy told the story of The Stooges, asking plaintively, 'Where are you now when I need your noise?'

Still, *The Idiot* was hugely influential. The jump from *Raw Power* to this suppressed, inhibited style resonated with British post-punk bands like Magazine and Joy Division. Recorded at Château d'Hérouville in France and finished off at Munich's Musicland, *The Idiot* served as a preparation for Bowie's own giant step forward with *Low*, the first of his 'Berlin Triptych' albums. 'Poor Jim, in a way, became a guinea pig for what I wanted to do with sound,' Bowie admitted later. The border between the two albums was fuzzy, with some backing tracks and unfinished songs from the *Idiot* sessions going into Bowie's album.

This radical new direction had actually stirred before he and Iggy reached Europe. Bowie had been lined up to record an all-new score for *The Man Who Fell to Earth*, but this had fallen apart owing to various business wranglings, as well as doubts on the part of the director and other executives about the early demo tracks Bowie laid down. The score was ultimately provided by John Phillips, formerly of The Mamas and the Papas. But the tentative direction pursued for the abortive Bowie soundtrack – 'slow and spacey cues with synth, Rhodes and cello' and 'a couple of weirder, atonal cues using synths and percussion', according to Paul Buckmaster, who worked on the sessions – would blossom with *Low*.

Bowie's ambition was signalled by the record's working title: *New Music Night and Day*. The line-up was an augmented version of the *Station to Station* team: guitarist Ricky Gardiner and pianist Roy Young joined Carlos Alomar, George Murray and Dennis Davis. Tony Visconti produced. But the crucial X-factor at work on the album was a figure whose musical function was shifting and imprecise: Brian Eno. In those songs where he directly contributes, Eno generally plays a different instrument or set of instruments each time, some of them bearing faintly fantastical names. (What's a 'Splinter Mini-Moog'?) Sometimes he reverts to a role like the one he played in early Roxy Music, providing 'guitar treatments'; on another song, he just sings backing vocals. But Eno's most crucial contribution to *Low* – something that assumed even more importance on the two other Berlin albums, *"Heroes"* and *Lodger* – is as aesthetic adviser and accomplice in sonic adventure, a genial catalyst for Bowie to go further out-there.

In a funny sort of way, Eno provided the 'German' element that Bowie originally intended to get directly through collaborating with musicians like Edgar Froese (who was invited to a recording session, hung around for hours, but mystifyingly never got the call to the studio). Eno had already, in 1974, studio-jammed with Harmonia, the supergroup formed by Neu!'s Michael Rother and Cluster's Dieter

Moebius and Hans-Joachim Roedelius. Later, he would collaborate
with Cluster on a trilogy of brilliant albums.

When it came to his post-Roxy solo work, Eno was operating from
a similar headspace as the Germans: phasing out vocals or relegat-
ing them to a low-in-the-mix textural role, exploring structures and
instrumental line-ups and rhythms that increasingly had nothing to
do with rock. He had started out with two song-oriented solo LPs,
Here Come the Warm Jets and *Taking Tiger Mountain (By Strategy)*,
that in retrospect form the historical thread between Syd Barrett-
style psychedelic whimsy and the geeky-goofy side of new wave.
Eno's image, especially on the cover of *Warm Jets*, was still glammy:
lipstick, long fair hair, a shiny choker around his throat. But by
1975's *Another Green World*, he'd shaved his balding hair short and
started wearing non-flashy clothes of the kind a visual artist might
wear for a day's messy activity in the studio. And the music he was
making was sound-painterly: mostly instrumental, captivating the
ear with its textures and atmosphere more than its rhythm-drive or
melodic insistence. The studio was where it was at for Eno, where
the magic happened; a brief, nerve-shredding tour to promote the
solo debut, backed by a high-energy outfit called The Winkies, had
convinced him that live performance did not agree with him.

The path Eno chose – jettisoning pop stardom for a cult-figure
career as a nomadic experimentalist – showed Bowie an alluring
alternative to his current existence. He loved what Eno had done
on *Another Green World*, which joined the German groups as his
favoured listening while touring in America. He also dug *Discreet
Music*, on which Eno used tape-loop delay systems to create a
subtly shifting cloud of sound. Music that essentially played itself,
Discreet Music's evacuation of ego appealed to Bowie's Buddhist
side. It was a step towards ambient music – background sound as
an atmospheric tint, a mood-vapour – which Eno would invent on
1978's *Music for Airports*. A radical break with pop's demand for

faces, focus, energy, events, Eno's music pointed to a way forward and a life beyond glam.

Bowie's and Eno's separate evolution as artists overlapped in various ways. For his solo LPs, Eno convened motley line-ups of artists drawn from across the genre landscape rather than setting out with a sonic concept and then choosing musicians to fulfil it. His creativity took the form of organising social-musical encounters that generated unforeseen 'aural outcomes'. Bowie took a similar approach with the three Berlin LPs: according to Eno, 'David knew that putting certain players together would create an over-all context *automatically.*'

During the Berlin recordings, Bowie would try other techniques that Eno had come up with, like his ruses to push highly trained players out of their comfort zone. Instead of asking them to play specific notes or riffs or keys (something beyond him as a non-musician), Eno triggered their imaginations by suggesting they 'play' landscapes, animals, weather patterns or surreal scenarios. This didn't always go down well with the professionals: guitarist Alomar, in particular, was derisive about some of these ploys. Another Eno invention that came into play on *"Heroes"* and *Lodger* was Oblique Strategies: a pack of cards with open-ended instructions or advice ('Honour thy error as a hidden intention'; 'Is it finished?') designed to help artists out of creative blocks or jolt them into making arbitrary decisions. Eno described the Strategies and various other structures/strictures that he set up as 'tricks and subterfuges that I use to create an accidental situation . . . to defeat bits of me, or amplify bits of me . . . I'm looking to reduce my conscious intervention and get the intuitive parts of me going.'

Bowie and Eno had also ended up in the same place when it came to the role of words, though for different reasons. Mild in temperament, fundamentally well adjusted, methodical in his creative practice, Eno struggled with his lack of . . . well, *struggle*: there weren't any emotional or social-political statements that he felt a burning need to vent. He confessed to the *NME* that song lyrics were 'a problem in that I didn't have anything to say. I didn't have a message and I didn't have experiences that I felt strongly enough to want to write about.' Eno sidestepped this deficit by generating what he called 'picture-lyrics', often dreamy landscapes in which oddly passive characters seemed drained of will and agency. Or he'd emit nonsense syllables that he gradually formed into words that sounded good and were fun to sing but didn't necessarily make any sense.

Quite different from Eno in disposition – a tortured Romantic who swung between grandiosity and self-loathing – Bowie like-wise found himself 'literally stuck for words', but for other reasons: depression and inner emptiness. Leaving Los Angeles, he realised 'how little I knew, how little I had to say'. Where his earlier albums were crammed with lyrics (*Diamond Dogs* contained over 2,000 words), *Low* was virtually aphasic: Bowie scholar Hugo Wilcken points out that it has only 410 words on its lyric sheet. Over half of the album consisted of instrumentals or near-instrumentals featur-ing wordless vocals. Even the supposedly song-oriented first side starts and ends with an instrumental. 'Sound and Vision', the single off the album – an unexpectedly big hit in the UK, reaching #3 – takes a minute and a half before Bowie even opens his mouth.

Abandoning his previous modes – the character song, the mini-screenplay song, the digest-of-esoteric-reading song – Bowie here seems naked, unable to hide behind masks or personae. *Low* is a scatter of emotional shards, the broken vessel of a man. According to psychoanalytic theorist Julia Kristeva, melancholia disables lan-guage, makes it difficult to verbalise emotions and thus manage them; depressive speech falters, trails off unfinished, struggles against sinking into the silent black. Bowie's singing style also changed on *Low*: mostly sticking to a lower register, it doesn't soar or show off. 'Be My Wife', subdued and artless in its naked ache, is a long way from the mannered dramatics of 'Wild Is the Wind'.

For all its glum disorientation, *Low*'s first side is energetic and brisk: 'seven quite manic disco numbers' is how Eno described it to the *NME*. But the groove and ease of *Young Americans* tunes like 'Right' or *Station*'s 'Golden Years' and 'TVC-15' has been left behind. *Low* exists in a new era; it somehow invents post-punk before punk even got properly started.

The album's nervous, brittle feel comes in large part from its legendary drum sound, created using a machine called the Eventide Harmoniser. Producer Tony Visconti oversold the device to Bowie with the claim that 'it fucks with the fabric of time'. Basically, it alters the pitch of instruments in real time, rather than using after-the-event slowing down or speeding up of tape. The effect as used on *Low* texturises the drums in a way that makes them jut obtrusively through the mix, a snap and crash perfect for songs sung by a man who seems to have no skin.

Sometimes these songs lose a little of their intrigue when you find out the humble specificity of what inspired them. 'Breaking Glass', a snapshot of relationship conflict, warns 'don't look at the carpet': apparently that's an allusion to a Kabbalistic diagram drawn by Bowie on the floor. (I prefer my three-decades-old mishearing of the lyric as 'I've done something awful on it.') Likewise 'Always Crashing in the Same Car' works better as a vague image of someone caught in a life-loop, repeating addictive-obsessive behaviours with the same outcome, rather than the literal truth, which is something to do with Bowie ramming his Mercedes over and over into the car of a devious drug dealer.

But with 'Be My Wife' the transparently autobiographical misery is affecting. 'I've lived all over the world / I've left every place,' Bowie sings, but 'sometimes it gets so lonely', so please 'share my life'. After this emotional abyss, the only way is up: side one of *Low* goes out with the frail optimism of 'A New Career in a New Town', a painfully bright and brisk instrumental flashing by like a landscape through train windows.

The brilliance of *Low*'s first half is no preparation for the 'expressionist mood pieces' (Bowie's phrase) that make up side two. Here's where the promise of the working title's 'New Music' is really fulfilled. These four anguished atmospheres are a tantalising glimpse of what the score to *The Man Who Fell to Earth* could have been. (Bowie sent *Low* to Roeg with a note saying, 'This is what I wanted to do for you.') You could even imagine this music as the album *in* the movie that we never get to hear, made by alien Thomas Jerome Newton's alter ego, The Visitor. Certainly there are precious few terrestrial precedents for the genre Bowie invents here.

When Eno joined Bowie and his team at Hansa Studio 1, near the Berlin Wall, much of *Low*'s first side had been partially laid down in sessions at the Château d'Hérouville. So it was on the second side that Eno's X-factor really came into play. Using a variety of synths (including the Chamberlin, a tape-based playback keyboard in the Mellotron mode, and the EMS AKS, a synth in a briefcase that you controlled with a joystick), Eno draped glistening swathes of gloomy texture over tracks like 'Art Decade' and 'Warszawa'. The former's title sounds like a nod to the twenties, the period of German culture that obsessed Bowie, but 'decade' also suggests 'decayed' – just right for the piece's dank twilight sound. 'Warszawa' was inspired by 'the very bleak atmosphere' Bowie had picked up when his train made its stop–start progress through Poland's capital on the way to the Soviet Union.

Most of the *Low* side-two tracks have real-world correlates: 'Weeping Wall', as you'd probably guess, was inspired by the Berlin Wall ('the misery of it', Bowie told *Record Mirror*), while 'Subterraneans' is meant to evoke the plight of those inhabitants 'who got caught in East Berlin after the separation'. But listeners will irresistibly – and rightfully – generate their own mind-pictures in response to these three-dimensional soundscapes. Although *Low*'s second side is generally thought of as instrumental music, three of the four tracks feature Bowie's voice. But on 'Warszawa' his singing is wordless, its ecstatic mournfulness influenced by a record of a Balkan boys' choir that Eno had brought to Berlin. 'Subterraneans' features recognisably English words that make no sense: 'Share bride failing star / Care-line care-line care-line care-line.' Bowie's twinkling vocal makes them seem more like a lost or invented language, a magical incantation or centuries-old children's nonsense rhyme.

The album's title obviously signifies low spirits, the state of being laid low. 'I was at the end of my tether physically and emotionally and had serious doubts about my sanity,' Bowie said of this period. *Low* also suggests 'low profile', an escape from the limelight into the shadows, as 'Golden Years' had proposed. Bowie's move to Berlin was meant to bring him back down to earth, ground him in mundane realities, like having to buy his own food from Turkish grocers. Not that he would have been doing a huge amount of shopping for provisions: according to Eno, Bowie was surviving on a single raw egg per day, cracked straight into his mouth after coming home from all-night studio sessions.

Still, part of the restorative effect of Berlin was that he was able to walk or cycle around the city unrecognised, or politely ignored. The people of Berlin, Bowie told *Rolling Stone*, were 'very matter-of-fact about celebrities . . . It makes it a very good place for someone like me to live, because I can be incredibly anonymous. You never get stopped here. They don't seem particularly joyful about seeing a famous face.' This compared favourably with LA's 'killing kind of sycophancy'.

In his essay 'On Narcissism', Freud writes that paranoia's symptoms include 'delusions of being noticed' and 'delusions of being watched'. But if you're famous, all these things are actually happening: reality itself is driving you mad. Bowie's time in Germany provided respite from the public's gaze. 'Berlin was my clinic,' he recalled. 'It brought me back in touch with people. But I would still have days when things were moving round the room even when I was sober. It took two years to cleanse my system.' He was effectively in rehab, recovering from both drugs and fame. It was very much like those rest cures for neurasthenia and other ailments that the wealthy once took in coastal resorts or high-altitude retreats – except that Bowie picked a harsh urban environment and worked non-stop as his route back to psychic and physical health.

Yet there was a sense in which Bowie's Berlin was still a narcissistic projection, a stage for the self. 'As a city, it seemed to be a macrocosm of my own state of mind,' he said. 'I thought it would be a good thing to place myself in a context resembling myself and see what came of it.' Berlin, he said in a 1979 TV interview, offered 'the kind of friction' he was looking for: people there 'lived with the idea of collapse at any minute', and as a result didn't 'tolerate flippancy . . . It's a very tight life.'

Writing about Bowie-in-Berlin in his book *Heroes*, Tobias Rüther observes that the areas of the city in which the singer lived and worked amounted to 'a cross-section of his world of images'. Bowie's apartment in Schöneberg was a kilometre and a half from the Nollendorfplatz area where Isherwood had lived – a neighbourhood associated since the twenties with gay life, a location for *Kabarett* nightclubs like Eldorado. Schöneberg was also where Marlene Dietrich grew up. But Berlin as a whole was also encrusted with historical traces of the Third Reich. 'It's such an ambiguous place – it's hard to distinguish between the ghosts and the living,' Bowie told *Vogue* in 1978.

Just as Bowie had semi-consciously constructed his experience of Los Angeles, he was selective when it came to what Berlin had to offer. In the seventies, the city was a hive of counterculture. Bowie had minimal interaction with this longhair, left-wing side of Berlin. Perhaps it was too much like things he had encountered in the late sixties – arts labs, communes, squats, free festivals – and ultimately rejected.

He was out of step with late-seventies Berlin in other ways: it's hard to imagine that his 'strong leaders' spiels of that era would have endeared him to a radical generation whose entire cultural outlook was organised around the promotion of an anti-fascist life. For the most militant West German youth, their protests against militarism were linked to a feeling that de-Nazification had not been thorough-going enough. Third Reich fellow travellers had resurfaced in authority positions in post-war public life, like industrialist Hanns Martin Schleyer, a former SS officer and Nazi party member who by the seventies was president of the Confederation of German Employers' Associations.

Avoiding the hippy radicals and the new punk clubs, which he found boring, Bowie was drawn to the elements in Berlin life that most corresponded to his Weimar fantasies – such as the cabaret scene reigned over by his new muse, the drag queen Romy Haag. The latter's club, Chez Romy Haag, was located in a bar that had been more or less intact since the twenties: according to Angie Bowie, stepping inside was 'like going back decades, the Berlin of Christopher Isherwood, the glory days of avant cabaret before Adolf'.

Bowie was also drawn to German Expressionism, frequently visiting the Brücke Museum to see work by artists like Ernst Ludwig Kirchner, Fritz Bleyl and Emil Nolde. He took up painting himself, imitating the stark strokes of these painters, who were influenced by primitivist art and medieval woodcuts. The Expressionist obsession fed into the black-and-white artwork for his next album, "Heroes", where Bowie's angular gestures and autistic stare were reminiscent of Erich Heckel's portrait of Kirchner, his colleague in Die Brücke movement.

"Heroes" was the only one of the Berlin triptych to be recorded from start to finish in the city. The album is dominated, eclipsed even, by its title track. It was recorded in Hansa's large, wood-floored Studio 2 (Bowie nicknamed it the Big Hall by the Wall), whose reverberant properties helped to create the track's feeling of epic scale. Against the backdrop of golden-guitar streaks and silver-synth swirls, Bowie's vocal is poised at first – matching the stately glide of the rhythm – but then vaults into drama. His voice sounds wrenched and overwrought, verging on off-key – the first sign of an impulse to uglify his vocals that would become a painful, too-sharp screech on parts of *Lodger* and *Scary Monsters*. But here, on '"Heroes"', it works, resulting in a sort of uplifting dirge.

The influence of Neu! is overwhelmingly present. Bowie must have known about their track 'Hero' on *Neu! 75*: an exhilarating blast and blare of chord-strum and wind-tunnel vocals. The song's protagonist hurtles – on a motorbike or in a car, it's not clear – across the city, pained by some kind of romantic injury: 'just another hero riding through the night'. The billowing agitation of the guitars on Bowie's '"Heroes"' also *sounds* like the 'flaming heart' of Michael Rother's 1977 solo album *Flammende Herzen*. Bowie had actually contacted the ex-Neu! guitarist with a view to him playing on *"Heroes"*. There was mutual interest, but this never transpired. So on '"Heroes"' the tapestry was a three-weave mesh of Robert Fripp's controlled feedback, Carlos Alomar's melodic stitch-work and Eno's tremolo-juddering synth (so crucial he earned a co-credit on the song). Fripp flew in for a two-day, no-sleep burst of creativity and, straight off the plane, did three takes of '"Heroes"'; Tony Visconti blended all three together in the mix.

Recalling the session later in 1977, Eno told the *NME* that he had only been involved on the backing track, which was laid down before Bowie conceived the melody and lyric (the method used for all the song-based tunes on *"Heroes"*, in fact). 'When I left, I already had a feeling about that track – it sounded grand and heroic. In fact, I had that very word in mind.' When Bowie brought the finished album to Eno's London home to play it, he heard the line 'we can be heroes' with a cold rush of retroactive clairvoyance: 'I was absolutely . . . It was such a strange feeling . . . I just shivered with . . . When you shiver, it's a fear reaction, isn't it?'

Bowie said he found his theme when he observed the regular meetings of a boy and girl through the Hansa Studio windows. Every lunch break the couple would rendezvous at the foot of the Berlin Wall. In Bowie's mind, these were clandestine trysts: 'They were obviously having an affair. And I thought of all the places to meet in Berlin, why pick a bench underneath a guard turret on the wall?' Projecting more than a little (after all, the place might just have been equidistant between their respective work places), Bowie decided that the couple chose to meet there 'to cause the affair to be an act of heroism'. (Another more banal version has it that it was actually Visconti furtively meeting a woman who was not his wife.)

Kissing in the shadow of the Wall was a dramatic staging of life, taking something commonplace and giving it grandeur by 'facing that kind of reality' – Berlin as a city split in twain by geopolitical, world-historical forces – 'and standing up to it' by getting on 'with life'. This was pure Bowie, a new flowering of his long-running, con-flicted desire to be extraordinary. 'I always had a repulsive sort of need to be something more than human,' he confessed to Cameron Crowe in 1975. 'I felt very very puny as a human. I thought, "Fuck that. I want to be a superman."' In another interview, he talked about the dread of being insignificant, which meant he could never be happy being just 'a good person . . . just another honest Joe. I want to be a supersuperbeing.'

These comments – and the use of the word 'repulsive', indicat-ing self-disgust and shame – suggest Bowie was aware of the anti-egalitarian aspect of this titanic impulse. In *The Image*, Daniel

Boorstin connects an obsession with the Hero – both the lionising of heroes and the desire to be heroic yourself – with 'a contempt for democracy'. One example Boorstin cites is Thomas Carlyle, whose 1841 book *On Heroes, Hero-Worship, and The Heroic in History* is a rousing celebration of prophets, poets and philosophers, but also leaders like Cromwell and Napoleon. Carlyle's authoritarian paeans to *Hero*archy, as he punningly dubbed it, are regarded by some as having laid the intellectual foundations for fascism. But even a socialist like George Orwell recognised the emotional appeal of hero rhetoric. Fascism, he wrote, is 'psychologically far sounder than any hedonistic conception of life', swaying the people with ennobling offers of 'struggle, danger, and death' rather than raised standards of living or 'a good time'.

Bowie had gone down this road recently with his 'strong leader' spiels. The song '"Heroes"' scales down to a democratic revision of what heroism could be: small acts of defiance or self-sacrifice that puncture the passing of time with flashes of transitory glory. But why the strange scare quotes around "Heroes" in the song and album titles? They imply a sceptical irony – that the girl and boy at the foot of the Berlin Wall aren't really heroes, except in their own self-aggrandising minds. Besides, Bowie could never really settle for anything as small as being an 'ordinary Joe' paired with an ordinary Jill, both of them feeling like king and queen 'just for one day'. Bowie would always crave something grander – the ubiquity of stardom, the immortality of having made a uniquely original achievement.

In *The Denial of Death*, cultural anthropologist Ernest Becker writes about the individual's desire to be 'an object of primary value in the universe' as the hallmark of immaturity. 'He must stand out, be a hero, make the biggest possible contribution to world life, show that he *counts* more than anything or anyone else.' Hero systems like faith, patriotism, causes and creeds of every kind, support 'self-esteem maintenance' by enabling the individual to participate in something larger than himself. But all these 'immortality projects' were now in decay, leaving humans vulnerable to insignificance.

Heroic fantasy was Bowie's defence against feeling 'puny' as a human speck. It was also a way of warding off depression. The dream was to live perpetually on the higher slopes, far from the commonplaceness and baseness of human existence – the 'steam and filth of human lowlands', as Nietzsche put it. Oh to dwell for ever amid 'mountains on mountains' and 'sunbirds to soar with', as Bowie sang on 'Station to Station'.

Looking around for heroes, Bowie venerated the fearlessness of artists who put themselves on the line, from Iggy to Chris Burden. Celebrated on the *"Heroes"* track 'Joe the Lion', Burden pushed performance art to the limit by undergoing physical ordeals: his 'works' included getting nailed to the top of a Volkswagen and having an assistant fire a bullet through his arm.

'"Heroes"', released as a single in the autumn of 1977, was a surprisingly modest hit for Bowie. It peaked at a lowly #24 in the UK and flopped completely in America. Perhaps it was out of step with punk's anti-heroism. Quite coincidentally, The Stranglers scored a much bigger hit at almost the same time with 'No More Heroes', a half-ironic, half-wistful song that listed exemplars of the vanished breed, such as Trotsky and Lenny Bruce. According to Strangler Hugh Cornwell, the ultimate message was 'don't have heroes. Be your own hero.'

Although it only made a small impression at the time, '"Heroes"' has swollen to become one of Bowie's best-loved songs. It's a classic wheeled out for just about any context that calls for a bit of ennobling: weddings, televised sporting events – you name it. The lyrical sentiments are universal, easily slotted into a wide range of circumstances by all sorts of ordinary mortals. Which brings into relief an odd thing about Bowie's songbook: a surprising lack of what you might call 'humanly useful' songs. '"Heroes"' is one of the few Bowie songs that could be filed in the same 'universally relatable' folder that holds Boston's 'More Than a Feeling', John Cougar Mellencamp's 'Jack and Diane', Van Halen's 'Jump', Talking Heads' 'Once in a Lifetime', The Smiths' 'How Soon Is Now' and 'There Is a Light That Never Goes Out' . . .

Like a mountain peak, the song '"Heroes"' casts a shadow over the rest of *"Heroes"* the album. Eno claimed that everything on the record apart from 'Sons of the Silent Age' was 'evolved on the spot in the studio', and more than that, was a first take. Like *Low*, there are Eno-esque instrumentals, but they don't have the desolate ache that's so affecting on the earlier album. 'V-2 Schneider' is Bowie reciprocating Kraftwerk's gift of 'Trans-Europe Express', but the title is the most interesting thing about the track. It cheekily compacts Florian's surname with the V-2 rocket, Hitler's last-chance miracle weapon, which whooshed to just outside the Earth's atmosphere before falling silently onto London in the final year of the Second World War (the 'V' stood for *Vergeltung*: vengeance). The album's mixture of strained songs like 'Blackout' and sound-paintings like 'Moss Garden' goes by in a blur until the gorgeous closer of 'The Secret Life of Arabia'. Its disco-funk exoticism looks ahead to *Lodger*, the final album in the Berlin trilogy (although actually mostly done in Switzerland), where the loose theme is tourism and the downsides of life as a transient.

RCA came up with great slogans for the *"Heroes"* press campaign: 'There's New Wave, There's Old Wave, and There's David Bowie' and 'Tomorrow Belongs to Those Who Can Hear It Coming' (a cheeky echo of *Cabaret*'s 'Tomorrow Belongs to Me'). But these would have been better used for the flawless masterpiece and true breakthrough into virgin hinterlands that was *Low*. The soul that was bared on that album is now barricaded again on *"Heroes"*, which is opaque and evasive.

Before recording *Lodger*, Bowie brought his romance with Berlin to an anticlimactic end with the movie *Just a Gigolo*. When he first moved to the city, there had been talk of making a movie scripted by Christopher Isherwood. Later on, he had discussed being involved in a cinematic adaptation of Brecht's *Threepenny Opera*, to be directed by Rainer Werner Fassbinder, or taking the lead role in a film about painter Egon Schiele, to be shot in Vienna. But in the event, his Weimar obsession sputtered out with *Gigolo*, the brainchild of actor David Hemmings, who enticed Bowie with the prospect of starring alongside Marlene Dietrich. She agreed to come out of retirement but baulked at returning to Germany for the filming. Her scenes were shot in Paris and spliced together with Bowie's.

He plays a Prussian officer, Paul Ambrosius von Przygodski, who is first seen arriving at the trenches during the First World War. Asked by his superior officer what he expects to find on the front line, von Przygodski replies, 'Fame and glory, of course . . . Heroism is my destiny.' In fact, he ends up in hospital, then drifts fecklessly through Weimar Germany, falling in with veterans who've formed a proto-Nazi paramilitary group. By the end of the movie he is being carried to his tomb under a swastika flag. *Gigolo*'s credits announce 'and with pride MARLENE DIETRICH', but it's unlikely she felt the same way. Bowie, for his part, described it as 'my 32 Elvis Presley movies rolled into one'.

In 1979, Bowie released *Lodger*. Made under the working title 'Planned Accidents', it was an erratic album – less groundbreaking than *Low*, more compelling in places than *"Heroes"*. Bowie had lived in Berlin for three years, but now he was in the process of leaving. The theme of life-as-a-tourist runs through a number of songs, like 'Fantastic Voyage' and 'Move On', and echoes through the exotic allusions of 'African Night Flight' and 'Yassassin (Turkish for: Long Live)' too.

But the album's most memorable tracks plunge us back into Bowie's long-running preoccupations with fame and sexual identity. 'Boys Keep Swinging', the first single off the album, romps through all the clichés of masculinity, its checklist of privilege deliciously mismatched with the video, in which Bowie drags up as female glamour archetypes, including Lauren Bacall and Marlene Dietrich. At each transition, he wipes the lipstick across his face in a savage smear, while ripping off the wig – a gesture nabbed from Romy Haag's cabaret routine. (Some say it was a cruel kiss-off, Haag having been indiscreet about their relationship to the newspapers.)

'D.J.', the underrated second single, failed to match the UK Top 10 success of 'Boys'. It's the lament of the disc jockey, someone who presents to an audience the work of others, yet accrues unearned glory through association. 'I am what I play,' mumbles the disconsolate character, adding, 'I got believers believing me.' The fact that the song is titled 'D.J.' – and not the customary rendering for disc jockey as either DJ or deejay – adds strength to the pet theory advanced by some Bowieologists that the abbreviation stands for David Jones. At the end of the video, Bowie graffiti-sprays the letters – his initials – onto a mirror. It's a song that captures the hollowed-out melancholy of an artist committed to constant change, cramming himself with new input to maintain his output levels.

Bowie's bedraggled whimper in the last verse of 'D.J.' – 'I've got believers in me' – suggests a star exhausted by fame who feels his voraciously demanding and expectant audience to be a burden. It's a straight-from-the-heart confession of confusion from a man with no answers. At the start of the decade, with 'Song for Bob Dylan', Bowie had sensed a 'leadership void' in rock and moved in to claim the role: 'Okay, Dylan, if you don't want to do it, I will,' is how he characterised his thinking, looking back from the vantage point of the midseventies. But by the end of that decade, being a weathervane artist, someone that people 'tell the time by', had wrung him out.

Along the way, he had taken on so many personae that David Jones – aka D.J. – had got lost in the shuffle. In 1976, journalist Jean Rook asked Bowie about 'David Jones'. Bowie replied, 'I like him.

I'd still like him if I could only get in touch with him. We've been apart for a long time, and I've so many more changes to make. Jones is real. Bowie isn't real. There's nothing real about standing up in front of 7000 people. I suppose that doing that is a bit sinister when you think about it but, if it is, the only person I brainwash and scare stiff is myself.'

That same year he confessed to *Playboy*, 'I honestly don't know where the real David Jones is. It's like playing the shell game. Except I've got so many shells I've forgotten what the pea looks like . . . Being famous helps put off the problem of discovering myself.'

Having pulled himself back from the LA edge and partially reconstituted himself in Berlin, Bowie could have withdrawn into serene seclusion, or at least negotiated a more sane, low-profile form of creativity. 'I keep telling myself every time I finish one of these forays into the public eye, never again,' Bowie told Gordon Burn in 1980. Yet once again, the bipolar rhythm that marked his career – relentless pursuit of the limelight alternating with shattered retreat from it; feeling like a hero versus feeling like a zero – would swing to the manic once more. Bowie was not ready to close down his 'little corporation of characters' and take himself off the pop market. Far from it: he was about to lunge for super-fame even bigger than before.

AFTERSHOCKS:

A Partial Inventory of Glam Echoes
and Reflections

August

John Lydon auditions for the Sex Pistols, singing along to
Alice Cooper's 'I'm Eighteen' on the jukebox at McLaren and
Westwood's boutique SEX. He gets the job less for the power of his
pipes than for his grimaces and gestures. Matching his green hair,
Lydon's green teeth inspire his new bandmates to call him 'Johnny
Rotten'. Using this stage name, Lydon creates one of rock's great
dramatis personae, welding together aspects of his real-life personality and presence (withering sarcasm, piercing stare) with menace-
projection learnt from Cooper, Alex Harvey, Ian Dury – and from
Laurence Olivier in his 1955 role as *Richard III*. A Shakespeare
buff, Lydon loved how the great English thesp 'made Richard
III riveting in his excessive disgust'. In his 1994 memoir, Lydon
reveals that 'Johnny Rotten definitely has tinges of Richard III in
him. I saw it a long time before I conceived Rotten. No redeeming
qualities. The worst of everything to excess.' That Lydon drew on
such an un-American source as Olivier – all stage craft and technical precision, a million miles from Method mumbling – may explain
why 'Johnny Rotten' is such an awesomely original creation within
rock. It also echoes a foundational moment in the history of British
rock presentation: Jack Good coaching Gene Vincent to play up his
Richard III limp to mesmerise TV audiences.

1977

September

Poised for a comeback, Marc Bolan looks leaner and keener than
he has in years. Presenting his own pop show, *Marc*, which airs

during the late-afternoon children's TV slot, Bolan delights in
hosting new-wave groups, whose tight attack he finds energising.
For the last episode of *Marc*'s first series the star guest is Bowie:
the old friends jam together (although the reunion is marred by
an offstage tiff). The show is recorded on 7 September, but by
the time it airs on the 20th, Bolan is dead, killed in a car crash on
Barnes Common, south-west London. Lover Gloria Jones was at
the Mini's wheel – Marc never learnt to drive.

October

A few weeks after '"Heroes"' dents the Top 30, the Berlin Wall
crops up again as a chart single's *mise en scène* with the Sex Pistols'
'Holidays in the Sun'. Halfway through, Rotten starts ranting about
'This third rate B-movie stuff / Cheap dialogue, cheap essential
scenery' – as though the divided city has been revealed as just a
flimsy stage for his private psychodrama. Then Rotten fourth-walls
like Alice in 'School's Out': instead of 'we can't think of a word that
rhymes', he bleats, 'I don't understand this bit at all,' sounding
genuinely panicked by his own paranoid vision.

1978

February

Kate Bush's debut album *The Kick Inside* kicks off with 'Moving',
a tribute to Lindsay Kemp, with whom she studied after seeing his
troupe's version of Genet's *Flowers*. Kemp, she later tells *Sounds*,
'opened up my eyes to the meanings of movement. He makes you
feel so good . . . He fills people up, you're an empty glass and glug,
glug, glug, he's filled you with champagne.' The mime master is
not Bush's only connection to Bowie. Although her early music
sits somewhere ornate and decorous at the crossroads of singer-
songwriter and prog's lighter side, glam is a large part of Bush's
make-up. A fan of the first four Roxy albums and Steve Harley, she

also witnessed the final Ziggy Stardust concert. She hails from the same edge-of-south-London suburbia as Bowie (Welling rather than Bromley) and has similar spiritual-seeker leanings: Gurdjieff is namechecked in her Top 10 hit 'Them Heavy People'. Bush's expressive movements make her 'a completely audio-visual artist', proclaims EMI's Bob Mercer, who vows that the company will break her in America through television rather than radio. That never happens, but the British public embrace her: 'Wuthering Heights', the 1977 debut single, goes to #1. Punk-minded critics and hipsters, though, find her stratospheric warbling and romantic-fantastic lyrics hopelessly deficient in street cred. Although only nineteen, she's filed with the old wave, aka 'boring old farts'. Some BOFs are indeed Bush's mentors and friends: David Gilmour, Roy Harper, Peter Gabriel. EMI have signed her as the first female exponent of that well-arranged, art-pop style they've done so well with, from The Beatles to Cockney Rebel. Soon, though, seizing the potential of both pop video and the recording studio, Bush will stake a strong claim to be the female Bowie.

October

Johnny Rotten, now going by his real name John Lydon, has a new band: Public Image Ltd. The inspiration comes from Muriel Spark's 1968 novel *The Public Image*, about a film actress who – embroiled in scandal – can only escape ruin by leaving the business of image-production altogether. 'I'm not interested in promoting an image,' Rotten tells journalist Vivien Goldman. 'I'm not going to dress up in pantomime outfits to please the public.' In the Pistols, Lydon tired of touring ('just like theatre, repeated night after night'), chafed as persona hardened into shtick and got sick of people trying to out-Rotten him (whether it was his friend turned cartoon psycho Sid Vicious, or hostile strangers looking to test him). In PiL's debut single, 'Public Image', Lydon asserts both his ownership of 'Johnny Rotten' and his right to discard the suit of character armour – just like Bowie shed Ziggy. The persona was 'my entrance' onto the stage of pop culture, he sings grandly; now he's staging 'my grand finale'. The song starts with a 'hello' greeting his punk following and ends with 'goodbye'. But alongside recriminations at those who only saw the surface (clothes, hair colour) there's self-reproach: 'somebody had to stop me' – a confession that Lydon-as-Rotten had become an alter-ego-maniac. That's why the band's called Public Image *Ltd*. 'The limited applies to egos,' Lydon tells Goldman. 'It was egos that bust up the Pistols, mainly Malcolm's . . .' That 'mainly' is an admission: as King Punk, Rotten had become – as McLaren tauntingly accused – a spiky-haired Rod Stewart. Just another rock star.

October

Hi-gloss guitar dazzling your ears like light glancing off a mirror-ball, Japan's 'Adolescent Sex' is one of glam's lost classics. Lost, because its raunchy disco-rock is tragically out of synch with the punky times. The group's androgynous beauty cuts no ice with the music papers, who mock Japan as glam stragglers with zero street cred. Yet they ought to be rolling in the stuff: they hail from Catford, south London, and have impeccably working-class origins. Singer David Sylvian and his drumming brother Steve Jansen are sons of a manual labourer; keyboard player Richard Barbieri has a hotel-waiter dad; bassist Mick Karn's father is a butcher. But rather than exploit their humble backgrounds, Japan renounce them; singer and drummer shed their paternal surname (Batt) and rename themselves in transparent homage to Sylvain and Johansen from the New York Dolls. The initial spark for Japan was not the Dolls, though, but Bowie: after seeing 'Starman' on *Top of the Pops*, they all went out and got Ziggy-style mullets.

October

Staged at the Roseland dance space in New York, 'Below the
Belt' is the first collaboration between Jean-Paul Goude and
Grace Jones, who's destined to vie in the eighties with Kate Bush
and Madonna as a female Bowie. Jamaican-born Jones started
out as a model and became a disco diva, but – like Bowie – her
true ambition was always acting: 'I modelled in order to support
myself while I went on cattle calls for theatre and film jobs,' Jones
recalled in 1987. 'In a way I geared the musical career to bring
me back there . . . that's why I staged it with all the theatrics and
the visuals.' Jones became a disco cult figure with Tom Moulton-
produced covers of Piaf's 'La Vie en Rose' and show tunes like
'Send in the Clowns and *Annie*'s 'Tomorrow'. But it was her gay
crowd-pleaser 'I Need a Man' that electrified Goude when he saw
Jones do a club PA. 'The ambiguity of her act was that she herself
looked like a man,' Goude recalled. 'I could see how the average
guy could get a little scared by her physical appearance.' A self-
confessed 'heterosexual cissy', Goude thrilled to Jones's dominatrix
aura. He became her stylist, radically overhauling her stage presentation and record artwork, but also became her lover. Goude
accentuated Jones's monumental physique with big-shouldered
garments that anticipated eighties-style female power-dressing
and gave her a geometric, cropped hairstyle, inspired by boxers
like Muhammad Ali and Jack Dempsey. 'Below the Belt' was
originally intended to take place on the West Side waterfront of
New York, Goude recalled, inside the trucks 'where the most
hardcore homosexuals copulate' – an echo of *Wayne County at
the Trucks*. But the weather's too wintry, so Goude and Jones take
over Roseland for Halloween. 'Blinding lights and wind machines'
are deployed to 'rape the audience . . . show them who was boss'.
Jones performs inside a boxing ring, throwing punches and doing
the Ali shuffle, surrounded by professional boxers skipping ropes

in 'beat-up headgear' and 'dirty handwraps'. Boxing represents African American pride. More problematically, another part of the show involves Jones dressed as a tiger. Goude sees Jones as a new Josephine Baker – hence the provocative play with images of Africa and savagery.

November

On X-Ray Spex's debut album, *Germfree Adolescents*, Poly Styrene's roar of anguished defiance shreds consumerism, sexual role play and media-promoted images. Of Scottish-Irish-Somalian extraction, Marianne Elliott-Said picked Poly Styrene as her name as 'a send up of being a pop star . . . like a little figure, not me . . . a lightweight disposable product . . . that's what pop stars are meant to be'. There's an echo here of Bowie's 'plastic soul' and Ziggy as 'plastic rocker'. As is the case with much punk, glam-turned-inside-out is what you get on the glorious *Germfree Adolescents*: tunes like 'Art-I-Ficial' cry out with a sort of jubilant bitterness, Poly unloosing her emptiness vengefully upon a world that has made her generation inauthentic and soulless. 'Obsessed with You' blasts advertisers for whom every kid is 'just another fig-ure for the sales machine', but also the impressionable, mouldable kids. 'I Am a Cliché' and 'I Am a Poseur' reflect back at society its own worst nightmare of youth-gone-wrong. 'Let's Submerge' and 'Warrior in Woolworths' lampoon the concepts of rebellion and the underground on which punk itself is based. 'The Day the World Turned Day-Glo' and 'Plastic Bag' are hallucinatory con-sumer phantasmagorias – 'I eat Kleenex for breakfast and use soft hygienic Weetabix to dry my tears,' '1977 and we are going mad! 1977 and we've seen too many ads!' – like 'Virginia Plain', soured and psychotic. 'Art-I-Ficial' rails against cosmetic notions of femi-ninity: 'the pretty little mask's not me'.

Early in '79 comes *Who Is Poly Styrene?* – a BBC2 *Arena* arts documentary made by Alan Yentob, the man who directed the Bowie documentary *Cracked Actor*. Alternating between snapshots of X-Ray Spex on tour and interludes of Poly at home, it's an oddly subdued portrait. Two years after taking on the Poly Styrene alter ego, the strain is showing. 'It isn't normal for people to be surrounded with people telling them they're great . . . to be up onstage and people jumping all over you and ripping your clothes off,' Styrene complains softly. Touring is a treadmill of peak experiences with throngs of complete strangers, 'one lot of hysterical people to the next lot of hysterical people'. Styrene frets about how 'I'm like an actress – onstage I'm one thing, and offstage I'm something else.' *Who Is Poly Styrene?* ends on a Garbo-esque 'I vant to be alone' note: Marianne Elliott-Said by herself, playing the piano.

'Identity', X-Ray Spex's greatest song, confronts the contradictions of commodified rebellion. The climactic knot of images involve a mirror smashed and wrists slashed with a shard. But there's one further blade-twist of irony: 'Did you do it for fame? / Did you do it in a fit? / Did you do it before you read about it?' 'Identity' is a premonition of crisis for Poly. A gentle hippy-like spirit, deep down Styrene isn't into punk's destructive nihilism. Increasingly disoriented, exhausted by touring, unsettled further by a sexual trauma, Styrene suffers a breakdown. After hallucinating a UFO through a hotel window, she's hospitalised and misdiagnosed with schizophrenia. Ultimately, she quits for a quieter life and quieter music: Hare Krishna and the placid solo LP *Translucence*. But in a further ironic fold to the story, Poly is the fairly transparent basis for 1980's *Breaking Glass*, a movie about a punkette who becomes a star with her anti-consumerism, anti-authority songs, then cracks up and ends up in a mental ward.

Winter

Skipping gaily past mounds of uncollected garbage bags in central London, a tribe of extravagantly costumed youths wend their way towards Billy's, a club. It's the 1978–9 Winter of Discontent, when the bin men, along with many other unions, strike, ultimately bringing down the Labour government and bringing down on themselves the nemesis of Thatcherism. But the young people – the seeds of a subculture soon confusingly known as New Romantics, Futurists, and Blitz Kids – are blithely unconcerned. They are heading to Billy's regular Tuesday 'Bowie Night', whose flyer proclaims: 'Fame, Fame, Fame Jump Aboard the Night Train'. Indeed, many of the regulars are destined for pop stardom – Boy George, Marilyn, Martin Degville and Tony James of Sigue Sigue Sputnik, Jeremy Healy of Haysi Fantayzee – while others become leading style journalists, photographers, fashion designers. As the poky club grows packed, it moves to a larger venue in Covent Garden and gets a new name, Blitz. To enter was 'like walking onto a film set', claimed one regular. Really, it's like a scrambling of multiple different films, as if the Blitz kids had ransacked the costume departments of disparate movie productions, mix-and-mismatching eras and countries. 'Futurist' fits the soundtrack, which is electronic and danceable, but not really the look, which raids history's wardrobe as well as Boots' cosmetics counter. If there's a unifying thread, it's un-America and unrock, a *Mittel Europa* atmosphere derived second-hand via Bowie-in-Berlin.

Among the Blitz scene's future stars are Martin and Gary Kemp. Bowie and Roxy fiends, until recently they called their group The Gentry (shades of *Country Life*). But journalist pal Robert Elms supplies them with something more exotic and cryptically sinister that he saw scrawled in a Berlin nightclub toilet: Spandau Ballet. It's the ghoulish name for the twitching of corpses hit by

machine-gun fire during the First World War, but it also evokes
the prison to which Rudolf Hess and other Nazi war criminals
were condemned. 'Musclebound', their second single, drifts further eastward with a video that mingles Cossack and Soviet imagery – warrior cavalry, peasants strenuously hewing with sickles and
hammers. *Journeys to Glory*, the debut LP, has Speer-of-destiny
typography, a heroic statue of a Roman athlete's torso and a sleeve
note by Elms exalting the group's 'strident elitism': Spandau's
word-of-mouth shows mean that 'unless your ears are pinned
firmly to the "right" ground your chances of seeing them are at
present slim'. Guitarist/songwriter Gary Kemp salutes Spandau's
stylish in-crowd following for co-creating the atmosphere of their
gigs and describes the group's music as 'applause to the audience'.

1979

March
Siouxsie and the Banshees' second single, 'The Staircase
(Mystery)', features a cover of T. Rex's '20th Century Boy' as its
B-side. The Banshees are glam to the core. Both from Bromley,
Bowie's old neck of the woods, Siouxsie Sioux and Steve Severin
actually met at Wembley, at a 1974 Roxy concert. Sonically and
visually, the Banshees are glam elegance filtered through punk
brutality. Their aesthetic of beauty-through-cruelty is based
around the four As: angularity, androgyny, artifice, aristocracy.
Six As, if you bung in 'assault' and 'authoritarianism'. Siouxsie
started dressing to distress aged fifteen: 'I used to go out of my
way to have very unattractive hairstyles . . . geometrically very
ugly, cropped and very frightening to the opposite sex . . . I think I
always knew the way I wanted to live was completely as a fascist. I
call myself a fascist personally, I like everything my own way.' *Join
Hands*, the Banshees' second album, released later in '79, features
'Regal Zone': Siouxsie imagines 'standing alone', an untouchable

and intimidating ice queen, striking her vassals dumb and numb with cold awe. Her beauty is forbidding, promising neither sensuality nor even tactility, offering only worship from afar. White face slashed across with black Cleopatra eyeshadow, spikey raven hair, uncurvy, jagged in her movements, Siouxsie is androgynous without being tomboyish. Seduction without reproduction: instead of Rotten's Richard III, imagine her as Lady Macbeth – 'unsex me here, and fill me from the crown to the toe topful of direst cruelty! . . . Come to my woman's breasts, and take my milk for gall.' A triumph of will over and against nature, Siouxsie turns herself into an art object; flash not flesh, she's all surface, like a masque or sculpture. As she shrieks in one song, 'Metal will rule in my master scheme.'

April

'The Tour of Life' is Kate Bush's inner dream world brought to the stage for twenty-four concerts. Her one and only tour, it's a fully choreographed, large-ensemble affair, with two male dancers gyrating around the singer and ten others onstage. During the seventeen costume changes, there's mime, magic and poetry readings to keep the audience diverted. Kate sings some songs from inside a three-dimensional egg, lined with red satin and symbolising the womb; for others, she's garbed as a Second World War pilot, a gangster, a magician, and more. The tour is technologically innovative, too: her sound engineer rigs up a groundbreaking wireless head mic, freeing Kate's movements. *Melody Maker* hails it as 'the most magnificent spectacle' rock's ever seen. But for the *NME*, the maximalist production is out of step with post-punk's gaunt aesthetics. Reviewer Charles Shaar Murray scorns the Bush fantasia as a regression to 'all the unpleasant aspects of David Bowie in the MainMan era . . . Tony Defries would've loved you seven years ago, Kate, and seven years ago maybe I would've too. But these days I'm past the stage of admiring people desperate to dazzle and bemuse.' Along with the mixed reviews and the physical and financial strain of such an ambitious endeavour, a terrible shadow is cast by the accidental death of lighting engineer Bill Duffield. Bush retreats from live performance for thirty-five years.

May

Roxy Music have reformed and scored a huge hit with #2 single 'Dance Away'. In '76, they'd disbanded, mutually exhausted, creatively dry and in financial difficulties. After three years of solo floundering, they reunite to continue the smoothing-out and crossing-over process they started with *Country Life* and *Siren*, with a renewed determination to crack America, where the real killings are made. *Manifesto* and *Flesh + Blood* spawn a string of UK hit singles: the blandly attractive art-disco of 'Angel Eyes'; the golden shimmer of 'Oh Yeah'; the #1 Lennon tribute cover 'Jealous Guy'. Best of the bunch is 1980's 'Same Old Scene': its glinting synth-shivers and nervous funk, as Roxy biographer Paul Stump notes, provide much of the template for Duran Duran's sound.

December

David Bowie appears on *Saturday Night Live*, accompanied by downtown NYC performers Klaus Nomi and Joey Arias. They actually *carry* Bowie onstage – he's encased in a plastic tuxedo and bow tie, an immobilising plane of black-and-white material that makes him look 2D – before backing him on versions of 'The Man Who Sold the World' and 'Boys Keep Swinging'. A Berlin transplant to New York's late-seventies clubland, Nomi's own act merges Queen/Sparks-style popera, Kraftwerk's Germanic formality and Zolar X's extraterrestrial image. Nomi first made a name for himself as the closing act at 'New Wave Vaudeville', a postmodern take on the variety revue staged in 1978. Appearing onstage amid clouds of dry ice and the sounds of a landing spaceship, he sang an aria from Saint-Saëns' *Samson et Dalila*. Transfixed by his 'transcendent, peculiar, inexplicable but undeniably otherworldly artistic vision', Kristian Hoffman of The Mumps introduces himself to Nomi after the performance. Soon Hoffman has become his musical director, pulling together a backing group and developing a set of original songs penned by himself ('Nomi Song', 'Total Eclipse', 'Simple Man', 'After the Fall') and covers (Lou Christie's 'Lightning Strikes', Lesley Gore's 'You Don't Own Me', Marlene Dietrich's 'Falling in Love Again'), plus baroque pieces by the likes of Purcell. The closest Nomi ever got to proper opera was working as an usher at the Deutsche Oper Berlin, but in the rough-edged context of New York post-punk, his pipes are astonishingly pure and celestial. 'With that voice, and that eerie amorphous charisma, Klaus would be OUR Bowie,' Hoffman believes. Nomi adapts Bowie's stylised black-and-white tux and tie from the *SNL* performance and makes it his own signature look, a stage suit whose very wide, straight shoulders create a triangle as they taper sharply into the waist before flaring out with a tutu-like effect. In combination with his snow-white foundation, dark lipstick in silent-movie bow shape and stylised black-dyed hair (huge brow, extreme widow's peak, angular tufts sculpted like the fins on a fifties car), the overall effect is startling, like Nomi's been scooped out of a black-and-white science-fiction movie from the twenties and dropped into the garish present. A discussed Bowie collaboration never transpires, but Nomi signs to Bowie's old label, RCA. Despite TV appearances, the pop breakthrough never happens, though, and in 1983 he becomes one of the first figures in the entertainment world to succumb to AIDS.

1980

May

The first issue of a new monthly magazine called *The Face* comes out. Launched by former *NME* editor and ex-mod Nick Logan, at the start *The Face* is pretty much the *NME* with better photographs. Simon Frith observes that '*The Face* is, essentially, a picture paper; it has the best musician photos there have ever been.' The mag's initial focus is on post-punk and 2-Tone, but gradually that shifts towards club culture and fashion. Writing about the New Romantics for *The Face* – in his role as resident punk-mourner – Jon Savage grouches that 'all this posing naturally favours photographers, not journalists'. Logan and his team soon have company and competition: rival 'style mags' like *iD*, *Blitz* and *New Sounds, New Styles*, all of which share *The Face*'s pictorial emphasis and London-centric slant. Another significant publication at this time is *ZG*, a large-format, sharply designed periodical with issues themed around topics like 'Heroes' or 'Icons & Idols'. *ZG* is written by art-school academics and brainy pop writers who take 'all this posing' seriously. You might fairly critique *iD* and the others for privileging style over substance, but for the *ZG* writers, style *is* substance: something to decode as much as ogle.

August

Despite Bowie's dominance of the seventies, 'Ashes to Ashes' is amazingly only his second UK #1. An oblique self-portrait of a falling star who's hit 'an all-time low', the song takes the melancholy electronic swirls of *Low*'s second side and turns them into pop, via Chuck Hammer's synthesized layers of 'guitarchitecture'. Blending self-mythology and self-admonishment, 'Ashes to Ashes' reflects back on Bowie's career and life-journey so far, with references to Major Tom (revealed as a junkie), a veiled dig at his mother and the video appearance of Bowie-as-Pierrot – a nod to both Lindsay Kemp and 'The Mask' (Bowie's mime allegory about the price of fame). The lyrics recycle common criticisms of the artist as calculated and cold, now internalised as self-lacerating doubts and reproaches: 'never done anything out of the blue'; 'want an axe to break the ice'. Graced with his most exquisitely winding extended melody since 'Ziggy Stardust', this might be the most gloomy single ever to make #1. But it relaunches Bowie as a pop star, preparing the ground for his biggest stretch of fame ever. Craftily co-opting the New Romantics, the video features the garishly made-up visage of Blitz doorman Steve Strange, along with three other 'faces' from the club. It's a timely reminder that Bowie is the glamdaddy of all this eighties dress-up-box pop.

'Ashes' is the first single off Bowie's post-Berlin album *Scary Monsters (and Super Creeps)*, which everybody – even the diehards – knows deep down was the Last Great Bowie Album (at least until the very last one). Highlights: the parched and jagged funk of second single and huge hit 'Fashion', a sister song to 'Fame', with Bowie equating the meaningless oscillations of style with the left/right swings of politics and sounding grimly fatalistic about the public's capacity for obedience in either domain. And fourth single (and flop) 'Up the Hill Backwards', where the fatalism is existential: life itself is the diktat, the unwanted gift. Yet from the opening lines onward – 'The vacuum created by the arrival of freedom / And the possibilities it seems to offer' – Bowie sounds fraught and serene, burdened and buoyant all at once.

October
Swept along by New Romanticism – although they try to keep their distance – Japan score their first chart entry with 'Gentlemen Take Polaroids'. The swagger of 'Adolescent Sex' has mutated into svelte electronic funk: a meshwork of Karn's fretless bass and Jansen's

sinuous un-rock rhythms, draped with Barbieri's calligraphic synth and Sylvian's languid, lacquered croon. 'Gentlemen Take Polaroids' could almost be a lost Roxy Music song or LP title, managing to evoke aristocracy and aestheticism, with hints of voyeurism, emotional distance, kinky sex. Developing within minutes, the Polaroid image creates instant nostalgia, freeze-framing memories; Bryan Ferry's starry-eyed male gaze turned into a machine – or the cellphone selfie decades ahead of schedule. Although Bowie had been the initial spur for Japan, Ferry's vibrato is the model for Sylvian's mannered poise. After five years of perseverance and half a million of manager Simon Napier-Bell's own money, Japan become stars with early-eighties hits like 'Ghosts', 'Life in Tokyo' and 'Visions of China', plus the successful album *Tin Drum*. In '84, Sylvian does the art-pop star thing and mounts an exhibition of his Polaroid work, which involves a self-devised image-distortion technique.

October

Prince releases his third album and first classic, *Dirty Mind*. On the back cover he poses languidly in black thigh-high stockings, bikini briefs and little else: an invitation to the kinkiest of reveries. The *NME*'s Barney Hoskyns hails the album as a 'glam-funk *Let's Get It On*' and describes an early-'81 NYC gig at the Ritz Ballroom as 'like seeing Marc Bolan and Jimi Hendrix in the same body'. But others are perturbed by this purple-clad imp of the polymorphously perverse. Self-described 'punk-funk' freak Rick James is affronted by Prince's unmanly aura (while also shrewdly perceiving the commercial threat posed, Prince threatening to make James's bad-boy macho posturing look old-fashioned). In an increasingly one-sided feud, James rails against Prince for 'faking the funk' and, exhibiting absurdly hypocritical prudery, for being a bad role model: 'He's a mentally disturbed young man . . . He sings songs about oral sex and incest.' Recalling a 1980 tour on which Prince

played support, James later claims to have felt 'sorry' for 'this little
dude wearing hi-heels' who took off his trench coat at the end of
the set to reveal 'little girl's bloomers . . . The guys in the audience just booed the poor thing to death.' Prince's prancing goes
down equally poorly when he supports ageing androgynes The
Rolling Stones on their 1981 tour: rockist audiences pelt him with
cabbages.

1981

April

The UK pop sensation of 1981, Adam Ant scores his first #1 with
'Stand and Deliver'. Among the most glam-indebted of the first-
wave punks, Adam and the Antz had built up a following with
decadently kinky Nazi-chic ditties like 'Whip in My Valise', 'Beat
My Guest', 'Deutscher Girls' and the debut album, *Dirk Wears
White Sox* (a reference to Bogarde as a former SS officer in *The
Night Porter*). Deciding, like Bolan before him, that 'cult figure'
was a euphemism for 'loser', Adam crosses over with a ruthlessly
catchy – yet thrillingly, abrasively odd – sound that mixes African
Burundi drums with swashbuckling guitar licks and Apache war-
whoop melodies. Image-wise, Adam and his band patch together
scraps from children's storybook adventures and Hollywood action
genres: pirates, cowboys and Indians, knights in shining armour
. . . and in 'Stand and Deliver', a 'dandy highwayman'. In the
song, Adam declares that he's tired of deep-and-meaningful but
image-poor post-punk, 'where only showbiz loses'. In the video,
he prances impishly as a Dick Turpin-esque figure, stopping stage
coaches and robbing swanky nobles armed with a flintlock in one
fist and a hand mirror in the other. Captured, he's placed in the
gallows, but escapes the noose and runs off gleefully with his gang
through a field of giant-size mirrors with gilt frames.

May

Grace Jones's *Nightclubbing* is released and becomes the hip-
ster's choice for album of '81. Jones is like a Roxy cover girl who's
stepped out of the photograph and seized control of the microphone. Model turned diva, she's become the art-pop equivalent
of a project, the focus of a team of male mentors who musically
and visually stage-manage her shift to a more challenging sound
and image. But all the framing would amount to nothing without
Jones's charisma: the imperious, if inflexible voice; the imposing
physical presence. Tall, angular, ebony-skinned, she suggests a geographical paradox: an ice queen from Africa's dark heart.

The art-ification of Jones began with 1980's *Warm Leatherette*,
when Island boss Chris Blackwell enlisted Jamaica's top rhythm
section, Sly & Robbie, and co-produced the album with Alex
Sadkin. *Leatherette* and *Nightclubbing* resemble Bryan Ferry's
first two solo albums: most of the songs are covers, tailored to her
scary-sexy image. Chrissie Hynde's 'Private Life' could almost
have been purpose-built: a cold-hearted take-down of an emotionally needy man with a menstruating heart. 'That's so wet,' sneers
Jones, scorning his pathetic notions of attachment and commitment, boasting, 'I'm very superficial.' The song is a UK hit; on the
B-side, Jones covers Joy Division's 'She's Lost Control'. At this
time, she also does an unreleased version of nu-glamdroid Gary
Numan's 'Me! I Disconnect from You'. The album's title track,
'Warm Leatherette', is The Normal's electro-punk novelty with
lyrics inspired by *Crash*, J. G. Ballard's novel about the eroticism
of auto accidents. Alongside the post-punk, there's glam in the
mix: a cover of Roxy's 'Love Is the Drug'. All are delivered with
a unique scowling sensuality and are embedded in reggae-funk
that sounds simultaneously laidback and uptight. Sade for de Sade
readers, *Nightclubbing* includes the bespoke-written Sting tune
'Demolition Man' (Jones as vengeful death machine), a cover of

the Iggy/Bowie dirge 'Nightclubbing' and Australian new-wave oddity 'Walking in the Rain', with its gender-bent lines 'Feeling like a woman / Looking like a man.'

Meanwhile, Goude exacerbates the race/gender mayhem with the punningly titled *One Man Show*, which is closer to performance art or a runway fashion show than a pop concert. The 1981 tour involves set pieces like Jones dressed as a gorilla and wearing a grass skirt while playing the bongos. For 'Demolition Man', there's 'an army of marching Grace Joneses – soldiers, same size, wearing perfect masks of her face, goose-stepping in formation across the stage', recalls Goude. That same year, he publishes the photo book *Jungle Fever*. Its cover is an infamous image of Jones naked, snarling on all fours in a cage, with a bloody chunk of raw gnawed meat at her feet. But inside she's just one of several black women – at once girlfriends, muses, protégées and fetish objects – dubiously exoticised by Goude. Jones is the culmination of his mounting obsession with statuesque black women. To him she seems 'a demi-goddess . . . her face something more than just pretty . . . more like an African mask'. Deciding 'deliberately to mythologize Grace Jones', Goude uses photographic trickery to distend her body into unnatural and unrealistic postures. 'I cut her legs apart – lengthened them, turned her body completely to face the audience like an Egyptian painting.' He then paints over the print to create 'the illusion that Grace Jones actually posed for the photograph and that only she was capable of assuming such a position . . . If you really study it, the pose is anatomically impossible.' For other images, Goude paints Jones blue-black so that she looks 'barely human. She is more like a strange, menacing alien.' What started for Goude as an already problematic obsession with blackness as the realer-than-real thing spirals into a disturbed fantasy. As Jones becomes 'the threatening . . . male–female, erotic menace I wanted her to be', Goude confesses that he is 'no longer sure what I fell in love with, Grace or my idea of what Grace should be'. His obsession becomes all-consuming – 'there was nothing else in my life' – and the relationship combusts.

May

Steve Strange launches the even bigger Club for Heroes in Baker Street, London. By this point he is a pop star in his own right, fronting Visage. A stylised and faintly exotic synonym for 'face', it's the perfect name for a group in the Video Decade. Singles like 'Fade to Grey' layer ashen-voiced Bowie-in-Berlin melancholy over a brisk electro-disco pulse. For 'The Damned Don't Cry', the big hit off 1982's *The Anvil*, Visage make a thirties mini-movie of a video that's the missing link between Kraftwerk's 'Trans-Europe Express' promo and Visconti's *The Damned*. Strange stands on a wintry train platform, then travels by steam locomotive, peering into compartments where decadent revellers in fedoras and diamante headdresses clink champagne glasses.

September

Number 1 for four weeks, Adam and the Ants' 'Prince Charming' is a nu-glam manifesto, beseeching his followers, 'Don't you ever stop being dandy, showing me you're handsome,' and assuring them that 'ridicule is nothing to be scared of'. A twist on *Cinderella*, the video shows Adam as both a downtrodden male Cinderella and as the magically transformed Prince Charming who gatecrashes the ball. In a final dizzying sequence, we see Adam guised as a one-man gallery of his own heroes – Clint Eastwood, Alice Cooper, Rudolph Valentino, Marlon Brando, with each actor garbed in their most famous role. The song's lurching rhythm – somewhere between waltz and Navajo war dance – is accompanied by a stop–start dance whose frozen poses, haughty and erect, parallel the vogueing style then emerging at drag-queen balls in New

York's gay underground. In these gladiatorial dress-up-and-dance contests, the competitors move between 'stills' inspired by the fashion spreads in glossy magazines. 'A ball is to us . . . as close to reality as we're going to get, to all that fame and fortune and stardom and spotlights,' one voguer explains, while another describes the experience for participant and spectator alike as 'like crossing into the looking glass, into Wonderland'. In the 'Prince Charming' video, Adam smashes a giant mirror, a cracking of the (public) image that's like a portent of the psychological crack-up that would claim the ex-idol in later years.

October

Prince releases *Controversy*, his fourth album. Unlike *Dirty Mind*, the cover sees him fully clothed, but still very much the dainty dandy: sporting eyeliner and blush, he's clad in a mauve coat, wing collar and cravat. On the title track/lead single 'Controversy', the racially/sexually ambiguous singer presents himself as the Enigma at the roiling centre of a vortex of discourse, parroting back the fascinated confusion of his audience: 'Am I black or white? Am I straight or gay?' *Dirty Mind's* rave reception, which saw rock critics anointing him as the genre-crossing, gender-bending, races-uniting saviour of modern music, has clearly put Prince's head in a swirl. By 1983's *Purple Rain*, his mass-market breakthrough album/movie, Prince sounds positively messianic: renaming his backing band The Revolution, he sings, in 'I Would Die 4 U', about how 'I'm not a woman, I'm not a man / I am something that you'll never understand.'

1982

May

The final Roxy Music album, *Avalon* could also be taken as the ultimate Roxy album, arriving at the dream of a perfected existence that the earlier records gestured towards. *Avalon* is literally the sound of money. Its patina of perfectionism and professionalism exudes a glossy 'n' classy aura of no-expense-spared. Released a few months before the first compact discs reach the record stores, the wispily detailed mist of tingling overdubs seems tailor-made for this new era of hi-fi. A real studio-as-instrument affair, *Avalon* is 'raised to a sort of sublimity by Bob Clearmountain's mix', says Andy Mackay. Immaculate back-ground music, *Avalon* can be seen as Ferry's own version of Eno's ambient; an 'I can do that too' riposte, even. Indeed, the album's co-producer, Rhett Davies, worked on *Another Green World* and *Music for Airports*. Ferry's presence in this sound is as just another texture and mood-tone, rather than a singing personality in the usual pop sense. His debonair croon evokes a faded and jaded gentility; the haiku-like words of songs like 'More Than This' and 'Avalon' are a world away from the florid verbosity of 'If There Is Something' and 'Beauty Queen'.

Avalon establishes the template and the shackle for Ferry's solo future. Nineteen eighty-five's *Boys and Girls* features many of the same session hirelings that augmented Roxy's rump on *Avalon*. *Avalon* had effectively erased the musical personalities of Manzanera and Mackay; now they're simply dispensed with. Ferry succeeds in asserting definitively that Roxy Is Not Really a Band After All. But the victory is barren. In English legend, Avalon is where King Arthur, defeated, goes to die. Perhaps Ferry sub-consciously knew this when he chose the name, sensing that the album's soundscape – aristocracy as ambience – would be where he would 'die' as a creative force. Or at least come to rest, eking out half-lives languidly for the rest of his career.

The cover – an armour-clad medieval noble whose wrist sports a crested falcon – seems like a break with Roxy tradition. Actually, it *is* another girl, but for the first time you can't see the model's face.

Ferry doesn't want to share it, because it's his posh fiancée Lucy Helmore, gazing out over the lake near her parents' holiday home on the west coast of Ireland. The message, opaque to almost everybody who saw it at the time, is: 'I've made it. This is my lady.' As Ferry tells the *Observer*, he's become 'the first rock star to join the English aristocracy'. Helmore is almost too perfect a Ferry paramour: a model, but also a socialite. Impeccably upper class, with one foot in the City (Lloyd's insurance broker for a father) and the other in the country life (she grew up around horses and hunting), she's so pale-skinned you can almost see the blue blood.

Around this time, chez Ferry gets profiled in the decor magazine *Interiors*. Where his previous London flats and houses had been cutting edge in their ironic Pop Art-infused taste, the new living quarters disappoint Ferry-watchers with their staid selection of antiques and watercolours of horses and dogs. But Ferry has twigged that your actual upper-class types aren't trendy; the true mark of the proper nob is tweedy-traditional taste. As Peter York noted with a trace of wistfulness, Ferry's style now was 'backwards into the future, forwards into the past, and perhaps a little step to the right'. Postmodernism has often been accused by those on the left of being in cahoots with conservatism. 'Everything you do has to relate to the past, probably,' Ferry mused back in '74, talking to *Melody Maker*. 'I don't really see myself as capable of devising a totally new musical form, or a new form of dress or any sort of appearance.' Such aesthetic neoconservatism elides smoothly into the political kind. But as a scion of the toiling classes, Ferry never concealed his desire for wealth and all the finer things it procures: collectable art, vintage wine, exquisite furnishings, exquisiter women.

Ferry and Helmore marry on 26 June 1982. They put their first-born – Charles Frederick Otis, the first of four sons – down for Eton as soon as he pops out.

June

The hit single 'Fireworks' is the first of a string of Siouxsie micro-manifesto anthems – others include 'Painted Bird' and 'Dazzle' – for goth, the post-punk subculture that's emerged in the Banshees' wake. Goth represents the breaking away of punk's arty-glam wing from the social-realist factions. For this tribe apart, the streets aren't a source of credibility or authenticity, but a stage on which to dramatise oneself as strange and separate. 'Fireworks' exalts goth's sepulchral version of glamour as a pyrotechnic protest against dowdy and dour normality: 'We are fireworks burning shapes into the night'. The female contingent of goth, in particular, is made in Siouxsie's image: each of her looks is in turn copied by a legion of lookalikes. She becomes the most influential female fashion icon of the alternative eighties.

In July, as 'Fireworks' drops from the chart sky, the Batcave opens in London's Soho. The soundtrack is new goth, old glam and The Cramps; the vibe is dark and sleazy; the look is Banshees meets Bauhaus meets *Rocky Horror Show*. Defining itself against other London clubs of the sort that *The Face* covers, Batcave has a strict 'No Funk, No Disco' policy; effectively, it's 'No Synths' too, eschewing New Romantic sounds for guitar groups only. But really goths versus New Romantics is just one set of Bowie's children fighting another set of Bowie's children; almost like different phases of his discography set against each other (*Ziggy Stardust/Aladdin Sane* versus *Young Americans/Low*). It's sibling rivalry, or the narcissism of small differences. Boy George and Andi from Sex Gang Children even shared a squat at one point.

But as goth codifies itself into a defined style and sound, the Banshees drift away from it. Released in November '82, *A Kiss in the Dreamhouse* is lush and texturally sophisticated, its reference points shifting from the trashy B-movie horror of '81's *Juju* to voluptuous *fin de siècle* decadence – Baudelaire, Huysmans,

Beardsley, Klimt. The title comes from a documentary about a forties Los Angeles brothel called The Dreamhouse, where the hookers had plastic surgery to look like Hollywood stars.

September
Kate Bush's *The Dreaming* bemuses critics and bypasses the
public, but it's her unfettered mistresspiece. Having abandoned
live performance altogether, Bush plunges deeper into the studio,
exploring its capacities for illusion spinning: a theatricality of the
mind's eye, conjured through sound. Armed with state-of-the-art
machines like the Fairlight sampler, Bush pushes her existing
maximalist tendency over the brink – an intricate excess of layers,
details, twists, treatments. Particularly arresting are all the new
warped ways in which Bush is using her voice. 'Pull Out the Pin'
and 'Suspended in Gaffa' writhe with exaggerated accents and
jarring phrasings, like she's dementedly putting on and taking off
vocal costumes. Deranged thespian emphasis is placed on particular words or even syllables, while Bush develops a new vocabulary
of throat-scorched shrieks and yelps. Emotions clash and fuse into
alloys impossible to parse as normal everyday human feelings.
She lets rip with the studio effects and the stereophonic trickery.
'Leave It Open' teems with birds-on-helium twitters and plaits the
phased main vocal into infolded shapes. Pretentious in the best
sense of the word, Bush no longer seems like a pre-punk throwback but a sort of posh cousin to the goths, not just paralleling
Cocteau Twins and *Dreamhouse* Siouxsie, but surpassing them.

October
Bauhaus's single of 'Ziggy Stardust' lands the goth group on *Top
of the Pops*, where Peter Murphy re-enacts Bowie and Ronson
in the form of some stylised homoerotic interplay with guitarist
Daniel Ash. On the B-side, there's another glam homage: a cover

of Eno's proto-punk rampage 'Third Uncle'. But this isn't even
their first glam tribute: in 1980, Bauhaus put out a single of Bolan's
'Telegram Sam'. Speaking to *Seconds* magazine, Ash recalls how
he and Murphy worshipped Ziggy-era Bowie: 'It wasn't a sexual
thing, it was aesthetic, a beautiful thing to look at . . . It was like I'd
never seen that before, some sort of alien – is it male or female?'
Bauhaus and their idol soon coexist in the same filmic fantasy
space thanks to *The Hunger*. The 1983 movie opens with Bauhaus
performing their foundational goth track 'Bela Lugosi's Dead' in a
New York nightclub, into which vampire lovers John and Miriam
– Bowie and Catherine Deneuve – prowl in search of prey. The
credits roll over Murphy's gaunt beauty, intercut with Bowie and
Deneuve's faces as they silently and coldly select a pair of pretty
things on the club floor to lure home. Backdropped by Bauhaus's
contorted poses, one credit is for 'Make-Up Illusions' – a perfect
glam–goth moment.

1983

March

Seems like half the UK is ripping off *Young Americans*' plastic soul
'n' funk – complete with Bowie's wedge haircut of the time – so
he decides to repeat it himself with *Let's Dance*. The urban/R&B
coordinates are updated – Chic's Nile Rodgers produces – but
the strategy is the same: conquer America with a stylish, white-
face version of its own black music. Another modish element is
postmodernism. 'Let's Dance', the single and megahit, feels like a
response to ABC's *Lexicon of Love*, an exercise in meta-romance
that exploits and acknowledges the power of clichés. That's how
I've always taken the references to 'serious moonlight' and lines
like 'put on your red shoes and dance the blues'. The justly celebrated video has nothing to do with the song, arguably even
undercuts it: filmed in New South Wales, it's an oblique homage

to Nicolas Roeg's *Walkabout*, showing an indigenous Australian couple who are seduced by Western urban sophistication. But at the end they stomp a pair of red women's shoes (symbol of elegance, glamour, high society) into the dust, turn their backs on the city and head back to the bush. Number 1 in nine nations, 'Let's Dance' is Bowie's most poppy song since 'Young Americans' – except that his voice sounds strangely haggard, in places wracked with desperation. But the next single, 'Modern Love', is bouncy, refurbished Motown, with a video that displays Bowie looking healthy, tanned, eager to please. Many original fans regard this as the big betrayal: a cleaned-up Bowie cleaning up in the Reagan-era marketplace. In interviews, he expresses bemusement at the 'I'm gay' era, claims he doesn't know where his head was at in those days. As packed stadiums across America testify, Bowie's newfound extroversion and optimism are perfectly attuned to the eighties' just-say-no/make-it-big ethos.

June
In the video for Eurythmics' 'Who's That Girl?', Annie Lennox ups the gender-confusion ante, playing female and male characters – a blonde nightclub singer and a sideburned rock'n'roller – who, in a climactic piece of video trickery, kiss each other. Cross-dressing pop star Marilyn appears in the promo, as Dave Stewart's companion.

September
Kiss remove their make-up. Paul Stanley persuades Gene Simmons that it's high time they proved they're a real band with no need for gimmicks, and on 18 September they appear in public unmasked for the first time. Meanwhile, a whole new wave of metal bands are caking on the cosmetics. Among them are Twisted Sister, from Long Island, New York. Fronted by Dee Snider, they

are outright drag rock, wearing fright wigs and frocks, but they play it for panto-dame grotesquerie rather than androgynous allure. Luckily, Twisted Sister have learnt from glam sonics as well as theatrics, puking up a pair of shouty brat-rock minor classics with 'We're Not Gonna Take It' and 'I Wanna Rock'.

October

The Smiths score their first hit with 'This Charming Man'. As seen on *Top of the Pops*, Morrissey's dancing leaves some viewers rapt and raptured converts, but confuses the vast majority. Walking a thin line between entrancing and embarrassing, his blend of grace and awkwardness resembles the self-loving pirouettes of a bedroom-bound teenager alone but for a record player and a mirror – private moments suddenly propelled onto the most public stage of British pop. As further hits come – 'Heaven Knows I'm Miserable Now', 'William It Was Really Nothing' – along with a self-titled debut album, The Smiths take on the role of opposition to the pop mainstream, a righteous rejection of garish videos, synth pop, faux-soul sounds and the high-life imagery of yachts and Roxy-cover models brandished by Duran Duran and their like. When they first emerge, The Smiths vow never to use a synth or make a video. Their ambition gets the better of them when it comes to the promo prohibition, but their jangly guitar-based sound sticks out in the glossy, hi-tech chart-pop context of drum machines and sequencers. From their dressed-down image to the deliberate ordinariness of the group's name, The Smiths represent the common people, all those marginalised or left behind in the enterprise-culture eighties. They are intensely polarising: disliked by radio DJs and mocked by mainstream media, but consistently voted best band by the readership of the rock press. Rushing out to buy the new single by The Smiths to make sure it goes straight into the charts (only to drop down after Morrissey's disconcerting dancing on *TOTP*) is a sort of aesthetic protest vote against the neo-glam pop of Thatcher's second term. In a sense, against the Bowie-fied and Roxy-fied eighties.

And yet glam is a huge element of Morrissey's make-up. As a teenager, he'd been president of the New York Dolls fan club (a passion he shared with Japan and the young Nick Rhodes, later of Duran Duran) and had even published a short book about the band. He loved Sparks and Bolan (traces of T. Rex creep into a couple of Smiths singles). And while he didn't name-drop Bowie and Roxy in the eighties – an indication of how both had come to seem like the enemy because of their progeny but also their own drift to the centre – young Morrissey loved them too. Post-Smiths, Morrissey will enlist Mick Ronson to produce his 1992 solo album *Your Arsenal*.

Morrissey's glam keeps the androgyny and the Wildean wit, but baulks at the fashion-forward idea of perpetual change. His idea of style is more like Quentin Crisp's: decide who you are, then perpetuate it. His image never changes in the eighties: jeans, simple shirt, timeless fifties rockabilly quiff.

Following Wilde, Morrissey revives the original idea of the dandy, as opposed to the fancy-dress notion promoted by Adam Ant and Steve Strange. True dandies were elegant but relatively restrained; their clothes manifest above all a sharpness of mind. Growing up in a dilapidated working-class neighbourhood of Manchester during the sixties and seventies, Morrissey developed the ideal of a hard-edged personality, standing out and apart from the mediocre mass. There is a war being waged here between the bored and the boring: as Morrissey put it in his 2013 memoir, '*the monotonous in life must be protected at all costs*. But protected from what? *From you and I.*' The dandy self is a monstrous eruption of sheer freakish difference, innately against nature and against the grain. But it's also a persona that's been zealously cultivated and shaped to goad the small-minded; a self fashioned, in Morrissey's case, out of fragments of poets (Stevie Smith, Auden, Housman), dramatists (Shelagh Delaney), actors (James Dean) and a select group of pop precursors (the Dolls, Buzzcock Pete Shelley, Sandie Shaw).

The irresolvable contradiction in The Smiths is the clash between Morrissey's belief in himself as extraordinary, destined for some kind of peculiar greatness, and his commitment to social realism and his working-class roots. Describing the photographs on the Smiths' record sleeves, Morrissey said his intent was 'to take images that were the opposite of glamour and to pump enough heart and desire into them to show ordinariness as an instrument of power – or, possibly, glamour'. But is it really possible to be both a dandy and loyal to the common people? That was the impossible balancing act Morrissey tried to pull off: on the one hand, preaching fatalistic humility in songs like 'Accept Yourself' and mocking the royal family in 'The Queen Is Dead'; on the other, self-preening and almost regal in songs like 'Still Ill', which decreed 'England is mine and she owes me a living'. In 'Frankly Mr Shankly', he sings about the 'hideous tricks' fame plays on the mind, while confessing he'd 'rather be famous than righteous or holy'.

Another facet to Morrissey's improbable blend of puritanism and dandyism is his sexuality – or lack of it. His vaunted and flaunted celibacy is seen by some as a mask for closeted homosexuality. Songs like 'This Charming Man' and 'Reel Around the Fountain' drip with homoeroticism. So does cover artwork like the photograph of actor George O'Mara's bare buttocks on the debut single 'Hand in Glove' or the debut LP's still of a bare-chested Joe Dallesandro from the Andy Warhol/Paul Morrissey film *Flesh*. Asserting that he was pansexual in theory but inactive in practice, Morrissey combined asceticism and ambiguity in a way that maximised his appeal across the spectrum: straight males, girls looking for a sensitive and non-thrusting heart-throb, gay men decoding what they were sure was his true orientation through the scattered visual and lyrical clues. But Morrissey's claims to sex-exempt status are also a cunning form of one-upmanship, of sticking out at a time when Boy George makes being gay harmless and Jimmy Somerville renders it worthy. In 1983, Morrissey's stance is as provocative as Bowie's 'I'm gay and always have been' was in 1972, marking him out as elusive, confusing, undecidable, someone beyond or outside either the normative closure of hetero coupling or the pride of defined gay identity.

1984

April

Queen's video for 'I Want to Break Free' has the entire band in drag, with a storyline based on long-running British soap *Coronation Street*. Freddie, naturally, is the brassy barmaid Bet Lynch, albeit keeping his thick black moustache. There are ballet segments too, with Mercury – moustache-less – recreating Nijinsky in *L'Après-midi d'un faune*.

September

'Blue Jean', the first single off *Tonight*, the follow-up to the blockbusting *Let's Dance*, comes with a twenty-minute mini-film directed by Julien Temple. Bowie plays two roles in *Jazzin' for Blue Jean*: uncool nonentity Vic and self-preening rock star Screaming Lord Byron. This provides an opportunity for some amusing self-mockery, as Vic accuses the Bowie-like Byron of being a 'conniving, randy, bogus-Oriental old queen! Your record sleeves are better than your songs!' The song, alas, is the merest afterthought, while the album might be the most desultory thing Bowie ever recorded (although there'll be other contenders in the second half of the decade). The record sleeves are ghastly too.

1985

January

A new London club night called Taboo takes the next logical step
in the glam>>New Romantic escalation: concentrating on visual
shock and sidelining music almost completely. Its host, Aussie
expatriate Leigh Bowery, hopes to become 'the Andy Warhol of
London', with a menagerie of superstar freaks. Bowery is a fan of
Huysmans's *Against Nature*: like that novel's Jean des Esseintes,
he dedicates his entire existence to monstrosity and artifice. His
whole week is spent conceiving and creating the hallucinatory
kitsch of his costume, hair and make-up for the next night of
Taboo. Bowery looks like 'modern art on legs', as Boy George puts
it. He also performs onstage: one infamous routine involves giving
messy birth to a giant-size baby (actually his female companion
curled up upside down inside Bowery's voluminous costume).
Uncontrollably druggy and bitchy, Taboo's atmosphere is 'extreme,
severe, intense, nasty', recalls scenester Matthew Glammore, who
claims he used to vomit on people for a laugh. Unlike the Blitz or
the Batcave, no bands or pop stars emerge from the Taboo scene,
although Bowery does later front the outfit Minty. But music is
strictly a background soundtrack to the exhibitionism.

1986

April

David Bowie has a supporting role in Julien Temple's movie musical *Absolute Beginners*. The *Great Rock 'n' Roll Swindle* director
sent Bowie a copy of Colin MacInnes's 1959 cult novel – a snapshot of the late-fifties dawn of the Teen Age in Britain – followed
by an early draft of the script. Bowie agreed to write and sing the
theme tune, but only if he could play the part of the advertising
executive Vendice Partners. He models the character on ad men

he'd encountered during his brief stint at the Hirst agency in the early sixties, copying the way they flitted back and forth between a buzzed-up faux-American accent and the grey rasp of a native-born Englishman. 'Vendice Partners' sounds like a pun on vendors and the notion of salesmanship, but also a company name (Bowie's 'corporation of characters' perhaps). It also echoes Vance Packard, whose *The Hidden Persuaders* Bowie devoured as a youth. One of Packard's revelations concerned Madison Avenue's development of subliminal advertising: images flickering too briefly to be consciously perceived but which could motivate people to crave products. In 1976, Bowie enthused about the banned technique: 'If it hadn't been outlawed, it would have gone out of advertising very quickly and straight into politics. I would have excelled at it.'

Along with the *Absolute Beginners* theme, Bowie writes and performs another song, 'That's Motivation', which accompanies the film's most striking song-and-dance routine – equal parts eighties promo video and Gene Kelly flashback. Sharp-suited Partners escorts the movie's central character, eighteen-year-old photographer Colin, through a bustling office where copy-writers shout out buzzwords – 'DAZZLING!', 'RADIANT!', 'KING-SIZE!' – at Partners's finger-snap command. Ad man and cameraman dance on top of a massive typewriter, scale an Everest of frozen food, jive on the polar top of a spinning globe that symbolises the Jet Age, and groove on a giant-size 45 rpm single. Motivation figures in the song as the electrical current of capitalist existence – what drives the general public to products or politicians ('Now you has mass motivation,' exults Partners), but also what propels the individual forward in confident anticipation of success. During the dance routine, Partners drop-kicks Colin across the floor and into a mirror. The two stare at their own reflections in the cratered glass; Partners croons, 'Then you learn to fall in love with yourself,' before abruptly shoving Colin right through the cracked mirror. 'That's Motivation' could almost be a time capsule of advice beamed back to the young, struggling David Jones by his successful older self: a manual for self-manufacture. The lyrics are positive-visualisation mantras: Partners instructs Colin to ask himself each morning, 'Why am I so exciting? / What makes me dramatic?'

Like most retro culture, *Absolute Beginners* addresses its present as much as the historical past: it's about the early eighties even more than the late fifties. Hyped by the style magazines for a good two years before the lavish spectacle finally reached the screens, *Absolute Beginners* uses the UK's pop past to hold up a flattering mirror to its pop present: the London demi-monde of video directors, club promoters, stylists, clothes designers and ex-art-school bands, all of whom had learnt the art of posing from Bowie and Ferry. Profuse with pop-star wannabes singing in ersatz American, *Absolute Beginners* confirms the new orthodoxy of the style press: British pop genius lies not in musical creativity per se, but in repackaging the danceable sounds of black America – *tarting them up*, to use the phrase Bowie had wielded back in '72. But the movie – abysmal apart from the bits with Bowie and Ray Davies – is an absolute bust, ultimately serving as a gravestone-shaped bookend to an era.

1987

March

Running out of aesthetic steam, Siouxsie and the Banshees release a treading-water/taking-stock album of cover versions paying homage to formative influences. A third of them are glam: Roxy Music, Sparks, Iggy, Kraftwerk ('Hall of Mirrors', what else?). The album's title: *Through the Looking Glass*.

May

For 'If I Was Your Girlfriend' – the second single off his master-piece double album *Sign '⊕' the Times* – Prince transgenders his vocal, pitching it up to become the feminine alter ego Camille. This gender-morph is the vehicle for a delirious fantasy of some-how becoming his girl's best female friend: helping her pick out clothes, confiding and advising, hanging out without the hang-ups caused by the sexual divide. 'Would you run to me if somebody hurt you even if that somebody was me?' 'If I Was Your Girlfriend' comes from an unreleased album created entirely around the Camille character. Prince-ologists claim the name was inspired by nineteenth-century French intersex person Alexina Barbin, who was raised as a girl, got reclassified as male aged twenty-two, and used the gender-indeterminate name Camille thereafter. Prince might have encountered Barbin's rediscovered memoir, published in 1980, or seen or read about the 1985 movie *Mystère Alexina*. Alexina/Camille grappled externally with uncomprehending med-ical and religious institutions, and internally with persistent feel-ings of not belonging – 'vague sadness', 'inexpressible uneasiness', 'strange perplexity' – culminating in suicide aged thirty. Prince's embrace of Camille adds strength to the contemporary view of him as an inherently queer artist (if rampantly hetero in his private life). As does his later career-damaging gesture of swapping his given name for an unpronounceable glyph composed out of the male and female symbols.

September

Filed under pop metal, Def Leppard are really glam. Fans and aspirants to The Sweet's ultra-produced sound, they find their own Phil Wainman in Mutt Lange, who's rumoured to record each power chord individually, retuning after each plectrum impact because the strings go minutely out of tune. From the mega-selling

Hysteria, the dub-cratered single 'Pour Some Sugar on Me' is as sonically radical as David Essex's 'Rock On' – a song they'll cover, and make a decent fist of, two decades later.

1988

June
The Decline of Western Civilization Part II is Penelope Spheeris's documentary about what's generally known as hair metal. But the scene's true aficionados simply call it glam. The links are clear and even direct sometimes: W.A.S.P.'s Blackie Lawless, originally from Staten Island, was actually in the New York Dolls for half a minute, replacing Johnny Thunders during the group's last tour, and later he was in the group Killer Kane with Arthur Kane. For other hair-metal bands, the Dolls-y and glammy influence is mediated by the shockingly pretty Finnish group Hanoi Rocks. Flouncy-scarf-wearing Aerosmith and Kiss are in the mix too. Boot camp for many key players on the Sunset Strip glam-metal scene was an outfit with the overtly Anglophile name London, which existed from 1978 to 1981 and then again in the late eighties: alumni include Nikki Sixx (later in Mötley Crüe), W.A.S.P.'s Blackie Lawless, Guns N'Roses guitarist Izzy Stradlin and Fred Coury of Cinderella.

By the time Spheeris rolls up to the Strip with her camera crew, glam metal's been going a while and has made commercial incursions with Ratt, Quiet Riot (covering Slade's 'Cum on Feel the Noize'), Mötley Crüe, Poison, Warrant and many more. 'Hair metal' catches on because the hair is long, well conditioned, blow dried, often dyed golden blond or streaked. But it could just as well have been called 'make-up metal': eyeliner and mascara are de rigueur, with some going as far as eyeshadow, pink gloss lipstick, blusher. Essentially, hair-metal dudes dress to look like the women in the audience they hope to have sex with. Beneath the flash throbs basic raunch'n'roll that's hooky and hip-grinding: good for shouting along and dancing to. Which is not something you can say about thrash, death, speed, crust or any of the other dark 'n' doomy genres that together make up a gathering force of resistance to pretty-boy pop metal during the eighties. Just about the only thing overground and underground metal retain in common is screeching, emotional-content-devoid guitar solos, but glam at least keeps 'em concise.

Probably the glammest thing about glam metal is its obsession with stardom and the beyond-parody lifestyle of sleazy excess it promises. Watching *Decline of Western Civilization*, what's striking – but also unsettling – is the absolute unwavering self-belief of the bands. Every last one – no matter how patently talent-free – is convinced it's going to happen for them. Not one has a back-up plan. Failure is inconceivable. Fame is their manifest destiny, a matter not of 'if' but 'when' – just so long as they want it hard enough.

1989

May

The eighties started out looking like they were going to be the Bowie Decade, both in terms of his own full-spectrum dominance (album sales and tours, but also starring roles in films like *Merry Christmas Mr Lawrence* and an acclaimed Broadway performance as the lead in *The Elephant Man*) and his influence being legion. But by the mid-decade point, it all went very wrong: *Tonight*, the Live Aid 'Dancing in the Street' video team-up with Jagger, the preposterously overblown 'Glass Spider' tour, *Never Let Me Down*, the flop Jim Henson movie *Labyrinth* . . . Bowie later recalled being unhappy and directionless for much of the late eighties, while his friend Julien Temple spoke of the singer's struggle with the 'gruelling nature of reinvention . . . the huge creative surge required to do that again and again. It takes its toll, psychically.'

Bowie-ism itself has gone out of style, with a shift towards underground rock and anti-glamour. Bowie's antennae, sharp as ever, detect this. Although he has sometimes mocked the notion of himself as a chameleon, pointing out that the lizard changes colour to be inconspicuous, to not stand out from its surroundings – hardly Bowie's MO or desire! – 'chameleonic' fits with what he does when he forms Tin Machine. Influenced by alt-rock groups like Pixies and Sonic Youth, who'd been developing the template for what would later reach the mainstream as grunge, Bowie subsumes himself for the first time within the band format. Tin Machine, at least in theory, is a democracy: on the self-titled debut's front cover, Bowie appears as just one bloke among four equals. The album is recorded live, with no overdubs, a raw blast of guitar, bass, drums and voice that is intended, says guitarist Reeves Gabrels, as a two-fingered gesture to all that dance crap on the radio. Tin Machine songs are 'screaming at the world', adds Gabrels – and note how the interviews pointedly involve the entire band, not just the star frontman. In another first, Bowie grows a beard – a sign of the coming times, anticipating the facial hair soon to be rife among alt-rock and grunge bands.

1990

March
Madonna's black-and-white retro-glamour video for 'Vogue' either pays tribute to or co-opts New York's gay subculture of balls and costumed competition, to create an anthem of escape-through-fantasy and magical masquerade. Learn from the screen gods and goddesses who 'gave good face', advises Madge; 'strike a pose, there's nothing to it'.

December

In the winter of '91/2, music undergoes one of its periodic phase-shifts, swinging violently from glam to anti-glam. The vainglory of hair metal gets swept away by the grunge mudslide. Grunge is literally glamour's opposite, signifying 'dirt' and, by extension, society's rejected and dejected: burn-outs, slackers, the born-to-lose. MTV switches allegiance with indecent haste. The effect is like somebody's turned down the brightness on your television: garish, euphoric videos by Poison and Warrant give way to sallow-lit, dingy-looking promos by Pearl Jam, Stone Temple Pilots, Alice in Chains, Kyuss, Helmet. Grunge groups are 'anti-image' but the look – concertedly unkempt, hair almost as long as glam-metal groups but greasy and tangled – is distinct and easily copied. Alternative's anti-fashion spills into the malls, which are soon selling ripped denim, flannel shirts, even grunge-exploitation cosmetic brands like Urban Decay (makers of Asphyxia Lip Gunk), with their slogan: 'Does pink make you puke?' The visual dimension to pop is demoted nonetheless: grunge and its UK cousin shoegaze exalt overpowering sound and there's not much to look at onstage. Rituals like crowd-surfing and stage-diving collapse the distance between band and audience, subsuming all within a raucous community of equals.

And yet . . . Nirvana wear dresses in the video for 'In Bloom'. Anti-macho and pro-weirdo, Kurt Cobain sings 'Everyone is gay' in 'All Apologies'. During their *MTV Unplugged* performance, the group covers 'The Man Who Sold the World'. Less literally, you might say that Cobain was torn between glam and anti-glam impulses: tortured by his guilty desire for stardom, longing to return to the dark womb of the underground community.

1992

May

Suede's debut single, 'The Drowners', is a sensation. Brett
Anderson's swoony petulance fuses Bowie and Morrissey just like
Bernard Butler's crisp, flouncy riffs fuse Ronson and Marr. Dizzy
with homoeroticism ('We kiss in his room / To a popular tune'), the
song speaks of a longing to be ravished and engulfed. Anderson
is obsessed with erotic and emotional surrender, or as critic Barry
Walters put it more bluntly, with the idea of being the bottom.
Yet as the singer admits, his 'gayness' exists purely in the realm of
his imagination: he hasn't experimented even to the extent Bowie
had in the years leading up to 'I'm gay'. Famously – notoriously
– Anderson describes himself as 'a bisexual man who has never
had a homosexual experience'. For which he's roundly mocked,
but nonetheless he makes a persuasive case for the defence: just
because he'd 'never had someone's cock up my arse', that doesn't
make him a poseur or fraud. 'The sexuality you express is not limited to things you've experienced . . . If you're a virgin, does that
make you asexual?' When I speak with Anderson in '92, the singer
says, 'I just don't feel like I'm a fully-fledged member of the male
sex. But I think lots of men feel like that.'

1993

March

The Manic Street Preachers put out a T-shirt proclaiming 'ALL
ROCK'N'ROLL IS HOMOSEXUAL'. 'Tis a pity their sound –
their ambition is Clash meets Guns N'Roses, the result closer to
The Alarm meets Bon Jovi – is so straight-down-the-line: rousing,
combat-rocky, not the least bit fey or fantastical.

1995

June

Mirrorball is the possibly ironic title of an album by Neil Young that features Pearl Jam as his backing group. From their muddy churn to their symphony-of-brown clothes, Pearl Jam are as unglam as alt rock gets, and the team-up makes sense: Young is grunge's godfather. He's the anti-Bowie, from his unchanging sound (ragged-glory guitar plus yearning folky singing) to unchanging image (faded denim, flannel, beat-up sneakers and straw-like hair that's seemingly a stranger to conditioner). Young is the icon of the rock-reborn nineties, representing a true-grit ideal of unyielding integrity. No serial self-reinvention for ol' Neil; he sticks to his guns, like the decrepit outlaws of Peckinpah's *The Wild Bunch*.

Meanwhile, Bowie is having a bad decade. Give or take a Suede, he's disappeared as an influence/reference point, and his own profile as an active music-maker just keeps slipping. After reuniting with Nile Rodgers for the *Let's Dance* redux of *Black Tie White Noise*, he makes another attempt to revisit fruitful phases of his own past: the conceptually and sonically overcooked *Outside*, released in September, is the first time he's made music with Eno since 1979.

November

On the 25th, *Melody Maker*'s front cover is a report on Romo – a renaissance of eighties New Romanticism that's very much a reaction to unglam grunge and laddish Britpop. Journalistic champions Simon Price and Taylor Parkes pen a brilliant Romanifesto, but the majority of the bands – Plastic Fantastic, DexDexTer, Viva, Sexus – fall a good way short of the rhetoric. Romo peters out quickly. The main problem is that it is premature, breaking the twenty-year revival rule by trying to stage an early-eighties resurrection a half-decade ahead of schedule.

1996

October

Antichrist Superstar is the breakthrough album for Marilyn Manson, making them into the new Alice Cooper. Like Alice, it's the name of the band and the singer simultaneously; like Alice, he's a non-singer who's not much of a looker either but who triumphs by transforming himself into a figure of fascination–repulsion, a bête noire for Middle America's parents and an anti-hero for Middle America's kids. Unlike Alice, though, there's not much in the way of killer (or *Killer*) tunes 'n' riffs in evidence.

1997

January

Earthling is an endearing – if only semi-successful – attempt by Bowie to hitch a ride on the new vanguard of drum and bass. 'Little Wonder', the single, works beautifully: bobbing amid the churning thicket of chopped-up breaks, Bowie's frail vocal flashes all the way back to 'The London Boys'. He's done his jungle homework, talking knowledgeably about labels like Congo Natty and Kemet. Perhaps the mod in him responds to the blackness and the sheer speediness of this new London sound. But there's still the sense of running-on-empty. In truth, the most cutting-edge thing Bowie did in '97 – in the entire nineties, really – was to float his life's work on the stock market. Using innovative and then little-known financial instruments called asset-backed securities, he issued Bowie Bonds and earned an instant fortune ($55 million) by effectively selling the rights to his future royalties. Just the kind of fiddly finagling and magical-thinking speculation that brought down the world's markets just over a decade later. Classic Bowie: always the early adopter.

1998

September
On *Mechanical Animals*, industrial-metal freak show Marilyn
Manson strip away the generic-nineties ugly-noise to reveal their
inner glam. 'The Dope Show', the lead single, is modelled on Iggy
and Bowie's 'Nightclubbing', admits primary music man Twiggy
Ramirez, with some T. Rex bump 'n' grind added. For the video,
the singer replays *The Man Who Fell to Earth* in the Hollywood
Hills, costumed as a hermaphroditic alien with white latex, nip-
pleless breasts and an ambiguous crotch pouch. Falling into the
clutches of rock-biz manipulators, the starman becomes a star:
fronting Omega and the Mechanical Animals, he sports red-gloss
platform boots and Ziggy-esque glitter on his forehead, while cops
in pink uniforms French kiss in front of the stage. 'We're all stars
now in the dope show,' rasps the chorus. 'I was making a mockery
of what I was, taking a shot at myself,' Manson says of the album
years later. The heavy-handed Warholian critique of celebrity
culture resumes on 'I Don't Like the Drugs (But the Drugs Like
Me)', whose video features Manson crucified on a cross made of
television sets. One good wisecrack, though: reality TV is everyone's chance at 'fifteen minutes of shame'.

2000

April
After 857 Off-Broadway performances, award-winning cult musical *Hedwig and the Angry Inch* closes, and soon after production
starts on the movie version. Written by John Cameron Mitchell
and Stephen Trask, it's the tale of a trans rock star (played by
Mitchell) who survives botched male-to-female surgery, leaving
just the title's 'angry inch' of gender-indeterminate flesh behind.
The rock musical has an extremely chequered history, but Trask's

tunes are the most convincingly rocking specimens of the form
since *Rocky Horror*.

November

Marilyn Manson are back with *Holy Wood (In the Shadow of the
Valley of Death)*. Influenced heavily by the Columbine school
shootings – in which Manson's music was alleged to have been a
corrupting influence on the killers – it's a garbled concept album
about death and fame based around the idea of an imaginary city
where Celebritarianism is the religion. Garbling it further is the
fact that it's part of a trilogy of conceptual rock operas, but one that
runs in reverse: '96's *Antichrist Superstar* was the final instalment,
and *Holy Wood* is the start.

2001

March

'Clint Eastwood' by Gorillaz – Damon Albarn and pals hiding
behind cartoon alter egos – and the anime-style videos for Daft
Punk's 'One More Time' and 'Aerodynamic' refloat The Archies'
idea of the imaginary pop group. It's a sideways recognition of
the increasingly fantastical turn taken by pop video, with stars
approaching the status of figments spun into existence by teams of
technicians: make-up artists, hair stylists, lighting crews, video and
audio post-production units. Singing itself has become hyper-real:
vocal deficits compensated for, or strengths drastically boosted, by
the chopping up and restitching of lines or even single words from
different takes, with the composited performance further tinted
and perfected using pitch-correction technology. The audio signature of twenty-first-century pop is set to become the superhuman
glisten glazed across the radioscape by Auto-Tune and Melodyne.
As similarly intensive processes of editing and computer-generated
imagery weave their way into video, the borderline between a

human star and an animated creation gets decidedly blurry.

You could call it digital glam, or digi-glam for short. It's the logical extension of pop video's non-realistic and non-sequential traits. (A significant threshold was crossed in the late eighties with the multiple costume changes and senselessly shifting backdrops in promos like Whitney Houston's 'I Wanna Dance with Somebody' and Madonna's 'Express Yourself' and 'Vogue'.) Just like sound in the Pro Tools era, moving images have become a mouldable goo of binary code to be recombined in Frankenstein fashion. As the twenty-first century unfurls, scenes in film and TV lose integrity as real-world spaces, with material composited to improve the compositional balance – why not drop a church in the background? Post-production technicians known as graders or colourists tweak the visual palette dramatically, contrasting hues to make figures 'pop' out of their surroundings. Film it flat and fix it in the mix – that's the ethos now. The kind of Photoshop trickery long used in fashion photography becomes routine in video, with 'motion retouching' applying a perfect sheen to singers with blemished complexions (often by 'sampling' skin-tissue pixels from elsewhere), removing lipstick from teeth or shaving down the nose of a very famous pop star who appears later in this epilogue.

Daft Punk sing about 'Digital Love' in 2001. But by decade's end, they've fallen out of it and are analogue curmudgeons decrying the very techniques they'd exalted and excelled at. On 2013's *Random Access Memories*, they implore 'Give Life Back to Music'. *Trop tard, mes amis*: pop has entered the uncanny valley of no return.

October

The first Electroclash festival takes place in Williamsburg, New York. All through the grunge and gangsta nineties, authenticity and 'real-ness' had been the metrics that counted. NWA talked of 'reality rap' and 'street knowledge'; as recreated in the movie *Straight Outta Compton*, the group told a press conference that 'our art is a reflection' of what they see outside their front door, which 'ain't glamorous'. Escapist compared to gangsta and grunge, nineties rave nonetheless represented a mass secession from the mainstream in favour of underground sounds and faceless collectivity. But electroclash – a better-timed Romo, an attempted eighties resurrection bang on the twenty-year anniversary – is an early sign that glitzy fantasy is about to stage a comeback, an indication of a renewed appetite for pop that basically says, 'This *isn't* me.'

Fischerspooner are prime movers in the New York scene. Presenting themselves as harbingers of the New Pretentiousness, the duo Warren Fischer and Casey Spooner stage performances involving costume changes, choreography, video backdrops and up to thirty extras. Another crucial figure is Larry Tee, the DJ-producer-promoter who coined the term 'electroclash', runs the club Berliniamsburg and wrote the hit 'Supermodel' for drag-queen star RuPaul. Electroclash reaches glam through its eighties replay: synths, stiff drum-machine beats, cold souls and frozen poses. Equal parts Visage and *Liquid Sky*, the attitude is crystallised in Sophia Lamar's 'Fake': 'No hearts for you to break / We are the fake / The fake machines pretend to live on TV screens.'

Despite a big record deal for Fischerspooner and excitement about acts like Peaches and Miss Kittin, electroclash crumbles quickly: the songs aren't strong enough, the personalities too muted. But its influence will resurface: Lady Gaga is basically Fischerspooner with tits – and hits.

2004

September

Bryan Ferry's sons Otis and Isaac have grown up to be fanatical fox hunters. Outraged by the Labour government's ban on these ancient blood rites of the English aristocracy, Otis – a member of the Countryside Alliance and joint master of the South Shropshire Hunt – joins a storming of the House of Commons. There's a pattern here that causes Bryan's boys to be labelled 'the feral Ferrys': two years earlier, Isaac got suspended from Eton after sending an abusive email to an anti-hunting campaigner. Their father, meanwhile, continues his drift rightwards, alluding quietly in interviews to having Conservative political views, in between more lively talk of wine connoisseurship, pheasant shooting with the Earl of Arundel and his growing collection of paintings by the Bloomsbury Group.

2007

October

The flyer for New York Street Revival and Trash Dance promises 'burlesque pop. rock n roll. glam. metal'. A series of Thursday parties at the Slipper Room, they're conceived and hosted by performance artist Lady Starlight and a performer who's only just started calling herself Lady Gaga. The party's name pays homage to 1974's Hollywood Street Revival and Trash Dance festival. But where that event was an ironically winking wake for the Death of Glitter, the New York Street Revival really *is* a revival – the self-conscious announcement of glam's rebirth on the Lower East Side.

October

Britney Spears's *Blackout* is a digi-glam dystopia. It's like Britney became her own paparazzi, taking intrusive snapshots of a star's life slipping out of control and exposing them to the whole wide world. *Blackout* is – at least in part – a sonic souvenir of her *annus horribilis*: the head-shaving, the rehab, the messy divorce from Kevin Federline, the out-of-it performance at MTV's Video Music Awards. The title/hook of the second single, 'Piece of Me', invites you to hear it or think it as a 'piece of meat'. Throughout the album, the drastic vocal processing and editing applied to Britney's vocals dramatise the effects of the media glare on her life and soul. You can almost hear Britney being chopped up by the cameras and morcellated by the meme-mill of social media, disseminated and disintegrated as millions of images, tweets, reblogs . . .

2008

August

The credits for Lady Gaga's 2008 debut, *The Fame*, make a point of thanking Andy Warhol and David Bowie. In interviews, she speaks of studying the work of Klaus Nomi, Grace Jones and Leigh Bowery. Gaga gives as good quote as she gives good face. But as you'd expect with an artist whose whole career feels like postmodernism's death rattle, or perhaps its zombie-like refusal to stay dead and buried, her patter often feels like déjà vu. 'I am not real. I am theater,' Gaga declaims. She feels like she's 'on a stage all the time . . . when I'm dancing, singing, making breakfast'. Arriving at an airport, getting out of a limo outside a club – everything is performed, made into an Event. 'I adore show business and don't ever want my fans to see me in any other way.' Echoing Oscar Wilde and Alice Cooper, Gaga speaks of 'lying profusely' and how 'music is a lie . . . art is a lie'. She flippantly flips the rockist attack lines – about style eclipsing substance – by wittily arguing that her music distracts and detracts from 'the performance art' of the videos, the stage shows and the public theatre of her fame.

Truthfully, the music – 'soulless electronic pop', Gaga calls it, with a wink to the Warholites and the anti-humanists out there – is just an efficient base for the visual provocations. Arriving with perfect timing to harness YouTube's access to global audiences, Gaga rides a revival of the pop-video form. It had gone into decline from its late-nineties big-budget peak because MTV had phased out music programming in favour of non-stop reality TV. Now pop is audio-visual like it's never been before, and Gaga's right there at the forefront. A YouTube native, she's the first real digi-glam superstar, her promos dizzy with digital FX and a frenzied turnover of costume/hair/make-up changes – the latter masterminded by an entourage of creative *consigliere* known as the Haus of Gaga.

November

Kanye West's *808s & Heartbreak* is a 'woke up this morning / got me the superstar blues' album in the tradition of Nirvana's *In Utero* and Puff Daddy's *Forever*. 'Welcome to Heartbreak', for instance, is the lament of someone who conquered the world but lost his life: West half wishes he could go back to being a regular nobody, because then his schedule wouldn't be so jam-packed that he turns up late for a relative's wedding, then has to leave before they cut the cake, nor would he have such difficulties in choosing which of his many girlfriends to take. *808s* oscillates in bipolar fashion from delusions of grandeur ('My reign is as far as your eyes can see,' proclaims 'Amazing') to whimpers of inner desolation, such as the navel-gazing nadir of 'Pinocchio Story'. Here Kanye bleats about the failure of luxury goods and worshipful fans to fill up his empty soul, mewling that 'I turn on the TV and see me / And feel nothing.' Kanye feels like Pinocchio because fame has made him unreal.

Self-reflexivity was West's shtick from the start, but at first it was fetching: 'Last Call', the protracted finale to his 2004 debut *The College Dropout*, related the saga of his ascent in a way that demystified the rap industry, detailing the career moves and games you have to play to make contracts and get breaks, and touchingly revealed the crises of confidence along the long winding route to the top. But as West becomes more and more of a public figure – accusing President Bush on live TV of not caring about black people during the post-Katrina New Orleans crisis, disrupting Taylor Swift's moment of glory at a video-music-award ceremony, marrying reality-TV star Kim Kardashian – his music increasingly seems like a by-product of, or sideshow to, the megalo-melodrama of his mediatised life. On songs like 'Monster' (from 2010's *My Beautiful Dark Twisted Fantasy*) and 'I Am a God' (2013's *Yeezus*) the blend of self-aggrandisement and self-loathing takes on a pathological edge. Kanye might still be regularly talking to Jesus, but he seems far from grace. On 2016's *The Life of Pablo* – the audio equivalent of his wife's photo book of selfies – the gospel framing of the album falls away rapidly to reveal a man addicted to attention and all the trophies and triumphs of worldly glory. 'Famous' is supposedly Kanye 'breaking up' with Fame (personified here by Rihanna) but still squeezes in instantly infamous jibes at Taylor Swift, along with a legion of haters 'mad they still nameless'. Equal parts scattershot genius and splattershit grotesquerie, *Pablo* suggested that West will continue to make exhibitionist art out of the impasses of 'living without limits' – at least until Twitter tires of him completely.

2009

September

Pop video as art form may be undergoing a rebirth, but at MTV's Video Music Awards ceremony the nominated promos get shown for just a few seconds. Live performance is what the VMAs are about these days, spectacular routines that increasingly blur the borders between pop and showbiz. Pink delivers a song while hanging upside down twirled around a vertical trapeze rope – probably not the most throat-relaxing posture for singing. Two years later at the 2011 VMAs, Chris Brown takes it even closer to Vegas or the circus, back-flipping from one end of the stage to the other by near-invisible levitating wires attached to his waist.

November

The Fame Monster is the deluxe expanded version of *The Fame*, issued to capitalise on Gaga's success, with eight new tracks – including her best and bestest-selling song 'Bad Romance' – tacked on. According to Gaga, 'the runway' directly inspired these songs: 'I wrote while watching muted fashion shows and I am compelled to say my music was scored for them.' Gaga videos often do resemble runway shows, except that the background scenery changes as frenziedly as the clothes. The end result is like Cindy Sherman meets Alexander McQueen, scored by a soundtrack of eastern European club music.

There's an odd fatalism about Gaga's tryst with that femme fatale Fame: not only does she know, from the abundant literature on the subject, that celebrity is soul-eroding, she's made that the major theme of her work. Trailing the VMAs performance of 'Paparazzi', Gaga proclaims her intent 'to say something very grave about fame and the price of it'. She starts the performance with the entreaty 'amidst all of these flashing lights I pray the fame won't take my life' and ends it by enacting her own death, with fake blood gushing from her breast and a feigned hanging hoisting her into the air.

Gaga even puts out a fragrance called Fame, a black perfume designed 'to smell slutty', like an 'expensive hooker'. Notes of belladonna evoke the toxic effects of stardom. 'Vanity can create a very cruel space for you if you don't know how to manage it,' Gaga warns. There's also 'Fame Kills', a tour with Kanye West that gets cancelled after the rapper withdraws from the public eye after his VMAs intervention. Gaga is wont to talk – melodramatically, but perhaps with genuine paranoia – of her fears that she might go the way of John Lennon or Princess Diana (with whom she particularly identifies), either assassinated by a stalker or hounded to death by paparazzi.

Yet despite all its costs, all its damage, Fame seems to be all there is to believe in. No ideology or faith – nor even a real-world love – can rival its promise of self-completion. Fame, as Gaga conceives it, isn't bestowed from outside; it's a sourceless inner conviction, what she calls 'feeling the fame'. It's just a matter of externalising this internal ego-image. 'I've always been famous, it's just no one knew it yet.' The star's duty then is inculcating the fans with self-love – which for Gaga equates not just with mere self-esteem but with the certainty of one's own extraordinariness. Her 'Monster Ball' tours are 'a pop cultural church', but rather than idolising Gaga, 'I'm teaching people to worship themselves.'

This fierce 'n' fabulous flame of self-belief is a magical defence against those who'd crush your ego – and perhaps your body. Gaga speaks for the misfits, the gender-confused, the bullied. In one interview, she recalls being thrown in a street-corner trash can at the age of fourteen by three boys, with girls looking on and laughing. She felt 'worthless. Embarrassed. Mortified.' Her only crime, she says, was being talkative and theatrical – too full of herself. In 2011, Gaga starts the Born This Way Foundation, an organisation to combat bullying.

Placing a definite article in front of 'fame' in the album's title is jarring, an alienation effect. 'The fame' sounds like a disease. The further conjunction of monstrosity – the Fame Monster – is even more unsettling. Is this fame as a monster ravaging the world landscape? Or Gaga herself as a monster spawned by the mutagenic effects on the human psyche of celebrity culture? Little Monsters is what Gaga calls her fans; she is Mother Monster.

'I used to pray every night that God would make me crazy,' Gaga confesses. 'That he would instill in me a creativity and a strangeness', of the kind that drove the artists she admired. But Gaga goes beyond the clichés of genius-as-madness. Fame lust itself is a maddening virulence, a deranged will to omnipresence and overexposure that precedes any specific gift or talent, and can exist in their absence. 'I want women – and men – to feel empowered by a deeper and more psychotic part of themselves. The part they're always trying desperately to hide,' Gaga declares. 'I operate from a place of delusion – that's what *The Fame* is all about. I used to walk down the street like I was a fucking star. I want people to walk around delusional about how great they can be and then to fight so hard for it every day that the lie becomes the truth.'

2010

January

Gaga has a rival for #1 New Female Star of America – Ke$ha. Her debut album, *Animal*, goes straight in at #1; 'TiK ToK', her smash single, sells 15 million. Ke$ha and Gaga have much in common. Both ride a club-friendly electro-pop sound. Both are straight but make public gestures of solidarity with LGBT youth: Gaga holding aloft her VMA trophy and declaring, 'This is for the gays!'; Ke$ha claiming that the 'suicide epidemic' among gay teens inspired her second #1 single, 'We R Who We R'. Both tour with theatrical stage spectaculars (Ke$ha's leaning less towards fashion-shock and more to puerile-surreal – dancing phalluses!). And both Gaga and Ke$ha are inspired by glam. In Ke$ha's case, her heroes are Bolan, Iggy and Alice Cooper rather than the arty Bowie–Roxy line. Glitter – the quintessence of cheap glamour – speckles her image, artwork and live performances.

Mixing exuberant carelessness and party-until-we-drop triumphalism, Ke$ha is rock'n'roll in every respect apart from her sound, which – crafted by producer Dr Luke – is contemporary dance-pop. On 'TiK ToK' she picks herself up the morning after the party the night before and uses Jack Daniel's for mouthwash. One verse she's name-dropping Mick Jagger, the next she's unfurling a wordless spiral of yodelling joy like Morrissey at his most unfettered. In between – arriving at another party – she drops the Zen couplet 'Ain't got no money in my pocket / But I'm already here.'

Another glam aspect to Ke$ha is her androgyny: talking trash like a twenty-first-century Suzi Quatro, rapping like a mall-chick version of The Beastie Boys. She describes her sound as 'balls over dance beats' and trails her second album, *Warrior*, with the slogan 'cock pop'. Treating boys like sex toys, chasing thrills with let's-get-wrecked recklessness, Ke$ha behaves – at least in song – like male rock stars have done for decades. And for this she becomes a lightning rod for contempt and condescension, the victim of hate blogs and slut-shaming tweets. There's also a clumsy satire by Princeton humorists, in which poet Paul Muldoon conducts a 'close reading' of 'TiK ToK' – a laboured spoof that has not one-tenth the wit, the flair for language, the wild-child spark of Ke$ha's own words and delivery.

March

Nickelodeon debuts *Victorious*, a popular teen sitcom about an aspiring singer at a performing-arts school. When I was a kid, children's television involved the adventures of anthropomorphic creatures or elves and trolls, ghost-story or science-fiction scenarios, or else it was simply realistic and mundane. Today's kids' TV – certainly in America – has a peculiar preponderance of comedy-dramas about children involved in entertainment. The trend started with *Hannah Montana* (a schoolgirl who's a pop star by night) and continued with *iCarly* (teen girls who create their own hit web TV show), *Austin + Ally* (friends who become a singing duo, then open a music school), *Big Time Rush* (the travails of a rising boy band), *Liv and Maddie* (twin sisters, one of whom is a celebrity) and *Gamer's Guide to Pretty Much Everything* (a world-famous gamer). Pumping out propaganda for the notion that nothing could be finer than a life in showbiz, these Disney and Nickelodeon programmes seem deliberately designed to work as recruitment drivers, ensuring a steady supply of raw young talent for the channels to sift for potential stars. And while most fade away after a few years of child celebrity, some go on to bigger things: the *Victorious* cast produces one of the biggest pop stars of the 2010s – Ariana Grande.

April

'Alejandro', the third single off *Fame Monster*, is perfunctory nothingness vaguely redolent of Madonna's 'La Isla Bonita'. But Steven Klein's promo is a tour de force of militaristic kitsch with a specialist-porn undertone. 'It's all about where I'm from and love of theater . . . love of the lie in art,' gushes Gaga. The 'where I'm from' probably refers to the Italian-American Catholic upbringing she shares with Madonna, figuring in the promo as compulsive blasphemy: Gaga as a nun in a red latex habit swallowing blood-red rosary beads. But *Cabaret* is in the mix too, and maybe *Evita*. The video oozes junta chic mingled with mood-tones from Tom of Finland. In yet another Madonna nod, Gaga wears a bra with machine-gun barrels jutting out as death nipples. Wrestlers from some between-the-wars military academy grapple homoerotically, clad in black shiny shorts and calf-length black boots. The whole 'Alejandro' promo is a visual tone-poem translation of the famous last sentences of Sontag's 'Fascinating Fascism': 'The color is black, the material is leather, the seduction is beauty, the justification is honesty, the aim is ecstasy, the fantasy is death.'

May

The ArchAndroid is the debut album from Janelle Monáe, ex-drama student and Afro(retro)futurist dandy. Her style blurs the lines between R&B, art pop and show tunes, while her videos and

tours are costumed and choreographed with regimental fastid-
iousness. *The ArchAndroid* is a sci-fi concept record and, like
its successor *The Electric Lady*, is part of the seven-part series
Metropolis.

June

Rappers have rhymed about fame's pleasures and pitfalls before:
Eminem with the stalker-fan song 'Stan', Kanye West . . . Drake
takes it to the next level by achieving fame with *Thank Me Later*,
an album about the process of becoming famous. Opening track
'Fireworks' boasts about 'looking down from the top' at streets
crowded with nobodies he's only just left behind. 'The Resistance'
and 'Over' address the disorientation of nascent stardom: sudden
fits of insecurity, a swarm of hangers-on he didn't know a year ago,
girls saying they love him. On 'Light Up' Jay-Z guest-raps about
how 'these bright lights turned me to a monster', while Drake
offers, 'Welcome to Hollywood, don't let this town ruin you.' A
child TV actor before he was a rapper, Drake has developed a
unique diffuse style that floats back and forth between rapping and
singing; likewise, his tone and lyrics waver between needy vulner-
ability and smug self-regard. Swaddled in gauzy folds of ambient
texture, Drake seems to leak out of the radio, making listeners feel
like they're inside his mind – a mind flitting woozily back and forth
'between psychotic and iconic'.

Drake follows *Thank Me Later* with another album largely about
fame, *Take Care*, which was swiftly followed by another album
largely about fame, *Nothing Was the Same*. He is pioneering a new
stage in rap's evolution, what might fairly be termed its decadence:
where the glitter flakes off all the prizes you've strived for, where
triumphalism fades to hollow inside. Perceiving the emptiness
doesn't discourage the sad rapper from filling the void with sex,
drugs and commodity fetishes. Even as he raps disconsolately

about how 'this is supposed to be what dreams are made of', Drake enthuses publicly about his plan to build the biggest residential swimming pool in the world. Thanks to Drake, a spiritual void and largesse tristesse become status symbols in rap, 'just what comes with the fame'.

June
Spinning off a pop career from being a popular and openly gay runner-up on *American Idol*, Adam Lambert kicks off his first major tour, titled 'Glam Nation'. His fans call themselves Glamberts. Later, Lambert fronts Queen and appears on *Glee* as Elliot 'Starchild' Gilbert. On shows like *Glee* and contests like *The X Factor*, pop history is being folded back into showbiz, the border between musical theatre and rock increasingly dissolved. All of it is there 'for your entertainment', as Lambert titles his debut album.

October
The spirit of 'School's Out' in the body of techno, Ke$ha's 'We R Who We R' is the greatest rave anthem of the twenty-first century – regardless of whether it's ever been played at a rave, which it probably hasn't. Like her follow-up smash 'Blow', it's a fight-for-your-right-to-party rally cry for the YOLO generation. Ke$ha's favourite trope is the apocalyptic scenario of time running out, the urgency of living like it's the last night of your life. This mood of embattled binge-hedonism underpins the desperate lust for life of 'Animal' and 'Till the World Ends', the Britney hit that Ke$ha co-wrote. With 'Die Young', the lead single off *Warrior*, it approaches self-parody.

October
Katy Perry's 'Firework' is not a cover of the Siouxsie song. It's an everybody-is-a-star anthem in which Perry encourages someone

who feels worthless (like a discarded 'plastic bag') to ignite her
inner spark and spectacularly reveal her glory to the world: 'Own
the night like the Fourth of July . . . Make 'em go "Oh, oh, oh".'
Self-affirmation imagery of this sort flickers through hits like Nicki
Minaj's 'Starships' ('twinkle twinkle little star' – that means you,
listener), Rihanna's 'Diamonds' ('shine bright like . . .'), Ke$ha's
'We R Who We R' ('you know we're superstars') and many others.
'Feminine incandescence' is the term used by critic Robin James
to describe these songs that often involve 'the transformation of
waste and melancholy into glowing potential'. Feminine incandescence is basically synonymous with Gaga's 'feeling the fame' –
inner certainty that you're destined for more.

What lies behind this spate of songs? Jean M. Twenge has an
idea or two. In her 2006 book *Generation Me* and 2009 sequel *The
Narcissism Epidemic* (co-authored with W. Keith Campbell) she
points the finger at parental practices and educational policies that
instil an unearned sense of specialness: 'inflated feedback', overly
positive reinforcement, praise spread equally regardless of actual
achievement. Because American schools don't allow hymns, secular 'uplift' anthems like 'Don't Stop Believing', 'Eye of the Tiger'
or 'Let It Go' (from *Frozen*) take up the slack, inculcating the
world view that David Smail called 'magical voluntarism' – 'if you
will it, it will come about'. In the chapter 'We Will All Be Famous'
Twenge points to surveys that show the effects of all the self-
esteem boosting and 'follow your dreams' ideology: a generation
that harbours unrealistic expectations of 'glamour jobs' (acting,
sports, music) and thinks 'being a celebrity' is 'the very best thing
in the world'. But this narcissism is brittle, liable to collapse on
contact with a real world where opportunities are shrinking. In the
chapter 'Raising Royalty', the title inspired by the vogue for kids'
T-shirts like 'My World, My Rules' and 'Little Princess', Twenge
and Campbell argue that today's 'softer' style of child rearing

– parents who act more like friends than authority figures – leads to weakened self-reliance and less firm ego boundaries, feeding into the culture of oversharing.

2011

January

Like her forefather Bowie, Gaga's acute self-consciousness and relentless self-curation don't discourage analysis by others, they incite it. Think pieces, blog essays, books (from bios to queer-theory works like J. Jack Halberstam's *Gaga Feminism*) erupt around her videography and discography, parsing and placing the densely encrusted references and allusions. Gaga practically pleads to be analysed using prisms like Baudrillardian hyper-reality, cyber-feminism and queer performativity. Academia always used to lag behind pop culture (punk studies went into overdrive during the eighties), but barely eighteen months into her stardom, the Lady Gaga and the Sociology of the Fame course is up and running at the University of South Carolina from spring 2011. Its creator, Professor Mathieu Deflem, becomes famous in his own right, leading him to write an academic paper on his experience of celebrity-by-association, 'Professor Goes Gaga'. In an interview, Deflem talks about the spiralling disorientation he felt: 'You kind of undergo it. You experience it. You do not really have any control.'

May

All this being-taken-so-seriously seems to affect Gaga: on *Born This Way*, the follow-up to *The Fame Monster*, she comes over like a pop stateswoman, addressing important issues, and in interviews talks about wanting to 'be at rallies with the fans, being a part of their voice, helping to mobilize and enforce change'. Conflating same-sex marriage rights and the plight of illegal immigrants to the US over a mariachi–HiNRG hybrid, 'Americano' blends the didactic and the tacky. Elsewhere on *Born This Way* there's a new bulk to the sound matching the weightier themes: stadium rock and eighties schlock add ballast and bombast to the clubby sound, flavours of Springsteen, Pat Benatar, Jim Steinman. 'The Edge of Glory' features E Street Band sax man Clarence Clemons; Brian May guests on 'Yoü and I'. The pomp-rock elements allow Gaga to flex her conventional musical prowess as pianist and singer. 'Born This Way', the lead single, is an all-purpose pride anthem for the LGBT community and anybody who feels weird, marginalised or 'culturally queer'. Brassy and blaring, the song 'not only plagiarizes Madonna, it super-sizes her', writes critic Pat Blashill, referring to the common perception that the song owes a lot to 'Express Yourself'. Advising 'don't be a drag, just be a queen' and asserting 'we are all born superstars', 'Born This Way' actually cuts against the glam principle of self-invention by effectively claiming that deviance isn't a choice but a fated, quasi-biological identity: God made me like this. But isn't it more radical – more glam – to say, 'I wasn't born this way, I'm choosing to go against nature'?

August

At the 2011 Video Music Awards, Gaga does a full-blown drag-king turn as her male alter ego Jo Calderone. The persona is seemingly modelled on bad boy Johnny in *The Outsiders* – greased-back hair, cigarette tucked behind the ear, lip-curled sneer – although other possibilities are Annie Lennox's turn as a sideburned fifties hood at the 1984 Grammys, and Anybodys, the tomboy who hangs around the Jets in *West Side Story*. Although her songs are mostly about hetero love-lust, Gaga plays the gender-confusion game as well as anybody since, well, Bowie. She propagates, or encourages, the rumour that she's a hermaphrodite, causing fans to scrutinise photos for suspicious bulges and rewind repeatedly the YouTube clip that seems to catch a 'penis' slipping out when she mounts a motorcycle in a skimpy skirt.

2012

February

At the 2012 Grammy Awards, rap star Nicki Minaj showcases new single 'Roman Reloaded' with an outlandish performance that combines stage spectacular and pre-recorded movie (*The Exorcism of Roman*, a pastiche of *The Exorcist*) and involves monk-robed dancers, a backdrop of giant stained-glass windows and Penn and Teller-style levitation illusions. The Roman in the title is Roman Zolanski – just one of fourteen alter egos used by Minaj in her songs and videos. Among the main ones are the super-cute, 'any colour so long as it's pink' anime-like doll Harajuku Barbie; the headscarf-wearing Nicki Teresa, aka the Healer; and Zolanski, described by Minaj as both her inner demon twin and her gay brother. There's also Roman's British mother Martha Zolanski, whose accent is precisely midway between Kate Bush and Siouxsie.

Some of Minaj's facility with voices and role-play comes from her studying theatre at Fiorello H. LaGuardia High School of Music & Art and Performing Arts – the setting for *Fame*. Alter egos aren't unprecedented in rap and R&B, either. Eminem's use of personae like Slim Shady paved the way both for Minaj and for Beyoncé's Sasha Fierce (an alter ego 'too aggressive, too strong, too sassy, too sexy!' for real-life Bey, she says). Commentators are quick to label Minaj the 'black Gaga', a comparison she vehemently rejects. She says the identity games started back in childhood as a form of fantasy escape from domestic turbulence. Whatever the source, the echoes of seventies glam and Bowie are evident. As one presenter on a pop-video channel puts it, 'There isn't a single "Nicki Minaj" . . . she says she's just being herself, but who she is *changes every day.*'

September

For half a decade now, Amanda Palmer's been pursuing an edgier
form of the resurgent pop theatricality of the twenty-first century in the duo The Dresden Dolls: darker and more European,
'Brechtian punk cabaret'. Now Palmer's controversially crowd-
funded solo album *Theatre Is Evil* breaks into the US Top 10.
Talking to *Alternative Press*, she comes across as a daughter of
Bowie, a hyper-productive polymath: 'I've wanted to do 15 artistic
projects at one time, and I didn't want anyone to fucking tell me
how to do them. I think being a rockstar was the easiest container
to pursue to do all the things I wanted to. Theater, film, music and
performance art all kind of fall under the umbrella of rock 'n' roll
. . . Because I grew up doing community theatre and watching
MTV . . . all signs pointed towards a life in rock 'n' roll.'

2013

January

In a brilliantly organised stealth attack, on the 8th of the month
David Bowie emerges from a decade's silence with 'Where Are
We Now?' The single is a wistful reverie of his Berlin years, the
singer describing himself as a 'man lost in time near KaDeWe'
(a reference to a famous department store) who's reached that
twilight time of life when memory-ghosts are constant companions. Strolling through Berlin, Bowie's 'just walking the dead'.
The Next Day album follows, its contents shadowed by his brush
with mortality (the massive 2003 heart attack that precipitated his
undeclared retirement), and earns his best reviews for a couple
of decades. The cover is the original front sleeve of *"Heroes"* but
with a white square that almost but not quite obliterates Bowie's
face – a symbol of Time obliterating even the most heroic of
artistic achievements? Blank space of another sort, the *tabula rasa*
of possibility, is celebrated by 'David Bowie Is', the title of the

concurrent retrospective at the Victoria and Albert Museum. His whole career has been about filling in that blank, then wiping the slate clean and starting again.

February

Beyoncé's half-time performance at the Super Bowl is the victory lap capping off her global superstardom. Planned for months, costing millions, involving 500 local volunteers to erect the stage in addition to Beyoncé's own crew, the fifteen-minute mini-concert is a celebration of Queen Bey's remorseless flawlessness. It starts with a taped speech of football manager Vince Lombardi gravely exhorting the pursuit of excellence 'with all of one's might'. The glamour and clamour, Lombardi intones, are just the exterior testament to what really matters: an implacable inner drive to dominate, 'the spirit, the will to excel, the will to win'. Beyoncé literally erupts onto the stage, to the sound of her hit 'Run the World'. For the next fourteen minutes she flexes her vocal training and rehearsed flair amid what seems like hundreds of lights blaring thousands of watts. It's a fiesta of feminine incandescence – jets of fire, guitars with Roman candles ejaculating sparks from either end of the instrument – with special FX mirroring that 'clones' a mini-army of Beyoncés.

Beyoncé at the Super Bowl is like the panopticon in reverse: surveillance turned inside out, 'all eyes on me'. A hundred and ten million watch it in real time; many more worldwide catch it later on the Internet. 'All minds on me' too: the performance generates 300,000 tweets per minute. Swooning reviewers pay tribute like bedazzled courtiers. *Rolling Stone*, for instance, gushes that the set's supposed absence of crowd-pleasing favourites indicates that '*she's Beyoncé and Beyoncé can get away with doing whatever Beyoncé feels like doing*'.

The Beyoncé spectacular is nominated in multiple technical

categories at the Emmys. But it wins for just one: 'Outstanding Lighting Design/Lighting Direction'. Deservedly, as it's the overkill climax of an illumination escalation that has seen awards ceremonies and arena shows get more audience-stunning and retina-bruising with each year. Historically, light and power have always been linked, from the candle power that only lords and kings could afford, to the splendour of bright dyes and glittering gems that shone out in a world of murk and squalor. Beyoncé at the Super Bowl is where bling and blitz converge, a tour de force of shock and awe.

March

South Korean group GLAM – it stands for Girls Be Ambitious – release their third single, 'In Front of the Mirror'. They're just one of scores of K-pop acts whose sound mashes together elements of R&B, rap and Euro club sounds. Video-wise, there's a similar whirl of decontextualised signifiers: dance moves and clothing and fetish objects drawn from skateboarding, goth/emo, Disney, ballet, ghetto fabulous, dystopian science fiction, fetish wear, retro vintage and a dozen more style dialects. Luxury rubs against the militaristic; American sports juxtapose with Japanese imperial uniforms. Androgyny is a big element in K-pop – but only for the boys, whose already-perfect skin is digitally sanded to a ceramic glisten. The girls are as hyper-femme as Minaj's Harajuku Barbie (probably inspired by K-pop or its Japanese counterpart, J-pop). Perhaps the most intriguing thing about K-pop's cachet with a select bunch of Western hipsters is its *lack* of exoticism. Barely perceptible quirks of cultural distance creep in here and there, but for the most part it's a mirror image of Britney- and One Direction-type pop, a simulation of a simulation of a simulation. Half sweatshop, half sweetshop, South Korea's audio-video industry churns out the ultimate in digi-glam: eye/ear candy so denatured and ultrabrite it's hard to hold onto the idea that there is a 'real' behind the pixie-dust pixels flickering over your eyeballs. Watching G-Dragon or 2NE1 miniaturised on a smartphone or tablet, it feels even more like transmissions from some fairy-tale world.

June

An out-of-the-blue worldwide hit in 2013, Lorde's 'Royals' recalls '"Heroes"' (and fancy that, the LP it's on is called *Pure Heroine*). It revolves around the idea of cash-poor kids from nowhere towns who'll 'never be royals' but still manage to achieve moments of glory in their ordinary lives, far from the limelight and 'the lux'. Lorde sings about being a queen bee (or is it Queen Bey?) with just the one subject: her boyfriend. Critics, some pro and some con, take the song as an explicit rebuke to the regality of recent rap: in the video for 'Bow Down', Beyoncé is draped in crown jewels; her consort Jay-Z records an album with Kanye West called *Watch the Throne*; in 'Moment 4 Life' Nicki Minaj proclaims, 'it's my empire . . . In this very moment I'm king,' while guest rapper Drake demands foes and hoes 'bow down' to 'a young king'. But I like to imagine that Lorde might have also been inspired by an episode from the 2007 series *I'm from Rolling Stone*, an unlikely and unsuccessful reality-TV show about aspiring rock writers competing for a salaried job. One contestant, Krystal, loiters outside a red-carpet event for the launch of Paris Hilton's album. When the heiress and pop-star wannabe turns up with her mom, Krystal gushes uncontrollably about how honoured she feels to be in the presence of 'the iconic family . . . royalty to me'. Mrs Hilton looks disdainfully at the peasant and turns away without a word.

October

Sia's op-ed 'My Anti-Fame Manifesto' is published in *Billboard*. For years a hugely successful songwriter for hire but a not very successful singer, Sia Furler has decided she'll only perform with her features hidden behind an oversize Warhol-esque platinum-blonde wig. The ruse – turning glamour into a shield against the public gaze – results in a peculiar form of faceless stardom. For videos such as breakthrough single 'Chandelier' Sia goes even further, recruiting the child dancer Maddie Ziegler as her stand-in persona; at concerts, Ziegler cavorts around the stage while Sia sings with her back to the audience. In the *Billboard* manifesto – for which she appeared on the front cover with a paper bag over her head – Sia describes the social-media scrutiny suffered by stars she's worked alongside as a self-esteem-eroding onslaught: a million 'sharp-tongued' mother-in-laws creating 'never dreamed of' insecurities. 'So me and fame will never be married.' As heard on 2014's *1000 Forms of Fear* and its 2016 follow-up *This Is Acting*, Sia's music is a ruthlessly efficient hook-machine of Euro-club beat-bombast and soaring-yet-groaning vocals in the Gaga–Rihanna style – *The Fame Monster* without the art trappings. And without the fame.

November
After *Born This Way*'s bombast, Gaga takes the fatal step further into hubris with *ARTPOP*. The fanfare for the album (plus related transmedia activity) claims that Gaga will 'bring art culture into pop in a reverse Warholian expedition' – only forty years after Bowie accomplished that mission. 'I live for the applause applause applause,' Gaga proclaims on the lead single 'Applause' – only to be met with resounding silence from the global pop audience.

2014

August
Ending two decades of reclusive semi-retirement only sporadically interrupted by low-key album releases, Kate Bush returns to the

stage with a twenty-two-concert run at the London Apollo, triggering non-stop coverage and rejoicing on mainstream and social media alike. 'Before the Dawn' is her first live show since 1979's 'Tour of Life', and the fans are ecstatic, many watching it with tears streaming down their faces. Barely a voice can be heard dissenting from the coronation of Kate as National Treasure. Yet somehow in my gut I know my friend Samantha is right when she privately reveals her disappointment as a long-time Bush fan who coughed up nearly £300 for a pair of tickets: 'The show was little more than a prog-rock *Jackanory* . . . an excruciating panto . . . wish this concert had never happened to us.'

August

K-pop already approaches the state of animation. Digi-glam's next frontier comes with the label PC Music and its roster of semi-imaginary pop stars: Lipgloss Twins, Princess Bambi, Hannah Diamond. Co-produced by PC mastermind A. G. Cook, QT's 'Hey QT' (released on XL) sounds like four-year-old Lola from the UK cartoon series *Charlie and Lola*, now grown up enough for first crushes and texting. Wittily playing on the idea of Auto-Tune-era pop as an artificial buzz, QT is linked to a fictitious energy drink called DrinkQT. The highly polarising PC is much discussed in hip circles, but the motivations behind its ultra-brite sound remain shadowy. What's the point, exactly? Not satire or parody, says Cook. Sympathetic observers identify the PC aesthetic as 'post-irony': a simulation of the mainstream that is very slightly askew, replacing critique and commentary 'with ambiguity and uncanniness'.

September

And then the strategic retreat: Gaga makes the classic hip-to-be-square switch. First she sings a *Sound of Music* medley at the Academy Awards. Then she partners with crooner Tony Bennett

for the best-selling *Cheek to Cheek* album and tour. A deliberate echo of Bowie's 'Peace on Earth/Little Drummer Boy' duet
with Bing Crosby for that 1977 TV special? Or just a shrewd, safe
career move?

October

Jeffrey Osbourne's animated video for Nicki Minaj's 'Only' recalls
the Pathé newsreel-like fantasies in the movie version of *Billy Liar*
– Fisher's dreams of being the dictator of Ambrosia. Presented as
something like a cross between a Führer and a pharaoh, Minaj is
fanned by vassals and flanked by banners bearing a swastika-like
symbol. The animation is styled to look like a thirties propaganda
film, with digitally faked scratches on the celluloid. The colour
palette is totalitarian – black, red, white, grey. Clad in a shiny black
bodysuit, Minaj appears with an entourage of ministers and mar-
shals. All maintain the same static, rigid posture – commanding
and haughty. Serried ranks of stormtroopers get inspected by their
leader; images unfurl of tanks, Speer-style pseudo-classical architecture, missile gantries, gas masks, V-2-like rockets, explosions and
surveillance cameras. Drake, guest rapping, appears as some kind of
cardinal, or maybe the Pope. The video causes an outcry and Minaj
apologises, insisting that 'I'd never condone Nazism in my art.'

October

True fans always understood that 'Ke$ha' was a persona, but it *felt*
real, rooted in Kesha Sebert's actual self. *Animal* and *Cannibal*,
she said, presented an amped-up cartoon of the fairly feral lifestyle
she led in Los Angeles in the immediate pre-fame years. 'Ke$ha'
was Kesha Sebert's actual personality multiplied by ten. That's
what she said at the height of her success, anyway. Then came
2013's *Warrior* – which flopped, I think, because you could tell
Kesha's heart wasn't in it. She sounded like she'd been hired for

the job of being 'Ke$ha'; like she was impersonating herself, and wanly. In truth, her real desire with *Warrior* had been to release a full-blown rock record, but she'd been persuaded out of the idea by her radio-conscious minders. Out of all the jams she'd recorded with alt-rockers such as Flaming Lips, only 'Dirty Love' – a raunchy duet with a bemused-sounding Iggy Pop – made *Warrior's* final cut. But going along with Dr Luke's 'advice' about sticking with the winning formula didn't pay off: the formula stopped winning. The career crisis turned personal when Ke$ha checked into a rehab facility in early 2014 to recover from bulimia. Her mother and songwriting partner Peba claimed Luke had triggered this by telling Ke$ha she was overweight.

Then, in October of that year, Ke$ha stunned the pop world by suing Dr Luke for sexual and emotional abuse dating back to the early years of their long involvement. The alleged misconduct included plying her with drugs, rape (when she was a virgin), emotional abuse and general domination of her musical direction. In her account, Luke had been something like Kim Fowley to Ke$ha's one-girl Runaways. Luke counter-sued for defamation, claiming that Sebert was making a transparent attempt to break loose from her contract. The ensuing free-fire of accusations and litigation froze Ke$ha's career dead, preventing her from releasing new music and spawning the 'Free Kesha' movement.

In the court of public opinion, Dr Luke was instantly judged guilty. It makes sense that people would side instinctively with Ke$ha. Not only is she more endearing than the shadowy Svengali, it's also the feminist thing to do. It didn't hurt that Ke$ha's claims coincided with a flurry of historic sex-crime cases involving male abusers in the entertainment world: Jimmy Savile, Gary Glitter, Bill Cosby and many more. But the sad truth is that either scenario is a lose–lose for Ke$ha fans. If Dr Luke's contention turned out to be true, then our heroine would be exposed as having invented a reputation-sliming story to weasel out of the legally binding partnership with the man who made her a superstar. But equally, if Ke$ha's accusations are just, her music is forever stained: the Ke$ha persona would be revealed not simply as an act, but as the absolute opposite of her lived reality. Far from the unbridled libertine of her music and performance (see also the reality-TV show and book *My Crazy Beautiful Life*), Kesha Sebert would turn out to have been bridled, demeaned, joylessly coerced at every step of the process.

Pop fans, motivated primarily by pleasure, easily ignore the conditions in which the products they enjoy are made. (That goes for sneakers and iPads, as well as entertainment.) If we took backstories into account, we'd never be able to listen comfortably to the records Tina Turner made while professionally and romantically entangled with Ike. Writing this book I listened to 'Cherry Bomb' with a thrill only slightly marred by the fresh revelations about Kim Fowley's treatment of Jackie Fox. Perhaps one day I'll be able to hear 'TiK ToK' or 'We R' and feel the rush, take delight again in the fiction of 'Ke$ha'. The question is: should I?

2016

January
Lady Gaga wins a Golden Globe for her role in *American Horror Story*. Dressed in a black-velvet, bare-shouldered, cleavage-plunging Atelier Versace gown – 'the pinnacle of retro glamour', the style blogs gush – she gives an overcome-by-emotion acceptance speech that is perfect down to the last lip-tremor. Gaga informs the audience of her new peers that 'I wanted to be an actress before I wanted to be a singer, but music worked out first.' The fame monster completes her metamorphosis into an all-American entertainer.

10 January

Where were *you* when David Bowie died?

I was right here. Sitting at this computer, approaching the end of this book. In fact, I was listening to *Outside*, Bowie's experimental record from 1995, a concept album largely about death, when the first tweets started to come through.

How did *you* feel when you heard David Bowie was dead?

My nine-year-old daughter Tasmin, who barely knows who David Bowie is but knows what's been keeping me so busy the last couple of years, asked my wife: 'Is Dad okay?' I wasn't stunned or even surprised somehow. Having written about *The Next Day* when it came out, I was aware that death had been impinging heavily on Bowie's consciousness. Calling the next album *Blackstar* and giving songs titles like 'Lazarus' seemed like the extension of that apprehensive, twilight-descending mood. And having immersed myself so intensely in his life's work, and his whole era, as a historian, he had curiously come to seem like history to me.

What did impact me were the shockwaves of awe and grief and celebration that followed in the next forty-eight hours, and in the weeks that followed. So many people with such different versions of Bowie, each one changing their lives or representing something inspirational for them. So much reflection, and so many varied reflections – people's lives intersecting with one phase or another of his work, setting off an endless chain of private earthquakes.

So often it felt like people were mourning themselves, grieving the passing of their moment. Which now suddenly and painfully felt like a distinct era with a looming cut-off point; a historical curio, as somebody put it, that people a hundred years, or maybe even as soon as thirty years, from now would struggle to understand. The much-circulated statement, mistakenly attributed to Simon Pegg – 'If you're sad today, just remember the Earth is over four billion years old and you somehow managed to exist at the same time as David Bowie' – caught the tone and struck a chord with its mixture of gratitude and self-congratulation. Cosmically parochial, yes . . . but it's how people in every age have felt about their era, that it was *special* (even if only for its decline, disorder, corruption). 'May you live in interesting times,' goes the not-actually-Chinese proverb. For many, Bowie more than anybody else made the late twentieth century an interesting time to be alive. Partly he did that through being so *interested* – ravenously hungry for stimulation, relentlessly pursuing a succession of cutting edges – and communicating that to his fans, both in terms of his specific obsessions at various points but also a general attitude of adventurous curiosity. Almost infecting them with the disease of mental unrest.

One effect of Bowie's death was an instant feast, a glut of information, analysis, reaction . . . images, video clips, obscure tracks from every stage of his long career. Over the course of a week or two, so many tangents and back-stories got dropped on the banqueting table of the Internet. It was an extreme example of the way our archival culture can flatten the history out of things: you lose not just the sense of events happening in a sequence, but the improvised and random quality to that sequence. It all looks more magisterial and planned out than it was – as if ordained.

One thing I've been trying to do here is recreate that sequence of events – history as one thing after another – and the fact that nobody, least of all Bowie or the other protagonists of glam, knew what was coming next. Multiple times during his career, critics and fans wondered if Bowie was all done, worried that he had nothing more to give and nowhere to go. Bowie himself thought that a bunch of times. He was doing a cultural high-wire act, without any idea of where the wire led or how long he could stay on it.

Probably the most commonly voiced theme in the celebration of Bowie that week was the identification of him with possibility, constant change, continual self-reinvention . . . along with the related idea that Bowie 'gave us permission to be weird'. 'His songs were secret encryptions for freaks the world over to communicate by,' wrote Kari Krome in one testimonial.

Many other facets emerged that were unexpected. The black fan's Bowie, but also Bowie as a fan and supporter of black music (that clip of Bowie on MTV confronting the station about its failure to programme videos by African American artists). Bowie as New Yorker, obsessed with the city but also living there quietly for a long period in the last phase of his life. Bowie as a passionate, knowledgeable but low-profile art-world figure: a contributor/editorial board member at *Modern Painters*; the founder of an art-book publisher.

But certainly in my corner of the Internet and social media, Bowie as shapeshifter was the dominant theme. The values he exemplified – flexibility, adaptability, mobility – are articles of faith for the creative and media classes for a good reason: the ideal of perpetual self-reinvention emerges as an occupational by-product of living with the ever-present likelihood of having to rebrand yourself or switch careers. Bowie is a touchstone for creatives because of their uneasy intermediary place in the scheme of things: midway between the class that runs and owns the world, and the working masses. Creatives invest in aesthetics and taste so heavily because it's their edge of difference: what makes them feel superior to the philistine finance-minded, but also elevates them from the sluggish majority whose lives are still largely bound by origins and surroundings. In a way Bowie-ism is an aesthetic version of the principles of modern finance: the mobility of capital as it divests and reinvests at mercurial speed, disruptive innovation . . .

Bowie came along at a time when the idea of revolution or alternative ways of living proposed in the sixties began to fade. The big trade-off that ensued was the shunting of 'revolution' out of the social-political domain and into the commercial-aesthetic zone (convulsions in style and entertainment), as well as into private life (sexual/spiritual exploration). Lots of ch-ch-changes – of the kind that also generated ch-ch-ching in the marketplace of commodified desire – but not change to the basic structures that organise life. Bowie is the emblem for this individualised, privatised form of revolution.

Looking at the span of Bowie's career – the work but also the interviews and appearances – it's clear that underneath the vaunted identity changes lay a surprising degree of consistency: a core personality of English decency. Except for a bonkers phase for a couple of years in the mid-seventies, through it all Bowie is *himself* – charming, courteous, curious, generous, funny, sometimes a little dry and coolly distanced, but so often erupting in enthusiasm. In a very English way, Bowie was a fan of things that took him out of his Englishness – black music, German modernism, New York bohemia. But the Englishness remained through it all. By all accounts, he was a real gent – and despite his best efforts to put himself in jeopardy, fundamentally sane.

One of the many endearing things to emerge in the flood of shared memories was Eno talking about how he and Bowie communicated in a comic banter straight out of Peter Cook and Dudley Moore's routines. Another is the story of the video shoot for 'Ashes to Ashes' – specifically, a beach scene involving Bowie dressed as Pierrot. The filming was interrupted by an old man walking his dog in a very leisurely way. When the director gestured at Bowie – sitting patiently to one side – and asked the old man, 'Do you know who this is?' the fellow replied, 'Of course I do. It's some cunt in a clown suit.' Bowie observed many years later, 'That was a huge moment for me. It put me back in my place and made me realize, "yes I'm just a cunt in a clown suit."'

'Ashes to Ashes' takes its title from the burial service in the

Church of England's Book of Common Prayer. 'Earth to earth, ashes to ashes, dust to dust' is a reminder of transience, the vanity of worldly ambition. In Bowie's song, the title chorus evokes futility and barrenness. 'Ashes to Ashes' is about despair – 'hitting an all-time low' – and depression is a kind of death-in-life.

Death stalked Bowie's work, from the debut album's 'Please Mr Gravedigger', through the cover of Brel's 'My Death' to the macabre apocalypse of *Diamond Dogs* ('corpses rotting on the slimy thoroughfare') and *Outside*'s 'The Hearts Filthy Lesson', with its imagery of 'a fantastic death abyss'. That song, Bowie explained, was about being confronted with 'the fact that life is finite. That realization, when it comes, usually later in life, can either be a really daunting prospect or it makes things a lot clearer.' The whole album – subtitled 'The Ritualistic Art Murder of Baby Grace – A Non-Linear Gothic Drama Hyper-Cycle' – is about a future where murder is a sanctioned form of artistic expression.

'Confront a corpse at least once,' Bowie instructed readers of *Esquire* in 2004. 'The absolute absence of life is the most disturbing and challenging confrontation you will ever have.' Death was unusually vivid for him following 2003's massive heart attack and the surgery that followed. Debilitated, Bowie withdrew from public life for a decade. When he returned, it was with a literally morbid album, *The Next Day*. The title itself seems to be about the way we all of us carry on in the assumption that there will always be a next day – right up until there isn't one; about how hard it is to live in full awareness of the urgency of time passing, to live up to the challenge of *carpe diem*.

Most of the songs on *The Next Day* concerned two braided themes: stardom and death. In the video for the album's second single, 'The Stars (Are Out Tonight)', Bowie and Tilda Swinton played an elderly couple persecuted by a pair of vampiric celebrities who stalk them, invade their house and manipulate them like marionettes. The concept came from a line about how 'we will never be rid of these stars', though the song itself was less literal, portraying stars as an overlord class who 'burn you with their radiant smiles', but also as faintly pitiable creatures, jealous of the quiet lives and grounded existence of nonentities. 'But I hope they live for ever,' Bowie sings, a gesture of bitter solidarity with both dead stars and stars still living (and still chasing the fantasy of immortality).

Elsewhere, '(You Will) Set the Earth on Fire' was the sales pitch of a Svengali to a potential starlet, while 'How Does the Grass Grow' reads now like a premonition, with its imagery of gazing defeated at the stars: 'The light in my life burned away / There will be no tomorrow.' The closing 'Heat' saw Bowie impersonating Scott Walker – brilliantly – and intoning cryptically about missions grown dark and worlds ending, before confessing, 'I don't know who I am' and 'I am a seer / But I am a liar.'

At the time of making *The Next Day* Bowie didn't know he had cancer, but you wonder if perhaps he sensed something. When it came, the bad news spurred a burst of creativity – and risk taking. His determination to deliver a final statement as immaculately as possible – despite the sapping chemo sessions and a reported half-dozen heart attacks – resulted not just in the final album *Blackstar*, but also the stage musical *Lazarus*, the carefully curated box set *Nothing Has Changed* (with its Bowie-in-the-mirror artwork) and various posthumous releases said to be lined up for 2017 and beyond.

Warhol – whom Bowie played in the 1996 movie *Basquiat* – believed that fame could 'keep at bay' Death, or so claims the art critic Donald Kuspit. All Bowie's preparations for keeping himself in our eyes and ears, hearts and charts, could also seem like a desperate and superstitious attempt to cheat death – a kind of media afterlife.

Blackstar, though, seems like an attempt to stare into the abyss – to come to terms with the fact that however often you reinvent yourself, Death, the Great Uninventor, will catch up with you. The title – rendered graphically as ★ – has been interpreted variously as a type of cancer lesion, a symbol in alchemy (the *sol niger* or black sun), a reference to an Elvis song and an allusion to the black-music influences on the album (Kendrick Lamar's socially conscious hip hop, Bowie's first love jazz, the skittery drum patterns that recall his late-nineties dalliance with jungle).

The simplest meaning, though, seems to be the most telling: a black star is a dead star, a bright light in fame's firmament that's been snuffed out. According to the album's cover designer, Jonathan Barnbrook, the use of the graphic ★ rather than the word was intended to communicate 'a sort of finality, a darkness, a simplicity' – the punctuating starkness of the ultimate full stop. It's the perfect closure to a career, a stardom, that began with 'Space Oddity' and the character of Major Tom, serenely fatalistic as he drifts off into the black void of space.

Bowie, Barnbrook further revealed, also wanted the connotation of 'a black hole sucking in everything'. A black hole – a supermassive star that collapses at the end of its life cycle – exerts immense gravitational attraction and, according to Stephen Hawking's astrophysical theories, emits a form of radiation. Likewise with dead pop or film stars: our obsession can take on even more plangent obsessiveness once they've passed, as with the cults of Marilyn Monroe, Ian Curtis and Jim Morrison. Certain stars have an uncanny afterlife, as though the ending of their lustreless late period of decline is really a blessing, allowing their mythic dimension – based on their early perfection – to blossom again in their absence, propagating itself in all kinds of ways (Elvis being a prime example). Dead stars continue to radiate, fade away never . . .

The dead star is a void, but perhaps in another sense the living star is a void too, at least the kind of star Bowie was. Running on emptiness, a hunger for attention and inspiration – this was what propelled Bowie at such speed. 'I had given my life away – to work, to extremism, to jumping into taboos,' is how he described the fastest part of his public life, from Ziggy to the Thin White Duke – a comment made in the context of having wrenched himself out of that pattern in order to spend more time with his young son.

'Spiritually starving' is a phrase Bowie also used, but less to describe an artistic type, and more as a general comment on Western civilisation after the death of God. One surrogate that has filled the vacuum is fame. For aspirants, it holds out the promise of both heaven on earth and a kind of immortality; for admirers, it offers something to worship and emulate. Replacing religion and perhaps even eclipsing romantic love, fame is today's opiate of the people. It is an endlessly seductive fantasy solution to whatever problems and limitations you face, whether rooted in personal deficiency or social origins. Fame is the mirage of a wholeness and prestige that will be attained once you've achieved ubiquity, a flaring up of the self in the spotlight-blazing gaze of the entire world.

'There must be a hole in a man who gets up on a stage and cries, "Look at me! Look at me!"' mused Anthony Newley in a 1963 interview. 'I am still a paramount egotist forever watching myself. Why? A kid needs all the attention, all the affection. He works for it. He was born with an engaging little face and nothing more. So he uses his cuteness to get love . . . He sharpens and hones that ability until it is an art. Acting, when you boil it down, is just a plea for approval, for love.'

But hunger for admiration and adoration is only part of what drove Bowie. He hungered to admire and adore, lusting after and chasing inspiration tirelessly. During the mass remembrance in the immediate wake of his death, an old piece written by Bowie resurfaced: an annotated list of twenty-five of his favourite records, chosen out of the thousands he owned. The selections were often surprising, the comments touching, insightful and funny. It was one of the only things I read during that whole period that made me feel, truly, the loss of a human being: this was Bowie as fellow record nerd, rather than mythical superbeing.

One entry was about Richard Strauss's *Four Last Songs*, the bulk of which were inspired by the composer's proximity to death, and which were premiered posthumously and given their titles by Strauss's friend Ernest Roth. Stressing that we should listen to Gundula Janowitz's interpretation, Bowie wrote that the music 'aches with love for a life that is quietly fading'. Presumably written not long before his own first big brush with death, the 2003 piece ran in *Vanity Fair*, that almanac of worldly glory. At the close of the novel *Vanity Fair*, Thackeray writes, 'Ah! *Vanitas Vanitatum!* Which of us is happy in this world? Which of us has his desire? Or, having it, is satisfied?'

Blackstar is Bowie's Seven Last Songs, the singer rising to the occasion of his own ending. The long opening title track is one of the best things he's ever done. He sounds like a pained angel, a wavering after-image of himself, already half not there any more. In the lyric he defines 'blackstar' negatively – not a film star, not a pop star, not a marvel star (perhaps a reference to Marvel and the endless succession of superhero movies Hollywood churns out, blockbusting nothingnesses that reduce actors to components of CGI spectacle). 'Lazarus', as others have observed, is a self-epitaph, a valedictory wave from the afterlife ('Look up here, I'm in heaven'). The last track, 'I Can't Give Everything Away', imitates – or samples – the harmonica from *Low*'s 'A New Career in a New Town', accessing its brittle hopefulness about the next destination. What if there is an afterlife, after all?

The videos made for the album's singles seem to make reference to the seventeenth-century painting genre of the *vanitas* – the still life whose arrangements of objects mean to remind the viewer of the ephemeral nature of earthly achievements and earthy pleasures, often involving symbols like the human skull. Alongside its palsied scarecrows twitching in a field, 'Blackstar' features a dead astronaut on the Moon's surface. An androgynous figure with a cat's tail opens the helmet and finds a skull decorated with glittering gemstones. In the even more creepy and gorgeous video for 'Lazarus', a skull lurks on the desk at which Bowie writes frenziedly – the artist trying to outrun Death with a last burst of delirious creativity, brain fizzing with final thoughts.

More than a horror of the skull beneath the skin, though, Bowie seemed troubled by the idea of physical decay. He was keenly aware of the constant potential of the body – the flesh machine that houses consciousness – for abjection: that's why, on *Outside*, the heart's lesson is 'filthy'. *The Next Day*'s title track includes lines about being not quite dead, 'my body left to rot in a hollow tree'. In his farewell email to Eno, who only realised it was a goodbye message after Bowie was gone, the singer wrote: 'Thank you for our good times, Brian. They will never rot.' That word again, jarring and revealing. The hope here is that these intense shared moments are somehow immune to decay. That's the most any of us could hope for – to have lived intensely, gloriously, lovingly, for molecules of time so radiant they simply have to be eternal. Perhaps that's another definition of glamour: lustrous images generated by organic, perishable beings that live on in personal and collective memory, long after their source has withered.

Bowie wanted no public funeral service; he was cremated without anyone in attendance, with his ashes later scattered by his family in Bali in a Buddhist ceremony. The absence of a public farewell seems to say: these remains aren't 'David Bowie'. The person you loved and admired is everywhere and anywhere but here, living on in millions of recordings and images, reverberations and reflections.

ACKNOWLEDGEMENTS

Thanks to my wife Joy Press for her guidance and patience through what turned out to be another 'long one'. She steered me away from various dead ends and the occasional cliff. As the book's first reader, she didn't mince her words (but she did mince mine), and as usual she was right she was right she was ALWAYS right. Love and gratitude.

Thanks and love also to my son Kieran and daughter Tasmin, who were virtually orphaned during the final stretch of *Shock and Awe*.

Thanks to my long-time agent Tony Peake and my new US agent Melissa Flashman for getting this project airborne.

Thanks to Lee Brackstone, my editor at Faber, for his support and flair. Thanks to Denise Oswald, who signed the book for Dey Street, and to Carrie Thornton for taking over the editing when Denise got an offer she couldn't refuse.

Thanks to David Watkins for his meticulous and wise close edit of the manuscript, and for his crucial involvement in the process of illustrating the book.

Thanks to Luke Bird for another wonderful Faber cover design.

Thanks to Ian Bahrami, Dan Papps, Kate Ward and everybody else at Faber involved in the production and promotion of the book.

Thanks to Heather Heisse for her contribution to the early research process, and to Jody Beth LaFosse for her fastidious transcription.

The seeds of this book go back at least as far as 1985, when as one of the team behind the 'pop journal' *Monitor* I got swept up in the collective enthusiasm for old glam and glitter records – excavated excitement that kept us buzzing through what was otherwise a pretty flat and dismal year for music. Big shout, then, to my old comrades: Paul Oldfield, whose brilliant article on 'Glitter' in *Monitor* issue 5 is a large influence on *Shock and Awe*; to Chris Scott and David Stubbs; and to Hilary Bichovsky, who might not have been so thrilled by the old Hello and Sweet singles as the boys but was a vital component of the vibe in those urgent days. Big shout to The Wilson Sisters, whoever the hell they might have been, whose warped homage to Mike Leander, '1972', was affixed as a flexi single to the front of *Monitor*'s final issue.

During the course of writing *Shock and Awe*, a bunch of people have steered me in good directions, or been a foil or sounding board, or been otherwise helpful. Big up to Phil Knight, Matthew Ingram, Nick Katranis, Kristian Hoffman, Stuart Swezey, Richard Cromelin, John Mendelssohn, Lisa Jane Persky, Andy Zax, Barney Hoskyns, Conrad Flynn, Carl Neville, Paul Kennedy, Droid, Sebastian Morlighem, Mike Krumper, Douglas Keeley. Apologies to anyone I have forgotten.

Big up to the music press of the early seventies and, in particular, *Melody Maker* – a fantastic resource for a historian, a time-travel trip for a fan. As a veteran of *Melody Maker* in a very different era, I was delighted to discover that well before my time it had been the best music paper in the world during a crucial phase of rock history, not just more illuminating than the competition, but more entertaining too.

Finally, I would like to thank Amanda Kirby, who has kept me company remotely during this long journey, and who influenced the book in ways she may not realise. Thank you for making me believe in magic.

BIBLIOGRAPHY

Auslander, Philip, *Performing Glam Rock: Gender and Theatricality in Popular Music* (Ann Arbor: University of Michigan Press, 2006)
—— 'Musical Personae', *The Drama Review*, vol. 50, no. 1 (spring 2006)
Baker, Roger, *Drag: A History of Female Impersonation in the Performing Arts* (New York: New York University Press, 1994)
Baker, Russell, 'Past Shock', *New York Times Magazine*, 4 May 1975
Bangs, Lester, 'Glitter Rock', in *Rock Revolution: From Elvis to Elton – The Story of Rock and Roll*, Eds Richard Robinson and the editors of *Creem* magazine (New York: Popular Library, 1976)
Barish, Jonas A., *The Antitheatrical Prejudice* (Los Angeles: University of California, 1981)
Barker, Hugh, and Yuval Taylor, *Faking It: The Quest for Authenticity in Popular Music* (New York: W. W. Norton & Company, 2006)
Baudelaire, Charles, *The Painter of Modern Life and Other Essays*, ed. and trans. Jonathan Mayne (London: Phaidon Press, 2001)
Becker, Ernest, *The Denial of Death* (New York: Simon & Schuster, 1973)
Beckett, Andy, *When the Lights Went Out: What Really Happened to Britain in the Seventies* (London: Faber & Faber, 2009)
Blake, Mark, *Is This the Real Life? The Untold Story of Queen* (New York: Da Capo Press, 2010)
Booker, Christopher, *The Neophiliacs: A Study of the Revolution in English Life in the Fifties and Sixties* (London: Wm. Collins, 1969)
—— *The Seventies: The Decade That Changed the Future* (New York: Stein and Day, 1981)
Boorstin, Daniel J., *The Image: A Guide to Pseudo-Events in America* (1962; New York: Vintage, 1992)
Bracewell, Michael, *Remake/Remodel: Art, Pop, Fashion and the Making of Roxy Music, 1953–1972* (London: Faber & Faber, 2007)
Braudy, Leo, *The Frenzy of Renown: Fame and Its History* (1986; New York: Vintage, 1997)
Brennan, J. H., *Occult Reich* (London: Futura Publications Limited, 1974)
Britton, Andrew, 'For Interpretation: Notes Against Camp', *Gay Left*, issue 7, winter 1978/9, reprinted in *Britton On Film: The Complete Film Criticism of Andrew Britton*, ed. Barry Keith Grant (Detroit: Wayne State University Press, 2008)
Brown, Mick, *Performance* (London: Bloomsbury, 1999)

Buckley, David, *Kraftwerk Publikation: A Biography* (London: Omnibus, 2012)

───── *The Thrill of It All: The Story of Bryan Ferry & Roxy Music* (Chicago: A Cappella Books, 2005)

Burns, Elizabeth, *Theatricality: A Study of Convention in the Theatre and in Social Life* (New York: Harper & Row, 1972)

Bussy, Pascal, *Kraftwerk: Man, Machine and Music* (Wembley: SAF Publishing, 1993)

Carlyle, Thomas, *On Heroes, Hero-Worship, and the Heroic in History* (London: James Fraser, 1841)

───── *Sartor Resartus*, originally published in *Fraser's* magazine (1833–84)

Cather, Willa, 'Paul's Case: A Study in Temperament' (1905), in *Willa Cather's Collected Short Fiction* (Lincoln: University of Nebraska Press, 1970)

Chambers, Iain, *Urban Rhythms: Pop Music and Popular Culture* (New York: St Martin's Press, 1985)

Cleton, Fabio (Ed.), *Camp: Queer Aesthetics and the Performing Subject: A Reader* (Ann Arbor: University of Michigan Press, 1999)

Cohn, Nik, *Awopbopaloobop Alopbamboom: Pop from the Beginning* (London: Weidenfeld & Nicolson Ltd, 1969)

Core, Philip, *Camp: The Lie That Tells the Truth* (London: Plexus, 1984)

County, Jayne, with Rupert Smith, *Man Enough to Be a Woman* (London: Serpent's Tail, 1995)

Crowley, Aleister, *Diary of a Drug Fiend* (1922; Newbury Port: Weiser Books, 2010)

Cunningham, Mark, *Good Vibrations: A History of Record Production* (Chessington: Castle Communications, 1996)

D'Aurevilly, Jules Barbey, *Of Dandyism and George Brummell* (1845), published as part of Walden, George, *Who's a Dandy?* (London: Gibson Square Books, 2002)

Dee, Simon, *The Simon Dee Book* (London: Purnell, 1968)

Dery, Mark, *All the Young Dudes: Why Glam Rock Matters* (Boing Boing, 2013)

Doggett, Peter, *The Man Who Sold the World: David Bowie and the 1970s* (New York: Harper Collins, 2012)

Doyle, Jennifer, Jonathan Flatley and José Esteban Muñoz (Eds), *Pop Out: Queer Warhol* (Durham and London: Duke University Press, 1996)

Dunaway, Dennis, and Chris Hodenfield, *Snakes! Guillotines! Electric Chairs! My Adventures in the Alice Cooper Group* (New York: St Martin's Press, 2015)

Dyer, Richard, *Stars* (London: British Film Institute, 1979)

Dyhouse, Carol, *Glamour: Women, History, Feminism* (London and New York: Zed Books, 2010)

Eco, Umberto, and Girocamo de Michele, *History of Beauty* (New York: Rizzoli, 2010)

Edelman, Lee, *No Future: Queer Theory and the Death Drive* (Durham and London: Duke University Press, 2004)

Fortune, Dion, *Psychic Self-Defense* (1930; Newbury Port: Weiser Books, 2011)

Fowler, Pete, 'Skins Rule', in Charlie Gillett and Simon Frith (Eds), *The Beat Goes On: The Rock File Reader* (London: Pluto Press, 1996)

Freud, Sigmund, 'On Narcissism', in *The Standard Edition of the Complete Psychological Works of Sigmund Freud, Volume XIV (1914–1916): On the History of the Psycho-Analytic Movement, Papers on Metapsychology and Other Works* (London: Hogarth Press/Institute of Psycho-Analysis, 1957)

Gergen, Kenneth J., *The Saturated Self: Dilemmas of Identity in Contemporary Life* (New York: Basic Books, 1991)

Gill, John, *Queer Noises: Male and Female Homosexuality in Twentieth-Century Music* (Minneapolis: University of Minnesota Press, 1995)

Gilman, Richard, *Decadence: The Strange Life of an Epithet* (New York: Farrar, Strauss, and Giroux, 1979)

Glitter, Gary, with Lloyd Bradley, *Leader: The Autobiography of Gary Glitter* (London: Ebury Press, 1991)

Goffman, Erving, *The Presentation of Self in Everyday Life* (New York: Anchor, 1959)

Goude, Jean-Paul, *Jungle Fever* (New York: Xavier Moreau, Inc., 1981)

Green, Martin, *Children of the Sun: A Narrative of 'Decadence' in England after 1918* (Mount Jackson: Axios, 1976)

Greene, Bob, *Billion Dollar Baby* (New York: Atheneum, 1974)

Grinspoon, Lester, and James B. Bakalar, *Cocaine: A Drug and Its Social Evolution* (New York: Basic Books, Inc., 1976)

Halberstam, J. Jack, *Gaga Feminism: Sex, Gender, and the End of Normal* (Boston: Beacon Press, 2012)

Hamelman, Steven L., *But Is It Garbage? On Rock and Trash* (Athens: University of Georgia, 2004)

Hawkins, Stan, *The British Pop Dandy: Masculinity, Popular Music and Culture* (Farnham: Ashgate, 2009)

Hermes, Will, *Love Goes to Buildings on Fire: Five Years in New York that Changed Music Forever* (New York: Faber & Faber, 2012)

Hewison, Robert, *Too Much: Art and Society in the Sixties: 1960–75* (London: Methuen, 1986)

Heylin, Clinton (Ed.), *All Yesterdays' Parties: The Velvet Underground in Print 1966–1971* (New York: Da Capo Press, 2006)

Hoberman, J., *Film After Film: Or, What Became of 21st Century Cinema?* (London and Brooklyn: Verso, 2015)

Hoskyns, Barney, *Glam!: Bowie, Bolan and the Glitter Rock Revolution* (London: Faber & Faber, 1998)

——— 'The Price of Fame: The Birth of Music from the Spirit of Tragedy', *New Musical Express*, 14 August 1982

Hunter, Ian, *Diary of a Rock 'n' Roll Star* (Frogmore, St Albans: Panther Books, 1974)

Hutcheon, Linda, *A Theory of Parody: The Teachings of Twentieth-Century Art Forms* (London: Methuen & Co. Ltd, 1985)

Hutchings, Peter, 'Little Ladies: *Rock Follies* and British Television's Dramatisation of Rock Music', in Ian Inglis (Ed.), *Popular Music and Television in Britain* (Farnham: Ashgate, 2010)

Huysmans, J. K, *Against Nature*, translated by Robert Baldick (1884; London: Penguin, 1959)

Isherwood, Christopher, *The Berlin Stories* (1945; New York: New Directions Publishing, 1963)

Kershaw, Miriam, 'Postcolonialism and Androgyny: The Performance Art of Grace Jones', *Art Journal*, vol. 56, no. 4 (winter 1997)

Koestenbaum, Wayne, *The Queen's Throat: Opera, Homosexuality, and the Mystery of Desire* (New York: Da Capo Press, 2001)

Kopkind, Andrew, 'Are Two Sexes Too Many?' *Boston Phoenix*, 10 October 1972, reprinted in *The Thirty Years' Wars: Dispatches and Diversions of a Radical Journalist 1965–1994* (London: Verso, 1995)

Kuspit, Donald, *The Cult of the Avant-Garde Artist* (Cambridge: Cambridge University Press, 1993)

——— *The Dialectic of Decadence* (New York: Stux Press, 1993)

Lachman, Gary, *Turn Off Your Mind: The Mystic Sixties and the Dark Side of the Age of Aquarius* (New York: Disinformation, 2001)

Laing, Dave, *One Chord Wonders: Power and Meaning in Punk Rock* (Milton Keynes: Open University Press, 1985)

Lasch, Christopher, *The Culture of Narcissism: American Life in an Age of Diminishing Expectations* (New York: W. W. Norton & Company, Inc., 1979)

Lenson, David, *On Drugs* (Minneapolis: University of Minnesota Press, 1995)

Levine, Laura, 'Men in Women's Clothing: Anti-theatricality and Effeminization from 1579 to 1642', *Criticism*, vol. 28, no. 2 (spring 1986)

Lombardi, John, 'Selling Gay to the Masses', *Village Voice*, 30 June 1975

Ludlam, Charles, *Ridiculous Theatre: Scourge of Human Folly – The Essays and Opinions of Charles Ludlam*, ed. Steven Samuels (New York: Theatre Communications Group, 1992)

MacCabe, Colin, *Performance* (London: British Film Institute, 1998)

MacDonald, Ian, *The People's Music* (London: Pimlico, 2003)

McDonnell, Evelyn, *Queens of Noise: The Real Story of The Runaways* (Boston: Da Capo Press, 2013)

McEwan, Ian, 'Dead as They Come', *Iowa Journal* (1977), collected in *In Between the Sheets* (1978; New York: Anchor, 1994)

Mackay, Andy, *Electronic Music* (Minneapolis: Control Data Publishing, 1981)

McLeod, Ken, 'Bohemian Rhapsodies: Operatic Influences on Rock Music', *Popular Music*, vol. 20, no. 2 (May 2001)

Melly, George, *Revolt into Style: The Pop Arts* (London: Allen Lane/Penguin Press, 1970)

Morin, Edgar, *The Stars*, trans. Richard Howard (1960; Minneapolis: University of Minnesota, 2005)

Morrissey, *Autobiography* (London: Penguin Classics, 2013)

Muñoz, José Esteban, *Cruising Utopia: The Then and There of Queer Futurity* (New York: NYU Press, 2009)

Munro, John Neil, *The Sensational Alex Harvey* (Edinburgh: Polygon, 2002)

Murray, Charles Shaar, *Shots from the Hip* (London: Penguin, 1991)

Napier-Bell, Simon, *You Don't Have to Say You Love Me* (London: New English Library, 1983)

Newton, Esther, *Mother Camp: Female Impersonators in America* (Chicago: University of Chicago Press, 1972)

Nietzsche, Friedrich, *The Will to Power*, trans. Walter Kaufmann and R. J. Hollingdale (New York: Vintage, 1968)

Nuttall, Jeff, *Bomb Culture* (London: Paladin, 1970)

O'Keefe, Daniel Lawrence, *Stolen Lightning: The Social Theory of Magic* (New York: Vintage Books, 1983)

Olds, Kirsten, '"Gay Life Artists": Les Petites Bonbons and Camp Performativity in the 1970s', *Arts Journal*, vol. 72, issue 2 (2013)

Oldfield, Paul, 'Glitter', *Monitor*, issue 4 (October 1985)

Otto, Rudolf, *The Idea of the Holy*, trans. John W. Harvey (1917; London: Penguin, 1959)

Paglia, Camille, *Sexual Personae: Art and Decadence from Nefertiti to Emily Dickinson* (London and New Haven: Yale University Press, 1990)

———— 'Theatre of Gender: David Bowie at the Climax of the Sexual Revolution', in *David Bowie Is* (London: V&A Publishing, 2013)

Palmer, Tony, *All You Need Is Love: The Story of Popular Music* (London: Penguin, 1977)

Payne, Jason, 'Hair and Makeup', *Log*, no. 17 (autumn 2009)

Paytress, Mark, *Bolan: The Rise and Fall of a 20th Century Superstar* (London: Omnibus, 2002)

Peellaert, Guy and Nik Cohn, *Rock Dreams*, introduction by Michael Herr (1973; New York: Roger & Bernhard, 1982)

Peraino, Judith A., 'Plumbing the Surface of Sound and Vision: David Bowie, Andy Warhol, and the Art of Posing', *Qui Parle: Critical Humanities and Social Sciences*, vol. 21, no. 1 (autumn/winter 2012)

Pih, Darren, *Glam: The Performance of Style* (Liverpool: Tate Liverpool, 2013)

Pitt, Kenneth, *Bowie: The Pitt Report* (London: Omnibus Press, 1983)

Postrel, Virginia, *The Power of Glamour: Longing and the Art of Visual Presentation* (New York: Simon & Schuster, 2013)

Pott, John, *A History of Charisma* (London: Palgrave Macmillan, 2009)

Praz, Mario, *The Romantic Agony* (1933; Oxford: Oxford University Press, 1970)

Ravenscroft, Trevor, *The Spear of Destiny: The Occult Power Behind the Spear Which Pierced the Side of Christ* (London: Neville Spearman Publishers, 1972)

Rechy, John, *City of Night* (New York: Grove Press, 1963)

Reed, Jeremy, *Waiting for the Man: The Life & Music of Lou Reed* (London: Omnibus, 2015)

Reynolds, Anthony, *Japan – A Foreign Place (The Biography 1974–1984)* (London: Burning Shed, 2015)

Rogan, Johnny, *Roxy Music: Style with Substance – Roxy's First Ten Years* (London: Star/W. H. Allen, 1982)

Royster, Francesca T., 'Feeling Like a Woman, Looking Like a Man, Sounding Like a No-No: Grace Jones and the Performance of Strange in the Post-Soul Moment', in *Women & Performance: A Journal of Feminist Theory*, vol. 19, no. 1 (March 2009)

Rüther, Tobias, *Heroes: David Bowie and Berlin* (London: Reaktion Books Ltd, 2014)

Savage, Jon, *The Kinks* (London: Faber & Faber, 1984)

Scott, Sir Walter, *Letters on Demonology and Witchcraft* (London: George Routledge and Sons, 1885)

Senelick, Laurence, *The Changing Room: Sex, Drag and Theatre* (London: Routledge, 2000)

Shapiro, Harry, *Waiting for the Man: The Story of Drugs and Popular Music* (New York: William Morrow and Company, Inc., 1988)

Shaviro, Steven, *Post-Cinematic Affect* (Ropley: Zero, 2010)

Sontag, Susan, 'Notes on "Camp"', in *Against Interpretation* (New York: Farrar, Straus, and Giroux, 1966)

———— 'Fascinating Fascism', *New York Review of Books*, 6 February 1975

———— *On Photography* (New York: Farrar, Straus, and Giroux, 1977)

Spark, Muriel, *The Public Image* (New York: Alfred A. Knopf, 1968)

Spengler, Oswald, *The Decline of the West* (1926; New York: Alfred A. Knopf, 1932)

Stevenson, Nick, *David Bowie: Fame, Sound and Vision* (Cambridge: Polity, 2006)

Strange, Richard, *Strange: Punks and Drunks and Flicks and Kicks – The Memoirs of Richard Strange* (London: Andre Deutsch, 2002)

Stump, Paul, *Unknown Pleasures: A Cultural Biography of Roxy Music* (London: Quartet, 1998)

Suzuki, D. T., 'Lectures on Zen Buddhism', in *Zen Buddhism & Psychoanalysis* (1959; New York: Harper Colophon, 1970)

Taylor, Ian, and David Wall, 'Beyond the Skinheads: Comments on the Emergence and Significance of the Glamrock Cult', in Geoff Mungham and Geoff Pearson (Eds), *Working Class Youth Culture* (London: Routledge & Kegan Paul, 1976)

Thompson, David, *Children of the Revolution: The Glam Rock Story 1970–75* (London: Cherry Red Books, 2010)

———— *Blockbuster! The Sweet* (London: Cherry Red Books, 2010)

Thompson, Jeremy, and Mary Blount, *Wired Up! Glam, Proto Punk, and Bubblegum – European Picture Sleeves 1970–1976* (London: Wired Up Media, 2012)

Thomson, Elizabeth, and David Gutman, *The Bowie Companion* (New York: Da Capo Press, 1996)

Tolkien, J. R. R., 'On Fairy Stories' (1939), in *The Tolkien Reader* (New York: Ballantine Books, 1966)

Tremlett, George, *Slade* (London: Futura Publications, 1975)

———— *The Gary Glitter Story* (London: Futura Publications, 1974)

———— *The David Essex Story* (London: Futura Publications, 1974)

Trynka, Paul, *David Bowie: Starman* (New York: Little, Brown and Company, 2011)

Turner, Jenny, 'Reasons for Liking Tolkien', *London Review of Books*, vol. 23, no. 22 (15 November 2001)

Twenge, Jean M., *Generation Me: Why Today's Young Americans Are More Confident, Assertive, Entitled – and More Miserable Than Ever Before* (New York: Free Press, 2006)

Twenge, Jean M. and W. Keith Campbell, *The Narcissism Epidemic: Living in the Age of Entitlement* (New York: Free Press, 2009)

Vermorel, Fred, *The Secret History of Kate Bush (& The Strange Art of Pop)* (London: Omnibus, 1983)

Vermorel, Fred, and Judy Vermorel, *Starlust: The Secret Fantasies of Fans* (London: Comet/W. H. Allen, 1985)

———— *Kate Bush: Biography* (London: Target, 1980)

Vernalis, Carol, *Unruly Media: YouTube, Music Video, and the New Digital Cinema* (Oxford: Oxford University Press, 2013)

Waksman, Steve, *This Ain't the Summer of Love: Conflict and Crossover in Heavy Metal and Punk* (Berkeley and Los Angeles: University of California Press, 2002)

Walden, George, *Who's a Dandy?* (London: Gibson Square Books, 2002)

Waldrep, Shelton, *The Aesthetics of Self-Invention: Oscar Wilde to David Bowie* (Minneapolis: University of Minnesota, 2004)

———— (Ed.), *The Seventies: The Age of Glitter in Popular Culture* (New York and London: Routledge, 2000)

Walker, Michael, *What You Want Is in the Limo: On the Road with Led Zeppelin, Alice Cooper, and The Who in 1973, the Year the Sixties Died and the Modern Rock Star Was Born* (New York: Spiegel & Grau, 2013)

Wareham, John, *Secrets of a Corporate Headhunter* (New York: Jove Books, 1981)

Warhol, Andy, *Popism: The Warhol Sixties* (New York: Harcourt Brace Jovanovich, 1980)

Waterhouse, Keith, *Billy Liar* (London: Michael Joseph, 1959)

Weber, Max, *On Charisma and Institution Building: Selected Papers*, ed. S. N. Eisenstadt (Chicago and London: University of Chicago Press, 1968)

Whittaker, Adrian, with Michael Bracewell, Moodies interview, *The Wire*, March 2010

Wilcken, Hugo, *Low* (New York and London: Continuum, 2007)

Wilde, Oscar, *The Picture of Dorian Gray*, in *Complete Works of Oscar Wilde* (London: Collins, 1948)

───── 'The Decay of Lying', in *Complete Works of Oscar Wilde* (London: Collins, 1948)

───── 'The Critic as Artist', in *Complete Works of Oscar Wilde* (London: Collins, 1948)

───── 'The Truth of Masks', in *Complete Works of Oscar Wilde* (London: Collins, 1948)

Willis, Ellen, 'Bowie's Limitations', *The New Yorker*, October 1972; reprinted in Nona Willis Aronowitz (Ed.), *Out of the Vinyl Deeps: Ellen Willis on Rock Music* (Minneapolis: University of Minnesota Press, 2011)

Willis, Paul, *Profane Culture* (London: Routledge & Kegan Paul, 1978)

Wollman, Elizabeth L., *The Theater Will Rock: A History of the Rock Musical, from* Hair *to* Hedwig (Ann Arbor: University of Michigan Press, 2006)

York, Peter, *Style Wars* (London: Sidgwick & Jackson, 1980)

───── *Modern Times* (London: William Heinemann Ltd, 1984)

───── 'So Different, So Appealing' (London: Frieze, March 2008)

INDEX

David Essex

ROCK FOLLIES

THE ROCKY HORROR PICTURE
SHOW

Steve Harley and Cockney Rebel

Sparks

Jet

Queen

Be-Bop Deluxe

The English Disco

Silverhead

Zolar X

Les Petites Bonbons

THE MAN WHO FELL TO EARTH

Heavy Metal Kids

The Sensational Alex Harvey Band

The Tubes

The Runaways

Doctors of Madness

Ultravox

Iggy Pop

Kraftwerk

Brian Eno